CW00531021

Finance Director's Handbook

Finance Director's Handbook

Fourth edition

Glynis D. Morris, BA FCA

and

Sonia McKay, LLB PhD
Andrea Oates, BSc

AMSTERDAM • BOSTON • HEIDELBERG • LONDON • NEW YORK • OXFORD
PARIS • SAN DIEGO • SAN FRANCISCO • SINGAPORE • SYDNEY • TOKYO
CIMA Publishing is an imprint of Elsevier

CIMA Publishing is an imprint of Elsevier
Linacre House, Jordan Hill, Oxford OX2 8DP, UK
30 Corporate Drive, Suite 400, Burlington, MA 01803, USA

First published as *Tolley's Finance Director's Handbook* 2001
Second edition 2002
Third edition 2003
Fourth edition 2007

British Library Cataloguing in Publication Data
A catalogue record for this book is available from the British Library

Library of Congress Cataloguing in Publication Data
A catalogue record for this book is available from the Library of Congress

ISBN–13: 978-0-7506-8129-2
ISBN–10: 0-7506-8129-2

For more information on all CIMA Publishing books
visit our website at http://books.elsevier.com

Typeset by Charon Tec Ltd (A Macmillan Company), Chennai, India
www.charontec.com

Printed and bound in Great Britain

07 08 09 10   10 9 8 7 6 5 4 3 2 1

Working together to grow
libraries in developing countries

www.elsevier.com | www.bookaid.org | www.sabre.org

ELSEVIER   BOOK AID
International   Sabre Foundation

Contents

Preface

The role of the finance director varies significantly between companies, depending to a large extent on the complexity and size of the business and the number of executives and managers available to share in the responsibilities. Whilst some finance directors will concentrate primarily on financial reporting, treasury and taxation issues, others will have a much wider remit and be expected to provide expertise and assistance in a variety of areas.

The field of financial reporting is becoming increasingly complex, particularly for listed companies, where the emphasis is now firmly on transparency and accountability. Accounting standards have become more conceptual in nature, underpinned by a requirement for preparers of accounts to apply the spirit and reasoning behind the detailed requirements. For listed companies, the requirement to prepare group accounts in accordance with International Accounting Standards (IASs) has created new challenges, and the Accounting Standards Board's plans to converge UK accounting practice with international requirements over the coming years, together with the adoption in the UK of International Standards on Auditing (ISAs), means that all companies are likely to feel the increasing impact of international harmonisation.

Listed companies also have significant additional reporting responsibilities under the Combined Code and, if they are registered with the US Securities and Exchange Commission (SEC), under the Sarbanes-Oxley Act 2002 and related SEC rules. The current reporting requirements in respect of internal control have focused attention on the issue of risk management and, whilst the detailed reporting requirements apply only to listed companies, there is nevertheless much in the related guidance that will be relevant to businesses of all sizes.

There are more changes to come in late 2006 or early 2007 as the recent review of UK company law culminates in new legislation. A revised draft Company Law Reform Bill was published in May 2006 and is currently progressing through Parliament. A number of areas are still under debate, including issues relating to narrative reporting in the annual directors' report and auditor liability. Meanwhile, the Financial Reporting Council continues to consider issues such as competition and choice in the UK audit market and the need to improve the quality and security of accounting information filed at Companies House.

These are all areas in which the finance director's input to discussions and decisions is likely to be significant. I therefore make no apology for the fact that the chapters on audit, corporate governance, financial reporting and investor relations are the most substantial sections of this book. However, in addition to guidance in these key areas, this handbook is intended to provide an overview of other business issues and activities that may fall within the remit of the finance director. The book is intended as an initial source of advice and guidance rather than as a comprehensive manual, and sources of further information are indicated where appropriate.

This edition is based on legal and other requirements in force as at 30 June 2006. In the fast moving world of today, very little stands still for long and an indication of known or expected future developments is therefore given where appropriate. No reference work can be comprehensive in this complex and fast changing environment, or take account of the specific circumstances of each particular case, and finance directors should therefore always seek appropriate professional advice.

I am particularly grateful to Sonia McKay and Andrea Oates who have contributed the chapters on 'Employment law' and 'Health and safety' respectively, and to the editorial team at Elsevier for their help and support.

Glynis D. Morris
Chartered Accountant

Abbreviations and References

Legislation

CA 1985	=	Companies Act 1985
CA 1989	=	Companies Act 1989
COSHH	=	Control of Substances Hazardous to Health Regulations 1999
ERA 1996	=	Employment Rights Act 1996
HSWA 1974	=	Health and Safety at Work etc. Act 1974
RIDDOR 1995	=	Reporting of Injuries, Diseases and Dangerous Occurrences Regulations 1995
TULRCA 1992	=	Trade Union and Labour Relations (Consolidation) Act 1992
TUPE	=	Transfer of Undertakings (Protection of Employment) Regulations 1981

Bodies

ACAS	=	Advisory, Conciliation and Arbitration Service
ACCA	=	Association of Chartered Certified Accountants
APB	=	Auditing Practices Board
ASB	=	Accounting Standards Board
ASC	=	Accounting Standards Committee
CAC	=	Central Arbitration Committee
CIMA	=	Chartered Institute of Management Accountants
CIPFA	=	Chartered Institute of Public Finance and Accountancy
CRE	=	Commission for Racial Equality
EAGGF	=	European Agricultural Guidance and Guarantee Fund
EMAS	=	Employment Medical Advisory Service
EOC	=	Equal Opportunities Commission
ERDF	=	European Regional Development Fund
ESF	=	European Social Fund
FIFG	=	Financial Instrument for Fisheries Guidance
FRC	=	Financial Reporting Council
FRRP	=	Financial Reporting Review Panel
FSA	=	Financial Services Authority
HMRC	=	HM Revenue and Customs
HSC	=	Health and Safety Commission
HSE	=	Health and Safety Executive
IASB	=	International Accounting Standards Board
ICAEW	=	Institute of Chartered Accountants in England and Wales

ICAI	=	Institute of Chartered Accountants in Ireland
ICAS	=	Institute of Chartered Accountants of Scotland
ICC	=	Incident Contact Centre
ICSA	=	Institute of Chartered Secretaries and Administrators
LEC	=	Local Enterprise Council
NACOSS	=	National Approval Council for Security Systems
NAPF	=	National Association of Pension Funds
OPRA	=	Occupational Pensions Regulatory Authority
PIRC	=	Pensions and Investment Research Consultants Limited
PRAG	=	Pensions Research Accounting Group
PSO	=	[Inland Revenue] Pension Schemes Office
TEC	=	Training and Enterprise Council
UITC	=	Urgent Issues Task Force

Publications

ACoP	=	Approved Code of Practice
FRED	=	Financial Reporting Exposure Draft
FRS	=	Financial Reporting Standard
FRSSE	=	Financial Reporting Standard for Smaller Entities
IAS	=	International Accounting Standard
IFRS	=	International Financial Reporting Standard
ISA	=	International Standard on Auditing
OFR	=	Operating and Financial Review
SAS	=	Statement of Auditing Standards
SORP	=	Statement of Recommended Practice
SSAP	=	Statement of Standard Accounting Practice

Miscellaneous abbreviations

ACT	=	advance corporation tax
AESOP	=	all-employee share ownership plan
AGM	=	annual general meeting
ASP	=	Application Service Provider
B2B	=	Business to Business
B2C	=	Business to Consumer
B2G	=	Business to Government
C2G	=	Consumer to Government
CEO	=	chief executive officer
CFC	=	controlled foreign company
CIC	=	close investment-holding company
CTSA	=	corporation tax self-assessment
E & OE	=	errors and omissions excepted
EDI	=	Electronic Data Interchange
EE/ET	=	Employee's Earnings Threshold
EGM	=	extraordinary general meeting
EHO	=	environmental health officer
EMI	=	Enterprise Management Incentive

ER/ET	=	Employer's Earnings Threshold
ETO	=	economic, technical or organisational
ISP	=	Internet Service Provider
JWG	=	Joint Working Group
MA	=	Maternity Allowance
PAYE	=	Pay As You Earn
plc	=	public limited company
PPE	=	personal protective equipment
S2P	=	State Second Pension
SERPS	=	State Earnings Related Pension Scheme
SMP	=	Statutory Maternity Pay
SSP	=	Statutory Sick Pay
UEL	=	Upper Earnings Limit
VAN	=	Value Added Network
VAT	=	value added tax
VDU	=	visual display unit
WFTC	=	Working Families Tax Credit

Law report references

ICR	=	Industrial Cases Reports
IRLB	=	Industrial Relations Law Bulletin
IRLR	=	Industrial Relations Law Reports

1

Audit

1 Audit

1.1 The External Audit Requirement

Under *section 384(1)* of the *Companies Act 1985 (CA 1985)*, every company must appoint an auditor or auditors. The only exceptions to this, set out in *section 388A* of *CA 1985*, are for dormant companies and certain small companies, which are exempt from the obligation to appoint auditors if they are exempt under *sections 249AA* and *249A* respectively from the provisions of *CA 1985* on the annual audit of accounts.

1.2 Audit Exemption for Dormant Companies

At a Glance
* A dormant company is usually exempt from the requirement to appoint auditors and have its annual accounts audited.
* The definition of 'dormant' for these purposes is set out in *CA 1985*.
* Certain companies are ineligible for the exemption even if they meet the definition.
* Members of a dormant company can require an audit to be carried out in any financial year by following the procedure laid down in *CA 1985*.
* The directors must make a formal statement in the accounts in order for the exemption to be available.
* A dormant company that acts as an agent for another party must disclose this fact in its annual accounts.

A company that is dormant, as defined in *CA 1985*, is usually entitled to exemption from an annual audit. The exemption has been available for some time, but the process for taking advantage of it was changed by the *Companies Act 1985 (Audit Exemption) (Amendment) Regulations 2000 (SI 2000/1430)*, which came into effect for accounting periods ending on or after 26 July 2000. Prior to this, a dormant company had to pass a special resolution exempting itself from the audit provisions of *CA 1985* and the appointment of auditors. The exemption is now automatically available to those companies that meet the conditions set out in

CA 1985. The exemption granted by *section 249AA* of *CA 1985* relates only to the annual audit requirement – a dormant company must still prepare annual accounts in accordance with the accounting provisions of the legislation and deliver a copy to the Registrar.

1.3 Definition of 'Dormant'

A company is dormant for any accounting period during which it does not have a 'significant accounting transaction'. This is defined in *CA 1985* as any transaction requiring an entry to be made in the accounting records, other than:

- the taking up of shares by a subscriber in pursuance of an undertaking given by him/her in the Memorandum of Association;
- a fee payable to the Registrar on a change of the company's name;
- a fee payable to the Registrar on the re-registration of the company (ie on a change in status from private to public, or vice versa);
- a penalty under section *242A* of *CA 1985* for failure to deliver accounts; and
- a fee payable to the Registrar for registration of the company's annual return.

The last four of these were introduced by the *Companies Act 1985 (Audit Exemption) (Amendment) Regulations 2000* (*SI 2000/1430*). A company that is dormant ceases to be so as soon as a significant accounting transaction occurs.

1.4 Eligibility for Audit Exemption as a Dormant Company

A company is not entitled to audit exemption as a dormant company if it is a banking or insurance company, or an authorised person for the purposes of the *Financial Services and Markets Act 2000*. In other cases, a dormant company is eligible for audit exemption for a financial year if it has been:

- dormant since its formation; or
- dormant since the end of the previous financial period; and
  - is entitled to prepare its individual accounts in accordance with *section 246* of *CA 1985* (or would have been so entitled if it had not been a public company or a member of an ineligible group), and
  - is not required to prepare group accounts for that financial year.

The directors must also make a formal statement in the accounts that the company is entitled to the exemption (see **1.6** below). The exemption for dormant companies that are public companies or members of an ineligible group is set out in *section 249AA(2)(a)*, which cross refers to *sections 247A(a)(i)* and *247A(b)*. For accounting periods beginning on or after 1 April 2005, these two sections were removed by the *Companies Act 1985 (Operating and Financial Review and Directors' Report etc.) Regulations 2005* (*SI 200/1011*) and equivalent provisions are now set out in *sections 247A(1B)(a)* and *247A(1A)(b)* respectively.

In February 2006, the DTI issued an interpretation confirming that there was no intention to change the audit exemption provisions for dormant companies as a result of the implementation of *SI 2005/1011* and that the cross-references will be corrected when a suitable opportunity arises. In the meantime, they should be interpreted as relating to the new provisions of *section 247A*.

1.5 Members Requiring an Audit to be Carried Out

Any member or members of a dormant company holding not less than 10 per cent of the issued share capital, or of any class of share capital, can require an audit to be carried out for any financial year by depositing a written notice to this effect at the company's registered office no later than one month before the end of the relevant financial year. Where a company does not have a share capital, not less than 10 per cent of the members in number terms can require an audit to be carried out.

1.6 Directors' Statement

The exemption from the annual audit is only available to a dormant company if the balance sheet in the company's accounts includes a statement by the directors that:

- for the year in question, the company is entitled to the exemption in *section 249AA(1)* of *CA 1985*;
- no notice has been deposited under *section 249B(2)* of *CA 1985* requiring an audit to be carried out for that financial year; and
- the directors acknowledge their responsibilities for:
  - ensuring that the company maintains accounting records that comply with *section 221* of *CA 1985*, and
  - preparing accounts which give a true and fair view of the state of affairs of the company at the end of the financial year, and of the profit or loss for that year, in accordance with *section 226* of *CA 1985*, and which comply with the relevant accounting requirements of *CA 1985*.

The statement must be given above the signature of the director on the balance sheet.

1.7 Dormant Company Acting as Agent

The *Companies Act 1985 (Audit Exemption) (Amendment) Regulations 2000 (SI 2000/1430)* also introduced a new requirement for a dormant company that acts as an agent for another party to disclose this fact in its annual accounts. The requirement applies for accounting periods ending on or after 26 July 2000 and *Schedule 4 (para 58A)*, *Schedule 8 (para 51A)* and *Schedule 8A (para 9A)* to *CA 1985* have all been updated to incorporate the new disclosure. The details must therefore also be given in abbreviated accounts if the company chooses to prepare these for filing purposes.

1.8 Audit Exemption for Small Companies

At a Glance
* Exemption from an annual audit is available to companies that qualify as small under the size criteria set out in *CA 1985*.
* Certain companies are ineligible for qualification as a small company, even if they meet the size criteria.
* Special provisions apply to dormant subsidiaries and to small groups who would otherwise be ineligible for the exemption.
* Separate total exemption conditions apply for charitable and non-charitable companies.
* A charitable company that does not meet the total exemption conditions may be exempt from a full audit if it meets the report conditions – in this case a special report on the accounts must be prepared by a reporting accountant.
* Members of a small company can require an audit to be carried out in any financial year by following the procedure laid down in *CA 1985*.
* The directors must make a formal statement in the accounts in order for the exemption to be available.

Exemption from an annual audit for certain small companies was originally introduced by the *Companies Act 1985 (Audit Exemption) Regulations 1994 (SI 1994/1935)*, which inserted *sections 249A* to *249E* into *CA 1985*. The provisions in these sections have been updated on a number of occasions since they were first introduced.

The details below set out the latest position and generally apply for accounting periods ending on or after 30 March 2004.

1.9 Eligibility for Exemption

Audit exemption is only available to companies that qualify as small under *CA 1985* – the qualification criteria are explained in detail at **3.48 COMPANY LAW**. Certain companies are ineligible for qualification as a small company and are therefore not entitled to audit exemption. *Section 249B(1)* of *CA 1985* also specifies that the following are not eligible for audit exemption even if they fulfil the conditions set out in the legislation:

* a public company;
* a parent or subsidiary undertaking (except in the specific circumstances explained at **1.10** below);

- a person with permission under *Part 4* of the *Financial Services and Markets Act 2000* to carry on a regulated activity;
- a person who carries on an insurance market activity;
- an appointed representative within the meaning of *section 39* of the *Financial Services and Markets Act 2000*, other than an appointed representative whose scope of appointment is limited to activities that are not regulated activities for the purpose of that Part of the Act (see below);
- a special registered body as defined in *section 117(1)* of the *Trade Union and Labour Relations (Consolidation) Act 1992* or an employers' association as defined in *section 122* of that Act.

The exception for certain appointed representatives applies for accounts delivered to the Registrar on or after 5 September 2005 and generally enables small companies involved in insurance mediation or mortgage advisory activities to take advantage of audit exemption. The Financial Services Authority (FSA) has also issued a consultation paper outlining proposals to bring all small firms and appointed representatives within the scope of audit exemption, on the basis that adequate alternative arrangements are already in place to protect consumers who deal with these small companies. The FSA notes that the proposals are supported by the DTI and, if they meet with general acceptance, the relevant legal changes could be implemented by the end of 2006.

1.10   Small Groups and Dormant Subsidiaries

Audit exemption is generally not available to parent and subsidiary undertakings, although special provisions have now been made for dormant subsidiaries and small groups. A subsidiary that has been dormant (see **1.3** above) throughout the financial year will be exempt from an annual audit if it satisfies the other exemption conditions. Also, a parent or subsidiary undertaking will not be regarded as ineligible for audit exemption if, throughout the period that it was a parent or subsidiary, it was a member of a group that qualifies as a small group under *section 249* of *CA 1985* for the financial year covering that period (or would so qualify if all bodies corporate in the group were companies) and was not at any time within that year an ineligible group as defined in *section 248(2)* of *CA 1985*, and:

- if the company is not a charity, the group has an aggregate turnover in that year of not more than £5.6 million net or £6.72 million gross;
- if the company is a charity, the group has an aggregate turnover in that year of not more than £350,000 net or £420,000 gross; and
- the group has an aggregate balance sheet total for that year of not more than £2.8 million net or £3.36 million gross.

A parent or subsidiary that meets these criteria will therefore be eligible for audit exemption provided that it also satisfies the other conditions set out in *CA 1985*. Gross figures are those before the set-offs and adjustments normally made when preparing consolidated accounts and net figures are those after these adjustments have been made. There is no requirement for the turnover and balance sheet limits to be considered on the same basis. The rules and definitions set out in *section 249* of *CA 1985* apply (see **1.12** below). The draft Company Law Reform Bill published in May 2006 includes a proposal to increase the group turnover threshold to £700,000 net or £840,000 gross in the case of a small charitable company registered in England and Wales. Separate arrangements will apply for a small charitable company registered in Scotland.

1.11   Conditions for Audit Exemption

Section 249A of *CA 1985* sets out two separate categories of conditions for audit exemption – total exemption conditions and report conditions. A company that meets the total exemption conditions in a financial year is not required to have its accounts for that year audited. A company that meets the report conditions for a financial year is not required to have its accounts for that year audited, provided that the directors arrange for a special report on the accounts to be made by a reporting accountant. For practical purposes, the report conditions now only apply in the case of a company that is a charity.

1.12   Total Exemption Conditions

A company that is not a charity will satisfy the total exemption conditions for a financial year if:

- it qualifies as a small company for that year under *section 246* of *CA 1985*;
- its turnover for the year is not more than £5.6 million; and
- its balance sheet total for the year is not more than £2.8 million.

All three conditions must be met for the company to be eligible for audit exemption. If the financial period is more or less than one year, the turnover limited must be adjusted proportionately. The balance sheet total is the aggregate of the amounts shown as assets in the company's balance sheet, before the deduction of any liabilities. The directors must also make a formal statement in the accounts that the company is entitled to the exemption for that financial year (see **1.17** below).

1.13   Charitable Companies

A company that is a charity will satisfy the total exemption conditions if:

- it qualifies as a small company for that year under *section 246* of *CA 1985*;
- its gross income for the year is not more than £90,000; and
- its balance sheet total for the year is not more than £2.8 million.

All three conditions must be met for the company to be eligible for audit exemption. Gross income is defined as 'income from all sources, as shown in the company's income and expenditure account' and the limit is adjusted proportionately if the financial period is more or less than one year. The balance sheet total is the aggregate of the amounts shown as assets in the company's balance sheet, before the deduction of any liabilities. The directors must also make a formal statement in the accounts that the company is entitled to the exemption for that financial year (see **1.17** below). It should be noted that, in the case of total audit exemption, the balance sheet threshold was increased to £2.8 million by the *Companies Act 1985 (Accounts of Small and Medium-sized Enterprises and Audit Exemption)(Amendment) Regulations 2004 (SI 2004/16)* for charitable companies as well as for other companies, although the DTI had originally indicated that there was no intention to do so. This creates the slight anomaly that, for a charitable company, the balance sheet threshold for total audit exemption is significantly higher than the equivalent threshold under the report conditions (see **1.14** below).

1.14   Report Conditions

These conditions are now only relevant for a company that is a charity. A charitable company will satisfy the report conditions if:

- it qualifies as a small company for that year under *section 246* of *CA 1985*;
- its gross income for the year is more than £90,000 but not more than £250,000; and
- its balance sheet total for the year is not more than £1.4 million.

All three conditions must be met for the company to be eligible for the exemption and the same definitions and rules apply as for the total exemption conditions. Note that, although the balance sheet threshold for total audit exemption has been increased to £2.8 million, the equivalent threshold for the report conditions remains at £1.4 million. The draft Company Law Reform Bill published in May 2006 proposes certain changes to the audit exemption provisions for charitable companies to help achieve consistency with charity law (or proposed charity law). In particular:

- references to the report conditions and the reporting accountant will be replaced with the terms 'independent examination in lieu of audit' and 'independent examiner'; and
- the upper gross income threshold will be increased to £500,000 for charitable companies registered in England and Wales – separate arrangements will apply for companies registered in Scotland.

1.15   Special Report by Reporting Accountants

For a charitable company which meets the report conditions to be exempt from the annual audit, the directors must arrange for a special report to the members to be made by a reporting accountant. *Section 249D* of *CA 1985* specifies those who are eligible to act as the reporting accountant. The reporting accountant may be an individual, a body corporate or a partnership and must be:

- a member of one of the following bodies:
  - Institute of Chartered Accountants in England and Wales,
  - Institute of Chartered Accountants of Scotland,
  - Institute of Chartered Accountants in Ireland,

- ○ Association of Chartered Certified Accountants,
- ○ Association of Authorised Public Accountants,
- ○ Association of Accounting Technicians,
- ○ Association of International Accountants,
- ○ Chartered Institute of Management Accountants,
- ○ Institute of Chartered Secretaries and Administrators; and
- entitled to engage in public practice under the rules of the relevant body.

The same rules on independence apply as in the case of auditors (see **1.27** below). The reporting accountant must express an opinion:

- on whether the accounts are in agreement with the company's accounting records;
- on whether the accounts are drawn up in a manner consistent with the relevant provisions of *CA 1985*;
- that the company satisfies the report conditions set out in *section 249A* of *CA 1985*; and
- that the company did not at any time during the year fall within any categories not entitled to audit exemption.

1.16   Members Requiring an Audit to be Carried Out

Any member or members of a company holding not less than 10 per cent of the issued share capital, or of any class of share capital, can require an audit to be carried out for any financial year by depositing a written notice to this effect at the company's registered office no later than one month before the end of the relevant financial year. Where a company does not have a share capital, not less than 10 per cent of the members in number terms can require an audit to be carried out.

1.17   Directors' Statement

The exemption from the annual audit is only available if the balance sheet in the company's accounts includes a statement by the directors that:

- for the year in question, the company is entitled to the exemption granted by *section 249A(1)* or *(2)* of *CA 1985*;
- no notice has been deposited under *section 249B(2)* of *CA 1985* requiring an audit to be carried out for that financial year; and
- the directors acknowledge their responsibilities for:
  - ○ ensuring that the company maintains accounting records that comply with *section 221* of *CA 1985*, and
  - ○ preparing accounts which give a true and fair view of the state of affairs of the company at the end of the financial year, and of the profit or loss for that year, in accordance with *section 226* of *CA 1985*, and which comply with the relevant accounting requirements of *CA 1985*.

The statement must be given above the signature of the director on the balance sheet.

Audit

SMALL COMPANY AUDIT EXEMPTION FLOWCHART

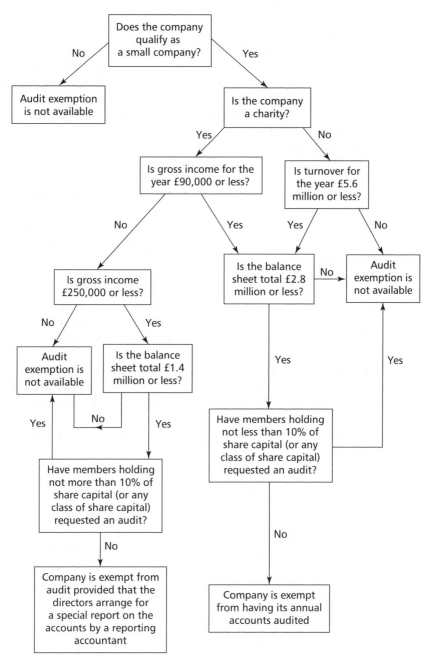

1.18   Appointment of External Auditors

At a Glance
* The first auditors may be appointed by the directors at any time before the first general meeting of the company at which accounts are laid.
* In subsequent years, auditors must be appointed at each general meeting at which accounts are laid.
* In each case, separate provisions apply where a private company elects to dispense with the laying of accounts.
* A private company may elect to dispense with the annual appointment of auditors, in which case the auditors are deemed to be reappointed each year.
* If a company fails to appoint auditors, the Secretary of State may appoint a person to fill the vacancy.
* Either the directors or the company in general meeting can appoint auditors to fill a casual vacancy or if the company ceases to be eligible for audit exemption.
* An individual or firm is only eligible for appointment as a company auditor if they are a member of a recognised supervisory body as defined in *CA 1989* and if they are independent of the company.
* The rules on auditor independence were subject to intense scrutiny as part of the post-Enron review and a number of changes have been put into place.
* An auditor who becomes ineligible for appointment must vacate the office immediately and given written notice to the company.
* The Secretary of State may require a second audit to be carried out if an auditor has acted whilst ineligible for appointment.

1.19   Appointment of First Auditors

Under *section 385(3)* of *CA 1985*, the first auditors may be appointed by the directors at any time before the first general meeting of the company at which accounts are laid and they hold office until the conclusion of that meeting. Separate provisions are set out in *section 385A(3)* of *CA 1985* for a private company which elects to dispense with the laying of accounts. In this case, the first auditors may be appointed by the directors at any time before:

* the end of the period of 28 days beginning with the day on which copies of the company's first annual accounts are sent to members under *section 238* of *CA 1985*; or
* if notice is given by a member or auditor under *section 253(2)* of *CA 1985* requiring the laying of accounts before the company in general meeting, the beginning of that meeting.

Once appointed, the auditors hold office until the end of that 28-day period or, where relevant, the conclusion of the meeting. If the directors do not make an appointment under *section 385(3)* or *385A(3)* of *CA 1985*, auditors may be appointed by the company in general meeting.

1.20 Appointment in Subsequent Years

Section 385(2) of *CA 1985* requires auditors to be appointed at each general meeting of the company at which accounts are laid. The auditors appointed hold office from the conclusion of the meeting until the conclusion of the next general meeting at which accounts are laid. In the case of a private company which elects to dispense with the laying of accounts, *section 385A(2)* of *CA 1985* requires auditors to be appointed by the company in general meeting before:

- the end of the period of 28 days beginning with the day on which copies of the company's annual accounts for the previous financial year are sent to members under *section 238* of *CA 1985*; or
- if notice is given by a member or auditor under *section 253(2)* of *CA 1985* requiring the laying of accounts before the company in general meeting, the conclusion of that meeting.

The auditors hold office from the end of the 28-day period (or, where relevant, the conclusion of the meeting) until the end of the time for appointing auditors for the next financial year. If auditors are in office when a private company elects to dispense with the laying of accounts, they continue to hold office until the end of the time for appointing auditors for the next financial year, unless the company in general meeting decides otherwise. Similarly, if auditors are in office when such an election ceases to have effect, they continue to hold office until the conclusion of the next annual general meeting of the company.

1.21 Election to Dispense with the Annual Appointment of Auditors

Under *section 386(1)* of *CA 1985*, a private company can elect to dispense with the obligation to appoint auditors annually. In practice, private companies who elect to dispense with the laying of accounts will usually wish to dispense with the annual appointment of auditors as well, to avoid the need to hold a general meeting of the company each year. Where such an election is in force, the auditors in office are deemed to be reappointed for each succeeding financial year unless:

- the directors have taken advantage of the exemption from audit conferred by *section 249A* or *249AA* of *CA 1985*; or
- a resolution has been passed under *section 393* of *CA 1985* to the effect that the auditors' appointment should be brought to an end.

If the election ceases to have effect, the auditors continue to hold office until the conclusion of the next general meeting of the company at which accounts are laid or the end of the time for appointing auditors for the next financial year, depending on whether *section 385* or *section 385A* of *CA 1985* applies.

1.22   Failure to Appoint Auditors

Under *section 387(1)* of *CA 1985*, if a company fails to appoint or reappoint auditors, or they are not deemed to be reappointed, before the end of the time for appointing auditors, the Secretary of State may appoint a person to fill the vacancy. The legislation requires the company to notify the Secretary of State that this power has become exercisable. This must be done within one week of the end of the time for appointing auditors, and companies and officers who fail to comply with this requirement are liable to a fine.

1.23   Casual Vacancies

Under *section 388(1)* of *CA 1985*, either the directors or the company in general meeting may appoint auditors to fill a casual vacancy in the office of auditor. *Section 388(2)* of *CA 1985* allows any surviving or continuing auditor to continue to act during such a vacancy. For example, if a company has appointed joint auditors and a casual vacancy arises in the office of one of the joint auditors, the other auditors would be able to continue to act during the vacancy.

1.24   *Resolutions in Respect of Casual Vacancies*

Section 388(3) of *CA 1985* requires special notice to be given for any resolution at a general meeting of the company to:

- fill a casual vacancy in the office of auditor; or
- reappoint as auditor a retiring auditor who was appointed by the directors to fill a casual vacancy.

Immediately on receipt of such notice, the company must send a copy to the person proposed to be appointed and, if the casual vacancy was caused by the resignation of an auditor, to the auditor who resigned.

1.25   Change in Eligibility for Audit Exemption

Where a company ceases to be eligible for audit exemption (for example, because it is no longer dormant or because it has exceeded the audit exemption criteria), the directors are allowed to appoint auditors as follows:

- if *section 385* of *CA 1985* applies, at any time before the next meeting of the company at which accounts are laid; or
- if *section 385A* of *CA 1985* applies, at any time before:
  - the end of the period of 28 days beginning with the day on which copies of the annual accounts are next sent to members under *section 238* of *CA 1985*, or

    ○ if notice is given under *section 253(2)* of *CA 1985* requiring the laying of accounts before the company in general meeting, the beginning of that meeting.

Once appointed, the auditors hold office until the conclusion of the meeting or the end of the 28-day period, as appropriate. If the directors do not make an appointment under these sections, auditors may be appointed by the company in general meeting.

1.26   Eligibility for Appointment as Company Auditor

Under *section 25* of the *Companies Act 1989* (*CA 1989*), either an individual or a firm may be appointed as a company auditor, but they will only be eligible for appointment if they are a member of a recognised supervisory body (as defined in *section 30* of *CA 1989*) and eligible for appointment under the rules of that supervisory body. Specific requirements on recognised supervisory bodies are set out in *Schedule 11* to *CA 1989*. The supervisory bodies currently recognised in relation to the appointment of company auditors are:

* Institute of Chartered Accountants in England and Wales;
* Institute of Chartered Accountants of Scotland;
* Institute of Chartered Accountants in Ireland;
* Association of Chartered Certified Accountants;
* Association of Authorised Public Accountants.

Special provisions apply to certain individuals who qualified for appointment as a company auditor prior to 1 January 1990 other than by membership of one of these bodies.

1.27   Auditor Independence

Under *section 27* of *CA 1989*, a person is ineligible for appointment as auditor of a company if he or she is:

* an officer or employee of the company; or
* a partner or employee of such a person, or a partnership of which such a person is a partner; or
* ineligible by virtue of either of the above for appointment as auditor of any associated undertaking of the company – in this context, an associated undertaking is defined as:
  * ○ a parent undertaking of the company,
  * ○ a subsidiary undertaking of the company, or
  * ○ a subsidiary undertaking of any parent undertaking of the company.

The rules therefore encompass the widest group of which the company is a member. For the purpose of this section, an auditor is not regarded as an officer or employee of the company. *Section 744(1)* of *CA 1985* defines an officer of the company as including a director, manager or secretary – an individual or firm therefore cannot act as both auditor to and secretary of the same company.

1.28   *Professional Requirements on Independence*

Historically, professional requirements on auditor independence have been set by the recognised supervisory bodies. However, the various post-Enron reviews in the UK concluded that responsibility for standards on auditor independence should be transferred to an independent body. In December 2004, the Auditing Practices Board (APB) published the following five Ethical Standards for Auditors:

- ES 1 *Integrity, objectivity and independence*
- ES 2 *Financial, business, employment and personal relationships*
- ES 3 *Long associations with the audit engagement*
- ES 4 *Fees, economic dependence, remuneration and evaluation policies, litigation, gifts and hospitality*
- ES 5 *Non-audit service provided to audit clients*

These are available from the APB website at http://www.frc.org.uk/apb/ publications/ethical.cfm and are effective for financial periods beginning on or after 15 December 2004 (and, in certain cases, contractual arrangements accepted after 5 October 2004). They generally impose more stringent requirements than the previous professional guidance in the UK. In developing the standards, the APB has attempted to comply with both the IFAC *Code of Ethics for Professional Accountants* and the EC Recommendation 'Statutory auditors' independence in the EU: A set of fundamental principles' and, where these two documents differ, has adopted the more stringent recommendations. The APB has also imposed its own more stringent requirements where it considers this to be necessary.

1.29   *Ethical Issues and the Smaller Company*

The consultation process for the new Ethical Standards raised a number of concerns that they would prevent smaller practices from providing a mix of audit, accountancy and tax services to the same client. After considering the responses to the consultation, the APB concluded that the principles set out in the standards should be maintained for all audits, but issued a further standard allowing limited exemptions in the case of smaller entities. Auditors taking advantage of the reliefs offered by the Ethical Standard 'Provisions Available for Small Entities' (PASE) must make this fact clear in their audit report. The reliefs offered include allowing the audit firm to provide additional non-audit services to an audit client in specific circumstances and allowing the firm to continue as auditors where a former partner in the firm joins an audit client as a director or key manager. The need for additional safeguards must be properly considered and actioned in each situation where the reliefs are applied. A major problem with the reliefs currently offered is that they apply only to companies that come within the *CA 1985* definition of a small company, and to equivalent entities in specialised sectors. Consequently, most of these entities are already exempt from the statutory audit requirement. The practical concerns for accountancy practitioners and their clients relate mainly to companies that

Audit

are small, owner-managed businesses but still require an annual audit, and no exemptions are currently available in these cases.

1.30   *Annual Disclosures on Independence*

The auditors of listed companies are required by the UK and Ireland version of International Standard on Auditing 260 (ISA 260) 'Communication of audit matters with those charged with governance' to disclose at least annually in writing to the audit committee all relationships between the auditor firm (and its related entities) and the client (and its related entities) that may reasonably be thought to affect the independence of the audit firm and the objectivity of the audit team, together with the related safeguards that are in place. The auditors must also confirm in writing to the audit committee each year:

- that, in their professional judgement, the audit firm is independent within the meaning of regulatory and professional requirements and that the objectivity of the audit team is not impaired;
- that the firm has complied with the APB's Ethical Standards; and
- the total amount of fees charged to the client and its affiliates by the auditor and its network firms, analysed into appropriate categories and with separate disclosure of any future services that have been contracted or for which a written proposal has been submitted.

Any concerns over independence and objectivity that are raised in these disclosures should also be discussed with the audit committee. As part of its series of guidance booklets for non-executive directors serving on an audit committee, the Institute of Chartered Accountants in England and Wales (ICAEW) published *Reviewing Auditor Independence* in November 2003. This is available free of charge from the ICAEW website at www.icaew.co.uk.

1.31   *Post-Enron Developments*

Auditor independence was also considered in detail by the DTI as part of the post-Enron review. The report of the Co-ordinating Group on Audit and Accounting Issues (CGAAI) published in January 2003 made the following points:

- UK requirements should continue to be based on principles rather than detailed, prescriptive rules but there need to be tougher and clearer safeguards, particularly on the provision of non-audit services to an audit client.
- Audit firms should be provided with improved guidance on threats arising from economic dependence on a single audit client (which can arise at the level of the firm as a whole, an individual office or an individual partner).
- For periods starting on or after 1 January 2003, audit firms with listed and other public interest clients should voluntarily publish an annual report including whole firm financial information, details of their organisational structure and reward systems, information on how quality is achieved and monitored, and their policies and procedures for managing threats to their independence.

- Audit firms with listed and public interest clients should disclose in that annual report any fees representing more than 5 per cent of total fees and should also ensure that the audit committee or board of the relevant audit client is aware of their potential economic dependency on the appointment.
- The responsibility for setting standards on independence should be transferred from the regulatory bodies to an independent body.
- The unit responsible for monitoring the performance of audit firms with listed clients should continue to develop inspection themes (such as auditor independence) and should publish annual information on how it monitors the independence requirements and aggregate information on the effectiveness of the management of such matters by the major audit firms.

The review decided against the mandatory rotation of audit firms on the grounds that this may have a negative impact on audit quality and effectiveness, particularly in the early years of an audit appointment, would create significant additional costs, especially in terms of management time and has had no strong positive impact in countries where it has been introduced. The review group concluded that there were sensible and effective alternatives to mandatory rotation. These include giving the audit committee specific responsibility for periodic consideration of whether a change of external auditors is needed and professional requirements on the rotation of key audit partners on a regular basis.

1.32   *Provision of Non-Audit Services*

There has been considerable debate in recent years over whether auditor independence is impaired by the provision of additional services (such as taxation services and consultancy advice) to audit clients and the Combined Code now recommends that audit committees should keep the nature and extent of any additional services under review. APB Ethical Standard ES 5 deals in detail with the provision of non-audit services to an audit client and sets out comprehensive guidance on what is and is not acceptable in terms of the provision of the following services:

- internal audit;
- the design and implementation of IT systems;
- valuation and actuarial valuation services;
- taxation;
- litigation support and other legal work;
- corporate finance and other transaction related services; and
- accounting assistance.

The *Companies (Audit, Investigations and Community Enterprise) Act 2004* also introduced new provisions on the disclosure of other services provided by the auditors and the related remuneration received by them, and new disclosure requirements under these provisions were introduced for accounting periods beginning on or after 1 October 2005 (see **1.99** below). The main reason given for the changes was that the provision of non-audit services to an audit client could undermine the auditors' independence, and that shareholders and others need to be given sufficient and appropriate information to be able to assess this potential threat and to make relevant comparisons between companies. Although many companies were already giving more than the previous statutory minimum disclosure, there were continuing concerns that a voluntary approach to disclosure was resulting in a lack of comparability.

1.33   Rotation of Audit Partners

APB Ethical Standard ES 33 sets out the latest requirements on the rotation of audit partners. Generally, firms which audit listed companies are expected to have policies and procedures to ensure that:

- no individual acts as audit engagement partner or independent partner for such an engagement for a continuous period of more than five years;
- where the independent partner becomes the audit engagement partner, the combined period of service in those positions does not exceed five years;
- an audit engagement partner or independent partner who has acted in that role, or in a combination of the roles, for a period of five years (either continuously or in aggregate) does not hold any further position of responsibility in relation to the audit until a further period of five years has elapsed;
- no one acts as the key audit partner for a continuous period of more than seven consecutive years;
- where a key audit partner becomes the audit engagement partner, the combined period of service in these roles does not exceed seven years; and
- an individual who has acted as a key audit partner for a period of seven years (either continuously or in aggregate) does not hold any further position of responsibility in relation to the audit until a further period of two years has elapsed.

Similar rotation requirements may also need to be applied to certain other cases (eg audits of other public interest entities). ES 3 generally applies for accounting periods beginning on or after 15 December 2004 but a limited degree of flexibility is permitted for financial periods beginning on or before 15 December 2006 where rotation might otherwise impair the quality of the audit. The guidance also allows for some flexibility in situations where partner continuity is particularly important (eg where the business is undergoing significant management changes or is involved in a takeover). Audit firms are expected to have policies and procedures to monitor the length of time that individuals serve in a senior role on any audit engagement that is not subject to the above rotation requirements, and ES 3 notes that serving as an audit engagement partner for a continuous period of more than 10 years may lead a reasonable and informed third party to conclude that the firm's independence is impaired. Although continuity of audit partner and audit staff can be helpful, companies should therefore expect their auditors to plan for changes over time.

1.34   *Regulation of Auditors*

Although the supervision and qualification of company auditors is governed by a statutory framework, the professional accountancy bodies, as recognised supervisory bodies, are responsible for the training, qualification, authorisation and monitoring of registered auditors, and for dealing with complaints and disciplinary matters. Certain changes to the regulatory framework were made as a result of the UK post-Enron reviews, although the stated intention was to preserve the principles of the existing arrangements, which were generally considered to have worked well in practice. However, certain new conditions of recognition have been imposed on the recognised supervisory bodies, including:

- having arrangements for ethical standards on integrity and independence to be set by an independent body;
- participation in a demonstrably independent audit inspection process for listed companies and other public interest entities; and
- participation in a demonstrably independent disciplinary process for serious public interest cases.

Provisions incorporating these changes were included in the *Companies (Audit, Investigations and Community Enterprise) Act 2004* and came into effect on 6 April 2005. Also, until recently the DTI has been responsible for monitoring the activities of the recognised supervisory bodies but this role has now been taken on by the Professional Oversight Board (POB), a subsidiary of the Financial Reporting Council. As a result, POB is now responsible for:

- independent oversight of the regulation of the auditing profession by the recognised supervisory bodies;
- monitoring the quality of the auditing function in relation to economically significant entities; and
- independent oversight of the regulation of the accountancy profession by the professional accountancy bodies.

1.35   Action when Auditor becomes Ineligible for Appointment

If an auditor becomes ineligible for appointment during his term of office, *section 28* of *CA 1989* requires him to vacate the office immediately and give written notice to the company that he has vacated the office for this reason. Any auditor who continues to act in contravention of this section, or who fails to give written notice that he has vacated the office of auditor, is guilty of an offence and liable to penalties, unless he can demonstrate that he did not know and had no reason to believe that he was or had become ineligible for appointment. The requirements of *section 394(1)* of *CA 1985* (see **1.49** below) apply when the auditor vacates office as a result of ineligibility.

1.36 Power of the Secretary of State to Require a Second Audit

Under *section 29* of *CA 1989*, where a person appointed as auditor of a company was ineligible for appointment for any part of the period during which the audit was conducted, the Secretary of State can require the company to engage the services of someone who is eligible for appointment as auditor to:

* audit the relevant accounts again; or
* review the original audit and report on whether a second audit is required – this report must give reasons to support the conclusion reached.

The company must comply with the Secretary of State's direction within 21 days of its being given and, where the second option is used, the company must send a copy of the report to the Registrar of Companies within 21 days of receiving it. If the report recommends a second audit, the company must immediately take the necessary steps to arrange this. A company that fails to comply with these requirements is guilty of an offence and liable to a fine. However, if a person has accepted appointment as auditor or continued to act as auditor when he knew he was ineligible, the company may recover from him any costs incurred in complying with *section 29* of *CA 1989*.

1.37 Changes in External Audit Appointments

At a Glance

* It is normal practice for companies to review their external audit arrangements on a regular basis.
* Auditors may resign from office by depositing a written notice at the company's registered office or can cease to hold office by not seeking reappointment.
* Auditors can be removed from office by an ordinary resolution with special notice, or by the company choosing not to reappoint them once their term of office has expired.
* Auditors who have resigned, been removed or not been reappointed are given certain rights to make the members of the company aware of any circumstances connected with their resignation or removal.
* Special provisions apply in the case of a private company which has elected to dispense with the annual appointment of auditors.
* Auditors who cease to hold office must make a formal statement of any circumstances that they consider should be brought to the attention of the members or creditors of the company, or a statement that there are no such circumstances.
* Professional standards require the new auditor to communicate directly with the outgoing auditor before accepting appointment.

1.38   Regular Review of Audit Arrangements

Changes in audit appointments may come about when auditors resign, do not seek reappointment or are not reappointed by the company because they wish to appoint new auditors. Broadly similar rules apply under *CA 1985* whatever the reason for the change. It is normal practice for companies to review their audit arrangements on a regular basis. This may be particularly important as a business develops and expands and its overall needs change. Issues to be considered might include the following:

- Do the auditors have the appropriate degree of industry knowledge and experience?
- Is the independence of the auditors still assured?
- Can the auditors provide the necessary geographical coverage?
- How effective has the audit service been in recent years?
- How well do the auditors communicate with company management on significant business issues and any material weaknesses identified in the systems of internal control?
- Does the audit provide value for money?
- Are the auditors able to provide the full range of services that the company requires?

From time to time, the company may wish to invite other firms to submit a proposal and fee quote for undertaking the audit. This may result from a positive decision to appoint new auditors (for instance, if the company is not satisfied with the audit service it is currently receiving, or if expansion of the business means that the current auditors are no longer able to provide the level of service that the company requires) or it may be done simply to confirm that the company is receiving value for money under its present arrangements. The process can involve a considerable amount of management time and will therefore not usually be undertaken more regularly than once every three to five years.

As explained below, *CA 1985* already requires specific disclosures to be made whenever an auditor ceases to hold office. The draft Company Law Reform Bill published in May 2006 proposes certain additional notification requirements that will apply to all listed companies and other public-interest entities, irrespective of why the auditor ceases to hold office, and in any other case where an auditor ceases to hold office before the end of his term of office. The draft Bill also includes a provision to enable the members of a quoted company to require publication on the company's website of a statement setting out any matter that they propose to raise at the next accounts meeting in relation to the audit of the company's accounts or to any circumstances connected with the auditor ceasing to hold office since the previous accounts meeting.

1.39   Resignation of Auditors

Under *section 392* of *CA 1985*, auditors may resign from office by depositing a written notice to that effect at the company's registered office. However, this notice is not valid unless it is accompanied by a statement of any circumstances connected with their resignation which they consider should be brought to the attention of the members or creditors of the company, or a statement that there are no such circumstances (see **1.49–1.51** below). Provided the relevant conditions are met, the auditors' resignation is effective from the date on which the notice is deposited or from any later date specified in the notice. The company is required to send a copy of the notice to the Registrar of Companies within 14 days of its being deposited at the registered office. Failure to comply with this requirement may result in a fine.

1.40   *Rights of Resigning Auditors*

Where the auditors' notice of resignation is accompanied by a statement of circumstances connected with their resignation which they consider should be brought to the attention of the members or creditors of the company, the auditors are given certain rights by *section 392A* of *CA 1985*. The auditors may:

- deposit with the notice a signed requisition calling on the directors to convene an extraordinary general meeting of the company to receive and consider any explanations of the circumstances connected with their resignation that the auditors wish to place before the meeting; and/or
- request the company to circulate to its members a written statement of reasonable length on the circumstances connected with their resignation – the auditors may request that this statement be circulated before a meeting convened by the directors at the auditors' request (as explained above), or before any general meeting at which their term of office would otherwise have expired or at which it is proposed to fill the vacancy caused by their resignation.

The statement referred to here is not the one that the auditors are required to issue along with the notice of their resignation, but in practice it is likely to be based on this and to cover the same points. The auditors are also entitled to receive notice of, and copies of all communications relating to, any of the meetings referred to above, and are entitled to attend the meeting and be heard on any part of the business that concerns them as former auditors.

1.41   *Obligations of the Company and its Directors*

Where the auditors deposit a notice requesting the directors to convene an extraordinary general meeting as explained above, the directors are required to act on the notice within 21 days from the date of its deposit, and to convene a meeting on a date not more than 28 days from the date of the notice convening it. Every director who fails to take all reasonable steps to comply with these requirements is guilty of an offence and liable to a fine. Where the auditors request the circulation of a statement on the circumstances connected with their resignation, the company must:

- state in the notice of the meeting that such a statement has been made; and
- send a copy of the statement to every member of the company to whom the notice of the meeting has been, or is being, sent.

If the auditors' statement is received too late for the company to comply with these requirements, or if the company simply fails to comply with them, the auditors can require their statement to be read out at the meeting. This is without prejudice to the auditors' right to speak at the meeting on any part of the business that concerns them as former auditors. Special provisions allow the statement not to be sent out or read out where the court is satisfied that the rights conferred by *section 392* of *CA 1985* are being abused.

1.42   Auditors Not Seeking Reappointment

In most cases, the auditors' term of office will expire automatically at the conclusion of the general meeting at which accounts are laid or, in the case of a private company that has elected to dispense with the laying of accounts, at the end of the time for appointing auditors. Auditors who have completed the annual audit and do not seek reappointment for a further term can therefore cease to hold office without resigning. However, auditors who do not seek reappointment are still required to make a statement of any circumstances connected with their decision that they consider should be brought to the attention of the members or creditors of the company, or a statement that there are no such circumstances (see **1.49–1.51** below).

1.43   Removal of Auditors During Term of Office

Under *section 391* of *CA 1985*, auditors may be removed from office by an ordinary resolution of the company in general meeting. This applies regardless of any agreement between the auditors and the company. However, special notice must be given for any resolution to remove auditors before their term of office has expired. Where such a resolution is passed, the company must give notice to the Registrar in the prescribed form (Form 391) within 14 days. Auditors who are removed from office are still required to make a statement of any circumstances connected with their ceasing to hold office that they consider should be brought to the attention of the members or creditors of the company, or a statement that there are no such circumstances (see **1.49–1.51** below).

1.44   Failure to Reappoint Retiring Auditors

As noted above, the auditors' term of office will usually expire at the conclusion of the general meeting at which accounts are laid or, in the case of a private company that has elected to dispense with the laying of accounts, at the end of the time for appointing auditors. The company can therefore effectively remove the auditors by choosing not to reappoint them once their term of office has expired. However, as with the removal of auditors during their term of office, *CA 1985* requires special notice to be given of any resolution to appoint as auditors someone other than the retiring auditors. Also, auditors who are not reappointed at the end of their term of office are still required to make a statement of any circumstances connected with their ceasing to hold office that they consider should be brought to the attention of the members or creditors of the company, or a statement that there are no such circumstances (see **1.49–1.51** below). If the company passes a written resolution to appoint as auditors someone other than the retiring auditors, a copy of that resolution must be sent immediately to the outgoing auditors.

1.45   Rights of Auditors Who Have Been Removed or Not Reappointed

The rights of auditors who are removed from office or not reappointed are set out in *section 391A* of *CA 1985*. As explained above, special notice is required of any resolution to remove auditors or to appoint a person other than the retiring auditor. When a company receives this notice (which, under *section 379* of *CA 1985* must be given at least 28 days before the meeting at which the resolution is to be moved), a copy must be sent immediately to the auditors to be removed, or to the retiring auditors and the person proposed for appointment. The auditors who are to be removed, or not reappointed, may make written representations of a reasonable length and request the company to notify these to the members. Auditors who are to be removed are also entitled to receive notice of, and copies of all communications relating to, any general meeting at which their term of office would otherwise have expired or at which it is proposed to fill the vacancy caused by their removal, and are entitled to attend the meeting and be heard on any part of the business that concerns them as former auditors. The *Companies Act 1985* also specifically notes that nothing in the provisions of *section 391* of *CA 1985* is to be taken as depriving auditors who are removed from office of any compensation or damages that might be payable in connection with the termination of their appointment as auditors, or any other appointment that terminates at the same time.

1.46   *Obligations of the Company and its Directors*

Where auditors who are to be removed or not reappointed make written representations and request the company to notify these to the members, the company must:

- state in the notice of the meeting the fact that such representations have been made; and
- send a copy of the representations to every member of the company to whom the notice of the meeting has been, or is being, sent.

If the auditors' representations are received too late for the company to comply with these requirements, or if the company simply fails to comply with them, the auditors can require the representations to be read out at the meeting. This is without prejudice to the auditors' right to speak at the meeting on any part of the business that concerns them as former auditors. Special provisions allow the statement not to be sent out or read out where the court is satisfied that the rights conferred by *section 391A* of *CA 1985* are being abused.

1.47   *Termination of Appointment Where Auditors are Not Appointed Annually*

Where an election is in force under *section 386* of *CA 1985* to dispense with the annual appointment of auditors, the auditors in office are deemed to be automatically reappointed each year. Under *section 393(1)* of *CA 1985*, any member of the company can deposit a written notice at the company's registered office proposing that the appointment of the auditors be brought to an end – however, no member may deposit more than one such notice in any financial year. If a notice is deposited under this section, the directors are required to:

* convene a general meeting of the company for a date not more than 28 days after the date on which notice was given; and
* propose at that meeting a resolution in a form that enables the company to decide whether the auditors' appointment should be brought to an end.

If the company decides to end the appointment, the auditors are not deemed to be reappointed when they next would have been under the normal rules. If the notice is deposited in the period of 14 days beginning with the day on which the company's annual accounts are sent to the members, any deemed reappointment which has already taken place for the financial year following the year to which the accounts relate ceases to have effect. In other circumstances, the auditors continue in office until the end of the time for appointing auditors under the normal rules. The rights and duties of auditors in these circumstances are the same as in any other situation where a retiring auditor is not reappointed (see **1.45** above). Under *section 381D* of *CA 1985*, if the company passes a written resolution to bring the auditors' appointment to an end, a copy of that resolution must be sent immediately to the outgoing auditor. The provisions of *section 393* of *CA 1985* are not affected by any other agreement between the company and the auditors, and the auditors are not entitled to any compensation or damages as a result of their appointment being terminated under this section.

1.48   *Additional Rights of Member Who Deposited Notice*

Under *section 393(4)* and *(5)* of *CA 1985*, if within 14 days from the date of the deposit of the notice the directors have not taken action to convene a meeting, the member (or members) who deposited the notice may convene the meeting, provided that:

* the meeting is held within three months of the date of the deposit of the notice; and
* it is convened in the same manner (as far as possible) as the directors are required to convene meetings.

Reasonable expenses incurred by the member in convening the meeting are to be reimbursed by the company, and the company should then recover them out of the fees or remuneration payable to any of the directors who were in default.

1.49 Statement Required from Auditors Ceasing to Hold Office

Section 394(1) of *CA 1985* requires any auditors who cease to hold office to deposit at the company's registered office:

- a statement of any circumstances connected with their ceasing to hold office that they consider should be brought to the attention of the members or creditors of the company; or
- a statement that there are no such circumstances.

This statement is required in every situation where auditors cease to hold office, including resignation, not seeking reappointment, removal from office, not being reappointed when their term of office expires or becoming ineligible for appointment. Where the auditors resign, the statement must be deposited along with the notice of resignation. Where the auditors do not seek reappointment, the statement must be deposited not less than 14 days before the end of the time allowed for appointing auditors. In all other cases, the statement must be deposited within 14 days of the date that the auditors cease to hold office.

1.50 *Action Required by the Company*

If the auditors' statement details circumstances connected with their resignation that they consider should be brought to the attention of members and creditors, the company has 14 days in which to:

- send a copy to every person who is entitled to be sent copies of the accounts under *section 238* of *CA 1985*; or
- apply to the court, in which case they must notify the auditors of this application.

If the court is satisfied that the auditors are not using the statement to secure needless publicity, the company must, within 14 days of the date of the court's decision, notify the auditors of that decision and send a copy of the auditors' statement to every person entitled to receive copies of the accounts. If the court considers that the auditors are using the statement to secure needless publicity for defamatory matter, it will direct that the statement need not be sent out and may direct the auditors to meet all or part of the company's costs in making the application. In this case, the company has 14 days in which to send a statement of the effect of the court order to every person entitled to receive a copy of the company's accounts. The company and its officers are liable to a fine for failure to comply with these requirements.

1.51 *Action Required by the Former Auditor*

If the auditors have not received notice of an application to the court 21 days after the day that their statement was deposited with the company, they must send a copy of their statement to the Registrar of Companies within the next seven days (ie within 28 days of the date on which the statement was originally deposited with the company). It is not entirely clear whether this requirement only applies where there are circumstances which the auditors consider need to be brought to the attention of the members and creditors, or whether it applies equally to statements that there are no such circumstances. Auditors are therefore generally advised to send copies of all statements to the Registrar, unless they have been notified of an application to the court. If the company applies to the court and the court decides that the auditor is not using the statement for needless publicity, the auditors must send a copy of their statement to the Registrar within seven days of receiving notice of the court's decision from the company. Auditors who fail to comply with these requirements are liable to a fine, although it is a defence for the auditors to show that they took all reasonable steps and exercised all due diligence to prevent the offence.

1.52   Professional Requirements on a Change of Auditor

Where a company proposes to appoint new auditors, professional standards require the new auditor to communicate directly with the outgoing auditor before accepting appointment. The new audit firm will usually seek written permission from the company to communicate with the outgoing auditor and will ask the company to give written authority to the outgoing audit firm to discuss the matter freely with the proposed new auditor. If this permission is refused, the proposed new auditor will generally not be able to accept nomination or appointment. If an issue of conflicting viewpoints between the company and the existing auditor becomes apparent, the prospective audit firm is required to discuss the conflict with the company and satisfy themselves either that the company's view is one which they can accept as reasonable, or that the company accepts that the new auditor might have to express a contrary opinion (for instance, that the issue might result in a qualified audit report).

1.53   Rights and Duties of External Auditors

At a Glance
* Auditors are entitled to receive notices and communications relating to all general meetings of the company, to attend such meetings and to speak on certain issues.
* Auditors have a statutory right of access at all times to the company's books and records and to information and explanations from the company's officers.
* The auditors of a parent company also have a statutory right to require information and explanations from a subsidiary undertaking and its auditors.
* Auditors have a right to receive copies of any written resolutions that are proposed by a private company.

* Auditors have a duty to report to members on all annual accounts of the company and to consider whether the directors' report is consistent with the accounts.
* Auditors are required to report by exception on certain aspects of the accounting records and if they have not received all the information and explanations they require.
* Auditors have a duty to include in their report on the accounts any undisclosed information on directors' remuneration and benefits.
* If the directors incorrectly claim exemption from the preparation of group accounts, the auditors have a duty to state this fact in their report.
* In highly regulated sectors, the auditors may also have a duty to report directly to the regulator.
* Under the *Proceeds of Crime Act 2002* and the *Money Laundering Regulations 2003* auditors have a duty to report knowledge or suspicions of money laundering.

1.54   Rights in Respect of General Meetings

Under *section 390(1)* of *CA 1985*, the auditors are entitled to receive all notices of, and other communications relating to, any general meeting of the company which a member of the company is entitled to receive. They are also entitled to attend any general meeting of the company and to be heard at any meeting they attend on any part of the business which concerns them as auditors. Specific provisions also apply in the case of auditors who have resigned, or who have been removed from office or are not to be reappointed (see **1.37–1.51** above).

1.55   Rights to Information

The auditors' statutory rights to information and explanations are set out in *section 389A* of *CA 1985*. The provisions were updated by the *Companies (Audit, Investigations and Community Enterprise) Act 2004*, with the changes coming into effect for accounting periods beginning on or after 6 April 2005. *Section 389A(1)* grants the auditors a right of access at all times to the company's books, accounts and vouchers and creates a statutory duty for the following persons to respond to enquiries by the auditors:

* any officer or employee of the company;
* any person accountable for the company's books, accounts or vouchers;
* any subsidiary incorporated in Great Britain, together with its officers, employees, auditors and any persons accountable for its books, accounts or vouchers; and
* any persons who fell within one or more of the above categories at the time to which the auditors' enquiries relate.

It is an offence for any of the above to fail to respond, or to delay responding, to the auditors' enquiries. It is also an offence for them to knowingly or recklessly make an oral or written statement to the auditors that is misleading, false or deceptive in any material respect. Furthermore, where the company's accounts are subject to audit, *section 234ZA* of *CA 1985* requires the directors' report to include a formal statement that, at the date on which the report is approved, no director has withheld information from the auditors which he or she knows, or ought to know, would be relevant to the audit. Information is covered by this requirement if:

- a director is aware of the information, or it would be reasonable for him or her to obtain it by making enquiries;
- the director knows, or ought to know, that the auditors are not aware of it; and
- the director knows, or ought to know, that the information is relevant to the audit.

As with similar company law provisions, whether a director ought to know a matter is to be assessed on the basis of whether it would be known by a reasonably diligent person with the knowledge, skill and experience expected of a person carrying out the functions of a director and also the specific knowledge, skill and experience that the individual director has. This disclosure requirement applies for accounting periods beginning on or after 1 April 2005 and ending on or after 6 April 2005.

1.56   *Rights in Relation to Overseas or Unincorporated Subsidiary Undertakings*

The auditors' rights in relation to subsidiaries incorporated in Great Britain are covered by *section 389A(1)* as explained above. In the case of a subsidiary undertaking that is not a body corporate incorporated in Great Britain (for instance, a subsidiary incorporated overseas or an unincorporated UK entity, such as a partnership), *section 389A(3)* gives the auditor the right to require the parent to obtain from the following persons any information or explanations reasonably needed for the purpose of the audit:

- the undertaking itself;
- any officer, employee or auditor of the undertaking;
- any person accountable for the undertaking's books, accounts or vouchers; and
- any persons who fell within one or more of the above categories at the time to which the auditors' enquiries relate.

The parent has a statutory duty to take all steps reasonably open to it to obtain the necessary information or explanations, and it is an offence for the company or its officers to fail to comply with the auditors' request.

1.57   Rights in Relation to Written Resolutions

Private companies are permitted by *section 381A* of *CA 1985* to act by means of a written resolution rather than by a resolution of the company in general meeting or by a resolution of a meeting of any class of members of the company. Under *section 381B* of *CA 1985*, a director or secretary of the company who knows that it is proposed to seek agreement by means of a written resolution, and who knows the terms of the resolution, has a duty to arrange for a copy of the resolution to be sent to the auditors at or before the time that it is sent to the members for signature. There are penalties for failure to comply with this requirement, although is it a defence to demonstrate that it was not practicable to comply or that there were reasonable grounds to believe that the auditors had been informed of the proposed resolution. Failure to comply with the requirement does not invalidate the resolution. The auditors also have the right to receive all communications relating to a written resolution that must be supplied to a member of the company under *Schedule 15A* to *CA 1985*. The recent company law review recommended simplification of the procedures for written resolutions and the draft Company Law Reform Bill published in May 2006 no longer includes a requirement for the directors to send a copy of a proposed written resolution to the auditors. However, the clauses on the duties and rights of auditors retain the auditors' right to receive all communications relating to a written resolution that are supplied to members of the company.

1.58   Duty to Report on the Annual Accounts

The auditors are required by *section 235(1)* of *CA 1985* to report to the members on all annual accounts of the company that are to be laid before the company in general meeting during their term of office. This is considered in more detail below (see **1.65–1.84** below). *Section 235(3)* of *CA 1985* also requires the auditors to state in their report whether the information given in the directors' report is consistent with the accounts for that financial year (see **1.78** below).

1.59   Duties in Respect of Accounting Records

In carrying out their audit, the auditors have a duty to carry out appropriate investigations to enable them to form an opinion on whether:

- proper accounting records have been kept by the company;
- proper returns adequate for audit purposes have been received from any branches not visited by them; and
- the company's individual accounts are in agreement with the accounting records and returns.

If the auditors are not satisfied on any of these issues, they must state this fact in their report on the annual accounts. If they are satisfied on the above issues, no mention of this needs to be made in their report.

1.60   Duty in Respect of Information and Explanations Not Received

As explained at **1.55** above, the auditors are entitled to receive all the information and explanations that they consider necessary in order to perform the audit. If they are not able to obtain all of the information or explanations that they consider necessary, they are required to state this fact in their report.

1.61 Duty in Respect of Disclosure of Directors' Remuneration and Benefits

If the accounts or, where relevant, the auditable part of the directors' remuneration report do not include all of the required disclosures in respect of directors' emoluments and other benefits, or transactions between the company and its directors or other officers, the auditors have a duty to include a statement of the missing details in their audit report, so far as they are reasonably able to do so. In the case of listed companies, the Financial Services Authority (FSA) also requires the auditors to review certain disclosures in respect of directors' remuneration required by the UK Listing Rules, and to provide details of any missing information in their report, although many of the disclosures required under the Listing Rules now overlap with the *CA 1985* requirements in respect of the directors' remuneration report.

1.62 Duty in Respect of Exemption from Preparing Group Accounts

If the directors have taken advantage of *section 248* of *CA 1985*, which relieves small and medium-sized companies from the requirement to prepare group accounts, but in the opinion of the auditors the company is not entitled to this exemption, the auditors must state this fact in their report on the company's accounts.

1.63 Duty to Report Directly to Regulators

In highly regulated sectors, such as the banking and financial services sectors, auditors may be required to report directly to the regulator on certain matters specified in legislation or by the relevant regulator. They also have a duty to report directly to the regulator information which comes to their attention during the course of their work if there is reasonable cause for them to believe that this information may be of material significance to the regulator in carrying out his functions. Detailed guidance on this duty to report is provided in a separate section of the UK and Ireland version of International Standard on Auditing 250 (ISA 250) *Consideration of Laws and Regulations in an Audit of Financial Statements* (copies can be downloaded from the publications section of the Auditing Practice Board website at http://www.frc.org.uk/apb/publications/).

1.64 Duty to Report Known or Suspected Money Laundering

Under the *Proceeds of Crime Act 2002* and the *Money Laundering Regulations 2003* (which came into effect in March 2004), accountants – and thus auditors – have a duty to report to the Serious Organised Crime Agency (SOCA) knowledge or suspicions of money laundering, which is given a very broad definition encompassing the possession, handling or concealment of the proceeds of any criminal activity. Fraud, tax evasion and the breach of other legislation will potentially come within the reporting requirement (for instance, money saved by failing to comply with health and safety requirements will be deemed to constitute the proceeds of crime) and there is no de minimis limit, so every offence will need to be considered, regardless of the amount involved.

1.65   Statutory Reporting by External Auditors

At a Glance
* Auditors must express an opinion on all annual accounts laid (or sent out) during their term of office.
* Auditors must also express an opinion on whether the directors' report is consistent with the financial statements for the relevant accounting periods.
* The UK and Ireland version of International Standard on Auditing 700 (ISA 700) 'The Auditor's Report on Financial Statements' sets out detailed requirements on the form and content of an audit report.
* The audit report must be dated on the day on which it is actually signed by the auditors.
* Auditors must express a qualified opinion if they disagree with any aspect of the accounts or if the scope of their work has been limited in any way.
* If the accounts disclose a fundamental uncertainty, the auditors must draw attention to this in their report.
* A special report from the auditors must be included in any summary financial statements issued by the company.
* The usual requirements apply to the accounts of a small company (unless it is exempt from audit), but a different auditors' report is required on abbreviated accounts prepared for filing purposes.
* A special auditors' report is also required if the annual accounts or directors' report are revised.
* If their report on the annual accounts is qualified, the auditors must make a written statement on whether the matter is material in determining whether a proposed distribution is permissible under *CA 1985*.
* *CA 1985* requires the auditors to make a formal report in certain other circumstances that may arise from time to time.

1.66   Report on Annual Accounts

The auditors are required to report to the members on all annual accounts of the company that are to be laid before the company in general meeting during their term of office. If the company has elected to dispense with the laying of accounts, the auditors are required to report on all annual accounts sent to the members and others during the auditors' term of office. For accounting periods beginning on or after 1 January 2005, *section 235* of the *CA 1985* specifies that the auditors must state whether, in their opinion:

- the annual accounts have been properly prepared in accordance with *CA 1985* and, where relevant, with the IAS Regulation;
- the accounts give a true and fair view in accordance with the relevant financial reporting framework:
  - ○ in the case of an individual balance sheet, of the state of affairs of the company at the end of the financial period,
  - ○ in the case of an individual profit and loss account, of the profit or loss of the company for the financial year, and
  - ○ in the case of group accounts, of the state of affairs of the undertakings included in the consolidation as a whole, and of the profit or loss of those undertakings for the financial year, so far as concerns the members of the company;
- for accounting periods beginning on or after 1 April 2005, the information given in the directors' report is consistent with the accounts for the relevant financial year; and
- in the case of a quoted company, the auditable part of the directors' remuneration report has been properly prepared in accordance with *CA 1985*.

A parent company that is required to prepare group accounts need not publish its own profit and loss accounts, although it must still prepare one, and the auditors are not required to report on this. The auditors' report must also:

- identify the accounts on which the auditors are reporting and the financial reporting framework under which they have been prepared;
- describe the scope of the audit and identify the auditing standards in accordance with which the audit has been conducted;
- be either qualified or unqualified, and include a reference to any matters to which the auditors wish to draw attention by way of emphasis without qualifying their report.

Most of the above requirements were introduced by the *Companies Act 1985 (International Accounting Standards and Other Accounting Amendments) Regulations 2004 (SI 2004/2947)* and the *Companies Act 1985 (Operating and Financial Review and Directors Report etc.) Regulations 2005 (SI 2005/1011)*. Prior to this, the legislation included similar requirements for the auditors to express an opinion on whether the accounts showed a true and fair view and had been properly prepared in accordance with *CA 1985* and for the auditors of quoted companies to report on certain elements of the directors' remuneration report but, in the case of the directors' report, required the auditors to report only on any inconsistency with the accounts. The legislation did not refer in any way to the financial reporting framework used, the audit scope or the auditing standards adopted.

1.67   *The True and Fair View and IAS Accounts*

Following implementation of the IAS Regulation, which requires listed companies to prepare group accounts in accordance with International Accounting Standards (IASs) and gives most companies the option of adopting IASs in place of UK accounting standards, the Financial Reporting Review Panel (FRRP) and Financial Reporting Council (FRC) have published two documents on the true and fair view in the context of IAS accounts:

- a legal opinion by Freshfields Bruckhaus Deringer on the effect of the IAS Regulation on the requirement for accounts to show a true and fair view – this concludes that, for companies preparing IAS accounts, references to the 'true and fair view' in the legislation are references to the requirement under IASs for accounts to achieve a fair presentation;
- a paper entitled 'The implications of new accounting and auditing standards for the true and fair view and auditors' responsibilities', which concludes that the concept of the true and fair view remains a cornerstone of financial reporting and auditing in the UK and that there has been no substantive change in the objectives of an audit and the nature of auditors' responsibilities.

1.68   *Names of the Auditors*

Every copy of the auditors' report that is laid before the members in general meeting, or otherwise circulated, published or issued, must state the names of the auditors. The company and every officer who fails to comply with this requirement is guilty of an offence and liable to a fine.

1.69   *Signature of the Report*

The auditors' report must be signed and dated by the auditors and the copy of the accounts delivered to the Registrar must carry a manuscript signature on the auditors' report. A new *section 707B* inserted into *CA 1985* by the *Companies Act 1985 (Electronic Communications) Order 2000 (SI 2000/3373)* allows documents to be delivered to the Registrar using electronic communication, provided that delivery is in the form and manner directed by the Registrar, and states that where a signed document is required, it must instead be authenticated in the manner directed by the Registrar. This opens the way for annual accounts and auditors' reports to be delivered to the Registrar electronically in due course, but the detailed procedures for this have not yet been put into place by Companies House.

1.70   *Requirements of Auditing Standards*

For accounting periods beginning on or after 15 December 2004, detailed requirements on the form and content of an auditor's report are set out in the UK and Ireland version of ISA 700 'The auditor's report on financial statements'.

For earlier accounting periods, similar requirements were set out in Statement of Auditing Standards 600 (SAS 600). Under ISA 700, an auditor's report must include the following basic elements:

- a title;
- details of the person(s) to whom the report is addressed;
- an opening or introductory paragraph which:
  - identifies the financial statements that have been audited,
  - explains the respective responsibilities of the entity's management and the auditors in respect of the financial statements;
- a scope paragraph which:
  - refers to the auditing standards in accordance with which the audit has been conducted,
  - describes the work that the auditor has performed;
- an opinion paragraph which:
  - refers to the financial framework used to prepare the financial statements,
  - expresses an opinion on the financial statements;
- the date of the auditor's report;
- the address of the auditors; and
- the signature of the auditors.

Although the ISA includes illustrative wording for audit reports, the APB issued Bulletin 2005/4 *Auditor's Reports on Financial Statements in Great Britain and Northern Ireland* in November 2005 and this sets out the latest examples of auditors' reports on the accounts for use in the UK. These reports reflect the following recent developments:

- the requirement for EU listed companies to prepare group accounts in accordance with International Financial Reporting Standards (IFRSs) for accounting periods beginning on or after 1 January 2005;
- the option for most other companies to adopt IFRSs from the same date;
- recent changes to the requirements of *CA 1985*; and
- the adoption in the UK of International Standards on Auditing (ISAs) for accounting periods beginning on or after 15 December 2004.

However, the illustrative reports in Bulletin 2005/4 do not reflect the auditors' new reporting responsibility in respect of consistency between the accounts and the directors' report. This applies for accounting periods beginning on or after 1 April 2005 and is covered instead in ISA (UK and Ireland) 720 (revised) which was published in April 2006.

1.71   *Financial Framework*

One of the key issues considered in Bulletin 2005/4 is the requirement to refer in the audit report to the financial framework that has been used to prepare the accounts and to state whether the accounts give a true and fair view in accordance with that framework. The example reports originally described the financial reporting framework in the paragraph dealing with the directors' responsibilities in respect of the accounts as:

- 'in accordance with applicable law and with IFRSs as adopted for use in the European Union' where IFRSs have been adopted; and
- 'in accordance with applicable law and with United Kingdom Generally Accepted Accounting Practice' where UK accounting standards have been adopted.

Similar wording was also used in the paragraph setting out the auditors' opinion. However, in December 2005 the APB issued a press release explaining that the Accounting Regulatory Committee of the European Commission had subsequently indicated its support for the expression 'in accordance with IFRSs as adopted by the EU'. There was concern that the wording 'as adopted for use in the EU' may imply that the standards are only for use in the EU which is not necessarily the case. The APB noted that the difference was not regarded as sufficiently significant to warrant revision of Bulletin 2005/4 at this stage, but the EC wording has been added as a footnote to the electronic version of the document and auditors can use it if they wish. A similar illustrative audit opinion is given for small companies adopting the FRSSE, although in this case the auditor's opinion refers to UK GAAP 'applicable to Smaller Entities'.

1.72   *Compliance with Full IFRSs*

Not all current IFRSs have been adopted for use in the EU as yet, but in many cases a company adopting IFRSs will be in a position of complying with both full IFRSs and those adopted by the EU. Where such a company requests the auditor to express a 'true and fair' opinion in relation to full IFRSs, the APB notes a preference for this to be given as a separate opinion to avoid any confusion and to leave intact the opinion that is required by UK company law.

1.73   *Parent Company's Individual Accounts*

Another complexity arises from the fact that a parent company preparing IFRS group accounts may prepare its own accounts in accordance with IFRSs or in accordance with UK GAAP. The illustrative example reports therefore cater for both situations. The guidance notes that, where such a parent company prepares its own accounts in accordance with UK GAAP, it may choose to present these in a separate section of the annual report. In these circumstances, the APB suggests that a separate auditors' report should be provided on each set of accounts. Where this approach is adopted, it is also suggested that the auditors' opinion in respect of the company's corporate governance disclosures is given in the report on the group financial statements, but the opinion on the directors' remuneration report is given in the report on the parent company's financial statements. There may be further complications for the auditor's report where advantage is taken of the exemption in *section 230* of *CA 1985* from publication of the parent company's own profit and loss account and certain related information.

1.74   *'Bannerman' Wording*

Following a judgement in the Scottish Court of Sessions (*Royal Bank of Scotland v Bannerman Johnstone Maclay and others*), the professional account-ancy bodies issued a recommendation to their members that the following add-itional paragraph should be included in an auditor's report as protection against potential exposure to claims by third parties:

> 'This report is made solely to the company's members, as a body, in accordance with sec-tion 235 of the Companies Act 1985. Our audit work has been undertaken so that we might state to the company's members those matters we are required to state to them in an audi-tor's report and for no other purpose. To the fullest extent permitted by law, we do not accept or assume responsibility to anyone other than the company and the company's members as a body for our audit work, for this report, or for the opinions we have formed.'

It has therefore become normal practice for this to be included in all auditors' reports.

1.75   *Date of Auditors' Report*

ISA (UK and Ireland) 700 (see **1.70** above) also sets out detailed requirements on the dating and signature of the audit report. Auditors should not sign their report until the financial statements and annual report have been approved by the directors, and the date on the audit report should be the date on which the auditors physically sign to express their opinion on the financial statements.

1.76   *Qualified Opinions, Adverse Opinions and Disclaimers*

Under ISA (UK and Ireland) 700 (see **1.70** above), auditors are required to express a qualified opinion when:

- they disagree with the treatment or disclosure of an item in the financial state-ments; or
- there has been a limitation on the scope of their work (eg where there is inad-equate evidence to support a figure in the accounts); and
- in the auditors' opinion, the effect is, or may be, material to the financial statements.

An adverse opinion must be issued when the effect of a disagreement is so material that the auditors conclude that the financial statements are seriously misleading or incomplete, and a disclaimer of opinion must be expressed when the possible effect of a limitation in scope is so material that the auditors are unable to express an opinion on the financial statements.

1.77   *Significant Uncertainty*

ISA (UK and Ireland) 700 (see **1.70** above) also considers the situation of a signifi-cant uncertainty which is adequately accounted for and disclosed in the financial statements (for instance, where the outcome of a significant litigation issue is still unclear, or the negotiation of bank facilities is still in progress). In these circumstances the auditors should consider adding an explanatory paragraph to their report, drawing attention to the uncertainty but making clear that their opinion is not qualified in this respect. The standard specifically requires such a paragraph to be added to the auditor's report where the significant uncertainty involves a going concern problem.

1.78   Directors' Report

For accounting periods beginning on or after 1 April 2005, there is a specific requirement for the auditors' report to include a separate opinion on whether or not the directors' report is consistent with the accounts. As a result, the APB has published a revised version of International Standard on Auditing (UK and Ireland) 720 which applies for accounting periods beginning on or after 1 April 2005 and ending on or after 31 March 2006. The material in the original version of the standard now forms Section A, entitled 'Other Information in Documents Containing Audited Financial Statements' whilst a new Section B, entitled 'The Auditor's Statutory Reporting Responsibility in Relation to Directors' Reports' sets out requirements on this new reporting requirement. Auditors are required to read the information given in the directors' report, including any that is incorporated by means of a cross-reference, and consider its consistency with the accounts. They are also required to agree the details to their working papers or to the entity's accounting records. Where financial information in the directors' report has been prepared on a different basis to that used in the accounts, the auditors must consider whether this fact has been adequately disclosed and should check the reconciliation of the information to that given in the accounts. Inconsistencies between the directors' report and accounts are defined as including:

- differences between amounts or narrative appearing in the two documents;
- differences in the bases of preparation of related items which have not been adequately disclosed; and
- contradictions between figures in the accounts and narrative explanations of those figures in the directors' report.

Any inconsistencies should generally be resolved through discussion and appropriate amendments to the disclosures. Where the auditor has unresolved concerns relating to disclosures in the directors' report, any material inconsistencies should be described in the auditors' report and reflected in the auditors' opinion on the directors' report.

1.79   Summary Financial Statements

Section 251 of *CA 1985* enables companies to issue summary financial statements to their members, rather than copies of the full accounts, provided that certain conditions are properly observed (see **11 FINANCIAL REPORTING**). Summary financial statements must be derived from the annual accounts and other reports, and must comply with the requirements of *section 251* of *CA 1985* as regards their form and content. Summary financial statements are specifically required to include:

- an opinion from the auditors on whether the summary financial statements are consistent with the full accounts and (in the case of a quoted company) with the directors' remuneration report and, where the statement includes information derived from the directors' report, with that report or review;
- an opinion from the auditors on whether the statement complies with *section 251* of *CA 1985* and any regulations made under that section;
- a statement on whether the auditors' report on the full accounts and, where relevant, the auditable part of the directors' remuneration report was qualified or unqualified – if it was qualified, the report must be set out in full, together with any additional information needed to understand the qualification (eg a particular note to the accounts);
- a statement on whether the auditors' report on the full accounts contained a statement under *section 237(2)* of *CA 1985* (inadequate accounting records or returns, or accounts not in agreement with the accounting records or returns) or under *section 237(3)* of *CA 1985* (failure to obtain all information and explanations the auditors considered necessary) – if such a statement was included, the auditors' report on the full accounts must be set out in the summary financial statements.
- for accounting periods beginning on or after 1 April 2005, a statement on whether the auditors' opinion on consistency between the directors' report and the accounts was qualified or unqualified – where the opinion was qualified, it must be set out in full, together with any additional material needed for the qualification to be understood.

Guidance on the procedures that the auditors should undertake, is set out in APB Bulletin 1999/6 *The Auditors' Statement on the Summary Financial Statement* and the latest example of an auditors' report on summary financial statements is set out in APB Bulletin 2002/2 *The United Kingdom Directors' Remuneration Report Regulations 2002* (copies can be downloaded from the publications section of the Auditing Practice Board website at http://www.frc. org.uk/apb/publications/). The APB is currently consulting on whether Bulletin 1999/6 should be updated to take account of the recent legislative changes in respect of summary financial statements or whether a UK and Ireland version of ISA 800 'The Independent Auditor's Report on Summary Audited Financial Statements' should be adopted in its place.

1.80   Shorter Form Accounts

Certain companies that qualify as small are permitted under *section 246* of *CA 1985* to prepare annual accounts in accordance with *Schedule 8* to *CA 1985* rather than *Schedule 4* (see **3.51 COMPANY LAW**). This essentially condenses some of the balance sheet information and detailed disclosures that would otherwise need to be given in the accounts. Accounts prepared under these provisions are usually referred to as 'shorter form accounts'. Shorter form accounts are still required to show a true and fair view, even though they are not required to give all of the disclosures set out for other companies. Auditors are therefore still required to express an opinion on whether the shorter form accounts show a true and fair view, unless the company is eligible for audit exemption (see **1.1–1.17** above).

1.81   Abbreviated Accounts

Companies that qualify as small or medium-sized are permitted by *sections 246* and *246A* of *CA 1985* to deliver abbreviated accounts to the Registrar (see **3.56** and **3.68 COMPANY LAW**). Abbreviated accounts are not required to show a true and fair view and in practice will not do so. Where a company takes advantage of the option to file abbreviated accounts, the accounts must be accompanied by a special report from the auditors, unless the company is exempt from an audit (see **1.1–1.17** above). The auditors are required to state that, in their opinion:

- the company is entitled to deliver to the Registrar abbreviated accounts prepared in accordance with *section 246(5)* or *246A(3)* of *CA 1985*; and
- the abbreviated accounts are properly prepared in accordance with the relevant section.

The latest guidance on reporting on abbreviated accounts, together with example reports, is set out in APB Bulletin 2006/3 *The Special Auditors' Report on Abbreviated Accounts in the United Kingdom* (copies can be downloaded from the publications section of the Auditing Practice Board website at http://www.frc.org.uk/apb/publications/). This includes guidance on the dating and signature of the report. The legislation does not allow for the auditors' special report on abbreviated accounts to be qualified, so if the auditors are not able to provide a positive opinion on the two matters set out in the legislation, the company will not be able to file abbreviated accounts.

1.82   *Impact of Qualified Audit Report on the Full Accounts*

The fact that the auditors' report on the full accounts is qualified does not in itself affect the company's ability to file abbreviated accounts, but the auditors will need to consider whether the subject of the qualification could affect the company's status as a small or medium-sized company, in which case they may not be able to give a positive opinion on the company's entitlement to deliver abbreviated accounts. If the company is still entitled to file abbreviated accounts, *section 237B(3)* of *CA 1985* sets out the following requirements:

- the special auditor's report on the abbreviated accounts must include the full text of the qualified audit report on the full accounts, together with any further material needed to understand the qualification; and

- if the auditors' report on the full accounts contained a statement under *section 237(2)* of *CA 1985* (inadequate accounting records or returns, or accounts not in agreement with the accounting records or returns) or under *section 237(3)* of *CA 1985* (failure to obtain all information and explanations the auditors' considered necessary), the special auditors' report on the abbreviated accounts must set out that statement in full.

The legislation does not cover the situation where the auditors' report on the full accounts refers to a significant uncertainty, but APB Bulletin 2006/3 (see **1.81** above) notes that the details set out in the legislation are minimum disclosure requirements that do not preclude the inclusion in the report of other information that the auditor considers important for a proper understanding of the report. In particular, the APB considers it necessary for the auditor to include any emphasis of matter paragraph from the full audit report in the special report, together with any further material needed to understand this. The Bulletin also includes guidance on the inclusion of an 'other matter' paragraph in the auditors' report (for instance, the auditors' opinion on consistency between the directors' report and the financial statements) and whether this should be repeated in the special report.

1.83   Revised Annual Accounts

Where revised annual accounts are issued under *section 245* or *245A* of *CA 1985* and the *Companies (Revision of Defective Accounts and Report) Regulations 1990* (*SI 1990/2570* as amended by subsequent SIs), the auditors are required to state whether, in their opinion:

- the revised accounts have been properly prepared in accordance with the provisions of *CA 1985* as they have effect under the Regulations;
- a true and fair view, seen as at the date on which the original annual accounts were approved, is given by the revised accounts with respect to the matters set out in *section 235(2)* of *CA 1985* (see **1.66** above); and
- the original annual accounts failed to comply with the requirements of *CA 1985* in the respects identified by the directors.

An example report is given in APB Practice Note 8 *Reports by Auditors under Company Legislation in the United Kingdom* (copies can be downloaded from the APB website at www.frc.org.uk/apb/publications/). If there has been a change of auditors, the directors can resolve that the report on the revised accounts be made by the auditors who reported on the original accounts, provided that they agree to make this report and that they would still be eligible for appointment as auditors.

1.84   Revised Directors' Report or Directors' Remuneration Report

Where a revised directors' report is issued under *section 245* or *245A* of *CA 1985* and the *Companies (Revision of Defective Accounts and Report) Regulations*

1990 (SI 1990/2570 as amended by subsequent SIs), the auditors are required to state whether, in their opinion, the information given in the revised report is consistent with the annual accounts for the relevant year. That year must be specified in the auditors' report. An example report is given in APB Practice Note 8 (see **1.83** above). If there has been a change of auditors, the directors can resolve that the report on the revised directors' report should be made by the auditors who reported on the accounts issued with the original directors' report, provided that they agree to make this report and that they would still be eligible for appointment as auditors. Where the directors' remuneration report has been revised, the auditors are required to express an opinion on whether any auditable part of the revised report has been properly prepared.

1.85   Distribution Where the Audit Report is Qualified

Where a company intends to make a distribution and the auditors have issued a qualified audit report on the last annual accounts, *section 271(4) of CA 1985* requires the auditors to make a written statement on whether, in their opinion, the matter in respect of which their report is qualified is material for the purpose of determining whether the proposed distribution contravenes the requirements of *sections 263* to *265* and *270 of CA 1985* on profits available for distribution. The auditors can make this written statement either simultaneously with their report on the annual accounts or at a later date, but it must be laid before the company in general meeting before the distribution is made. An example report is given in APB Practice Note 8 (see **1.83** above). The report can only be made by the auditors who qualified their report on the relevant accounts.

1.86   Distribution by Public Company Based on Initial Accounts

Where a company wishes to make a distribution during its first accounting reference period, or before the accounts for that period have been laid before the members or delivered to the Registrar, initial accounts must be prepared to support the distribution. In the case of a public company, *section 273 of CA 1985* requires initial accounts to be:

- properly prepared in accordance with the normal accounting requirements of *CA 1985*;
- approved and signed by the directors; and
- delivered to the Registrar.

The auditors are required to report whether, in their opinion, the initial accounts have been properly prepared (which is specifically defined as showing a true and fair view of the state of the company's affairs at the balance sheet date and the profit or loss for the relevant period, and complying with the relevant accounting provisions of *CA 1985*). An example report is given in APB Practice Note 8 (see **1.83** above). If the report is qualified, the auditors must also state whether, in their opinion, the matter in respect of which their report is qualified is material for the purpose of determining whether the proposed distribution contravenes the requirements of *sections 263* to *265* and *270* of *CA 1985* on profits available for distribution. The auditors' report (and the statement, where relevant) must be delivered to the Registrar of Companies with the initial accounts before the distribution takes place.

1.87 Re-registration of a Private Company as a Public Company

A private company that wishes to re-register as public must deliver certain documents to the Registrar of Companies, including an audited balance sheet and related notes as at a date not more than seven months before the application to re-register. The auditors are required to make an unqualified written statement that, in their opinion, this balance sheet shows that the amount of the company's net assets (as defined in *section 264(2)* of *CA 1985*) at this balance sheet date was not less than the aggregate of its called-up share capital and undistributable reserves. An example report is given in APB Practice Note 8 (see **1.83** above). If the company's last audited accounts covered a period ending more than seven months before the application, an updated balance sheet will need to be prepared by the company and audited by the auditors.

1.88 Redemption or Purchase of Own Shares Out of Capital

Where a private company redeems or purchases its own shares wholly or partly out of capital, the directors are required by *section 173* of *CA 1985* to make a statutory declaration specifying the amount of the permissible capital payment for the shares in question and setting out their opinion that:

- there are no grounds on which the company could be found unable to pay its debts immediately following the payment out of capital; and
- the company will be able to continue to carry on business as a going concern throughout the year immediately following the date of the payment and will be able to pay its debts as they fall due.

The form and content of this declaration, and the issues that the directors must take into account when making it, are specified in the legislation. When the declaration is delivered to the Registrar, it must have attached to it a report by the auditors, addressed to the directors, stating that:

- they have enquired into the company's state of affairs;
- in their opinion, the amount specified in the declaration as the permissible capital payment has been properly determined in accordance with *sections 171* and *172* of *CA 1985*; and
- they are not aware of anything to indicate that the opinion expressed by the directors in the declaration is unreasonable in all the circumstances.

An example report is given in APB Practice Note 8 (see **1.83** above). The legislation makes no provision for this report to be qualified, so if the auditors are unable to make these statements the redemption or purchase cannot proceed.

1.89   Financial Assistance for the Purchase of Own Shares

Financial assistance for the purchase of own shares can only be given in very specific circumstances. Before the assistance is given, the directors must make a statutory declaration setting out details of the proposed financial assistance and expressing their opinion that there are no grounds on which the company could be found unable to pay its debts immediately following the giving of the financial assistance; and that either:

- the company will be able to pay its debts as they fall due during the year immediately following the giving of the assistance; or
- if it is intended to commence the winding up of the company within twelve months, the company will be able to pay its debts in full within twelve months of the commencement of the winding up.

The form and content of this declaration, and the issues that the directors must take into account when making it, are set out in *section 156* of *CA 1985*. When the declaration is delivered to the Registrar, it must have attached to it a report by the auditors, addressed to the directors, stating that:

- they have enquired into the state of affairs of the company; and
- they are not aware of anything to indicate that the opinion expressed by the directors in the declaration is unreasonable in all the circumstances.

An example report is given in APB Practice Note 8 (see **1.83** above). Once again, the legislation makes no provision for this report to be qualified, so if the auditors are unable to make these statements, the directors cannot proceed with the proposed financial assistance.

1.90   Allotment of Shares by a Public Company Other Than for Cash

Where a public company proposes to allot shares for consideration in a form other than cash, it is usually required by *section 103* of *CA 1985* to obtain a report on the value of the assets to be received as consideration for the shares. This report must be obtained in the six months before the date of allotment and must be made by independent accountants who may, but need not, be the auditors of the company. If they are not the auditors, they must be qualified to act as auditors (see **1.26–1.27** above). Under *section 108* of *CA 1985*:

- the independent accountants may rely on a valuation made by another specialist who appears to them to have the requisite knowledge and experience, and who is not associated with the company (eg as an officer or employee of the company or group) – in practice they will have to follow the detailed guidance in the UK and Ireland version of International Standard on Auditing 620 (ISA 620) 'Using the Work of an Expert' if they wish to adopt this approach (copies can be downloaded from the APB website at http://www.frc.org.uk/apb/publications/);

- their report must state:
  - the nominal value of the relevant shares,
  - the amount of any premium payable on the shares,
  - a description of the consideration,
  - if they have valued part (or all) of the consideration themselves, a description of that part, the method of valuation and the date of valuation, and
  - where all or part of the consideration has been valued by another person, a statement of this fact, the valuer's name, knowledge and experience, a description of the consideration, and the method and date of valuation; and
- the report must also contain, or be accompanied by, a note by the independent accountants that:
  - where a valuation has been carried out by another person, it appeared reasonable to them to arrange or accept this,
  - the method of valuation was reasonable in all the circumstances,
  - it appears to them that there has been no material change in the value of the consideration since the valuation, and
  - on the basis of the valuation, the value of the consideration together with any cash to be paid, is not less than the aggregate of the nominal value of the shares and any premium to be treated as paid up.

An example report is given in APB Practice Note 8 (see **1.83** above). The legislation makes no provision for the independent accountants' report to be qualified. Additional requirements apply under *section 108(7)* of *CA 1985* where the consideration for the transfer of a non-cash asset is only partly satisfied by the allotment of shares.

1.91   Transfer of Non-cash Assets to a Public Company by a Member of the Company

In the first two years following registration or re-registration as a public company, *section 104* of *CA 1985* requires a company to obtain approval by an ordinary resolution of the company if it wishes to purchase from a subscriber to the company's memorandum a non-cash asset for consideration worth one-tenth or more of the nominal value of the company's issued share capital. In addition, a valuation report similar to that required on the allotment of share for non-cash consideration must have been made to the company in the six months immediately preceding the transfer. The report must be made by independent accountants qualified to act as auditors (although they need not be the auditors) and the same rules apply on accepting a valuation carried out by another person as for the allotment of shares by a public company other than for cash (see **1.90** above). In addition, under *section 109* of *CA 1985*, the independent account-ants' report must:

- state the consideration to be received and given, describing the assets and specifying any amounts to be paid or received in cash;
- state the method and date of valuation; and
- contain, or be accompanied by, a note by the independent accountants that:
  - where a valuation has been carried out by another person, it appeared reasonable to them to arrange or accept this,
  - the method of valuation was reasonable in all the circumstances,
  - it appears to them that there has been no material change in the value of the consideration since the valuation, and
  - on the basis of the valuation, the value of the consideration to be received by the company is not less than the value of the consideration to be given.

The legislation makes no provision for the independent accountants' report to be qualified. Additional requirements apply under *section 109(3)* of *CA 1985* where the consideration is given only partly for the transfer of a non-cash asset.

1.92   Other Reporting by External Auditors

At a Glance
- Auditors will usually report formally to management on any significant systems weaknesses and other issues that have come to their attention during the audit.
- The FSA *Listing Rules* require the auditors of listed companies to review and report on certain aspects of the corporate governance disclosures recommended in the *Combined Code.*
- Auditors may review and report on the interim report issued by a listed company, but there is no formal requirement for them to do so.

1.93   Reporting to Management

During the audit, or at the conclusion of their work, the auditors will usually report formally to the directors or senior management on:

- any significant weaknesses in the accounting or internal control systems that have come to their attention during the audit, together with their recommen-dations for improvements;
- any significant business issues that have come to their attention during the audit, together with their advice (eg potential economies or improvements in efficiency); and
- any significant errors identified during the audit and comments on any indi-vidual accounting policies or practices that they consider need to be drawn to the attention of the directors or senior management.

If the company has an audit committee, these issues may be reported to the directors through the committee (see **1.135–1.168** below). Auditing standards require auditors to report significant weaknesses in accounting and internal control systems to the directors or senior management on a timely basis, unless the weakness has already been identified by the entity and appropriate corrective action taken. The auditors will usually ask directors or senior management to respond to the points raised in their report, indicating the actions to be taken. Less significant issues will usually be discussed at a meeting with the directors or senior management and the points raised documented for future reference, together with any action agreed. It is normal practice for auditors to follow up all the issues that have been reported, usually during their subsequent audit, to confirm that the action agreed in response to the points raised has actually been taken.

1.94   *Scope of Report*

The auditors' work is carried out on a test basis and will normally be concentrated on those areas that present the highest risk of material error or misstatement in the accounts. The nature of the work therefore means that the auditors' report to management cannot be a comprehensive statement of all weaknesses which may exist in the accounting and internal control systems, or of all improvements that could be made. The auditors' formal report will therefore usually emphasise that it covers only those issues that have come to their attention during the course of the audit, and may give an explanation of the audit approach to help the directors understand the scope of the work undertaken.

1.95   *Confidentiality of Reports*

The reports that auditors issue to the directors or senior management are confidential documents and the auditors will therefore usually include in the report a statement that it has been prepared solely for the use of the company's management and should not be disclosed or quoted to another party without the prior written consent of the auditors. Similarly, the auditors will not usually provide a copy of the report to another party without the prior written consent of the directors. However, in certain regulated industries (such as the banking and financial services sectors) and in the public sector, auditors will often have a duty to provide copies of their reports to the relevant regulatory body or funding council.

1.96   Reporting Under the Combined Code

The FSA *Listing Rules* require the directors of listed companies to make statements in the annual report on compliance with the best practice provisions of the *Combined Code* and ongoing concern. These requirements are considered in more detail in **6 CORPORATE GOVERNANCE**. Where the FSA requires the directors to make such statements, the *Listing Rules* stipulate that they must also be reviewed by the auditors. In the case of the compliance statement, the auditors' review is only required to cover those aspects of the Code that can be verified objectively. There is no requirement under the *Listing Rules* for the auditors to prepare a formal report on the results of their review, or for such a report to be published. The latest APB guidance now requires the extent of the auditors' review of the corporate governance statements to be explained in the section of the audit report that explains the auditors' responsibilities. Examples can be found in APB Bulletin 2005/4 *Auditor's Reports on Financial Statements in Great Britain and Northern Ireland* (copies can be downloaded from the APB website at http://www.frc.org. uk/apb/publications/). If the auditors are not satisfied with the adequacy of the corporate governance disclosures and cannot resolve the problems through discussion with the directors, they are required to report their concerns in a separate paragraph as part of their opinion on the financial statements, but this will not constitute a qualification of their report on the annual accounts.

1.97 *Agreement of Scope of Review*

It is important that the respective responsibilities of the directors and the auditors in relation to the corporate governance statements, and the scope of the auditors' work on the statements, are clarified at an early stage to prevent any potential misunderstandings. The intention of the present *Listing Rules* is to ensure that auditors provide some assurance on the directors' corporate governance disclosures, but to avoid substantial additional audit work and the consequent financial implications that this would have for companies. The scope of the auditors' work in respect of corporate governance statements should be set out in a formal engagement letter between the company and the auditors. This can be dealt with as a stand-alone document or as a separate section of the engagement letter for the statutory audit. APB Bulletin 2004/3 *The Combined Code on Corporate Governance: Requirements of Auditors under the Listing Rules of the Financial Services Authority* sets out guidance on the detailed procedures that auditors should normally undertake when reviewing corporate governance statements (copies can be downloaded from the APB website at http:// www.frc.org.uk/apb/publications/).

1.98 Reporting on Interim Reports

Listed companies are required by the FSA *Listing Rules* to issue an interim report each year, giving details of their results for the first half of the financial year. There is currently no formal requirement for auditors to review or report on interim reports before they are published. APB Bulletin 1999/04 *Review of Interim Financial Information* sets out guidance on the procedures that should be undertaken where auditors are asked to review an interim report, although it notes that the directors (or, where relevant, the audit committee – see **1.135–1.168** below) may ask the auditors to carry out specific agreed procedures as an alternative to this. Where an interim report is reviewed in accordance with the APB guidance, the FSA *Listing Rules* require the auditors' review report to be published as part of the interim report. The Accounting Standards Board ('ASB') Statement *Interim*

Reports also recommends disclosure of the extent to which the information given in the interim report has been audited or reviewed (for information on obtaining copies see the ASB website at www.frc.org.uk/asb/publications/). The latest guidance on the wording of the review report can be found in APB Bulletin 2001/02 *Revisions to the Wording of Auditors' Reports on Financial Statements and the Interim Review Report* (copies can be downloaded from the APB website at www.frc.org.uk/apb/publications/). Because the recommended review work is limited in scope, and does not constitute an audit, the auditors will normally report in terms of 'negative assurance' – in other words, they report that nothing has come to their attention to indicate that material modification is required to the information presented in the report. APB Bulletin 1999/04 recommends that, where the scope of the work agreed between the directors and auditors is less than that set out in the Bulletin, the directors should describe the interim report as 'neither audited nor reviewed'.

1.99 Remuneration of External Auditors and their Associates

At a Glance
* *CA 1985* generally provides for the remuneration of the auditors to be fixed by whoever appoints them.
* The remuneration received by the auditors for their services as auditors must be disclosed in the annual accounts.
* In most cases, the accounts must also disclose details of any non-audit services provided by the auditors and their associates to the company and its associates, and the remuneration received for these.
* Significant changes have been made to the disclosures requirements for accounting periods beginning on or after 1 October 2005.

1.100 Remuneration for Services as Auditors

Section 390A of *CA 1985* provides for the remuneration of the auditors to be fixed as follows:

* where the auditors have been appointed by the company, their remuneration should be fixed by the company in general meeting, or in any other way decided by the company in general meeting (in practice, most companies resolve to give the directors authority to agree the auditors' remuneration);
* where the auditors have been appointed by the directors, their remuneration should be fixed by the directors; and
* where the auditors have been appointed by the Secretary of State, their remuneration should be fixed by the Secretary of State.

The legislation defines remuneration as including amounts paid in respect of expenses and any benefits in kind, but in practice, professional and ethical

Audit

requirements will usually prevent auditors from accepting benefits in kind from the company.

1.101   Disclosure of Remuneration for Services as Auditors

For accounting periods beginning before 1 October 2005, *section 390A of CA 1985* requires the remuneration paid to the auditors in respect of their work as auditors to be disclosed in the notes to the annual accounts. The amount to be disclosed should include the audit fee, any amounts payable in respect of expenses and the estimated money value of any benefits in kind received by the auditors in respect of their services as auditors. The nature of any benefits in kind should also be disclosed. However, professional and ethical requirements will usually prevent auditors from accepting benefits in kind from the company. For accounting periods beginning on or after 1 October 2005, a revised *section 390B of CA 1985* gives the Secretary of State new powers to make regulations on the disclosure of remuneration received or receivable by the auditors, and detailed requirements are now set out in the *Companies (Disclosure of Auditor Remuneration) Regulations 2005 (SI 2005/2417)*. These supersede the previous regulations on the disclosure of auditor remuneration and cover fees for both audit and non-audit work. The changes relate primarily to the disclosure of fees for non-audit work, and the requirement to give separate disclosure of the auditors' remuneration as auditors continues to apply to all companies, as does the requirement to include (and disclose) any related benefits in kind. However, the new disclosure requirements do make a number of changes in respect of the disclosure of audit fees in group accounts. In particular:

- the amount to be disclosed is the fee receivable by the auditor of the parent company in relation to the audit of the individual accounts of that company and the audit of the consolidation, including any work carried out by the parent company auditors on consolidation returns prepared by the subsidiaries;
- any fees receivable by the parent company auditors in respect of statutory audit work for one or more of the individual subsidiaries (i.e. separate from the audit work on the group accounts) do not form part of this disclosure and should instead be included in the first disclosure category for fees for non-audit services (i.e. the auditing of accounts of associates of the company pursuant to legislation), together with any similar fees receivable by the auditors' associates – this represents a significant change from the previous requirements, where audit fees for companies included in the consolidation were aggregated for disclosure in the notes to the group accounts; and
- where a subsidiary is audited by a firm that is not associated with the parent company auditors, this audit fee will no longer be included in the group accounts disclosures.

These issues are highlighted in draft guidance on the practical implications of the new disclosure requirements published by the ICAEW as TECH 04/06 'Disclosure of Auditor Remuneration' which can be downloaded from the ICAEW website at http://www.icaew.co.uk. The guidance document leads the reader through a series of 44 questions on the disclosure requirements and provides as an Appendix a comprehensive worked example of how the detailed requirements might be met in practice. Comments on the draft guidance were invited by 4 July 2006 and it will be published in final form after consideration of the responses.

1.102   *Adjustments to Fees in Respect of Previous Years*

The amount to be disclosed is the remuneration payable in respect of the current year. This will usually be an estimate of the amount to be charged for the audit (including expenses). The legislation does not consider a situation where the actual fee in respect of any year is different to the amount provided for (and thus disclosed) in the accounts for that year. Minor adjustments to the figure are not usually disclosed but if the audit fee for a particular year has effectively been under-/overstated by a material amount, it will usually be appropriate to disclose the adjustment separately in the following year's accounts.

1.103   Remuneration for Non-audit Services

For accounting periods beginning before 1 October 2005, *section 390B* of *CA 1985* gives the Secretary of State the power to require the disclosure of remuneration paid to the auditors or their associates in respect of non-audit services provided to the company or group, and to define remuneration, associates and associated undertakings for this purpose. Disclosure requirements in respect of non-audit fees were originally introduced by the *Companies Act 1985 (Disclosure of Remuneration for Non-audit Work) Regulations 1991* (*SI 1991/2128*) and were updated by the *Companies Act 1985 (Disclosure of Remuneration for Non-audit Work) Amendment Regulations 1998* (*SI 1995/1520*). However, a revised *section 390B* was introduced by the *Companies (Audit, Investigations and Community Enterprise) Act 2004*. As a result, *CA 1985* now specifies that the Secretary of State may make provision for disclosure of the nature of any services provided by the auditors and require the details to be given by a particular class or description, and may require the disclosure of the separate amounts received by the auditors and their associates, or the disclosure of aggregate amounts. Regulations can also specify that disclosure should be given in the notes to the accounts, the directors' report or the auditors' report. The *Companies (Disclosure of Auditor Remuneration) Regulations 2005* (*SI 2005/2417*) were laid before Parliament in August 2005 and supersede the previous disclosure requirements for accounting periods beginning on or after 1 October 2005.

1.104   *Disclosures Prior to 1 October 2005*

For accounting periods beginning before 1 October 2005, the figure to be disclosed is the aggregate amount of remuneration in respect of work carried out during the financial year, regardless of whether it has been billed to the company. Comparative figures must also be given. Once again, remuneration specifically includes the estimated money value of benefits in kind, and both the nature and the estimated money value of any benefits must be disclosed, although these are unlikely to arise in practice. Where the auditors (or their associates) are also the auditors of any UK subsidiary undertaking of the company (as defined in *section 258* of *CA 1985*), any amounts in respect of services to the subsidiary must be included in the aggregate remuneration. The regulations specifically require the auditors to provide the company with the information that it needs to be able to comply with the disclosure requirements. Where more than one auditor has held office during the year, separate disclosure is required in respect of each auditor and their associates.

1.105 *Associates of Auditors Prior to 1 October 2005*

The definition of associates for this purpose is very complex but it broadly includes:

- any partnership in which the auditors are a partner or with which the auditors have a partner in common;
- any body corporate in the same group as the auditors;
- any directors of the auditors;
- any body corporate in which the auditors, a partner of the auditors or a director of the auditors controls the exercise of 20 per cent or more of the voting rights, or any other body corporate in the same group as such a body corporate.

If such a relationship exists at any time during the financial year, the entity is regarded as an associate of the auditors for that year. Reference should be made to the regulations if there is any doubt over whether an entity should be treated as an associate of the auditors. Amendments were made to the regulations in 1995 to specifically exclude entities that might otherwise have been treated as associates of the auditors as a result of insolvency and receivership appointments.

1.106 *ICAEW Guidance on Additional Disclosure*

Guidance on more extensive disclosure of the nature and value of non-audit services provided by auditors was published by the ICAEW in July 2003. This was based on EC recommendations and recommended that full and transparent disclosure should be made of all fees due to the audit firm and its network firms in relation to work performed during the period for the audit client and all entities controlled by that client alone. In the case of joint audits, the same disclosures should be given for each principal audit firm. The disclosures should cover both the nature and extent of the services provided and the review and approval process followed, and should provide sufficient information to enable a user of the accounts to judge whether the potential for conflicts of interest has been satisfactorily addressed. However, this guidance on voluntary additional disclosure has been superseded by the new statutory disclosure requirements for accounting periods beginning on or after 1 October 2005.

1.107   *Disclosures from 1 October 2005*

The *Companies (Disclosure of Auditor Remuneration) Regulations 2005* (*SI 2005/2417*) set out new disclosure requirements on the remuneration of auditors for accounting periods beginning on or after 1 October 2005. They require companies to give separate disclosure in the notes to the accounts for each type of service specified in Schedule 2 to the regulations and the amount paid to the auditors and their associates for that service, with no de minimis exemptions. The following categories are specified for disclosure:

- auditing the accounts of associates of the company pursuant to legislation;
- other services provided under legislation;
- other services relating to taxation;
- services relating to information technology;
- internal audit services;
- valuation and actuarial services;
- services relating to litigation;
- services relating to recruitment and remuneration;
- services relating to corporate finance transactions; and
- other services.

Where a service could fall within more than one of the specified categories, it should be treated as falling within the first one listed. As under the previous disclosure requirements, remuneration includes any benefits in kind (although these should be rare in practice) and the nature and estimated money value of such benefits must be separately disclosed. The auditors are also required to provide the directors with any information needed to comply with the disclosure requirements. Where more than one person has acted as auditor during the year, separate disclosure is required for each auditor and their associates.

1.108   *Disclosure Exemptions*

Small and medium-sized companies and groups continue to be exempt from the detailed disclosures in respect of non-audit services, although they must continue to disclose the remuneration paid to the auditors in respect of the audit of the company's accounts. There is also no requirement for the disclosures in respect of non-audit services to be given in the individual accounts of a parent company, or of its subsidiaries, when the parent prepares group accounts under *CA 1985*, provided that the individual accounts state that the relevant disclosures are required to be given in the group accounts. These exemptions are considered in some detail in the ICAEW's TECH 04/06 (see **1.101**) which concludes that the exemptions will not be available to:

(i) a parent that voluntarily prepares group accounts in addition to individual accounts;

(ii) a parent that is exempt from the requirement to prepare group accounts because it is itself a subsidiary of a foreign parent – this is on the basis that the foreign parent is not required to prepare group accounts under the Act

and so is not required by the legislation to provide the relevant disclosures in its own group accounts; or
(iii) the subsidiaries of such parent companies.

1.109   *Associates of the Company from 1 October 2005*

The disclosure requirements cover services provided to the company and its associates. A company's associates include any subsidiary, other than one in respect of which severe long-term restrictions substantially hinder the exercise of the company's rights, and any associated pension scheme, which is defined as a scheme for the provision of pension and similar retirement or death benefits to directors and employees (or former directors and employees) of the company or any subsidiary, where either:

- a majority of trustees are appointed by the company or a subsidiary (or a person acting on their behalf); or
- the company or a subsidiary exercises a dominant influence over the appointment of the auditor to the scheme.

Overseas entities are included within the definition. For each service category identified above, separate details must be given for services provided to the company and its subsidiaries, and services provided to any associated pension schemes.

1.110   *Associates of Auditors from 1 October 2005*

Under the new regulations, the following are included within the definition of associates of the auditors:

- any person controlled by the auditors or by an associate of the auditors (unless the control arises solely as a result of an insolvency or receivership appointment);
- any person or group of persons which controls the auditors;
- any person using a common or similar trading name to the auditors, if the auditors' intention in using that name is to create the impression of a connection between them;
- any party to an arrangement with the auditors under which costs, profits, quality control, business strategy or significant professional resources are shared; and
- any partnership which has a partner in common with the auditors, or any body corporate which has a director in common with the auditors.

The regulations also cover a number of more complex situations involving links and associations with other partnerships and bodies corporate. Overseas entities are also included within the definition of associates. The draft ICAEW guidance in TECH 4/06 (see **1.101**) notes that the revised definition of auditors' associates is comprehensive and will capture a wide range of individuals and organisations with connections to the auditor. Auditors will therefore need to apply careful judgement in assessing whether a particular individual, partnership, body corporate or other entity falls within the new definition.

1.111   Internal Audit

At a Glance
* The primary role of internal audit is to assist management in identifying potential risk and to provide assurance that the company's system of internal control is effective in reducing risk to an acceptable level.
* There are significant differences between the roles of internal and external auditors.
* It is important that internal audit remains independent of the company's operating functions.
* A strong internal audit function can help management to demonstrate that they are taking their corporate governance responsibilities seriously.
* Internal audit may also carry out special assignments and investigations on behalf of management.
* The internal audit function may be resourced in-house or may be subcontracted to an appropriate external organisation.
* Terms of reference should be established to clarify the purpose, authority and scope of work of internal audit.
* The internal audit function should be headed and staffed by individuals with appropriate professional expertise.
* The scope of internal audit work should generally be unrestricted and should cover all aspects of the company's system of internal control.
* The work of the internal audit function should be carefully planned, and progress should be monitored as the year progresses.
* Internal audit should issue a formal report on each system or operational area that has been subject to audit and should prepare summary reports and an annual report for presentation to management.
* Good liaison between internal auditors and external auditors can help both to operate more efficiently and prevent unnecessary duplication of work.

1.112   Role of Internal Audit

The role of internal audit has altered considerably over the years, reflecting the changing needs of business and management. This has been especially true in recent years, as corporate governance issues have been given an increasingly high profile. Directors and senior management are much more aware of their responsibilities for the control of business risk and for the establishment of systems and controls to safeguard assets, prevent fraud and irregularity, and enhance the efficient operation of the business. The primary role of an internal audit function is to assist management in identifying potential risk and to pro-vide assurance that the company's system of internal control is effective in reducing business risk to an acceptable level. It also acts as a useful source of information for management on what is actually happening in practice within the business, and provides support and advice by identifying needs and recom-mending policies, procedures and controls to resolve potential problems as they are identified. In the case of a public company, the work of internal audit will usually be a significant factor in enabling the directors to report on internal con-trol as required by the *Combined Code* (see **6 CORPORATE GOVERNANCE**). The Code also recommends that companies that do not have an internal audit function should consider annually whether there is a need for one.

1.113   Distinction Between External Audit and Internal Audit

There are significant differences between the roles of external auditors and internal auditors. External auditors are appointed by the shareholders and report to them by expressing an independent opinion on whether the com-pany's annual accounts show a true and fair view of the state of affairs of the company at the balance sheet date and of its profit or loss for the financial year. The work of the external auditors is therefore directed towards identifying any potentially material misstatement in the annual accounts, and confirming that the accounting treatments and disclosures required by the legislation and by accounting standards have been properly dealt with. Internal audit is a service function of the company, focusing its efforts on the effectiveness of the com-pany's systems of internal control and reporting any weaknesses and concerns to management. Companies' legislation generally requires every UK company to appoint external auditors (the only exceptions being dormant companies and certain small companies as explained at **1.1–1.17** above), but management can choose whether or not to establish an internal audit function.

The principal distinctions between external and internal audit can there-fore be summarised as follows:

	External auditors	Internal auditors
Appointed by	Shareholders	Management
Report to	Shareholders	Management
Role defined by	Statute	Management
Primary function	Independent opinion on the annual accounts	Assisting management with the identification and control of business risk

Although the roles of external auditors and internal auditors are quite distinct, good liaison between the two can help both to operate more efficiently.

1.114   How Not to Use Internal Audit

Historically, there has been a considerable degree of confusion over the precise role of internal audit. It is important to recognise that internal auditors are not responsible for designing and implementing systems and procedures, nor are they responsible for the prevention and detection of fraud and irregularity. These are, and must always remain, the responsibility of management. Internal auditors have an important role to play in assisting management to fulfil their responsibilities, and they will frequently recommend changes to systems and procedures, or new controls that should be introduced. However, if they were to become directly involved in designing and implementing systems and procedures, their independence from the operating functions could be seriously impaired. For the same reason, it is essential that internal auditors are not seen as a floating resource who can be used to cover for the unexpected departure or long-term absence of accounting and other staff.

1.115   Benefits of Internal Audit

The heightened profile of corporate governance issues, and public reporting on aspects such as internal control under the *Combined Code* (and its predecessor Codes), has generally increased management's awareness of their responsibilities and encouraged them to reconsider how these responsibilities can best be fulfilled in practice. Internal audit has had a relatively high profile within the public sector for some years, but has generally been slower to develop within the private sector, except in the largest organisations. In the past, internal audit departments tended to be given a low status within the organisation, but the benefits of a well-organised and high calibre internal audit function are now becoming clearer to companies of all sizes. Management always retains the responsibility for identifying business risk and introducing procedures and controls to reduce risk to an acceptable level. However, establishing a strong internal audit function to assist with this can enable management to demonstrate clearly that they have paid due attention to the relevant issues, and that the procedures and controls that have been put in place are being subjected to continual scrutiny. This is particularly important as the business develops – without regular independent scrutiny, the procedures and controls can easily become out of date and fail to provide adequate cover in new areas of operation.

1.116   Areas Usually Covered by Internal Audit

Internal audit will usually provide assurance on:

- safeguarding of the company's assets;
- the completeness and accuracy of the company's accounting and other records;
- the adequacy and effectiveness of measures to prevent fraud and other irregularity; and
- the overall efficiency of the operations.

The internal auditors should develop a strong, in-depth knowledge of the company's operating systems, coupled with their own professional expertise, and they are therefore in a good position to advise management on the assessment of risk and the implementation of procedures and controls. If there is no internal audit function, the external auditors will usually need to carry out some review and testing of the company's systems and controls, but as their focus is the material accuracy of the annual accounts, their work will concentrate on financial controls rather than the company's overall system of internal control. The level and extent of their review and testing will also be lower, as the level of assurance needed for external audit purposes will not be as extensive as that required for effective management of the business.

1.117   Special Assignments

As well as assisting with the assessment and control of business risk, internal auditors often carry out special assignments and investigations to assist management in the achievement of business objectives, such as value for money reviews and more extensive investigations of specific business areas (for instance, a review of the effectiveness and efficiency of an individual part of the business operation, or of a particular service function, such as catering or maintenance). The areas selected for review may have been identified by management as needing investigation, or may have been highlighted by the internal auditors during their other work, or by the external auditors.

1.118   Establishing an Internal Audit Function

An internal audit function is a service department within the organisation, assisting management to fulfil its responsibilities. In larger entities, there will usually be a separate internal audit department, its staffing levels being dependent on the size and complexity of the organisation and the level of work required throughout the year. In the case of a group, one internal audit department will normally serve all locations and subsidiaries within the group. In a smaller organisation, there may be insufficient work to justify a fully staffed internal audit department, or it may be that the department would be so small (eg requiring only one or two members of staff) that it would be difficult for it to command the necessary authority within the business. However, this does not mean that it is totally impractical for a small company to operate an internal audit function. It should be possible to sub-contract internal audit work to an external organisation with the necessary skills and experience (eg a firm of accountants with internal audit expertise). The fact that the function is an internal one does not prevent it being provided from an outside source, although particular care may be needed in defining the terms and scope of the work.

1.119   Terms of Reference

The purpose, authority and scope of work of the internal audit department should be set out in a formal document. This will help to give the internal auditors the high profile within the organisation that is necessary if they are to function effect-ively. It should also clarify the independence of the internal auditors from the other parts of the business and the remit of internal audit, ensuring in particular that this is not restricted in any way and covers all aspects of the business. Where internal audit work is sub-contracted, these matters will normally be dealt with in an engagement letter between the parties. In all cases, the terms of reference for the internal audit function should be regularly reviewed and updated (through the audit committee where appropriate – see **1.135–1.168** below).

1.120   Head of Internal Audit

It is important that the internal audit function, however it is organised, is headed up by an individual who has the necessary professional expertise and carries the respect, confidence and support of other members of the senior management team. He or she should preferably have an appropriate professional qualifica-tion, relevant experience and the personal skills needed to deal with individuals throughout the organisation and to handle potentially difficult and sensitive issues. There needs to be a close working relationship between the head of internal audit and the executive directors and also, where relevant, good communication between the head of internal audit and the audit committee (see **1.135–1.168** below). If the internal audit function is a separate department within the organ-isation, the head of internal audit will be a management appointment. If internal audit work is sub-contracted, the person with overall responsibility for the work (eg a partner in a firm of accountants) is in effect the head of internal audit, and it will be important to ensure that the necessary relationships can be put into place quickly and effectively. Where the company has an audit committee, this committee will usually participate in the appointment. The head of internal audit should have a direct line of communication to the chairman of the audit commit-tee, to enable sensitive issues to be raised and discussed without executive man-agement being present where necessary, and to demonstrate and strengthen the independence of the internal audit function.

1.121   Staffing

If the internal audit department is to achieve the necessary degree of respect and confidence within the organisation, it is essential that it has adequate resources to carry out its work. Wherever possible, internal audit staff should be suitably trained and professionally qualified. This does not necessarily mean that everyone needs to hold the same qualifications. The department should be viewed as a team and the skills and expertise available should be appropriate for the range of work that the department is expected to cover. The skills needed will inevitably vary, depending on the nature and complexity of the business. As well as financial expertise, the internal audit function may need skills in areas such as computing, logistics or environmental issues. On occasions it may be appropriate to second high calibre staff with particular skills from elsewhere in the organisation to assist with specific internal audit projects. This can be valuable in increasing general awareness and understanding of the internal audit function within the company, and can help to raise the profile of internal audit. It is important to remember that internal audit staff will need to deal with individuals throughout the organisation, and that they may sometimes be required to handle potentially difficult and sensitive situations. All internal audit staff need to have strong inter-personal and communication skills and to be confident in dealing with senior management.

1.122   Independence and Objectivity

Internal auditors must be genuinely independent of the systems and operations that they review and report on. Without a high degree of professional independence and objectivity, the internal audit function will not achieve the status and level of authority necessary for it to become a strong and effective management resource, and it will not command the respect and confidence of management and staff. There is also a risk that internal audit staff will not be able to make genuinely unbiased and impartial judgements if they have a close involvement in the detailed operations. It is essential that the head of internal audit is not given additional executive responsibilities within the organisation and that audit staff are not involved in the day-to-day operations of other parts of the business. This does not preclude the secondment of staff from other departments to assist with specific internal audit assignments as explained above, but long-term internal audit staff should not have a regular involvement in other departments. It is particularly important that internal auditors are not seen as a floating resource who can be used to cover for the unexpected departure or long-term absence of key members of staff.

The ability of the head of internal audit to communicate directly with the chairman of the audit committee (see **1.135–1.168** below) whenever he or she considers it necessary helps to demonstrate the independence of the internal audit function from the executive management. The audit committee (or management where there is no audit committee) should satisfy themselves each year that appropriate procedures are operating to safeguard the independence and objectivity of the internal audit function.

1.123   Scope of Internal Audit Work

The scope of the internal auditors' work should generally be unrestricted and should cover the full spectrum of the company's system of internal control. The scope of the work undertaken by the internal auditors will vary depending on the circumstances of the company and should be discussed and agreed by the board. Where appropriate, this will be dealt with initially by the audit committee (see **1.135–1.168** below), who will then submit detailed proposals to the board for consideration and formal approval. The scope of internal audit work will usually include:

- understanding and assessing the key business risks and reviewing the procedures used to identify and manage these;

- reviewing the adequacy and effectiveness of controls over financial and other operational information;
- reviewing the adequacy and effectiveness of the procedures established by management to safeguard the company's assets and resources, and to prevent fraud and irregularity;
- reviewing the adequacy and effectiveness of procedures designed to ensure compliance with law and regulations that are central to the business;
- reviewing the adequacy and effectiveness of procedures designed to ensure that the policies and plans agreed by management are brought into effect; and
- reviewing the efficiency and effectiveness of particular aspects of the business.

1.124   Internal Audit Needs Assessment and Strategic Plan

The initial stage in planning internal audit work will usually be to develop an internal audit needs assessment. This will identify all the aspects of the company's operations that will be subject to review by the internal auditors. In most organisations it will not be practical for all areas to be covered by internal audit in one year. It is normal practice for internal auditors to operate on a three- or four-year cycle, ensuring that all systems and operations are covered during the three- or four-year period. In some cases, all the work on a particular system or operational area may be carried out in one year – in other cases, work on an individual system or operation may be spread over the full audit period, so that some aspects are covered in each year of the cycle. Where a system or operational area is considered to be particularly critical to the business, it may be deemed necessary for it to be covered by internal audit each year. The overall audit needs assessment must therefore be developed into a strategic audit plan to demonstrate how full coverage will be achieved over the audit cycle (ie the three- or four-year period). In order to prepare a strategic audit plan, there will need to be some prioritisation of internal audit work over the audit cycle. Areas that are identified as high risk will generally be covered earlier in the audit cycle, and may be covered on more than one occasion during the cycle; areas that are deemed medium or low risk will generally be covered later in the audit cycle. Both the internal audit needs assessment and the strategic audit plan should be developed by the internal auditors in discussion with management and should be formally approved by the board (through the audit committee where appropriate – see **1.135–1.168** below).

1.125   Annual Review

The internal audit needs assessment and strategic audit plan must be reviewed and updated annually. There are very few situations where the needs assessment and strategic plan developed at the beginning of an audit cycle will not need to be adapted during the course of the cycle. Changes may be needed to:

- incorporate new systems and operations as the business develops;
- amend priorities because changes in circumstance have increased or reduced the risk associated with a particular aspect of the business; and/or

- amend priorities on the basis of the results of internal audit work already completed.

Both the internal auditors and management should be involved in the review and update of the internal audit needs assessment and the strategic audit plan, and the revised documents should be approved by the board (through the audit committee where appropriate – see **1.135–1.168** below).

1.126   Detailed Internal Audit Plan

Once the internal audit needs assessment and strategic audit plan have been approved, the internal audit department must develop a detailed audit plan for the current year, setting out the areas to be covered, the proposed timing of the work and the proposed reporting timetable. The plan should include adequate time for following up points raised in the reports on previous audits to confirm that the agreed action has in fact been taken and that the problem originally identified has been resolved as far as is practicable. The detailed audit plan for the year should also be approved by the board (through the audit committee, where appropriate – see **1.135–1.168** below).

1.127   Monitoring Work as the Year Progresses

The head of internal audit should report regularly to management on the progress of audit work against the plan for the year and explain any significant variations. Reporting will be dealt with through the audit committee where appropriate (see **1.135–1.168** below).

1.128   Reports on Individual Systems and Operations

Internal audit will issue individual reports on each system or operational area that has been subject to audit. Their reports will normally draw an overall conclusion in respect of that system or area, and will concentrate on highlighting any potentially serious weaknesses or concerns identified during the audit, along with the internal auditors' recommendations for changes and improvements. The recommendations will normally be discussed with management and the agreed action noted for each item. It is usually helpful to agree a standard structure for internal audit reports – for instance:

- executive summary;
- the overall conclusions drawn by the auditors; and
- the detailed findings and recommendations for improvement, divided into:
  - major weaknesses and concerns, and
  - other issues.

It is important that weaknesses and concerns are rigorously followed up by internal audit later in the year (or, where appropriate, later in the audit cycle), to confirm that the agreed action has actually been taken and that the potential problem originally identified has been satisfactorily resolved.

1.129　Summary Reports

Summary reports should be prepared and presented formally to management (through the audit committee where appropriate – see **1.135–1.168** below) by the head of internal audit on a regular basis during the year. This reporting will normally take place on two or three occasions each year and may be combined with reports on the progress of audit work against the annual audit plan. A specific timetable for this level of reporting should be agreed at the beginning of the year.

1.130　Annual Report

The head of internal audit may also be asked to prepare an annual report summarising the work completed during the financial year and the overall conclusions drawn on the operation of the company's system of internal control. This will be particularly relevant for directors of listed companies who are required under the *Combined Code* to state in the annual report that they have reviewed the effectiveness of the company's system of internal control. An annual report from the head of internal audit will be one source of supporting information that the audit committee (see **1.135–1.168** below) and board of directors will usually wish to review when considering the various directors' statements relating to compliance with the *Combined Code*.

1.131　Liaison with External Auditors

Although the roles of external auditors and internal auditors are quite distinct, good liaison between the two can help both to operate more efficiently and prevent any unnecessary duplication of work. Liaison normally works best when there are regular meetings and continuous dialogue between the two groups of auditors, and each has a good understanding of the audit approach adopted by the other. The most crucial aspect is to ensure that there is good communication each year at the planning stages of both internal and external audit work. If the external auditors are consulted when internal audit work is being planned, this may help to increase the usefulness of the results for external audit purposes and enable the external auditors to reduce the extent of their detailed audit testing. This does not mean that the external auditors should in any way decide the scope or nature of the internal audit work – this must remain a management responsibility – but by discussing and agreeing issues such as the timing of the work, the methods of sample selection and the documentation of results, it should be possible to ensure that the work of the internal auditors is of maximum benefit to the external auditors as well as to management. Similarly, when the detailed external audit work is being planned, it will be important for the external auditors to take full account of the extent and results of internal audit work. Where appropriate, the audit committee (see **1.135–1.168** below) will usually be responsible for the overall monitoring of liaison between the two groups of auditors.

1.132 Impact of Internal Audit Work on External Audit Procedures

The external auditors retain sole responsibility for the independent audit opinion on the annual accounts, for deciding the nature and extent of the audit procedures to be carried out in support of that opinion and for all matters of judgement in relation to the audit opinion. However, as part of their work, the external auditors will need to obtain assurance on the completeness and accuracy of the company's accounting records (which will form the basis for the annual accounts) and the adequacy and effectiveness of the company's internal financial controls. Where the company has an internal audit function, the external auditors may be able to place reliance on the work of the internal auditors to help them achieve the level of assurance they require for external audit purposes, and this in turn may enable them to reduce the extent of some of their detailed audit testing. The external auditors will usually need to be satisfied that the internal audit function is adequately resourced, appropriately staffed and independent of those on whom it is reporting; that the work of the internal auditors is properly planned, supervised and documented; and that the recommendations made by the internal auditors carry appropriate weight within the organisation. Their procedures to assess these issues will usually include reviewing the reports and working papers of the internal audit department.

1.133 Impact of External Audit Work on Internal Audit Procedures

There is generally less scope for internal auditors to make detailed use of the work of the external auditors. However, regular feedback on weaknesses and irregularities identified during external audit work can be helpful in directing the work of internal audit to areas of potential business risk. The external auditors may also highlight operational areas where value for money reviews, efficiency reviews or other special investigations may usefully be incorporated in the internal audit work programme.

1.134 Additional Guidance

In November 2003, the Audit and Assurance Faculty (AAF) of the Institute of Chartered Accountants in England and Wales (ICAEW) published *Evaluating the Effectiveness of Internal Audit* to help audit committee members monitor the effectiveness of internal audit. The guidance recommends that monitoring is carried out by means of a regular review of internal audit reports during the course of the year and an annual review, which will usually comprise some form of self-assessment by the head of internal audit, together with supporting feedback from management, the external auditors and any other relevant bodies (such as regulators). The guidance also draws attention to the standards developed by the Institute of Internal Auditors, which recommend that an independent review of the internal audit function is carried out at least every five years. The AAF has also published *The Power of Three: Understanding the Roles and Relationships of Internal and External Auditors* and *Audit Committees and Obtaining Value from Internal Audit*. These booklets are available free of charge to members of the AAF and can be purchased by non-members for £7.50 a copy (www.icaew.co.uk/aafac or 020 7920 8493). Also, as part of its series of guidance booklets for non-executive directors serving on an audit committee, the ICAEW published *The Internal Audit Function* in March 2004. This is available free of charge from the ICAEW website at www. icaew.co.uk.

1.135   Audit Committees

At a Glance
* A well-constituted and well-run audit committee can bring considerable benefits.
* The Smith Guidance sets out additional recommendations on the role and activities of an audit committee.
* The audit committee should be formally constituted and should have written terms of reference.
* The *Combined Code* includes specific provisions on the membership of the audit committee.
* Appointments to the audit committee should generally be by recommendation of the nomination committee and should be for a fixed term.
* Audit committee members must disclose any potential conflicts of interest.
* The company should provide an induction programme and ongoing training and support for audit committee members.
* Management must provide the audit committee with all the information that it needs to discharge its responsibilities.
* The precise role of the audit committee should be tailored to the circumstances of the company.
* The audit committee should review all financial reporting documents before publication.
* The audit committee should review the company's internal control and risk management systems, and the procedures for whistleblowing.
* The audit committee should monitor and review the activities of the internal audit function.
* The audit committee has primary responsibility for making a recommendation on the appointment, reappointment or removal of the external auditors.
* The audit committee should approve the terms of engagement and remuneration of the external auditor.
* The audit committee should assess the independence and objectivity of the external auditors each year.

* The audit committee should agree with the board the company's policy on:
  o The employment of former partners and employees of the external audit firm, and
  o the provision of non-audit services by the external auditors.
* The audit committee should agree the scope of external audit work each year.
* The audit committee should review the results of the external audit in conjunction with the annual report and accounts.
* The audit committee should consider the auditor's report to management, together with management's response to the points raised.
* At the end of the audit cycle, the audit committee should assess the effectiveness of the external audit process.
* The audit committee should meet sufficiently often to be able to review and monitor major issues, and at least three times each year.
* Only audit committee members are entitled to be present at meetings, but other individuals may attend by invitation.
* The audit committee chairman should report regularly to the main board.
* The annual report should include a separate section describing the role and responsibilities of the audit committee and the actions taken to discharge those responsibilities.
* The effectiveness of the audit committee should be reviewed annually by the main board.

1.136 Benefits of an Audit Committee

Audit committees have become an important aspect of corporate governance in recent years, partly as a result of the recommendations set out in the *Combined Code* but also because companies have begun to appreciate the benefits that an effective audit committee can bring in terms of providing additional assurance on the adequacy of the company's system of internal control and on the quality of its financial information (for both internal and external use) and of its financial decision-making. Although the *Combined Code* applies primarily to listed companies, the principles underlying the recommendations apply to every company and all directors are therefore encouraged to follow them. The recommendations are equally relevant for non-profit organisations, particularly where there is a high degree of public interest in their activities, eg charities and public sector bodies. The potential benefits of an audit committee include:

* improved quality of financial reporting and increased public confidence in the credibility and objectivity of financial statements;
* the creation of a climate of discipline and control, which can help to reduce the opportunity for fraud;
* the opportunity for non-executive directors to contribute their independent judgement and play a positive role within the company;

- the provision of a forum for the finance director to raise issues of concern and instigate appropriate action;
- the provision of a strong channel of communication between the external auditors and the board, enabling them to raise issues of concern and assert their independence in the event of a dispute with management;
- the strengthening of the internal audit function, by increasing its independence from management.

1.137   Potential Drawbacks

However, there are some potential difficulties that companies need to be aware of when establishing and operating audit committees:

- the existence of an audit committee can result in the main board abdicating its collective responsibilities in respect of the audit and the review and approval of the annual accounts;
- the audit committee can become a barrier between the external auditors and the executive directors of the company; and
- the audit committee will not function effectively if it lacks the necessary understanding to deal with the accounting and auditing issues that will be brought to its attention.

Careful planning can prevent these becoming real issues in practice.

1.138   The Smith Guidance

As part of the UK Government's response to the collapse of Enron, a small working group was appointed by Financial Reporting Council, under the chairmanship of Sir Robert Smith, to develop further the initial guidance on audit committees included in the original *Combined Code*. The resulting report 'Audit Committees: Combined Code Guidance', commonly referred to as the *Smith Report*, was published in January 2003. The introduction to the report emphasises that the audit committee has a particular role, acting independently from the executive, in ensuring that the interests of shareholders in relation to financial reporting and internal control are properly protected. However, this is in no way intended to create a departure from the UK principle of the unitary board – all directors continue to have the same legal responsibility for the company's affairs and any disagreements must be resolved at board level. The report included the draft of a revised section of the *Combined Code* on audit committees, together with supplementary guidance intended to assist boards in establishing and operating an audit committee and also to assist directors who serve as members of an audit committee. The draft set out certain essential requirements for audit committees in bold text in the guidance and noted that compliance with these was considered necessary in order to achieve compliance with the *Combined Code*. The revised *Combined Code*, published by the Financial Reporting Council in July 2003, changed this approach slightly. In addition to the provisions on the role, responsibilities and membership of the audit committee, four of the 'bold text' items from the *Smith Report* have become *Combined Code* provisions – these cover the audit committee's work in relation to:

- reviewing the company's whistleblowing procedures;
- reviewing the effectiveness of internal audit (or the need for an internal audit function where the company does not have one);
- the appointment of external auditors; and
- the provision of non-audit services by the external auditors.

For accounting periods beginning on or after 1 November 2003, listed companies must confirm their compliance with these provisions or explain any departures. Other aspects of the *Smith Report* originally highlighted as being essential have simply become part of the supplementary guidance, which is published as an appendix to the Combined Code along with the Turnbull Guidance and other recommendations on good practice. Relevant issues from the Smith Guidance are discussed in the following sections.

1.139   Constitution and Terms of Reference

An audit committee should be constituted formally as a sub-committee of the main board, to ensure that there is a clear relationship between the two. The audit committee should report regularly to the main board and be answerable to it. The *Combined Code* also recommends that the board should provide written terms of reference for the audit committee and make them publicly available (eg on the company's website or by request), and that the annual report should include a separate section describing the work of the audit committee in discharging its responsibilities during the year (see **1.166** below). The *Smith Report* included an example terms of reference under the following headings (although this has not been reproduced in the Smith Guidance attached to the revised *Combined Code*):

- constitution;
- membership;
- attendance at meetings;
- frequency of meetings;
- authority;
- responsibilities; and
- reporting procedures.

A further example, based on that set out in the *Smith Report*, is given in Appendix 2 to this chapter. However, this is not intended to be prescriptive and companies are encouraged to develop and tailor it to suit their own circumstances. In particular, the example is drafted from the perspective of an individual company and will need adapting to cover the specific circumstances of a group. Terms of reference should be realistic and should give the committee sufficient resources and authority to perform its role effectively. The Smith Guidance recommends that the audit committee should carry out an annual review of its terms of reference and recommend to the board any changes that are considered necessary.

1.140   Membership of the Audit Committee

Membership of the audit committee is a critical issue – any committee can only be as good as the people that serve on it. In particular, the effectiveness of the audit committee often depends on a strong, independent chairman who has the confidence of both the board and the external auditors, and on the quality of the non-executive directors. The size and complexity of the company, and the size of the board of directors, will usually have a direct bearing on the size and membership of the audit committee. The *Combined Code* recommends that:

- the audit committee should have at least three members (or two members in the case of smaller companies), all of whom should be independent non-executive directors (see **6.17**); and
- the board should satisfy itself that at least one member of the audit committee has recent and relevant financial experience (the *Smith Report* suggested that this might be as an auditor or a finance director of a listed company) and the Smith Guidance notes that this member should preferably hold a professional accountancy qualification.

The chairman of the company should not be a member of the audit committee. The members of the audit committee should be identified in the annual report.

1.141   Skills, Experience and Training

There should normally be wide consultation before recommending that an individual is appointed as a member of the committee. The Smith Guidance suggests that appointments should be by recommendation of the nomination committee (where there is one), in consultation with the audit committee chairman. Qualities that will commonly be taken into account in assessing an individual's suitability for membership of the audit committee will include:

- breadth of general business experience;
- knowledge of the company's operations, finances and accounting;
- understanding of the roles of external and internal auditors and familiarity with the main concepts of Auditing Standards;
- knowledge and understanding of the key aspects of financial reporting;
- personal qualities; and
- commitment (including the amount of time that the individual can make available).

The audit committee will usually function as a team and it may therefore be appropriate to consider the balance of experience and abilities across the membership as a whole. The nature of the audit committee's activities makes it particularly important for the committee as a whole to have an adequate understanding of the management of business risk, accounting and financial reporting and internal control. Additional relevant skills may be needed, depending on the nature of the company's activities – for instance, where it is involved in specialised financial activities. Members of the company's executive management team should not be appointed to the audit committee as their attendance at every meeting could inhibit others from raising sensitive issues. However, their input to audit committee discussions may be needed from time to time, and there should be a facility for them to attend audit committee meetings by invitation (see **1.163** below).

1.142   Appointing a Chairman

The Cadbury Committee emphasised the importance of the chairman in ensuring the effective operation of the audit committee and the *Smith Report* highlighted the need for a frank and open relationship, and a high level of mutual trust, between the audit committee chairman and the board chairman, chief executive and finance director. The chairman of the audit committee will usually be appointed by the board as a whole. Particular qualities that will need to be assessed in appointing a chairman include:

- strength of personality;
- experience of the role of chairman;
- attitude to business risk management and control, and related ethical issues;
- attitude towards the audit function (both external and internal); and
- commitment (including the amount of time that he/she can make available).

1.143   Length of Appointment to Audit Committee

The long-term nature of the activities of the audit committee mean that a certain degree of continuity of membership is helpful. However, this needs to be balanced against the need for fresh input and a new outlook from time to time. The Smith Guidance recommends that appointments should be for a period of up to three years, extendable by no more than two additional periods of three years, provided that the individual continues to be sufficiently independent. From a practical point of view, it is often helpful for the appointment periods of the individual members to end in different years so that the company is not faced with a loss of significant audit committee experience by two or three members retiring at the same time.

1.144   Avoiding Conflicts of Interest

Individuals recommended for appointment to the audit committee should be required to confirm their independence at the time of appointment. Once appointed they are responsible for ensuring that their entry in the register of directors' interests is kept up to date and for declaring any potential conflict of interest in respect of agenda items at meetings of the audit committee. They should not vote on any item in respect of which they have a potential conflict of interest.

1.145   Training and Support for Audit Committee Members

The Smith Guidance recommends that an induction programme is provided for each new audit committee member, covering:

- the role of the audit committee and its terms of reference;
- the expected time commitment; and
- an overview of the company's business, including the main business and financial dynamics and risks.

It may also be helpful to provide new members with summaries of the issues raised in recent reports from both external and internal auditors. Ongoing training should be provided to all audit committee members to enable them to keep up to date with issues relevant to their role. This training might cover:

- principles and developments in financial reporting and related company law;
- understanding financial statements, applicable accounting standards and recommended accounting practice;
- the regulatory framework for the company's business;
- the role of external and internal audit; and
- risk management.

The Smith Guidance notes that both induction programmes and ongoing training might take a variety of forms, including attendance at formal courses and conferences, internal seminars and briefing sessions led by external advisers. The audit committee should also be given the facility, and the funding, to obtain independent legal, accounting or other advice where it reasonably considers this to be necessary.

1.146   Information Provided to Audit Committee

The Smith Guidance emphasises that management has an obligation to ensure that the audit committee is kept properly informed and to provide the information that it needs to fulfil its role. Management is expected to take the initiative in providing information to the committee, rather than waiting to be asked for it, and to make clear to all directors and employees that they must co-operate with the audit committee and provide any information requested.

1.147   Role and Activities of the Audit Committee

The role of audit committees has become increasingly diverse as they have become more common. The detailed role and activities of the audit committee must be tailored to the needs of the individual company, but the principal role of the audit committee is summarised as providing assurance that the board's collective responsibility for financial matters and internal control is rigorously discharged. The Smith Guidance summarises the role and responsibilities of the audit committee under the following headings:

- financial reporting;
- internal controls and risk management systems;
- whistleblowing;
- the internal audit process;
- the external audit process:
  - ○ appointment,
  - ○ terms and remuneration,
  - ○ independence, including the provision of non-audit services, and
  - ○ the annual audit cycle.

In the case of a group of companies, the parent board should ensure that there is adequate co-operation within the group, and with the external and internal auditors of each company within the group, to enable the audit committee to discharge its responsibilities. The Smith Guidance also emphasises that the work of the audit committee is wide-ranging, time-consuming and sometimes intensive – it is therefore important that members of the committee are able to make the appropriate amount of time available for the task and that they receive appropriate recompense for this, and that companies make appropriate resources available.

1.148   Financial Reporting

The audit committee's responsibilities in relation to financial reporting cover:

- the interim statement;
- the preliminary announcement;
- the company's financial statements;
- the operating and financial review (OFR);
- the company's corporate governance statements; and
- the summary financial statement (where one is prepared).

Wherever practical, the audit committee should also review other statements containing financial information which require board approval prior to publication – for instance, the release of price sensitive information, or financial reports to regulators. Management are responsible for preparing accounts which show a true and fair view, and for meeting relevant accounting and disclosure requirements, and the audit committee's review should focus in particular on:

- comparisons with the previous year and the explanations for any significant variances;
- the significant accounting policies, estimates and judgements, and whether these are appropriate;
- any changes in accounting policies and their disclosure in the accounts;
- any adjustments necessary as a result of the work carried out by the external auditors;
- going concern;
- disclosure of any significant commitments or contingent liabilities;

- impact of any significant events since the balance sheet date;
- compliance with accounting standards and other reporting requirements (including, where appropriate, those laid down by the FSA);
- the clarity and completeness of the disclosures, and whether they are set properly in context; and
- the results of the external audit.

In particular, management should explain the accounting treatment of any significant or unusual transactions, particularly where the treatment is open to different approaches, and the committee should consider whether the approach adopted is appropriate. Following their review, the audit committee should submit the relevant financial statements to the board with their recommendations on approval. If the committee is not satisfied with any aspect of the company's financial reporting, it should report its views to the board.

1.149   Internal Controls and Risk Management Systems

The audit committee should review the company's internal financial controls (ie the systems used to identify, assess, manage and monitor financial risks) and, in the absence of other specific arrangements (for instance, the establishment of a separate risk committee of independent directors) should review the company's internal control and risk management systems. Management should report to the committee on the effectiveness of the systems that they have established and, in particular, the results of any testing carried out by the internal and external auditors. Following their assessment, the audit committee should review and approve the directors' statements in the annual report in respect of internal control and the management of risk (see **6.66** below).

1.150   Whistleblowing

The audit committee should review the arrangements in place to enable company staff to raise, in confidence, concerns about possible improprieties in respect of financial reporting or other issues, and should consider whether these provide for proportionate and independent investigation and follow-up of the matters raised (see also **12 FRAUD**).

1.151   The Internal Audit Process

Where the company has an internal audit function, the audit committee should monitor and review the effectiveness of internal audit activities. This process should normally include:

- reviewing and approving the remit of the internal audit function;
- confirming that there is appropriate liaison between external and internal auditors, to prevent duplication of work and make the most effective use of the available resources;
- confirming that the head of internal audit has direct access to the board chairman and to the audit committee, and is accountable to the audit committee;

- ensuring that the internal audit function is adequately resourced, maintains a suitable degree of independence from other functions within the company, has appropriate standing within the company and is given access to the information that it needs in order to fulfil its remit;
- reviewing the proposed annual programme of internal audit work before this is submitted to the board for approval;
- monitoring progress against the plan during the year;
- reviewing the results of internal audit work, together with management's response to the points raised; and
- monitoring and assessing the role and effectiveness of the internal audit function in the context of the company's risk management system.

The Smith Guidance also notes that the audit committee should approve the appointment, or termination of appointment, of the head of internal audit. Where the company does not have an internal audit function, the *Combined Code* recommends that the audit committee should consider annually whether there is a need to establish one and make a recommendation to the board on this. Where an internal audit function is not considered necessary, the audit committee should explain the reasoning behind this decision in the relevant section of the annual report.

1.152   Appointment of External Auditors

The Smith Guidance notes that the audit committee is responsible for overseeing the company's relationship with the external auditors, and for overseeing the selection process where the appointment of new auditors is being considered. Technically, the annual appointment of the external auditors is a matter for the shareholders, but the board of directors will usually put forward recommendations for the shareholders to consider. Under the *Combined Code*, the audit committee should have primary responsibility for making a recommendation on the appointment, reappointment or removal of the external auditors. The recommendation should be made initially to the board, and then to the company's shareholders. If the board does not accept the recommendation of the audit committee, the annual report must include a statement from the audit committee explaining its recommendation and why the board has taken a different view. The audit committee's recommendation each year should be based on an assessment of the qualifications, expertise, resources, effectiveness and independence of the external auditors. The assessment should cover all aspects of the audit service and, as part of their review, the audit committee should obtain a report on the audit firm's own internal quality control procedures. If the external auditor resigns, the audit committee should investigate any issues giving rise to the resignation and consider whether any further action is required.

1.153   *Terms and Remuneration of External Auditors*

The audit committee should approve the terms of engagement and the remuneration to be paid to the external auditor in respect of audit services. The committee should review the audit engagement letter at the start of each audit and confirm that it has been updated to deal with any new issues or requirements and any other changes in circumstances since the previous year. Where the audit committee considers the scope of the audit to be inadequate, it should arrange for additional work to be undertaken. The committee should also satisfy itself that the remuneration payable to the auditors is appropriate for the service provided and that an effective audit can be carried out for that fee.

1.154 *Independence*

The audit committee should have procedures to assess the independence and objectivity of the external auditors each year, taking into account relevant professional and regulatory requirements. The assessment should cover all relationships between the company and the audit firm, including the provision of non-audit services. In the case of listed companies, professional auditing standards require the auditors to make certain disclosures in respect of their independence each year (see **1.30** above) and the Smith Guidance also recommends that the audit committee should seek annual information from the audit firm on the policies and processes that it adopts to maintain independence and monitor compliance with relevant professional requirements, including the requirement under APB Ethical Standards (see **1.28** and **1.33** above) for the appointment of the audit engagement partner to be rotated at least every five years and that of other key audit partners to be rotated at least every seven years, and current UK guidance on fee dependency. Factors to consider when assessing independence include:

- undue financial dependence on the audit client;
- actual or threatened litigation in respect of the audit client;
- personal or family relationships;
- beneficial interests in shares and other investments;
- involvement of the audit firm as trustee;
- provision of other services to the audit client;
- a partner or senior member of staff joining the audit client.

1.155 *Employment of Auditor's Former Employees*

The Smith Guidance recommends that the audit committee should agree with the board the company's policy on the employment of former partners and employees of the audit firm, especially any who were part of the audit team and moved directly to the company. The policy should take into account relevant ethical guidance within the accountancy profession. The committee should then monitor the application of the policy and should consider in particular the number of such individuals currently employed in senior positions within the company and whether this could impair, or be perceived to impair, the independence of the audit firm. Detailed guidance is now set out in APB Ethical

Standard for Auditors 2 (ES 2) (see **1.28** above) which includes consideration of the following situations:

- a partner or employee of the audit firm working for an audit client on a temporary or 'loan' basis;
- a partner joining an audit client;
- another member of the audit engagement team joining an audit client;
- a close family member of a partner and/or other senior individual within the audit firm joining an audit client; and
- a director or senior employee of the audit client joining the audit firm.

1.156   *Provision of Non-audit Services*

The audit committee should develop and recommend to the board the company's policy on the provision of non-audit services by the audit firm, the objective being to ensure that the provision of such services does not impair the independence or objectivity of the auditor. Issues to be considered by the audit committee include:

- whether the audit firm is a suitable supplier of the services – for instance, as a result of its skills and experience;
- whether appropriate safeguards are in place to prevent any threat to independence or objectivity in the conduct of the external audit;
- the nature of the non-audit services and the related fee levels, individually and in aggregate, relative to the audit fee; and
- the criteria which govern the compensation of the individuals performing the audit.

Other issues to consider in the context of the provision of non-audit services are summarised in **1.28–1.32** above. The company's formal policy should specify the types of work for which the external auditors can be engaged without formal approval, those from which the external auditors should be excluded, and those which require formal referral to the audit committee for a decision. The committee may also wish to set fee limits in general or for specific classes of work. In principle, the audit committee should not agree to the auditors providing non-audit services which:

- result in the external auditor auditing the work of its own firm;
- result in the external auditor making management decisions for the company;
- create a mutuality of interest between the external auditor and the company; or
- put the external auditor into the position of advocate for the company.

The *Combined Code* recommends that the annual report to shareholders should explain how the company's policy provides appropriate protection of auditor independence and objectivity. For accounting periods beginning on or after 1 October 2005, more stringent requirements have been introduced on the disclosure of non-audit services provided by the auditors and their associates, and the related remuneration received (see **1.107–1.110** above).

1.157   Agreeing the Scope of the External Audit

Before the detailed audit work commences each year, the audit committee should discuss and agree with the auditors the scope of their work and the overall work plan, including planned materiality levels and proposed resources to carry out the plan. In the case of a group with a complex structure or overseas interests, more than one firm of auditors may be involved, and the audit committee will need to be satisfied that proper co-ordination between the various auditors can be achieved. This meeting with the auditors will also provide a suitable opportunity to consider recent changes in accounting standards and reporting requirements and the potential impact for the company. Where additional information needs to be prepared or collated as a result of these changes, early consideration of the issues should help to ensure that the company has sufficient time to put the necessary procedures in place. It will also be important to consider any changes that have taken place within the business, or are planned for the near future, and their impact for the annual accounts and the audit (for instance, new business activities or potential closures). The aim should be to identify any likely problem areas at this stage, so that solutions can be identified in good time. If the company has an internal audit function, it will be important to ensure that there is good liaison between the internal and external auditors, to avoid any potential duplication of work and make the most effective use of all the available resources. In the case of listed companies, the auditors will often have additional reporting responsibilities in respect of the interim report and corporate governance issues, and the nature and scope of their work in these areas also needs to be considered and agreed.

1.158   Reviewing the Results of the External Audit

The results of the external audit should be reviewed in conjunction with the annual report and accounts, as the two are inextricably linked. In particular, the audit committee should:

- discuss with the auditors any issues identified during the course of their work, distinguishing those that have been resolved and any that remain unresolved, and any reservations that the external auditors have in respect of the annual report and accounts;
- review the key accounting and audit judgements; and
- review the level of errors identified during the audit and obtain explanations from management and the auditors for any that remain unadjusted.

The audit committee should also review the audit representation letter before it is signed by management, and consider whether the information given is complete and appropriate, based on the committee's own knowledge. In particular, the committee should explore any non-standard issues raised in the representation letter. Other issues that may need to be considered at this stage include:

- adequacy of the company's accounting records and systems of internal control;
- any breakdowns in systems and controls identified during the audit;

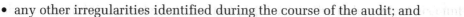

- any other irregularities identified during the course of the audit; and
- where relevant, the auditors' opinion on the company's statement of compliance with the *Combined Code* and the consistency of the company's statements on going concern and internal control with the knowledge gained by the external auditors during the course of their work.

This will usually be an appropriate time for the audit committee to discuss the actual audit costs with the auditors and to begin thinking about any changes to the audit approach that may be needed for the following year – planning for the next year will usually be most effective when the successes and difficulties of the current year are fresh in the mind.

1.159   Reviewing the Auditors' Report to Management

At the conclusion of the audit, the auditors will usually issue a formal written report on:

- any significant weaknesses in the accounting or internal control systems that have come to their attention during the audit, together with their recommendations for improvements;
- any significant business issues that have come to their attention during the audit, together with their advice (for instance, potential economies or improvements in efficiency); and
- any significant errors identified during the audit and comments on any individual accounting policies or practices that they consider need to be drawn to the attention of the directors or senior management.

The audit committee should consider this report, together with management's response to the points raised. This is considered in more detail at **1.93–1.95** above.

1.160   Assessing the Effectiveness of the External Audit

At the end of the audit cycle, the audit committee should assess the effectiveness of the external audit process and review:

- any significant changes from the original audit plan and the reasons for these;
- the robustness and perceptiveness of the auditors in handling the key accounting and auditing judgements identified, and in responding to questions from the audit committee;
- feedback from key individuals (eg finance director, head of internal audit) on the conduct of the external audit; and
- the content of the management letter and any commentary on the systems of internal control, to assess whether these demonstrate a good understanding of the business, whether any recommendations have been acted upon and, where relevant, the reasons why no action has been taken.

1.161   Frequency and Timing of Audit Committee Meetings

In practice, most audit committees meet between two and four times a year, depending on the complexity of the company's activities. The Smith Guidance now recommends that there should be no fewer than three meetings each year, timed to coincide with key dates in the financial reporting cycle, although it also notes that most committees will need to meet more frequently than this. The important point is for the committee to meet sufficiently often to be able to review and monitor major issues. The terms of reference may provide for additional meetings to be held in emergencies (for instance, where a prompt decision is needed) or for specific purposes. It is also important to consider the timing of audit committees' meetings in relation to:

- the scheduled meetings of the main board, so that the audit committee can report and put forward its recommendations in a timely manner; and
- the company's financial timetable – in the case of quoted companies, this will need to take into account the publication of the interim report, preliminary announcement and annual report and accounts so that the audit committee can make its input at the appropriate point.

Sufficient time should be allowed between audit committee and main board meetings to enable issues requiring further work to be properly followed up and reported to the board where appropriate. Meetings should be planned well in advance to encourage a good attendance by committee members and so that finance staff, external auditors and internal auditors have plenty of notice of when information will need to be presented. In larger organisations, it may be appropriate for the location of the meetings to be varied, to give audit committee members the opportunity to visit key operational sites. The Smith Guidance also notes that the audit committee chairman and, to a lesser extent, other committee members will usually want to keep in touch on a continuing basis with key individuals within the company and with the external audit lead partner.

1.162   Agendas

The annual accounts production and audit schedules will often provide a useful starting point when scheduling meetings of the audit committee and agreeing agendas. A suitable schedule of meetings for a quoted company might be as follows:

Timing	Main agenda items

Approximately five months into the financial year	• Consideration of the scope of the external auditors' work on the interim report;
	• Consideration of the report from the Head of Internal Audit, covering:
	  ○ progress with the planned work programme,
	  ○ issues arising since the first report,

(continued)

Timing	Main agenda items
	○ follow up of significant points raised in the previous report; ● Self-assessment of the committee's effectiveness and review of the terms of reference for the committee to confirm these are still appropriate or to identify changes to be put to the board for consideration.
Approximately seven months into the financial year	● Consideration of recent or imminent developments in financial reporting and their impact for the company; ● Review of the interim report prior to its release; ● Consideration of the results of the external auditors' work on the interim report; ● Discussion with the external auditors on the proposed audit approach and the audit plan; ● Consideration of the proposed external audit fee.
Approximately ten months into the financial year	● Consideration of the report from the Head of Internal Audit, covering: ○ progress with the planned work programme, ○ issues arising since the last report, ○ follow up of significant points raised in the previous report; ● Consideration of the scope of internal audit work for the next financial year.
Prior to the release of the preliminary announcement	● Consideration of the annual report and accounts; ● Review of the results of the external audit; ● Review of external audit costs; ● Review of the service provided by the external auditors, and their independence, and recommendation on appointment (or reappointment) of auditors; ● Consideration of annual report from the Head of Internal Audit, covering: ○ summary of the work completed for the previous financial year and comparison with the planned work programme, ○ issues arising since the last report, ○ follow up of significant points raised in previous report, ○ progress of the work planned for the current financial year.

Where the company has an internal audit function, the review of reports from this department may be dealt with as separate agenda items at the meetings dealing with external audit issues (as suggested above), or may be covered in separate meetings. For instance, in the case of an unquoted company, there will not usually be an interim report and it may therefore be appropriate to schedule four audit committee meetings during the year to deal alternately with internal audit and external audit issues.

1.163 Other Attendees

The Combined Code states that no one other than the relevant committee chairman and members is entitled to be present at meetings of the main board committees (ie audit, remuneration and nomination), and the Smith Guidance reinforces this point in respect of the audit committee. However, other individuals may attend by invitation of the committee, and the finance director, the head of internal audit and the external auditors will usually be invited to attend. Depending on the circumstances, they may only need to attend for part of the meeting. The Smith Guidance recommends that the audit committee should meet at least once each year with the external and internal auditors without management present, to ensure that the auditors have an opportunity to raise any issues of concern. In practice, this can usually be arranged to take place at the conclusion of one of the regular audit committee meetings.

1.164   Attendance Records

It is good practice to keep detailed attendance records for audit committee meetings and for the board of directors to review these on an annual basis to confirm that each committee member is making an appropriate contribution to the work of the committee. Attendance information will also need to be retained in future for inclusion in the annual report on the committee's activities (see **1.166** below).

1.165   Reporting to the Main Board

The agendas for meetings of the main board should include a report from the chairman of the audit committee as a regular item. This enables the audit committee to report to the board on the main points arising from its discussions with both external and internal auditors and also to put recommendations to the board when appropriate. The board has collective responsibility for the annual accounts and for internal control within the company, but will usually look to the audit committee for advice on issues relating to financial reporting, internal controls and the financial aspects of corporate governance. The audit committee will also have responsibility for making recommendations to the board on the appointment or reappointment of auditors and the agreement of the external audit fee. Minutes of the meetings of the audit committee will usually be circulated to all board members for information. The Smith Guidance notes that, where there is disagreement between the audit committee and the board, adequate time should be made available for discussion, and hopefully resolution, of the issue. If the matter cannot be resolved, the audit committee should have the right to report the issue to the shareholders within the annual report on its activities.

1.166   Reporting to Shareholders

The Smith Guidance recommends that the annual report includes a separate section each year describing the actions taken by the audit committee in fulfilling its responsibilities, as set out in the committee's terms of reference. The suggested contents of the report include:

- a summary of the role of the audit committee;
- the names of all members of the audit committee during the period (with appointment and resignation dates where appropriate) and details of the relevant qualifications, expertise and experience of each member;
- the number of audit committee meetings and the attendance by each member;
- the actions and procedures carried out to:
  - monitor the integrity of the financial statements,
  - review the integrity of the company's internal financial control and risk management systems,
  - review the independence of the external auditors, including disclosure of the company's policy on the provision of non-audit services and an explanation of how this protects auditor independence,
  - oversee the external audit process, including confirmation that its effectiveness has been assessed.

Other areas that may need to be covered include:

- an explanation of the recommendation to the board on the appointment of the external auditors and, where applicable, the process adopted to select a new auditor;
- confirmation that the plans and work of the internal audit department have been reviewed or, if there is no internal audit function, an explanation of the committee's consideration of the need to establish one;
- details of the remuneration policies for members of the audit committee (or a cross-reference to the directors' remuneration report); and
- details of any dedicated resources available to the committee.

The *Smith Report* included an outline of such a report, but this is not reproduced in the guidance attached to the revised *Combined Code*. The audit committee chairman should also be present at the AGM to answer questions, through the board chairman, on this report and on any other matters that come within the scope of the audit committee's responsibilities.

1.167 Self-Assessment and Appraisal

The *Combined Code* recommends that the board should undertake a formal and rigorous annual evaluation of the effectiveness of each board committee. In the case of the audit committee, this might include considering developments generally in the role and activities of audit committees and discussing the extent to which the audit committee is considered to have fulfilled the various aspects of its terms of reference. Feedback might also be sought from the head of internal audit and the external auditors on these points. Specific questions to consider might include:

- Are there appropriate procedures for appointing committee members?
- Does the committee have the appropriate mix of knowledge and skills?

- Is the amount and nature of training and administrative support appropriate?
- Are the committee's terms of reference appropriate?
- Does the committee adequately fulfil its role?
- Is the frequency and timing of committee meetings appropriate?
- Are agendas and appropriate supporting information circulated to committee members in good time?
- How effective are the committee's relationships with management, internal audit and the external auditors?
- Does the committee's workload require a change of emphasis?
- Does the committee need subsidiary committees to deal with significant or overseas business units?
- If subsidiary committees are already in place, are the arrangements working effectively?
- What significant issues does the committee need to address in the coming year?

The appendices to the revised *Combined Code* also include a performance evaluation checklist, setting out questions that may be relevant to an assessment of the performance of the board and of individual non-executive directors.

1.168   Additional Guidance

Since the introduction of the revised *Combined Code* in 2003, the ICAEW has published a series of guidance booklets designed to help directors, and in particular non-executive directors who are members of an audit committee, to meet their responsibilities. The following publications may be of particular interest to finance directors and audit committee members:

- *Company Reporting and Audit Requirements* (November 2003)
- *Evaluating Your Auditors* (November 2003)
- *Reviewing Auditor Independence* (November 2003)
- *Monitoring the Integrity of Financial Statements* (March 2004)
- *Whistleblowing Arrangements* (March 2004)
- *The Internal Audit Function* (March 2004)

All of the above are available free of charge from the ICAEW website (www.icaew.co.uk). The APB has also published an updated Briefing Paper 'Effective Communication between Audit Committees and External Auditors', which provides guidance for non-executive directors on the implications of formal reporting by auditors under professional auditing standards. This is available from the APB website (www.frc.org.uk/apb/publications). Details of additional publications dealing specifically with internal audit matters can be found at **1.134** above.

Appendix 1

Useful Websites on Audit Related Matters

Financial Reporting Council	www.frc.org.uk
Financial Reporting Review Panel	www.frc.org.uk/frrp
Auditing Practices Board	www.frc.org.uk/apb
Professional Oversight Board	www.frc.org.uk/pob
Accountancy Investigation and Disciplinary Board	www.frc.org.uk/aidb
Institute of Chartered Accountants in England and Wales	www.icaew.co.uk
ICAEW Audit and Assurance Faculty	www.icaew.co.uk/aafac
Institute of Internal Auditors (UK and Ireland)	www.iia.org.uk

Appendix 2

Specimen Terms of Reference for an Audit Committee

These specimen terms of reference are for guidance only and are based on the example published in the *Smith Report* (see **1.138** above). Terms of reference should be developed and adapted to suit the specific circumstances of the company or group.

1   Constitution

1.1   The board hereby resolves to establish a committee of the board, to be known as the audit committee ('the committee').

2   Membership

2.1   The committee shall be appointed by the board. All members of the committee shall be independent non-executive directors of the company. The committee shall consist of not less than three members. Two members shall comprise a quorum at any meeting of the committee.

2.2   The chairman of the committee shall be appointed by the board from amongst the independent non-executive directors.

3   Attendance at Meetings

3.1   The finance director, the head of internal audit and a representative of the external auditors shall attend meetings at the invitation of the committee.

3.2   The chairman of the board and other board members shall attend meetings if invited by the committee.

3.3   There shall be at least one committee meeting, or part of a meeting, each year where the external auditors and internal auditors attend without management present.

3.4   The company secretary shall be the secretary to the committee.

4   Frequency of Meetings

4.1   Meetings shall be held not less than three times each year and, where appropriate, shall coincide with key dates in the company's financial reporting cycle.

4.2   Additional meetings shall be held as required, and the external auditors or internal auditors may request a meeting if they consider that one is necessary.

5   Authority

5.1   The committee is authorised by the board to:
- investigate any activity within its terms of reference;
- seek any information that it requires from any employee (and all employees are directed to co-operate with any request made by the committee); and
- obtain external legal or other independent professional advice and request advisers to attend meetings as necessary.

6   Responsibilities

6.1   The responsibilities of the committee shall be:
- to consider the appointment of the external auditor and assess the independence of the external auditor, ensuring that key partners are rotated at appropriate intervals;
- to oversee the process for selecting the external auditor and make appropriate recommendations, through the board, to the shareholders for consideration at the AGM;
- to recommend the audit fee to the board and pre-approve any fees in respect of non-audit service provided by the external auditor, and to ensure that the provision of non-audit services does not impair the independence or objectivity of the external auditor;
- to discuss with the external auditor, before the audit commences, the nature and scope of the audit, and any additional assurance or reporting that may be required, and to review the auditor's quality control procedures and the steps taken to respond to changes in regulatory and other requirements;
- to consider whether there is appropriate liaison and co-ordination between the internal and external auditors;
- to review the external auditor's management letter and management's response;
- to review the internal audit programme and ensure that the internal audit function is adequately resourced and has appropriate standing within the company;
- to consider management's response to any major internal audit or external audit recommendations;
- to approve the appointment or dismissal of the head of internal audit;
- to review the company's procedures for handling allegations from whistleblowers;
- to review reports from management and the internal auditors on the effectiveness of the systems for internal financial control, financial reporting and risk management.

- to review, and challenge where necessary, the actions and judgements of management in relation to the interim report, annual financial statements and other formal reports on the company's financial performance before submission to the board, paying particular attention to:
  - critical accounting policies and practices and any changes in them,
  - decisions requiring a major element of judgement,
  - the extent to which the financial statements are affected by any unusual transactions in the year, and how they are disclosed,
  - the clarity of disclosures,
  - significant adjustments resulting from the audit,
  - the going concern assumption,
  - compliance with accounting standards, and
  - compliance with stock exchange and other legal requirements;
- to review the company's statements on compliance with the *Combined Code*, going concern and the review of the effectiveness of the company's system of internal control prior to endorsement by the board, and in particular to review:
  - the policies and processes for identifying and assessing business risks and the management of those risks by the company,
  - the company's policies for ensuring compliance with relevant legal and regulatory requirements,
  - the company's policies for the prevention and detection of fraud, and
  - the effectiveness of such policies and procedures in practice;
- to discuss any problems and reservations arising from the external audit and any matters that the external and internal auditors may wish to discuss (in the absence of management where necessary);
- to consider other topics and issues, as defined by the board.

7   Reporting Procedures

7.1   The secretary shall circulate the minutes of meetings of the committee to all members of the board.

7.2   The chairman of the committee, or as a minimum another member of the committee, shall attend the board meeting at which the annual accounts and reports are approved.

7.3   The committee's responsibilities and activities during the year shall be disclosed in the annual report and accounts.

7.4   The chairman of the committee shall attend the AGM and answer questions, through the chairman of the board, on the committee's responsibilities and activities.

8   Terms of Reference

8.1   The committee shall conduct an annual review of its terms of reference and make recommendations to the board.

Cashflow Management

2 Cashflow Management

2.1 Overview

> **At a Glance**
> * Business growth always puts pressure on cashflow, but careful management can help to minimise working capital requirements.
> * The objective of managing working capital is to ensure that sufficient funds are available to meet the day-to-day cashflow needs of the business.
> * There are a number of common weaknesses that need to be addressed when managing working capital.

2.2 Importance of Cashflow Management

In developing any business, it is important to appreciate the relationship between growth and cashflow. A company's trading performance controls the amount of cash that flows in and out of the business, but the rate at which that cashflow takes place depends on the efficiency with which the company's assets and liabilities are managed. Business growth always puts pressure on cash resources because of the inevitable delays between the timing of payments (cash outflow) and receipts (cash inflow). Good management of cash, debtors, creditors and stock helps to minimise working capital requirements and either reduces borrowing costs or releases funds for other profitable investment. Even the most profitable of companies can fail if its cashflow is not properly managed.

2.3 Managing Working Capital

The main objective of working capital management is to ensure that sufficient cash is available to meet the day-to-day cashflow needs of the business. These will include making payments on time to:

* management and staff, in the form of wages and salaries;
* those who supply goods and services to the company;
* central and local government, in the form of VAT, corporation tax, business rates etc.

In order to manage working capital and cashflow effectively, management needs to have regular and reliable information on what is happening in every aspect of the business.

2.4 Common Weaknesses

The more common weaknesses in managing a company's working capital requirements include:

- failure to prepare cashflow forecasts, or to use and update them on a regular basis once they have been prepared – this usually results in the business encountering regular cash crises and relying heavily on expensive short-term borrowings;
- failure to budget in terms of the balance sheet as well as the profit and loss account – without this, there is no benchmark against which to measure the effectiveness of the company's asset management;
- failure to control debtors effectively, thus missing the best opportunity for releasing working capital for other purposes;
- attempts to increase cash resources by not paying suppliers, without considering the damage that this might do to relationships and the consequent effect on supplies or other aspects of the company's business;
- failure to appreciate the true cost of holding unnecessarily high levels of stock.

2.5 Managing Cash Resources

At a Glance
- A detailed medium-term cashflow forecast should be prepared to identify when surplus cash is likely to arise and when additional cash is likely to be required.
- This requires the preparation of realistic monthly forecasts for all items of income and expenditure for a period of at least twelve months.
- Assumptions made in preparing the forecast should be consistent and clearly thought through, and should be documented for future reference.
- It is helpful to incorporate a measure of sensitivity into the forecast, so that the potential effect of unexpected events can be assessed.
- Prompt action should be taken to deal with any potential cash shortages identified by the forecast.
- Actual cashflow should be compared with the forecast on a regular basis (usually monthly).
- Bank charges should be subjected to regular monitoring and review.
- Guidelines should be established for the investment of surplus funds as they arise.
- Controls should be established to achieve an acceptable degree of security over the company's cash resources.

2.6   Key Aspects

The key aspects of the management of cash resources are:

- regular preparation and updating of cashflow forecasts;
- regular monitoring of cash balances;
- prompt investment of surplus funds; and
- development of good internal control over cash.

2.7   Need for Cashflow Forecasts

Every business will need to prepare short-term cashflow forecasts (eg an informal projection of the cash requirements over the next week) to confirm that the immediate cash needs can be met from existing resources or facilities, but in order to manage cash resources effectively a more detailed, medium-term forecast will need to be developed. The objective is to identify:

- when surplus cash is likely to arise, so that returns on this can be maximised; and
- when additional cash is likely to be required, so that appropriate borrowings can be arranged at the lowest available cost – bank overdrafts are usually one of the most expensive forms of borrowing, so if the cashflow forecast indicates a longer-term need for a particular level of finance, it will be advisable to try to arrange a cheaper alternative.

The completed forecast will provide a useful benchmark against which to measure actual cashflow performance. A detailed cashflow forecast will also be an important element of the information that the directors need in order to assess whether the business is a going concern (see **6 CORPORATE GOVERNANCE** and **11 FINANCIAL REPORTING**).

2.8   Preparing a Detailed Cashflow Forecast

The preparation of a detailed medium-term cashflow forecast will involve the collation of information from a variety of sources within the business. In particular, it will require the preparation of sensible monthly forecasts of all items of income and expenditure, based on projections of:

- sales;
- other income (eg investment income);
- staff wages and salaries;
- other direct costs and overheads;
- fixed asset purchases and disposals;
- financing charges;
- taxation, including VAT; and
- any other payments that the business is committed to making (eg repayment of loan finance).

These projections must take into account the expected timing of the related cashflows. For instance, in the case of sales, as well as predicting the total amount of goods or services to be sold over the period, it will also be necessary to assess when the company's customers will actually pay for the goods and services that they have received, taking into account the company's standard payment terms and also past experience of business with those customers. The projections should cover a minimum period of twelve months. Depending on the nature of the business it may be possible or advisable to prepare cashflow forecasts for a longer period. Another useful option is to prepare the forecast on a rolling basis, so that projections for an additional period are added on a monthly or quarterly basis as appropriate and the detailed forecast always looks ahead for a period of twelve months. An example layout of a detailed cashflow forecast is given overleaf.

2.9   *Assumptions*

The preparation of a cashflow forecast will inevitably involve the use of assumptions. These should be clearly thought through and documented for future reference. It is also of critical importance that the assumptions used in different aspects of the forecast are consistent with one another – for instance, that the projections for direct costs are based on the same sales volumes as the sales projections.

2.10   *Sensitivity Analysis*

It is usually helpful to incorporate a measure of sensitivity into the cashflow forecast. For instance, what will happen to the overall cash position if a significant order fails to materialise as predicted, or if a customer suddenly doubles his order requirements (with a consequent effect on direct costs, which may need to be paid before the additional income comes in from the increased sales)? Will there be sufficient flexibility in the available cash resources to cope with this? It is also important to consider the impact that fixed overhead costs will have on cashflow if the predicted sales income is not achieved or is achieved later than originally expected.

2.11   Using a Cashflow Forecast

Having put time and effort into preparing a cashflow forecast, it is vital that the end result is put to good use. If the forecast indicates a serious cash shortage at certain times of the year, the first step is to consider whether some of the projected expenditure could be rescheduled – for instance, delaying the purchase of some fixed assets for a month or two may avoid the cash shortage without serious detriment to the business operations. Inevitably, many payments cannot be delayed and if it is not possible to avoid the cash shortage by rescheduling expenditure, the options for obtaining some additional finance should be explored at an early stage.

Example: Cashflow forecast

	Jan	Feb	Mar	Apr	May	Jun	Jul	Aug	Sept	Oct	Nov	Dec
Receipts												
Sales												
Investment income												
Loans received												
Other												
Total receipts												
Payments												
Wages and salaries												
PAYE and NI												
Direct costs:												
Materials												
Power												
etc.												
Overheads												
Insurance												
Travel												
Rates												
Leasing												
Bank charges												
etc.												
Fixed assets												
VAT												
Loan repayments												
Corporation tax												
Total payments												
Surplus/(deficit) for month												
Opening bank balance												
Closing bank balance												

Cashflow Management

2.12   Regular Comparison of Actual with Forecast

Actual cashflows should be compared with the forecast on a regular basis (usually monthly) and any significant variations should be investigated, so that remedial action can be taken if necessary. This exercise involves comparing actual receipts and payments against the original forecast, so that differences can be identified and explained. The forecast for the remainder of the period should then be updated to reflect the impact of any receipts and payments that were projected to arise at an earlier date but which are still outstanding. The overall projected cash position will need to be checked again to confirm that it is still within the facilities available, or to identify when additional arrangements will need to be put into place. These steps should help management to constantly refine and improve their forecasting procedures, and also help to clarify exactly what is happening within the business.

2.13   Relationship with Bank

If the updated forecast indicates that an agreed overdraft limit is likely to be breached for a short time, this should be discussed with the bank manager at the earliest opportunity. If the forecast indicates that the present overdraft limit is likely to be inadequate in the longer term, further action will be needed, either to obtain additional finance from other sources or to approach the bank for an increase in the overdraft. A business is more likely to get a positive response from the bank if it can demonstrate that it has working capital, and in particular cashflow, under good control than if it gives the impression of living from day to day and dealing with the surprises as they happen. Regular communication with the bank when things are going well will put useful relationships in place for the time when additional help and support is needed.

2.14   Monitoring Bank Balances

As well as keeping a regular check on cashflows, and comparing actual with forecast, it is also important to be aware of the current bank position and in particular to understand exactly what the bank is charging the business for the facilities that it provides. Issues to be considered include the following.

- Do you understand the extent and implications of the various elements of the charges that the bank makes and when these will be charged to your account?
- Do you understand the interest arrangements in respect of the account?
- Do you predict what the charges will be, compare this with the amount actually charged and immediately follow up any apparent overcharging?

Smaller businesses in particular, and especially those that are new and growing, are often in a difficult position when it comes to negotiating with their bankers, but it is advisable to try to ensure that terms are reviewed on a regular basis and that the bank is offering the best deal available.

2.15 Investment of Surplus Funds

Guidelines should be established in advance for the investment of surplus funds as they arise – leaving money idle in a bank account costs the business money in terms of lost income. There will usually be a cost to transferring surplus funds to a deposit or money market account and it is therefore important to establish that the return will be worthwhile. It should be relatively straightforward to establish the minimum amount that needs to be invested in order to achieve a return and thus to set a sensible guideline above which funds should be considered for investment. The period of time for which the funds can be invested will depend on the company's financial commitments. An up-to-date cashflow forecast should be helpful in establishing when the surplus funds will need to be available for other purposes.

2.16 Internal Controls Over Cash

Controls should be established to achieve a sensible degree of security over the company's cash and to ensure that receipts and payments are recorded promptly in the accounting records. In a more complex organisation, and particularly where extensive use is made of electronic payments and receipts, additional controls may need to be introduced. Basic cash controls will usually include procedures to ensure that:

- duties in this area are segregated as far as is practicable;
- all payments are supported by appropriately authorised documentation, which should be presented to the person signing the cheque (or equivalent);
- all receipts are banked at the earliest practical opportunity;
- any amounts received in cash are banked in tact (ie some or all of the cash is not used for other business purposes);
- detailed reconciliations are prepared monthly (at least) for each bank account and are subject to regular review – and any unusual, or long outstanding, items are promptly investigated.

In particular, staff should be made aware of the need to bank funds promptly. In a smaller operation it may be appropriate for banking to take place once or twice a week as a general rule, but in a larger company daily bankings will usually be needed. Even where banking takes place only on set days, special arrangements should be made to ensure that large cheques are banked as soon as they are received rather than being held until the next regular banking. Customers should also be encouraged to make use of bank transfers and other electronic payment methods as much as possible, as this speeds up the process of cleared funds reaching the company's bank account.

Cashflow Management

2.17   Managing Debtors

At a Glance
* Effective management of debtors can be one of the quickest and easiest ways to release cash for other purposes.
* Specific consideration should be given to payment terms when negotiating and agreeing orders or contracts.
* Procedures should be established to ensure that invoices are raised promptly, and to deal with any customer queries and disputes that may arise.
* Credit terms should be stated on all relevant documentation – standard credit terms should be subject to regular review, including comparison with those offered by other businesses.
* The potential benefits to be gained by offering incentives for prompt payment should be weighed against the potential costs.
* Credit limits should be established for individual customers and should be subject to regular review.
* A clear system should be established for following up unpaid invoices and for monitoring overall debtor days.
* Debt factoring and invoice discounting may be useful ways of releasing cash in certain circumstances.
* Businesses are entitled to charge interest on overdue debts.

2.18   Prompt Conversion into Cash

Debtors can make a heavy demand on working capital, especially when a business is growing, but effective management of debtors can be one of the quickest and easiest ways to release cash for other purposes. The aim of a successful business should be to convert stock (where relevant) to debtors and then to cash in the shortest possible time – having capital tied up in debtors leads to increased borrowing costs or the lost opportunity of investing the additional cash more profitably elsewhere. The two key elements of effective debtor management are a good system of internal control and regular and effective reporting.

2.19   Deposits and Interim Payments

The first step is to think about the timing of payments for an order or contract at the time that it is negotiated and agreed. In some cases (eg where goods are being made to order), the customer may be willing to pay a deposit with the order. In other cases, particularly in the services field where work may be carried out over a period of time, it should be possible to agree a schedule of interim payments during the course of the project – the aim should be to bill for each phase of the work as soon as it has been completed rather than to wait until completion of the whole contract. Once a payment schedule has been agreed, procedures should be put in place to ensure that invoices are raised at the appropriate time.

2.20   Invoicing

The next step is to ensure that invoices are raised promptly for all goods and services delivered to customers. The ideal situation is for the invoice to be raised on the same day as delivery, although this may not always be possible for other administrative reasons. If immediate invoicing is not possible, staff should be set a sensible target (for instance, that all sales are invoiced within four days of delivery) and regular checks should be made to confirm that this is being achieved or to identify and resolve any problems that are causing delays. Where a contract involves invoices being raised at regular intervals (eg monthly for an ongoing supply of services), special control systems may need to be set up to ensure that the documentation is raised promptly and that the need to raise the invoice is not overlooked. It is also worth establishing the customer's approach to the payment of invoices – for instance:

- does the date of payment depend on when the invoice is posted onto the customer's accounting system? If so, raising the invoice a few days earlier may result in payment being received a month earlier;
- does the customer hold invoices until a statement has been received and checked, and then pay on the basis of the statement? If so, the timing of issue of the statement could have a significant impact on when payment is actually received.

It is also advisable to ensure that the invoice gives all the details that the customer needs to be able to make payment – for instance, many companies now include details of their bank account so that payment can be made by bank transfer. At the very least, the invoice should include a remittance slip with clear details of who to make cheques payable to and where to send them.

2.21   Disputed Items

Every possible step should be taken to ensure that invoice details are clear, accurate and unambiguous, and in particular that the correct price is charged when an invoice is raised, especially if discounts or other price incentives have been agreed in certain cases. Some customers will use any excuse to delay payment and minor errors in pricing, calculations and other invoice details, or something as simple as failure to quote their order reference number, can present them with a golden opportunity. Furthermore, if the customer makes payments on the basis of statements rather than individual invoices, a query on a single invoice can be used to delay payment of every other invoice listed on the statement. Inevitably, genuine queries will arise from time to time and it is important to have set procedures for dealing with these, and for recording the discussions with the customer and the action taken. Good communication between departments is essential. For instance, if a query over a small number of defective or damaged goods is holding up the payment of a substantial batch of invoices, the staff dealing with the technical query need to be aware of the importance of resolving it quickly – it may appear to them to be a relatively trivial matter unless they have been told of the full implications.

2.22 Customer Credit Terms

Most companies operate standard credit terms, the most common being:

- *net monthly* – the disadvantage of this method is that it may provide customers with the opportunity to exclude invoices towards the end of the month from their processing and in effect double the credit period taken on these sales;
- *net 30 days*; and
- *settlement by (say) the 21st day of the following month* – this allows time to follow up any outstanding amounts, with the aim of securing payment before the end of the month.

It is advisable to ask all customers to sign a credit application form as formal confirmation that they accept the agreed credit terms. It can also be useful at this stage to obtain the name of the person who will approve invoices for payment, so that if any problems arise they can be referred directly to that person. The agreed credit terms should also be stated clearly on each quotation, order form or order acknowledgement, invoice and statement. Even where standard terms operate for most sales, separate arrangements will often be made with a small number of customers. Where separate credit terms are agreed, these need to be sufficiently competitive to attract and maximise sales but at the same time limit the risk of the company incurring unpaid debts and the potential impact of slow payment on the company's cashflow. No company should offer extended credit terms if its cashflow forecast shows that it cannot afford to do this. Credit terms should also be subject to regular review and should be compared with those offered by other businesses.

2.23 Incentives for Prompt Payment

It may be possible to negotiate favourable payments terms with some customers by guaranteeing delivery within a tight timescale or in accordance with a schedule to meet their particular business needs. Discount schemes can also be used to encourage prompt payment or payment by convenient methods, such as direct debit. However, it should always be borne in mind that discount schemes can require a considerable amount of administrative time and effort and can be difficult to control, especially if a variety of discounts are in operation at any one time, or if different discount arrangements are made with individual customers. Problems can also arise where customers take the discount even though they fail to make the payment on time and a decision then needs to be taken on whether to pursue the matter or let it go for the sake of good customer relations. The potential benefits need therefore to be weighed carefully against the potential costs.

2.24 Use of Customer Credit Limits

Credit control is an important function within the business, both in terms of assessing the credit-worthiness of customers and potential customers, and in the prompt collection of debts. Alongside normal procedures for checking the credit-worthiness of customers and potential customers, it is usually advisable to operate a sensible system of credit limits for individual customers. Credit limits should not be regarded as fixed limits, but should act as guidelines to indicate when the continued supply of goods and services to a particular customer should be referred to an appropriate member of senior management. It may be commercially justifiable to allow sales to be made over and above the agreed credit limit, provided that this decision is taken by someone with the authority to commit the company to the additional risk involved. Credit limits should also be subject to regular review – a customer who trades reliably within an established limit may be a good source of additional business (although it is not unknown for a business to pay several small invoices on time and then default on a substantial invoice), but if there are signs that a customer is getting into financial difficulties, the company's potential exposure should be monitored more carefully by lowering the credit limit.

2.25 Effective Debt Collection Procedures

Effective debt collection requires regular and reliable information on sales ledger balances and a clear system for following up older outstanding items. The budgeting process should include a projection of expected debtor days and the actual position should be compared regularly against budget to confirm that everything is in order or to identify where additional action is needed. If a substantial proportion of income comes from a small number of major customers, it may be worth setting up separate procedures for monitoring these accounts – regular personal contact can be invaluable in keeping the accounts in good order as well as developing closer relationships for the future. It is often useful to establish a standard system of sending out statements and chasing letters at regular intervals, but the most effective debt collection tool is the telephone – one telephone call can bring results much more quickly than standard letters if that call is made to the right person. If persistent problems are encountered over the collection of amounts owing from a particular customer it may be necessary to put a stop on further supplies until the balance is cleared and consider a policy of cash with order for any future supplies.

2.26 Debt Factoring and Invoice Discounting

In some cases, debt factoring or invoice discounting may be a useful way of releasing cash for other purposes, particularly for small and growing businesses, but these can also be expensive methods of obtaining finance and the details of any proposed agreement need to be carefully reviewed as they do vary widely. Debt factoring usually involves the transfer of specific debtors to the factor and the company is then able to draw up to a fixed percentage of the face value of the debts transferred. The amount advanced is usually repaid as the underlying debts are collected. Depending on the precise terms of the agreement, control over the debtors ledger and responsibility for collecting the amounts due (and for any bad debts that arise) may be taken over by the factoring company or may remain with the company. Where invoice discounting is used, funds are advanced against the company's outstanding invoices, and the company retains control over, and responsibility for, collection of the amounts owing. In both cases, interest will be charged on the amounts advanced and various service charges may also be payable. Fees may be fixed in advance or may be subject to adjustment to reflect the actual level of debt collection. The precise terms of the factoring or discounting agreement will determine the accounting treatment that needs to be adopted in the company's accounts. For those adopting UK accounting practice, this is covered in detail in Application Note C to FRS 5 *Reporting the Substance of Transactions* (for information on obtaining copies see the Accounting Standards Board website at www.frc.org.uk/asb). However, for entities adopting FRS 26 'Financial Instruments: Measurement', Application Note C is superseded by the recognition and derecognition requirements set out in an amendment to FRS 26 published in April 2006 and which applies for accounting periods beginning on or after 1 January 2007, although earlier adoption is permitted. Entities adopting international accounting standards will need to comply with the requirements of IAS 39 'Financial Instruments: Recognition and Measurement'.

2.27   Charging Interest on Overdue Debts

The *Late Payment of Commercial Debts (Interest) Act 1998* permits a company to charge interest on the late payment of business debts. Initially, charges could only be made by small companies to larger companies and government organisations but this was extended from November 2000 so that charges could also be made to other small businesses. The legislation was extended again from November 2002 so that businesses of any size, and also public sector bodies, now have a statutory right to charge interest on unpaid debts. Companies that wish to charge interest on overdue balances are advised to draw attention to this fact when discussing and agreeing terms with their customers. The Better Payment Practice Group provides useful guidance documents on the late payments legislation and general issues relating to payment practice (for further information, see the Group's website at www.payontime.co.uk/).

2.28   Managing Creditors

At a Glance
* The objective should be to take as much advantage as possible of the credit period offered by suppliers without damaging the business relationship.
* Procedures should be established to control the placing and authorisation of purchase orders and the recording of related liabilities, and to monitor the overall creditor position.

* Clear rules should be drawn up on the payment of individual suppliers' accounts.
* The potential benefits of discounts offered by suppliers should be weighed against the potential cashflow cost of early payment.
* Particular care should be taken over liabilities such as tax and VAT, where the penalties for late payment may be severe.

2.29   Relationship with Suppliers

Delaying payments to creditors can provide a cheap source of short-term finance and thus reduce the company's overall working capital requirement, but it is a step that should be taken with extreme care. The objective should always be to take as much advantage as possible of the credit period allowed by each individual supplier, but to avoid damaging the relationship with those suppliers. Damaged relationships can have an adverse impact on future supplies and potentially on the company's entire business if it is unable to meet its commitments to its own customers as a result. The usual signs of potential difficulties with suppliers include:

* reduced co-operation from the supplier;
* less flexibility over prices, or the imposition of sudden price increases;
* a tightening in credit terms; and
* delayed deliveries (leading eventually to supply stoppages).

Once again, good communication between different departments is critical. The purchasing department will usually be the first to become aware of the changes in the supplier's attitude, but if they do not have first-hand knowledge of the payment position on the account, they may not be able to interpret the signs until it is too late. Signs of a deterioration in the relationship should always generate prompt action to identify the cause and try to repair the damage as soon as possible.

2.30   Internal Control Over Purchases and Expenses

As with sales and debtors, a good system of reporting is critical to the maintenance of tight control over purchases and creditors. Invoices should be registered, authorised and posted promptly to the ledger. This will help to prevent liabilities being overlooked and then emerging unexpectedly. The internal control system should be designed to ensure that:

* all orders are authorised at an appropriate level, and prices are agreed at the time that the order is placed;
* the company pays only for goods and services that it has ordered and which were received in good condition (eg where relevant, invoices should be matched with orders and goods received records before being authorised for payment);

Cashflow Management

- the company pays the price that was agreed with the supplier; and
- the company only pays once for the goods and services that it has received.

Particular care should also be exercised over the setting up of new accounts with suppliers and over the terms of trade that are agreed with them – both the opening of the account and trading terms should be authorised at an appropriate level. There should also be a formal tendering process for all major purchases so that the company can ensure that it receives the best deal possible, and regular checks should be carried out to confirm that the tendering process is being used in practice.

2.31   Regular Monitoring of Creditors

Detailed records should be kept of the maximum length of credit that can be taken from each supplier and payment rules should be drawn up on the basis of this information. Management should receive regular reports on the overall creditor position, including details of creditor days (analysed into categories, if appropriate) and the total outstanding in value terms, with comparisons against budget in each case.

2.32   Taking Advantage of Discounts

Discounts offered for early payment also require careful attention. The level of discount offered should be measured against the cost of early payment in terms of the cashflow impact and the additional administrative cost of arranging separate payment for these accounts. If the discount proves worthwhile, there should be a separate system for identifying these invoices when they arrive and ensuring that payment is processed in time to obtain the discount.

2.33   Other Creditors

Other amounts payable such as VAT, PAYE, National Insurance Contributions and corporation tax will often represent substantial liabilities, and delaying the payment of these items will sometimes seem attractive in cashflow terms. However, it can be very costly, both in terms of the penalties and interest that will be charged, and the damage that may be done to the company's standing with the relevant authorities.

2.34   **Managing Stock**

> **At a Glance**
> * The investment in stock can make heavy demands on working capital and stock levels therefore require careful monitoring.
> * Stock levels should be monitored in both physical and value terms, and action plans developed to deal with any apparently excessive holdings.

> * Realistic order and reorder levels should be established for each principal stock line.
> * Regular physical checks should be carried out to confirm the accuracy of the underlying stock records.

2.35 Costs of Holding Stock

For a company whose business involves the supply of goods rather than services, the need to hold stock is readily apparent. Customers are becoming increasingly concerned with speed of delivery and a company needs to hold sufficient finished goods in stock to be able to meet this demand. Similarly, sufficient stocks of raw materials will usually need to be held in order to maintain production at efficient levels. The investment in stock can make heavy demands on working capital and stock levels should therefore be closely monitored to achieve a careful balance between the potential cost of stock shortages (which is often difficult to quantify in absolute terms) and the cost of holding excess stock, which will usually include:

- warehousing and storage costs;
- handling costs;
- control and administration costs, including insurance;
- stock obsolescence; and
- financing charges (or loss of potential interest receivable) on the working capital invested.

2.36 Monitoring and Control

Management should constantly monitor the extent of the company's investment in stock and be aware of the level of stock, in both physical and value terms. The regular reports received might cover the following information:

- overall stock levels;
- stock shortages or excesses arising;
- level of customer service achieved;
- stock turnover, or days' usage held in stock;
- summary of slow-moving and potentially obsolete items; and
- wastage levels.

Depending on the nature and complexity of the business, it may be appropriate to analyse this information by stock product, stock category or location. The detailed information should be used by management to compare actual stock levels with budget or expected levels and to devise clear action plans to deal with any apparently excessive stock holdings. It is important that those with day-to-day responsibility for stock understand management's objectives – most people tend to be cautious by nature and, without this understanding, instinct will often prompt them to hold slightly more stock than is necessary or to retain items just in case they should be needed at some point in the future. Sensible order quantities and reorder levels should be established for each principal stock line, based on up-to-date information on usage levels and delivery times, and these should be kept under review. A system should be established to identify and monitor slow-moving and potentially obsolete items, so that they can be disposed off as quickly and effectively as possible.

2.37 Physical Stock Checks

It is also important to confirm that the stock information reported to management, and on which they will base their decisions, is accurate and complete. This will usually involve carrying out regular physical checks to confirm that the underlying stock records are accurate. A detailed check will always be required at the year end for accounts purposes (unless a fairly sophisticated system of cyclical checking is in place) but this may not be sufficient to ensure the accuracy of stock information throughout the year. Regular checks need not be time-consuming – a small number of key stock items will often represent a high proportion of stock in value terms and a system of regular checks on these items (on a cyclical basis if appropriate) should be relatively easy to establish. Annual checks will often suffice for the less significant stock lines, on the basis that any potential discrepancies here would not be sufficiently large to influence management decisions.

Appendix 1

Useful Websites on Cashflow Management and Related Issues

Better Payment Practice Group	www.payontime.co.uk
Institute of Credit Management	www.icm.org.uk/
Association of Corporate Treasurers	www.treasurers.org/
The Factors and Discounters Association	www.thefda.org.uk/
ICAEW Finance & Management Faculty	www.icaew.co.uk/fmfac
Business Link	www.businesslink.gov.uk
Federation of Small Businesses	www.fsb.org.uk
UK Insolvency Helpline	www.insolvencyhelpline.co.uk

Cashflow Management

Company Law

Company Law

3 Company Law

3.1 Maintenance and Retention of Accounting Records

At a Glance
* *CA 1985* includes specific provisions on the accounting records that a company must keep.
* Accounting records should be updated on a regular basis and supporting documentation retained in an orderly manner for future reference.
* Memorandum records should be maintained of any adjustments that are not entered into the accounting records until the end of the financial year (eg provisions for bad debts).
* If the preparation of accounting records is outsourced, care should be taken to ensure that the arrangements achieve compliance with the *CA 1985* requirements.
* A parent company must also take all reasonable steps to ensure that its subsidiaries keep appropriate accounting records.
* *CA 1985* also prescribes where accounting records should be kept and for how long they should be retained.
* Where accounting records are computerised, care is needed to ensure that the information remains accessible for the full retention period, especially if the underlying systems change.

3.2 Legal Requirement to Keep Accounting Records

Under *section 221(1)* of the *Companies Act 1985* (*CA 1985*), every company must keep accounting records which:

* are sufficient to show and explain the company's transactions;
* disclose with reasonable accuracy the financial position of the company at any point in time; and
* enable the directors to ensure that any balance sheet and profit and loss account prepared under *CA 1985* complies with the accounting provisions of that Act.

Being able to establish the financial position of the company at any point in time is particularly important in the context of the wrongful trading provisions of the

Insolvency Act 1986 – it is essential that the directors of the company always have access to accurate information on which to assess the company's solvency.

3.3 Interpretation of the Requirement

The usual interpretation of the above requirement is that the accounting records do not necessarily need to show the overall financial position of the company at a particular point in time, but that all relevant financial information should be entered into the accounting records promptly, so that the overall financial position can be established if required. The accounting records should therefore be updated on a regular basis and supporting documentation should be retained in an orderly manner for future reference. The accounting records should also clearly show the date of each transaction. It is not acceptable to keep records in the form of a bundle of documents to be converted into formal accounting records at the end of the financial period.

3.4 Impact of Provisions and Adjustments

When financial accounts are prepared, a number of adjustments will usually need to be made to the information shown in the accounting records in order to comply with the accounting requirements of *CA 1985* and of accounting standards. For instance, provision may need to be made for potential bad debts or for other expected losses and liabilities. These items will not usually be incorporated into the detailed accounting records until the end of the financial year, but it is advisable for the directors to keep a memorandum note of such items as they arise during the year so that they can be taken into account in preparing financial information for management purposes and also if the financial position of the company needs to be formally established at a particular point during the period.

3.5 Outsourcing

It is becoming increasingly common for businesses to outsource certain functions or activities. Where the preparation of detailed accounting records is outsourced, steps should be taken to ensure that the company can still be regarded as keeping accounting records (as opposed to causing them to be kept). The contractual arrangements should establish the company's legal ownership of the accounting records and should provide access to them at all times by the company's directors, officers and auditors.

3.6 Contents of Accounting Records

The general requirement to keep accounting records is expanded by *section 221(2)* and *(3)* of *CA 1985*, which require the accounting records to include:

- entries from day to day of all sums of money received and paid, together with details of the matters to which they relate;
- a record of the assets and liabilities of the company; and

- in the case of a company dealing in goods:
  - ○ statements of stock held at the end of each financial year,
  - ○ statements of stocktakings from which the statements of stocks held are prepared, and
  - ○ except for goods sold in the ordinary retail trade, statements of all goods sold and purchased, in sufficient detail to enable the buyers and sellers to be identified.

Specialised businesses (eg insurance brokers and other financial services businesses) may also have to comply with additional requirements laid down in relevant legislation.

3.7 *Statements of Stock and Stocktakings*

No specified form is laid down for statements of stock or stocktakings. The requirement is usually interpreted as relating to the stock sheets and related summaries that support the stock figure shown in the annual accounts, but where stocks are extensive and some reliance is placed on interim stocktakes carried out at other times of the year, or stocktakes are carried out on a continuous or cyclical basis throughout the year, documentation for these should also be retained.

3.8 Additional Duties of Parent Company

Under *section 221(4)* of *CA 1985*, a parent company is required to take all reasonable steps to ensure that a subsidiary undertaking keeps accounting records that enable the directors of the parent to prepare accounts which comply with the requirements of *CA 1985*, even where the subsidiary is not subject to a legal requirement to keep such records. A parent must therefore ensure that all the necessary information is available from its subsidiaries to enable the preparation of consolidated accounts for the group as a whole. This should not be a problem where the subsidiaries are companies based in the UK, and are therefore subject to the same requirements as the parent, but specific action may need to be taken where a parent has unincorporated or overseas subsidiaries.

3.9 Location and Inspection of Accounting Records

Under *section 222(1)* of *CA 1985*, the accounting records must be kept at the company's registered office, or at any other place that the directors consider appropriate, and they must be open to inspection by the officers of the company. *Section 389A(1)* of *CA 1985* also gives the auditors a right of access to the company's accounting records at any time. If the accounting records are kept outside Great Britain, accounts and returns must be sent to, and kept in, a place in Great Britain and must be open to inspection by the officers of the company. These accounts and returns must:

- disclose with reasonable accuracy the financial position of the business at intervals of not more than six months; and

Company Law

- enable the directors to ensure that balance sheets and profit and loss accounts for the company are prepared in accordance with the requirements of *CA 1985*.

3.10   Retention of Accounting Records

Section 222(5) of *CA 1985* specifies that accounting records must be retained as follows:

- in the case of a public company, for a period of six years from the date on which they were made; and
- in the case of a private company, for a period of three years from the date on which they were made.

The retention periods laid down in *CA 1985* should be regarded as minimum periods and, in practice, it will usually be advisable to retain certain items for a longer period. Other legislation may also require the adoption of longer retention periods – for instance, employers operating a PAYE scheme are required to keep records of payments to employees for three years after the end of the relevant tax year and VAT legislation generally requires accounting records and related documents (eg tax invoices, import/export documentation) to be retained for six years. Particularly significant records and documents may need to be retained indefinitely. As a general rule, directors are recommended to keep other accounting records for at least six years from the end of the relevant accounting period.

3.11   What Needs to be Retained?

It is difficult to find definitive guidance on exactly which records need to be retained. As regards the *CA 1985* retention requirements, accounting records are the records and documents that show the financial position of the company at any point in time, give details of the sums received and paid and record details of the company's assets and liabilities. The requirement is therefore usually interpreted as covering the records of prime entry and related documentation, such as:

- the nominal ledger, sales ledger, purchase ledger and journal;
- sales invoices and credit notes and any related transactions listings or day books;
- purchase invoices and credit notes and any related transactions listings or day books;
- register of fixed assets;
- cash book; and
- bank statements.

As explained above, there is also a specific requirement to retain stock summaries and stocktaking documentation. The situation is less clear-cut in the case of secondary documentation such as order and delivery documentation. The information in these documents will usually have been transferred onto other documents and records, such as purchase and sales invoices, and secondary documents are therefore not usually considered to be covered by the *CA 1985* retention requirement.

3.12 Computerised Records

Most businesses now maintain their accounting records in computerised rather than in hard-copy format and this raises additional issues. As well as retaining the relevant disks or files for the requisite period, it is also important to ensure that any hardware or software needed to retrieve or access the stored information is also retained, or that arrangements are in place to enable all information retained in non-legible form to be accessed. This is a point that can easily be overlooked when computer systems are upgraded or replaced.

3.13 Documents Retained in Other Forms

Records and documents, especially those relating to significant business transactions, should be retained in their original form wherever practicable. However, lack of space will often make it impractical for a company to retain all of its primary accounting documentation in original form for the requisite period. It will therefore usually be acceptable to retain documents in another form, such as microfilm, provided that procedures are put in place to ensure that:

- all documents are copied properly;
- the microfilm versions are stored securely; and
- the microfilm versions continue to be accessible and can be authenticated if necessary.

3.14 Consequences of Non-compliance

Each provision of *CA 1985* on the maintenance, content, retention and location of accounting records notes that every officer of the company who fails to comply with the legal requirements is guilty of an offence and liable to imprisonment or a fine, or both. However, it is a defence for an officer of the company to show that he/she acted honestly and that the default was excusable in the circumstances in which the company's business was carried on.

3.15 Requirement to Prepare Annual Accounts

At a Glance
* *CA 1985* requires the directors to prepare a balance sheet and profit and loss account for the company for each financial year.
* A parent company must prepare consolidated group accounts as well as its own individual accounts.
* Certain small and medium-sized companies are exempt from the requirement to prepare group accounts.
* A parent company that is the subsidiary of an undertaking established under the law of another EC State may also be exempt from the requirement to prepare group accounts, provided that certain conditions are met.

Company Law

> * Special provisions on the preparation of accounts apply to an oversea company (ie a limited company incorporated outside the UK but with a branch or place of business here).
> * A company's financial year is determined by its accounting reference date – *CA 1985* includes detailed provisions on determining, and changing, the accounting reference date.

3.16   Individual Company Accounts

Section 226 of *CA 1985* sets out the requirement for the directors of every company to prepare accounts for each financial year. For accounting periods beginning before 1 January 2005, these accounts had to comply with the detailed form and content requirements set out in the legislation. However, for accounting periods beginning on or after 1 January 2005, *section 226* is amended by the *Companies Act 1985 (International Accounting Standards and Other Accounting Amendments) Regulations 2004 (SI 2004/2947)* to give the directors of most companies the option of preparing either:

- Companies Act accounts, by following the form and content requirements of the legislation and UK accounting standards; or
- IAS accounts, by preparing the accounts in accordance with international accounting standards (IASs) – in this case, the detailed provisions in *CA 1985* on the form and content of annual accounts no longer apply.

The only exception is charitable companies, which must always prepare Companies Act accounts. The directors of a parent company are also encouraged to ensure consistency in the adoption of IASs within the group, unless there are good reasons against this. Under *section 226A* of *CA 1985*, Companies Act accounts must comprise:

- a balance sheet as at the last day of the financial year; and
- a profit and loss account for the financial year.

The balance sheet must give a true and fair view of the state of affairs of the company at the end of the financial year and the profit and loss account must give a true and fair view of the profit or loss for the year. Companies Act individual accounts must also comply with the detailed requirements of *Schedule 4* to *CA 1985*. There are no detailed provisions in the legislation on the form and content of IAS accounts, but similar requirements to those set out above will generally apply under the requirements of IASs. Also, under *section 235* of *CA 1985*, the auditors' report is required to include an opinion on whether the accounts show a true and fair view in accordance with the relevant financial accounting framework adopted by the company, and this requirement applies to both Companies Act accounts and IAS accounts. Certain additional disclosure requirements are set out in other Schedules to *CA 1985* (for instance, those relating to directors' remuneration and interests in related undertakings) and these continue to apply to both Companies Act and IAS accounts. The preparation of individual accounts is considered in more detail in **11 FINANCIAL REPORTING**.

3.17   Group Accounts

Section 227 of *CA 1985* sets out the requirement for a parent company to prepare group accounts for each financial year, in addition to its own individual accounts. For accounting periods beginning before 1 January 2005, these accounts had to comply with the detailed form and content requirements set out in the legislation. However, for accounting periods beginning on or after 1 January 2005, *section 227* is amended in the same way as *section 226* (see **3.16** above) to give the directors of most parent companies the option of preparing either:

- Companies Act group accounts, by following the form and content requirements of the legislation and UK accounting standards; or
- IAS group accounts, by preparing them in accordance with international accounting standards (IASs) – in this case, the detailed provisions in *CA 1985* on the form and content of group accounts no longer apply.

A parent company that is a charity must always prepare Companies Act group accounts, and a listed company must always prepare IAS group accounts under the requirements of the EU IAS Regulation. The London Stock Exchange has also announced that AIM companies will be expected to report under IASs for accounting periods beginning on or after 1 January 2007. Under *section 227A* of *CA 1985*, Companies Act group accounts must comprise:

- a consolidated balance sheet setting out the state of affairs of the parent company and its subsidiary undertakings as at the last day of the financial year; and
- a consolidated profit and loss account dealing with the profit or loss of the parent company and its subsidiary undertakings for the financial year.

The consolidated balance sheet must give a true and fair view of the state of affairs of the group at the end of the financial year, and the profit and loss account must give a true and fair view of the profit or loss of the group for the year, so far as concerns the members of the parent company. Companies Act group accounts must also comply with *Schedule 4A* to *CA 1985*. This sets out detailed requirements on the form and content of group accounts, including general rules on consolidation and requirements in respect of acquisition and merger accounting. There are no detailed provisions in the legislation on the form and content of IAS group accounts, but similar requirements to those set out above will generally apply under the requirements of IASs. Also, under *section 235* of *CA 1985*, the auditors' report is required to include an opinion on whether the group accounts show a true and fair view in accordance with the relevant financial accounting framework adopted by the parent company for the group accounts, and this requirement applies to both Companies Act group accounts and IAS group accounts. The preparation of group accounts is considered in more detail in **11 FINANCIAL REPORTING**.

Company Law

3.18   Exemption from Group Accounts Requirement

Certain small and medium-sized groups are exempt from the requirement to prepare group accounts (see **3.47–3.74** below). A parent company is also generally exempt from the requirement to prepare group accounts if it is itself a subsidiary of a parent undertaking established under the law of an EEA State and:

- it is wholly owned by that parent; or
- the parent undertaking holds more than 50 per cent of the shares and notice requesting preparation of group accounts has not been served on the company by shareholders holding more than half of the remaining shares or 5 per cent of the total shares in the company.

A number of specific conditions (relating mainly to the preparation, audit and filing of group accounts by the ultimate parent or an intermediate parent) are laid down in *section 228(2)* of *CA 1985* and all of these must be met for the exemption to be available. The exemption is also not available to any company whose shares are listed on a stock exchange in any EEA State. For accounting periods beginning on or after 1 January 2005, the *Companies Act 1985 (International Accounting Standards and Other Accounting Amendments) Regulations 2004* (*SI 2004/2947*) extend this exemption to an intermediate parent company which is a subsidiary of a parent established outside the EEA, provided that the parent prepares audited consolidated accounts in a manner equivalent to that required by the *EC Seventh Company Law Directive*. The conditions under which the exemption is available are broadly identical to those set out above for intermediate parent companies within an EC group. The Urgent Issues Task Force (UITF) has issued a draft Abstract on whether financial statements prepared in accordance with International Financial Reporting Standards (IFRS) or Generally Accepted Accounting Principles (GAAP) in other countries meet the requirement for equivalence with the EC Seventh Directive. This was published in UITF Information Sheet No 79 and sets out the UITF's view that:

- accounts prepared in accordance with IFRSs adopted by the EU will meet the equivalence requirement;
- accounts prepared in accordance with full IFRSs will meet the equivalence test, subject to the need to consider why the EU has not adopted a particular standard or interpretation;
- accounts prepared using other GAAPs closely related to IFRSs will meet the equivalence test, subject to the need to consider any differences from IFRSs adopted by the EU;
- accounts prepared in accordance with US GAAP, Canadian GAAP and Japanese GAAP will meet the equivalence test, subject to:
  - ensuring that the scope of entities included in the consolidation is consistent with the EC Seventh Directive;
  - ensuring that consistent accounting policies have been used for all entities included in the consolidated accounts; and
  - evaluating the effect of any exemptions or modifications to the GAAPs allowed by any specialised industry standards that have been applied; and

- accounts prepared using other GAAPs should be assessed for equivalence with the requirements of the EC Seventh Directive.

Comments on the draft Abstract were requested by 23 June 2006.

3.19 Oversea Companies

An oversea company is a limited company incorporated outside the United Kingdom and Gibraltar but which has a place of business or a branch here. A different regime applies, depending on whether the UK presence is a place of business or a branch (see **3.21** below). An oversea company with a place of business in the UK is required by *section 700* of *CA 1985* to prepare a balance sheet and profit and loss account for each financial period in exactly the same way as a company formed and registered under *CA 1985*. The Secretary of State is given the power to modify this requirement and to exempt an oversea company from the requirement. There is a slight anomaly at present in that the *Oversea Companies (Accounts) (Modifications and Exemption) Order 1990* (*SI 1990/440*) requires the accounts of an oversea company to be prepared in accordance with *CA 1985, Part VII, Sch 9* as they stood before the legislation was amended by the *Companies Act 1989*. There is no requirement for an auditors' report or a directors' report and the Order grants exemptions from certain disclosures that would otherwise need to be given in the accounts.

3.20 *Delivery of Accounts to Registrar*

The accounts must be delivered to the registrar within 13 months of the end of the accounting period and, if they are prepared in a language other than English, a certified translation must be attached. If the company's first accounting reference period is more than 12 months, the accounts must be delivered within 13 months of the first anniversary of the date on which the company established a place of business in the UK. Failure to comply with the requirement constitutes an offence and the company and every director is liable to a fine and to a daily default fine for continued contravention. However, it is a defence for a director to demonstrate that he/she took all reasonable steps to achieve compliance, although failure to prepare the accounts cannot be used as a defence against failure to deliver them.

3.21 *Company with Branch in the UK*

Different requirements apply to an oversea company with a branch in the UK under:

- *section 699A* of *CA 1985* for credit or financial institutions to which the EC Bank Branches Directive applies; and
- *section 699AA* of *CA 1985* for other oversea companies.

The detailed requirements on the preparation and delivery of annual accounts are set out in *Schedules 21C* and *21D* to *CA 1985* respectively. Broadly, these enable the entity to deliver the accounts and reports that it is required to

Company Law

prepare under the laws of its home state. If the home state does not have accounts requirements, the entity must prepare and deliver accounts as if it were an oversea company to which *section 700* applied (see **3.19** above).

3.22   *Proposed Changes*

A DTI consultation document issued in 1999 considered the anomalies that arise from having similar, but slightly different, requirements for oversea companies with branches and other places of business in the UK. The current situation causes confusion and uncertainty and is further complicated by the need for complex provisions covering a change from a branch to a place of business and vice versa. The document therefore recommended the introduction of a single registration scheme for oversea companies, based on the present branch requirements. The DTI document *Modern Company Law for a Competitive Economy: Final Report* issued in July 2001 reiterates most of these proposals, with minor amendments in some cases. The main recommendations are that:

- the present requirements should be replaced with a single registration scheme for oversea companies, based on the requirements of the EC *Eleventh Directive*;
- the framework for the new regime should be set out in primary legislation, with the details implemented by secondary legislation;
- companies incorporated in Northern Ireland and Gibraltar which establish a place of business in Great Britain will be required to register under the new regime (the earlier consultation document had proposed that the regime should apply only to companies registered outside the UK and Gibraltar);
- where an oversea company operates in Great Britain from a number of locations within a common management structure, only one registration will be required;
- the oversea company will be required to file the annual accounts and reports which its home State requires it to prepare and publish; and
- where the home State does not have accounts requirements, the Secretary of State should be given the power to require the filing of accounts prepared in accordance with prescribed regulations (the report includes simplified illustrative requirements).

The Government has confirmed its intention to proceed on this basis and the draft Company Law Reform Bill published in May 2006 includes clauses to enable the Secretary of State to make appropriate provisions by means of regulations.

3.23   Accounting Reference Date

A company's financial year is determined by its accounting reference date. Under *section 224(2)* of *CA 1985*, the company can choose its accounting reference date, provided that notice is given to the Registrar of Companies in the prescribed form within nine months of incorporation. If the company does not give such notice, its accounting reference date will be the end of the month in which the anniversary of its incorporation falls.

Example 1

Company incorporated on	20 December 2005
Accounting reference date (unless a	
different date is notified)	31 December
First accounting period ends	31 December 2006

3.24   First Financial Period

The company's first financial period begins on the date of incorporation, even though the company may not start to trade until a later date. The first financial period ends on the accounting reference date and, under *section 224(4)* of *CA 1985*, must be a period of more than six months, but not more than 18 months.

Example 2

Company incorporated on	14 March 2005
Chosen accounting reference date	31 December
First accounting period ends	31 December 2005
(ie the first financial period will be 9.5 months)	

Example 3

Company incorporated on	14 March 2005
Chosen accounting reference date	31 May
First accounting period ends	31 May 2006
(ie the first financial period will be 14.5 months)	

Where the first financial period is more than twelve months, there are special rules on the period allowed for delivering accounts to the Registrar of Companies (see **3.37** below).

3.25   Subsequent Financial Years

Each subsequent financial year begins on the day immediately following the accounting reference date and lasts for twelve months, ending on the next accounting reference date. However, *section 223* of *CA 1985* permits the directors to use a date not more than seven days before or after the accounting reference date as the financial year end if this is more convenient. For instance, this can be used to ensure that the financial year end falls at a weekend to simplify stocktaking procedures.

3.26 Change of Accounting Reference Date

Section 225 of *CA 1985* sets out the rules for changing a company's accounting reference date. A change of date can generally be effective for the current accounting period and subsequent periods, or for the previous accounting period and subsequent periods. However, the accounting reference date for the previous accounting period cannot be changed if the time allowed for delivering accounts for that period to the Registrar has already expired. The accounting reference date is changed by submitting Companies House Form 225 to the Registrar. An accounting reference period can be shortened or lengthened by a change of accounting reference date, subject to certain rules:

- an accounting reference period cannot be extended to a period of more than 18 months (except where an administration order is in force under *Part II* of the *Insolvency Act 1986*); and
- any notice extending an accounting reference period is ineffective if it is given within five years of the end of an earlier accounting period that was extended, regardless of whether or not that extended period was more or less than twelve months.

There are exceptions to the second requirement where:

- the company is a subsidiary or parent of another EEA undertaking and the change is to bring its accounting reference date into line with that of its parent or subsidiary;
- an administrative order is in force under *Part II* of the *Insolvency Act 1986*; or
- the Secretary of State directs that the notice of change of accounting reference date is to be effective.

The directors must specify on Form 225 whether the accounting period is to be shortened or extended as a result of the change of accounting reference date.

Example 4

Company's existing accounting reference date	31 August
Last accounts made up to	31 August 2005
New accounting reference date	31 December

Form 225 must specify whether the current accounting period is to be shortened to four months (ie the next accounts will be prepared to 31 December 2005) or extended to 16 months (ie the next accounts will be prepared to 31 December 2006).

There are special rules on the period allowed for delivering accounts to the Registrar of Companies when an accounting reference date is changed (see **3.38** below).

3.27 Shortened First Financial Period

Although *section 224(4)* of *CA 1985* specifies that a company's first accounting period must be at least six months, the legislation does not give a minimum length for a shortened accounting period. As *section 224* is subject to the provisions of *section 225* of *CA 1985*, it appears that the procedure for changing an accounting reference date can be used to achieve a first accounting period of less than six months if required.

Example 5

Date of incorporation	15 May 2005
Chosen accounting reference date	31 August
Under normal rules, first accounts must be for the period of 15.5 months to	31 August 2006

If the company wants its first accounting period to end on 31 August 2005, it seems that it can achieve this by initially notifying a later accounting reference date (say 31 December) and then notifying a change to 31 August and electing to shorten the current accounting period – the first accounting period would therefore end on 31 August 2005 (ie an accounting period of 3.5 months).

3.28 Laying and Delivering Accounts

At a Glance
* *CA 1985* requires the directors to lay copies of the annual accounts, directors' report and auditors' report before the company in general meeting within a specified period each year.
* Copies of these items must also be sent out to the members and other entitled persons in advance of the meeting – special provisions now allow this to be done electronically.
* The Government has issued proposals for reducing the time allowed for distributing copies of the annual accounts and reports and delivering a copy to the registrar.
* A member or debenture holder has the right to be given a single copy of the last accounts and reports.
* A private company can elect to dispense with the laying of annual accounts and reports, but the members retain the right to require them to be laid.

* The directors must deliver copies of the annual accounts and reports to the registrar within a specified period each year.
* Companies House lays down strict specifications on the quality of documents delivered to them for filing purposes.
* *CA 1985* permits the amounts shown in the annual accounts to also be disclosed in euros.
* Certain unlimited companies are exempt from the requirement to deliver their annual accounts and reports to the Registrar.

3.29   Laying of Accounts

Under *section 241* of *CA 1985*, directors are required to lay before the company in general meeting copies of the annual accounts, directors' report and auditors' report for each financial year. The period for laying the accounts and reports before the members is defined in *section 244* of *CA 1985* as seven months from the end of the accounting reference period for a public company and ten months from the end of the accounting reference period for a private company. Different deadlines may apply for the first accounting period and following a change of accounting reference date. As explained in **3.32** below, the Government proposes in due course to remove the statutory requirement for the annual accounts and reports to be laid before the members in general meeting. At present, there are penalties for failing to comply with the requirement, although it is a defence for a director to demonstrate that he/she took all reasonable steps to achieve compliance by the due date. However, failure to prepare the accounts in time cannot be used as a defence against the failure to lay them before the members by the due date.

3.30   Requirement to Send Out Accounts

Under *section 238(1)* of *CA 1985*, a copy of the annual accounts, directors' report and auditors' report (and, in the case of a quoted company, the directors' remuneration report) must be sent to every member of the company, every holder of the company's debentures and every person entitled to receive notice of general meetings not less than 21 days before the date of the meeting at which copies of those documents are to be laid. If copies are sent out less than 21 days before the date of the meeting, they are deemed to have been duly sent if all the members entitled to attend and vote at the meeting agree to this. As explained in **3.32** below, the Government has issued proposals which change the timing of the distribution of the annual accounts and reports to the members and other persons entitled to receive them.

3.31   Use of Electronic Communication

The *Companies Act 1985 (Electronic Communications) Order 2000* (*SI 2000/3373*) came into force on 22 December 2000 and inserts new *subsections 4A to 4E* into *section 238* of *CA 1985*. These clarify that references to sending accounts and reports to those entitled to receive them include:

- sending copies by electronic communication to the address notified to the company for that purpose by the person entitled to receive the documents; or
- where the company and the person entitled to receive the accounts so agree, publishing the documents on a website, notifying the person in the manner agreed that they have been published in this way and providing him/her with both the address of the website and details of where and how the documents may be accessed on the website.

Any provision in the articles that would prevent the company from taking up the option is rendered void by the Order. Where the information is published on a website, it must remain on the website throughout a period beginning at least 21 days before the date of the meeting at which the accounts are to be laid and ending at the conclusion of the meeting, and the notification to the person entitled to receive the information must be given not less than 21 days before the date of the meeting. Where the information is available for only part of the period as a result of circumstances that the company could not reasonably be expected to prevent or avoid, the failure to comply with the legal requirement will not invalidate the proceedings of the meeting. (See also **11.128** ICSA GUIDANCE ON ELECTRONIC COMMUNICATION.)

3.32 Proposed Changes

Based on the results of the recent company law review, the Government White Paper *Modernising Company Law* issued in July 2002 proposed changes to reduce the period allowed for distributing the annual accounts and reports to the members and delivering a copy to the registrar. In future, the legislation will assume that the accounts and reports will not be formally laid before the members in general meeting (on the basis that, under other proposals in the White Paper, most private companies will in future be free from the requirement to hold an Annual General Meeting (AGM), although the present requirement will generally be retained for public companies). Under the proposals in the White Paper:

- a private company would be required to distribute the annual accounts and reports to members, and to deliver a copy to the registrar, within seven months of the end of the financial reporting period;
- a public company would be required to distribute its annual accounts and reports to the members, and to deliver a copy to the Registrar, within six months of the end of the accounting reference period.

However, the draft Company Law Reform Bill published in November 2005 reduced the filing period for a private company by just one month, to nine months after the end of the accounting period, although it retained the proposed filing period of six months for public companies. The situation was then changed again by a consultation document published jointly by HM Revenue & Customs and Companies House in December 2005. This sets out proposals to align filing dates for company accounts and tax returns as far as possible, and notes a preference for a normal filing period of seven months. If this is accepted, the Bill is likely to be amended to introduce a seven month filing period for private company accounts but retain the proposed period of six months for public companies. In effect, this would reinstate the proposals in the White Paper. There will be an additional requirement for quoted companies to publish their annual accounts and reports on the internet as soon as practicable after they have been approved, and in any event no later than four months after the end of the financial reporting period. Where an AGM is to be held, this will have to be done within six months of the financial year-end in the case of a public company and within ten months of the financial year-end in the case of a private company. In effect, the period allowed for distributing documents to the members of a public company will therefore be reduced by the notice period for the AGM. Additional provisions will apply where an AGM is held before the statutory deadline for distribution of the accounts and reports. The White Paper also proposes removing the requirement to send the annual accounts and reports to the holders of debentures first issued after the revised legislation comes into force, on the basis that debenture holders should be able to obtain any information they require under the terms of the debenture.

3.33   Right to Demand Accounts

Section 239 of *CA 1985* gives any member of a company and any holder of the company's debentures a right to be given on demand, and without charge, a single copy of the company's last annual accounts, directors' report and auditors' report. If the company does not comply within seven days, the company and every officer is guilty of an offence and liable to a fine. If the contravention continues, a daily default fine applies.

3.34   Special Election for Private Companies

A private company may elect under *section 252* of *CA 1985* to dispense with the requirement to lay the accounts and reports before the members in general meeting. This must be done by elective resolution in accordance with *section 379A* of *CA 1985*. Such an election is effective for the accounts and reports for the financial year in which the election is made and for subsequent financial years. Similarly, where such an election ceases to have effect, the requirements of *section 241* of *CA 1985* apply to the accounts and reports for the financial year in which the election ceases to have effect and to those of subsequent financial years. When an election is in force, any reference in *CA 1985* to the laying of accounts before the members is to be read as a requirement to send copies to the members of the company and to others entitled to receive them under *section 238(1)* of *CA 1985*. Under *section 253(1)* of *CA 1985*, copies of the accounts and reports must be sent out not less than 28 days before the end of the period allowed for laying and delivering them, and those sent to the members of the company must be accompanied by a notice informing them of their right to require the accounts and reports to be laid before the company in general meeting.

In the case of default, the company and every officer who is in default is guilty of an offence and liable to a penalty. The draft Company Law Reform Bill includes changes that will automatically free most private companies from the requirement to hold an Annual General Meeting and will remove the statutory requirement for the annual accounts and reports to be laid before the members (see **3.32** above).

3.35   Members' Right to Require Accounts to be Laid

Under *section 253(2)* of *CA 1985*, any member or auditor of the company may require a general meeting to be held for the purpose of laying the accounts and reports by depositing a written notice at the company's registered office within the period of 28 days beginning with the day on which the accounts are sent out under *section 238(1)*. If the directors do not proceed to convene a meeting within 21 days of the deposit of the written notice, the member who deposited the notice may convene the meeting. Such a meeting must be held not more than three months after the date of deposit of the written notice and must be convened, as far as possible, in the same manner as meetings are convened by the directors. Any reasonable expenses incurred by the person who deposited the notice as a result of the directors' failure to convene the meeting are to be reimbursed by the company and recouped by the company from directors' fees or remuneration. Under the legislation, the directors are also deemed not to have convened a meeting if they convene it for more than 28 days after the date of the notice convening it.

3.36   Delivering Accounts to the Registrar

The directors are required by *section 242(1)* of *CA 1985* to deliver a copy of the annual accounts, directors' report and auditors' report for each financial year to the Registrar of Companies. In the case of a public company, these documents must be delivered within seven months of the end of the accounting reference period, and in the case of a private company they must be delivered within ten months of the end of the accounting reference period. Different deadlines may apply for the first accounting period and following a change of accounting reference date. As explained in **3.32**, the Government intends to reduce the period allowed for delivering a copy of the annual accounts and report to the registrar. Penalties apply where the directors fail to comply with the delivery requirements, although it is a defence for a director to prove that he/she took all reasonable steps to achieve compliance by the due date. However, failure to prepare the accounts and reports on time cannot be used as a defence against failure to deliver them by the due date. The company is also liable to a civil penalty as set out in *section 242A* of *CA 1985*. The penalties escalate where the default continues for three months, six months, twelve months or more beyond the due date for delivery. Subject to the provisions of *section 710B(6)* of *CA 1985*, which allow certain documents to be delivered in Welsh, if any part of the annual accounts and reports is in a language other than English, a certified translation must be attached.

Company Law

3.37   *First Accounting Period*

Under *section 244(2)* of *CA 1985*, if the company's first accounting reference period lasts for more than twelve months, the due date for laying and delivering the first accounts and reports is the later of:

- seven months (public company) or ten months (private company) from the first anniversary of incorporation; or
- three months from the end of the first accounting reference period.

Example 6

Private company incorporated on	15 March 2005
Chosen accounting reference date	31 July
First accounting reference period ends	30 July 2006

The due date for laying and delivering the accounts will be the later of:

- ten months from the first anniversary of incorporation – 15 January 2007; or
- three months from the end of the first accounting period – 31 October 2006.

The due date will therefore be 15 January 2007.

If the first accounting period is twelve months or less, the normal rules apply for establishing the due date for laying and delivering the accounts.

Example 7

Private company incorporated on	15 March 2005
Chosen accounting reference date	31 December
First accounting reference period ends	31 December 2005

The due date for laying and delivering the first accounts is ten months after the end of the first accounting reference period – 31 October 2006.

3.38   *Change of Accounting Reference Date*

When changing an accounting reference date, it is important to recognise that this may alter the due date for laying and delivering the annual accounts and reports. Under *section 244(4)* of *CA 1985*, when an accounting reference period is shortened on a change of accounting reference date, the due date for laying and delivering the accounts is the later of:

- seven months (public company) or ten months (private company) from the new accounting reference date; or
- three months from the date of the notice of the change of accounting reference date.

3.39 *Business Interests Outside UK*

For accounting periods beginning before 1 January 2005, the directors of a company that carried on business or had interests outside the UK, Channel Islands and the Isle of Man were permitted to apply for a three-month extension to the period allowed for laying and delivering the annual reports and accounts. This was removed for subsequent accounting periods by the *Companies Act 1985 (International Accounting Standards and Other Accounting Amendments) Regulations 2004* (*SI 2004/2947*), on the basis that extension was no longer justifiable in the current climate of rapid global communication.

3.40 *Strict Interpretation of Due Date*

Companies House currently interprets the due date for delivery of accounts and reports very strictly. For instance, if an accounting reference period ends on 28 February, the accounts must be with the Registrar of Companies by 28 September for a public company and by 28 December for a private company. Delivery by 30 September or 31 December respectively will not be sufficient to avoid a penalty. However, the draft Company Law Reform Bill published in May 2006 includes a welcome change, by proposing that the filing period should normally end with the date corresponding to the accounting date, but where this is the last day of the month, the due date for filing should be the last day of the appropriate month – so, in the above examples, the filing dates would become 30 September and 31 December respectively. Also, the accounts must be accepted as correct in order to meet the delivery requirement. If they are delivered by the due date but are subsequently returned by Companies House for amendment, and the corrected accounts cannot be delivered by the due date, penalties will be incurred. Common errors that result in accounts being rejected by Companies House include:

- errors in the company's name or registered number;
- accounts made up to the incorrect accounting reference date;
- signatures omitted on the directors' report, balance sheet and/or auditors' report; and
- failure to include exemption statements where appropriate.

3.41 *Document Quality*

Much of the information held by Companies House is now scanned to produce an electronic image and strict specifications are therefore laid down for the quality of documents delivered to them. These requirements have recently been reinforced following the introduction of an internet enquiry service by Companies House and the need to ensure that text is relatively quick for users to download and does not take up too much memory space. Key points to remember when filing annual accounts and reports are:

- they must be printed in black on good quality white paper;
- the paper should have a matt finish;
- the documents should be of A4 size with a good margin;

- letters and figures should be clear, legible and of uniform density – in particular, they should not be less than 1.8 mm high or have a line width of less than 0.25 mm;
- there should be no shaded areas on photographs; and
- the company's registered number must be shown prominently on the front page.

The Registrar may reject accounts that are delivered in a format that does not permit straightforward electronic capture. Whilst problems arise most frequently with the accounts of larger companies (which are more likely to include photographs and complex graphics), difficulties have also been caused by some of the standard accounts production packages frequently used by smaller companies, particularly where these automatically shade comparative figures.

3.42   *Signatures*

Under *section 233* of *CA 1985*, the annual accounts must be approved by the board of directors and the balance sheet must be signed by one or more directors on behalf of the board. The name of the person who signed the balance sheet must be included on every copy of the accounts that is laid before the company in general meeting or otherwise published, circulated or issued. Financial Reporting Standard 21 (FRS 21) 'Events after the balance sheet date' also requires the following details to be disclosed:

- the date on which the financial statements were authorised for issue;
- who gave that authorisation; and
- where the entity's owners, or others, have the power to amend the financial statements after issue, a statement of that fact.

The date on which the accounts were authorised for issue is usually given alongside the directors' signature on the balance sheet, but may alternatively be disclosed in the notes to the accounts. *Section 234A* of *CA 1985* requires the directors' report to be similarly approved and signed either by a director or by the company secretary, on behalf of the board, and *section 234C* sets out equivalent requirements in respect of the directors' remuneration report prepared by a quoted company. Under *sections 233, 234A, 234C* and *236* of *CA 1985*, the copies of the annual accounts and reports that are delivered to the Registrar must include manuscript signatures on the balance sheet, directors' report, directors' remuneration report (where relevant) and auditors' report.

3.43   *Delivery by Electronic Means*

The *Companies Act 1985 (Electronic Communications) Order 2000* (*SI 2000/3373*) inserts a new *section 707B* into *CA 1985*, under which any requirement under the legislation to deliver a document to the Registrar of Companies can be satisfied by using electronic communications, provided that the delivery is made in the form and manner prescribed by the Registrar. In due course, this will enable annual accounts and reports to be filed electronically. The detailed procedures for this have not yet been put in place by Companies House, although arrangements are expected to be introduced later in 2006 to enable small companies and dormant companies to file unaudited accounts electronically as the first stage in the e-filing project for company accounts.

3.44   Preparation of Accounts in Euros

Section 242B of *CA 1985* permits the amounts shown in the annual accounts to also be disclosed in euros. A company may also deliver to the Registrar an additional copy of the accounts in which the amounts shown have been translated into euros. In either case, the amounts must have been translated at the relevant exchange rate prevailing at the balance sheet date and the exchange rate used must be disclosed in the notes to the accounts. Where an additional copy of the accounts is delivered and the company is subject to audit, the additional accounts must also be accompanied by a copy of the auditors' report.

3.45   Unlimited Companies

Under *section 254* of *CA 1985*, an unlimited company is exempt from the requirement to deliver a copy of its annual accounts and reports to the Registrar, provided that it was not, at any time during the relevant accounting reference period:

- a subsidiary undertaking of a limited undertaking;
- an undertaking that would have been a subsidiary undertaking if the rights exercisable by or on behalf of two or more limited undertakings had been exercised; or
- a parent company of a limited undertaking.

The exemption is not available to an unlimited company that is a banking or insurance company, the parent company of a banking or insurance group, or a qualifying company within the meaning of the *Partnerships and Unlimited Companies (Accounts) Regulations 1993* (*SI 1993/1820*), or to an unlimited company that carries on business as the promoter of a trading stamp scheme within the *Trading Stamps Act 1964*.

Annual Reporting Timetable

	Listed companies	Other public companies	Private companies
Issue interim statement (see **11.97** INTERIM REPORTS)	Within 90 days of the period end (although the ASB encourages issue within 60 days of the period end).	Not required.	Not required.
Issue preliminary announcement (see **11.110** PRELIMINARY ANNOUNCEMENTS)	Within 120 days of the year end (although the ASB encourages issue within 60 days of the year end).	Not required.	Not required.

(*continued*)

Annual Reporting Timetable (*continued*)

	Listed companies	Other public companies	Private companies
Distribute annual accounts and reports to the members and other persons entitled to receive them	Not less than 21 days before the date of the meeting at which copies are to be laid before members.	Not less than 21 days before the date of the meeting at which copies are to be laid before the members.	Not less than 21 days before the meeting at which copies are to be laid.*
Lay annual accounts and reports before the members in general meeting	Within seven months of the end of the accounting period.	Within seven months of the end of the accounting period.	Within ten months of the end of the accounting period.*
Deliver annual accounts and reports to the Registrar	Within seven months of the end of the accounting period.	Within seven months of the end of the accounting period.	Within ten months of the end of the accounting period.

* A private company may elect to dispense with the requirement to lay the annual accounts and reports before the members in general meeting. In this case, copies must be sent out not less than 28 days before the end of the period allowed for laying and delivering the accounts and reports (see **3.34** above).

3.46   Small Companies and Groups

> **At a Glance**
> * A company must meet at least two out of three qualifying conditions in order to qualify as a small company under *CA 1985*.
> * A small company can choose to prepare 'shorter form' annual accounts for the members and/or abbreviated accounts for filing with the registrar.
> * Certain companies are ineligible for the exemptions, even if they meet the qualifying conditions.
> * Shorter form accounts have slightly simpler formats for the balance sheet and reduced disclosures in the notes to the accounts.
> * A small company can also choose to adopt the Financial Reporting Standard for Smaller Entities (FRSSE) rather other applicable accounting standards.
> * A small company is also permitted to prepare a modified directors' report.
> * Filing abbreviated accounts enables a small company to preserve some degree of confidentiality about its affairs, but against this must be weighed the cost of preparing two sets of accounts each year.
> * The rules on qualification as a small group are similar to those for qualification as a small company, although different qualifying conditions apply.
> * A small group is exempt from the requirement to prepare group accounts, and a small company that prepares shorter form individual accounts can take advantage of the reduced disclosure requirements when preparing group accounts.
> * Certain groups are ineligible for the exemption from preparing group accounts, even if they meet the qualifying conditions.

3.47   Qualification as a Small Company

Under *section 247* of *CA 1985*, a company generally qualifies as a small company for a financial year if it meets the qualifying conditions set out in *CA 1985* in both the financial year under consideration and the previous financial year. A company that meets the qualifying conditions in its first financial year qualifies as a small company for that year. A company is also treated as qualifying as small if:

- it qualified as small in the previous financial year, or was treated as qualifying as small in that year; or
- it qualifies as small in the current financial year and was treated as qualifying as small in the previous financial year.

These rules can appear very complicated, but the effect is to enable a company to continue to qualify as small even though it exceeds the qualifying conditions in one financial year. If it exceeds the criteria for two consecutive financial years, then it no longer qualifies as a small company under *CA 1985*.

3.48   Qualifying Conditions – Small Company

In order to qualify as small, a company must meet at least two of the following conditions:

- turnover not more than £5.6 million;
- balance sheet total not more than £2.8 million;
- number of employees not more than 50.

If the accounting period under review is more or less than one year, the turnover limit is adjusted proportionately. The expression 'balance sheet total' is defined as the total of the amounts shown as assets in the balance sheet, before any deduction for liabilities. The number of employees is to be calculated by adding together the number of persons employed by the company each month (regardless of whether they were employed for the full month) and dividing this by the number of months in the financial period. The financial limits have been updated on a number of occasions since the small company provisions were first introduced. The above limits were introduced by the *Companies Act 1985 (Accounts of Small and Medium-sized Enterprises and Audit Exemption) (Amendment) Regulations 2004 (SI 2004/16)* and generally apply for accounting periods ending on or after 30 January 2004 (subject to certain transitional conditions). For accounting periods beginning on or after 1 January 2005, qualification can be assessed on the basis of either Companies Act or IAS accounts (see **3.16** above).

3.49   Accounts Exemptions for Small Companies

Two main accounts exemptions are available to a small company under *CA 1985*:

- it can prepare annual accounts under *Schedule 8* to *CA 1985* rather than *Schedule 4* – accounts prepared under *Schedule 8* are usually referred to as

Company Law

FLOWCHART – QUALIFICATION AS A SMALL COMPANY

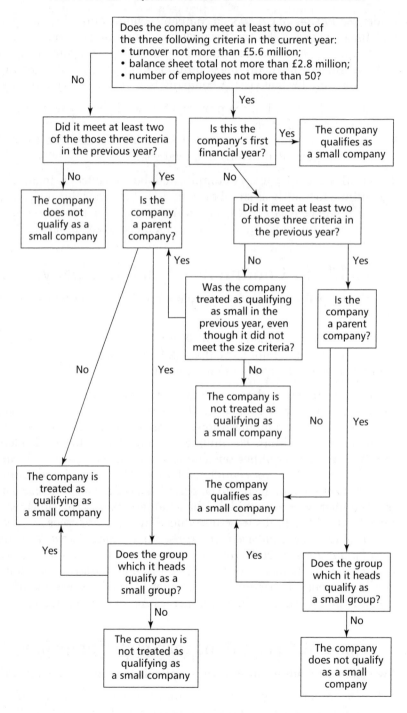

'shorter form accounts', reflecting the less detailed requirements of *Schedule 8*; and

- it can file abbreviated accounts with the Registrar (although full or shorter form accounts must still be prepared for the members).

Both exemptions are optional and a small company can continue to prepare and file full accounts if it wishes, or can file shorter form accounts if it does not wish to prepare abbreviated accounts for filing purposes. For accounting periods beginning on or after 1 January 2005, the option to prepare shorter form accounts and the full abbreviated accounts regime apply only where the company prepares Companies Act accounts (see **3.16** above). However, certain filing exemptions continue to apply to small companies preparing IAS accounts (see **3.56** below).

3.50   Ineligible Companies

The accounts exemptions referred to above are not available to the following, even if they meet the qualifying conditions set out in *CA 1985*:

- a public company;
- a person who has permission under *Part 4* of the *Financial Services and Markets Act 2000* to carry on a regulated activity;
- a person who carries on an insurance market activity; or
- a member of an ineligible group – this is defined in *section 247A(2)* of *CA 1985* as a group where any of the members is:
  - a public company,
  - a body corporate that has the power to issue shares or debentures to the public,
  - a person who has permission under *Part 4* of the *Financial Services and Markets Act 2000* to carry on a regulated activity, or
  - a person who carries on an insurance market activity.

In this context, a group means a parent and its subsidiary undertakings. In the case of an intermediate parent company it is therefore necessary to consider the wider group and not just the group headed by the intermediate parent. A UK subsidiary of a foreign parent will be a member of an ineligible group if the foreign parent has the power to issue shares or debentures to the public (and it is the power to issue such shares or debentures, rather than their actual issue, that is the deciding factor). However, a minor relaxation has been introduced for accounting periods beginning on or after 1 January 2005, so that a small company is now permitted to prepare a modified directors' report even if it is a member of an ineligible group (see **3.55** below). It should also be noted that, under *section 247A(3)* of *CA 1985*, a parent company is not treated as a small company unless the group which it heads qualifies as a small group (see **3.60–3.61** below).

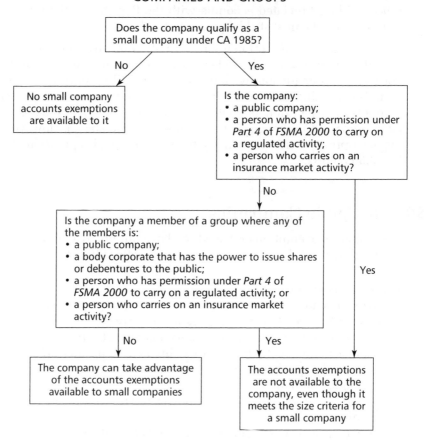

ACCOUNTS EXEMPTIONS AVAILABLE TO SMALL
COMPANIES AND GROUPS

Does the company qualify as a small company under CA 1985?

No → No small company accounts exemptions are available to it

Yes → Is the company:
• a public company;
• a person who has permission under *Part 4* of *FSMA 2000* to carry on a regulated activity;
• a person who carries on an insurance market activity?

No → Is the company a member of a group where any of the members is:
• a public company;
• a body corporate that has the power to issue shares or debentures to the public;
• a person who has permission under *Part 4* of *FSMA 2000* to carry on a regulated activity; or
• a person who carries on an insurance market activity?

No → The company can take advantage of the accounts exemptions available to small companies

Yes → The accounts exemptions are not available to the company, even though it meets the size criteria for a small company

Yes → The accounts exemptions are not available to the company, even though it meets the size criteria for a small company

3.51   Shorter Form Accounts

Section 246(2) of *CA 1985* permits a small company preparing Companies Act accounts (see **3.16** above) to prepare shorter form accounts by following the requirements of *Schedule 8* to *CA 1985* rather than those of *Schedule 4*. Essentially, the balance sheet formats in *Schedule 8* are less detailed than those in *Schedule 4*, and certain note disclosures normally required by *Schedule 4* are not repeated in *Schedule 8*. There is no change to the profit and loss account formats. A small number of additional exemptions are set out in *section 246(3)* of *CA 1985* – these cover disclosures normally required by *Schedule 5* in respect of related undertakings and by *Schedule 6* in respect of directors' emoluments and other benefits. For accounting periods beginning on or after 1 January 2005 and ending on or after 1 October 2005, they also include an exemption from the disclosure of employee costs and numbers required by *section 231A* of *CA 1985* (although a small company adopting Format 2 or 4 for the profit and loss account must still disclose staff costs as part of the Format).

3.52 *Directors' Statement – Shorter Form Accounts*

Shorter form accounts must include a statement in a prominent position on the balance sheet, above the signature of the director(s), that they are prepared in accordance with the special provisions of *Part VII* of *CA 1985* relating to small companies.

3.53 *True and Fair View – Shorter Form Accounts*

Shorter form accounts are still required by *CA 1985* to show a true and fair view, even though they may not include all the detailed disclosures required in full accounts. In certain circumstances, additional disclosures may be needed in order to achieve a true and fair view. For instance, shorter form accounts must still be prepared in accordance with applicable accounting standards and detailed disclosures required by those standards will therefore need to be given in shorter form accounts even if they are not specifically required by *Schedule 8* to *CA 1985*. Small companies are exempt from the requirement to disclose whether the accounts have been prepared in accordance with applicable accounting standards, but not from the requirement to adopt appropriate standards.

3.54 Financial Reporting Standard for Smaller Entities ('FRSSE')

A Financial Reporting Standard for Smaller Entities ('FRSSE') was first published in November 1997 and came into immediate effect (for information on obtaining copies see the ASB website at www.frc.org.uk/asb). Various revised versions of the FRSSE have been issued since then, the latest being effective for accounting periods beginning on or after 1 January 2005. The purpose of the FRSSE is to combine simplified accounting requirements for smaller entities into one document and regular updates are therefore needed to bring the requirements into line with current accounting practice. The contents of the FRSSE are based on the requirements of other accounting standards and UITF Abstracts, but the definitions and measurement requirements are included in simplified form and many of the detailed disclosure requirements are omitted. The current version of the FRSSE is also a 'one-stop shop' document, encompassing all of the company law accounting requirements that apply to small companies as well as those from accounting standards and related pronouncements. Company law requirements are distinguished from other aspects of the FRSSE by being set out in small capitals in the text. Only the most common balance sheet format is included in the FRSSE but small companies continue to have the option of adopting the alternative format if they wish. However, in the case of the profit and loss account, only Formats 1 and 2 from *CA 1985* are now available to companies adopting the

FRSSE. The FRSSE may be applied to financial statements that are intended to give a true and fair view of the results and financial position of:

- small companies and groups, as defined in *CA 1985*; and
- entities that would qualify as small if they were incorporated under *CA 1985*.

Adoption of the FRSSE is optional and, where it is adopted, this fact must be disclosed in the accounts. If a small company chooses not to adopt the FRSSE, its accounts must be prepared in accordance with all other applicable accounting standards.

3.55 Modified Directors' Report

A small company is also permitted to prepare a modified directors' report. Under *section 246(4)* of *CA 1985*, the following details need not be given:

- fair review of the business and the principal risks and uncertainties it faces (normally required by *CA 1985, s 234ZZB*);
- amount recommended to be paid as dividend (normally required by *CA 1985, s 234ZZA*);
- market values of certain fixed assets (normally required by *CA 1985, Sch 7, para 1(2)*);
- important events since the balance sheet date (normally required by *CA 1985, Sch 7, para 6(a)*);
- likely future developments in the business (normally required by *CA 1985, Sch 7, para 6(b)*);
- details of research and development activities (normally required by *CA 1985, Sch 7, para 6(c)*);
- details of the existence of branches outside the UK (normally required by *CA 1985, Sch 7, para 6(d)*); and
- details of employee involvement (normally required by *CA 1985, Sch 7, para 11*).
- for accounting periods beginning on or after 1 January 2005, disclosures in respect of the use of financial instruments (normally required by *CA 1985, Sch 7, para 5A*).

Also, for accounting periods beginning on or after 1 January 2005 and ending on or after 1 October 2005, small companies within the size criteria which do not generally qualify for SME exemptions simply because they are part of an ineligible group are now granted the same directors' report exemptions as other smaller companies, although the position remains unchanged in respect of other accounts exemptions. Where advantage is taken of any of these exemptions, the directors' report must include a statement in a prominent position, above the signature of the director or secretary, that it is prepared in accordance with the special provisions of *Part VII* of *CA 1985* relating to small companies. This requirement does not apply where the directors have taken advantage of the audit exemption conferred on dormant companies by *section 249AA* of *CA 1985*, as a different statement is required in this case. The exemptions in respect of the accounts and the directors' report operate independently, but in practice a small company will usually take advantage of both or neither.

3.56   Abbreviated Accounts

Section 246(5) of *CA 1985* permits a small company to file abbreviated accounts with the Registrar, although full or shorter form accounts must still be prepared for presentation to the members. Abbreviated accounts enable a small company to preserve some degree of confidentiality about its activities, although against this must be weighed the disadvantage of having to prepare two sets of accounts each year. The following exemptions apply to abbreviated accounts for small companies and are set out in *section 246(5)* of and *Schedule 8A* to *CA 1985*:

- the directors' report and profit and loss account need not be filed;
- the balance sheet is only required to show items that are assigned a Roman number in the standard formats – detailed analyses of the totals are therefore not generally required, although debtors and creditors due after more than one year still have to be shown separately;
- the notes to the accounts are only required to disclose:
  - the accounting policies adopted,
  - details of share capital,
  - details of share allotments during the year,
  - movements in fixed assets (but only by main headings),
  - details of borrowings,
  - the basis of any foreign currency conversion,
  - comparative figures, and
  - in the case of a dormant company that has acted as an agent for another party, a statement of that fact.

Section 246(6) of *CA 1985* grants further exemptions from disclosures normally required by *Schedule 5* (related undertakings) and *Schedule 6* (directors' emoluments and other benefits). For accounting periods beginning on or after 1 January 2005, a small company that chooses to prepare IAS accounts can continue to take advantage of the exemption from filing its profit and loss account and directors' report, but the exemptions in respect of the balance sheet and related notes apply only where Companies Act accounts are prepared. The disclosure exemptions granted by *section 246(6)* of *CA 1985* also continue to apply to IAS accounts. The recent company law review considered abolishing the abbreviated accounts regime, but the DTI's latest proposal is to retain the regime but require all companies to disclose turnover in their published accounts.

3.57   *Directors' Statement – Abbreviated Accounts*

Where a small company takes advantage of the option to prepare and file abbreviated accounts, the accounts must include a statement in a prominent position on the balance sheet, above the signature of the director(s), that they are prepared

Company Law

in accordance with the special provisions of *Part VII* of *CA 1985* relating to small companies.

3.58   *Auditors' Statement – Abbreviated Accounts*

If the company's full or shorter form accounts have been audited, the abbreviated accounts delivered to the Registrar must be accompanied by a special report from the auditors stating whether, in their opinion:

- the company is entitled to deliver abbreviated accounts; and
- the abbreviated accounts have been properly prepared in accordance with *section 246(5)* and *(6)* of *CA 1985*.

The full text of the auditors' report on the full or shorter form accounts must also be included if this report was qualified, or included a statement under *section 237(2)* of *CA 1985* (inadequate accounting records or returns, or accounts not in agreement with the records or returns) or under *section 237(3)* of *CA 1985* (failure to obtain all the information and explanations that the auditors considered necessary). The latest Auditing Practices Board guidance on reporting on abbreviated accounts, set out in Bulletin 2006/3 *The Special Auditors' Report on Abbreviated Accounts in the United Kingdom*, also requires any emphasis of matter paragraph from the full audit report to be included in the special report, together with any further material needed to understand this. The Bulletin also considers whether an 'other matter' paragraph in the auditors' report should be repeated in the special report. It gives as an example a situation where the auditor draws attention to an inconsistency between the directors' report and the accounts and concludes that there would generally be no requirement to include this in the special report on a small company as the company is not required to file the directors' report.

3.59   *True and Fair View – Abbreviated Accounts*

Abbreviated accounts are not required to show a true and fair view and in practice they will not do so because they will not include the detailed disclosures normally considered necessary to achieve this. However, they are in effect an extract of the full or shorter form accounts, which do need to be prepared in accordance with applicable accounting standards. In the case of abbreviated accounts, therefore, a distinction is effectively made between the measurement and disclosure requirements of accounting standards, in that the abbreviated accounts must still follow all of the measurement requirements of accounting standards (or the FRSSE) adopted in the full or shorter form accounts, but the additional disclosures normally required by accounting standards (or the FRSSE) need not be given.

3.60   Qualification as a Small Group

The rules on qualification as a small group are similar to those for qualification as a small company. Under *section 249(1)* of *CA 1985*, a group (which in this case means a parent company and its subsidiary undertakings) qualifies as small if it meets the qualifying conditions in both the financial year under consideration and the previous financial year. A group that meets the qualifying conditions in the parent company's first financial year qualifies as a small group for that year. A group is also treated as qualifying as small if:

- it qualified as small in the previous financial year, or was treated as qualifying as small in that year; or
- it qualifies as small in the current financial year and was treated as qualifying as small in the previous financial year.

As with individual companies, this means that a group continues to qualify as small even though it exceeds the qualifying conditions in one financial year. If it exceeds the criteria for two consecutive financial years, then it no longer qualifies as a small group under *CA 1985*.

3.61   Qualifying Conditions – Small Group

In order to qualify as small, a group must meet at least two of the following conditions:

- turnover not more than £5.6 million net (or £6.72 million gross);
- balance sheet total not more than £2.8 million (or £3.36 million gross);
- number of employees not more than 50.

The same definitions and rules apply as for small companies (see **3.48** above). Gross figures in the financial limits are those before the adjustments and set-offs normally made when preparing consolidated accounts and net figures are those after such adjustments. The option of using gross figures enables a group to demonstrate that it meets the criteria without the need to go through the mechanics of consolidation. There is no requirement in the legislation for the turnover and balance sheet limits to be considered on the same basis. The financial limits have been updated on a number of occasions since the provisions were first introduced, and the above limits generally apply for accounting periods ending on or after 30 January 2004 (subject to certain transitional conditions). For accounting periods beginning on or after 1 January 2005, qualification can be assessed on the basis of either Companies Act or IAS accounts (see **3.17** above).

3.62   Accounts Exemptions Available to Small Groups

Two main accounts exemptions are available to small groups:

- under *section 248* of *CA 1985*, the parent company of a small group is exempt from the requirement to prepare group accounts (unless the group is an ineligible group); and
- under *section 248A* of *CA 1985*, a small company that prepares shorter form accounts and is preparing group accounts for the same financial year is permitted to prepare the group accounts in accordance with *Schedule 8* to *CA 1985*.

Company Law

For accounting periods beginning on or after 1 January 2005, the second exemption is only available where the company prepares Companies Act group accounts (see **3.17** above). A parent company is not entitled to the exemption from the requirement to prepare group accounts if the group which it heads is an ineligible group. This is defined in *section 248(2)* of *CA 1985* as a group where any of the members is:

- a public company;
- a body corporate that has the power to issue shares or debentures to the public;
- a person who has permission under *Part 4* of the *Financial Services and Markets Act 2000* to carry on a regulated activity; or
- a person who carries on an insurance market activity.

FRS 2 *Accounting for Subsidiary Undertakings* requires certain disclosures to be given in the accounts where the parent company of a small group takes advantage of the exemption from the requirement to prepare group accounts (for information on obtaining copies see the ASB website at www.frc.org. uk/asb).

QUALIFICATION AS A SMALL GROUP

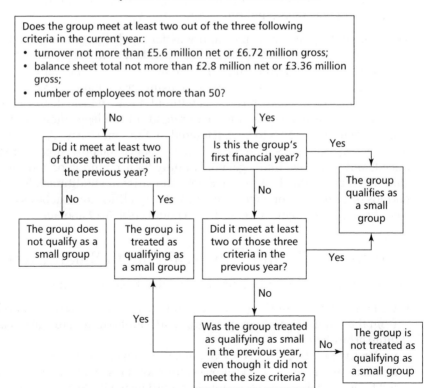

3.63   Medium-sized Companies and Groups

At a Glance
* A company must meet at least two out of three qualifying conditions in order to qualify as a medium-sized company under *CA 1985*.
* A medium-sized company can choose to prepare abbreviated accounts for filing with the registrar.
* Certain companies are ineligible for this exemption, even if they meet the qualifying conditions.
* Filing abbreviated accounts enables a medium-sized company to pre-serve a limited degree of confidentiality about its affairs, but against this must be weighed the cost of preparing two sets of accounts each year.
* The rules on qualification as a medium-sized group are similar to those for qualification as a medium-sized company, although different quali-fying conditions apply.
* A medium-sized group is generally exempt from the requirement to pre-pare group accounts, although certain groups are ineligible for this exemption even if they meet the qualifying conditions.

3.64   Qualification as a Medium-sized Company

Under *section 247* of *CA 1985,* a company generally qualifies as a medium-sized company for a financial year if it meets the qualifying conditions set out in *CA 1985* in both the financial year under consideration and the previous financial year. A company that meets the qualifying conditions in its first finan-cial year qualifies as a medium-sized company for that year. A company is also treated as qualifying as medium-sized if:

* it qualified as medium-sized in the previous financial year, or was treated as qualifying as medium-sized in that year; or
* it qualifies as medium-sized in the current financial year and was treated as qualifying as medium-sized in the previous financial year.

The effect of this is to enable a company to continue to qualify as medium-sized even though it exceeds the qualifying conditions in one financial year. If it exceeds the criteria for two consecutive financial years, then it no longer quali-fies as a medium-sized company under *CA 1985*.

3.65   Qualifying Conditions – Medium-sized Company

In order to qualify as medium-sized, a company must meet at least two of the following conditions:

* turnover not more than £22.8 million;
* balance sheet total not more than £11.4 million;
* number of employees not more than 250.

Company Law

If the accounting period under review is more or less than one year, the turnover limit is adjusted proportionately. The expression 'balance sheet total' is defined as the total of the amounts shown as assets in the balance sheet, before any deduction for liabilities. The number of employees is to be calculated by adding together the number of persons employed by the company each month (regardless of whether they were employed for the full month) and dividing this by the number of months in the financial period. The above limits were introduced by the *Companies Act 1985 (Accounts of Small and Medium-sized Enterprises and Audit Exemption) (Amendment) Regulations 2004* (*SI 2004/16*) and generally apply for accounting periods ending on or after 30 January 2004 (subject to certain transitional conditions). For accounting periods beginning on or after 1 January 2005, qualification can be assessed on the basis of either Companies Act or IAS accounts (see **3.16** above).

3.66 Accounts Exemption for Medium-sized Companies

The main accounts exemption permitted to a medium-sized company is that it can file abbreviated accounts with the Registrar, but the permitted abbreviations in this case are very limited. Full accounts must continue to be prepared each year for the members. The exemption is optional and a medium-sized company can continue to file full accounts if it wishes. A medium-sized company is also exempt from the requirement to disclose whether its accounts have been prepared in accordance with applicable accounting standards (but not from the requirement to adopt appropriate standards). Also, for accounting periods beginning on or after 1 April 2005, medium-sized companies are granted limited exemptions in respect of some of the detailed directors' report disclosures introduced by the *Companies Act 1985 (Operating and Financial Review and Directors' Report etc.) Regulations 2005* (*SI 2005/1011*). As a result, the business review prepared by a medium-sized company need not include analysis using key performance indicators (KPIs) in respect of non-financial information (for instance, employee matters and environmental issues) although financial KPIs must still be presented. Companies that meet the size criteria for a medium-sized company but do not generally qualify for SME exemptions simply because they are members of an ineligible group can also take advantage of this exemption in respect of the directors' report.

3.67 Ineligible Companies

The exemptions are not available to the following, even if they meet the qualifying conditions set out in *CA 1985*:

- a public company;
- a person who has permission under *Part 4* of the *Financial Services and Markets Act 2000* to carry on a regulated activity;
- a person who carries on an insurance market activity; or

- a member of an ineligible group – this is defined in *section 247A(2)* of *CA 1985* as a group where any of the members is:
  - a public company,
  - a body corporate that has the power to issue shares or debentures to the public,
  - a person who has permission under *Part 4* of the *Financial Services and Markets Act 2000* to carry on a regulated activity, or
  - a person who carries on an insurance market activity.

In this context, a group means a parent and its subsidiary undertakings. In the case of an intermediate parent company, it is therefore necessary to consider the wider group and not just the group headed by the intermediate parent. A UK subsidiary of a foreign parent will be a member of an ineligible group if the foreign parent has the power to issue shares or debentures to the public (and it is the power to issue such shares or debentures, rather than their actual issue, that is the deciding factor). Also, under *section 247A(3)*, a parent company is not treated as a medium-sized company unless the group which it heads qualifies as a medium-sized group (see **3.72–3.73** below). However, as explained at **3.66** above, for accounting periods beginning on or after 1 April 2005, a company that qualifies as medium-sized can still take advantage of the limited exemptions in respect of the directors' report, even if it is not entitled to other accounts exemptions because it is a member of an ineligible group.

3.68   Abbreviated Accounts

Section 246A(3) of *CA 1985* permits a medium-sized company to file abbreviated accounts with the Registrar, although full accounts must still be prepared for presentation to the members. Abbreviated accounts enable a medium-sized company to preserve a limited degree of confidentiality about its activities, although against this must be weighed the disadvantage of having to prepare two sets of accounts each year. The following exemptions apply to abbreviated accounts for a medium-sized company:

- the company may file a profit and loss account that begins with 'gross profit or loss', being a combination of the figures for turnover, cost of sales and other operating income (or the equivalent figures under the alternative standard formats); and
- the notes to the accounts need not analyse turnover by class of business and geographical market (normally required by *paragraph 55* of *Schedule 4* to *CA 1985*).

There are no exemptions for the balance sheet or directors' report. For accounting periods beginning on or after 1 January 2005, the exemptions apply only where the company prepares Companies Act accounts (see **3.16** above). The recent company law review considered abolishing the abbreviated accounts regime, but the DTI's latest proposal is to retain the regime but require all companies to disclose turnover in their published accounts.

3.69   *Directors' Statement – Abbreviated Accounts*

Where a medium-sized company takes advantage of the option to prepare and file abbreviated accounts, the accounts must include a statement in a prominent position on the balance sheet, above the signature of the director(s), that they are prepared in accordance with the special provisions of *Part VII* of *CA 1985* relating to medium-sized companies.

3.70   *Auditors' Statement – Abbreviated Accounts*

Where abbreviated accounts are delivered to the Registrar, they must be accompanied by a special report from the auditors stating whether, in their opinion:

- the company is entitled to deliver abbreviated accounts; and
- the abbreviated accounts have been properly prepared in accordance with *section 246A(3)* of *CA 1985*.

The full text of the auditors' report on the full accounts must also be included if this report was qualified, or included a statement under *section 237(2)* of *CA 1985* (inadequate accounting records or returns, or accounts not in agreement with the records or returns) or under *section 237(3)* of *CA 1985* (failure to obtain all the information and explanations that the auditors considered necessary). The latest Auditing Practices Board guidance on reporting on abbreviated accounts, set out in Bulletin 2006/3 *The Special Auditors' Report on Abbreviated Accounts in the United Kingdom*, also requires any emphasis of matter paragraph from the full audit report to be included in the special report, together with any further material needed to understand this. The Bulletin also considers whether an 'other matter' paragraph in the auditors' report should be repeated in the special report. It gives as an example a situation where the auditor draws attention to an inconsistency between the directors' report and the accounts and concludes that this would also need to be repeated in the special report on the abbreviated accounts of a medium-sized company, on the basis that there is a requirement to file the directors' report in this case.

3.71   *True and Fair View – Abbreviated Accounts*

Abbreviated accounts are not required to show a true and fair view and in practice they will not do so because they will not include the detailed disclosures normally considered necessary to achieve this. However, they are in effect an extract of the full accounts, which do need to be prepared in accordance with applicable accounting standards. In the case of abbreviated accounts, therefore, a distinction is effectively made between the measurement and disclosure requirements of accounting standards, in that the abbreviated accounts must still follow all of the measurement requirements of accounting standards adopted in the full accounts, but the additional disclosures normally required by accounting standards need not be given. However, it should be noted that some accountants take the view that, because the permitted abbreviations for medium-sized companies are so limited, the additional disclosures required by accounting standards should be given in the abbreviated accounts as well as in the full accounts.

3.72   Qualification as a Medium-sized Group

The rules on qualification as a medium-sized group are similar to those for qualification as a medium-sized company. Under *section 249(1)* of *CA 1985,* a group (which in this case means a parent company and its subsidiary undertakings) qualifies as medium-sized if it meets the qualifying conditions in both the financial year under consideration and the previous financial year. A group that meets the qualifying conditions in the parent company's first financial year qualifies as a medium-sized group for that year. A group is also treated as qualifying as medium-sized if:

- it qualified as medium-sized in the previous financial year, or was treated as qualifying as medium-sized in that year; or
- it qualifies as medium-sized in the current financial year and was treated as qualifying as medium-sized in the previous financial year.

As with individual companies, this means that a group continues to qualify as medium-sized even though it exceeds the qualifying conditions in one financial year. If it exceeds the criteria for two consecutive financial years, then it no longer qualifies as a medium-sized group under *CA 1985.*

3.73   Qualifying Conditions – Medium-sized Group

In order to qualify as medium-sized, a group must meet at least two of the following conditions:

- turnover not more than £22.8 million net (or £27.36 million gross);
- balance sheet total not more than £11.4 million (or £13.68 million gross);
- number of employees not more than 250.

The same definitions and rules apply as for medium-sized companies (see **3.65** above). Gross figures in the financial limits are those before the adjustments and set-offs normally made when preparing consolidated accounts and net figures are those after such adjustments. The option of using gross figures enables a group to demonstrate that it meets the criteria without the need to go through the mechanics of consolidation. There is no requirement in the legislation for the turnover and balance sheet limits to be considered on the same basis. The financial limits have been updated on a number of occasions since the provisions were first introduced. The above limits generally apply for accounting periods ending on or after 30 January 2004 (subject to certain transitional conditions). For accounting periods beginning on or after 1 January 2005, qualification can be assessed on the basis of either Companies Act or IAS accounts (see **3.17** above).

3.74 Accounts Exemptions Available to Medium-sized Groups

Under *section 248* of *CA 1985,* the parent company of a medium-sized group is exempt from the requirement to prepare group accounts, unless the group which it heads is an ineligible group. This is defined in *section 248(2)* of *CA 1985* as a group where any of the members is:

- a public company;
- a body corporate that has the power to issue shares or debentures to the public;
- a person who has permission under *Part 4* of the *Financial Services and Markets Act 2000* to carry on a regulated activity; or
- a person who carries on an insurance market activity.

FRS 2 *Accounting for Subsidiary Undertakings* requires certain disclosures to be given in the accounts where the parent company of a medium-sized group takes advantage of this exemption (for information on obtaining copies see the ASB website at www.frc.org.uk/asb). During the course of the recent company law review, views have been divided on whether or not the exemption should be retained, and it should be noted that the draft Company Law Reform Bill published in May 2006 includes a requirement for all parent companies, other than those that qualify as small, to prepare consolidated accounts unless they qualify for one of the other exemptions under *CA 1985* (see **3.18** above).

3.75 Banking and Insurance Companies and Groups

At a Glance
* A banking company must prepare annual accounts in accordance with *Part I* of *Schedule 9* to *CA 1985* (rather than in accordance with *Schedule 4*).
* The parent company of a banking group (as defined in *CA 1985*) must prepare group accounts in accordance with the special provisions of *Part VII* of *CA 1985*, as modified by *Part II* of *Schedule 9* to *CA 1985*.
* An insurance company must prepare annual accounts in accordance with *Part I* of *Schedule 9A* to *CA 1985* (rather than in accordance with *Schedule 4*).
* The parent company of an insurance group (as defined in *CA 1985*) must prepare group accounts in accordance with the special provisions of *Part VII* of *CA 1985*, as modified by *Part II* of *Schedule 9A* to *CA 1985*.

3.76 Banking Companies

A banking company is defined in *section 742B* of *CA 1985* as a company which has permission under *Part 4* of the *Financial Services and Markets Act 2000* to accept deposits, except where such permission is given only for the purpose of carrying on another regulated activity. A banking company is required to prepare its individual accounts in accordance with the provisions set out in *Part I* of *Schedule 9* to *CA 1985* rather than with *Schedule 4*. The accounts must state that they are prepared in accordance with the special provisions of *Part VII* of *CA 1985* relating to banking companies. The accounts are still required to show a true and fair view and the requirements of accounting standards therefore continue to apply, as do the recommendations in SORPs issued by the British Bankers' Association/Irish Bankers' Federation. The general rules for presenting accounts are broadly the same as for other companies, but the balance sheet and profit and loss account formats are adapted to allow for the special circumstances of banking companies. However, it should be noted that banking companies are specifically excluded from the exemptions available to small and medium-sized companies. For accounting periods beginning on or after 1 January 2005, the option to prepare IAS accounts applies equally to banking companies (see **3.16** above).

3.77 Banking Groups

A banking group is defined in *section 255A(4)* of *CA 1985* as a group where:

- the parent is a banking company; or
- the parent does not carry on material business (other than the acquisition, management and disposal of subsidiary undertakings) and its principal subsidiary undertakings are wholly or mainly credit institutions (ie undertakings whose business is to receive deposits or other repayable funds from the public and to grant credits for its own account).

The parent company of a banking group is required to prepare group accounts in accordance with *Part VII* of *CA 1985* as modified by *Part II* of *Schedule 9* to *CA 1985*. The group accounts must state that they are prepared in accordance with the special provisions of *Part VII* of *CA 1985* relating to banking groups. The normal rules on the preparation of group accounts apply, including the requirement for the group accounts to show a true and fair view, but the group account formats are amended in a similar way to those for banking companies. However, banking groups are specifically excluded from the group accounts exemptions currently available to small and medium-sized groups. For accounting periods beginning on or after 1 January 2005, the provisions on the preparation of IAS group accounts apply to banking groups in the same way as to other groups (see **3.17** above).

3.78 Insurance Companies

An insurance company is defined in *section 742C* of *CA 1985* as a person (whether incorporated or not) who:

(a) has permission under *Part 4* of the *Financial Services and Markets Act 2000* to effect or carry out contracts of insurance;

(b) carries on insurance market activity; or

(c) may effect or carry out contracts of insurance under which the benefits provided are exclusively or primarily benefits in kind in the event of accident to or breakdown of a vehicle, but who does not fall within (a) above.

Company Law

A friendly society within the meaning of *section 116* of the *Friendly Societies Act 1992* is specifically excluded from this definition.

An insurance company is required to prepare its individual accounts in accordance with *Part I* of *Schedule 9A* to *CA 1985* rather than with *Schedule 4*. The accounts must state that they are prepared in accordance with the special provisions of *Part VII* of *CA 1985* relating to insurance companies. The accounts are still required to show a true and fair view and the requirements of accounting standards therefore continue to apply, as do the recommendations in the SORP *Accounting for Insurance Business* developed by the Association of British Insurers. The general rules for presenting accounts are broadly the same as for other companies, but the balance sheet and profit and loss account formats are adapted to allow for the special circumstances of insurance companies. However, it should be noted that insurance companies are specifically excluded from the exemptions available to small and medium-sized companies. For accounting periods beginning on or after 1 January 2005, the option to prepare IAS accounts applies equally to insurance companies (see **3.16** above).

3.79   Insurance Groups

A insurance group is defined in *section 255A(5)* of *CA 1985* as a group where:

- the parent is an insurance company; or
- the parent does not carry on material business (other than the acquisition, management and disposal of subsidiary undertakings) and its principal subsidiary undertakings are wholly or mainly insurance companies.

The parent company of an insurance group is required to prepare group accounts in accordance with *Part VII* of *CA 1985* as modified by *Part II* of *Schedule 9A* to *CA 1985*. The group accounts must state that they are prepared in accordance with the special provisions of *Part VII* of *CA 1985* relating to insurance groups. The normal rules on the preparation of group accounts apply, including the requirement for the group accounts to show a true and fair view, but the group account formats are amended in a similar way to those for insurance companies. However, insurance groups are specifically excluded from the group accounts exemptions currently available to small and medium-sized companies. For accounting periods beginning on or after 1 January 2005, the provisions on IAS group accounts apply to insurance groups in the same way as to other groups (see **3.17** above).

3.80   Publication of Accounts

At a Glance
* Publication of a document is defined in *CA 1985* as publishing, issuing or circulating it or otherwise making it available for public inspection – this is usually deemed to include issue to a specific group of individuals as well as to the public at large.

> * Statutory accounts are defined as those that are required to be delivered to the registrar.
> * The auditors' report must always be included when statutory accounts are published.
> * Non-statutory accounts (as defined in *CA 1985*) must include a formal statement that they are not the company's statutory accounts and certain details about the statutory accounts for the financial period covered by the non-statutory accounts.

3.81   Definition of Publication

Publication of a document is defined in *section 240(4)* of *CA 1985* as publishing, issuing or circulating it, or otherwise making it available for public inspection in a manner calculated to invite members of the public generally, or any class of members of the public, to read it. The legal definition of 'public' is very wide and the definition of publication is usually deemed to cover the issue of documents to specific groups of individuals, such as the company's employees.

3.82   Statutory Accounts

Statutory accounts are defined in *section 240(5)* of *CA 1985* as the individual or group accounts for a financial year that are required by *section 242* of *CA 1985* to be delivered to the Registrar. For small and medium-sized companies, the term consequently includes abbreviated accounts if these can be delivered in place of full accounts. Where statutory accounts are published in other documents (eg publicity brochures), *section 240(1)* of *CA 1985* specifies that the auditors' report must always be included.

3.83   Non-statutory Accounts

Non-statutory accounts are defined in *section 240(5)* of *CA 1985* as:

• any balance sheet or profit and loss account relating to, or purporting to deal with, a financial year of the company; or
• an account in any form purporting to be a balance sheet or profit and loss account for the group (ie the company and its subsidiary undertakings) relating to, or purporting to deal with, a financial year of the company.

A balance sheet or profit and loss account that forms part of the statutory accounts is specifically excluded from this definition. A document will therefore constitute non-statutory accounts if it contains financial information covering a company's normal accounting period and balance sheet information as at the company's normal financial year end. There is no definitive guidance on what level of detail constitutes a profit and loss account for these purposes, but it seems that the publication together of figures for (say) turnover and profit for the year might be deemed to be a profit and loss account for that year. The following will usually constitute non-statutory accounts:

- interim reports issued by listed companies (given that they will usually include comparative figures for a full financial year);
- preliminary statements issued by listed companies;
- summary financial statements, if they are made available to a wider group than 'entitled persons' (for instance, by publication on a website);
- summarised reports (eg for issue to employees);
- financial information published on a company website.

3.84   Formal Statement in Non-statutory Accounts

Whenever a company publishes non-statutory accounts, *section 240(3) of CA 1985* requires the document to include a statement indicating:

- that they are not the company's statutory accounts;
- whether statutory accounts for any financial year covered by the non-statutory accounts have been delivered to the Registrar;
- whether the auditors (or, where relevant, the reporting accountants) have reported on the statutory accounts for any financial year covered by the non-statutory accounts (although *section 240(3) of CA 1985* specifically prohibits publication of this report in the non-statutory accounts);
- whether the auditors' report (or the reporting accountants' report) was qualified or contained a statement under *section 237(2) of CA 1985* (inadequate accounting records or returns, or accounts not in agreement with the records and returns) or *section 237(3) of CA 1985* (failure to obtain all the information and explanations the auditors considered necessary); and
- for accounting periods beginning on or after 1 January 2005, whether the auditors drew attention to any other matters by way of emphasis in their report without qualifying the report.

If the published document includes information for two financial years (for instance, a preliminary announcement with figures for both the current and the previous financial year), the statement must give the relevant details for each year.

3.85   Revision of Defective Accounts and Reports

> **At a Glance**
> * Directors are permitted to prepare revised annual accounts and a revised directors' report and/or directors' remuneration report where the original versions did not comply with the requirements of the legislation – the revision must be restricted to correction of the original.
> * Two methods of revision are offered – complete replacement of the original accounts and/or report, or the issue of a supplementary note.

* *CA 1985* specifies the disclosures that must be given in each case and sets out detailed requirements on the circulation, laying and delivery to the registrar of the revised accounts and/or report.
* It may also be necessary to consider the impact of the revision on other documents, such as summary financial statements or abbreviated accounts.
* The Secretary of State has the power to raise with the directors any matters which suggest that the annual accounts may not comply with the requirements of *CA 1985* and to apply to the court for an order requiring revision of the accounts.
* The Financial Reporting Review Panel (FRRP) is authorised to apply directly to the court for an order requiring revision of the accounts without first raising the matter with the directors, but this power is rarely used in practice.
* Where the court orders the revision of annual accounts, it has wide powers to give directions on the audit of the revised accounts, the revision of related documents, the manner of drawing attention to the revision and who should bear the costs of the application and the revision.

3.86   Voluntary Revision by the Directors

Section 245 of *CA 1985* permits the directors to prepare revised annual accounts and a revised directors' report and/or directors' remuneration report where the original versions did not comply with the requirements of *CA 1985*. For accounting periods beginning on or after 1 January 2005, the *Companies Act 1985 (International Accounting Standards and Other Accounting Amendments) Regulations 2004 (SI 2004/2947)* amend *section 245* to allow specifically for the voluntary revision of a summary financial statement, regardless of whether the underlying accounts and reports also require revision. If the original accounts and reports have already been laid before the members, or delivered to the Registrar, the revisions must be confined to the correction of the aspects that did not meet those requirements, together with any necessary consequential alterations. No other adjustments should be made. The *Companies (Revision of Defective Accounts and Report) Regulations 1990 (SI 1990/2570* as amended by subsequent SIs) offer directors a choice of two methods for making any necessary corrections:

* completely replacing the original report and/or accounts; or
* issuing a supplementary note.

The directors are free to choose whichever method seems most appropriate in the circumstances. The revised document(s) must be prepared as at the date that the original version was approved by the directors – in other words, no account should be taken of events between that date and the date on which the revision is made.

Company Law

3.87   Disclosure Requirements

Where the directors' report, directors' remuneration report or accounts are completely replaced, and the original version has already been sent out to entitled persons, laid before the members or delivered to the Registrar, the revised version must give details of the adjustment(s) made and contain a prominent statement that:

- they replace the original report and/or accounts and, in the case of revised accounts, that they are now the statutory accounts of the company for that financial year; and
- they have been prepared as at the date of the original report or accounts.

Where the revision is done by means of a supplementary note, the note must include a prominent statement that it revises certain aspects of the original accounts, that it is to be treated as part of those accounts, and that the revision has been made as at the date of the original report or accounts. If the company's accounts are subject to audit, the auditors are required to report on the revisions, regardless of which revision method is adopted (see **1.83–1.84** above).

3.88   Circulation of Revised Accounts and/or Report

The requirements of *sections 233, 234A and 234C* of *CA 1985* on the signature of the annual accounts, directors' report and directors' remuneration report apply equally to the revised accounts and/or report and, where revision is done by means of a supplementary note, the signing requirements apply to that note. Where copies of the original report and/or accounts have already been sent to an entitled person, the directors must, within 28 days of the revision, send that person a copy of the revised report and/or accounts (or a copy of the supplementary note), together with the relevant report from the auditors. A copy must also be sent, within the same timescale, to any individual who is entitled to receive copies of the report and accounts at the date of the revision, even if they did not receive copies of the original report and/or accounts, unless the company is entitled at that date to send that person a summary financial statement.

3.89   Laying and Delivering Revised Accounts and/or Report

Where the original report or accounts have already been laid before the members, a copy of the revised accounts and/or report, together with the report from the auditors, must be laid before the next general meeting of the company at which annual accounts for a financial year are laid, unless the revised report and/or accounts have already been laid at an earlier general meeting. Where the original report or accounts have already been delivered to the Registrar, the directors must, within 28 days of the revision, deliver to the Registrar a copy of the revised report and/or accounts (or the supplementary note), together with the report from the auditors.

3.90   Impact on Other Documents

The directors may also need to consider the impact of the revision on any related documents, such as summary financial statements or abbreviated accounts – the revision may affect disclosures given in those statements or accounts, or, in the case of abbreviated accounts, may mean that the company is no longer eligible for the exemption from filing full accounts (eg if the revision takes figures above the financial limits in the qualifying conditions). If revisions are needed to a summary financial statement that has already been issued, the directors must prepare a further summary financial statement, including a short explanation of the revisions made, and send this, within 28 days of the revision of the report and/or accounts, to every person who received the original summary financial statement and to any other person entitled to receive a copy of such a statement at the date of the revision. If no revision of the summary financial statement is necessary, the directors must instead send out a note stating that the annual report and/or accounts have been revised, but that there is no bearing on the summary financial statement. If the auditors' report on the revised report and/or accounts is qualified, a copy must be attached to the note. If revisions are needed to abbreviated accounts that have been delivered to the Registrar, or if the company is no longer eligible to deliver abbreviated accounts, the directors must deliver appropriate revised accounts to the Registrar within 28 days of the revision of the full or shorter form accounts. If no revision to the abbreviated accounts is necessary, the directors must deliver to the Registrar:

- a note stating that the annual accounts have been revised, but that this has no bearing on the abbreviated accounts already delivered; and
- a copy of the auditors' report on the revised accounts.

3.91   Compulsory Revision of Accounts

Section 245A of *CA 1985* gives the Secretary of State the power to raise with the directors any matters which suggest that the annual accounts may not comply with the requirements of *CA 1985*. The directors have one month in which to respond to the queries, or in which to prepare revised accounts. If no response is received or the accounts are not revised, the Secretary of State may apply to the court for an order requiring the directors to prepare revised accounts. Also, under *section 245B(1)* of *CA 1985*, a person authorised by the Secretary of State may make direct application to the court for an order requiring revision of the accounts, without first raising the matter with the directors. The Financial Reporting Review Panel (FRRP) is currently authorised to do this, although in practice their approach is to try to resolve matters with the directors without resorting to this power. Notice of the application to the court must always be given to the Registrar, regardless of whether the application is made by the Secretary of State or by another authorised person. For accounting periods beginning on or after 1 January 2005, *sections 245–245C* of *CA 1985* are amended by the *Companies Act 1985 (International Accounting Standards and Other Accounting Amendments)*

Regulations 2004 (SI 2004/2947) to apply the same requirements to IAS accounts as to Companies Act accounts. The *Companies (Audit, Investigations and Community Enterprise) Act 2004* also makes minor amendments to *section 245C* and adds new *sections 245D–245G* which:

- widen the powers of authorised persons to obtain information from the company and its officers, employees and auditors;
- establish a gateway to enable the Inland Revenue to disclose relevant information to an authorised person to assist with the identification of defective accounts;
- establish gateways to enable an authorised person to disclose certain information to bodies such as the DTI, Treasury, Bank of England, Financial Services Authority and Inland Revenue to assist them in carrying out their legal functions; and
- restrict the use or disclosure of information under other circumstances.

These provisions came into effect on 6 April 2005. The *Companies Act 1985 (Operating and Financial Review and Directors' Report etc.) Regulations 2005 (SI 2005/1011)* make further changes to *CA 1985* to bring directors' reports within the scope of the provisions on compulsory revision and within the remit of the FRRP for accounting periods beginning on or after 1 April 2006.

3.92   Powers of the Court

Where the court orders the revision of accounts, it has wide powers to give directions on the audit of the revised accounts, the revision of the directors' report or any summary financial statements, the steps to be taken by the directors to ensure that the revision is brought to the attention of any persons likely to rely on the original accounts, and any other matters that the court thinks fit. It can also order that the costs of the application to the court, and of the preparation of revised accounts, should be borne by some or all of the directors who approved the original accounts. For this purpose, every director is regarded as having been a party to the approval of the accounts, unless it can be shown that he/she took all reasonable steps to prevent the original accounts being approved.

3.93   **Dividends and Distributions**

At a Glance
- * A company can only make a distribution out of distributable reserves available for that purpose.
- * Separate rules on distributable reserves apply for private and public companies.
- * Certain reserves will always be undistributable.
- * Detailed guidance on realised profits and losses has been issued by the Institute of Chartered Accountants in England and Wales.

> * Particular care is needed in the case of linked, circular or artificial transactions.
> * The classification of a profit or loss as realised or unrealised may change over time.

3.94 Distributable Reserves

CA 1985 does not often use the term 'dividend' but refers instead to a 'distribution' which it defines as any distribution of a company's assets to its members, in cash or in any other form, except distributions by way of:

- an issue of fully paid or partly paid bonus shares;
- the redemption or purchase of the company's own shares out of capital, the proceeds of a fresh issue of shares, or unrealised profits;
- the reduction of share capital by extinguishing or reducing the liability of any members in respect of share capital not paid up, or paying off paid up share capital; or
- a distribution of assets to members on the winding up of the company.

Under the Act, a distribution can only be made if the company has sufficient distributable reserves available. The legislation specifies which accounts should be used to determine a company's distributable reserves and special considerations apply if the audit report on those accounts was qualified (see **1.85** above). This is a highly complex area and only a brief outline of the issues is given here. Legal advice should always be sought in cases where there is any doubt over the potential availability of reserves for distribution.

3.95 Profits Available for Distribution

A company may only make a distribution out of profits that are available for that purpose and these are defined in *section 263(3)* of *CA 1985* as:

- accumulated, realised profits, to the extent that these have not been previously distributed or capitalised; less
- accumulated, realised losses to the extent that these have not previously been written off in a reduction or reorganisation of capital.

Separate rules apply in the case of investment companies. Reference should also be made to the company's memorandum and articles of association, as these may contain additional, more restrictive rules on the distribution of the company's profits. Additional rules also apply in the case of public companies. A public company may only make a distribution if:

- at the time of the distribution, the amount of its net assets is not less than the aggregate of its called up share capital and undistributable reserves; and
- the distribution does not reduce the amount of its net assets to less than that aggregate.

Company Law

Again, separate rules apply to investment companies. In this context, net assets is defined as the aggregate of the company's assets less the aggregate of its liabilities. Uncalled share capital cannot be treated as an asset for this purpose and liabilities specifically include any provisions for liabilities and charges. The effect of these provisions is that a public company must take account of unrealised losses when establishing profits available for distribution. A private company needs only to consider realised profits and realised losses.

3.96   Undistributable Reserves

No company, whether public or private, can distribute the following reserves:

- the share premium account;
- the capital redemption reserve;
- the excess of accumulated, unrealised profits over accumulated, unrealised losses (to the extent that profits have not been previously capitalised and losses have not been previously written off in a reconstruction or reorganisation – in this context, a transfer to the company's capital redemption reserve made on or after 22 December 1980 is not regarded as a capitalisation of reserves);
- any other reserve which the company is prohibited from distributing by its memorandum or articles of association or by any other enactment.

3.97   Definition of Realised Profit and Losses

The interpretation of realised profits and losses is covered by *sections 262(3)* and *742(2)* of *CA 1985*. Realised profits and losses are the profits and losses that fall to be treated as realised, in accordance with the principles generally accepted for determining realised profits and losses for accounting purposes, at the time the accounts are prepared. FRS 18 *Accounting Policies* considers the issue of realised profits in the context of the *CA 1985* requirements and notes that profits are to be treated as realised for these purposes only when they have been realised in the form of cash or of other assets the ultimate cash realisation of which can be assessed with reasonable certainty. Additional guidance can be found in TECH 7/03 *Guidance on the determination of realised profits and losses in the context of distributions under the Companies Act 1985* published by the Institute of Chartered Accountants in England and Wales (ICAEW) in March 2003. This supersedes the guidance previously set out in two technical releases (TR 481 and TR 482) issued by the ICAEW in 1982 and can be found on the ICAEW website at http://www.icaew.co.uk. This document reflects the law at 31 December 2002 and accounting standards in issue at that date. It should not be used to question the lawfulness of earlier distributions, but directors may need to re-examine reserves balances in the light of the new guidance before making or recommending future distributions. Under this guidance, all losses should be regarded as realised, except to the extent that the law, accounting standards or the ICAEW guidance provide otherwise. A profit is to be regarded as realised when it arises from:

- a transaction or event where the consideration received is qualifying consideration;
- an event which results in the company receiving qualifying consideration without giving any consideration;
- proper use of the marking to market method of accounting;
- the translation of a monetary asset comprising qualifying consideration, or of a liability, denominated in a foreign currency;
- the reversal of a loss previously regarded as realised;
- an appropriate proportion of a profit previously regarded as unrealised becoming realised as a result of:
  ○ consideration previously received becoming qualifying consideration,
  ○ the disposal of the related asset for qualifying consideration,
  ○ recognition of a realised loss on the disposal or scrapping of the asset,
  ○ recognition of a realised loss on the write-down of the asset for depreciation, amortisation, diminution in value or impairment, or
  ○ the distribution in specie of the related asset;
- a court-sanctioned reduction or cancellation of capital, unless the court directs, or the company undertakes, that the amount credited to reserves is not to be treated as a realised profit; or
- in the case of an unlimited company, a reduction or cancellation of capital which results in a credit to reserves, to the extent that the consideration received meets the criteria set out in the guidance.

The guidance provides practical examples of transactions and events that will normally give rise to realised profits and realised losses. A separate section of the guidance deals with marking to market in the context of banking companies and their subsidiaries and other market makers and investment dealers.

Since the publication of TECH 7/03, the ICAEW has issued additional guidance on realised and distributable profits in the following Technical Releases:

- TECH 50/04 – *Guidance on the effect of FRS 17 'Retirement Benefits' and IAS 19 'Employee Benefits' on realised profits and losses.*
- TECH 64/04 – *Guidance on the effect on realised and distributable profits of accounting for employee share schemes in accordance with UITF Abstract 38 and revised UITF Abstract 17.*
- TECH 21/05 – *Distributable profits: Implications of IFRS.* This sets out draft guidance on the implications of the transition to international accounting standards (IASs). It is presented as a supplement to TECH 7/03 and deals with issues that did not arise under UK accounting practice at the time that the original guidance was developed. In particular, it considers issues arising from fair value accounting, hedge accounting and other aspects of recent changes in the accounting treatment of financial instruments. The ICAEW also emphasises that neither the law on distributions nor the basic principles in TECH 7/03 have changed as a result of the new company law provisions on the preparation of IAS accounts.

- TECH 57/05 – *Distributable profits: Implications of IAS 10 and FRS 21 for dividends*. This was issued as an interim measure to enable companies to take action where necessary to deal with certain matters that came to light as a result of work on finalising the draft guidance published in TECH 21/05.

Copies can be downloaded from the ICAEW website at www.icaew.co.uk.

3.98 Qualifying Consideration

Qualifying consideration is defined in the ICAEW guidance as:

- cash;
- an asset for which there is a liquid market (as defined in the guidance);
- the total or partial release, settlement or assumption by another party of a liability of the company, unless:
  - the liability arose from the purchase of an asset that does not meet the definition of qualifying consideration and has not been disposed of for qualifying consideration, and
  - the purchase and release are part of a group or series of transactions or arrangements that are artificial, linked or circular;
- an amount receivable in any of the above forms, where:
  - the debtor is capable of settling the amount within a reasonable period of time,
  - it is reasonably certain that the debtor will be capable of settling when called upon to do so, and
  - there is an expectation that the amount will be settled.

3.99 Linked Transactions

The ICAEW guidance emphasises that a series of artificial, linked or circular transactions and arrangements, designed to achieve an overall commercial effect, should be viewed as whole when assessing whether a profit has been realised. A realised profit will only arise where the end result for the company meets the criteria set out in the guidance. Appendix A to the guidance considers the application of this principle to certain intra-group transactions, including:

- group treasury functions and cash pooling arrangements;
- dividends received or receivable from subsidiaries;
- asset sales between a parent and its subsidiaries, and between fellow subsidiaries;
- dividends in specie; and
- returning a capital contribution to the donor.

Additional guidance was issued in December 2005 in ICAEW TECH 57/05 on the implications of the requirements of FRS 21 *Events After the Balance Sheet Date* and the equivalent international accounting standard (IAS 10) on accounting for proposed dividends. In particular, the guidance considers:

- the need for subsidiary companies to pay interim dividends to the parent company before the end of the financial year to enable the parent to record these as income in its own accounts – this may be necessary to ensure that the parent has sufficient distributable profits to meet its own proposed final dividend;

- what constitutes payment in the case of an interim dividend.

3.100   Changes in Circumstances

The classification of a profit or loss as realised or unrealised is not fixed and may change as a result of a change in the realisation principles, a change in the law, accounting standards or UITF Abstracts, or some other change in circumstances (eg where an amount receivable no longer meets the definition of qualifying consideration). The guidance explains in detail how to establish which profits should be treated as previously distributed when a profit initially regarded as realised is reclassified as unrealised. When considering the payment of an interim dividend, directors should assess the effect of any known or likely changes on the expected level of profits available for distribution at the year end – for instance, the potential impact of a new accounting standard that requires the recognition of additional liabilities or provisions in the accounts.

3.101   Deferred Tax, Exchange Gains and Goodwill

The ICAEW guidance includes specific consideration of issues relating to deferred tax, goodwill, asset exchanges, hedging transactions and foreign exchange profits and losses. A provision for deferred tax should generally be regarded as a realised loss, except that deferred tax relating to an unrealised gain on a revalued asset should be treated as a reduction of that gain. Unless there are doubts about the convertibility or marketability of the currency in question, foreign exchange profits arising on the translation of monetary items should be regarded as realised, irrespective of the maturity date of the asset or liability. Goodwill becomes a realised loss over its useful economic life. Where it was eliminated against reserves under SSAP 22 *Accounting for Goodwill* and remains eliminated under the transitional provisions of FRS 10 *Goodwill and Intangible Assets*, the write-off does not constitute an immediate realised loss, but should be treated as becoming realised on a systematic basis over the useful economic life of the goodwill (ie giving the same effect on reserves as when goodwill is capitalised and amortised through the profit and loss account over its useful economic life). Negative goodwill credited directly to reserves under SSAP 22 similarly becomes a realised profit on the same basis as if it had been accounted for under FRS 10.

3.102   Pension Liabilities

FRS 17 *Retirement Benefits* was published in November 2000 and is fully effective for accounting periods beginning on or after 1 January 2005, although additional disclosures must be given in the accounts in the intervening years if the standard is not adopted early. Under this standard, a deficit arising in a defined benefit pension scheme will usually need to be included as a liability in the accounts of an employer. This might inhibit the ability of the company to pay a dividend – for instance, where the defined benefit liability is so large that it reduces distributable reserves below the level needed to cover a proposed distribution. Appendix IV to the standard notes that this situation is not expected to arise very often in practice. It was therefore not considered appropriate to deal with it in the standard, and companies who do encounter the problem are advised to discuss the matter with their legal advisors. Additional guidance can also be found in TECH 50/04 *Guidance on the effect of FRS 17 Retirement Benefits and IAS 19 Employee Benefits on Realised Profits and Losses* which was issued by the ICAEW in November 2004.

3.103   Depreciation Charged on Revalued Assets

Provisions for depreciation should generally be regarded as realised losses. However, if an asset has been revalued and depreciation is charged on the revalued amount (in accordance with present accounting requirements), only depreciation based on the original cost of the asset is treated as a realised loss for distribution purposes. This is on the basis that the additional depreciation is matched by the unrealised profit arising from the revaluation.

3.104   Development Costs

Under *section 269* of *CA 1985,* any development costs shown as an asset in a company's accounts are to be treated as a realised loss, with the following exceptions:

- if the costs have been revalued, any element that represents an unrealised profit need not be treated as a realised loss;
- if there are special circumstances which justify the directors' decision not to treat the costs as a realised loss, and the note to the accounts on development costs:
  - states that the costs are not to be treated as a realised loss, and
  - explains the circumstances relied on by the directors to justify their decision.

It is usually acknowledged that the carry forward of development costs in accordance with SSAP 13 *Accounting for Research and Development* will justify a decision by the directors not to treat the costs as a realised loss for distribution purposes, provided that appropriate disclosures are made in the accounts.

3.105   ESOP trusts

UITF Abstract 38 *Accounting for ESOP trusts* requires the sponsoring company of an ESOP trust to recognise in its own accounts the assets and liabilities of the trust over which it has *de facto* control. Under the Abstract, the consideration paid for any shares in the company that are held by the ESOP trust should be deducted in arriving at shareholders' funds, until those shares vest unconditionally in employees. The previous Abstract on this issue required such shares to be shown within fixed assets or current assets as appropriate. The Abstract includes consideration of the legal aspects of its accounting requirements and notes that deducting the consideration from shareholders' funds does not imply that the shares have been purchased by the company as a matter of law or that they are required to be cancelled. The UITF has also received legal advice that the acquisition of shares in the company by an ESOP trust does not of itself affect the amount of the company's realised profits or realised losses, although other related transactions (eg a loan to the ESOP trust to fund the acquisition of the shares) may do so. However, the accounting treatment required by UITF Abstract 38 will reduce the aggregate value of the company's net assets (because own shares held will be deducted from shareholders' funds rather than shown as assets) and this may have implications for a public company as a result of the additional rules on the maintenance of share capital and reserves (see **3.95** above). Additional guidance can also be found in TECH 64/04 *Guidance on the effect on realised and distributable profits of accounting for employee share schemes in accordance with UITF Abstract 38 and revised UITF Abstract 17* which was issued by the ICAEW in December 2004.

3.106   Implications of Adoption of IASs

The ICAEW has also issued draft guidance on the implications of the transition to international accounting standards for the determination of realised profits and losses in the context of distributions. TECH 21/05 was published in June 2005 and comments were invited by early September 2005. The ICAEW is currently in the process of finalising the guidance. The issues are considered primarily in the context of companies that are required to adopt IASs and those who opt to prepare IAS accounts (see **3.16** above), but certain aspects will also be relevant companies continuing to prepare Companies Act accounts, given the ASB's plans to converge UK accounting practice with international requirements. The draft guidance is presented as a supplement to TECH 7/03 *Guidance on the determination of realised profits and losses in the context of distributions under the Companies Act 1985* and deals with issues that did not arise under UK accounting practice when that guidance was developed. In particular, it considers issues arising from fair value accounting, hedge accounting and other aspects of recent changes in the accounting treatment of financial instruments. The ICAEW emphasises that neither the law on distributions nor the basic principles in TECH 7/03 have changed as a result of the new *CA 1985* provisions on the preparation of IAS accounts. A number of issues that came to light during work on finalising this guidance prompted the ICAEW to publish a separate statement on the practical implications of the requirements of FRS 21 and IAS 10 *Events after the balance sheet date* in respect of proposed dividends (see **3.99** above).

Appendix 1

Useful Websites on Company Law Issues

Companies House	www.companieshouse.gov.uk
DTI – Corporate Law and Governance Directorate	www.dti.gov.uk/cld
Office of Public Sector Information (for online legislation)	www.opsi.gov.uk/legislation/
Company Law Reform Bill	www.dti.gov.uk/cld/facts/clr.htm

4

Company Secretarial

Company Secretarial

4 Company Secretarial

4.1 Role of Company Secretary

At a Glance
* *CA 1985* currently requires every company to appoint a company secretary.
* The company secretary may also be a director of the company, except where the company has only one director.
* The company's articles of association will usually set out detailed provisions on the appointment and removal of the company secretary.
* The *Combined Code* recommends that any change in the appointment of the company secretary should be a matter for the board as a whole to decide.
* In the case of a public company, the directors must take reasonable steps to ensure that the person appointed has the requisite knowledge and experience to fulfil the role.
* The company secretary is an officer of the company and may be held criminally liable for any defaults committed by the company.
* The precise duties of the company secretary are not generally prescribed by statute – they will usually need to be set out in his/her contract of employment.

4.2 Appointment of Company Secretary

Section 283(1) of the *Companies Act 1985* (*CA 1985*) requires every company to appoint a company secretary. The company secretary may, but need not, be a director of the company, although a sole director is specifically prohibited from being appointed as the company secretary. A person or firm is also prohibited by *section 27(1)* of the *Companies Act 1989* from appointment as both auditor and company secretary. The company's articles of association will usually set out provisions on the appointment and removal of the company secretary. In most cases, the power to appoint and remove the company secretary will rest with the directors. In the case of listed companies, the *Combined Code* recommends that any change in the appointment should be a matter for the board as a whole to decide (see **6.11 CORPORATE GOVERNANCE**). The company may appoint an assistant or deputy secretary, and the office of company secretary may also be held jointly between two or more individuals or corporations. The recent company law review recommended that the requirement for a private company to appoint a company secretary should be removed and the draft Company Law Reform Bill published in May 2006 reflects this proposed change.

4.3   Qualifications of Company Secretary

In the case of a public company, the directors are required to take all reasonable steps to ensure that the company secretary appears to have the requisite knowledge and experience to fulfil the role. The person appointed must:

- be a member of one of the following bodies:
  - the Institute of Chartered Accountants in England and Wales ('ICAEW'),
  - the Institute of Chartered Accountants of Scotland ('ICAS'),
  - the Institute of Chartered Accountants in Ireland ('ICAI'),
  - the Association of Chartered Certified Accountants ('ACCA'),
  - the Institute of Chartered Secretaries and Administrators ('ICSA'),
  - the Chartered Institute of Management Accountants ('CIMA'), or
  - the Chartered Institute of Public Finance and Accountancy ('CIPFA'); or
- be a barrister, advocate or solicitor called or admitted in any part of the UK; or
- have held the office of secretary (or assistant or deputy secretary) of the company on 22 December 1980; or
- have held the office of company secretary of a company (other than a private company) for at least three out of the last five years immediately before his/her appointment as secretary; or
- be a person who appears to the directors to be capable of carrying out the functions of company secretary, because he/she holds, or has held, any other similar position or is a member of any other body.

No formal requirements are laid down in the case of a private company, but directors should still bear the above points in mind, although the level of knowledge and experience required in this case will usually depend on the size and complexity of the company and the precise role that the company secretary is expected to have.

4.4   Duties of Company Secretary

The *Companies Act 1985* does not specify any formal role for the company secretary, although various sections allow for documentation to be signed by the company secretary – for instance, *section 234A of CA 1985* permits the directors' report to be signed on behalf of the board by a director or by the company secretary. Under *CA 1985*, the secretary is an officer of the company and may be held criminally liable for any defaults committed by the company. The secretary may also be required to prepare a statement of the company's affairs if an administrative receiver or provisional liquidator is appointed, or if an order is made for the company to be wound up. The other duties of the company secretary will usually be set out in his/her contract of employment. Depending on the size and complexity of the business, the role of company secretary may be a full-time post or may be combined with another role within the organisation. The duties undertaken by the company secretary usually include:

- maintaining the statutory books and registers and arranging any inspections that are requested (see **4.4–4.23** below);
- ensuring that statutory forms and returns are prepared and filed on time (see **4.24–4.26** below);
- preparing and circulating notices of meetings, together with detailed agenda papers where appropriate (see **4.27–4.39** below);
- preparing minutes of general meetings and directors' meetings and sending copies of relevant resolutions and agreements to the Registrar (see **4.27–4.39** below);
- retaining any other formal documentation required by companies' legislation and controlling the use of the company seal, if one is held (see **4.40–4.51** below).

4.5 Statutory Books and Registers

At a Glance
* *CA 1985* requires every company to keep a number of statutory books and registers – the required items must be kept even if there are currently no entries to be made in them.
* Statutory books and registers need not be maintained in bound format, provided that adequate measures are taken to prevent or detect any falsification.
* Every company must keep a register of members, updated to reflect changes in membership and any notified changes of address.
* Where appropriate, the register of members must include a formal statement that the company has only one member.
* The register of members should generally be kept at the company's registered office – the Registrar must be notified if the register is kept elsewhere or if its location changes.
* There is no requirement to keep a register of debenture-holders, but specific requirements apply to any such register that is kept voluntarily.
* Every company must keep an up-to-date register of directors and secretaries at the company's registered office.
* Every company must keep a register of directors' interests in the shares and debentures of the company or any other company in the same group.
* Every public company must keep a register of notified interests in its shares – this must be kept in the same location as the register of directors' interests.
* Every limited company must keep a register of charges affecting the company's property and floating charges over the company's undertaking or property.
* All registers must generally be open to inspection.

4.6   Requirement to Keep Statutory Books and Registers

The *Companies Act 1985* requires every company to keep a number of statutory books and registers. Some of these, such as the register of members and the company minute book, form an important part of the company's original records, but most are only needed to make certain information about the company available to the public, and the details recorded are generally not of significance for other purposes. *Section 722* of *CA 1985* permits the statutory books and registers to be maintained by making entries in bound record books or by recording the information in any other manner, provided that adequate measures are taken to prevent or detect any falsification. *Section 723* of *CA 1985* permits the records to be maintained on a computer, provided that they can be reproduced in legible form if required. The requirement to keep the registers applies even if there are currently no entries to be made in them, as the absence of an entry may still provide useful information to someone inspecting the register (ie by confirming that there are no registrable items). The company and every officer who fails to comply with the requirements (including those relating to inspection of the registers) is liable to a fine and also to a daily default fine for continued contravention. Table 1 opposite summarises the registers and other statutory books that must be maintained.

4.7   Register of Members

Section 352 of *CA 1985* requires the following details to be entered in the register of members:

- names and addresses of all members;
- date on which each person was registered as a member;
- date on which any person ceased to be a member;
- if the company has share capital, the following information must be entered with the names and addresses of the members:
  - the shares held by each member, distinguishing each share by its number and, if the company has more than one class of share, by its class,
  - the amount paid or agreed to be considered as paid on the shares of each member; and
- if the company does not have share capital but has more than one class of member, the class to which each member belongs must be shown with the names and addresses.

An entry relating to a former member may be removed from the register 20 years after the date on which he/she ceased to be a member. If the company has more than 50 members, it must keep an alphabetical index of the members' names unless the register is itself alphabetical. The index must be kept with the register and must be updated within 14 days of any change in the register which affects the index. The register should be kept up to date to reflect changes in membership and shareholdings and also any changes of address that have been notified. *Section 355* of *CA 1985* specifies how entries relating to share warrants should be

Table 1: Statutory books and registers to be maintained

Register/book	Location	Public right of inspection	Sections of CA 1985	Further information
Register of members	Registered office or other location notified to Registrar	Yes	ss 352–353	see 4.7–4.13
Register of directors and secretaries	Registered office	Yes	ss 288–290	see 4.15–4.17
Register of directors' interests in shares and debentures	Registered office or with register of members	Yes	s 325	see 4.18–4.20
Register of interests in shares (public companies only)	With register of directors' interests	Yes	s 211	see 4.21–4.23
Register of charges (limited companies only)	Registered office	Yes	ss 411–412	see 4.24–4.25
Minute books (general meetings)	Registered office	No	ss 382–383	see 4.41–4.43
Minute books (board meetings)	As directors determine	No	ss 382–383	see 4.44

dealt with. The register is regarded as *prime facie* evidence of matters authorised or directed by *CA 1985* to be included in it. A company with a share capital, and whose objects include doing business in the countries or territories set out in *Schedule 14* to *CA 1985* (broadly Northern Ireland and any of Her Majesty's domains outside the UK, Channel Islands and Isle of Man), may keep a separate overseas branch register of the members who are resident in that country or territory, provided that it complies with the detailed requirements set out in *section 362* of *CA 1985*.

4.8 *Single Member Companies*

A public company must always have at least two members, but a private company can be a single member company. If the number of members in a private company falls to one, an entry must be made in the register, alongside the name and address of the sole member, stating that the company has only one member and giving the date on which this situation arose. If the membership of a single member company increases to two or more, a statement that the company has ceased to have only one member, and the date on which this occurred, must be entered alongside the name and address of the person who was formerly the sole member.

4.9 *Location of Register of Members*

The register of members should usually be kept at the company's registered office, but:

- if it is written up at another office of the company, it may be kept at that location; or
- if the company arranges for the register to be written up by another person, it may be kept at the office where this work is done.

This is subject to an overriding requirement that the register must always be kept in the country where the company is registered (ie England and Wales, or Scotland as appropriate). Unless the register has at all times been kept at the registered office, the company must notify the Registrar, using the prescribed form (Form 353), of the place where it is kept and of any changes in that location.

4.10 *Inspection of Register of Members*

The register of members, together with the index, must be open to inspection by any member of the company without charge and by any other person on payment of the prescribed fee, except where the register has been officially closed (see **4.11** below). Any person may ask for a copy of the register, or any part of it, on payment of the prescribed fee, and the company must send the copy within ten days from the day following the date of the request. Failure to allow inspection of the register, or to provide a copy of the register, constitutes an offence and the court can also compel the company to allow an immediate inspection of the register and index or to send the required copies to the person requesting them.

4.11   *Closure of Register of Members*

Section 358 of *CA 1985* enables the company to close the register for a period or periods not exceeding 30 days in total in each year, although this is rarely done in practice. Notice of the closure must be given by placing an advertisement in a newspaper circulating in the area where the company's registered office is situated.

4.12   *Rectification of Register of Members*

Section 359 of *CA 1985* sets out the procedure for applying to the court for rectification of the register in the following circumstances:

- where the name of any person has been incorrectly entered in, or omitted from, the register; or
- there is a default or unnecessary delay in entering in the register the fact that any person has ceased to be a member.

The application may be made by the person concerned, by any member of the company or by the company itself. The court may refuse the application, or may order rectification of the register and, where appropriate, payment by the company of any damages suffered by the person concerned.

4.13   *Notice of Trust*

In the case of companies registered in England and Wales, no notice of any trust (whether expressed, implied or constructive) can be entered in the register of members. The beneficiaries of a trust holding shares in a company, therefore, have no direct connection with, or rights against, the company.

4.14   Register of Debenture-holders

There is no statutory requirement for a company to keep a register of debenture-holders, but if it chooses to do so, *sections 190* and *191* of *CA 1985* impose similar requirements to those for the register of members as regards the location of the register (including notification to the Registrar), inspection of the register and the provision of copies of all or part of the register.

4.15   Register of Directors and Secretaries

Every company is required to keep a register of its directors and secretaries at the company's registered office. Under *section 289* of *CA 1985*, the register

Company Secretarial

must show the following details for each director (including any shadow directors):

(*a*) his/her present Christian name, or other forename, and surname (in the case of a peer or titled individual, the title may be given instead of, or as well as, these details);

(*b*) any former name, except that the following need not be given:
  (i) in the case of a peer or titled individual, the name used before adoption of, or succession to, the title,
  (ii) a name changed or disused before the individual reached the age of 18,
  (iii) a name which has been changed or disused for 20 years or more, and
  (iv) in the case of a married woman, the name by which she was known before marriage;

(*c*) usual residential address – although from 2 April 2002, the *Companies (Particulars of Usual Residential Address) (Confidentiality Orders) Regulations 2002 (SI 2002/912)* allow individuals who can demonstrate actual or serious risk of violence or intimidation to apply to the Secretary of State for permission not to reveal their usual residential address on the Companies House public record or the company's public record;

(*d*) nationality;

(*e*) business occupation (if any);

(*f*) other directorships currently held or held during the previous five years (there are exemptions for directorships of dormant companies and companies in the same group); and

(*g*) date of birth.

Where a corporation (or Scottish firm) is appointed as a director, the register should record the corporate (or firm) name and its registered or principal office.

  Section 290 of *CA 1985* requires the following details of secretaries to be recorded in the register:

- his/her present Christian name, or other forename, and surname;
- any former name; and
- usual residential address (see (*c*) above).

The same rules on names apply as in the case of directors. If a corporation or Scottish firm is appointed as secretary, the register should show the corporate (or firm) name and its registered or principal office. Where joint secretaries are appointed, the required details must be given for each individual except that, where all the partners in a firm are joint secretaries, only the name and principal office of the firm needs to be shown.

4.16   *Changes in Directors and Secretaries*

Any changes in directors or secretaries, or any changes to the details recorded in the register for an existing director or secretary, must be notified to the Registrar within 14 days of the change, using the prescribed form (Form 288a, 288b or 288c as appropriate). Where the change involves the appointment of a new director or secretary, the form must be signed by the individual to indicate their consent to the appointment. Where a corporation is appointed, the form should be signed by an officer on behalf of the corporation. The changes must also be recorded in the register of directors and secretaries.

4.17   *Inspection of Register of Directors and Secretaries*

The register of directors and secretaries must be open to inspection by any member of the company without charge and by any other person on payment of the prescribed fee. Refusal to allow inspection of the register is an offence, and the court can compel the company to allow an immediate inspection of the register.

4.18   Register of Directors' Interests

Section 325 of *CA 1985* requires every company to keep a register of directors' interests in the shares and debentures of the company or another company in the same group. The definition of 'interests' for this purpose is very wide and is specifically extended by *section 328* of *CA 1985* to include interests held by the director's spouse and children. Each director and shadow director has a duty under *section 324* of *CA 1985* to give the company written notification of these interests, and the company is required to record the details against the director's name in the register of interests, together with the date of the entry. The company is also obliged to enter the following details against a director's name in the register whenever it grants him/her a right to subscribe for shares in, or debentures of, the company:

- date on which the right is granted;
- period during which, or time at which, the right is exercisable;
- consideration for the grant or, if there is no consideration, a statement of that fact; and
- description of the shares or debentures involved, the number or amount of them and the price (or consideration) to be paid for them.

Whenever such a right is exercised by a director, the company must record the following details against the director's name in the register:

- the fact that the right has been exercised;
- the number or amount of shares or debentures in respect of which it is exercised; and
- the fact that they were registered in the name of the director, or the name(s) in which they were registered (showing the number or amount of shares or debentures against each name).

All details must be recorded in the register within three business days of the day on which the obligation to make the entry arises.

4.19   *Location of Register of Directors' Interests*

Detailed provisions on the location of the register of directors' interests are set out in *Part IV* of *Schedule 13* to *CA 1985*. The register must be kept either at the

Company Secretarial

company's registered office or, if the register of members is kept elsewhere, with the register of members. Unless the register has at all times been kept at the registered office, the company must notify the Registrar, using the prescribed form (Form 325), of the place where it is kept and of any changes in that location. The company must also keep an index of the names in the register, unless the register itself constitutes an index. The index must be kept with the register and must be updated within 14 days of the entry of a name in the register.

4.20 *Inspection of Register of Directors' Interests*

The register of directors' interests must be open to inspection by any member of the company without charge and by any other person on payment of the prescribed fee. Any person may request a copy of all or any part of the register on payment of the prescribed fee and the company must send the copy within ten days of the day on which the request is received. The register must also be produced at the start of the annual general meeting and must remain open and accessible throughout the meeting to any person attending. It is an offence to refuse inspection of the register, and the court can compel the company to allow an immediate inspection of the register or to send a copy to any person who has requested one.

4.21 Register of Interests in Shares

Every public company is required by *section 211* of *CA 1985* to keep a register of interests in shares. There is no similar provision for private companies. Any information disclosed to a public company under *Part VI* of *CA 1985* (disclosure of interests in shares) must be entered into the register against the name of that person, together with the date of the entry. All entries must be made within three business days of the day on which the obligation to make the entry arises. Where a company receives notification that a person is no longer acting 'in concert' with others in relation to the acquisition of shares, it is obliged to record this information against that person's name wherever it appears in the register as a party to the agreement. Entries against each name in the register must appear in chronological order and the company must keep an index of the names in the register, unless the register itself constitutes an index. The index must be kept with the register and must be updated within ten days of a name being entered on the register. The company must also record, in a separate part of the register, information that it receives as a result of an enquiry made under *section 212* of *CA 1985*, which enables a company to seek formal confirmation of interests that it reasonably believes a person to be holding. In this case, the following information must be recorded against the name of the registered holder of the shares:

- the fact that the company gave written notice under *section 212* of *CA 1985*;
- the date on which the notice was given; and
- any information received by the company as a result, to the extent that this relates to the present interests held by any persons in the share capital of the company.

4.22 Removal of Entries from Register of Interests in Shares

Section 217 of *CA 1985* permits entries to be deleted from the register of interests in shares in the following circumstances:

- more than six years have elapsed since the date of the entry and either:
  - ○ that entry recorded the fact that the person in question had ceased to have a notifiable interest in the share capital of the company, or
  - ○ the entry has been superseded by a later entry made under *section 211* of *CA 1985* against the same person's name;
- the company received details under *Part VI* of *CA 1985* of a notifiable interest held by another person – it must within 15 days notify that person of the entry made in the register and that person may apply to the company to have his/her name removed from the register on the grounds that the entry was incorrect; and
- a person identified in the register as acting 'in concert' with others in the acquisition of the company's shares may apply to have the information recorded that he has ceased to be a such a party.

Entries in the register of interests in shares cannot be removed in any other circumstances. If the company fails to make an alteration requested under *section 217* of *CA 1985*, the applicant can apply to the court, who can order that the amendment be made. Where an entry is removed from the register, the index must also be updated within 14 days.

4.23 Location and Inspection of Register of Interests in Shares

The register of interests in shares, together with the index, must be kept at the same location as the register of directors' interests (see **4.19** above). The register must be available for inspection by any person without charge. Any person can also request a copy of the register, or any part of it, on payment of the prescribed fee. It is an offence to refuse inspection of the register and the court can compel the company to allow an immediate inspection of the register or to send a copy to any person who has requested one. However, the register or index should not be made available for inspection if it contains information about a company which is entitled to exemption under *section 231(3)* of *CA 1985* from the disclosure of certain of its shareholdings if such disclosure would be harmful to the business of the company.

4.24 Register of Charges

A company has a duty under *section 399* of *CA 1985* to send to the Registrar details of certain charges that it creates (see **4.52–4.56** below), but the person benefiting from the charge may also apply for it to be registered. *Section 407* of *CA 1985* also requires every limited company to keep a register of charges at its registered office and to enter into that register all charges affecting property of the company and all floating charges on the company's undertaking or any of

Company Secretarial

its property. Entries in this register are therefore not restricted to charges that are notifiable to the Registrar. Each entry must give:

- a short description of the property charged;
- the amount of the charge; and
- other than in the case of securities to bearer, the names of the persons entitled to it.

Any officer who knowingly or wilfully authorises or permits the omission of a required entry in the register is liable to a fine. The company must also keep at its registered office a copy of every instrument creating a charge that requires entry in the register of charges. If a charge is satisfied, this should also be recorded in the register.

4.25 *Inspection of Company Register of Charges*

The register of charges maintained by the company and the copies of instruments creating registrable charges must be open to inspection by any member or creditor of the company, without charge, for at least two hours during the normal business day. The register must also be open to inspection by any other person on payment of a fee not exceeding 5 pence for each inspection. It is an offence to refuse inspection of the register, and the court can compel the company to allow an immediate inspection.

4.26 **Returns and Forms**

At a Glance
- ✳ Certain details are put on public record by requiring every company to make formal submissions to the registrar.
- ✳ A change in the location of the company's registered office takes effect from the date that it is registered by the registrar, although documents can be validly served at the previous address for a further 14 days.
- ✳ Every company must prepare and deliver an annual return made up to the company's return date.

4.27 Information Available to the Public

Certain company information is made available to the public through the statutory right of inspection of company registers, but other details are put on public record by requiring each company to make regular submissions to Companies House. Significant changes in the company's constitution or affairs must be notified to the Registrar on standard forms, and an annual return and a copy of the company's annual report and accounts must be delivered to the Registrar each year in accordance with a prescribed timetable. Table 2

Table 2: Principal company returns and forms

Event	Form or document to be filed	Sections of CA 1985	Further information
Company formation	Memorandum and articles of association; Forms 10, 12 and 224 (if required)	ss 10, 12, 13, 224	see 4.28
Change of registered office	Form 287	s 287	see 4.16
Appointment of director/secretary	Form 288a	s 288	see 4.16
Resignation of director/secretary	Form 288b	s 288	see 4.16
Change in personal details of director/secretary	Form 288c	s 288	
Increase in nominal capital	Form 123 (with copy of resolution)	s 123	
Allotment of new shares	Form 88(2) or 88(3)	s 88	
Change in capital structure	Form 122	s 122	
Special rights attaching to shares where not otherwise registrable	Form 128(1), 128(3) or 128(4)	s 128	
Financial assistance in connection with acquisition of own shares	Form 155(6)(a) (and 155(6)(b) where applicable)	s 155	see 4.29
Purchase of own shares	Form 169	s 169	
Annual return	Form 363	s 363	
Financial year-end	Annual report and accounts	s 242	see 11 FINANCIAL REPORTING
Change of accounting reference date	Form 225(1) or 225(2)	ss 225–226	see 11 FINANCIAL REPORTING
Passing of special, extraordinary or elective resolution, or other resolutions specified in CA 1985, s 380	Copy of resolution (and copy of memorandum or articles of association, where altered)	ss 18(2), 380	see 4.37–4.40 and 4.43
Removal of auditor	Form 391	s 391	see 1 AUDIT
Location of register of members	Form 353 or 353a	s 353	see 4.7–4.13
Location of overseas branch register (if kept)	Form 362 or 362a	s 362	see 4.7
Location of register of debenture-holders (if kept)	Form 190 or 190a	s 190	see 4.14
Location of register of directors' interests	Form 325 or 325a	s 325, Sch 13, Pt IV	see 4.18–4.20
Location of directors' service contracts	Form 318	s 318	see 4.46 and 6 CORPORATE GOVERNANCE
Creation of charge or acquisition of property subject to a charge	Form 395 or 397	ss 395–400	see 4.52–5.49
Satisfaction and release of property from charge	Form 403a or 403b	s 403	see 4.56

Company Secretarial

overleaf summarises the principal requirements for supplying information to Companies House.

4.28   Change of Registered Office

A company must always have a registered office to which all communications and notices can be sent. The location of the registered office must be included on the statement sent to the Registrar at the time of incorporation. Any subsequent change in location must be notified to the Registrar on the prescribed form (Form 287). The change takes effect on registration by the Registrar, but a document may be validly served at the previous registered address during the 14 days after registration of the change.

4.29   Annual Return

Section 363 of *CA 1985* requires every company to prepare and deliver to the Registrar in each calendar year an annual return made up to a date no later than the company's return date. The return date is either:

- the anniversary of the company's incorporation (for the first period); or
- the anniversary of the date to which the last annual return was made up.

The return date may be brought forward by reducing the period between annual returns to a period of less than twelve months, but there is no facility to extend the return period for more than twelve months. The annual return must be signed by a director or by the company secretary and must be delivered to Companies House within 28 days of the return date, together with the prescribed filing fee (currently £15). A shadow director is not deemed to be a director for the purpose of signing the annual return. A computer-generated form is now issued to each company, shortly before its return date, pre-printed with the details currently held by the Registrar. The directors or secretary must check these details (and amend them if appropriate) and complete any remaining sections of the form before signing and returning it to the Registrar. Companies House also offers a facility for online filing of the annual return, although certain companies (for instance, those with more complex structures and those in receivership or liquidation) are currently excluded from this option. Use of the service requires prior registration so that a security code and authentication code can be issued to the company. The filing fee remains the same irrespective of which filing method is used. Further information on online filing can be found on the Companies House website (www.companieshouse.gov.uk).

 Failure to deliver the annual return is an offence, and the company is liable to a fine and to a daily default fine for continued contravention. Every director and secretary is similarly liable unless he/she can demonstrate that all reasonable steps were taken to avoid the offence.

4.30   Meetings

At a Glance
* *CA 1985* makes provision for three types of meeting of members of the company and prescribes when each of these should be held. Further provisions may be included in the company's memorandum and articles of association.
* A company must hold its first annual general meeting (AGM) within 18 months of incorporation, and then must hold an AGM in each calendar year, not more than 15 months after the previous AGM.
* A private company may elect to dispense with the requirement to hold an AGM, although members retain the right to require one to be held.
* An extraordinary general meeting (EGM) will generally only be held to deal with urgent business.
* In certain circumstances, the members or the auditors can require the directors to convene an EGM.
* The directors of a public company are required to convene an EGM if the net assets of the company fall below half of its called up share capital or if the court orders that an EGM be held.
* *CA 1985* prescribes the notice period for each type of meeting and the contents of the notice of the meeting.
* Decisions may be made by ordinary resolution, extraordinary resolution or special resolution – *CA 1985* prescribes when each form of resolution should be used.
* Special notice must be given for certain ordinary resolutions proposed at a general meeting.
* The elective regime enables private companies to dispense with formal meetings and to act by means of written resolutions.
* Minutes must be prepared for all general meetings and copies of certain resolutions must be delivered to the Registrar.
* Minutes must also be prepared for all meetings of the directors.

4.31   General Meetings of the Company

The *Companies Act 1985* makes provision for three types of meeting of the members of a company – annual general meeting, extraordinary general meeting and separate general meeting of a class of shareholder – and sets out the circumstances in which each of these should be held. Separate meetings by class of shareholder are usually only required in company reconstructions or where the rights of the shareholders are to be otherwise varied. A company's memorandum and articles of association may include additional provisions on the holding of general meetings of the members and on practical issues such as how many members constitute a quorum. In the absence of any provision in the articles, *section 370(4)* of *CA 1985* states that two members personally present are deemed to constitute a quorum. In the case of a sole member private company, *section 370A* of *CA 1985* deems that one member present in person or by proxy is a quorum. A single member may also constitute a quorum (if so directed) in the case of:

- a meeting called by the Secretary of State under *section 367* of *CA 1985* (default in holding an annual general meeting); and
- a meeting ordered by the court under *section 371* of *CA 1985*.

4.32   Annual General Meeting

Under *section 366* of *CA 1985*, a company's first annual general meeting ('AGM') must be held within 18 months of incorporation. Thereafter, the company must hold an AGM in each calendar year, and each meeting must be held not more than 15 months after the previous meeting. Under the elective regime, a private company may dispense with the requirement to hold an AGM (see **4.39** below). The legislation does not prescribe the business to be transacted at the AGM, but it might include:

- consideration of the annual report and accounts;
- reappointment of the auditors;
- declaration of a final dividend;
- approval of directors' remuneration;
- authorisation for the directors to allot shares up to a specified level;
- disapplication of pre-emptive rights for the allotment of shares up to a specified level.

A private company may also deal with the passing of elective resolutions under *section 379A* of *CA 1985* (see **4.39** below). Under *section 376* of *CA 1985*, members representing not less than one-twentieth of the total voting rights, or not less than 100 members holding shares on which there has been paid up an average of £100 per member, may submit written details of a resolution to be moved at the AGM and a statement of not more than 1,000 words to be circulated with the notice of the meeting. For listed companies, the *Combined Code* includes a number of recommendations on the conduct of the AGM (see **6.39 CONSTRUCTIVE USE OF THE AGM**).

4.33   *Proposed Changes*

Based on the recent company law review, the Government White Paper *Modernising Company Law* issued in July 2002 proposes freeing private companies from the requirement to hold an AGM, although the members will be able to decide by ordinary resolution to continue to hold them. The statutory requirement to hold an AGM will be retained for public companies, although it will be possible for the members to decide unanimously to dispense with this requirement. Where an AGM is held, the timing will be linked to the financial reporting cycle. The proposal is that the AGM of a public company should be held within six months of the financial year end and that the AGM of a private company should be held within ten months of the financial year end. It is also proposed that the minimum notice period for all general meetings should be 14 days. The Government also intends to enhance the existing powers of proxies at general meetings, enable members to demand (and vote on) a poll in advance of the meeting, and give members the right to require scrutiny of any poll. These proposals are now incorporated in the draft Company Law Reform Bill published in November 2005.

4.34   Extraordinary General Meetings

Any general meeting of all the members that is not the annual general meeting is deemed to be an extraordinary general meeting ('EGM'). The articles will usually give the directors the right to call an EGM whenever they wish, but in practice they will generally do so only to deal with urgent business that cannot wait for the next AGM. The following individuals can also require the directors to convene an EGM:

- members holding not less than one-tenth of the paid up share capital carrying voting rights at general meetings or, if the company does not have share capital, members representing not less than one-tenth of the total voting rights of all the members with a right to vote (*CA 1985, s 368*);
- a resigning auditor who considers that there are circumstances connected with his resignation that need to be drawn to the attention of the members (*CA 1985, s 392A*).

The directors of a public company must also convene an EGM within 28 days of becoming aware that the net assets of the company are half or less of its called up share capital (*CA 1985, s 142*) or where the court so orders under *section 371* of *CA 1985*.

4.35   Notice of Meetings

Formal written notice of a general meeting must be given to each person entitled to attend. Under *section 369* of *CA 1985*, the minimum notice period is:

- 21 days for an annual general meeting;
- 21 days for a general meeting at which a special resolution is to be proposed; and
- 14 days for other general meetings.

The company's articles of association may increase these notice periods but cannot reduce them. However, a meeting called by shorter notice will still be valid if:

- in the case of an annual general meeting, the shorter notice has been agreed to by all the members entitled to attend and vote at the meeting; and

- in the case of other general meetings, the shorter notice has been agreed to by a majority of members holding not less than 95 per cent of the nominal value of the shares giving the right to attend and vote at that meeting (or, if the company does not have a share capital, members representing not less than 95 per cent of the total voting rights at that meeting of all the members).

Under the elective regime for private companies, the minimum percentage for agreeing to shorter notice for meetings other than the annual general meeting may be reduced to not less than 90 per cent, provided that all the members agree to this (see **4.39** below).

4.36　Contents of Notice of Meeting

The formal written notice of a general meeting should give:

- the name of the company;
- the date, time and place of the meeting;
- the business to be transacted, in sufficient detail for this to be understood and setting out clearly the full text of any proposed resolutions; and
- for a company with a share capital, a statement that a member entitled to attend and vote at the meeting has the right to appoint a proxy to attend and vote on his/her behalf (*CA 1985, s 327(3)*).

The notice of the annual general meeting is required by *section 366(1) of CA 1985* to specify this fact. Similarly, if it is intended to propose a special, extraordinary or elective resolution at the meeting, the resolution must be clearly identified as such in the notice of the meeting.

4.37　Resolutions

Decisions of the company as a whole are made by the members passing resolutions in general meeting. There are three types of resolution under companies' legislation.

- *Ordinary resolution.* This is the normal method of seeking the approval of the members and is normally carried by a simple majority. Any resolution that is not an extraordinary resolution or a special resolution is deemed to be an ordinary resolution. An ordinary resolution will suffice for most business, unless *CA 1985* or the company's articles specify that an extraordinary or special resolution is required.
- *Extraordinary resolution.* An extraordinary resolution is required in only two situations under the law:
  - on the voluntary winding up of the company under *section 84(1)(c) of the Insolvency Act 1986*, and
  - at a meeting of the holders of a class of shares to approve a variation of the rights attaching to those shares (*CA 1985, s 125*).

  The resolution must be described as an extraordinary resolution in the notice of the meeting and it must be passed by a majority of at least three-quarters of the votes cast. No particular notice period is specified for an extraordinary resolution, so the notice period is the same as that for the meeting at which it is to be proposed (ie 14 days if it is to be proposed at an EGM). Based on the recent company law review, the Government White Paper *Modernising Company Law* issued in July 2002 proposes abolishing the extraordinary resolution as a separate category. Where an enhanced majority is justified, it is proposed to replace the current requirement for an extraordinary resolution with a requirement for a special resolution. These changes are reflected in the draft Company Law Reform Bill published in May 2006.

- *Special resolution.* The *Companies Act 1985* requires a special resolution to be used for:
  - alteration of the objects clause in the company's memorandum of association (*CA 1985, s 4*),
  - alteration of the articles of association (*CA 1985, s 9*),
  - disapplication of pre-emption rights (*CA 1985, s 95*),
  - reduction of capital, subject to court confirmation (*CA 1985, s 135*),
  - change of company name (*CA 1985, s 28*),
  - provision of financial assistance for the purchase of own shares (permitted only for a private company) (*CA 1985, s 155*),
  - purchase of own shares (*CA 1985, s 164*), and
  - alterations of the company's status by re-registration (eg from private to public – *CA 1985, s 43*).

The articles may require a special resolution to be used in other circumstances. The resolution must be described as a special resolution in the notice of the meeting and 21 days' notice of the meeting must be given. The resolution must be passed by a majority of at least three-quarters of the votes cast. Based on the recent company law review, the Government White Paper *Modernising Company Law* issued in July 2002 proposes reducing the notice period for a special resolution to 14 days consistent with the proposed minimum notice period for all general meetings (see **4.33** above). This change is reflected in the draft Company Law Reform Bill published in May 2006.

4.38   *Ordinary Resolution with Special Notice*

Under *CA 1985*, special notice must be given to the company for certain ordinary resolutions that are to be proposed at a general meeting (note that special notice of an ordinary resolution is totally different from a special resolution). Special notice must be given of any proposed resolution to:

- appoint as director of a public company or its subsidiary a person aged 70 or over (*CA 1985, s 293*);
- remove a director before his term of office has expired (*CA 1985, s 303*);
- fill a casual vacancy in the office of auditor (*CA 1985, s 388*);
- re-appoint a retiring auditor appointed by the directors to fill a casual vacancy (*CA 1985, s 338*);

- remove an auditor before his term of office has expired (*CA 1985, s 391A*); and
- appoint an auditor other than the retiring auditor (*CA 1985, s 391A*).

Notice of the resolution must be given to the company at least 28 days before the meeting at which it is to be proposed, although it is deemed to have been properly given if the meeting is called for a date 28 days or less after the giving of the special notice. Notice of the resolution must be given to the members at the same time, and in the same manner, as the notice of the meeting. Where this is not practicable, notice may be given in a newspaper with an appropriate circulation, or in any other manner permitted by the articles, at least 21 days before the meeting. The draft Company Law Reform Bill published in May 2006 includes a proposal to reduce this period to 14 days consistent with proposed changes to other notice periods. Where relevant, notice of the resolution must also be given to the director or auditor affected.

4.39   *Elective Resolutions*

Under *section 379A* of *CA 1985*, a private company may pass an elective resolution to:

- dispense with the requirement to lay reports and accounts before the members in general meeting;
- dispense with the requirement to hold an AGM;
- dispense with the requirement to appoint auditors annually;
- reduce the majority needed to consent to short notice of a general meeting; or
- give the directors authority to allot shares for a period of more than five years.

However, a member still retains the right to require the laying of the report and accounts, the holding of an AGM and consideration of the termination of the auditors' appointment at a general meeting. At least 21 days' written notice must be given of a meeting at which an elective resolution is to be proposed, unless all the members entitled to vote at the meeting agree to shorter notice. As an alternative, the company may use the option of a written resolution (see **4.40** below). An elective resolution may be revoked by an ordinary resolution to that effect and is automatically revoked if a private company re-registers as a public company.

4.40   *Written Resolutions*

Written resolutions are available only to a private company. Under *section 381A* of *CA 1985*, anything that a private company can do by a resolution in general meeting (or in a separate meeting of a class of shareholder) may be done instead by means of a written resolution signed by or on behalf of all the members who would have been entitled to attend and vote at a general meeting at the date of the resolution. The *Companies Act 1985* specifically permits written resolutions to be used even where the company's articles would otherwise prevent this. However, under *Part I* of *Schedule 15A* to *CA 1985*, a director or auditor may not be removed during their term of office by means of a written resolution. The members' signatures need not all be on one document, provided that each document that has been signed includes an accurate statement of the resolution. No previous notice is required and the date on which the resolution is passed is the date on which the last member signs. For certain resolutions (principally those involving the company's share capital and arrangements with directors), specific procedural requirements set out in *Part II* of *Schedule 15A* to *CA 1985* must be followed. In all cases where a written resolution is used, a copy must be sent to the auditors (or they must be otherwise informed about its contents) at or before the time that the resolution is sent to the members. Based on the recent company law review, the Government White Paper *Modernising Company Law* issued in July 2002 includes proposals to allow a private company to pass a written ordinary resolution with a simple majority of the eligible votes and to pass a written special resolution with 75 per cent of the eligible votes, rather than requiring unanimity for all written resolutions. These changes are reflected in the draft Company Law Reform Bill published in May 2006.

4.41   Minutes of General Meetings

Every company is required by *section 382* of *CA 1985* to keep minutes of the proceedings of its general meetings. If it fails to do so, the company and every officer who is in default is liable to a fine and to a daily default fine for continued contravention. In the case of a private company, written resolutions agreed under *section 381A* of *CA 1985* must be recorded in the same way as minutes of a general meeting. A minute signed by the chairman of the meeting, or by the chairman of the next meeting, constitutes *prima facie* evidence of the proceedings.

4.42   *Location and Inspection of Minute Books*

The minutes of general meetings must be kept at the company's registered office and must be open to inspection by the members of the company without charge. A member may also request a copy of any minutes on payment of the prescribed fee and the company must make this copy available within seven days of the request. If inspection is refused, the company and every officer who is in default is liable to a fine and to a daily default fine for continued contravention. The court can also compel the company to allow an immediate inspection or to send a copy of the minutes to any member who has requested one.

4.43   Delivery of Resolutions to Registrar

A signed copy of any ordinary resolutions on the following issues must be sent to the Registrar:

- an increase in the company's authorised capital (*CA 1985, s 123*);
- authority for the directors to allot shares (*CA 1985, s 80*); and
- the voluntary winding up of the company under *section 84(1)(a)* of the *Insolvency Act 1986* (*Insolvency Act 1986, s 84*).

Company Secretarial

In addition, a signed copy of every extraordinary resolution, every special reso-lution and every elective resolution passed by the company must be delivered to the Registrar. The requirement to deliver resolutions to the Registrar con-tinues to apply where a private company takes the relevant decision by means of a written resolution. In each case, the signed copy must be delivered within 15 days of the date on which the resolution was passed.

4.44   Directors' Meetings

The company secretary will usually play a key role in ensuring that meetings of the board of directors are well planned and organised and that the proced-ures agreed by the board are actually followed in practice. He/she may also be expected to provide guidance to the directors on their responsibilities as direct-ors and how these should be discharged. Further information on the conduct of directors' meetings can be found in **6 CORPORATE GOVERNANCE**. The company sec-retary should attend all board meetings and should prepare minutes of those meetings. *Section 382* of *CA 1985* requires each company to keep minutes of the meetings of its directors and managers, but members are not given any right to inspect these minutes and the legislation does not specify where they should be kept.

4.45   Other Administrative Matters

At a Glance

* A company must retain copies of the service contracts agreed with directors (and, where relevant, with the directors of its subsidiaries), or written memoranda of the terms of appointment if there is no formal contract, and make them available for inspection to members of the company.
* *CA 1985*, the *Business Names Act 1985* and common law place certain restrictions on the names that can be used by companies and other businesses.
* The company's name must be displayed in easily legible form outside every office or place of business.
* Specific requirements must be followed when a company wishes to change its name.
* The company's name must appear in legible form on all business sta-tionery and other official documents, including letters and forms trans-mitted by electronic means.
* Certain charges created by the company must be formally registered with the registrar.
* There is no statutory requirement for a company seal but where one exists, the articles will usually prescribe how and when it can be used.

4.46 Directors' Service Contracts

Section 318 of *CA 1985* requires a company to retain copies of the service contracts agreed with its directors (and, where relevant, with the directors of its subsidiaries), or written memoranda of the terms of appointment if the directors do not have formal contracts. These must be available for inspection by any member of the company, without charge, for at least two hours during each normal business day. If the company refuses to allow a member to inspect a contract or memorandum, the court can require immediate inspection. Prior shareholder approval is required for certain service contracts for directors. Further information on these requirements, and on directors' service contracts in general, is given in **6 CORPORATE GOVERNANCE.**

Company Names

4.47 *Restrictions on use of Certain Names*

Certain restrictions are placed on the use of company and business names by *CA 1985*, the *Business Names Act 1985* and common law. *Section 26* of *CA 1985* prevents a company using:

- the words 'limited' or 'unlimited' and the expression 'public limited company' other than at the end of its name;
- a name that already appears on the index of company names maintained by the Registrar (proposed names should always be checked against this index); or
- a name which, in the opinion of the Secretary of State, would constitute a criminal offence or be considered offensive.

There are also restrictions to prevent the use of a name that might imply a connection with the government or with a local authority. *Section 28* of *CA 1985* gives the Secretary of State power to require a company to change its name if it appears to be too similar to the name of another company, although this power is only available in the twelve months after registration. Under *section 32* of *CA 1985*, the Secretary of State can require a company to change its name at any time if, in his opinion, it gives a misleading indication of the nature of the company's activities and could cause harm to the public. *Section 30* of *CA 1985* exempts certain private companies limited by guarantee from the need to include 'limited' in the company name. The *Business Names Act 1985* regulates the situation where a company wishes to carry on business under a name other than the company name.

4.48 *Display of Company Name*

Section 348 of *CA 1985* requires a company to paint or affix its name, in a conspicuous and easily legible form, outside every office or place from which it carries on business. The company and every officer who is in default is liable to a fine for failure to comply with this requirement, and to a daily default fine for continued contravention.

Company Secretarial

4.49   *Change of Company Name*

Section 28 of *CA 1985* permits a company to change its name by special resolution of the members. The availability and acceptability of the proposed new
name must be checked beforehand (as for the name of a new company), and a
copy of the resolution must be sent to the Registrar within 15 days of the date on
which it was passed, together with payment of the prescribed fee. If the change
of name is approved, the Registrar will issue a Certificate of Incorporation on
Change of Name and the new name becomes effective from the date on which
this certificate is issued.

Business Stationery and Other Documentation

4.50   *Company Details*

Under *section 349* of *CA 1985*, a company's name must appear in legible form on:

- all business letters;
- all notices and other official publications;
- all bills of exchange, promissory notes, endorsements, cheques and orders for
  money or goods purporting to be signed by or on behalf of the company; and
- all bills of parcels, invoices, receipts and letters of credit.

Section 351 of *CA 1985* also specifies that the following details must be shown
in legible form on a company's business letters and order forms:

- place of registration (ie England and Wales, or Scotland);
- registered number;
- address of the registered office;
- if the company is exempt from the obligation to use the word 'limited' as part
  of its name, a statement that the company is limited (eg 'a company limited
  by guarantee'); and
- if the company is an investment company (as defined in *section 266* of *CA
  1985*), a statement of that fact.

Business letters and forms sent by electronic means should also comply with
these requirements. A company that fails to comply is liable to a fine, as is
every officer who issues, or authorises for issue, documentation without the
relevant details.

4.51   *Other Information*

There is no legal requirement to show the names of the company's directors on
business stationery, but if a company chooses to give this information, *section
305* of *CA 1985* requires the names of all the directors to be given, including
those of any shadow directors. Similarly, there is no requirement for the amount
of the company's share capital to be stated on business stationery but if this
information is given (and this is very rare in practice), *section 351* of *CA 1985*
requires the amount shown to be the company's paid-up share capital.

Registration of Charges

4.52 *Requirement to Register Certain Charges*

Section 396 of *CA 1985* sets out details of charges created by the company that must be registered. These are:

- a charge for the purpose of securing any issue of debentures;
- a charge on uncalled share capital of the company;
- a charge created or evidenced by an instrument which, if executed by an individual, would require registration as a bill of sale;
- a charge on land (wherever situated) or any interest in it, but not including a charge for rent or any other periodical sum issuing out of the land;
- a charge on the company's book debts;
- a floating charge on the company's undertaking or property;
- a charge on calls made but not paid;
- a charge on a ship or aircraft, or any share in a ship; and
- a charge on goodwill or any intellectual property.

For these purposes, a charge includes a mortgage. *Section 399* of *CA 1985* requires the company to send to the Registrar details of every such charge created by the company within 21 days of its creation using the prescribed form (Form 395), together with any instrument creating or evidencing the charge. The person benefiting from the charge may also apply for it to be registered, and may recover from the company any fees paid to the Registrar. Special provisions apply under *section 397* of *CA 1985* where a series of debentures is issued. Failure to comply with the registration requirement means that the company and every officer in default is liable to a fine, and to a daily default fine for continued contravention. The charge also becomes void against a liquidator or administrator and any creditor of the company, and the loan secured by the charge becomes immediately repayable.

4.53 *Charges Already Existing on Property Acquired*

Under *section 400* of *CA 1985*, if a company acquires property that is subject to a registrable charge, it must send to the Registrar within 21 days of the acquisition the prescribed particulars of the charge and a certified copy of the instrument (if any) by which the charge was created or is evidenced. Additional time is allowed where the property is situated, and the charge was created, outside Great Britain.

4.54 *Role of the Registrar*

The Registrar must keep a register for each company showing all the charges requiring registration under *CA 1985*, and must enter into it the following details:

- for a series of debentures:
  - the total amount secured by the whole series,
  - dates of the resolutions authorising the issue of the series and the date of the covering deed (if any) by which the security is created or defined,

- ○ general description of the property charged, and
- ○ names of the trustees (if any) for the debenture-holders;
- for other charges:
  - ○ the date on which the charge was created or, where appropriate, the date on which the property subject to the charge was acquired by the company,
  - ○ the amount secured by the charge,
  - ○ short particulars of the property charged, and
  - ○ the persons entitled to the charge.

The Registrar must also issue a certificate of registration of the charge, showing the amount secured. The register maintained by the Registrar is open to inspection by any person.

4.55   *Rectification of Register*

Section 404 of *CA 1985* enables the court to order the rectification of the register for an omission or misstatement, or to extend the time allowed for registration, if it is satisfied that the error or omission was accidental or inadvertent or is not of a nature to prejudice the position of creditors or shareholders of the company, or if it is just and equitable to do so.

4.56   *Satisfaction and Release of Charges*

The Registrar may enter in the register a memorandum of satisfaction, in whole or in part as appropriate, on receipt of a statutory declaration in the prescribed form (Form 403a or 403b), verifying that:

- the debt for which the charge was given has been paid or satisfied in whole or in part;
- part of the property or undertaking charged has been released from the charge or has ceased to form part of the company's property or undertaking.

Where the entry constitutes a memorandum of satisfaction in whole, a copy must be sent to the company.

4.57   Company Documents and Deeds

Changes to rules on the execution of company documents and deeds have been made by the *Regulatory Reform (Execution of Deeds and Documents) Order 2005* (*SI 2005/1906*) which came into force on 15 September 2005. *Section 36A* of *CA 1985* has been amended to deal only with the execution of company documents, and a new *section 36AA* has been inserted on the execution of company deeds. *Section 36A* of *CA 1985* states that a document is executed by a company by the affixing of its common seal, but then goes on to say that a company need not have a common seal and that a document signed by a director and secretary of the company, or by two directors, and expressed to be executed by the company (in whatever form of words) has the same effect as if it had been executed under the company's common seal. A document that purports to be signed by a director and secretary of the company, or by two directors, is deemed to have been duly executed, but where a document is to be signed by one individual as director or secretary of more than one company it is not deemed to be duly signed unless that individual has signed it separately in each capacity. A document that makes clear on its face that it is intended to be a deed has effect as a deed. Under *section 36AA*, a document is validly executed as a deed if it has been duly executed by the company and is delivered as a deed, and a document is presumed to have been delivered upon its being executed unless a contrary intention is proved. Simultaneous changes to the *Law of Property (Miscellaneous Provisions) Act 1989* clarify that the fact that a document has been executed under seal does not mean that it has been executed as a deed. Guidance on the impact of the operation of these rules has been published by the Department for Constitutional Affairs (see their website at www.dca.gov.uk). If the company does have a seal, the articles will usually provide that this can only be used with the authority of the directors. A company which has a common seal may also have:

- an official seal, in the form of a facsimile of the common seal with the additional word 'Securities', for use in sealing securities issued by the company and documents creating or evidencing such securities; and
- an official seal for use in an overseas territory – this must be a facsimile of the common seal with the addition of the name of every territory, district or place where it is to be used.

Company Secretarial

Appendix 1

Useful Websites on Company Secretarial Issues

Institute of Chartered Secretaries and Administrators	www.icsa.org.uk/
Companies House	www.companieshouse.gov.uk
DTI – Corporate Law and Governance Directorate	www.dti.gov.uk/cld
Department for Constitutional Affairs	www.dca.gov.uk
Office of Public Sector Information (for online legislation)	www.opsi.gov.uk/legislation/
Company Law Reform Bill	www.dti.gov.uk/cld/facts/clr.htm

Contracts

5 Contracts

5.1 Overview of Contract Law

> **At a Glance**
> * In order to create a contract, there must be clear agreement between the parties on four separate issues: consideration, certainty, intention, and offer and acceptance.
> * A verbal contract can be just as binding as a written one, but it will often be more difficult to establish that the necessary elements were in place in the absence of written confirmation.
> * Implied terms (or statutory rights) may apply in addition to any written terms for a specific contract.
> * The onus is on the buyer to clarify any specific requirements before the contract terms are finalised.
> * The legal view on what constitutes acceptance of an offer may vary between countries.
> * A product catalogue is usually considered to be an invitation to treat rather than an offer for sale, but care is needed where priced order forms are included.
> * The seller will not usually be entitled to correct pricing errors made when preparing estimates or proposals.
> * Action to enforce a contract should only be taken after careful consideration of all the surrounding issues.
> * The inclusion of third party redress may be a significant issue, especially where groups of companies are involved.

5.2 What Creates a Contract?

Although there is UK legislation in place dealing with contract law, many of the requirements are based on case law and can therefore be difficult to identify without specialist knowledge. Particular protection measures for employees and consumers have been introduced in recent years as a result of the need to implement EU requirements, but these do not generally apply to transactions between businesses. In order to create a legally enforceable contract, there must be clear agreement between the parties on four separate issues.

- *Consideration:* Consideration is something of value and will usually take the form of an obligation to pay an agreed amount of money. However, a promise to provide something in return is an equally valid form of consideration. In effect, there must be something in the arrangement to benefit both parties.
- *Certainty:* Certainty means that there must be unambiguous agreement on what is expected of each party to the arrangement. Both the buyer and the seller must be clear about what is being bought and sold, on what terms the transaction will take place and when the transaction will take place. Other aspects of the arrangement may need to be specified if they are significant. For example, if the seller agrees to repair any goods sold to the buyer under the arrangement, it must be clear whether this commitment will be invalidated by any particular action by the buyer, and also for how long the seller's obligation to repair the goods will continue.
- *Intention:* There must be an intention on the part of all the parties involved to create a legally binding relationship between them. It is generally assumed that an arrangement between two or more independent businesses is intended to be legally binding, especially if it is related to their normal business activities. However, a business may wish to clarify this intent to avoid any doubt over the position.
- *Offer and acceptance:* The basic rules of offer and acceptance apply to all contracts, although in the case of transactions with consumers they are now supported by a substantial body of other laws and regulations designed to protect the interests of the consumer. Transactions between businesses are generally not covered by this type of protection. An offer may be made by either the buyer or the seller and must be accepted by the other party in order to create a contract. For example, if the seller offers to carry out a service for a set fee, the buyer may respond with an acceptance of that offer or with a counter-offer (eg an agreement to buy the service but at a reduced fee). The counter-offer does not constitute an acceptance and there will be no contract unless the seller indicates acceptance of the counter-offer. If the seller responds with another counter-offer, the process continues until a final offer and acceptance has been put into place. There is a general rule that an acceptance needs to be communicated to the party making the offer in order to create a contract. However, the communication may be express or inferred (for instance, delivery of the goods or services by the seller will usually infer acceptance of the last offer made by the buyer).

5.3   Verbal Contracts and Written Contracts

There is no requirement for an agreement to be made in writing in order to create an enforceable contract. However, if problems are encountered over an informal, verbal business arrangement, it will usually be much more difficult to demonstrate that the four elements needed to create an enforceable contract (see **5.2** above) were in place. The existence of the contract would need to be demonstrated from the surrounding circumstances, and following through the sequence of events and finding other parties able to confirm what was said may not be a straightforward task. It is therefore always advisable to confirm verbal agreements in writing. There are, however, certain contracts which must always be made in writing. Any contract relating to an interest in land must be in writing, as must a consumer credit transaction (in order to comply with relevant legislation).

5.4 Implied Contract Terms

Implied terms (or statutory rights) will sometimes apply in addition to the detailed terms set out in the contract. Once again, many of these have been established to protect the consumer. For instance, there is an implied term under the *Sale of Goods Act 1979* that all products supplied are of satisfactory quality and fit for the purpose for which they are purchased, and the buyer will therefore have a statutory right of replacement for any defective goods.

5.5 Specific Requirements of the Buyer

If the buyer has any specific requirements in respect of the goods and services to be supplied (for instance, the format in which they are to be supplied, or the material from which they are to be constructed), the onus is on him to make these clear before the terms of the contract are finalised. If this is not done, the seller is free to fulfil the contract as he sees fit. The fact that a buyer considered his requirements to be obvious and not in need of specific comment in the contract is unlikely to provide a good defence.

5.6 Acceptance of an Offer

Where the acceptance of an offer is made in writing and sent to the other party by post, the rule in the UK is that this satisfies the requirement for the acceptance to be communicated, even if the other party never receives the letter. It is worth nothing that in many countries, especially in the EU, the acceptance must be physically received by the other party to create a contract. Additional issues can arise where trading takes place over the internet, and particularly where the parties to the contract are based in different jurisdictions. It is therefore advisable to state clearly in any contract how the acceptance of an offer should be communicated and which laws will apply to the contract created by that acceptance.

5.7 Product Catalogues

Questions sometimes arises over whether product catalogues constitute an offer and whether the seller is therefore committed to any prices quoted in the catalogue. A product catalogue is usually considered to be an invitation to treat (in other words, an invitation for a prospective buyer to offer to buy) rather than an offer for sale. The seller should therefore be able to respond to the buyer's offer by explaining any change in pricing and making a counter-offer to sell at the latest price. However, a priced order form enclosed with the catalogue might be regarded as an offer to sell, in which case the seller would be committed to the price quoted. It seems unlikely that a catalogue or order form that was clearly out of date would be regarded as binding on the supplier. It is therefore advisable to include an expiry date on each catalogue and order form, and to state that any prices quoted are subject to change.

5.8 Correction of Pricing Errors

A catalogue or price list will not usually constitute an offer (see **5.7** above), and it should therefore be possible to correct any pricing errors before a contract is concluded. By contrast, an estimate or proposal will be an offer and a seller is unlikely to be able to correct a pricing error made in such a document. There may an exception to this general rule if the buyer was clearly aware of the error and tried to rely on it unfairly. Sellers sometimes add the expression 'errors and omissions excepted' ('E & OE') to a quotation or proposal to try to gain protection in these circumstances, but this is unlikely to be effective in law and may contravene the unfair contract terms legislation unless it is reasonable in the circumstances and has been drawn to the attention of the prospective buyer. Once a contract has been put into place, the terms of the contract stand – any error made when raising a related invoice can therefore be corrected to bring it in line with the underlying contract.

5.9 Enforcing a Contract

Action to enforce a contract that has run into problems should only be taken after careful consideration of all the surrounding issues. In most cases, discussion and compromise, or use of the alternative dispute resolution procedures, will produce a better result than taking the matter to court. Particular points to consider if legal action is proposed include:

- whether the business has met every aspect of its own commitments under the contract;
- whether any relevant termination clauses have been correctly followed;
- whether fulfilment of the contract is the main objective, or whether compensation or damages would suffice.

Legal proceedings can be time-consuming and expensive and should generally be undertaken only when all other options have failed.

5.10 Third Party Redress

The *Contracts (Rights of Third Parties) Act 1999* changed the previous principle that a contract under English law could only bind someone who was a party to that contract and could consequently only be enforced by a party to the contract. The new legislation allows a third party to benefit under a contract where:

- the contract expressly provides that they may benefit in this way; or
- a term of the contract purports to confer a benefit on them.

However, it is also possible for a contract to state expressly that a non-party to the contract cannot obtain any such benefit, in which case the enforcement position will remain as before. Many businesses have amended their standard contract terms to prevent the possibility of third party redress, but buyers may want to try to negotiate for this to be reinstated. The issue may be particularly relevant where the goods or services purchased may be used by more than one company (eg by several companies within a group). With third party redress, each company would be able to seek compensation for any loss suffered if problems should arise. Without this, only the company that contracted for the goods or services would be able to make a claim. Certain contracts (including bills of exchange and employment contracts) are specifically exempt from the changes.

5.11 Standard Terms of Business

At a Glance
* Every business should prepare standard terms of business before entering into transactions with other parties, taking care not to infringe the unfair contract terms legislation.
* Standard terms should be developed in the context of the company and the nature of its business – it is generally inadvisable to use terms developed by another business as a model.
* It is also important to review the standard terms of business adopted by suppliers and other trading partners, and to clarify any ambiguous issues.

5.12 Need to Prepare Standard Terms

Every business should prepare standard terms of business before entering into transactions with other parties. Such a document provides evidence that the other party was made fully aware of the terms of the agreement and that a legally enforceable contract has been put into place. It therefore gives considerable protection to the seller if problems arise over the transaction. However, care should be taken to ensure that the terms decided on do not contravene the unfair contract terms legislation. It is also important to ensure that:

- the terms are clear and unambiguous;
- the print size indicates that the terms are intended to be read and understood; and
- the terms are drawn to the attention of the customer.

It is always advisable to seek professional help when preparing standard terms of business.

Contracts

5.13 Contents

It is important that the standard terms of business are developed in the context of the company and the nature of its business. It can be particularly dangerous to base them on standard terms developed by another business, which does not trade in the same way or is unlikely to be faced with the same potential problems. It is also unwise to rely solely on any terms established by the other party. In some cases, specific terms will be drafted for each contract or arrangement – for instance, professional services firms will usually set out precise terms for each engagement that they accept, although these will usually be based on standard wordings. However, in many businesses, standard terms will suffice and once they have been drafted can be applied to all, or most, contracts. Issues that will be relevant to most businesses include:

- what products or services are to be supplied, and when;
- how payment is to be made;
- what will happen in the event of late payment (especially if interest is to be charged);
- whether reservation of title applies (see **5.16–5.18** below);
- what will happen if the goods prove to be faulty, or the services unsatisfactory;
- what will happen in the event of a dispute;
- which country's laws apply to the contract.

Additional considerations will usually apply if, for instance, the business sells to consumers or makes use of factors or agencies. If, in exceptional circumstances, changes to the standard terms are agreed for an individual contract, the amended terms should be communicated in writing and a copy retained for future reference.

5.14 Suppliers' Standard Terms of Business

It follows that it is equally important to review and understand the standard terms adopted by suppliers and other trading partners, as the business will be contractually bound by these. If any aspects are ambiguous, clarification should be sought before the contract is signed. If this is dealt with initially over the telephone, it is advisable to ensure that the discussions are followed up by written confirmation and that this is retained for future reference.

5.15 Reservation of Title

At a Glance
* Reservation of title can be used to provide a degree of protection against a customer going into receivership or liquidation before making payment for goods received.
* Legal advice should be taken when drafting reservation of title clauses, to ensure that they are effective in achieving the required result.

* Reservation of title may not offer the best solution if there are serious concerns over the solvency of a customer.
* Where the impact of reservation of title is material, certain disclosures should be given in the notes to the accounts.
* The security given to creditors who have supplied goods under reservation of title may impact on other loan covenants.

5.16   Protection Afforded by Reservation of Title

The principal effect of trading with reservation of title is that the seller retains legal title to the goods until the buyer has paid for them. This can be helpful if the buyer goes into receivership or liquidation before payment has been made, as the seller is then entitled to reclaim the goods from the buyer's premises, provided that they can be appropriately identified. If the goods have been sold on by the buyer to a third party, it is also possible for the proceeds of these sales to be regarded as being held in trust for the original seller. Inevitably, the position of any other creditors of the company will be adversely affected by the reservation of title and a receiver or liquidator may try to contest the claim. It is therefore essential to obtain professional legal advice when drafting reservation of title clauses to ensure that they are effective in achieving the desired result. The precise wording used will often be of critical importance. Even with a carefully drafted reservation of title clause, there is always a risk that the goods cannot be identified (eg if they have been used in production) and that the clause cannot be enforced. Whilst reservation of title may be a useful protection in some cases, other solutions (eg payment in advance of delivery) may be more effective if there are serious concerns over the solvency of the customer.

5.17   Accounting Issues

A recommendation entitled 'Accounting for goods sold subject to reservation of title' was issued in 1976 by the Institute of Chartered Accountants in England and Wales ('ICAEW'). This considers when goods should be treated as sold for accounting purposes if they are subject to reservation of title. The paper concludes that such a transaction should be accounted for on the basis of its substance rather than its legal form – the goods should therefore be treated as sold by the seller, and as purchased by the buyer, even though the seller may still hold legal title to them. Where the accounts are materially affected by the accounting treatment adopted for sales and purchases subject to reservation of title, the treatment used should be disclosed in the accounts. The buyer will also need to disclose the fact that the creditor in respect of those goods may in effect be secured, with quantification of the amount involved where practicable. If it is not practicable to do this (for instance, because of the number of suppliers seeking to reserve title or doubts about the legal effectiveness of some clauses), the situation should be explained in the notes to the accounts.

Contracts

5.18   Impact for Other Borrowings

A business which holds goods that are subject to reservation of title will also need to consider the potential impact on any other borrowings, and in particular whether the security in effect given to the creditor results in any breaches of covenants or other requirements set out in loan or finance agreements.

Appendix 1

Useful Websites on Contract Law and Related Issues

Office of Fair Trading	www.oft.gov.uk
Business Link	www.businesslink.gov.uk
Law Society	www.lawsociety.org.uk
Department of Trade and Industry	www.dti.gov.uk/
Office of Public Sector Information (for online legislation)	www.opsi.gov.uk/legislation/
European Database: Case Law – Unfair Contract Terms	www.adns.cec.eu.int/CLAB/

6

Corporate Governance

6 Corporate Governance

6.1 The Combined Code

> **At a Glance**
> * The first detailed guidance on corporate governance was set out in the *Cadbury Code of Best Practice*.
> * Corporate governance was defined in the Cadbury Report as the system by which companies are directed and controlled.
> * Good corporate governance is based on the principles of openness, integrity and accountability.
> * Additional guidance was set out in the *Greenbury Code of Best Practice* and all existing guidance was then drawn together in the *Combined Code*.
> * The *Combined Code* was revised again as part of the UK post-Enron review and the new Code came into effect for accounting periods beginning on or after 1 November 2003.
> * The Financial Reporting Council made a small number of additional amendments to the *Combined Code* in June 2006 and companies are encouraged to comply with the updated version for accounting periods beginning on or after 1 November 2006.
> * The *Combined Code* sets out principles of good governance and also best practice provisions for the adoption of those principles.
> * Listed companies must disclose each year how they have applied the principles set out in the *Combined Code* and whether they have complied with the best practice provisions, with an explanation for any areas or periods of non-compliance.

6.2 The Cadbury Code of Best Practice

Corporate governance became a high profile issue in December 1992, with the publication of the *Cadbury Code of Best Practice* and the *Report of the Committee on the Financial Aspects of Corporate Governance* (the 'Cadbury Report'). This Committee, chaired by Sir Adrian Cadbury, had been formed in 1991 at a time of general concern over standards of financial reporting and accountability, particularly in the light of the BCCI and Maxwell cases, and when controversy was beginning to develop over levels of directors' remuneration. The Committee's report was based on the premise that company directors should have the freedom to develop their companies and drive them forward, but that they should do so within an effective framework of accountability. The Committee's recommendations therefore focused primarily on the structure of the board, its control and reporting functions, and the role of the external auditors, and drew on principles that were already being widely followed. Although the recommendations were aimed mainly at listed companies, the Committee's objective was to raise the overall standards of corporate governance and the general level of public confidence in financial reporting. All entities were therefore encouraged to follow the recommendations in the *Cadbury Code of Best Practice*.

6.3 Definition of Corporate Governance

Corporate governance was defined in the Cadbury Report as 'the system by which companies are directed and controlled'. The role of the shareholders is to appoint the directors and the external auditors, and to satisfy themselves that an appropriate governance structure is in place. The directors are responsible for setting the company's strategic aims, providing the leadership to put these into effect, supervising the management of the business and reporting to shareholders on their stewardship. The financial aspects of corporate governance are identified as the way in which the board sets financial policy and oversees its implementation (including the use of financial controls) and the process of reporting to the shareholders on the activities and development of the company.

6.4 Openness, Integrity and Accountability

The *Cadbury Code of Best Practice* was based on the principles of openness, integrity and accountability, which were described as follows in the Cadbury Report:

- *openness* is the basis for the confidence that must exist between a business and those who have a stake in its success – an open approach to the disclosure of information contributes to the efficient working of the market economy, prompts boards to take effective action and allows shareholders and other interested parties to scrutinise companies more closely;
- *integrity* means straightforward dealing and completeness – financial reporting should be honest and should present a balanced view of the company's affairs;
- *accountability* – the board of directors is accountable to the shareholders and effective accountability is achieved through the quality of information provided by the board to the shareholders and by the willingness of the shareholders to exercise their responsibilities as owners of the business.

6.5 Subsequent Developments

The Cadbury Committee addressed those aspects of corporate governance that it considered were most in need of immediate attention. However, they noted in their report that the situation was continually evolving, through the Accounting

Standards Board's programme of new accounting standards, the development of best boardroom practice and the possibility of increased regulation through European Community initiatives. The Committee therefore emphasised the importance of keeping corporate governance guidance up to date and recommended that a further committee should be appointed within the following two to three years to examine progress on compliance with the *Cadbury Code of Best Practice* and consider the need to revise and update the recommendations in the light of emerging issues. The successor committee, under the chairmanship of Sir Richard Greenbury, developed new recommendations on the setting and disclosure of directors' remuneration in the *Greenbury Code of Best Practice* and a further committee, under the chairmanship of Sir Ronald Hampel, developed a new *Combined Code* which built on (and superseded) the recommendations set out in the Cadbury and the Greenbury Codes. The main remit of the Hampel Committee was to review the implementation of, and levels of compliance with, the two Codes that had resulted from the work of the Cadbury and Greenbury Committees. The Hampel review resulted in the development of a new *Combined Code*, which drew together elements of the existing Codes and set out the broad principles of corporate governance, together with detailed guidance on the application of these principles in practice. The Hampel Report advocated a flexible approach to reporting on compliance with the Code, leaving directors free to choose how to explain their corporate governance policies in the light of the specific circumstances of the company or group. The new *Combined Code* was published in June 1998 and became fully effective for accounting periods ending on or after 22 December 2000 (although earlier implementation was required for aspects other than reporting on internal control).

6.6 The Higgs Review

As part of the UK Government's response to the issues raised by Enron and other high profile accounting scandals, the DTI commissioned Derek Higgs to lead a short independent review of the role and effectiveness of non-executive directors. The Higgs Report was published in January 2003 and set out recommendations to increase rigour and transparency in the appointment process for non-executive directors and to widen the spread of experience in UK boardrooms. The Report also set out the draft of a revised *Combined Code*, incorporating these recommendations, which was intended to become effective from 1 July 2003. A separate working group was appointed by the Financial Reporting Council (FRC), under the chairmanship of Sir Robert Smith, to develop further the guidance on audit committees included in the *Combined Code*. The resulting report *Audit Committees: Combined Code Guidance* (commonly referred to as the Smith Report) was published in January 2003, at the same time as the Higgs Report, and included the draft of a revised section of the *Combined Code* on audit committees, together with supplementary guidance intended to assist boards in establishing and operating an audit committee and also directors who serve as members of an audit committee. The report identified certain essential requirements for audit committees, which were set out in bold text, and noted that compliance with these would be necessary to achieve compliance with the *Combined Code*. The detailed guidance in the Smith Report and the new section of the *Combined Code* was also intended to be effective for accounting periods beginning on or after 1 July 2003.

6.7 Finalisation of New Combined Code

In May 2003, the FRC announced the setting up of a working group of its members to produce a revised version of the *Combined Code*, taking into account comments raised during the consultation period on the draft that resulted from the Higgs and Smith Reports. The new *Combined Code* was eventually published on 23 July 2003 and applies for accounting periods beginning on or after 1 November 2003. The document now notes that departure from the detailed Code provisions may be justified in particular circumstances, but it is still expected that listed companies will comply with them most of the time. Some specific relaxations are permitted for companies below the FTSE 350 although they are still encouraged to consider full compliance. The principles from the Higgs version were generally retained as 'main principles' (sometimes with some rewording) but some of the proposed best practice provisions became 'supporting principles' and the introduction to the Code notes that companies should report on how they have applied both the main and the supporting principles. This changed the nature and level of reporting in some areas. Changes were also made to the proposals in the Smith Report. A small number of the 'bold text' items became *Combined Code* provisions and must now be covered in the 'comply or explain' element of the company's reporting. Other aspects of the Smith Report previously highlighted as being essential simply became part of the supplementary guidance, which is included as an appendix to the Code along with the Turnbull Guidance (see **6.68** below) and other Higgs recommendations on good practice.

6.8 Ongoing Review of the Code

Following the UK post-Enron review, the Financial Reporting Council (FRC) assumed overall responsibility for the *Combined Code* and announced its intention to keep the Code under regular review, to ensure that it is working effectively and to identify any amendments that may be needed. In January 2005, the FRC reported that its initial informal assessment of the impact of the revised *Combined Code* had concluded that encouraging progress had been made. In particular, the FRC found that:

- both investors and companies thought that the corporate governance climate had improved over the previous years;
- investors reported an increased dialogue with companies and greater involvement by company chairmen on corporate governance issues; and
- issues such as performance evaluation and professional development are being taken more seriously.

However, the FRC also acknowledged that more time was needed for companies to plan and implement some of the new provisions, such as those relating to the number of independent non-executive directors and the balance of skills and experience within the board. The FRC began its first formal consultation on possible amendments to the *Combined Code* in January 2006 but proposed only two substantive amendments:

- a relaxation of the existing provisions to allow the chairman to sit on the remuneration committee; and
- the addition of new provisions to encourage companies to include a 'vote withheld' box on AGM proxy voting forms, as recommended by the Shareholder Voting Working Group, and to publish details of proxies lodged on resolutions where votes are taken on a show of hands.

An updated version of the *Combined Code*, reflecting these amendments was published in June 2006. In the Preamble to this version, the FRC notes that the Financial Services Authority is obliged by statute to carry out a separate consultation before listed companies can be required to disclose how they have applied the updated Code. This consultation is expected to begin in September 2006. In the meantime, the FRC encourages companies and investors to apply the revised Code voluntarily for reporting years beginning on or after 1 November 2006.

6.9 Structure of the Combined Code

The *Combined Code* was originally divided into two sections, the first setting out the principles of good governance under the key headings and the second giving the best practice provisions for each of those principles. The latest version of the Code has been restructured, so that the main principles, supporting principles and best practice provisions are set out together for each of the following headings:

- Section 1: COMPANIES
  A. Directors
  B. Remuneration
  C. Accountability and Audit
  D. Relations with Shareholders

- Section 2: INSTITUTIONAL SHAREHOLDERS
  E. Institutional Shareholders

6.10 Disclosure of Compliance with the Code

The *Listing Rules* of the Financial Services Authority (FSA) require every listed company to include in its annual report:

- a narrative statement of how it has applied the principles set out in the *Combined Code*, with explanations to enable the shareholders to evaluate how the principles have been applied; and
- a statement on whether or not it has complied throughout the accounting period with the best practice provisions set out in the *Combined Code*, with details of, and the reasons for, any areas or periods of non-compliance.

Other specific disclosures are required by certain sections of the Code and these are summarised in Schedule C to the new Code for ease of reference. Further details on reporting under the *Combined Code* are given in **6.60–6.64** below.

6.11 Directors

> **At a Glance**
> * The *Combined Code* sets out seven main principles in respect of directors.
> * The board has collective responsibility for the success of the company and for ensuring that obligations to shareholders are met.
> * There should be a clear division of responsibilities between the chairman and the chief executive, and these roles should not be undertaken by the same individual.
> * The board should include an appropriate balance between executive and non-executive directors and at least half of the board should comprise independent non-executives.
> * There should be a formal and rigorous procedure for making board appointments and the same process should be followed for both executive and non-executive directors.
> * Directors should be provided with all the information that they need to carry out their duties in an effective manner.
> * All directors should receive induction training when they join the board and should keep their skills and knowledge up to date.
> * The performance of the board, its committees and each individual director should be subject to formal evaluation each year.
> * All directors should be subject to re-election at intervals of not more than three years.

6.12 Main Principles

Section A of the new *Combined Code* sets out the following main principles in respect of directors:

* *The board*: every company should be headed by an effective board, which is collectively responsible for the success of the company.
* *Chairman and chief executive*: there should be a clear division of responsibilities at the head of the company between the running of the board and the executive responsibility for the running of the company's business. No one individual should have unfettered powers of decision.
* *Board balance and independence*: the board should include a balance of executive and non-executive directors (and in particular independent non-executive directors) such that no individual or small group of individuals can dominate the board's decision taking.
* *Appointments to the board*: there should be a formal, rigorous and transparent procedure for the appointment of new directors to the board.
* *Information and professional development*: the board should be supplied in a timely manner with information in a form and of a quality appropriate to enable it to discharge its duties. All directors should receive induction on

joining the board and should regularly update and refresh their skills and knowledge.

- *Performance evaluation*: the board should undertake a formal and rigorous annual evaluation of its own performance and that of its committees and individual directors.
- *Re-election*: all directors should be submitted to re-election at regular intervals, subject to continued satisfactory performance. The board should ensure planned and progressive refreshing of the board.

The supporting principles and best practice provisions in respect of each of the main principles are considered in more detail below.

6.13 The Board

The supporting principles explain that the board's role is to provide entrepreneurial leadership of the company within a framework of prudent and effective controls which enable risk to be assessed and managed. The board should set the company's strategic aims, ensure the availability of appropriate financial and human resources and review management performance. The board is also responsible for setting the company's values and standards and ensuring that obligations to shareholders are understood and met. All directors must take decisions objectively in the interests of the company. The role of the non-executive directors is summarised as follows in the supporting principles:

- to constructively challenge and help develop proposals on strategy;
- to scrutinise the performance of management in meeting goals and objectives;
- to monitor the reporting of performance;
- to satisfy themselves on the integrity of financial information and that financial controls and systems are robust and defensible;
- to determine appropriate levels of remuneration for executive directors;
- to have a prime role in appointing (and where necessary removing) executive directors and in succession planning.

The best practice guidance highlights the following points in relation to the board:

- the board should meet sufficiently regularly to discharge its duties effectively;
- there should be a formal schedule of matters specifically reserved for board decision;
- the annual report should:
  - include a high level statement on how the board operates, identifying the types of decision that are taken by the board and those that are delegated to management,
  - identify the chairman, deputy chairman (if there is one) and senior independent director, and the chairmen and members of the audit, nomination and remuneration committees,
  - give details of the number of board and committee meetings during the year and the individual attendance by directors;

- the chairman should meet with the non-executive directors without the executives present;
- the non-executive directors, led by the senior independent director, should meet at least once a year without the chairman present to appraise his/her performance, and on other occasions where deemed appropriate;
- where they have concerns about the way in which the company is being run or about a proposed course of action, directors should ensure that their concerns are recorded in the minutes;
- where a non-executive director resigns, he/she should provide the chairman with a written statement setting out the reasons, for circulation to the board; and
- companies should arrange appropriate insurance cover in respect of legal action against its directors.

6.14   Board Procedures

The Cadbury Report considered in greater detail the importance of an effective system of board structures and procedures and highlighted in particular the need to:

- appoint appropriate sub-committees of the main board (eg audit committee, remuneration committee, nomination committee) so that the work of the main board can be focused on key issues;
- recognise the importance of the finance function by making it the designated responsibility of a main board director – this director should be a signatory to the annual accounts and should have a direct right of access to the audit committee;
- maintain a formal and up-to-date schedule of matters to be decided collectively by the board, both to ensure that the control and direction of the company remains with the board as a whole and to safeguard against potential misjudgement or malpractice – this schedule was recommended to include as a minimum:
  - acquisition and disposal of material company assets (including subsidiaries),
  - investments,
  - capital projects,
  - authority levels,
  - treasury policies,
  - risk-management policies;
- lay down clear rules to determine materiality for any transaction and establish which transactions require more than one board signatory; and
- agree clear procedures to be followed in exceptional circumstances where decisions need to be taken between board meetings.

It is also considered good practice for the board to establish a code of ethics or statement of business practices and to ensure that all company employees are clear about the standards of conduct that are expected of them.

6.15   Chairman and Chief Executive

The Cadbury Report emphasised the significance of the role of the chairman and the need for him/her to accept fully the duties and responsibilities that the role entails. In particular, the chairman needs to have the ability to stand back from the detailed day-to-day operation of the business and to ensure that the board as a whole exercises appropriate control and leadership and is responsive to its obligations to the shareholders. The supporting principles in the *Combined Code* explain that the chairman is responsible for:

- leadership of the board;
- ensuring the board's effectiveness on all aspects of its role;
- setting the board's agenda;
- ensuring that the directors receive accurate, timely and clear information;
- facilitating the effective contribution of the non-executive directors;
- ensuring constructive relations between executive and non-executive directors; and
- ensuring effective communication with shareholders.

The related best practice provisions emphasise that the role of chairman and chief executive should not be carried out by the same individual and that the division of responsibilities should be clearly established, set out in writing and agreed by the board. Although there was a strong encouragement in the original Code for the roles of chairman and chief executive to be separated, there was an implied acceptance that combination of these roles might have been justified in certain circumstances. The present Code sets out much more stringent requirements and provides more detailed guidance on the specific responsibilities of the chairman. The best practice provisions also note that the chairman should meet the independence criteria (see **6.17** below) at the time of appointment and that a chief executive should not go on to become chairman of the same company. However, the Code does acknowledge that the board may decide on such a progression in exceptional circumstances, provided that:

- major shareholders are consulted in advance; and
- the reasons are set out to shareholders at the time of the appointment and also in the next annual report.

This was not included in the Higgs recommendations but was incorporated as a result of comments received during the consultation period for the new Code.

6.16   Board Balance and Independence

Legally, all directors are equally responsible for the decisions and actions of the board, regardless of whether their appointment is as an executive or non-executive. Whilst certain individuals may have particular responsibilities within the business, the board as a whole is responsible for ensuring that the company meets its obligations. The effectiveness of the board depends on how well the individual members work together as a team under the leadership of the chairman. The supporting principles in the new *Combined Code* note that:

- the board should not be so large as to be unwieldy but should be of sufficient size to achieve an appropriate balance of skills and experience and to allow changes to its composition to be managed without undue disruption;
- there should a strong element of both executive and non-executive directors to ensure that power and information are not concentrated in one or two individuals;
- when deciding the chairmanship and membership of committees, the board should pay due attention to the value of ensuring that membership is refreshed and that undue reliance is not placed on particular individuals; and
- no one other than the committee chairmen and members is entitled to attend meetings of the main board committees, but others may attend at the invitation of the committee.

Under the best practice provisions on board balance and independence, the non-executive directors that are considered to be independent (see **6.17** below) should be identified in the annual report, at least half the board (excluding the chairman) should comprise independent non-executive directors and the board should appoint one of the independent non-executives to be the senior independent director, to be available to shareholders if they have concerns which contact through the normal channels (ie chairman, chief executive or finance director) has failed to resolve or is deemed inappropriate. Smaller companies are required to have at least two independent non-executive directors (rather than having at least half of the board represented by independent non-executives). If the board considers a director to be independent despite the existence of relationships or circumstances which might appear to impair this independence, the reasons behind the board's decision should be explained in the annual report. There is consequently a significant emphasis on the board's collective responsibility for determining which directors are considered to be independent, and for justifying their decision to the shareholders.

6.17 *Independence*

Under the present guidance, a non-executive director is considered to be independent when the board determines that he/she is independent in character and judgement and there are no relationships or circumstances which could affect, or appear to affect the director's judgement. In particular, such relationships or circumstances arise where the director:

- has been an employee of the company or group within the last five years;
- has, or has had within the last three years, a material business relationship with the company either directly or as a partner, shareholders, director or senior employee of a body that has such a relationship with the company;
- receives (or has received) additional remuneration from the company apart from a director's fee, participates in the company's share option or performance-related pay scheme, or is a member of the company's pension scheme;

- has close family ties with any of the company's advisers, directors or senior employees;
- holds cross-directorships or has significant links with other directors through involvement in other companies or bodies;
- represents a significant shareholder; or
- has served on the board for more than nine years from the date of his/her first election.

6.18 *Role of Non-Executives*

Executive directors are expected to have an in-depth knowledge of the business, but the independent non-executives should bring a broader perspective as a result of their experience in other fields. The particular qualities usually required of non-executive directors include:

- wide experience of business practice and boardroom procedures;
- sound judgement and principles;
- the ability to take an objective view; and
- the ability to distinguish between governance and management.

Non-executive directors will usually sit on one or more of the three main board committees (audit, nomination and remuneration) and a non-executive director will chair these committees. They may also be required to take a lead where potential conflicts of interest arise – for instance, where conflict arises between the specific interests of the executive management and the company as a whole at the time of a takeover, or when considering boardroom succession. The *Combined Code* recommendations on the role of the non-executive director are considered in more detail in **6.13** above.

6.19 Appointments to the Board

The supporting principles in respect of appointments to the board note that appointments should be made on merit and against objective criteria, and care should be taken to ensure that appointees have enough time available for the role, especially if they are to act as chairman of one of the main board committees. The board is also required to satisfy itself that appropriate succession plans are in place for both the board and senior management to ensure a continuing balance of skills and experience. The best practice provisions recommend that:

- a nomination committee, with a majority of independent non-executive directors, should lead the process for board appointments and make recommendations to the board;
- the chairman or an independent non-executive director should chair the nomination committee (although the chairman should not chair the committee when it is dealing with the appointment of his/her successor);
- the nomination committee should make publicly available its terms of reference, explaining its role and the authority delegated to it by the board;

- the nomination committee should evaluate the balance of skills, knowledge and experience on the board and, in the light of this, prepare a description of the role and capabilities required for a particular appointment;
- for the appointment of a chairman, the nomination committee should prepare a job specification, including the time commitment expected, bearing in mind the need for availability in the event of a crisis;
- a chairman's other significant commitments should be disclosed to the board before appointment and in the annual report – any changes should be similarly reported as they arise;
- no individual should be appointed as chairman of two FTSE 100 companies;
- the terms and conditions of appointment of non-executive directors should be made available for inspection, the letter of appointment should set out the time and responsibility envisaged in the appointment and the non-executive directors should undertake that they will have sufficient time available to meet these expectations – any other significant commitments, including an indication of the time involved, should be disclosed to the board before appointment, and the board should be informed of any subsequent changes;
- the board should not agree to a full-time executive director taking on more than one non-executive directorship of a FTSE 100 company, or the chairmanship of such a company;
- the work of the nomination committee should be explained in a separate section of the annual report – this should include details of the process used in board appointments and an explanation if neither an external search consultancy nor open advertising has been used in the appointment of a chairman or non-executive director.

Although the nomination committee will deal with the detailed aspects of the selection process and then make a recommendation to the board, the actual appointment of a new director should be a matter for the board as a whole. The same appointment process should apply for both executive and non-executive directors. These provisions are aimed at ensuring that the appointment of each director is the result of an objective and transparent process.

6.20   *Formal Selection Process*

The main board should agree a formal selection process for new directors, together with formal terms of reference for the nomination committee. The selection process will usually involve the following steps by the nomination committee:

- identification of the need for a new director and the skills required from him/her;
- preparation of a job specification, including the time commitment expected and details of any board committees on which he/she will be expected to serve;
- preparation of a company information pack for issue to potential candidates;
- initial assessment of applicants and preparation of a short-list for interview;

- interviews and meetings with short-listed candidates and preparation of a recommendation to the main board.

The main board should then be given the opportunity to meet the recommended candidate before the matter is formally discussed by the main board and a decision on appointment is taken.

6.21 Information and Professional Development

The supporting principles in the present Code note that:

- the chairman is responsible for ensuring that directors receive accurate, timely and clear information – management has an obligation to provide such information, but directors should seek additional clarification and detail where necessary;
- the chairman should ensure that directors continually update their skills and their knowledge of the company to enable them to fulfil their role on the main board and its committees – the company should make the necessary resources available for this;
- under the direction of the chairman, the duties of the company secretary include:
  - facilitating induction,
  - assisting with professional development,
  - ensuring good information flows within the board and its committees;
  - ensuring good information flows between the non-executive directors and senior management; and
  - advising the board, through the chairman, on all governance matters.

The best practice provisions recommend that the chairman should ensure that new directors receive a comprehensive, formal and tailored induction on joining the board. Major shareholders should also be offered the opportunity to meet a new non-executive director. The board should ensure that all directors, and especially non-executives, have access to independent professional advice at the company's expense and that committees are provided with sufficient resources to undertake their duties. All directors should have access to the advice and services of the company secretary who is responsible for ensuring compliance with board procedures. Both the appointment and the removal of the company secretary should be a matter for the board as a whole.

6.22 *Induction*

The appendices to the *Combined Code* include an induction checklist, which is intended to serve as a guideline for the development of an in-house induction programme, tailored to the needs of the company and individual non-executive directors. The checklist recommends a combination of written information, presentations, meetings with senior management, site visits and informal meetings with employees, to give the new director a balanced overview of the company and its activities. The induction process should usually include coverage of:

- the company's constitution;
- board procedures and matters reserved for the board;
- major shareholders, and the company's policy on shareholder relations;
- group structures;
- the company's products or services, and major competitors;
- major customers and suppliers, and significant contracts;
- principal assets and liabilities;
- major risks, and the company's risk management strategy;
- key performance indicators; and
- regulatory requirements.

6.23   Organisation of Board Meetings

The chairman has overall responsibility for the management of board meetings but will need to work closely with the company secretary. They should plan the agenda for each meeting well in advance, often with input from the chief executive and finance director, and ensure that the board considers all the issues that ought to come before it. Most companies prepare an annual timetable of board and related committee meetings, built around key events in the business cycle (eg consideration and approval of strategic plans, consideration and approval of detailed budgets, publication of interim report, approval of annual report and accounts) and allowing for timely reporting from the committees to the main board. It is also important that:

- supporting papers are set out in an appropriate level of detail and are issued well in advance of the meeting so that all directors have adequate time to prepare and can make a constructive contribution to the discussions;
- the time available is allocated in an appropriate manner between individual agenda items – it will often be helpful to indicate on the agenda the nature of each item (eg report only, board decision required, formal board approval required) and how much time has provisionally been allocated for the related presentation and discussion;
- any differences of opinion that arise during meetings are dealt with in a mature, constructive and professional manner; and
- the minutes provide an accurate record of the proceedings and are circulated promptly to all those entitled to receive them.

6.24   Performance Evaluation

Performance evaluation was not included in the original *Combined Code*. There is just one supporting principle in the present Code, which notes that:

- individual performance evaluation should aim to show whether each director continues to contribute effectively and to demonstrate commitment to the role; and

- the chairman should act on the results of this evaluation by recognising the strengths and addressing the weaknesses of the board and, where appropriate, proposing new board members or seeking the resignation of directors.

The best practice provisions recommend that the board should state in the annual report how performance evaluation of the board, its committees and individual directors has been conducted and that the non-executive directors, led by the senior independent director, should evaluate the performance of the chairman, taking into account the views of the executive directors. The appendices to the *Combined Code* include a performance evaluation checklist. This notes that the process should be used constructively to improve overall board effectiveness, maximise strengths and tackle weaknesses. The results of the performance evaluation for the board as a whole should be communicated to the board, but the results of individual assessments should remain confidential to the chairman and the director concerned. The checklist includes questions that might be used to assess the effectiveness of the board, the contribution of the chairman and the performance of a non-executive director.

6.25   Re-election

There are no supporting principles in respect of re-election. The best practice provisions recommend that:

- all directors should be subject to election by the shareholders at the first annual general meeting after their appointment and to re-election thereafter at intervals of no more than three years;
- the names of directors submitted for election or re-election should be accompanied by sufficient biographical details and other relevant information to enable shareholders to make an informed decision;
- non-executive directors should be appointed for specified terms, subject to re-election and to *Companies Act 1985* provisions relating to the removal of a director;
- the board should set out in the papers accompanying the resolution to elect a non-executive director why they believe that individual should be elected;
- when a director is proposed for re-election, the chairman should confirm to shareholders that, following performance evaluation, the individual continues to make an effective contribution and to demonstrate commitment to the role;
- a proposal to re-elect a non-executive director for a term beyond six years (ie two terms of three years) should be subject to rigorous review and should take into account the need for progressive refreshing of the board;
- non-executive directors may serve for more than nine years, subject to annual re-election, but this could be relevant to the assessment of the director's independence.

6.26   Directors' Remuneration and Service Contracts

At a Glance
* Remuneration levels should be sufficient to attract, motivate and retain directors of the required quality, but the company should avoid paying more than is necessary.
* Comparison with the remuneration packages and relative performance of other companies may be helpful, but should be used with caution.
* Pay and conditions elsewhere within the company or group should also be borne in mind.
* Performance-related elements should form a significant proportion of the total remuneration package for executive directors, and performance conditions should be relevant, challenging and designed to enhance the business.
* New long-term incentive schemes should be subject to shareholder approval and awards under the schemes should usually be phased.
* The pension consequences of any changes in remuneration packages should be properly considered.
* Contract or notice periods should generally be limited to one year, and appropriate attention should be paid to compensation commitments in the event of early termination.
* *CA 1985* sets out detailed requirements on the retention and inspection of directors' service contracts.
* Changes may be made to the present company law provisions on directors' service contracts.
* A remuneration committee of independent non-executive directors should be established to make recommendations to the board on executive remuneration packages.

6.27   Main Principles

Section B of the *Combined Code* sets out the following main principles in respect of remuneration:

* *Level and make-up of remuneration*: Levels of remuneration should be sufficient to attract, retain and motivate directors of the quality needed to run the company successfully, but companies should avoid paying more than is necessary for this purpose. A significant proportion of executive directors' remuneration should be structured to link rewards to corporate and individual performance.
* *Procedure*: There should be a formal and transparent procedure for developing policy on executive remuneration and for fixing the remuneration packages of individual directors. No director should be involved in setting his/her own remuneration.

The original Code also included a section on the disclosure of directors' remuneration, but this has been removed following the implementation of the *Directors' Remuneration Report Regulations 2002* (*SI 2002/1986*) which apply for accounting periods ending on or after 31 December 2002 and introduce a statutory requirement for equivalent disclosures to those previously recommended in the Code. The disclosure requirements are considered in more detail in Chapter 23.

6.28   Level and Make-up of Remuneration

The supporting principle on the level and make-up of remuneration notes that the remuneration committee should judge where to position the company relative to other companies, but should use such comparisons with caution in view of the risk of increasing remuneration levels without a corresponding improvement in performance. They should also be sensitive to pay and employment conditions elsewhere in the group, especially when determining annual salary increases. The best practice guidance is divided into two sections – remuneration policy, and service contracts and compensation.

6.29   *Remuneration Policy*

The best practice provisions on remuneration policy include the following:

- performance-related elements should form a significant proportion of the total remuneration package for executive directors and should be designed to align their interests with those of the shareholder, and to give the directors a keen incentive to perform at the highest levels;
- in designing schemes of performance-related remuneration, the committee should follow the provisions set out in Schedule A to the *Combined Code* (see **6.30** below);
- executive share options should not be issued at a discount, except as permitted by Chapters **13.30** and **13.31** of the FSA *Listing Rules*;
- levels of remuneration for non-executive directors should reflect the time, commitment and responsibilities of the role and should not include share options; and
- where a company releases an executive director to serve as a non-executive director elsewhere, the remuneration report should state whether or not the director will retain earnings from the appointment and, if so, what the remuneration is.

The provisions do allow for share options to be granted to a non-executive director in exceptional circumstances, but note that shareholder approval should be sought in advance and any shares acquired through exercise of the options should be held for at least one year after the individual leaves the board. The holding of share options could also be relevant to the assessment of the director's independence (see **6.17** above).

6.30 *Performance-related Pay*

Schedule A to the *Combined Code* comprises the guidance originally set out in the *Greenbury Code of Best Practice* on directors' remuneration, with a number of minor wording changes. It recommends that:

- the remuneration committee should consider whether directors should be eligible for annual bonuses and, if so, performance conditions should be relevant, stretching and designed to enhance shareholder value – upper limits should be set and disclosed and there may be a case for part payment in shares to be held for a significant period;
- the remuneration committee should consider whether the directors should be eligible for benefits under long-term incentive schemes, and in establishing such schemes should:
  - weigh traditional share option schemes against other kinds of long-term incentive schemes,
  - generally ensure that shares granted and other forms of deferred remuneration do not vest, and options are not exercisable, in less than three years,
  - encourage directors to hold their shares for a further period after vesting or exercise, subject to the need to finance any costs of acquisition or associated tax liabilities;
- where new long-term incentive schemes are proposed, these should be approved by the shareholders and should preferably replace existing schemes, or at least form part of a well-considered overall plan incorporating existing schemes – the total rewards potentially available should not be excessive;
- payouts or grants under all incentive schemes (including new grants under existing share option schemes) should be subject to challenging performance criteria reflecting the company's objectives, and consideration should be given to criteria which reflect the company's performance relative to a group of comparator companies in certain key variables such as total shareholder return;
- grants under executive share option and other long-term incentive schemes should normally be phased rather than awarded in one large block;
- in general, neither annual bonuses nor benefits in kind should be pensionable; and
- the remuneration committee should consider the pension consequences and associated costs to the company of increases in basic salary and other changes in pensionable remuneration, especially for directors close to retirement.

6.31 *Service Contracts and Compensation*

The best practice guidance on directors' service contracts and compensation includes the following provisions:

- the remuneration committee should carefully consider what compensation commitments (including pension contributions and any other elements) the directors' terms of appointment would entail in the event of early termination – the aim should be to avoid rewarding poor performance and to take a robust line on reducing compensation to reflect a departing director's obligations to mitigate loss;

- notice or contract periods should be set at one year or less – if it is necessary to offer longer notice or contract periods to new directors recruited externally, these periods should reduce to one year or less after the initial period.

The original Code included a recommendation that the remuneration committee should consider the advantages of providing explicitly in the initial contract for compensation commitments other than in the case of removal for misconduct and, where compensation was not covered in a director's contract, should tailor their approach in the case of early termination to the wide variety of circumstances. These elements have now been removed from the best practice provisions. However, the present Code is more definite that notice or contract periods should be set at one year or less, or should reduce to one year or less as soon as possible.

6.32   *Service Contracts for Executive Directors*

An executive director is in effect an employee of the company and it is appropriate that the terms and conditions of his/her appointment should be set out in a written contract of service between the director and the company. A comprehensive service contract can help to prevent misunderstandings and provides a useful point of reference if problems arise. Non-executive directors have a very different role to executive directors and the terms and conditions of their appointment will usually be set out in a contract for services. A service contract for an executive director should normally include:

- specific duties of the director, including the amount of time to be spent on company activities (this may be particularly important where the individual also holds posts such as non-executive directorships in other businesses);
- remuneration, including details of any arrangements involving:
  - benefits in kind (eg private health cover, accommodation, company car),
  - bonus schemes,
  - long-term incentive plans,
  - share options;
- holiday entitlement;
- arrangements in the case of prolonged absence through illness;
- pension arrangements;
- required notice period, and procedures in the case of dismissal;
- compensation arrangements in the event of early termination of the contract; and
- confidentiality arrangements.

Other issues may need to be covered, depending on the circumstances. The Institute of Directors publishes a specimen contract of service for executive directors.

6.33   *Contracts for Services of Non-executive Directors*

The main role of non-executive directors is to make a positive contribution to the development of company strategy, and on matters such as company performance, standards of conduct and corporate governance issues. It is helpful to all parties for the terms of their appointment to be set out in a written contract for services. This will usually specify:

- the expected commitment, in terms of attendance at meetings of the board and its sub-committees; and
- fee arrangements.

Non-executive directors will usually be paid either a fixed fee, or a fixed retainer plus fees for attendance at specific meetings. The Cadbury Report emphasised the importance of striking an effective balance between recognition of the value of non-executive directors and their contribution to the company, and the need to ensure that any payments that they receive do not in effect undermine their independence. The fee arrangements should reflect the time commitment expected from the non-executive directors (which can often be quite considerable), and it can be helpful for them to take into account specific additional responsibilities, such as chairmanship of one or more of the sub-committees of the main board. It is not usually considered appropriate for non-executive directors to participate in company share option schemes, or to be provided with pension arrangements by the company.

6.34 *Companies Act 1985 Requirements*

Where a director has a written contract of service with the company, *section 318* of the *Companies Act 1985 (CA 1985)* requires the company to retain a copy of the contract at one of the following locations:

- the company's registered office;
- the place where the register of members is kept (if this is not the registered office); or
- the company's principal place of business (provided that this is in the part of Great Britain where the company is registered).

If a director does not have a written contract of service, the company must keep a written memorandum of the terms of his/her appointment. The same rules apply to a variation of a director's contract. A parent company is also required to keep copies of service contracts between its subsidiaries and their directors, or a written memorandum of the terms if these contracts are not in writing. Copies of all contracts and memoranda must be kept in the same place. If they are not kept at the registered office, the company must notify the Registrar of Companies of where they are held and of any changes in location. *Section 318(6)* of *CA 1985* emphasises that these arrangements apply equally in the case of shadow directors. Failure to comply can result in fines being charged on the company and on every officer who is in default.

Where a director of the company, or of one of its subsidiaries, is required under his/her contract to work wholly or mainly outside the UK, the company is not required to keep a copy of the contract, but it must keep a memorandum giving the director's name and the provisions of the contract relating to its duration. In the case of a contract for a director of a subsidiary, the name and place of incorporation of the subsidiary must also be recorded in the memorandum. These memoranda must be kept in the same place as the contracts and memoranda relating to the other directors.

However, there is no formal requirement for a company to retain a copy of a contract, variation or memorandum when the unexpired term is less than twelve months, or where the contract can be terminated by the company within the next twelve months without the payment of compensation.

6.35   Inspection of Contracts

Under *section 318(7)* of *CA 1985*, any member of the company is entitled to inspect the copies of the directors' contracts of service (or the memoranda where there is no written service contract) without charge. If the company refuses to allow a member to inspect a contract or memorandum, the court can require immediate inspection.

6.36   Shareholder Approval for Contracts for More Than Five Years

Under *section 319* of *CA 1985*, a director cannot be given the right of employment with the company (or, where relevant, with the group) for a period of more than five years under an agreement which does not allow the company to give unconditional notice at any time, unless this term of the contract has been first approved by the company in general meeting (or, in the case of a private company, by written resolution). By implication, a company is permitted to enter into an agreement giving a director employment for more than five years without prior shareholder approval, provided that the company is free to give unconditional notice at any time. Employment is defined as including employment under a contract for services. Where the director is also a director of the company's holding company, prior approval to the arrangement must normally be given by the shareholders of both the subsidiary and the holding company (unless the subsidiary is wholly-owned, in which case prior approval of the arrangement by the shareholders of the subsidiary is not required).

A written memorandum setting out the proposed agreement must be available for inspection by the members at the company's registered office for a period of at least 15 days before the meeting and at the meeting itself. In the case of a private company where agreement is to be by written resolution, a copy of the memorandum must be sent to each member before, or at the same time as, the resolution is provided for signature.

A term included in a director's contract in contravention of *section 319* of *CA 1985* is void, and the agreement is deemed to include a term entitling the company to terminate the agreement at any time by the giving of reasonable notice.

CA 1985 also includes special provisions to prevent a company entering into a series of shorter agreements with the same director in an attempt to avoid the requirement for shareholder approval of a contract that in effect extends for more than five years.

6.37   *Possible Areas for Change*

In June 2003, DTI issued a consultation document *Rewards for failure: Directors' remuneration – contracts, performance and severance.* This considered the linkage between directors' contracts, actual performance and compensation payments. In particular, the DTI raised the following issues:

- as a result of the *Combined Code* recommendations, notice periods of one year have become the norm and shorter periods are rare – this causes disparity between the treatment of directors and other company employees, who invariably have much shorter notice periods;
- confusion often arises between the terms 'contract period' and 'notice period' which are often used interchangeably in respect of directors' service contracts;
- the five year limit for service contracts under *CA 1985* (see **6.36** above) appears excessive in the light of the current best practice – a maximum contract period of three years on initial appointment and a maximum notice period of one year, might be more appropriate;
- rolling contracts, which are in effect renewed on a daily basis, are now more common than fixed term contracts and these may be used to circumvent the present statutory restrictions on the length of directors' service contracts – it may therefore be appropriate to bring rolling contracts within the scope of *section 319* of *CA 1985*;
- consideration should be given to prohibiting the use of specific covenants for severance payments where these provide for more compensation than would otherwise be payable under the one or three year contract; and
- the payment of compensation in instalments rather than as a single lump sum would give a company the ability to reduce or stop the payments when the former director takes up a new employment.

The draft Company Law Reform Bill published in May 2006 includes proposals that would require formal approval by the shareholders for any director's service contract that guarantees a term of employment that is (or may be) longer than two years and for any payment for loss of office made to a director.

6.38   Procedure for Developing Remuneration Policy

The supporting principles on the procedure for developing remuneration policy cover the following points:

- the remuneration committee should consult the chairman and/or chief executive about the proposals on the remuneration of other executive directors, and should have access to internal and external professional advice;
- the remuneration committee should be responsible for appointing any consultants in respect of executive remuneration;
- if executive directors or senior management are involved in advising or supporting the remuneration committee, care should be taken to recognise and avoid conflicts of interest; and

- the chairman of the board should ensure that the company maintains appropriate contact with its principal shareholders on remuneration issues in the same way as for other matters.

The best practice provisions include the following recommendations:

- the board should establish a remuneration committee of at least three independent non-executive directors (or two in the case of a smaller company);
- the committee should make available its terms of reference, explaining its role and the authority delegated to it by the board;
- where remuneration consultants are appointed, a statement should be made on whether they have any other connection with the company;
- the remuneration committee should have delegated responsibility for setting the remuneration of all executive directors and the chairman, including pension rights and any compensation payments;
- the committee should also recommend and monitor the level and structure of remuneration for senior management – the definition of senior management for this purpose should be decided by the board but should normally include the first layer of management below board level;
- the board (or the shareholders where the company's articles require this) should determine the remuneration of the non-executive directors – where the company's articles permit, the responsibility may be delegated to a small sub-committee, which might include the chief executive; and
- shareholders should be invited to approve all new long-term incentive schemes and significant changes to existing schemes, other than in the circumstances permitted by the *Listing Rules.*

The updated version of the Code published by the FRC in June 2006 (see **6.8**) includes a relaxation of these provisions to allow the company Chairman to sit on the remuneration committee (but not to chair it) if he/she was considered independent on appointment as Chairman. This is in addition to the recommended minimum number of independent directors noted above, and the principle that no director should be involved in setting his or her own remuneration continues to apply.

6.39   Accountability and Audit

At a Glance
- * The board's responsibility to present a balanced and understandable assessment of the company's financial performance and financial position extends to all forms of financial reporting.
- * The board should maintain a sound system of internal control.
- * The board should establish an audit committee of independent non-executive directors, at least one of whom should have recent and relevant financial experience.

6.40   Main Principles

Section C of the *Combined Code* identifies three main principles on account-ability and audit.

- *Financial reporting*: the board should present a balanced and understandable assessment of the company's position and prospects.
- *Internal control*: the board should maintain a sound system of internal con-trol to safeguard the shareholders' investment and the company's assets.
- *Audit committee and auditors*: the board should establish formal and trans-parent arrangements for considering how they should apply the financial reporting and internal control principles mentioned above, and for maintain-ing an appropriate relationship with the company's auditors.

The Cadbury Report discussed the presentation of a balanced and understandable assessment of the company's position in the context of recognised accounting practice. The accounts are required by law to show a true and fair view and they should give the highest level of disclosure consonant with presenting reports that are understandable, and without causing damage to the company's competitive position. The Cadbury Report also emphasised that balance involves dealing with setbacks as well as successes and that words are as important as figures. These issues are explored in more detail in **11 FINANCIAL REPORTING.**

6.41   Financial Reporting

The Code includes one supporting principle in respect of financial reporting which clarifies that the board's responsibility to present balanced and under-standable information extends to interim reports, other price-sensitive reports and reports to regulators. The related best practice provisions cover the follow-ing points:

- the directors should explain in the annual report their responsibility for preparing the accounts, and there should be a statement by the auditors about their reporting responsibilities; and
- the directors should report that the business is a going concern, with sup-porting assumptions or qualifications as necessary.

The statement of directors' responsibilities is considered in more detail in **11 FINANCIAL REPORTING.** Going concern is considered at **6.82** below.

6.42   Internal Control

There are no supporting principles on internal control and just one best practice provision which notes that the board should review the effectiveness of the com-pany's (or group's) system of internal control annually at least, and should report to shareholders that they have done so. The review should cover all material controls, including financial, operational and compliance controls and risk management systems. The Cadbury Code of Best Practice recommended that the directors should report on the effectiveness of the company's system of internal control, although the formal guidance issued subsequently required them to review and report only on internal financial control. The present requirements are considerably broader in scope and are considered in more detail at **6.66** below, together with the review of the need for an internal audit function.

6.43 Audit Committee and Auditors

There are no supporting principles in respect of the audit committee and auditors, but the Code includes the following best practice provisions:

- the board should establish an audit committee of at least three independent non-executive directors (or two in the case of smaller companies);
- the board should satisfy itself that at least one member of the audit committee has recent and relevant financial experience;
- the main role and responsibilities of the audit committee should be set out in written terms of reference and should include:
  - monitoring the integrity of the company's financial statements and any formal announcements relating to the company's financial performance, and reviewing significant financial reporting judgements contained in them,
  - reviewing the company's internal financial controls and, unless addressed by a separate risk committee of independent directors or by the board itself, the company's internal control and risk management systems,
  - monitoring and reviewing the effectiveness of the company's internal audit function,
  - making recommendations to the board (for it to put to the shareholders) on the appointment, reappointment or removal of the external auditor and approving the remuneration and terms of engagement of the external auditor,
  - monitoring and reviewing the external auditor's independence and objectivity and the effectiveness of the audit process, taking into account relevant UK professional and regulatory requirements,
  - developing and implementing policy on the engagement of the external auditor to supply non-audit services, taking into account relevant ethical guidance on this issue, and reporting to the board on any matter where the committee considers that action or improvement is needed;
- the audit committee should make available its terms of reference, explaining its role and the authority delegated to it by the board;
- the annual report should include a separate section describing the work of the committee in discharging its responsibilities;
- the audit committee should review the arrangements by which staff may, in confidence, raise concerns about possible improprieties in matters of financial reporting or other issues, with the objective of ensuring that arrangements are in place for proportionate and independent investigation and appropriate follow-up action;

- the audit committee should monitor and review the effectiveness of internal audit activities;
- where there is no internal audit function, the audit committee should consider annually whether there is a need for one and make a recommendation to the board – the absence of an internal function should be explained in the relevant section of the annual report;
- the audit committee should have primary responsibility for making a recommendation on the appointment, reappointment or removal of the external auditors – if the board does not accept the audit committee's recommendation, the annual report and any papers recommending appointment or reappointment should include a statement from the committee explaining its recommendation and setting out the reasons why the board has taken a different position; and
- if the external auditor provides non-audit services to the company, the annual report should explain to shareholders how auditor objectivity and independence is safeguarded.

All of these issues are considered in more detail at **1.137 AUDIT COMMITTEES.**

6.44   Relations with Shareholders

> **At a Glance**
> * The board should take steps to ensure that all directors develop a balanced understanding of the issues and concerns of the company's shareholders.
> * All proxy votes at the AGM should be counted and the level of proxies lodged, together with the balance for and against each resolution and any abstentions, should usually be reported.
> * A separate resolution should be proposed on each substantial issue.
> * The chairmen of the audit, remuneration and nominations committees should be available to answer questions at the AGM and all directors should attend the meeting.
> * The notice of the AGM, together with supporting papers should be issued to shareholders at least 20 working days before the meeting.

6.45   Main Principles

Section D of the *Combined Code* includes the following main principles in respect of the company's relations with its shareholders:

- *Dialogue with institutional shareholders*: there should be a dialogue with shareholders based on the mutual understanding of objectives. The board as a whole is responsible for ensuring that this dialogue takes place.
- *Constructive use of the AGM*: the board should use the AGM to communicate with private investors and encourage their participation.

6.46 Dialogue with Institutional Shareholders

The supporting principles in the Code note that, whilst recognising most shareholder contact will be with the chief executive and finance director, the chairman and where appropriate other directors (including the senior independent director) should maintain sufficient contact with shareholders to understand their issues and concerns, using whichever methods are most practical and efficient. The best practice provisions include the following recommendations:

- the chairman should discuss governance and strategy with major shareholders and should ensure that the views of shareholders are communicated to the board as a whole;
- non-executive directors should be offered the opportunity to attend meetings with major shareholders and should expect to attend if requested by the shareholders;
- the senior independent director should attend sufficient meetings with a range of major shareholders to listen to their views and develop a balanced understanding of their issues and concerns;
- the board should disclose in the annual report the steps taken to ensure that the members of the board, and the non-executive directors in particular, develop an understanding of the views of major shareholders about the company (eg through direct face-to-face contact, analysts' or brokers' meetings, surveys of shareholder opinion etc).

The introduction of recommendations on meetings between the non-executive directors and major shareholders has been an interesting development. Prior to the introduction of the present *Combined Code*, it was generally accepted that the chairman should be the main channel of communication with institutional investors on matters of concern and a direct approach to the senior independent director was seen as a last resort and an indication that something was seriously amiss. However, following its initial assessment of the impact of the present *Combined Code*, the FRC specifically noted that investors are reporting improved dialogue with companies (see **6.8** above).

6.47 Constructive Use of the AGM

There are no supporting principles on constructive use of the AGM, but the *Combined Code* includes the following best practice provisions:

- the company should count all proxy votes and, except where a poll is called, should indicate the level of proxies lodged on each resolution, the balance for and against the resolution and the number of abstentions, after the resolution has been dealt with on a show of hands;
- separate resolutions should be proposed on each substantially separate issue, and in particular a resolution should be proposed on the annual report and accounts;

- the chairman of the board should arrange for the chairmen of the audit, remuneration and nomination committees to be available to answer questions at the AGM and for all directors to attend; and
- the company should arrange for the notice of the AGM and related papers to be sent to shareholders at least 20 working days before the meeting.

These provisions have been expanded in the updated version of the Code published by the FRC in June 2006 (see **6.8**) so that the Code now recommends that:

- for each resolution, proxy appointment forms should enable shareholders to direct their proxy to vote for or against the resolution or to withhold their vote – both the form and any announcement of the results should make it clear that a 'vote withheld' is not a vote in law and will not be counted in the calculation of votes for and against the resolution;
- the company should ensure that all valid proxy appointments received for general meetings are properly recorded and counted; and
- after a vote has been taken (except where this is on a poll) the following information should be given at the meeting in respect of each resolution and should also be made available as soon as reasonably practicable on a website maintained by or on behalf of the company:
  - the number of shares in respect of which proxy appointments have been validly made;
  - the number of votes for the resolution;
  - the number of votes against the resolution; and
  - the number of shares in respect of which the vote was directed to be withheld.

Listed companies are encouraged to comply with these new recommendations on a voluntary basis for accounting periods beginning on or after 1 November 2006.

6.48   *Accountability to Shareholders*

The Cadbury Report summarised the relationship between the board and the company's shareholders as follows:

- the shareholders, as owners of the company, elect the directors to run the business on their behalf, and hold them accountable for its progress and development;
- the directors report to the shareholders on their stewardship of the company and its assets; and
- the shareholders appoint external auditors to provide an independent check on the company's financial statements.

The Cadbury Committee considered suggestions on how the accountability of directors to shareholders might be strengthened but concluded that shareholders should continue to make their views known to the board through direct communication and through attendance at annual general meetings. The Committee also noted that shareholder organisations set up to represent shareholder interests generally might provide an opportunity for individual shareholders to act collectively if they wish. Whilst shareholders cannot be involved in the detailed direction and management of their company, they are entitled to insist on a high standard of corporate governance, evidenced by compliance with the *Combined Code.*

6.49   *Government Proposals for Change*

The Government White Paper *Modernising Company Law* issued in July 2002 includes a number of measures designed to improve the quality of shareholder input at the AGM. In particular the following changes are proposed:

- in future, the timing of the AGM will be linked to the company's annual reporting cycle – public companies will be required to hold an AGM within six months of the financial year end and private companies who hold an AGM will have to do so within ten months of the financial year end;
- the annual accounts and reports will have to be sent to shareholders within six months of the end of the financial year end in the case of a public company and within seven months of the financial year end in the case of a private company – for public companies, the period allowed for distributing the accounts will in effect be reduced by the notice period for the AGM;
- quoted companies will be required to publish their accounts on a website as soon as practicable after approval and within four months of the financial year end at the latest – this is intended to give shareholders more opportunity to submit members' resolutions for inclusion in the notice of the AGM;
- members' resolutions and statements received by the company in time to be circulated with the notice of the meeting will have to be circulated to all members at the company's expense;
- quoted companies will also be expected to make any preliminary announcement of their results available to all members through the internet;
- the power of proxies at meetings will be enhanced, enabling them to speak, vote on a show of hands as well as in a poll and join with others in demanding a poll;
- members will be allowed to demand a poll in advance of a meeting and to vote on that poll without needing to attend the meeting or appoint a proxy;
- there will be a new right for a sufficient body of members to require an independent scrutiny of any poll; and
- quoted companies will be required to disclose on their websites and in their annual reports the results of polls at general meetings.

These changes are now incorporated in the draft Company Law Reform Bill published in May 2006.

6.50 Institutional Shareholders

At a Glance
* Institutional shareholders will usually have more access to boards than individual shareholders but companies must take steps to maintain parity between shareholders.
* There is a significant degree of common interest between individual shareholders and institutional shareholders.
* Detailed guidance for institutional investors is issued by the Institutional Shareholders' Committee (ISC) and other similar organisations.
* The *Combined Code* recommends that institutional shareholders' should apply the principles set out in the ISC's latest Statement of Principles.
* The *Combined Code* also includes a number of principles on the evaluation of corporate governance disclosures and shareholder voting.

6.51 Main Principles

The *Combined Code* includes the following main principles in respect of institutional shareholders.

* *Dialogue with companies*: institutional shareholders should enter into a dialogue with companies based on the mutual understanding of objectives.
* *Evaluation of governance disclosures*: when evaluating governance arrangements, particularly those relating to board structure and composition, institutional shareholders should give due weight to all relevant factors drawn to their attention.
* *Shareholder voting*: institutional shareholders have a responsibility to make considered use of their votes.

6.52 Communication with Shareholders

The Cadbury Report raised the following issues in respect of communication with shareholders:

* institutional shareholders will usually have more access to boards than individual shareholders, but there is still a need for companies to maintain parity between shareholders wherever possible – a board should therefore ensure that any significant statements concerning the company are made publicly so that they are equally available to all shareholders;
* in communicating with institutional shareholders, there is always a risk of the company disclosing inside information – price-sensitive information should only be disclosed with the prior consent of the shareholder (who will then be unable to deal in the company's shares until the information has been made public); and

- in order to develop long-term relationships, it is important for a company to communicate its strategy to the major shareholders – similarly shareholders should inform the company if they have concerns over particular aspects of the business.

6.53 Role of Institutional Shareholders

The Cadbury Report noted that institutional shareholders hold the majority of shares in listed companies, but emphasised that in many cases they hold them on behalf of individuals (eg as members of pension schemes or beneficiaries of insurance policies) and that there is a significant degree of common interest between individual shareholders and institutional shareholders. In particular, both have the same interest in standards of financial reporting and corporate governance. Since the publication of the Cadbury Report there has in fact been a rapid growth of active private investors. This is attributed to a variety of factors, including the interest generated by the growth of the dot.com industry (despite its subsequent problems), technological development (the internet has made it much easier to buy and sell shares) and the substantial growth of journalism on personal financial issues. However, there is no doubt that institutional investors continue to represent a very significant proportion of shareholders and are in a unique position to develop closer links with the companies in which they invest. The Cadbury Report drew attention to three key issues critical to the development of a constructive relationship between companies and their shareholders:

- the need for institutional investors to encourage regular contact at senior executive level to exchange views and information on strategy, performance, board membership and quality of management;
- the need for institutional investors to make positive use of their voting rights and to exercise their votes on a regular basis; and
- the need for institutional investors to take a positive interest in the composition of boards and the appointment of non-executive directors with appropriate experience and independence.

These issues were developed further by the Hampel Committee in the *Combined Code*, although the Committee did not put forward any disclosure requirements on compliance with the principles or provisions relating to institutional shareholders. However, they indicated their hope that these shareholders would disclose to the relevant companies, and possibly also to the public as a whole, the extent to which they are following the principles and provisions set out in the *Combined Code*.

6.54 Institutional Shareholders' Committee (ISC)

The Institutional Shareholders' Committee (ISC) represents the interests and concerns of institutional investors, with representatives from the Association of British Insurers (ABI), the National Association of Pension Funds (NAPF), the Association of Investment Trust Companies (AITC) and the Investment Management

Association (IMA). The ISC has issued guidance to institutional investors covering issues such as communication with boards, the use of voting rights, board composition, directors' remuneration and takeover bids. On the subject of shareholder voting, the guidelines note that institutional investors should support boards by positive use of their voting rights unless they have good reason for doing otherwise. Where an institutional investor considers it appropriate to vote against a particular proposal, the issue should be raised with the board in good time to allow for the problem to be considered and, if possible, a satisfactory solution found. If a solution proves impossible, it may be appropriate for a spokesperson to attend the meeting to explain why the proposal is being opposed. A poll should also be demanded in such cases, to ensure that the vote is properly recorded.

6.55   Dialogue with Companies

The *Combined Code* includes just one supporting principle on dialogue with companies, which notes that institutional shareholders should apply the principles set out in *The Responsibilities of Institutional Shareholders and Agents: Statement of Principles* which is published by the ISC and should be reflected in fund manager contracts. There are no best practice provisions on this issue. The ISC guidance makes the following points in respect of communication between companies and institutional investors:

- Institutional investors have a strong obligation to exercise their influence in a responsible manner. Many already have effective channels of communication, either directly or through advisers, with the boards of companies in which they invest. The ISC recommends that such channels should be developed more widely to make the communication process more effective.
- Formal methods of communication with shareholders (for instance, through the annual reports and accounts, shareholder circulars, and the right to attend meetings) may not be sufficient to establish the type of relationship which enables directors and shareholders to obtain a deeper understanding of each other's aims and requirements.
- Institutional shareholders should take positive steps to encourage regular and systematic contact, at senior executive level on both sides, so that views and information can be exchanged on strategy, performance, board membership and quality of management. This will enable shareholders to get a better understanding of management's objectives, the problems it is facing and the quality of those involved, and also focus the attention of management on the expectations and requirements of shareholders.
- Institutional investors do not wish to become insiders and price-sensitive information should generally not be transmitted during such regular contact. In exceptional circumstances, if a board needs to consult its institutional investors on issues which are price sensitive, the investors will need to accept that their ability to deal in the company's shares will be suspended. Companies must not make such disclosures inadvertently or without the consent of the institutional investor.

6.56　Evaluation of Corporate Governance Disclosures

The *Combined Code* includes the following supporting principles on the evaluation of corporate governance disclosures:

- institutional shareholders should consider carefully the explanations given for departures from the *Combined Code* and make reasoned judgements in each case;
- if they do not accept the company's position, institutional shareholders should give an explanation to the company in writing and be prepared to enter into a dialogue;
- a box-ticking approach to assessing corporate governance should be avoided; and
- when assessing corporate governance, institutional shareholders should bear in mind the size and complexity of the company and the nature of the risks and challenges that it faces.

The preamble to the *Combined Code* also highlights the importance of the evaluation of governance being carried out with common sense in order to promote partnership and trust, based on mutual understanding. Governance should not be evaluated in a mechanistic way and departures from the *Combined Code* should not automatically be treated as breaches.

6.57　Shareholder Voting

The *Combined Code* includes the following supporting principles on shareholder voting:

- institutional shareholders should take steps to ensure that their voting intentions are being translated into practice;
- on request, institutional shareholders should make available to their clients information on the proportion of resolutions on which votes were cast and non-discretionary proxies lodged; and
- major shareholders should attend AGMs where appropriate and practicable, and companies and registrars should facilitate this.

The original *Combined Code* also included a provision that institutional shareholders should endeavour to eliminate unnecessary variations in the criteria which each applies to the corporate governance arrangements and performance of companies in which they invest, but this is not included in the revised Code.

6.58　*Voting Guidelines*

Voting guidelines are regularly issued to institutional investors by organisations such as NAPF, ABI and Pensions Investment Research Consultants (PIRC), based on their assessment of the key current issues. Issues that have received most focus in recent times include directors' remuneration (including incentive schemes, service contracts and notice periods), the independence of non-executive directors and issues relating to the external audit (eg the level of non-audit services provided by the auditors, connections between the directors and auditors, reappointment or changes in the appointment of auditors, and the role and constitution of the audit committee). Directors are well advised to keep track of the current issues being raised by these organisations so that they can be forewarned of any difficulties that are likely to arise at the AGM. Relevant information can usually be found on their websites and in some cases will be circulated to larger listed companies in advance of the publication date for their annual reports and accounts.

6.59 Shareholder Voting Working Group Proposals

In February 2004, the Shareholder Voting Working Group published a report by its chairman, Paul Myners, following a review of the problems in the current UK system for shareholder voting and in particular the fact that a number of votes seem to be regularly 'lost' in the system. The main problems appear to stem from the system under which institutional investors appoint proxies to exercise their votes in UK companies and in particular:

- a complex chain of accountability, with a variety of other parties (eg custodian, investment manager, voting agency, registrar) between the issuer and the beneficial owner of the shares;
- reliance on a process that is still manually intensive and largely paper-based, requiring data to be printed and re-entered at various points; and
- a lack of transparency in the system.

The most important step to counteract these issues is felt to be the introduction of electronic voting. The report also considers the conscious withholding of votes as a mechanism for communicating reservations about a resolution without going as far as voting against it, although this is only meaningful if the company is made aware of the reason for taking this action. The report recommends that companies should provide a 'vote withheld' box on proxy forms, in addition to the 'for' and 'against' options (which would continue to form the basis for the legal decision on whether or not the resolution is carried). A progress report on shareholder voting issues, published in March 2005, showed that 85 per cent of FTSE 100 companies and 50 per cent of FTSE 250 companies had voluntarily offered a 'vote withheld' box on proxy forms in 2004. The FRC has also amended the *Combined Code* in June 2006 to incorporate additional provisions on the withholding of votes and the use of proxies (see **6.47**) and is encouraging companies to adopt these for accounting periods beginning on or after 1 November 2006. Other proposals raised in the report include:

- under electronic voting, a confirmation facility should be available to enable voters to check that their instructions have been received and their votes recorded correctly;
- as a matter of best practice, registrars should report the late receipt of instructions or explain why they have not been accepted;
- stocklending is important in maintaining market liquidity but lenders should automatically recall the stock when contentious resolutions arise, to prevent the system being used for the express purpose of acquiring votes;

- institutional investors should explain to the beneficial owners how a voting decision has been reached, especially where the issue is contentious;
- a poll should be called on all resolutions at company meetings; and
- company law should be amended to give more rights to proxies and to provide for the independent scrutiny of a poll if requested by shareholders – these issues are currently included in the draft Company Law Reform Bill (see **6.49** above).

6.60   Reporting Requirements

> **At a Glance**
> * Listed companies are required to make an annual statement on the extent of their compliance with the *Combined Code.*
> * The annual report of a listed company must include a statement from the directors on going concern.
> * The directors of listed companies must report to shareholders that they have reviewed the effectiveness of the company's system of internal control.
> * A separate directors' remuneration report must be prepared by all quoted companies.
> * The *Combined Code* includes recommendations on certain other disclosures which should be given in the annual report.

6.61   Statement on Compliance with the Combined Code

The Financial Services Authority (FSA) *Listing Rules* currently require each listed company to include in its accounts:

- a narrative statement of how it has applied the principles (both main and supporting) set out in the *Combined Code*, with explanations to enable the shareholders to evaluate how the principles have been applied; and
- a statement on whether or not it has complied throughout the accounting period with the best practice provisions set out in the *Combined Code*, with details of, and the reasons for, any areas or periods of non-compliance.

The preamble to the *Combined Code* emphasises that neither the form nor the content of the compliance statement has been prescribed. Directors are therefore given a free hand to explain their corporate governance policies in the light of the principles set out in the Code and any special circumstances that may have led the directors to take a particular approach. Certain aspects of the company's statement on compliance with the Code must be reviewed by the auditors (see **1.96** above).

6.62   Going Concern

Under the *Combined Code*, the directors should report in the annual report and accounts that the business is a going concern, with supporting assumptions or qualifications as necessary. This disclosure was originally recommended by the Cadbury Code of Best Practice but did not become fully effective until additional guidance was issued to directors in the document 'Going concern and financial reporting – guidance for directors of listed companies' published in November 1994. In the case of listed companies, the inclusion of a statement on going concern is now a direct requirement of the FSA *Listing Rules* and the statement must also be reviewed by the auditors. The going concern reporting requirement is considered in more detail at **6.83** below.

6.63   Internal Control

Under the *Combined Code*, the directors should conduct an annual review (as a minimum) of the effectiveness of the company's (or group's) system of internal control and report to shareholders that they have done so. The directors' statement on internal control must also be reviewed by the auditors. The directors' review should cover all aspects of internal control, rather than just internal financial control, but there is no longer a requirement for the directors to express an opinion on the effectiveness of the system. Guidance on reviewing internal control and reporting under the *Combined Code* was developed by a working party of the Institute of Chartered Accountants in England and Wales chaired by Nigel Turnbull. Their final report 'Internal Control – Guidance for directors on the *Combined Code*' (often referred to as the Turnbull Report) was published in September 1999 and is attached as an appendix to the *Combined Code*. Following a review of the recommendations, an updated version entitled *Internal Control: Revised Guidance for Directors on the Combined Code* was published by the FRC in October 2005 and applies for accounting periods beginning on or after 1 January 2006. Reporting in respect of internal control is considered in more detail at **6.66** below.

6.64   Remuneration of Directors

The original *Combined Code* recommended that details of the company's remuneration policy and extensive information on the remuneration received by each individual director should be disclosed in a separate directors' remuneration report. For accounting periods ending on or after 31 December 2002, the *Directors' Remuneration Report Regulations 2002* (*SI 2002/1986*) have amended *CA 1985* to require all quoted companies to publish a detailed report on directors' remuneration and to require auditors to report on certain aspects of the disclosures. The requirements are considered in more detail in **23 REMUNERATION**, which includes a checklist of the individual disclosures that must be given. The present Code does not include any provisions on the disclosure of directors' remuneration as this is now considered to be adequately covered by company law requirements.

6.65   Other Disclosures

The *Combined Code* also recommends the disclosure of certain other information in the company's annual report. These are summarised in Schedule C to the *Combined Code* and a checklist is attached as an appendix to this chapter. The FRC consultation document on possible changes to the *Combined Code* (see **6.8** above) also proposes that, where a Code provision requires information to be 'made available', placing the details on the company's website should be sufficient to satisfy the requirement. In the updated version of the Code published in June 2006 (see **6.8**), the FRC has added to Schedule C to the Code the additional disclosure requirements set out the *Listing Rules*, so that companies can find details of all relevant requirements in one place.

6.66   Internal Control

At a Glance
* Under the *Combined Code*, directors should review the effectiveness of the company's system of internal control at least annually and report to shareholders that they have done so.
* Guidance on reviewing and reporting on internal control is set out in *Internal Control: Revised Guidance for Directors on the Combined Code* (often referred to as the 'Turnbull Report').
* The guidance is based on the principle that companies will adopt a risk-based approach to establishing a system of internal control, and that the review of its effectiveness will be part of the normal process of managing the business.
* An effective system of internal control should provide reasonable assurance against business failure, material error, fraud or breaches of regulations.
* There should be a defined process for the board's review of the effectiveness of the internal control system each year, to provide adequate support for the directors' statement in the annual report.
* The annual statement should summarise the process that the board has applied, including where relevant the role of the audit committee, and acknowledge the board's responsibility for the system of internal control.
* The *Combined Code* recommends that companies without an internal audit function should review annually whether there is a need to establish one.
* In the case of listed companies, the auditors are required to review the directors' statement on internal control and to report any concerns in their report on the annual accounts.

6.67   The Combined Code

Provision C.2.1 of the revised *Combined Code* requires the directors to conduct an annual review (as a minimum) of the effectiveness of the company's (or group's) system of internal control and to report to shareholders that they have done so. Their review should cover all aspects of internal control, rather than just internal financial control. However, there is no longer a requirement for them to express an opinion on the effectiveness of the system.

6.68 Turnbull Guidance

Guidance on reviewing internal control and reporting under the *Combined Code* was developed by a working party of the Institute of Chartered Accountants in England and Wales chaired by Nigel Turnbull. Their final report *Internal Control – Guidance for Directors on the Combined Code* (often referred to as the 'Turnbull Report') was published in September 1999. The FRC issued an updated version of the guidance in October 2005 and this applies for accounting periods beginning on or after 1 January 2006. The guidance clarifies what is expected of the board of a listed company in terms of:

- applying *Principle C.2* of the *Combined Code* (maintaining a sound system of internal control to safeguard the shareholders' investment and the company's assets); and
- determining the extent of their compliance with the best practice guidance set out in *provision C.2.1* of the *Combined Code* (review of the effectiveness of the system of internal control).

The original document also included detailed guidance on dealing with *provision C.3.5* in respect of internal audit but this has been removed from the revised guidance on the basis that, under the present *Combined Code*, the annual review of the need for an internal audit function (if the company does not already have one) is part of the remit of the audit committee (see **6.81** below).

6.69 Aims of the Working Party

The objective of the original Internal Control Working Party was to develop guidance that:

- can be tailored to the circumstances of an individual company;
- identifies sound business practice, by linking internal control with risk management and placing emphasis on the key controls that a company should maintain;
- provides meaningful high level information and avoids extensive disclosure that does not add to a user's understanding; and
- will remain relevant and be capable of evolving with the business environment.

This approach is in line with the Preamble to the *Combined Code*, which emphasises that it is not the intention to prescribe the form or content of the various reporting statements required by the Code, but rather that companies should be free to explain their governance policies in the light of the principles set out in the Code and in the context of any special circumstances specific to the company. Following a formal review during 2005, the FRC reported the review group's conclusion that the guidance had helped to improve internal control in UK listed companies and that only limited changes were required to bring it up to date. In particular, the following changes were subsequently incorporated into the revised version of the guidance document:

- boards should review their application of the guidance on a continuing basis;

- boards should not be required to make a statement in the annual report and accounts on the effectiveness of the company's internal control system, but they should confirm that necessary action has been or is being taken to remedy any significant failings or weaknesses identified from the reviews of the effectiveness of the internal control system;
- boards should look on the internal control statement in the annual report and accounts as an opportunity to explain to shareholders how they manage risk; and
- in reaching their decisions on internal control issues, directors should apply the same standard of care as in the exercise of their other general duties as directors.

The review also concluded that there should be no extension of the external auditors' responsibilities in relation to the company's internal control statement.

6.70 Importance of Internal Control and Risk Management

Internal control is one of the main elements in the management of risk, along with the transfer of risk to third parties (eg through insurance arrangements), the sharing of risk (eg through participation in joint ventures) and contingency planning. The risks that any entity faces will inevitably change as the business develops and the environment in which it operates evolves. Companies must therefore regularly review and evaluate the risks to which they are exposed. The aim will usually be to manage and control business risk rather than to attempt to eliminate it completely. The Turnbull guidance is based on the principle that companies will adopt a risk-based approach to establishing of a system of internal control and to the regular review of its effectiveness. The review of the effectiveness of the internal control system should therefore be part of the normal process of managing the business rather than a specific exercise carried out only in order to comply with the recommendations of the *Combined Code.*

6.71 Group Perspective

The guidance notes specify that references to a company should be taken, where relevant, to refer to a group. The directors of a parent company are therefore responsible for reviewing the effectiveness of internal control from the perspective of the group as a whole and for reporting to the shareholders on this. Where the board's report does not cover any joint ventures or associates of the group, this fact should be disclosed.

6.72 Responsibility for the System of Internal Control

The detailed work involved in establishing, operating and monitoring a system of internal control should be carried out by individuals with the necessary skills, technical knowledge, objectivity and understanding of the business, its objectives, the industries and markets in which it operates and the risks that it faces. The detailed work will usually be delegated by the board to management and all employees are likely to have some responsibility for internal control as part of their accountability for achieving objectives. However, the board as a whole retains ultimately responsibility for the company's system of internal control. It must therefore set appropriate policies on internal control and satisfy itself on a regular basis that the system is functioning well in practice and that it is effective in managing the risks that the business faces.

6.73   Factors to Consider

A system of internal control can never provide absolute protection against business failure, material error, fraud or breaches of regulations, but it should be able to provide reasonable assurance against these problems. In determining policies on internal control and assessing what constitutes a good system of internal control in the particular circumstances of the company, the board should consider:

- the nature and extent of the risks that the company faces;
- the extent and categories of risk that it regards as acceptable for the company to bear;
- the likelihood of the risks crystallising;
- the company's ability to reduce the incidence, and impact on the business, of risks that do crystallise; and
- the costs and benefits of operating relevant controls.

The limitations on any system of internal control include human fallibility, management override of controls and the risk of unforeseen events and circumstances arising.

6.74   Definition of Internal Control

A system of internal control is defined in the guidance as encompassing the policies, processes, tasks, behaviours and other aspects of the company that, taken together:

- facilitate its effective and efficient operation by enabling it to respond appropriately to significant risks (including business, operational, financial and compliance risks);
- help to ensure the quality of internal and external reporting; and
- help to ensure compliance with applicable laws and regulations.

They include policies and processes to safeguard company assets from loss, fraud or inappropriate use, identify and manage liabilities, maintain proper records and generate information that is timely, relevant and reliable.

6.75   Elements of a Sound System of Internal Control

A sound system of internal control should reflect the company's control environment (see **6.76** below) and organisational structure, and should include:

- control activities;

- information and communication processes; and
- processes for monitoring the continuing effectiveness of the system.

The internal control system should be embedded in the company's operations and should form part of its culture. It must be capable of responding promptly to new risks as the business develops and should include procedures for reporting immediately to management when significant control weaknesses or failures are identified. The information provided to management might include regular reports on progress against the company's business objectives (eg by using agreed performance indicators) together with information on issues such as customer satisfaction and employee attitudes.

6.76   Control Environment

A company's control environment is usually considered to include:

- a commitment by directors, management and employees to competence, integrity and a climate of trust (eg leadership by example, development of an appropriate culture within the business);
- the communication to all managers and employees of agreed standards of behaviour and control consciousness, which support the business objectives and risk management and internal control systems (eg written codes of conduct, formal disciplinary procedures, formal procedures for the appraisal of performance);
- clear organisational structures, which help to ensure that authority, responsibility and accountability are clearly defined and that decisions and actions are taken by the appropriate individuals;
- clear communication to employees of what is expected of them, and of their freedom to act (eg in respect of customer relations, service levels, health and safety issues, environmental matters, financial and other reporting issues);
- allocation of sufficient time and resources to risk management and internal control; and
- provision of relevant training on risk and control issues, so that management and employees develop the necessary knowledge, skills and tools to support achievement of the company's objectives and the effective management of risk.

6.77   Reviewing the Effectiveness of Internal Control

The board may delegate to the audit committee or other board committees certain aspects of the review of the effectiveness of the system of internal control (for instance, those aspects that are particularly relevant to their activities), but the board as a whole should form its own view on the adequacy of the review after due and careful enquiry. In other words, it will not be sufficient for the audit committee alone to review the effectiveness of the system of internal control. The audit committee should report formally to the board, who should then take a collective decision on the adequacy of the review. The updated version of the Turnbull guidance emphasises that, in reaching their decisions on internal control issues, directors should apply the same standard of care as in the exercise of their other general duties as directors.

The precise role of the audit committee will vary between companies and will depend on factors such as the size, style and composition of the board and the nature of the principal risks that the business faces. The audit committee will usually consider financial controls, but may also be asked by the board to act as the focal point for reviews of the wider aspects of internal control. These issues should be considered by the board when the terms of reference for the audit committee are established and reviewed (see **1.137** AUDIT COMMITTEES).

6.78   *The Process of the Review*

There should be a defined process for the board's review of the effectiveness of the company's system of internal control, to provide adequate support for the statement made by the directors in the annual report. The board should take account of all the information available to it up to the date on which the annual report is approved and signed.

The board should not rely solely on the monitoring processes that form part of the business operations, but should receive and review regular reports on internal control, and should also carry out a specific annual exercise to support the statement in the annual report and to ensure that all significant aspects of internal control have been covered. The guidance suggests the following approach:

- there should be an agreed procedure for the board (or relevant committee) to receive and review regular reports on internal control from management or others qualified to prepare them (eg internal audit);
- the reports should provide a balanced assessment of the areas covered and should identify both the significant risks involved and the effectiveness of the internal control system in managing those risks;
- the board (or relevant committee) should:
  - consider the key risks and assess how they have been identified, evaluated and managed,
  - assess the effectiveness of the internal control system in managing those risks, taking into account the impact of any weaknesses or control failings that have been reported,
  - consider whether appropriate and prompt action is being taken to remedy weaknesses or failings,
  - consider whether the findings indicate a need for more extensive monitoring of the internal control system;
- the board should carry out a specific annual assessment to support the statement in the annual report – this assessment should cover:
  - changes since the last review in the nature and extent of significant risks,
  - the company's ability to respond effectively to change (both internal and external),
  - the scope and quality of the ongoing monitoring of the system of internal control, including where appropriate the internal audit function,

○ the extent and frequency of reporting to the board (or relevant committee) of the results of the monitoring process, enabling it to build up a cumulative assessment of the state of internal control and the effectiveness with which risk is managed,

○ the incidence of major control weaknesses or failings identified during the period and the extent to which they have resulted in unforeseen outcomes or contingencies that have had, could have had, or may in future have, a material impact on results,

○ the effectiveness of the year-end financial reporting process.

Where significant control weaknesses or failings are identified, the board should determine how these arose and should reassess the effectiveness of management's ongoing processes for designing, operating and monitoring the system of internal control.

6.79   The Annual Statement on Internal Control

The board's annual statement on internal control should provide users of the annual report and accounts with meaningful, high-level information. Particular care should be taken to ensure that the statement does not give a misleading impression. As a minimum, the board should disclose where applicable that:

- there is an ongoing process for identifying, evaluating and managing key risks;
- this has been in place for the year under review and up to the date of approval of the annual report and accounts; and
- this process accords with the relevant guidance on internal control and is regularly reviewed by the board.

The statement should also summarise the process that the board has applied in reviewing the effectiveness of the system of internal control, including where relevant the role of the audit committee or other committees, and confirm that necessary actions have been (or are being) taken to remedy any significant weaknesses or failings identified in the review. The board may also want to provide additional information to help users of the report and accounts understand the company's risk management processes and the internal control system.

If the board is unable to make any of these disclosures, this fact should be stated and the board should explain what action is being taken to rectify the situation. Where relevant, the board will also have to disclose that they have failed to conduct a review of the effectiveness of the company's system of internal control, or that they have not reviewed the need for an internal audit function if they do not already have one (see **6.81** below). Where weaknesses in internal control have resulted in significant problems which have been disclosed in the annual accounts, the board should describe the processes that it has applied to deal with the internal control aspects of the problems.

6.80   Acknowledgement of Responsibility

The statement should also include an acknowledgement that the board is responsible for the company's system of internal control and for reviewing its effectiveness, together with an explanation that such a system can only provide reasonable and not absolute assurance against material misstatement or loss.

6.81　Review of the Need for an Internal Audit Function

Provision C.3.5 of the *Combined Code* requires the audit committees of companies without an internal audit function to review annually whether there is a need to establish one. The original Code includes a more general recommendation on the need for a regular review of this issue and it was therefore covered in the first version of the Turnbull guidance. This also recommended consideration on an annual basis and suggested that the following factors might be taken into account:

- whether the board has other means of obtaining sufficient and objective assurance on the effectiveness of the company's system on internal control;
- whether there are any trends or current factors in the company's internal environment, markets or other aspects of its external environment that have increased, or are expected to increase, the risks faced by the company – for instance:
  - changes in organisational structure, reporting processes or information systems,
  - changes in key risks as a result of changes in products or services, entry into new markets, or changes in regulatory requirements,
  - adverse trends apparent from the monitoring of the internal control system, or
  - increased incidence of unexpected or unacceptable results.

Where there is an internal audit function, the board should review its remit, authority, resources and scope of work, also on an annual basis. The role of an internal audit function is considered in more detail at **1.111 INTERNAL AUDIT**.

6.82　Reporting by Auditors

Where directors are required by the FSA *Listing Rules* to include in the annual report and accounts a statement on compliance with the *Combined Code* and on going concern, the *Listing Rules* also require these statements to be reviewed by the auditors. In the case of the compliance statement, the auditors' review is only required to cover certain aspects, but these specifically include the directors' statement on internal control. Under the latest professional guidance, the auditors are required to explain this reporting requirement in the section of their report that sets out their responsibilities as auditors. If the auditors are not satisfied with the adequacy of the corporate governance disclosures and cannot resolve the problems through discussion with the directors, they are required to report their concerns in a separate paragraph as part of their opinion on the financial statements, but this will not constitute a qualification of their report on the annual accounts.

6.83 Additional Company Reporting under SEC Requirements

Non-US companies registered with the US Securities and Exchange Commission (SEC) are required by the *Sarbanes-Oxley Act 2002* and related SEC rules to comply with certain additional reporting requirements in respect of internal control. *Section 404(a)* of the Act requires judgements on the effectiveness of material controls over financial reporting to be made in the context of a suitable framework and the SEC has confirmed that the Turnbull Guidance is considered to provide such a framework. In December 2004, the FRC issued an additional guide for companies registered with the SEC on how the Turnbull guidance should be used in complying with the US reporting requirement. The guide can be downloaded from the FRC website at http://www.frc.org.uk/ corporate.

6.84 Going Concern

At a Glance

* Under the *Combined Code*, directors should report in the annual report and accounts that the business is a going concern, with supporting assumptions or qualifications where necessary.
* The document *Going Concern and Financial Reporting – Guidance for Directors of Listed Companies* sets out the principles that directors should follow in relation to a going concern.
* Going concern is defined as the hypothesis that the entity is to continue in operational existence for the foreseeable future.
* The term 'foreseeable future' is not defined, but additional disclosures should be given when the period considered by the directors is less than twelve months from the date on which the accounts are approved.
* When preparing the company's annual accounts, the directors should give formal consideration to the issue of going concern and should assess in particular whether there are any factors which cast doubt on the entity's ability to continue in operational existence.
* Factors to take into account include forecasts and budgets, cash flow and borrowing requirements, contingent liabilities, market developments and financial adaptability.
* The guidance includes illustrative wording for the directors' statement, depending on the company's circumstances.
* The directors' consideration of going concern should normally be updated when the interim report is formally reviewed by the board.

6.85 The Combined Code

The *Combined Code* recommends that the directors should report in the annual report and accounts that the business is a going concern, with supporting assumptions or qualifications as necessary. This disclosure was originally recommended by the *Cadbury Code of Best Practice* but did not become fully effective until additional guidance was issued to directors in the document *Going Concern and Financial Reporting – Guidance for Directors of Listed Companies,* published in November 1994. In the case of listed companies, the inclusion of a statement on going concern is now a direct requirement of the FSA *Listing Rules* and the statement must also be reviewed by the auditors.

6.86　Joint Working Group Guidance

The guidance set out in *Going Concern and Financial Reporting – Guidance for Directors of Listed Companies* was developed by a Joint Working Group ('JWG') and sets out the governance principles that directors should adopt in relation to going concern. The guidance is addressed primarily to listed companies, but it was hoped that the clarification of the concept of going concern would be of general benefit to all entities and would assist directors in meeting their obligations under *CA 1985*. The document has three main objectives:

- to explain the significance of going concern in relation to financial statements;
- to describe the procedures that an explicit statement on going concern may entail; and
- to recommend appropriate disclosures.

The directors of all companies are required to refer to the use of the going concern basis in the statement of their responsibilities in relation to the accounts (see **11.62 FINANCIAL REPORTING**).

6.87　Definition of Going Concern

FRS 18 *Accounting Policies* describes the going concern basis as the hypothesis that the entity is to continue in operational existence for the foreseeable future and notes that this basis will usually provide the most relevant information to users of the accounts (for information on obtaining copies see the Accounting Standards Board website at www.frc.org.uk/asb). The standard therefore requires directors to assess, when preparing accounts, whether there are any significant doubts about the entity's ability to continue as a going concern and requires the financial statements to be prepared on a going concern basis unless:

- the entity is being liquidated or has ceased trading;
- the directors intend to liquidate the entity or to cease trading; or
- the directors have no realistic alternative but to liquidate the entity or to cease trading.

In these circumstances the entity should prepare its financial statements on a different basis. The JWG guidance (see **6.86** above) emphasises that it will not usually be appropriate to adopt the going concern basis for the accounts if there is any intention or need to enter into a scheme of arrangement with the company's creditors, make an application for an administration order or put the company into administrative receivership or liquidation. However, the restructuring of a business, even on a major scale, is a relatively common practice these days and will not usually result in the going concern basis being an inappropriate basis for the preparation of the accounts.

6.88   Significance of the Going Concern Assumption

The use of the going concern basis for the preparation of accounts is of particular significance when assessing the appropriateness of the accounting policies adopted. Some items in the accounts would be unchanged if the entity was not considered to be a going concern, but others might be significantly affected by this. For instance, fixed assets are usually included in the accounts at cost or valuation, depreciated to reflect the proportion of the life of the asset that has been used up in the business to date. The balance sheet value of the assets essentially represents their value to the business as a going concern, but will not necessarily represent the amount that would be realised if the individual assets had to be sold. If an entity is being liquidated or has ceased trading, a different accounting treatment may therefore need to be adopted for these assets. Other costs and liabilities may also need to be included in the accounts – for instance, penalties for the breach or early termination of contracts such as leases and other rental agreements.

6.89   Foreseeable Future

Neither accounting standards nor *CA 1985* explain the term 'foreseeable future' and the JWG guidance (see **6.86** above) emphasises that it is not appropriate to set a minimum period to which the directors should pay particular attention when considering the issue of going concern. However, the guidance does make the following points:

- any consideration involving the foreseeable future involves making judgements about future events which are inherently uncertain;
- in general terms, the degree of uncertainty increases significantly the further into the future the consideration is taken;
- the judgement is valid only at the point in time at which it is made;
- in assessing going concern, the directors should take into account all the information of which they are aware at the time the judgement is made, and their statement on going concern should be made on the basis of the information that is known to them at the date on which they approve the financial statements.

Although no minimum review period is specified, the guidance does note that where the period considered by the directors has been limited, for example, to a period of less than one year from the date of approval of the financial statements, the directors should consider whether additional disclosure should be made to explain the assumptions underlying the adoption of the going concern basis. FRS 18 (see **6.87** above) now requires additional disclosures to be given in the accounts in these circumstances. Additional disclosures in the annual report and accounts are also required when the directors identify factors which cast doubt on the presumption that the company will continue in operational existence for the foreseeable future.

6.90 Procedures to be Carried Out

In order to be able to make the required statement on going concern each year, the directors will need to:

- give formal consideration to going concern each year;
- consider whether there are any factors which cast doubt on the entity's ability to continue in operational existence for the foreseeable future, and whether the going concern basis is appropriate for the financial statements;
- consider whether additional disclosure is necessary in the annual report and accounts;
- make a statement on going concern in the annual report and accounts.

It is not acceptable for directors to simply assume that the business can be treated as a going concern without carrying out any procedures to confirm this. However, many of the recommended procedures will already be carried out by directors and senior management for other purposes, such as the development of strategic plans, the preparation of budgets and forecasts, and risk management. All that may be necessary in these circumstances is to summarise the procedures already carried out, and the issues arising from them, and for the directors to consider whether any additional procedures need to be undertaken to cover any aspects that have not already been adequately dealt with. In practice, much of the work will be done prior to the approval of the accounts, but because the directors are required to make their assessment on the basis of the information known to them on the date on which the accounts are approved, they will need to update their review to take account of any changes in circumstances that have arisen since the detailed procedures were carried out.

6.91 Factors to Consider

Many different factors will be relevant to a consideration of whether a company or group is a going concern, and these will vary with the nature of the business under review. Some factors will be within the control of the directors – others may be external and therefore outside their direct control. Similar factors will need to be taken into account in preparing budgets and forecasts and the directors should therefore have a good understanding of the most significant issues for their company. The JWG guidance (see **6.86** above) sets out examples of major areas that directors will usually need to consider in order to identify whether they are, or could become, significant in relation to going concern – the list is not intended to be exhaustive but rather to indicate the sort of factors that should be taken into account when considering going concern. The areas identified in the guidance are:

- forecasts and budgets;
- borrowing requirements;
- liability management;
- contingent liabilities;
- products and markets;
- financial risk management;
- financial adaptability.

An appendix to the document sets out detailed procedures that may be followed, although the guidance emphasises that these should not be regarded as checklists, partly because not all of the procedures will be relevant in every case, and also because procedures which are not listed may be appropriate in certain circumstances. Each of the main areas is considered briefly below.

Additional guidance can be found in the UK and Ireland version of International Standard on Auditing 570 (ISA 570) *Going Concern* (copies can be downloaded from the APB website at www.frc.org.uk/apb/publications). Although this was developed to assist auditors when considering going concern, some of the issues raised may also be of help to directors when making their annual assessment of whether the company is a going concern. In particular the standard sets out illustrative summaries of financial, operational and other indicators of potential going concern difficulties.

6.92 Forecasts and Budgets

Budgets and cashflow forecasts should be prepared for at least the period to the next balance sheet date. Alternatively, they may be prepared on a rolling basis covering a twelve-month period. Subsequent periods will usually be covered by medium or long-term plans, giving a general indication of how the business is expected to perform. Budgets and forecasts will usually be supported by a detailed summary of the underlying assumptions and the directors will usually need to confirm that these are reasonable. Directors may also wish to carry out sensitivity analyses on the figures, particularly where the timing of cash receipts may be uncertain or the level of activity may vary significantly. Other factors that may need to be considered include:

- whether the budgets and forecasts need to be updated for changes in the assumptions or actual results to date;
- the interaction between assumptions;
- whether the budgets and forecasts provide adequately for rising costs;
- whether the budgets and forecasts take appropriate account of seasonal fluctuations;
- the accuracy of budgets and forecasts in previous years – it may be appropriate to document and analyse significant variances and consider whether these are likely to arise again in the current year.

6.93 Borrowing Requirements

The facilities available to the company should be reviewed and compared in detail to cashflow forecasts for at least the period to the next balance sheet date. It will often be appropriate to carry out sensitivity analyses on the critical assumptions when making this comparison, to identify whether facilities would be adequate even in a worst case scenario or whether covenants would be likely to be breached in these circumstances. The directors should seek to ensure that there are no anticipated shortfalls in facilities against requirements, no arrears of interest and no other breaches of covenants. There may be mitigating factors which would enable the directors to cope with any potential problems, for instance where they have scope to alter the amount or timing of significant cashflows. Any potential deficits, arrears or breaches that cannot be covered should be discussed with the company's bankers at an early stage to determine any action that needs to be taken and to prevent problems crystallising if possible. The onus is on the directors to be satisfied that appropriate and committed financing arrangements are in place.

6.94 Liability Management

The directors should ensure that the company's financial plans indicate appropriate matching of cash outflows with cash inflows. It is particularly important to ensure that cash outflows include all known liabilities, such as loan repayments, payments of tax and VAT, and any commitments which may be off-balance sheet (eg certain leasing commitments, or forward exchange contracts). It may also be appropriate to consider whether the company is particularly dependent on individual suppliers, and the impact that a failure in supply might have on the company's ability to meet its cash outflows.

6.95 Contingent Liabilities

The directors should review the company's exposure to contingent liabilities, including:

- liabilities experienced in the past and which might recur, such as legal proceedings, guarantees and warranties, and product liability claims not covered by insurance; and
- new contingencies that may arise in the future, such as environmental clean-up costs or future decommissioning costs.

6.96 Products and Markets

The directors should consider the size and strength of the market, the company's market share, and whether the market may change as a result of economic, political or other factors. In more complex businesses, this will usually need to be done by major product line. Depending on the nature of the business, this review may also need to take into account technical research and development, to confirm that this is adequate and can be maintained at an appropriate level for the foreseeable future. Other factors that may need to be considered include:

- product quality and expected life;
- the adequacy of the company's marketing strategy;
- the adequacy of the company's costing system, and in particular whether costs are updated on a regular basis;
- the customer mix, and in particular whether the business is dependent on a small number of significant customers – if so, the risk of losing one or more of them and the likelihood of finding alternative sales markets may also need to be assessed;

- the level of dependence on inter-group trading and the financial implications of this.

6.97   Financial Risk Management

Directors should identify which financial risks are most significant for their company and their current approach to managing these. For instance, financial risks might include exposure to fixed price contracts or to significant fluctuations in foreign currency exchange rates. Sensitivity analyses may need to be performed if assumptions on factors such as interest rates and foreign currency are particularly critical to the cashflow forecasts.

6.98   Other Factors

The JWG guidance (see **6.86** above) identifies a number of other factors that may need to be taken into account in particular circumstances, including:

- recurring operating losses or fluctuating profits and losses;
- the impact of dividend arrears;
- non-compliance with statutory capital requirements;
- the impact of labour difficulties;
- the potential impact of the loss of key management and staff, and the likelihood of finding suitable replacements quickly;
- the potential impact of the loss of a key patent or franchise;
- the impact of long-overdue debtors, or high stock levels;
- the impact of potential losses on long-term contracts;
- the potential impact of the company's fixed asset replacement policy (for instance, if funds are not available to replace assets regularly, there is the potential for increased maintenance costs, higher levels of down-time or quality control problems).

6.99   Financial Adaptability

Financial adaptability is the ability of the company to take effective action to alter the amounts and timings of cashflows to respond to unexpected needs or opportunities. Financial adaptability can help to mitigate any of the factors discussed above in relation to going concern. Consideration of financial adaptability might include reviewing:

- the ability to dispose of assets or postpone the replacement of assets, or to finance assets from other sources (eg leasing rather than outright purchase);
- the potential for obtaining new sources of finance;
- the possibility of extending or renewing loans, or restructuring debt;
- the possibility of raising additional share capital.

6.100 Going Concern Review

The checklist in Appendix 2 at the end of this chapter summarises the main steps that directors should take when carrying out an annual review of going concern. The checklist should not be regarded as comprehensive – other steps may need to be taken, depending on the specific circumstances of the company.

6.101 Overall Assessment and Conclusion

Once they have carried out all the individual procedures that they consider appropriate, the directors should determine the likely outcome by considering the range of potential outcomes and the probability of their occurrence and taking into account the implications of any interaction between the various factors. In practice, this will usually be evidenced by the board:

- considering a paper summarising the going concern position of the company;
- discussing the implications of the issues; and
- reaching a formal conclusion on going concern.

If the directors become aware of any factors that cast doubt on the ability of the entity to continue in operational existence for the foreseeable future, they will need to carry out additional detailed investigations to determine the extent of the problem and to decide how the company can best respond to it. They will also usually need to make additional disclosure in the annual report and accounts.

6.102 Making the Formal Statement

Having carried out appropriate procedures, the directors should be able to reach one of three possible conclusions:

- there is a reasonable expectation that the company will continue in operational existence for the foreseeable future, and the going concern basis is therefore appropriate for the financial statements;
- there are factors that cast doubt on the ability of the company to continue in operational existence for the foreseeable future, but the directors consider that it is still appropriate to use the going concern basis in preparing the financial statements; or
- it is unlikely that the company will continue in operational existence for the foreseeable future and it may therefore not be appropriate to use the going concern basis in preparing the financial statements.

The JWG guidance (see **6.86** above) sets out recommendations on disclosure in each of these circumstances.

6.103 *Going Concern Presumption Appropriate*

Where the directors conclude that there are no indications to suggest that the company will be unable to continue in operational existence for the foreseeable future, and that the going concern presumption is therefore an appropriate basis for the preparation of the accounts, the JWG guidance (see **6.86** above) suggests the following basic disclosure:

> 'After making enquiries, the directors have a reasonable expectation that the company has adequate resources to continue in operational existence for the foreseeable future. For this reason, they continue to adopt the going concern basis in preparing the accounts.'

The implication of this recommendation is that details of the 'supporting assumptions or qualifications as necessary' specifically required by the *Combined Code* only need to be given where there are some doubts or uncertainties over the continuation of the business. A number of companies have gone beyond the basic disclosure suggested in the guidance, and have given details of the steps that the directors have taken in reaching their conclusions, along the following lines:

> 'The directors have reviewed the company's budget for 200X and outline plans for the following two years. After taking into account the cash flow implications of the plans, including proposed capital expenditure and reorganisation costs, and after comparing these to the company's committed borrowing facilities, the directors are satisfied that it is appropriate to prepare the accounts on a going concern basis.'

6.104 *Going Concern Basis Used Despite Certain Doubts*

If there are some doubts or uncertainties over the appropriateness of the going concern basis for the accounts, the directors should explain the circumstances by giving details of:

- the factors that give rise to the problems (including any external factors that are beyond their control); and
- the action being taken to deal with the problem.

The JWG guidance (see **6.86** above) sets out the following example of a situation where the company has breached loan covenants and is in the process of renegotiating borrowing facilities as a result:

> 'The company is in breach of certain loan covenants at its balance sheet date and so the company's bankers could recall their loans at any time. The directors continue to be involved in negotiations with the company's bankers and as yet no demands for repayments have been received. The negotiations are at an early stage and, although the directors are optimistic about the outcome, it is as yet too early to make predications with any certainty. In the light of the actions described ... the directors consider it appropriate to adopt the going concern basis in preparing the accounts.'

6.105 *Going Concern Basis Not Appropriate*

Where the directors conclude that the company is unlikely to continue in operational existence for the foreseeable future, they will need to prepare accounts on an alternative basis, such as a break-up basis. This situation is expected to arise only rarely in practice, but in these circumstances the directors will have to state that, in their opinion, the company is no longer a going concern. They will usually need to take legal advice on the wording of such a statement. The fact that the company is not considered to be a going concern does not necessarily mean that it is insolvent, but the directors will need to give appropriate consideration to this and in particular to the wrongful trading provisions of the *Insolvency Act 1986*.

6.106 *Location of the Directors' Statement*

The JWG guidance (see **6.86** above) suggests that the directors' statement on going concern should be given in the Operating and Financial Review ('OFR') (see **11.89** ASB REPORTING STATEMENT 'OPERATING AND FINANCIAL REVIEW'), as the detailed discussion and analysis given in this review will usually help to put the going concern statement into context.

In practice, many companies present the going concern statement as part of a separate section of the annual report and accounts dealing with corporate governance issues rather than as part of the OFR. The accounts themselves may also need to refer to the use of the going concern basis in the note on accounting policies, especially if there are doubts or uncertainties over the going concern presumption. In these circumstances, it will usually be necessary to cross-reference the directors' statement to the details given in the accounts.

6.107 Application of the Guidance to Groups

In the case of a group, the JWG guidance (see **6.86** above) notes that the directors of the parent company should make a going concern statement in relation to both the parent company and the group as a whole. However, the statement in respect of the group should not be taken as implying that each of the individual companies within the group is considered to be a going concern.

6.108 Interim Reporting

Going concern will not usually be considered in the same level of detail in the context of an interim report as in the case of the annual report and accounts. However, the JWG guidance (see **6.86** above) notes that at the time that the interim report is approved, the directors should review their previous work on going concern and see whether any of the significant factors identified at that time have changed in the intervening period to such an extent as to affect the appropriateness of the going concern presumption. More information on the preparation of interim reports is given at **11.112** INTERIM REPORTS.

Appendix 1

Useful Websites on Corporate Governance Issues

Financial Reporting Council	www.frc.org.uk
Financial Services Authority	www.fsa.gov.uk
Institute of Directors	www.iod.com
Institute of Chartered Secretaries and Administrators	www.icsa.org.uk
Institute of Chartered Accountants in England and Wales	www.icaew.co.uk
Auditing Practices Board	www.frc.org.uk/apb

Appendix 2

Checklist – Combined Code Reporting Requirements

In addition to the overall statement on compliance (see **6.61** above), the *Combined Code* requires the following specific disclosures to be given in the annual report:

☐ A statement on how the board operates, including a high level statement on which types of decision are taken by the board and which are delegated to management [A.1.1]

☐ The names of the chairman, deputy chairman (where relevant), chief executive and senior independent director [A.1.2]

☐ The names of chairmen and members of the main board committees (ie audit, nomination and remuneration) [A.1.2]

☐ The number of meetings of the board and its main committees, and details of individual attendance by directors [A.1.2]

☐ The names of the non-executive directors whom the board considers to be independent [A.3.1]

☐ The reasons for considering a director to be independent if there are relationships or circumstances that might be deemed to affect this [A.3.1]

☐ The other significant commitments of the chairman and any changes to them during the year [A.4.3]

☐ A description of the work of the nomination committee, in a separate section of the report, including:

• the process used in respect of board appointments;
• an explanation if neither external consultancy nor open advertising has been used in the appointment of a chairman or non-executive director

[A.4.6]

☐ How performance evaluation of the board, its committees and the individual directors has been conducted [A.6.1]

☐ A description of the work of the remuneration committee as required by the *Directors' Remuneration Report Regulations 2002* (*SI 2002/1986*)

- ☐ Where an executive director serves as a non-executive elsewhere, whether or not the director will retain the relevant earnings and, if so, what the remuneration is [B.1.4]

- ☐ An explanation of the directors' responsibilities for preparing the accounts and a statement on the reporting responsibilities of the auditors [C.1.1]

- ☐ A statement from the directors that the business is a going concern, with supporting assumptions or qualifications as necessary [C.1.2]

- ☐ A report that the board has conducted a review of the effectiveness of the company's (or group's) system of internal control [C.2.1]

- ☐ A description of the work of the audit committee, in a separate section of the report [C.3.3]

- ☐ Where relevant, the reasons for the absence of an internal audit function [C.3.5]

- ☐ Where relevant, a statement from the audit committee explaining its recommendation on the appointment, reappointment or removal of the external auditor and the reasons why the board has taken a different position [C.3.6] (NB this should also be included in the papers sent out to shareholders on the appointment or reappointment of an external auditor)

- ☐ If the external auditor provides non-audit services, an explanation of how auditor independence and objectivity is safeguarded [C.3.7]

In addition, the following information is required to be made publicly available (eg by inclusion on the company's website):

- ☐ The terms of reference of the nomination committee [A.4.1]

- ☐ The terms of reference of the remuneration committee [B.2.1]

- ☐ The terms of reference of the audit committee [C.3.3]

- ☐ Where remuneration consultants are appointed, a statement on whether they have any other connection with the company [B.2.1]

The *Combined Code* also requires the following information to be made available:

- ☐ The terms and conditions of appointment of non-executive directors should be made available for inspection by any person at the company's registered office during normal business hours, for 15 minutes prior to the AGM and during the AGM [A.4.4]

☐ The papers sent out to shareholders in respect of a resolution to elect or re-elect a director should include:

- sufficient biographical details and any other relevant information to enable shareholders to make an informed decision [A.7.1]
- why the board considers that an individual should be elected as a non-executive director [A.7.2]
- in the case of re-election, confirmation from the chairman that, following formal performance evaluation, the individual continues to make an effective contribution and to demonstrate commitment to the role, including time for board and committee meetings and any other duties [A.7.2]

Checklist – Internal Control

This checklist summarises the issues that directors may need to consider in relation to internal control and is based on the ICAEW guidance document *Internal Control – Guidance for Directors on the Combined Code*. The checklist should not be regarded as comprehensive – directors may need to consider other issues, depending on the specific circumstances of the company.

☐ Does the company have clear business objectives and have these been communicated to all management and staff?

☐ Do the directors and senior management demonstrate an appropriate commitment to competence, integrity and the development of a climate of trust?

☐ Does the board adopt a professional approach to financial reporting?

☐ Has the company developed agreed standards of behaviour to support business objectives and risk management?

☐ Has it communicated these standards to all management and staff, for instance by means of:

- written codes of conduct;
- formal appraisal procedures;
- formal disciplinary procedures;
- performance reward schemes?

☐ Does the company have a clear organisational structure, with clearly defined lines of authority, responsibility and accountability?

☐ Are decisions and actions throughout the company properly co-ordinated?

- ☐ Does the organisational structure ensure that decisions are taken at an appropriate level and by appropriate individuals?

- ☐ Are sufficient time and resources allocated to risk management and internal control?

- ☐ Are management and staff provided with relevant training on business risk and internal control issues?

- ☐ Has the company developed a formal analysis of key risks, covering:
  - operational risk (both internal and external);
  - financial risk;
  - compliance risk;
  - other risks?

- ☐ Is business risk assessed on an ongoing basis and is the analysis of key risks regularly updated to take account of new developments, both within the business and externally?

- ☐ Have clear policies and strategies been developed to deal with significant risks identified in the assessment?

- ☐ Does management have a clear understanding of the level of risk that is regarded as acceptable to the board?

- ☐ Have appropriate communication channels been put into place to enable individuals to report suspected fraud, breaches of law or regulations, or other irregularities?

- ☐ Does the board receive regular reports on progress against business objectives and the related risk factors – for instance:
  - performance reports;
  - relevant performance indicators;
  - customer service levels;
  - quality control;
  - customer satisfaction;
  - employee attitudes?

- ☐ Does the board, or an appropriate committee, receive and review regular reports on internal control and:
  - consider how the key risks have been identified, evaluated and managed;
  - assess the effectiveness of the internal control system in managing those risks;
  - consider whether the company's financial and other information systems capture relevant, reliable and up-to-date information;
  - consider whether the company's financial and other information systems deliver appropriate information to the right individuals at the right time?

☐ Has the potential impact of identified internal control weaknesses or failures been properly established and considered?

☐ Has prompt and effective action been taken to deal with any internal control weaknesses or failures that have been identified?

☐ Are there appropriate procedures to confirm that agreed action is actually taken in practice?

☐ Has the board carried out a specific annual assessment to support the internal control statement in the annual report (see **6.77–6.79** above)?

☐ If the company has an internal audit function, has the board (or an appropriate committee) reviewed its remit, authority, resources and scope of work?

☐ If the company does not have an internal audit function, has the need to establish one been formally considered?

Checklist – Going Concern

This checklist summarises some of the issues that directors may need to consider when assessing whether the company is a going concern. Not every item will be relevant to every company. Similarly, the checklist should not be regarded as comprehensive – other factors may need to be taken into account, depending on the specific circumstances of the company.

A   Financial indicators of potential going concern difficulties

☐ Is the company incurring recurrent operating losses?

☐ Is the company experiencing fluctuating profits and losses?

☐ Is the company having difficulty in paying its debts (including tax, VAT and any off-balance sheet commitments) as they fall due?

☐ Are there any indications that the company's suppliers are withdrawing or reducing the terms of trade credit offered?

☐ Is the company experiencing significant liquidity or cashflow problems?

☐ Does the company have an excess of liabilities over assets?

☐ Does the company have net current liabilities?

☐ Has the company defaulted on the terms of existing loan covenants or breached the terms of existing loan agreements?

☐ Does the cashflow forecast indicate that the company will require additional borrowing facilities that have not yet been agreed?

☐ Is the company experiencing difficulty in meeting the interest cost on borrowings?

☐ Is a major restructuring of debt required?

☐ Does the company have a major debt repayment falling due without adequate facilities to cover this?

☐ Have major cashflow problems developed since the balance sheet date?

☐ Have significant losses arisen since the balance sheet date?

☐ Has the company been forced to sell substantial fixed assets without replacement?

☐ Does the company have significant exposure to fluctuations in exchange rates?

☐ Does the company have significant exposure to losses arising on fixed price contracts?

B   Operational indicators of potential going concern difficulties

☐ Is the company having difficulty in adapting to fundamental changes in the market?

☐ Is the company having difficult in adapting to fundamental technological changes?

☐ Is the company heavily dependent on limited range of products or services in a depressed market?

☐ Have recent technical developments rendered a key product or service obsolete?

☐ Has the company lost key customers?

☐ Has the company lost key suppliers?

☐ Has the company been forced to reduce the level of its operations (eg as a result of new legislation, environmental issues etc)?

☐ Has the company lost key members of management or staff?

☐ Is the company experiencing difficulties in recruiting the appropriate calibre and number of staff?

☐ Is the company encountering problems with labour-related organisations (eg trade unions)?

☐ Is the company experiencing quality control problems?

☐ Is the company experiencing significant uninsured warranty or product liability claims?

☐ Has the company lost significant patents, licences or franchises?

☐ Is the company incurring increased maintenance costs and downtime as a result of an inability to fund the replacement of fixed assets?

C   Other indicators of potential going concern difficulties

☐ Is the company involved in major litigation, where an adverse judgement may threaten the continuation of the business?

☐ Has the company given significant guarantees that are likely to be called upon?

☐ Are significant commitments likely to arise from environmental issues or new legislation?

Checklist – Going Concern Review

This checklist summarises the main steps that directors should take when carrying out an annual review of going concern. The checklist should not be regarded as comprehensive – other steps may need to be taken, depending on the specific circumstances of the company.

☐ Review the company's budgeting process and consider whether the resulting budget is appropriate for going concern review purposes – for instance, does the budget represent the best estimate of the results for the review period or has it been prepared with additional objectives in mind (eg to set performance targets) which might result in it being over-optimistic?

☐ Review the assumptions made during the budgeting process – for instance, those on:

- general issues such as inflation, interest rates and the economy;
- individual items of income and expenditure;
- customer demand;
- the availability of supplies and labour;
- the availability of finance;
- the incidence of product and warranty claims;
- the outcome and impact of contingent liabilities and guarantees.

Are the assumptions:

- realistic?
- consistent with each other?
- still valid at the time of the going concern review?

☐ Review the impact on the budget of changes in critical assumptions.

☐ Review the company's cashflow forecast and consider:

- whether adequate financing is already available or whether additional facilities need to be negotiated;
- if the term of any of the facilities is due to end within the period reviewed, whether confirmation should be sought of the likely continuation of that facility;
- the impact of any changes in critical assumptions.

☐ Consider whether any other factors cast doubt on the company's ability to continue operations for the foreseeable future (see Going Concern Checklist above).

☐ Consider whether the going concern assumption is appropriate and whether any additional disclosures need to be given in the accounts.

☐ Prepare a memorandum on going concern for formal consideration by the main board.

☐ Prepare a statement on going concern for inclusion in the annual report (listed companies only).

Corporate Transactions

Corporate Transactions

7.1 Acquisitions

At a Glance

* An acquisition may involve the purchase of shares in another company or the purchase of a trade and related net assets – the tax and accounting implications require careful research in each case.
* Clear parameters should be defined for the type of business that is being sought and the level and form of consideration that can be offered.
* Professional advisers or business brokers may be able to help in identifying potential targets – initial contact may be made by the company or by advisers.
* Efforts should be made to identify potential deal breakers at an early stage.
* The advisers to the potential acquirer will usually be responsible for preparing a first draft of the acquisition agreement.
* Investigating accountants should be engaged to carry out detailed due diligence work and prepare a written report on the target company.
* The projected profitability of the target and its net asset value (after appropriate adjustments) will usually form the basis for valuing the target business.
* Cashflow, gearing, legal and tax issues will need to be taken into account in deciding the form of the purchase consideration.
* Part of the consideration may be deferred and based on actual profitability over a specified period of time.
* Management buy-outs and management buy-ins are special types of acquisition.
* Company law and accounting standards set out detailed requirements on accounting for acquisitions.

7.2 Growth by Acquisition

At some stage in the development of a business, it may be appropriate to consider the acquisition of another business in order to progress the strategic plan – for instance, to open up new geographical areas or markets, to provide easier access to products or services that are currently being obtained from external sources, or to help with a planned diversification. The acquisition of a business may involve the purchase of shares in another company or the purchase of the trade and net assets representing all, or possibly just part, of another business. Each will have different accounting and tax implications which must be carefully researched beforehand. In either case, it is important that any acquisition should have a clear strategic purpose and that alternative options, such as organic growth, investment in an associate or setting up a joint venture, are also considered. In the case of listed companies, the FSA *Listing Rules* specify detailed disclosures that must be made to shareholders where substantial acquisitions are proposed – these reporting requirements should also be taken into account when planning an acquisition.

See Appendix 2 to this chapter for a checklist summarising the main issues to be considered when planning an acquisition.

7.3 Potential Targets

If the acquisition of another business has been identified as the most appropriate way forward, the directors must define clear parameters for the type of business or activity that they are seeking. This will enable the search to be more clearly focused and help to prevent management time being wasted on aborted efforts. It is worth taking the time to prepare a short written profile for the acquisition, covering issues such as:

- type of business, or particular product or service sought;
- any specific requirements on geographical location or market coverage;
- size of business;
- any particular requirements for the new business to provide a good match with the existing one (eg particular culture or management ethos);
- the maximum price;
- the form of consideration that will be offered (eg cash, shares, loan stock or some combination of these).

There are a number of routes to the identification of potential targets. For instance, some may be identified from existing business contacts or through the relevant trade press. It is advisable to make early contact with the company's professional advisers to discuss the details of the proposals – for instance, to ensure that the legal, accounting and tax implications of both the proposed acquisition and the suggested form of consideration are clearly identified and understood by all those involved. Professional advisers may also be able to help with the identification of potential acquisition candidates, either from their own business contacts or through an acquisitions and disposals database if the firm provides this service. Business brokers also specialise in identifying potential candidates and carrying out acquisition searches. Advertising in appropriate newspapers and trade journals may also be considered. It is important to consider how well any candidates match the profile prepared by the directors, so that the emphasis continues to be on finding a deal to match the requirements and not just acquiring the best of what appears to be available.

7.4 Initial Contact

Any potential candidates identified should be subject to some initial research, either in house or through a professional adviser, to establish their likely suitability and compatibility with the existing business – this might make use of a company search, marketing literature, and press and trade comment. If (one or more) potential acquisition targets are identified, an initial approach will usually be made through telephone contact with the chairman or senior director (who, in a private company, could also be the major shareholder), or with the board of the parent company if the entity is already a subsidiary of another business. This may be done by the directors or through a professional adviser, if anonymity is considered important at this stage, or if it would be helpful to make use of their expertise.

7.5 Preliminary Discussion

If both parties agree to pursue the matter further, preliminary discussions should take place to confirm that the target company appears to match the requirements and to identify any potential problems, or where relevant additional benefits. At this stage, it is important to try to identify anything that may seriously disrupt the negotiations or make the target company unacceptable (for instance, unacceptable risks or contingent liabilities that could give rise to serious problems in the future) to prevent unnecessary time and expense on an aborted deal. Clearly there may be an issue over confidentiality whilst the process is still at an exploratory stage, but it will be essential to have access to projections of turnover, profits and cashflow in order to carry out an initial assessment of the viability of the business and its value. The target business will usually want to put a confidentiality agreement into place in respect of any significant information disclosed during the discussions and negotiations, to provide protection if the deal should be aborted. Depending on the size and nature of the businesses, consideration may need to be given to whether the proposed deal might infringe competition law. The acquirer should also assess the potential impact of the acquisition on its own accounts and tax position.

7.6 Preliminary Negotiations

If, after the preliminary discussions, the directors consider the acquisition worth pursuing, preliminary negotiations should cover a draft acquisition agreement, the likely price for the deal and the nature of the consideration to be offered. The acquirer will normally be responsible for preparing a first draft of the acquisition agreement and should involve legal experts in this part of the acquisition process. The target company will then ask its own legal experts to review the draft

Corporate Transactions

and any differences of opinion on the various clauses will need to be resolved by negotiation. Letters of intent will usually be put into place, or heads of agreement reached, at this stage, subject to a satisfactory detailed review of the business. If there are still detailed elements of information that the target company is unwilling to make available (eg customer analysis, details of confidential research projects) this should be made clear so that the acquirer can assess the potential implications for the transaction. It is important that any significant issues that could potentially disrupt the negotiations are identified and tackled at the earliest opportunity.

7.7 Due Diligence

The directors will usually wish to involve accountants at this stage in the proceedings to carry out detailed due diligence work and prepare a written report on the target business. The accountants will need reasonably full access to the target business in order to carry out this work. If confidentiality is still an issue (for instance, the target company does not want its employees to know about the potential acquisition), this can usually be built into the arrangements, although certain key individuals at the target company will need to be made aware of what is happening so that they can provide relevant information and explanations to the investigating accountants. The scope of the accountants' work should be set out in a comprehensive engagement letter to ensure that there is no misunderstanding on individual responsibilities or the nature and scope of the work, and a detailed timetable and fee for the work should be agreed.

7.8 Detailed Assessment of the Business

The detailed assessment of the business should cover:

- brief history of the business;
- actual performance:
  - sales record in the last three to five years,
  - key customers and contracts,
  - market and competition,
  - pricing issues,
  - current order position,
  - actual costs in the last three to five years,
  - key suppliers and contracts,
  - production capacity and efficiency (where relevant),
  - research and development activities,
  - accounting policies,
  - profitability in the last three to five years;
- projected performance:
  - projected turnover for the next three to five years,
  - projected profitability for the next three to five years,
  - assumptions used (including an assessment of their reasonableness),

- cashflow projections for the next three to five years,
- sensitivity analysis;
- balance sheet:
  - analysis of fixed assets and significant movements in recent years,
  - any refurbishment or capital investment needed,
  - values attributed to any stocks, work-in-progress and long-term contracts,
  - recoverability of debtors,
  - reasonableness of creditors and provisions for liabilities and charges;
- taxation issues (including VAT):
  - outstanding liabilities,
  - deferred tax liabilities,
  - tax losses carried forward,
  - any unusual or unacceptable practices;
- management and staff:
  - key individuals,
  - any significant service contracts,
  - management culture and style,
  - salary levels,
  - bonus or incentive schemes and benefits packages offered,
  - pension arrangements (including any significant funding issues),
  - health and safety and employment law issues;
- contingent liabilities:
  - warranty or product claims,
  - environmental issues,
  - any outstanding litigation.

The accountants should prepare a detailed written report on the results of their due diligence work and highlight any particular concerns that have come to light. These will usually need to be discussed further with the target company and elements of the acquisition agreement renegotiated where necessary. The structure of the deal may also be relevant here – the potential risks in acquiring a company are usually greater than in acquiring just the assets of a business because any contingent liabilities will transfer with the company. The acquirer's legal advisers will also need to be involved throughout this part of the process, especially where warranties or indemnities need to be included in the final acquisition agreement to give the acquirer adequate protection on issues that have been identified during the due diligence work.

7.9 Valuing the Transaction

The value that the acquirer will put on the business will usually be based primarily on the projected profitability of the target business and its net asset value, adjusted for issues such as:

- the impact on the projected profitability of the target of any changes in accounting policy that will need to be made for consistency with the acquiring company or group;

- the financial impact of any changes in respect of staff issues that will need to be made to achieve consistency with the acquiring company or group – this might include salary levels, bonus or incentive schemes, benefits packages and pension arrangements (the latter in particular can often have significant ramifications);
- any opportunities for potential cost reductions and economies of scale;
- any increased valuations not reflected in the balance sheet of the target business (eg properties with a market value in excess of their balance sheet carrying value); and
- the availability of any unutilised tax losses.

The return on investment that the acquirer expects to achieve will also be relevant.

7.10 Consideration

The purchase consideration will usually take the form of cash, shares or other capital instruments of the acquirer, or a combination of these. Issues to consider include:

- the potential impact on the cashflow projections of the acquirer;
- the potential impact on shareholdings in the acquirer;
- the legal aspects of any share issues (eg *Companies Act 1985* and *Financial Services and Markets Act 2000* requirements, and also any provisions in the company's articles of association);
- the impact on gearing; and
- any potential tax implications.

Part of the consideration may be deferred until a later date, and may be based on the actual profits achieved over a specified period of time – say, the next two years. This form of deal, usually referred to as an earn-out, is particularly appropriate if the success of the target is felt to be dependent on the ongoing involvement and enthusiasm of the existing management team, there are concerns that the projected profitability levels may be over-optimistic, the level of asset backing is low because of the nature of the business, or there are other potentially significant risks, such as the possibility of losing a major customer once the deal becomes known. If an earn-out element is included in the deal, the acquisition agreement should be very specific on how the earn-out element will be calculated and in particular on issues such as:

- how profit is defined for these purposes and which accounting policies will be followed in establishing it;
- the impact of any additional costs, or reduced costs, as a result of the acquisition (eg changes in pension costs, directors' remuneration etc);
- the impact of any inter-group arrangements.

It will also be important to ensure that the profitability of the acquired business can be separately identified throughout the period of the earn-out – any plans for fuller integration with the existing business may therefore have to be deferred until the earn-out period has elapsed.

7.11   After the Acquisition

Once the deal has been finalised, arrangements will need to be made to inform employees, customers, suppliers and any other interested parties – this needs careful planning to ensure that all aspects are handled efficiently and effectively, bearing in mind that any change can give rise to feelings of uncertainty. Steps will then need to be taken to bring policies, procedures and controls in the new business into line with those in the acquiring company or group. These might include:

- budgeting and forecasting requirements;
- cash management and treasury policy;
- authorisation limits and procedures;
- accounting and reporting requirements; and
- internal control.

The extent of the changes needed may vary depending on whether the acquired business is to continue operating as a separate unit (initially at least) or whether it is intended to be fully integrated with the existing business as soon as possible.

7.12   Management Buy-outs and Management Buy-ins

A management buy-out is a particular form of acquisition, where some or all of the directors and senior managers of a business form a new company to buy out all or part of the existing business – for instance, a particular subsidiary or division of a group. As with any other acquisition, a management buy-out can take the form of a purchase of assets or a purchase of shares, each of which has different tax implications. A management buy-in is a similar arrangement, except that the acquiring team do not come from within the business to be acquired.

7.13   Accounting for an Acquisition

Under UK accounting practice, accounting for the acquisition of a trade and related net assets is relatively straightforward, although the transaction may still give rise to purchased goodwill if the consideration paid exceeds the underlying value of the individual assets and liabilities (if any) acquired. The practical aspects of reflecting the acquisition of a company in the financial statements of the acquirer are covered in detail in FRS 2 *Accounting for Subsidiary Undertakings*, FRS 6 *Acquisitions and Mergers* and FRS 7 *Fair Values in Acquisition Accounting*. Unless an acquisition meets the stringent criteria for a merger (see **7.16–7.19** below), it will be accounted for using the acquisition method of accounting, so that the assets and liabilities of the new company are brought into the consolidated balance sheet of the acquirer at their fair value at the date of acquisition.

Any difference between the aggregate fair values of the assets and liabilities acquired and the fair value of the consideration given in exchange represents goodwill (which must be accounted for in accordance with FRS 10 *Goodwill and Intangible Assets*). The detailed issues covered in the accounting standards include:

- the date on which control passes;
- measuring fair values for each type of asset or liability;
- measuring the fair value of the acquisition cost;
- the amounts to be reflected in the group profit and loss account in the year of acquisition;
- a prohibition on making provision for future operating losses and reorganisation costs resulting from an acquisition; and
- accounting for piecemeal acquisitions (eg where an associate becomes a subsidiary).

Extensive disclosure requirements also apply. FRS 1 *Cash Flow Statements* specifies how an acquisition should be reflected in the cashflow statement.

For information on obtaining copies of the above accounting standards see the Accounting Standards Board ('ASB') website at www.frc.org.uk/asb.

Similar requirements apply in IAS accounts, although with a number of significant differences, including in particular:

- a prohibition on the use of merger accounting;
- more stringent requirements on the separate identification of intangible assets;
- a different accounting approach where an acquisition takes place in stages;
- a different approach to accounting for subsequent adjustments to fair values; and
- a prohibition on the regular amortisation of goodwill, with a requirement for it to be subject to an annual impairment review instead.

Changes to the current requirements under IASs are expected to be implemented for accounting periods beginning on or after 1 January 2007, following completion of Phase II of a major IASB project on business combinations (see **7.14** below).

7.14   ASB Proposals for Change

The ASB published FRED 36 *Business Combinations and Amendment to FRS 2 Accounting for Subsidiary Undertakings* in July 2005. This Exposure Draft forms part of a package of proposed new standards (FREDs 36 to 39) arising from completion of the IASB's project on accounting for business combinations and is based on the latest proposals issued by the IASB for the revision of IFRS 3 *Business Combinations* and IAS 27 *Consolidated and Separate Financial Statements*. If implemented, the proposals will make wide-ranging changes to UK accounting practice and, in particular, to the way in which group accounts are prepared. The publication of this package of Exposure Drafts could be regarded as a critical point in the ASB's convergence project (see **11.7** below), not only because of the potential impact of the changes on UK accounting but also because it is very clear that the ASB itself has serious reservations over the merit of introducing new standards based on the latest international proposals. The principal concern is that the proposals fail to recognise the need for financial reporting to focus on the requirements of the parent entity's shareholders. A number of the proposed changes are controversial, and many conflict with current UK company law requirements. The ASB highlights its concerns in the preface to FRED 36 and expresses the view that some of the changes would not represent an improvement in UK financial reporting.

Under the latest proposals:

- group accounts would be required to reflect the fair value of an acquired business rather than the cost of the acquisition in the group accounts, with goodwill arising to the extent that this is more (or less) than the fair value of the identifiable assets and liabilities acquired;
- there would be a significant change to the way in which minority interests (renamed 'non-controlling interests') are accounted for, in that any outside equity interest in a subsidiary would be treated as part of the overall ownership interest in the group and changes in the parent's ownership interest which do not result in a change in control would be recognised as changes in equity, with no gain or loss recognised in the profit and loss account;
- goodwill would be treated as equivalent to any other asset and would be recognised in full, regardless of the level of the interest acquired by the parent;
- once recognised, goodwill would be measured at cost less impairment losses rather being subject to regular amortisation;
- any negative goodwill would be applied initially to reduce any related positive goodwill to zero, with any remaining excess recognised as a gain on acquisition; and
- expenses relating to an acquisition would be recognised as an expense in the profit and loss account in the year of acquisition.

At the time of publication, the ASB put forward a number of options on the timing of adoption of these standards for respondents to consider. These could have resulted in full or partial implementation of the changes for accounting periods beginning on or after 1 January 2007. However, the ASB is currently in the process of a more fundamental reconsideration of its convergence programme (see **11.7** below) and so implementation of the above changes seems likely to be deferred until a later date.

For information on obtaining copies of FREDs 36 to 39, see the ASB website at www.frc.org.uk/asb.

7.15 Mergers

At a Glance
* Company law and accounting standards set out stringent criteria that must be met before an acquisition can be classified as a merger.

> * Merger accounting seems likely to be prohibited in the not too distant future.
> * Under merger accounting, the accounts of the new entity are prepared as if the combining parties had always operated as a single entity.
> * The company law provisions on merger relief are completely independent of those on merger accounting and can be applied where the parent adopts acquisition accounting.

7.16   Use of Merger Accounting

Under UK accounting practice, FRS 6 *Acquisitions and Mergers* sets out five criteria, all of which must be met for an acquisition to be classified as a merger. The objective of the standard is that merger accounting should only be used for business combinations that genuinely represent an equal partnership between two or more entities. The criteria are therefore stringent, and few business combinations are likely to meet them in practice. Where a business combination does meet the criteria, merger accounting must be used (ie merger accounting is a requirement, not an option, in these circumstances). The specific requirements set out in *Companies Act 1985* in respect of a merger must also be met. Special arrangements apply under the Act in the case of group reconstructions. The use of merger accounting is prohibited in IAS accounts, and is likely to be prohibited under UK accounting practice if the ASB's proposals to converge UK requirements with international standards proceed (see **7.14** above).

For information on obtaining copies of FRS 6 see the ASB website at www.frc.org.uk/asb.

7.17   Criteria for a Merger

A merger is defined in FRS 6 (see **7.16** above) as:

> 'A business combination that results in the creation of a new reporting entity formed from the combining parties, in which the shareholders of the combining entities come together in a partnership for the mutual sharing of the risks and benefits of the combined entity, and in which no party to the combination in substance obtains control over any other, or is otherwise seen to be dominant, whether by virtue of the proportion of its shareholders' rights in the combined entity, the influence of its directors or otherwise.'

A business combination that does not meet this definition is classified as an acquisition. Under the standard, the specific criteria for a merger are that:

- no party to the business combination must be portrayed as being the dominant party or being dominated by another party to the combination;
- all parties to the combination must be involved in establishing the management structure of the combined entity and must reach a genuine consensus on the appointment of individuals to the agreed management posts;

- the relative sizes of the combining entities are not so disparate that one party dominates the combined entity by virtue of its relative size – where one party to the combination is substantially larger than any other party, it must be assumed that the larger party can and will dominate the combined entity and in such circumstances, the combination cannot be classified as a merger;
- under the terms of the combination, and taking into account acquisitions of equity shares in the two years before the combination:
  ○ the consideration received by the equity shareholders of each party to the combination, in relation to their equity holding, comprises primarily equity shares in the combined entity, and
  ○ any non-equity consideration (or equity shares with substantially reduced voting or distribution rights) represents an immaterial proportion of the fair value of the consideration received by the equity shareholders of that party;
- no equity shareholders of the combining entities retain any material interest in the future performance of only part of the combined entity.

7.18 Merger Accounting

The principle of merger accounting is that the accounts of the newly combined entity are prepared as if the parties had always operated as a combined entity. The accounts of the combining parties are therefore aggregated (subject to adjustments to achieve consistent accounting policies) and, in particular, all the reserves of the combining parties are included as reserves in the accounts of the combined entity, regardless of whether they arose before or after the actual merger took place. The profit and loss account and cashflow statement of the group include the results and cashflows of the combined entities for the whole of the financial year in which the combination takes place and all comparative figures must be restated so that they are presented on the same basis as the figures for the current year.

7.19 Merger Relief

The *Companies Act 1985* provisions on merger relief operate completely independently of the provisions on merger accounting and the related requirements of FRS 6 (see **7.16** above). It is therefore possible for a parent company to take advantage of the provisions on merger relief, but to account for the new subsidiary using the acquisition method of accounting. Separate considerations apply in the case of group reconstructions. The merger relief provisions apply where a company (the acquiring company):

- has obtained a holding of at least 90 per cent of the equity share capital of another company under an arrangement; and
- the arrangement requires the acquiring company to allot equity shares; and
- the consideration for the shares allotted by the acquiring company is:
  ○ the issue or transfer of shares in the other company to the acquiring company, or
  ○ the cancellation of any such shares not already held by the acquiring company.

Corporate Transactions

If the equity share capital of the other company is divided into different classes of shares, the 90 per cent holding must be obtained for each class of equity shares before the relief is available. Where the conditions are met, any premium on the shares issued by the acquiring company is not transferred to the share premium account, as would normally be the case. There are two possible treatments in the accounts of the parent company in these circumstances:

- the parent company can record only the nominal value of the shares issued – in this case, the investment in the subsidiary (or the relevant part of it) will also be recorded at this amount, plus the fair value of any additional consideration; or
- the parent company can record the investment at fair value and record the related premium on the shares in a separate reserve, usually described as a 'merger reserve' – this should be shown within 'other reserves' on the balance sheet.

If the investment is recorded at nominal value, and acquisition accounting is adopted for the group accounts, a consolidation adjustment will be required to create the merger reserve and the appropriate amount of goodwill in the group balance sheet when the net assets of the subsidiary are brought in at fair value as at the date of acquisition. If the investment is recorded at fair value in the parent company's accounts, the normal consolidation process will suffice. The relief is also extended to shares (in this case, either equity or non-equity) issued by the acquiring company in return for non-equity shares in the other company, if this is provided for in the agreement giving rise to the original merger relief. Merger relief is not available in respect of non-equity shares issued by the acquiring company in return for equity shares in the other company. In the case of piecemeal acquisitions, merger relief is only available in respect of the shares issued under the arrangement that brings the shareholding to or above the 90 per cent threshold, but prior holdings should be taken into account in assessing whether the 90 per cent threshold has been reached.

7.20   Disposals

At a Glance
- * It is important to clarify the reason for the disposal, the nature of the disposal (eg net assets or shares), the preferred type of buyer and the target price.
- * Preliminary work should be undertaken to confirm the values of any substantial assets to be disposed of (eg properties, intellectual property) and to assess the potential effect of the disposal on wider business issues (eg employee share schemes, pension schemes).
- * Professional advisers should be consulted so that tax, legal and accounting issues can be considered in conjunction with economic and commercial ones.

* Appropriate action should be taken to make the business attractive to a potential buyer.
* The directors should agree formally on the level of detailed information that will be made available and on any restrictions that will be put in place.
* Consideration should be given to the ways of identifying potential acquirers.
* Detailed information should be made available to a potential acquirer within a reasonable timescale – the advance preparation work should help with this.
* The draft acquisition agreement should be reviewed by the company's professional advisers at an early stage so that potential obstacles can be identified.
* The acquirer will normally want to arrange for investigating accountants to carry out detailed due diligence work on the business to be acquired.
* Professional advisers have an important role in ensuring that warranties and indemnities are kept to a minimum.
* Accounting standards set out detailed requirements on accounting for disposals.

7.21   Reasons for a Disposal

There are various reasons why the directors might decide to dispose of a business unit, or part of the existing business. There will invariably be a strategic element to the decision – for instance, a wish to withdraw from a particular market or geographical location, or the need to generate cash to fund new developments in the business. As with an acquisition, it is important to have a clear understanding of why a particular part of the business should be sold and why this is the best time to make the sale. This is often something that will be raised by a prospective purchaser, so it is worth thinking the issues through carefully beforehand. Other points to consider include:

* whether the disposal should be for cash or shares (or a combination of the two) – for instance, if a principal reason for the disposal is the need for an injection of cash into the remaining business, consideration in the form of shares will not be acceptable unless these are readily saleable;
* whether the intention is to dispose of business assets, or a business unit such as an operating subsidiary;
* the type of buyer preferred – for instance, another business, an individual or a management buy-out or management buy-in team;
* the target price;
* the market value of any substantial assets included in the disposal (eg properties);
* any intellectual property to be included in the transaction and how its value will be assessed;

- the potential impact on any employee share schemes and pension arrangements within the business.

All shareholders potentially affected by the deal should be made aware of, and should agree to, the proposed disposal before proceeding further.

7.22   Planning the Disposal

The timing of a disposal will not always be within the direct control of the vendor business, but the tax implications in particular should always be discussed with the company's professional advisers at an early stage in the process, so that any important timing factors can be taken into account. There may also be good economic and commercial reasons to support disposal at a particular point in time (eg onerous changes about to be introduced by new legislation) and it is always helpful if recent figures give a positive impression of the business. It is useful to draw up a timetable for the disposal process, so that it can be properly managed and to identify a projected date by which everything should have been completed. Steps should be taken to make the business attractive to a potential buyer – for instance:

- continuing to take action to monitor and improve margins and profitability;
- eliminating any unnecessary costs and expenses;
- reviewing the appropriateness of accounting policies;
- paying particular attention to key figures on the balance sheet (eg the age profile of debtors);
- ensuring that tax matters (including VAT issues) are kept up to date; and
- wherever possible, ensuring that any outstanding litigation is resolved.

The company's legal advisers should also be told of the intended disposal and asked to advise on any relevant legal issues, including the impact on any ongoing contracts and agreements. It is also worth considering the acquisition from the perspective of potential acquirers and the information that they are likely to request. Any concerns that the directors might have about disclosure can therefore be considered in good time and decisions taken on any restrictions to be applied in commercially sensitive areas. Once agreement has been reached on the detailed information that can be made available to potential acquirers, clear and concise summaries should be prepared setting out the principal information that is likely to be requested, so that the company is in a position to respond promptly when such requests are actually received.

See Appendix 2 to this chapter for a checklist summarising the main issues to be considered when planning a disposal.

7.23   Identifying Potential Acquirers

A detailed sale memorandum should be prepared and consideration should be given to the identification of potential acquirers. A significant factor here is likely to be whether the business is willing to make the proposed disposal publicly known at this stage, or whether confidentiality is considered important. Potential acquirers might be identified through existing business contacts, acquisition database services offered by the company's professional advisers, specialised business brokers, or press and trade advertisements. Advertising the business as being available for sale is usually regarded as a last resort when other avenues have failed, but may be worth considering if it can be done without revealing the identity of the business. It is important to put a confidentiality agreement in place with each potential acquirer before disclosing any significant business information, to protect the business in the event of an aborted deal.

7.24   The Negotiation Process

Once contact has been established with a potential acquirer, detailed information requested by them should be made available within a reasonable timescale. The advance preparation work already carried out should help with this. The aim should generally be to provide the minimum amount of detail necessary to progress the discussions, but without appearing to be too reluctant to release information, which creates concern that the business has something to hide. Contact should be maintained with the professional advisers throughout the process and their advice obtained on any significant issues that develop. The negotiation process is usually driven by the potential acquirer, who will be responsible for preparing a first draft of the acquisition agreement. This should be made available to the professional advisers for review and any potential obstacles identified as soon as possible in the negotiation process. Once the negotiations have progressed to letters of intent, or heads of agreement, the potential acquirer will usually want to make arrangements for their investigating accountants to examine the business in detail. This will involve detailed reviews of the accounting and other business records and discussions with members of the management team. If confidentiality below the level of senior management is considered important, arrangements can be put into place to secure this. The issues likely to be covered in the accountants' detailed report are summarised in **7.9** above.

7.25   Finalising the Deal

The potential acquirer will wish to discuss any issues that come to light as a result of the due diligence work carried out by the investigating accountants (eg additional contingent liabilities that have been identified) and to agree amendments to the draft agreement, including where appropriate the incorporation of warranties and indemnities. The professional advisers have an important role to play here in ensuring that warranties and indemnities are kept to a minimum, especially where reasonably full disclosure has already been made during the course of the due diligence work.

7.26   Accounting for Disposals

Under UK accounting practice, the practical aspects of reflecting the disposal of a company in the financial statements of the vendor are covered in detail in FRS 2 *Accounting for Subsidiary Undertakings*. The detailed issues covered in the standard include:

- the date on which control passes;
- the amounts to be reflected in the group profit and loss account in the year of disposal;
- calculating the gain or loss on disposal; and
- accounting for piecemeal disposals (eg where a subsidiary becomes an associate).

Extensive disclosure requirements also apply. FRS 1 *Cash Flow Statements* specifies how a disposal should be reflected in the cashflow statement.

For information on obtaining copies of the above accounting standards see the Accounting Standards Board ('ASB') website at www.frc.org.uk/asb.

Similar requirements apply in IAS accounts, although there are differences, in particular in the manner in which the gain or loss on disposal is calculated.

Appendix 1

Useful Websites on Corporate Transactions

Institute of Directors	www.iod.com
Business Link	www.businesslink.gov.uk
Chartered Institute of Personnel and Development	www.cipd.co.uk
Financial Services Authority	www.fsa.org.uk
Accounting Standards Board	www.frc.org.uk/asb
International Accounting Standards Board	www.iasb.org

Corporate Transactions

Appendix 2

Planning an Acquisition

This checklist summarises the main issues to be considered when planning an acquisition. It should not be regarded as comprehensive – additional factors may need to be considered, depending on the specific circumstances of the company or the transaction.

Checklist

☐ Define parameters for the type of business to be acquired and the level and nature of the consideration that can be offered – for instance:

- type of business sought;
- size of business sought;
- any specific requirements on geographical location and/or market;
- any specific requirements to fit with the existing business (eg culture, management style);
- nature of acquisition (eg shares or net assets);
- maximum price;
- form of consideration to be offered.

☐ Discuss the legal, tax and accounting implications with professional advisers.

☐ Consider whether there are any significant issues in relation to the timing of the transaction.

☐ In the case of a listed company, consider whether formal notification to the FSA and to shareholders is likely to be required – if so, clarify the precise requirements and put arrangements in place to ensure these are dealt with at the appropriate time.

☐ Consider the options for identifying potential targets – for instance:

- business contacts;
- professional advisers;
- business brokers;
- advertising.

☐ As potential targets are identified, carry out or arrange initial research to check whether they match the company's requirements.

☐ Decide whether initial contact should be made by the directors or by a third party (eg professional advisers).

☐ Use the preliminary discussions to identify possible obstacles or problem areas at an early stage.

☐ Consider whether the proposed deal might infringe competition law.

☐ Request projected financial information from the target business (subject to any confidentiality agreements that they may want to put into place).

☐ Obtain broad agreement on a price range for the deal and on the nature of the consideration – for instance:

- shares, loan stock, cash – or a combination of these;
- whether any element of the consideration should be deferred and subject to an earn-out clause.

☐ Arrange for the professional advisers to prepare a draft acquisition agreement – any issues raised on this document by the professional advisers of the target business will need to be resolved through negotiation.

☐ Put in place letters of intent, or heads of agreement, subject to a satisfactory detailed review of the business.

☐ Engage investigating accountants to carry out detailed due diligence work and prepare a written report on the target business – the precise scope of this work should be set out in formal terms of engagement with the investigating accountants.

☐ Assess the potential implications of:

- issues arising from the due diligence work;
- any restrictions on the detailed information that has been made available; and
- any issues arising from the proposed structure of the deal.

☐ In the light of the above, and in conjunction with the professional advisers, finalise:

- the details of the acquisition agreement, paying particular attention to warranties and indemnities;
- the value of the deal;
- the nature and terms of the consideration.

☐ Agree on the arrangements for informing employees, customers, suppliers and other interested parties.

☐ Plan appropriate action to integrate the acquired business into the existing company or group.

Corporate Transactions

Planning a Disposal

The checklist below summarises the main issues to be considered when planning a disposal. It should not be regarded as comprehensive – additional factors may need to be considered, depending on the specific circumstances of the company or the transaction.

Checklist

☐ Define the reasons for the disposal, any specific requirements of a potential purchaser and the nature of the consideration sought – for instance:

- reason for disposal (eg withdrawal from a specific market/location, need to generate cash etc);
- nature of the disposal (eg shares or net assets);
- type of buyer preferred (company, individual, management buy-out/buy-in);
- target price;
- acceptable form(s) of consideration.

☐ Discuss the legal, tax and accounting implications with professional advisers.

☐ Consider whether there are any significant issues in relation to the timing of the transaction.

☐ In the case of a listed company, consider whether formal notification to the FSA and to shareholders is likely to be required – if so, clarify the precise requirements and put arrangements in place to ensure these are dealt with at the appropriate time.

☐ Consider the potential impact of the disposal on wider business issues (eg company pension fund, employee share schemes etc).

☐ Obtain market values for any substantial assets (eg properties) to be included in the disposal.

☐ Consider how the value of any intellectual property included in the disposal is to be assessed.

☐ Plan any necessary action to make the business attractive to a potential buyer – for instance:

- action to monitor/improve margins and profitability;
- action to monitor/improve the balance sheet (eg age profile of debtors, level of current liabilities);
- elimination of unnecessary costs and overheads;
- review of accounting policies.

☐ Confirm that tax and VAT matters are up to date, and endeavour to resolve any outstanding litigation or similar issues.

☐ Agree on the detailed information to be made available and any restrictions to be imposed, and decide whether confidentiality agreements are required.

☐ Prepare a detailed sale memorandum.

☐ Consider the options for identifying potential purchasers – for instance:

- business contacts;
- professional advisers;
- business brokers;
- advertising.

☐ Decide whether initial contact should be made by the directors or by a third party (eg professional advisers).

☐ Use the preliminary discussions to identify possible obstacles or problem areas at an early stage.

☐ Obtain broad agreement on a price range for the deal and on the nature of the consideration.

☐ Arrange for professional advisers to review the draft acquisition agreement prepared by the potential purchaser – any issues raised will need to be resolved through negotiation.

☐ Put in place letters of intent, or heads of agreement, subject to a satisfactory detailed review of the business.

☐ Establish the detailed arrangements for a due diligence review by the potential purchaser or by investigating accountants appointed by the purchaser.

☐ In conjunction with the professional advisers, finalise:

- the details of the acquisition agreement, paying particular attention to warranties and indemnities;
- the value of the deal;
- the nature and terms of the consideration.

☐ Agree on the arrangements for informing employees, customers, suppliers and other interested parties.

Directors' Duties

8 Directors' Duties

8.1 General Duties

> **At a Glance**
> * The general rules on the role and duties of a company director are set out in common law and complex case law.
> * As part of the current modernisation of company law, the Government is proposing to introduce a statutory statement of the general principles by which all directors are bound.
> * A company director has fiduciary duties to the company (as a separate legal entity) and to its members as a whole, in addition to various legal responsibilities that apply to anyone running a business.
> * A director must act in accordance with the company's constitution and in the way most likely to promote the success of the company for the benefit of the members as a whole.
> * A director may not delegate his/her powers and must maintain independence of judgement.
> * A director must exercise appropriate care, skill and diligence.
> * A director should not enter into a transaction involving a personal interest unless he/she has disclosed that interest as required by company law.
> * A director or former director must not use company property or information for his/her own benefit unless such use has been properly authorised.
> * A director or former director must not accept any benefit conferred by a third party unless acceptance has been properly authorised, or the benefit is necessarily incidental to the proper performance of his/her role as director.
> * A company is permitted to provide indemnity insurance for its directors.

8.2 Statutory Position

The general rules on the role and duties of a company director are laid out not in companies' legislation itself but in complex and often inaccessible case law developed over many years and also in common law. This can make it difficult for directors, especially those in smaller companies, to gain a good understanding of their overall responsibilities. The Steering Group responsible for the recent review of company law therefore proposed the introduction of a statutory statement of principles on directors' general duties. The Government White Paper *Modernising Company Law* issued in July 2002 confirmed the intention to adopt this approach and included a draft Schedule setting out the principles which directors will be expected to follow. The latest version is set out in the draft Company Law Reform Bill published in May 2006 (see **8.5** below). The Steering Group suggested that the statement of directors' duties should also be given on Form 288a so that each director acknowledged his/her understanding of the role when signing to confirm acceptance of the appointment. However, the Government concluded that this might give a false impression that it was a comprehensive statement of directors' responsibilities, and also noted that the duties will apply, regardless of whether the director signs an acknowledgement of them. The current proposal is that Companies House should instead send a general information leaflet to all new directors. It is envisaged that there will be at least two versions of the leaflet (for private and public companies respectively), and that these will summarise all the duties and responsibilities imposed on directors by companies legislation and insolvency law.

8.3 General Legal Responsibilities

A variety of legal responsibilities apply to the directors of a company in the same way as to anyone else involved in running a business (eg a partner or sole trader) – for instance, the duty to comply with law and regulations in respect of employment, health and safety, public liability, consumer protection, VAT, excise duties and other taxes.

8.4 Fiduciary Duty

The position of a company director is, however, very different to that of someone running a business in partnership or as a sole trader, in that he/she is in a position of trust and consequently has a fiduciary duty both to the company (as a separate legal entity) and to the members who have invested in the company. This is a wide-ranging responsibility, but the main elements may be summarised as follows:

- the directors must comply with the company constitution and use their powers under it for proper purposes;
- the directors must run the company for the benefit of the members as a whole;
- the directors must always act in the interest of the company as a whole, and not for the benefit of an individual shareholder or creditor;
- the directors should act fairly as between members;

- a director should not profit personally from his/her position within the company and should avoid any conflict of interest – where a potential conflict of interest arises, the director has a duty to declare his/her personal interest to the company; and
- a director has an obligation to perform his/her duties with reasonable skill and care and must maintain independence of judgement.

8.5 Proposed Statutory Duties

The recent company law review recommended that a statement of directors' duties should be incorporated into company law, the intention being to clarify the present position by making the details more accessible and understandable, rather than to make significant changes to current law and practice. The draft Company Law Reform Bill published in May 2006 includes clauses setting out the proposed general duties of directors under the following headings:

- the duty to act within his/her powers;
- the duty to promote the success of the company;
- the duty to exercise independent judgement;
- the duty to exercise reasonable care, skill and diligence;
- the duty to avoid conflicts of interest;
- the duty not to accept benefits from third parties; and
- the duty to declare any interest in a proposed transaction or arrangement.

These general duties will apply to all directors, and the following duties will continue to apply to former directors after they have left office:

- the duty to avoid conflicts of interest in relation to the exploitation of property, information or opportunities of which he/she became aware whilst a director; and
- the duty not to accept benefits from third parties in relation to things done or omitted during the time that he/she was a director.

The company law review had also recommended the inclusion of special duties that would come into effect when a director knew, or should know, that the company was likely to be unable to meet its debts as they fall due, or that there was no reasonable prospect of the company avoiding going into insolvent liquidation. The Government has concluded that this would be a very finely balanced judgement and that the fear of personal liability might lead to excessive caution. It does not, therefore, propose to incorporate any aspects of insolvency law into the statutory statement of directors' duties, although attention will be drawn to the requirements of insolvency law in the guidance document for new directors (see **8.2** above).

8.6 *Acting within Powers*

Directors have an obligation to act in accordance with the company's constitution and with decisions taken under that constitution, and must only exercise their powers for the purpose for which they are conferred.

8.7   *Promoting the Success of the Company*

A director must act in good faith, and in the way that he/she considers will be most likely to promote the success of the company for the benefit of its members as a whole. However, in fulfilling this overriding duty, a director must also have regard to:

- the likely long-term consequences of any decisions;
- the interests of the company's employees;
- the need to foster business relationships with suppliers, customers and others;
- the impact of the company's operations on the local community and the environment;
- the desirability of the company maintaining a reputation for high standards of business conduct; and
- the need to act fairly between members.

8.8   *Exercise of Independent Judgement*

A director must not delegate any of his/her powers unless authorised to do so by the company's constitution or by a decision taken under that constitution. Directors must also maintain their independence of judgement and should not commit themselves to act in accordance with the wishes of another party. However, this duty is not infringed by a director acting in accordance with an agreement entered into by the company that restricts the exercise of discretion by the directors or in a way authorised by the company's constitution.

8.9   *Care, Skill and Diligence*

A director must exercise the care, skill and diligence which would be exercised by a reasonably diligent person with both:

- the general knowledge, skill and experience that may reasonably be expected of a person carrying out the functions carried out by the director in relation to the company; and
- the general knowledge, skill and experience which he/she has.

A higher standard may therefore be expected of a finance director than of (say) a non-executive director, although the particular level of competence and experience of each individual will also be taken into account.

8.10   *Conflicts of Interest*

A director should not authorise, permit or arrange for the company to enter into a transaction in which he/she has a personal interest unless that interest has been disclosed in accordance with company law. For instance, the company's constitution may permit directors to have a personal interest in company transactions provided that the interest is disclosed to the other directors. Similarly, a director should not enter directly into a transaction with the company unless that interest has been appropriately disclosed. The proposals in the draft Company Law Reform Bill emphasise that the duty to avoid conflicts of interest applies in particular to the exploitation of any property, information or opportunities, regardless of whether or the company could take advantage of them (see **8.11** below), and that a conflict of interest includes a conflict of duties.

8.11   *Personal Use of Company Assets*

A director should not receive any personal benefit as a result of his/her position as a director of the company. A director or former director must therefore not use for his/her own benefit, or for the benefit of another party, any property or information of the company, or any opportunities of the company of which he/she became aware whilst performing the role of director, unless:

- in the case of a private company, that use has been proposed to and authorised by the board and nothing in the company's constitution invalidates that authorisation; or
- in the case of a public company, the constitution includes a provision enabling the board to authorise such use, and the use has been proposed to and authorised by the board in accordance with the constitution.

In this context, the board means the board of directors acting without the participation of the director concerned.

8.12   *Benefits from Third Parties*

The draft legislation also prohibits a director or former director from accepting any benefit conferred as a result of his/her being a director, or doing (or not doing) anything as director. However, the duty is not infringed if the acceptance of such a benefit could not reasonably be regarded as likely to give rise to a conflict of interest, including a conflict of duties.

8.13   Indemnity and Insurance for Directors

The requirements of the *Companies Act 1985* on the provision of indemnities and insurance for directors were changed by the *Companies (Audit, Investigations and Community Enterprise) Act 2004*. The new provisions came into effect on 6 April 2005. A company is now permitted under *sections 309A* and *309B* to indemnify directors against proceedings brought by third parties. No indemnity can be provided against liabilities of the director to the company or to any associated company. The indemnity can generally cover both legal costs and the financial costs of any adverse judgement, but not:

- the legal costs of an unsuccessful defence of criminal proceedings;
- fines imposed in criminal proceedings; or
- penalties imposed by regulatory bodies.

Companies who provide an indemnity under the new provisions must disclose this fact in the directors' report and shareholders have the right to inspect any indemnification agreement. A company is also permitted to pay a director's defence costs as they are incurred. The director remains liable for the payment of any damages that are awarded to the company and, if the defence is unsuccessful, will be required to repay any costs that have been met by the company, except in the case of third party actions where the company has agreed to indemnify the director as discussed above. Companies are also permitted by *section 309A* to purchase indemnity insurance for directors of the company or of an associated company.

8.14   More Specific Duties

At a Glance
* A director has a duty to give the company written notification of any interests that he/she holds in shares or debentures of the company or group, and of any changes in those interests.
* Directors and other employees must ensure that they do not infringe provisions on insider dealing when entering into transactions involving the company's shares and debentures.
* A director has an obligation to disclose to the other directors any personal interest in a contract, transaction or arrangement involving the company – this requirement extends to interests held by persons connected with the director.
* Directors have a duty to provide appropriate information and explanations to the auditors.
* Where a private company intends to act by means of a written resolution, the directors have a duty to arrange for a copy of the resolution to be sent to the auditors.
* Directors have a duty to keep proper accounting records and to prepare annual accounts for the company or group.
* Under insolvency law, a liquidator can apply to the court for a director or former director to contribute personally to the company's assets if he/she knew, or should have known, that there was no prospect of the company avoiding going into insolvent liquidation.
* Any person who is knowingly a party to a company carrying on business for any fraudulent purpose, including an intent to defraud creditors, is guilty of an offence.

8.15   Disclosure of Interests in Shares and Debentures

Under *section 324* of *CA 1985*, each director and shadow director has a duty to give written notification to the company of any interest that he/she holds in the shares or debentures of the company or group, and the company is obliged to record these in a register of directors' interests which must be available for public inspection (see **4.18 COMPANY SECRETARIAL**). The definition of 'interests' for this purpose is very wide and is specifically extended by *section 328* of *CA 1985* to include interests held by the director's spouse and children. All interests, and any subsequent changes, must be notified to the company within five days of the interest arising or changing. Failure to comply with the requirements can result in imprisonment, or a fine, or both. Directors must take particular care when dealing in the company's shares and debentures that they do not infringe the rules on insider dealing set out in the *Criminal Justice Act 1993*. Directors and employees of listed companies should also comply with the Model Code that forms part of the FSA *Listing Rules*, or with any more stringent requirements adopted by the company in relation to dealing in the company's listed securities.

8.16   Disclosure of Interests in Contracts

Under *section 317* of *CA 1985*, a director has an obligation to disclose at a meeting of the directors any interest (whether direct or indirect) that he/she has in a contract, transaction or arrangement entered into by the company, or which the company proposes to enter into. The disclosure requirement extends to the interests of a person connected with the director, including:

- the director's spouse and children (including stepchildren);
- a body corporate with which the director is associated; and
- a trustee (acting in that capacity) of any trust which includes amongst the beneficiaries:
  - the director,
  - the director's spouse, children or stepchildren,
  - any body corporate with which he is associated,
  - a partner (acting in that capacity) of the director or of any person connected with him, and
  - a Scottish firm in which the director, or a person connected with him, is a partner.

The requirement to disclose specifically includes any loans, quasi-loans and credit transactions between the company and the director (see **8.23–8.35** below). The director must make the disclosure at the first meeting at which the proposed contract, transaction or arrangement is discussed, or at the first meeting after the director, or a person connected with him, has acquired a disclosable interest in a contract, transaction or arrangement with the company. A shadow director is required to give written notice to the directors of a disclosable interest before the meeting at which disclosure would otherwise have been required. Directors are also permitted to give general notice that they are connected with a particular company or firm and are therefore regarded as interested in any contract, transaction or arrangement with that entity. Whether the director can participate in any discussion or vote on the contract, transaction or arrangement will depend on the detailed provisions in the company's articles of association. If a director fails to disclose a notifiable interest, he/she is liable to a fine and may be prevented from retaining any private profits earned as a result of that interest. The contract, transaction or arrangement may also become voidable by the company.

8.17 Duty to Assist Auditors

Section 389A of *CA 1985* grants the auditors a right of access at all times to the company's books, accounts and vouchers and entitles them to require from the directors, officers and employees of the company the information and explanations that they consider necessary in order to perform their duties as auditors. It is an offence for a director, officer or employee knowingly or recklessly to make a statement to the auditors, either orally or in writing, which conveys (or purports to convey) information or explanations which the auditors are entitled to require and which is misleading, false or deceptive. A person who commits such an offence is liable to imprisonment or a fine or both. It is also an offence to delay responding to the auditors' enquiries. Further details on the duty to assist the auditors are given at **1.55** above. For accounting periods beginning on or after 1 April 2005, directors have an additional duty to volunteer information to the auditors and the directors' report must include a confirmation that each director has made appropriate enquiries and that all information relevant to the audit has been made available to the auditors. This statement is also considered in more detail at **1.55** above.

8.18 Use of Written Resolutions

Private companies are permitted by *section 381A* of *CA 1985* to act by means of a written resolution rather than by a resolution of the company in general meeting or by a resolution of a meeting of any class of members of the company. Under *section 381B* of *CA 1985*, a director or secretary of the company who knows that it is proposed to seek agreement by means of a written resolution, and who knows the terms of the resolution, has a duty to arrange for a copy of the resolution to be sent to the auditors at or before the time that it is sent to the members for signature. The auditors also have the right to receive all communications relating to a written resolution that must be supplied to a member of the company under *Schedule 15A* to *CA 1985*. There are penalties for failure to comply although is it a defence for a director or secretary to demonstrate that it was not practicable to comply or that there were reasonable grounds to believe that the auditors had been informed of the proposed resolution. The Government White Paper *Modernising Company Law,* issued in July 2002, confirmed the intention to simplify the present procedures for written resolutions and the draft Company Law Reform Bill published in May 2006 reflects this change.

8.19   Financial Responsibilities

The duties of the directors in respect of the maintenance of accounting records and the preparation of an annual report and accounts (including the need to make a formal statement of their responsibilities in respect of the accounts) are considered in detail in **11 FINANCIAL REPORTING.**

8.20   Wrongful Trading

Section 214 of the *Insolvency Act 1986* deals with the issue of wrongful trading. Where a company goes into insolvent liquidation, this section enables the liquidator to apply to the court for a person who is, or has been, a director of the company to contribute personally to the company's assets if he/she knew, or ought to have concluded, before the winding up of the company commenced, that the company had no reasonable prospect of avoiding going into insolvent liquidation. The legislation makes no specific reference to trading whilst insolvent, and it may therefore be acceptable for a company that is technically insolvent to continue trading if the directors consider that there is a genuine prospect of the company avoiding insolvent liquidation by doing so. In considering this issue, the facts that a director is expected to know, the conclusions that he/she is expected to reach and the steps that he/she is expected to take are those that would be known, reached or taken by a reasonably diligent person with both the general knowledge, skill and experience that may reasonably be expected of a person fulfilling that function, and the general knowledge, skill and experience that the director in question actually has. Once again, therefore, a higher level of skill, care and experience will usually be expected of a director with specific responsibility for financial and accounting matters. A director will not be personally liable in this way if he/she can demonstrate that, on first realising that insolvent liquidation was unavoidable, they took every step to minimise the potential loss to the company's creditors. A director is therefore advised to ensure that the minutes of board meetings include an accurate record of any concerns that he/she expresses in respect of the company's solvency.

8.21   Fraudulent Trading

Under *section 458* of *CA 1985*, every person who is knowingly a party to a company carrying on business with the intent to defraud creditors or for any fraudulent purpose, regardless of whether the company is solvent or not, is liable to imprisonment, or a fine, or both. Fraudulent trading is also covered in *section 213* of the *Insolvency Act 1986*. In this case, a liquidator is able to apply to the court for a person who is, or has been, a director of the company to contribute personally to the company's assets if, in the opinion of the liquidator, the director was knowingly a party to carrying on the company's business with the intent to defraud creditors or for any fraudulent purpose. Intent to defraud can include the company incurring additional debts when the directors were aware that there was no realistic prospect of the existing creditors being paid.

8.22 Loans to Directors

> **At a Glance**
> * *CA 1985* generally prohibits a company from making a loan to a director of the company or its holding company, and also from guaranteeing or providing security for such a loan.
> * In the case of a relevant company (broadly a public company or any member of a group including a public company), the prohibition extends to certain other transactions and arrangements.
> * For these purposes, 'director' includes a shadow director and any person occupying the position of director, regardless of his/her title.
> * The provisions also extend to persons connected with a director.
> * There are a number of specific exceptions to the general rules, principally covering small or short-term transactions and those carried out in the ordinary course of business.
> * With minor exceptions, all loans, quasi-loans and credit transactions involving directors must be disclosed in the annual accounts, regardless of whether or not they are permitted under the legislation.
> * If the required disclosures are not given, the auditors must give the information in their audit report, so far as they are reasonably able to do so.
> * There is no specific requirement under *CA 1985* to disclose the legality of a transaction.
> * It can be helpful to set up standard procedures to identify any illegal and disclosable transactions each year, and to keep them to a minimum.
> * Loans and similar transactions involving other officers of the company must also be disclosed in the annual accounts.

8.23 General Prohibition on Loans to Directors

Section 330(2) of *CA 1985* generally prohibits any company from:

* making a loan to a director of the company;
* making a loan to a director of the company's holding company;
* guaranteeing a loan to a director of the company or to a director of the company's holding company; and
* providing any security in connection with a loan to a director of the company or to a director of the company's holding company.

This is intended to provide a safeguard against the directors abusing their position within the company and using company assets for their personal benefit. Loans, quasi-loans and credit transactions are specifically included in the duty to disclose that is imposed on every director by *section 317* of *CA 1985* (see **8.16** above).

8.24 Additional Prohibitions for Relevant Companies

A 'relevant company' is a public company, a subsidiary of a public company, a fellow subsidiary of a public company or the holding company of a public company. In the case of relevant companies, the general prohibition on loans to directors extends to certain other transactions and arrangements. A relevant company is therefore also prohibited from:

- making a quasi-loan to a director of the company or to a director of the company's holding company, or to a person connected with any such director;
- guaranteeing a loan or quasi-loan, or providing any security in connection with a loan or quasi-loan to:
  - a director of the company, or a person connected with such a director, or
  - a director of the company's holding company, or a person connected with such a director;
- entering into a credit transaction as creditor for, or guaranteeing or providing security for a credit transaction made by any other person for:
  - a director of the company, or a person connected with such a director, or
  - a director of the company's holding company, or a person connected with such a director.

8.25   Quasi-loans

A quasi-loan is a transaction between two parties (the creditor and the borrower), where the creditor pays or agrees to pay a sum on behalf of the borrower, or reimburses or agrees to reimburse expenditure incurred by the borrower, on the terms that the borrower or a person on his behalf will reimburse the creditor, or in circumstances which create a liability for the borrower or person on his behalf to reimburse the creditor. The following are examples of quasi-loans:

- the purchase of any goods or services through the company, where the company becomes liable to pay the supplier and is subsequently reimbursed by the director;
- personal use of a company credit card by the director, where the company settles the liability and the director subsequently reimburses the company;
- a season ticket loan, if the company buys the ticket on behalf of the director and the director makes subsequent repayments, either in cash or by deduction from his salary;
- any personal costs paid by the company and subsequently reimbursed by the director (eg travel costs for a spouse who accompanies the director on a business trip).

8.26   Credit Transactions

A credit transaction is a transaction under which one party (the creditor):

- supplies goods under a hire purchase agreement or a conditional sale agreement;
- sells land under a hire purchase agreement or a conditional sale agreement;
- leases or hires goods in return for periodical payments;
- leases or hires land in return for periodical payments;
- otherwise supplies goods or services on the understanding that payment is to be deferred; or
- otherwise disposes of land on the understanding that payment is to be deferred.

Directors' Duties

8.27   Directors and Connected Persons

For these purposes, a director includes a shadow director and any person occupying the position of director, regardless of his/her actual title. The following are to be treated as persons connected with a director:

- the director's spouse;
- a child or stepchild under the age of 18 (including an illegitimate child);
- a body corporate with which the director is associated, and where the director and his/her connected persons are:
  - interested in at least 20 per cent of the nominal value of the equity share capital, or
  - entitled to exercise, or control the exercise of, more than 20 per cent of the voting power at a general meeting;
- the trustee of any trust, where the beneficiaries include:
  - the director,
  - his/her spouse,
  - his/her child (as defined above),
  - a body corporate with which he/she is associated (as defined above);
- the trustee of any trust whose terms confer on the trustees a power that may be exercised for the benefit of those noted (a person acting as trustee under an employee share scheme or a pension scheme is specifically excluded);
- a partner of the director or of any person connected with the director;
- a Scottish firm in which the director, or any person connected with him/her, is a partner or which has as a partner another Scottish firm in which the director, or a person connected with him/her, is a partner.

A person who is a director of the same company in his/her own right is not treated as a connected person of another director, even if the above criteria are met.

8.28   Exceptions to the General Prohibition

There are a number of specific exceptions to the general prohibition on making, guaranteeing or securing loans and quasi-loans to, and credit transactions with, directors or persons connected with directors, the main ones being:

- short-term quasi-loans (*CA 1985, s 332*);
- inter-company loans or quasi-loans within the same group (*CA 1985, s 333*);
- loans of small amounts (*CA 1985, s 334*);
- minor transactions and transactions in the ordinary course of business (*CA 1985, s 335*);
- transactions at the behest of the holding company (*CA 1985, s 336*); and
- funding of expenditure incurred in the performance of duties as a director of the company (*CA 1985, s 337*).

Special rules also apply in the case of banks and money-lending companies.

8.29 Disclosure of Loans to Directors

With a small number of specific exceptions, all loans and quasi-loans to, and credit transactions with, directors are disclosable in the annual accounts under *section 232* of, and *Schedule 6* to, *CA 1985* regardless of whether or not they are permitted under the legislation. The disclosure requirements specifically include any related guarantees and securities and must cover all transactions involving anyone who was:

- a director of the company at any time during the financial year;
- a director of the company's holding company at any time during the financial year; or
- a person connected with any such a director.

Under *paragraph 19* of *Schedule 6* to *CA 1985*, the fact that a transaction may have originated before an individual became a director of the company (or before a company became a subsidiary) will not exempt it from disclosure if there was an amount outstanding under that transaction during the year. For example, if an employee receives a loan from the company at the beginning of the year and repays it when he is appointed as a director of the company later in the year, details of the loan will still be disclosable in the accounts for that year. Similar considerations apply when individuals become connected persons during the year. Under *section 237(4)* of *CA 1985*, if the disclosure requirements have not been complied with, the auditors must include the relevant details in their audit report, so far as they are reasonably able to do so.

8.30 Detailed Disclosures

The following details must generally be given for each individual loan, quasi-loan, credit transaction or related arrangement:

- a statement that the transaction or arrangement was made or existed during the year;
- the name of the director involved, or where relevant the name of the connected person involved and the name of the director with whom he/she is connected; and
- the principal terms of each transaction, arrangement or agreement.

In the case of a loan, or an arrangement or agreement relating to a loan, the following information must be given:

- the amount of the liability in respect of principal and interest at the beginning of the year and at the end of the year;
- the maximum amount of the liability in respect of principal and interest during the year;
- the amount of any interest due which has not been paid; and
- the amount of any provision arising from the failure, or expected failure, of the borrower to repay all or part of the loan or to pay all or part of the interest.

Directors' Duties

In the case of a guarantee or security, or an arrangement relating to a guarantee or security, the following information must be given:

- the amount of the company's liability under the guarantee or security at the beginning of the year and at the end of the year;
- the maximum amount for which the company may become liable; and
- any amount paid and any liability incurred by the company, or by its subsidiary, in fulfilling the guarantee or discharging the security – this includes any loss incurred as a result of the guarantee or security being enforced.

In the case of a quasi-loan or credit transaction, or an arrangement or agreement relating to a quasi-loan or credit transaction, the accounts must disclose the value of the transaction or arrangement, or the value of the transaction or arrangement to which the agreement relates. The original value of the quasi-loan or credit transaction consequently remains disclosable each year up to and including the year in which full settlement or reimbursement is made.

8.31   Exceptions to Disclosure Requirement

There is no requirement to disclose a transaction or arrangement which was not entered into during the year and did not exist at any time during the year (ie transactions entered into and settled in earlier years do not continue to be disclosable). Also, credit transactions and related guarantees, securities and arrangements are not disclosable if the aggregate of the values of each transaction or arrangement for that director and his/her connected persons, after allowing for any reduction of the liabilities, does not exceed £5,000. Therefore, if an individual director, together with any connected persons, does not have more than £5,000 outstanding in respect of credit transactions, the details do not have to be disclosed. There is no *de minimis* disclosure exemption in respect of loans and quasi-loans to directors and connected persons. For accounting periods beginning before 1 January 2005, there was no requirement to provide comparative information in respect of loans to directors. However, the provisions of the *Companies Act 1985* on the disclosure of comparatives were amended by the *Companies Act 1985 (Investment Companies and Accounting and Audit Amendment) Regulations 2005* (*SI 2005/2280*) and the detailed requirements on the disclosure of comparatives are now set out in FRS 28 *Corresponding Amounts.* Although most of the specific exemptions previously set out in the legislation were retained, the ASB took the view that comparative information on loans to directors and other officers was readily available and would be useful to users of the accounts. FRS 28 therefore requires comparatives to be disclosed for accounting periods beginning on or after 1 January 2005 and ending on or after 1 October 2005. Similar requirements apply under the current version of the FRSSE, which was also updated by FRS 28. For information on obtaining copies of FRS 28, see the ASB website at www.frc.org.uk/asb.

8.32   No Disclosure on Legality

There is no requirement under *CA 1985* for the accounts to disclose whether a particular transaction or arrangement between a director and the company is legal or not. There is similarly no requirement for the auditors to express an opinion on the legality of any items disclosed in their audit report as a result of *section 237(4)* of *CA 1985* – they are simply required to make good any deficiencies in the disclosures required by the Act.

8.33 Company Procedures

Companies may find it helpful to develop a standard form for completion each year which requires every director to give formal confirmation that he/she has not been involved in any illegal or disclosable transactions or arrangements with the company, or to provide the relevant information. Such a form could include a summary of the requirements of *CA 1985* to remind the director of the importance of these matters. Company procedures might also include detailed guidance in the form of a directors' code of conduct to ensure that disclosable transactions are kept to a minimum. For instance, clear rules on the way in which company credit cards are to be used and how any purchases through the company should be dealt with, may help to ensure that disclosable transactions do not arise (for example, if purchases through the company are paid for by the director when the order is raised, the transaction should not come within the definition of a quasi-loan).

8.34 Legality of Loans and Similar Transactions with Directors

This summary gives an outline of the legal requirements in respect of loans and similar transactions with directors. Reference should be made to the legislation for precise details.

	CA 1985 section	Relevant companies	Other private companies
Loan to director or to director of a holding company	330 334	Permitted only where the aggregate of all outstanding amounts is not more than £5,000	Permitted only where the aggregate of the relevant amounts is not more than £5,000
Guarantee or security for loan to director or to director of holding company	330	Not permitted	Not permitted
Quasi-loan to director or to director of holding company	330 332	Permitted only where the aggregate outstanding is not more than £5,000 and reimbursement is required within 2 months	Permitted
Loan or quasi-loan to person connected with a director or with a director of holding company	330	Not permitted	Permitted

	CA 1985 section	Relevant companies	Other private companies
Guarantee or security for quasi-loan to director or director of holding company	330	Not permitted	Permitted
Guarantee or security for quasi-loan to person connected with a director or with a director of holding company	330	Not permitted	Permitted
Credit transaction with director or director of holding company	330 335	Permitted only where the aggregate of the relevant amounts is not more than £10,000	Permitted
Credit transaction with person connected with a director or with a director of holding company	330 335	Permitted only where the aggregate of the relevant amounts is not more than £10,000	Permitted
Guarantee or security for credit transaction involving the relevant director or director of holding company	330 335	Permitted only where the aggregate of the relevant amounts is not more than £10,000	Permitted
Guarantee or security for credit transaction involving person connected with a director or director of a holding company	330 335	Permitted only where the aggregate of the relevant amounts is not more than £10,000	Permitted

8.35   Loans to Other Officers of the Company

A company must also disclose in its annual accounts details of loans and similar transactions involving other officers of the company. Once again, there are separate rules in respect of banks and money-lending companies. There are, however, no prohibitions on making loans to officers of the company, provided that the individuals are not also directors. The detailed disclosure requirements are set out in *Part III* of *Schedule 6* to *CA 1985.* All definitions are the same as those for loans to, and similar transactions with, directors. There is also a similar requirement for the auditors to give any missing disclosures in their audit report, so far as they are reasonably able to do so. Comparative information on loans to other officers is now also disclosable under FRS 28 *Corresponding Amounts* (see **8.31** above).

8.36   Other Transactions with Directors

> **At a Glance**
> * *CA 1985* requires the annual accounts to include details of any transaction or arrangement in which a director had a material interest, either directly or indirectly.

* The board must act in good faith in deciding whether or not an interest is material for disclosure purposes.
* FRS 8 *Related Party Disclosures* also includes guidance on when a transaction should be regarded as material.
* The required details must be given individually for each director and for each relevant transaction or arrangement in the current year.
* If the required disclosures are not given, the auditors must give the information in their audit report, so far as they are reasonably able to do so.
* *CA 1985* sets out a number of exceptions to the general disclosure requirements, principally in respect of transactions between group companies and those involving only small amounts.
* Additional information may need to be given in respect of some transactions with directors, under the disclosure requirements of FRS 8 *Related Party Disclosures.*

8.37   Disclosure of Transactions

In addition to the detailed disclosures required for loans to directors, *CA 1985* also requires disclosure in the annual accounts of any transaction or arrangement in which a director had a material interest, either directly or indirectly. For these purposes, a director is treated as being interested in any transaction between:

* the company and the director, or a person connected with him/her; or
* the company's holding company and the director, or a person connected with him/her.

Only those transactions in which a director has a material interest are disclosable in the accounts and the interpretation of what constitutes a material interest is one of the most difficult aspects of this legislation. Paragraph **8.16** above considers in more detail the duty of each director to disclose to the other directors any interest that he has in a contract, arrangement or agreement involving the company. A substantial property transaction between the company and a director may also require prior shareholder approval under *section 320* of *CA 1985.*

8.38   Materiality

Paragraph 17(2) of *Schedule 6* to *CA 1985* provides that an interest is not material for disclosure purposes if the board of directors of the company are of the opinion that it is not material. It is generally accepted that the board must act in good faith in reaching this decision, although the legislation makes no specific statement on this. In this context, the board is defined as 'the directors of the company preparing the accounts, or a majority of those directors, but excluding in either case the director whose interest it is'. Therefore, the director involved in the transaction may not take part in the board's decision on whether or not it is material for disclosure purposes. The *Companies Act 1985* makes no mention of recording the board's decision, but it is usually advisable for the board's discussion and decision to be formally minuted. Two approaches to the interpretation of 'material' have developed:

- *the relevant view* – a transaction is material if knowledge of it might influence the decisions taken by the shareholders or users of the accounts, or be of specific interest to them; and
- *the substantive view* – a transaction is material if the director's interest in it is substantial, even though the transaction itself may be small.

One of the major problems with the substantive view is that a small interest in a major contract could be considered insubstantial and therefore not material (eg a commission of 1 per cent payable to a director on a company contract worth £1 million), whereas many people would consider that this is precisely the sort of arrangement that the shareholders would probably want to know about. The balance has tended, therefore, to favour the relevant view, but if there is any doubt over whether a transaction involving a director, or a person connected with him/her, is one in which the director has a material interest, legal advice should be taken.

8.39   FRS 8 Approach to Materiality

The Accounting Standards Board ('ASB') also adopted the relevant view in FRS 8 *Related Party Disclosures* but preserved some element of the substantial view in respect of transactions involving directors:

> 'Transactions are material when their disclosure might reasonably be expected to influence decisions made by users of general purpose financial statements. The materiality of related party transactions is to be judged, not only in terms of their significance to the reporting entity, but also in relation to the other related party when that party is:
>
> (a)   a director, key manager or other individual in a position to influence, or accountable for stewardship of, the reporting entity; or
>
> (b)   a member of the close family of any individual mentioned above; or
>
> (c)   an entity controlled by any individual mentioned in (a) or (b) above.'

For information on obtaining copies of FRS 8 see the ASB website at www.frc. org.uk/asb.

8.40   Detailed Disclosures under CA 1985

Where a director has a material interest in a transaction, the following information must be given in the notes to the accounts:

- a statement that the transaction or arrangement was made or existed during the year;
- the name of the director who has a material interest in the transaction and the nature of that interest;

- where relevant the name of the connected person involved in the transaction and the name of the director with whom he/she is connected;
- the value of the transaction or arrangement; and
- the principal terms of the transaction or arrangement (for instance, the rate of commission earned by the director in respect of a contract involving the company).

These details must be given individually for each relevant transaction during the year but comparatives for the previous year are not required. If the disclosure requirements have not been complied with, the auditors are required to include the relevant details in their audit report, so far as they are reasonably able to do so.

8.41   Value of a Transaction or Arrangement

The value of a transaction or arrangement is the price that could reasonably be expected to be obtained for the respective goods, services or land if they had been supplied in the ordinary course of business and on the same terms (apart from price) as they are supplied in the transaction under consideration – in other words, the price that would normally be obtained in an arm's length transaction. If the value of any transaction or arrangement cannot be expressed as a specific sum of money, for whatever reason, its value is deemed to exceed £100,000.

8.42   Exceptions to the General Disclosure Requirement

The *Companies Act 1985* sets out the following exceptions to the general disclosure requirements:

- a transaction between two companies does not need to be disclosed if the director's interest in the contract arises only from the fact that he is a director of both of the companies involved in the transaction;
- a contract of service between the company and director of the company, a director of the company's holding company, or a director of any of the company's subsidiaries does not require disclosure under these provisions of *CA 1985*;
- there is no requirement to disclose a transaction or arrangement which was not entered into during the year and did not exist at any time during the year (ie transactions entered into and settled in earlier years do not continue to be disclosable);
- an arm's length transaction between companies in the same group does not require disclosure under these provisions;
- disclosure of a transaction between group companies should only be necessary where the company has minority interests (although the wording of this part of the legislation is ambiguous); and
- disclosure is not required where the value of disclosable transactions or arrangements involving the director, including any outstanding amounts from previous years, did not at any time during the financial year exceed in aggregate £1,000 or, if more, did not exceed the lower of £5,000 or 1 per cent of the company's net assets at the end of the financial year – for this purpose,

a company's net assets are the aggregate of its assets, less the aggregate of its liabilities, including any provisions for liabilities and charges.

8.43   FRS 8 Disclosure Requirements

FRS 8 *Related Party Disclosures* requires the details disclosed in respect of material related party transactions (which include transactions with directors) to include the following:

- the names of the transacting parties;
- a description of the relationship between the related parties;
- a description of the transaction;
- the amounts involved;
- any other elements of the transaction necessary for an understanding of the financial statements;
- the amounts due to or from the related parties at the balance sheet date and any provisions for doubtful debts due from related parties at that date; and
- any amounts written off during the period in respect of debts due to or from related parties.

In the case of transactions with directors, some of these duplicate the disclosure requirements of *CA 1985*, but others may require additional information to be given in certain cases.

For information on obtaining copies of FRS 8 see the ASB website at www.frc.org.uk/asb.

The ASB issued FRED 25 *Related Party Disclosures* in May 2002 as part of its project to achieve convergence between UK accounting standards and international accounting standards. The Exposure Draft proposes replacing FRS 8 with requirements based on the revised IAS 24, although retaining the present UK requirement for an entity's controlling party to be named. The main changes proposed are:

- a number of changes to the current exemptions – in particular, the exemption for subsidiaries will in future only be available to wholly-owned subsidiaries, whereas entities that are 90 per cent owned are currently exempt from the disclosure requirements of FRS 8;
- no requirement to disclose the names of the transacting parties; and
- where amounts are due to or from related parties, a specific requirement to disclose the terms and conditions, the nature of the consideration and details of any related guarantees.

Appendix 1

Useful Websites on Directors' Duties and Related Issues

Institute of Directors	www.iod.com
Companies House	www.companieshouse.gov.uk
DTI – Corporate Law and Governance Directorate	www.dti.gov.uk/cld
Company Law Reform Bill	www.dti.gov.uk/cld/facts/clr.htm
Financial Services Authority	www.fsa.org.uk
Institute of Chartered Secretaries and Administrators	www.icsa.org.uk
Business Link	www.businesslink.gov.uk
Institute of Chartered Accountants in England and Wales	www.icaew.co.uk

Directors' Duties

E-commerce

9 E-commerce

9.1 E-commerce Strategy

At a Glance
* E-commerce opens up the possibility of new markets and opportunities but brings with it significant new areas of risk.
* The changes brought about by e-commerce are not just technological, but fundamental changes in the way in which a business operates and interacts with its customers, suppliers and employees.
* E-commerce business models are centred heavily around customer expectations and demands – businesses need to be aware of the potential effect of this on more traditional business methods and also on pricing and profitability.
* Management may face a number of barriers in considering whether or not to embrace e-commerce.
* The level of involvement in e-commerce can vary from the basic level of an e-mail address and static website to the extensive use of data exchange between businesses.

9.2 Impact of E-commerce

The arrival of the internet has already had a dramatic effect on business and has ongoing implications for management's approach to business strategy. It opens up the possibility of new markets and opportunities, but inevitably brings with it significant new areas of risk. A major risk for any business at the moment is the risk of being left behind. Few businesses can afford to ignore completely the potential impact of e-commerce, and directors must therefore begin to think about the company's e-commerce strategy even if they have no immediate plans to become directly involved. Even if a company does not wish to embrace the concept of e-commerce at this stage, the directors may find that it is forced on them by the demands of customers and suppliers, by the action of competitors or by environmental and technological developments. The development of e-commerce has been likened to a modern day equivalent of the industrial revolution, but with the added factor this time of an intense speed of change.

9.3   What is E-commerce?

E-commerce is usually defined as commercial activity that takes place over the internet by making use of digital technology. The three principal sectors of business, government and consumer are all affected by it, as highlighted by the range of new business models that have developed:

- *B2B (Business to Business)* – businesses buying and selling electronically across the whole of the supply chain;
- *B2G (Business to Government)* – businesses using electronic submission methods for documents such as corporation tax and VAT returns, or to file documentation with the Registrar;
- *B2C (Business to Consumer)* – a retail business selling directly to a consumer over the internet;
- *C2G (Consumer to Government)* – individuals using electronic submission for self-assessment tax returns.

9.4   Application to All Types of Business

The changes brought about by e-commerce are not just technological changes but fundamental changes in the way in which a business operates and interacts with its customers, suppliers and employees. The effect will be felt by businesses in all sectors, not just those that are considered to be internet businesses, but inevitably the benefits and threats will vary depending on the specific nature of each business. E-commerce may not be the best method of operation for every type of business – factors such as product characteristics, consumer style and demographic issues will also be relevant and some sections of the population will always prefer a more traditional approach to the purchase of goods and services. The first step in developing an e-commerce strategy will usually be to carry out or commission some relevant market research to review and analyse trends amongst customers and competitors, and then to establish the extent to which it will be appropriate or necessary for the company to become involved in e-commerce.

9.5   Customer Demands

Traditional business strategies generally do not fit well with the new e-commerce business models, which tend to be centred heavily around customer expectations and demands. Customers who purchase from a website increasingly expect goods and services to be delivered 24 hours a day and to arrive within a reasonably short space of time, regardless of which part of the world they come from. They also have much greater opportunity to compare prices on the internet and find the best possible deal. Businesses need to be aware of the impact that this can have on price levels and profitability, including the potential effect on existing customers buying through more traditional routes. E-commerce strategy cannot therefore be considered separately from general business strategy – the two need to be fully integrated.

9.6 Potential Barriers to E-commerce

Management may face a number of barriers in considering whether or not to embrace e-commerce, including:

- a general lack of awareness of what is happening in e-commerce;
- uncertainty about the potential benefits that e-commerce might bring;
- a lack of relevant management and technical skills – few directors and managers will have direct experience of change on this level and at this pace;
- the potential complexity and cost of setting up appropriate systems – a business that has been used to using standard system packages may find that it needs bespoke software in order to embrace fully the opportunities for e-commerce; and
- concerns over security and confidentiality.

9.7 E-commerce Terminology

In considering an e-commerce strategy, directors will need to be aware of the following expressions:

- *ASP (Application Service Provider)* – an ASP offers online access to standard packages (eg accounting, payroll, spreadsheets);
- *EDI (Electronic Data Interchange)* – a standard method of exchanging documents such as orders and invoices;
- *extranet* – the extension of a business's internal network to certain business partners;
- *firewall* – a security system which prevents and detects unauthorised access to a server or network, and may also prevent the transfer of unauthorised material;
- *hyperlink* – a coded reference to a document or another website, which enables a user to open up the document or site by clicking on the hyperlink;
- *ISP (Internet Service Provider)* – a host providing e-mail and website services;
- *VAN (Value Added Network)* – a network providing the technology platform for electronic data interchange.

9.8 Level of Involvement in E-commerce

The level of involvement that a business has in e-commerce can vary from the basic level of an e-mail address and static website to operations making extensive use of VANs and extranets to exchange data with other businesses. Companies may want to start at the basic level and then develop, or may want to begin their e-commerce involvement at one of the intermediate stages. The level of risk inevitably increases as the involvement becomes more complex. The various levels may be summarised as follows.

- *Business e-mail and static website.* The company uses an ISP to operate an e-mail account and maintain a static website. There is little risk of the business being seriously affected by prolonged downtime of the system, as communication can continue by other more traditional methods. However, computer viruses transferred by e-mail or through the internet may present a potential risk to the business. The main issues to consider will be:
  - selection of a reliable ISP;
  - ongoing costs of maintaining the website and e-mail service;
  - development of a company policy on e-mail (eg read and response times, e-mail courtesy, inclusion of company details, confidentiality issues, opening of attachments, policy on use for private purposes, prevention of e-mail abuse etc);
  - design of a well-presented website, which can be found easily by potential visitors (eg through registration with appropriate search engines) and meets their needs;
  - procedures for keeping website information up to date; and
  - procedures to monitor use of the website.
- *Business e-mail and interactive website.* The company uses an ISP to operate an e-mail account and an interactive website which can take orders from customers. The business is more dependent on the internet and the risk of losing business as a result of prolonged downtime is therefore increased. The business may also come under pressure from business partners to enter into B2B transactions. In addition to the issues mentioned above, the directors will need to consider:
  - internal systems, procedures and controls to deal with online orders;
  - the need to monitor ISP service levels even more closely;
  - the need to obtain a more detailed analysis of website usage; and
  - compliance with ISO 27001 (see **9.18** below).
- *Business e-mail and interactive website which accepts payment with order.* The company uses an ISP to operate an e-mail account and an interactive website which can take orders and also accept credit card payments from customers. In addition to the business risks above, the company will be reliant on the ISP to handle credit card transactions with customers. Additional issues that will need to be considered include:
  - general security of the site;
  - the need for secure software to authenticate and process credit card transactions;
  - the need for additional controls over the completeness and accuracy of the processing of this data; and
  - consideration of the use of an independent 'seal' to give customers confidence in the security of the site.
- *Business e-mail, interactive website and B2B activity.* In addition to the above, the company uses an extranet or VANs to exchange financial and other information with specific business partners and customers. The company's involvement

in e-commerce is now becoming quite complex and a major part of the overall business strategy. The ISP service levels are critical, with prolonged downtime representing a serious risk to the business. Additional issues to be considered include:

- the need for improved definition of ISP service levels and increased monitoring of actual performance;
- integration of EDI with the company's internal systems and controls;
- the need to preserve an audit trail for all transactions;
- security of information; and
- authorisation and internal control issues.

Level of activity	Issue to consider
Business e-mail address Static website	Identification of a reliable ISP Ongoing maintenance costs Company policy on use of e-mail Website design and procedures for updating Monitoring use of the website
Business e-mail address Interactive website	Identification of a reliable ISP and monitoring of service levels Ongoing maintenance costs Company policy on use of e-mail Website design and procedures for updating Systems and controls to deal with on-line orders Detailed analysis of website usage Compliance with ISO 27001 on security issues
Business e-mail address Interactive website accepting payment with order	Identification of a reliable ISP and monitoring of service levels Ongoing maintenance costs Company policy on use of e-mail Website design and procedures for updating Systems and controls to deal with on-line orders Detailed analysis of website usage Compliance with ISO 27001 on security issues Identification of secure software to deal with the processing of payments Controls over the accuracy and completeness of payment data Whether the site should carry an independent 'seal' to confirm security to users
Business e-mail address Interactive website accepting payment with order Use of extranets or VANs to exchange data with other businesses	Identification of a reliable ISP and monitoring of service levels Ongoing maintenance costs Company policy on use of e-mail Website design and procedures for updating Systems and controls to deal with on-line orders Detailed analysis of website usage Compliance with ISO 27001 on security issues Identification of secure software to deal with the processing of payments Controls over the accuracy and completeness of payment data Whether the site should carry an independent 'seal' to confirm security to users The need to preserve an audit trail for all transactions Authorisation and control issues for all electronic transactions

E-commerce

9.9 Security Issues

> **At a Glance**
> * When a business moves into e-commerce, it must review and adapt its system of internal control to cater for new aspects of the business.
> * Additional risks arising in an e-commerce environment include the risk of unauthorised access to information, the risk of unauthenticated or incorrect transactions being processed, and the risk of changes being made to a transaction during electronic transit.
> * The three principal components of good e-commerce security are confidentiality, integrity and dependability.
> * ISO 27001 provides a framework for establishing, maintaining and documenting systems to achieve security of information.

9.10 The Electronic Commerce (EC Directive) Regulations 2002

The *Electronic Commerce (EC Directive) Regulations 2002 (SI 2002/2013)* were laid before Parliament in July 2002 and generally came into effect on 21 August 2002. The only exception is *regulation 16*, which deals with stop now orders and is effective from 23 October 2002. The *Regulations* apply to anyone who:

* advertises goods or services on-line;
* sells goods or services on-line; or
* transmits or stores electronic content or provides access to a communication network (eg an internet service provider).

They are intended to encourage greater use of e-commerce across the EU and to boost consumer confidence by clarifying the rights and obligations of businesses and consumers. Any business involved in e-commerce, or contemplating becoming involved, needs to be aware of these requirements. The details are set out under three headings: information requirements, commercial communications and electronic contracting. The DTI has published detailed guidance on the operation of the *Regulations* – this can be accessed from the DTI website at www.dti.gov.uk/sectors/ictpolicy/. The *Regulations* themselves are available from the Office of Public Sector Information (www.opsi.gov.uk/si/si2002/20022013.htm).

9.11 *Information Requirements*

The principal requirements under this category are that end users should be provided with:

* the full contact details of the business;
* details of any relevant trade organisation to which the business belongs (eg name of the register and the business's registered number);

- details of any authorisation scheme relevant to the on-line business (eg registration with a professional body and how its professional rules can be accessed);
- the business's VAT number, if the on-line activities are subject to VAT; and
- a clear indication of prices, including any delivery or tax charges.

9.12   Commercial Communications

The principal requirements under this category are that end users should be provided with a clear indication of:

- any electronic communication designed to promote goods, services or image (either directly or indirectly);
- the person on whose behalf it is sent;
- any promotional offers advertised (eg discounts or promotional gifts), together with details of any related qualifying conditions; and
- any unsolicited commercial communications, so that recipients can identify them as such as soon as they receive them and can block them or choose not to open them.

9.13   Electronic Contracting

The principal requirements under this category are that end users should be provided with:

- a description of the various technical steps to be taken to conclude an on-line contract;
- an indication of whether a copy of the contract will be filed by the business, and whether this can be accessed;
- clear identification of the technical means by which the end user can correct any inputting errors that they make; and
- an indication of the languages offered in which to conclude the contract.

The related DTI guidance notes that the business should provide details of any relevant codes of conduct to which it subscribes, together with details of how end users can access the codes, and if end users are provided with the terms and conditions of their contract, they must be made available in a way that enables the user to store and reproduce them (eg by saving them onto a computer and printing them out). If an end user places an order with the business, receipt should be acknowledged without undue delay by electronic means.

9.14   Cross-border Trading

The *Regulations* also specify that online selling and advertising should generally be subject to the laws of the country in which the online trader is established, although the parties involved are free to decide that another law should apply to an on-line contract.

E-commerce

9.15   Continuing Need for Control

Under traditional business and accounting methods, management will usually have a comparatively high level of control over the input and output of financial and other information, particularly where systems require manual authorisation for certain transactions. An effective system of internal control will typically give good physical control over accounting data. When a business moves into e-commerce, it will need to review and adapt these controls to cater for new aspects of the business. The new controls that need to be introduced will not usually be significantly different in nature, but they will need to be designed to limit the company's exposure to different risks. The directors' responsibilities under the *Companies Act 1985* are the same in an e-commerce environment as in more traditional forms of business, but there is always a danger that management will fail to adapt the traditional and familiar controls to suit the new business models of e-commerce.

9.16   Security Issues

The main security issues in the context of e-commerce arise from:

- the risk of unauthorised access to information;
- the risk of processing unauthenticated or incorrect transactions; and
- the risk of a transaction changing whilst in electronic transit.

These risks are heightened where the level of use of e-commerce is more sophisticated and transactions are processed in real-time. For instance, without good controls a payment processed as £350 instead of £3,500 may only become apparent at a later stage.

9.17   Main Components of Good Security

The three main components of good security are confidentiality, integrity and dependability. Management will need to put appropriate procedures into place to ensure that information does not get into unauthorised hands, that only authorised data is processed and that processed data is accurate and complete. The company also needs to have good technical support and tried and tested recovery procedures. The process for developing good security systems will usually involve:

- establishing what needs to be protected;
- identifying the potential threats;
- analysing the risks; and
- on the basis of this information, developing appropriate security procedures which comply with any relevant laws and regulations – these might include:
  - the *Data Protection Act 1998*,
  - the *Computer Misuse Act 1990*,

- the *Health and Safety (Display Screen Equipment) Regulations 1992* (*SI 1992/2792*),
- the *Electronic Communications Act 2000,*
- the *Electronic Commerce (EC Directive) Regulations 2002* (*SI 2002/2013*) (see **9.10** above), and
- the *Privacy and Electronic Communications (EC Directive) Regulations 2003* (*SI 2003/2426*).

9.18   Information Security and ISO 27001

British Standard BS 7799 provided an initial framework for the establishment, maintenance and documentation of systems to achieve the security of information, but this has now been superseded by ISO 27001. Compliance with the standard should be seen as an ongoing objective rather than a one-off exercise, although more work will undoubtedly be needed on first implementation than in subsequent reviews. However, it is important that procedures are reviewed regularly, to confirm that they remain appropriate to the company's situation or that, where necessary, they are updated promptly to take account of changes in the nature of the company's activities and operations. Issues covered in the standard include:

- development of a company policy on information systems security;
- establishment of an appropriate organisational structure for information security, to ensure that relevant issues are considered, and systems and procedures updated, as the business develops;
- classification of the company's assets into four categories (information, software, physical assets and services) and consideration of the relative need for confidentiality, integrity and dependence in each case;
- consideration of personnel issues, including the dissemination of company policy on security, procedures for recording any breaches of security, and relevant staff disciplinary procedures;
- development of procedures to ensure the security and safety of company staff, premises and other assets (including information);
- development and use of operations manuals, including stringent controls over the electronic transfer of information and measures to prevent data corruption as a result of viruses and similar threats;
- development of strong access controls, including the authentication of transactions and users (through the use of passwords, data encryption, hash values etc);
- development and regular testing of back-up procedures and a recovery plan; and
- regular reviews for compliance with relevant laws and regulations, including procedures for keeping up to date with any changes in the requirements.

Even if the company does not wish to seek ISO 27001 accreditation, the required standards and controls should provide a useful benchmark against which to assess the company's systems and performance.

9.19   Risk Assessment and Management

> **At a Glance**
> * Management should assess the additional risks arising from an involve-
>   ment in e-commerce and develop procedures to limit any potential
>   adverse effect on the business.
> * Additional costs are likely to arise from the need to maintain a higher level
>   of technical support and to keep up to date with developing technology.
> * A website needs to be well designed, easy to use and up to date in order
>   to attract users.
> * Specific legal issues and commercial risks can arise when transacting
>   business through a website.

9.20   Additional Risks from E-commerce

The use of e-commerce brings with it a number of additional risks to the business, including:

* risks arising from increased dependence on technology;
* the risk of loss of business as a result of system downtime;
* the risk of the system not being able to expand in line with the development
  of e-commerce activities;
* the risk of damage to the reputation of the business; and
* additional security risks (as outlined at **9.15–9.18** above).

Management needs to assess each of these risks, categorise them as low,
medium or high and develop procedures to limit the potential adverse impact
on the business of the more significant risks crystallising in practice.

9.21   Potential Costs of E-commerce

As well as the problems and loss of business that may be caused by the occasional (or regular) failure of the relevant technology and equipment, companies
need to bear in mind the potential impact of the increased costs of involvement
in e-commerce. Additional costs might include:

* ongoing technical support, particularly if it is important for this to be available for 24 hours a day;
* the need to keep hardware and software up to date;
* the need to keep related security measures up to date; and
* the potential need to finance rapid expansion of the e-commerce activities.

9.22   Damage to Reputation

A badly designed website, or one that is difficult to use, can cause considerable
damage to the reputation of the business and result in loss of business. The

internet gives potential customers ample opportunity to find alternative sites that meet their requirements more quickly and easily. It can be tempting to use the quickest and easiest way of getting a presence on the internet, without thinking through the full implications. Issues to consider in relation to a company website, especially one that is intended to be interactive, include:

- users are more likely to be attracted to a company website if it is:
  - well designed,
  - easy to navigate,
  - quick to load,
  - up to date;
- users are less likely to use a website if:
  - they cannot order through the site (ie the site is a static one),
  - they have to give too much (and apparently unnecessary) detail on any order or other form that needs to be completed,
  - the site links to other sites which do not work (especially if transactions are meant to be completed via the second site), and
  - information on the site is clearly out of date.

9.23   Legal Issues

As noted at **9.17** above, there are various UK laws and regulations that may impact on a company carrying out business through the internet. It is important to have clear procedures and lines of responsibility for ensuring compliance with these, and also for keeping up to date with any changes in the requirements. Businesses also need to bear in mind the increased risk of fraud and money laundering being carried out through e-commerce transactions. Additional commercial risks may also arise, particularly where e-commerce gives rise to transactions in other parts of the world. For instance:

- there may be uncertainty over whether an e-commerce transaction has created a legally binding contract;
- it may be unclear which country's laws apply in the event of a dispute (although the *Electronic Communications (EC Directive) Regulations 2002 (SI 2002/2013)* should help to clarify this – see **9.10** above);
- digital signatures may not be acceptable in all countries;
- products that are acceptable in one country may be illegal in another;
- activities that are unregulated in one country may be regulated elsewhere; or
- the tax implications of a transaction may be unclear.

Each of these issues will need to be properly researched if the company intends to trade on a global basis.

E-commerce

Appendix 1

Useful Websites on E-commerce and Related Issues

BSI Group	www.bsi-global.com
Information Commissioner's Office	www.ico.gov.uk
Get Safe Online	www.getsafeonline.org
DTI	www.dti.gov.uk
ICAEW IT Faculty	www.icaew.co.uk/itfac
Business Link	www.businesslink.gov.uk
E-Commerce Innovation Centre	www.ecommerce.ac.uk
IT Governance Institute	www.itgi.org
Information Technology Infrastructure Library	www.itil.co.uk
IT Service Management Forum	www.itsmf.com

10

Employment Law

10 Employment Law

10.1 Types of Worker

At a Glance

* The standard test used to establish whether someone is an employee is whether their work is normally directed and under the control of their employer and there are mutual obligations to provide and perform work.
* Workers are self-employed where they provide their own tools and equipment, take a degree of financial risk, can profit from their own work management and control their own work.
* Whether workers are full or part-time does not affect their statutory employment rights; however, there is a legal duty on employers to ensure that part-time workers are treated no less favourably.
* Employees on temporary or fixed-term contracts have the right to be treated no less favourably than permanent workers.
* Employers are required to take particular account of young people's experiences and assess any specific risks related to inexperience in determining the work they are required to do.
* There is a general duty of care to the employee in relation to home-working contracts.

The legal responsibilities which an employer has to an individual depend on the nature of the employment relationship. An individual may be working:

* under a contract *of* service (employment) – directly employed by the employer – in legal terms defined as an 'employee';
* under a contract *for* services – working for an employer but not directed by the employer and able to arrange for substitutes – in legal terms usually defined as a 'worker';
* under a contractual relationship of *self-employment* – working for another party but taking their own financial risks, providing their own tools and so forth.

An employee, working under a contract of employment, has legal rights which extend beyond those appropriate for those working under a contract for services.

Additionally, employment rights may depend on the status of the employee, whether permanent or temporary, a young worker, teleworker or homeworker.

10.2 Employees

Most statutory employment rights protect employees, that is those working under a contract of employment. The standard test used to establish whether someone is an employee is whether their work is normally directed and under the control of their employer and whether there are mutual obligations to provide and perform work. If there is no right to offer work and no obligation to accept it, these mutual obligations cannot exist. Employees have a legal duty to obey lawful orders, work faithfully and with due diligence, give proper notice before ending their employment and pay their tax and National Insurance contributions. Employers are obliged to observe any statutory rights the employee has, pay wages due and make the appropriate tax and National Insurance deductions.

The fact that a contract includes a term which gives the worker the right to arrange for a substitute is likely to indicate a lack of employee status. However, this is dependent on the degree of choice available. If the substitute has to be selected from a panel chosen by the employers and paid by them it is more likely that there will be employee status (*MacFarlane v Glasgow City Council [2001] IRLR 7*).

10.3 Workers and the Self-employed

Someone working under a contract *of* service has the right to a restricted range of statutory employment rights – mainly the right to the National Minimum Wage together with the rights provided under the *Working Time Regulations 1998*, provided that there is a mutuality of obligations to work and be paid. Whereas an individual who is genuinely self-employed will not have access even to this more restricted range of statutory rights.

In some cases those working under a contract *of* service are termed 'self-employed workers', for example for tax purposes, and where the parties make it clear that it is their intention to create this form of contractual relationship. However, the ingredients of self-employment must exist, such as the method of payment, potential exposure to VAT and lack of consent to be an employee.

However, the fact that self-employed workers have fewer employment rights inevitably means that disputes arise where one party will allege that there is a contract of employment while the other states that the contract was for services. Where this occurs, the courts are more likely to decide that the individual is self-employed where they provide their own tools and equipment, take a degree of financial risk, can profit from their own work management and control their own work.

There are special rules regarding the payment of tax and National Insurance where workers supply their services to a client through a service company or partnership. If the worker would have been an employee if employed directly by the client, then IR 35 rules apply and tax and National Insurance is calculated as if the person was an employee (see **20.9 IR 35 AND PERSONAL SERVICE COMPANIES**).

10.4   Part-time Workers

The DTI defines a part-time worker as one who works less than 30 hours a week. Part-time workers must be given the same contractual rights, including access to bonuses, as enjoyed by full-time workers. Part-time workers can compare their terms and conditions with those of full-time staff, regardless of whether the latter are working under permanent or temporary contracts. Employers should not require part-time workers to have completed longer service than full-timers to get promotion. Whether workers are full or part-time does not affect their statutory employment rights, including rights to claim against unfair dismissal and redundancy.

Part-time workers may be able to establish rights based on sex discrimination, due to the fact that the overwhelming majority of them are women so that any difference in their treatment compared to that of full-timers affects proportionately more women than men.

The *Part-time Workers (Prevention of Less Favourable Treatment) Regulations 2000 (SI 2000/1551)* came into force on 1 July 2000. They place a specific duty on employers to consider giving access to part-time work for those workers who wish to undertake it, and establish a statutory right to no less favourable treatment with full-time workers doing the same work in the same establishment. This would include a right to contractual holiday and other contractual benefits, limited only by the fact that they can be provided pro rata. In addition, the *Occupational Pension Schemes (Equal Access to Membership) Regulations 1995 (SI 1995/1215)* prohibit discrimination between men and women in access to pension schemes. A person with responsibility for the upbringing of a child up to the child's sixth birthday must have a legal right to request flexible working arrangements, including the right to request a transfer to part-time work. If such a request is made the employer will have to concede it unless there are objectively justifiable reasons for refusing it.

There is no legal obligation to pay overtime rates to part-time workers until they have superseded the hours normally worked by full-timers.

10.5   Temporary Workers

An estimated 1.6 million workers are employed under temporary contracts and their number is growing at a faster rate than that of part-time workers.

Temporary or fixed-term employees can be those working for a specified period of time or working to complete a specified task.

The *Fixed-term Employees (Protection against Less Favourable Treatment) Regulations 2002 (SI 2002/2034)* impose a duty on employers to offer no less favourable treatment to employees on fixed-term contracts, compared to the treatment of permanent employees doing the same or similar work and with similar qualifications and skills. They cover all contractual terms, including pay and pensions, qualifying periods for employment benefits, opportunities to receive training and opportunities to secure permanent employment although the termination of a fixed-term contract does not itself amount to less favourable treatment (*Department for Work and Pensions v Webley [2005] IRLR 288*).

Although employers are not prevented from renewing fixed term contracts, the regulations state that they have a legal obligation to justify the renewal of any fixed term contract, once the employee has accumulated four years' employment. Additionally when a fixed-term contract comes to an end its non-renewal still amounts to a dismissal. If an employee is offered a series of temporary contracts there is likely to be a presumption of continuity between them. Combined service can be added together and where it comes to the necessary length to give the employee a statutory right, this will apply (*Flack and others v Kodak [1986] IRLR 255*).

10.6   Agency Workers

Agency workers, that is workers supplied by an external agency, are usually not regarded as employees of the company to which they are sent to work, although they are not excluded from pursuing discrimination rights against it (*BP Chemicals v Gillick [1995] IRLR 128*). Whether or not they are employees of the agency itself depends on the nature of the contract between them and the agency. However, as a result of the case of *Dacas v Brook Street Bureau (UK) Ltd [2004] IRLR 358 CA*, the employment status of agency staff has been explored. In that case the Court of Appeal held that while an individual employed through an agency was not its employee, there might have been an implied contract of employment between the worker and the organisation for which she worked.

10.7   Young Workers

There is little legislation which regulates the employment of young workers, other than for apprenticeship contracts which do strictly set down specific legal obligations on both sides. Employers are required to take particular account of young people's experiences and assess any specific risks related to inexperience in determining the work they are required to do. This risk assessment should be undertaken before the young person starts work.

Under *sections 32* and *33* of the *Teacher and Higher Education Act 1998*, young people aged 16 or 17 are entitled to take paid time off during work hours to undertake study or training leading to an academic or vocational qualification which is likely to enhance the employee's future employment prospects.

Local authorities have powers to issue byelaws aimed at the protection of children who are working. Under the *Children (Protection at Work) Regulations 1998 (SI 1998/276)*, children under the age of 16 have the right to a break of at least two weeks during the school holidays. Young workers (that is those under the age of 18) have the right to breaks after four and a half hours' work as well as to daily and weekly breaks. In addition the maximum working hours for young workers must not exceed eight hours a day or 40 hours a week, although they can be averaged over a longer period. Where a young person works for more than one employer the total hours worked must be aggregated and not average more than the maximum.

The maximum number of hours that a schoolchild can work in any week, when they are required to attend school, is twelve.

10.8 Homeworkers

When offering contracts to homeworkers employers need to establish whether these are contracts of employment or self-employed contracts for services. In the case of the former, the contract needs to take account of the general duty of care to the employee. This might include specifying breaks to be taken in the course of employment, carrying out risk assessments of the employee's home-working conditions and ensuring that terms and conditions do not result in discriminatory outcomes. Where a worker is employed in their home it is likely that all of the hours that they are at their employer's disposition will be taken into account in calculating entitlement under the *Working Time Regulations 1998* and the *National Minimum Wage Act 1988*, provided that they are at work (even if the workplace is their home), available for work if required and carrying out their activities or duties.

Workers posted to work in another EU State have the right to benefit from at least the minimum terms provided within that State.

10.9 Summary

Type of worker	Entitlement
Employees	Entitled to most statutory employment rights
Workers	Limited employment rights only: national minimum wage; working time rights, including statutory holidays
Part-time workers	Have the right to no less favourable treatment than available to full-time workers
Temporary employees	Have the right to no less favourable treatment than available to permanent employees
Agency workers	Have limited rights, dependent on their contractual status
Young workers	Right to have a risk assessment and to have their inexperience taken into account
Homeworkers	Employment rights depend on the individual's contractual status

Employment Law

10.10   Contracts of Employment

10.11   Offers of Employment

At a Glance
* Recruitment procedures should be gender and race neutral.
* An offer of a job and its acceptance creates a legally binding contract.
* Employment contracts can be in writing or oral, and can consist of statutory, implied and express terms.
* Employers must give all employees a 'principle statement' containing certain details of the contract in writing within two months of the commencement of employment.
* If an employer is intending to change contracts there must be consultation with the union (if recognised) or with employee representatives before the change is introduced.
* A contract is breached if one party proposes a fundamental change that is unacceptable to the other party.
* An employer can end an employment contract by giving contractual notice. After one month's continuous employment the minimum notice is one week. The maximum statutory notice (with twelve or more years' service) is twelve weeks.
* If an employer provides a reference there is a general duty of care to ensure that it is accurate and not misleading.

In seeking potential recruits and appointing individuals to new posts, employers need to guard against the risk of offending principles of discrimination law, specifically in relation to sex, race, disability, transsexuality, sexual orientation, religion or belief and trade union membership.

Recruitment procedures should be gender and race neutral and the conditions under which employment is offered (pay, holidays and so on) should not differ for discriminatory reasons. A guide, from the advisory service ACAS (see **10.70** below), *Recruitment and Induction*, gives advice to employers on how to ensure that their recruitment policies comply with the law (for information on obtaining copies see the ACAS website at www.acas.org.uk).

Prior to shortlisting it is important to draw up the criteria to be used for selection. Criteria can be 'essential' or 'preferred'. Care then needs to be taken to ensure that any employee selected for interview has met the 'essential' criteria if these have been set. A failure to do this leaves the employer at risk of discrimination claims, if the unsuccessful job applicant alleges that there has been unlawful discrimination (see **10.22–10.26** below).

Where a job applicant has a previous criminal record there is generally no obligation to disclose it provided it is 'spent'. However, under the *Police Act 1997*, standard and enhanced disclosures of criminal record certificates are to be available to employers from the Criminal Records Bureau. Enhanced certificates are required of employees seeking to work with children or vulnerable adults. However, administrative difficulties have forced the government to delay the introduction of the standard certificate.

An offer of a job and its acceptance creates a legally binding contract and if withdrawn there is potential for a damages claim by the individual to whom the job offer was made. An employer can, however, offer a job 'subject to a suitable reference'. Employers are not restricted in terms of where they seek references. In the absence of an express contractual term which says that only referees notified by the applicant will be approached, there is no implied term to that effect. Employers can seek and act upon references from any source which they deem appropriate. If references are normally provided for ex-employees, the refusal to provide one to an employee because they had previously alleged discrimination, will amount to unlawful victimisation.

It is important to draw up a job description which matches the requirements of the job on offer. There is a legal obligation to provide every employee with a job title or brief job description (*Employment Rights Act 1996, s 1(4)(f)*).

If a current or ex-employer does provide a reference, a general duty of care in negligence in relation to its contents is created (*Spring v Guardian Royal Exchange [1994] IRLR 460*). It must be 'accurate and not misleading' and although it does not have to be full and comprehensive, it must not give an unfair or misleading impression overall.

It is a criminal offence to employ someone aged over 16 unless they have a current and valid permission to be in the UK and have the right to work here. Employers should have carried out checks of documents, like passports, identity cards, to determine whether an individual has the right to work.

10.12 Employment Contracts

Employment relationships are based on contract and amount to an agreement between the parties, employer and employee with mutual obligations to work and to pay for the work. A contract can be in writing, in a standard form or by letter, but none of these are essential. An oral agreement between the two parties will still be a valid contract.

An employment contract consists of any implied terms (eg trust and confidence, custom and practice, statutory terms) and written and oral terms (commonly known as the express terms), together with those parts of any collective agreement whose terms are capable of being incorporated into the individual's employment contract. Discretionary terms cannot amount to custom and practice.

Employers have a legal obligation to have a 'dispute resolution procedure' which, as a minimum, must give the right to be informed on the nature of the charges and the opportunity to respond.

10.13 Statutory Contract Terms

Statutory contract terms include:

- minimum notice entitlement;
- statutory redundancy pay;

- maternity pay;
- statutory sick pay;
- equal pay;
- right to see personal stored data under the *Data Protection Act 1998* etc;

and will be implied into the contract even if unstated.

Certain employees have the statutory right to time off to perform certain duties. These include:

- those who hold certain public offices like Justices of the Peace, local authority members, tribunal members, health authority or school governors (*Employment Rights Act 1996, s 50*);
- safety representatives (*Safety Representatives and Safety Committee Regulations 1977 (SI 1977/500)*);
- trade union and employee representatives (*Trade Union and Labour Relations (Consolidation) Act 1992, s 168; Employment Rights Act 1996, s 61*);
- occupational pension fund trustees (*Employment Rights Act 1996, s 58*); and
- union learning representatives (*Employment Act 2002 (Commencement No 4 and Transitional Provisions) Order 2003 (SI 2003/1190)*).

Any term which seeks to contract the employee out of minimum statutory rights (eg those covering discrimination, equal pay, redundancy and unfair dismissal) is unenforceable. Contract terms, which are deemed to be unreasonable, may also be challenged under the *Unfair Contract Terms Act 1977*.

10.14   Express Terms – Contractual Terms and Conditions

In addition to these statutory rights, employees may also have legal entitlements to rights provided for in the contract. These contractual rights can cover:

- hours of work;
- holidays;
- pensions;
- life, personal accident and sickness insurance;
- long service awards;
- time off for medical appointments, stress counselling and pre-retirement procedures etc;
- competition, inventions and confidentiality;
- e-mail and internet use.

Employers are not prevented from monitoring, provided that employees know that this is taking place and that it is not so intrusive as to interfere with an employee's rights to privacy. Employees should be told if e-mails or internet use is being monitored or indeed if there is any other form of monitoring, whether by CCT or other surveillance methods. The Information Commissioner has issued codes of practice, which give guidance on the extent of the employer's duties in relation to monitoring at work.

10.15   Statement of Contract Terms

Under *section 1* of the *Employment Rights Act 1996* (*ERA 1996*) employers must give all employees a 'principal statement', containing certain details of the contract, in writing within two months of the commencement of employment. There is an absolute right by statute to be given their contract details in writing. If they are not provided, a tribunal can order that they must be or itself determine what the terms, at least as to notice, are.

The principal statement must include the following elements, all detailed in one document:

- the names of the employer and employee;
- the date when employment began and the period of continuous employment;
- the scale and rate of remuneration, pay intervals and its method of calculation;
- terms and conditions relating to hours of work and holiday entitlement (including public holidays); and
- the job title or description.

Employers must also provide a written statement indicating if the employment is permanent or not, whether there is a collective agreement in force and whether there is a requirement to work abroad.

In workplaces where, when the individual starts work, there are already 20 or more employees, a statement must also be given (or access to one provided) specifying any disciplinary rules or grievance procedures. *Section 10* of the *Employment Relations Act 1999* provides a right for workers to be accompanied to any disciplinary or grievance hearing. (See **10.45–10.47** below.)

Existing employees must also be given a statement of their written particulars, if they request one.

10.16   Altering Contractual Terms

Where an employer seeks to unilaterally alter contract terms and 21 or more workers are affected, there is an obligation to consult with the recognised union, or in its absence with employee representatives.

An employer can serve notice to change the contract. However, the legal effect of such notice may be to terminate the old contract and offer a new contract on different terms. If this happens, the employee may be able to argue that the contract has been breached and claim wrongful or unfair dismissal.

Just because the employee continues to report for work after the contract has been unilaterally changed does not mean that the change has been accepted by the employee. This is particularly so where the change has had no immediate impact on the way that the employee works and was not a necessary requirement of the job (*Aparau v Iceland Frozen Foods [1996] IRLR 119*). Employees whose contracts are significantly changed can continue to work while reserving their rights to pursue unfair dismissal claims.

The employment contract can be altered at any time with the agreement of both parties. With such agreement, a new statement, incorporating the altered terms, should be issued at the 'earliest possible opportunity' and not later than a month after the change.

10.17   Breach of Contract

A contract is breached if one party introduces a fundamental change which is unacceptable to the other party. It is up to the courts to decide whether a breach has occurred or not, but changes such as asking employees to move considerable distances to work, unless there is a term, express or implied, in the contract which allows the employer to transfer the employee, or significant changes in working hours or attempts to cut pay, could all amount to breaches of contract, opening the employer to damages claims. A reduction in working hours without agreement will always amount to a variation of contract and is capable of amounting to a breach.

An employee who claims damages for breach of contract has a legal obligation to mitigate (lessen) the loss by attempting to find alternative work.

As an alternative to pursing a breach of contract claim, employees may use the injunction to retain existing contractual rights. In one case, where the employer had decided no longer to follow the agreed disciplinary procedure, employees successfully obtained a court order (injunction) requiring that the original procedure be reinstated.

If the employee fundamentally breaches the contract then the employer can treat it as having been ended. However, if the employee continues to work following such a breach this is likely to amount to a waiver of the employee's right to act on the breach. Continuing to work also deprives the employee from asserting that the employer's breach is a justification for a refusal to obey legitimate orders. Special conditions apply where an employee resigns without giving the required notice and there is a contract clause that purports to give the employer the right to deduct pay equivalent to the notice that should have been given. In such cases employers only have the right to recoup money based on a pre-estimate of their anticipated loss due to the employee's breach. There is no general obligation on employees to tell their employer that they have breached their contracts. This does not amount to an employee's breach of an implied fiduciary duty to advance the employer's interests.

An employer too may sue for damages for breach of contract. Although normally the amount which can be claimed is limited to the actual financial loss attributable to the employee's breach, a sum that is often difficult to calculate, there may be circumstances when damages can be claimed from other sources. In the case of *Attorney-General v Blake [2001] IRLR 36*, the House of Lords held that an employer could claim as damages any profits made by the employee which came as a result of the employee's breach.

A breach of contract can be cumulative. What this means is that you can have a series of events, none of which in themselves is so crucial as to amount to a fundamental breach, but which when considered together do make up a fundamental breach of contract. While the breach has to be cumulative, it does not have to be continuous.

10.18 Ending the Contract

A contract can be terminated by dismissal. Employees have statutory rights against unfair dismissal and rights not to be dismissed for discriminatory reasons. In addition, they may also be able to pursue civil claims for wrongful dismissal.

An employer can end the contract without giving the notice required by offering pay in lieu of notice. The payment must at least equal the amounts which would have been earned, had the original notice period been worked. Pay in lieu is taxable. If neither notice nor pay in lieu is given, the employee may sue for breach of contract, claiming damages equal to the amount which would have been paid had the notice provisions been adhered to. However, this claim is subject to the general obligation on the party making the claim to mitigate the loss.

Employees too will usually have a contractual obligation to give notice to end the contract. Employers should, however, note that where an employee fails to give notice, or to give the appropriate amount of notice, it should not be assumed that the employer could deduct pay from any monies due to the employee. Even where a contract clause specifies that there will be a deduction where appropriate notice is not given, this will only be enforceable where the employer has made a pre-estimate of the anticipated financial loss attributable to the employee's breach and where the contractual clause reflects that amount. A general clause, which, for example, states that any money due will be withheld, is likely to be void.

The minimum statutory notice periods to be given by the employer are as follows.

Length of service	Notice period
Less than one month's continuous employment	No minimum period
Between one month and two years' continuous employment	One week's notice
More than two and up to twelve years' continuous employment	One week's notice for each complete year of continuous service
More than twelve years' continuous employment	Twelve weeks' notice

10.19 References for Ex-employees

Employers may be asked to provide references for ex-employees. Whilst there is no legal obligation under UK law to provide a reference on behalf of an ex-employee, the European Court of Justice has ruled that an employer who refuses this because the ex-employee has previously taken a sex discrimination claim, can be vulnerable to a fresh claim of victimisation on discriminatory grounds. The House of Lords, in the case of *Relaxion Group v Rhys-Harper [2003] UKHL 33*, has held that it is unlawful for employers to refuse to provide references for ex-employees if the reason for the refusal is because the employee, while in work, had taken or alleged any unlawful discrimination. The court held that any benefit that the employer applies generally to ex-employees should not be denied to someone on discriminatory grounds. The one exception where such a refusal would not give rise to a claim is where the reason for refusing to give a reference is due to the fact that the employer and employee are at the time involved in litigating a discrimination claim. If a current or ex-employer does provide a reference, a general duty of care in negligence in relation to its content is created (*Spring v Guardian Royal Exchange [1994] IRLR 460*). Any references provided must be 'accurate and not misleading' (*Kidd v Axa Equity & Law Life Assurance Society [2000] IRLR 301*).

10.20 *Whistleblowing*

The *Public Interest Disclosure Act 1998* gives employees who blow the whistle on their employers' fraudulent or criminal activities, statutory protection against victimisation. However, the employee must have a 'reasonable belief' in the allegation being made, even if it turns out to be untrue. But making a disclosure in bad faith, even where the disclosure is believed to be true, is not covered by the 1998 Act.

10.21 Summary

See the table below for a list of employers' duties in respect of contracts of employment.

Employers' duties	
On recruitment of new employees	Issue statement of written particulars within two months of starting work
Monitoring	Inform employees of any monitoring that is taking place and of the processes being used
On changing contracts	Issue statement of changes to contracts within a month of the change
Changing contractual terms	Consult with union (if recognised) or with employee representatives
On breach of contract	Right to sue for breach
On termination of contract	Give contractual/statutory notice

10.22 Discrimination

At a Glance
* Employers have a specific legal duty not to discriminate against employees on the grounds of their sex, marital status, race, transsexuality, sexual orientation, religion or belief or disability.
* Discrimination is unlawful if direct, indirect or by way of victimisation.
* Employers can be liable for acts of harassment carried out by employees where they have taken no or ineffective action to counter it. They are

also liable for any resulting physical or psychological injury resulting from the harassment.

* There is no upper-limit compensation in discrimination cases.
* Discrimination claims to tribunals must be submitted within three months of the discriminatory action.
* Employers should ensure policies are in place to address issues of harassment at work, whether based on sex, race, disability, sexuality, religion or belief, or transexuality.
* The *Disability Discrimination Act* covers all employers, regardless of size. Its definition of a 'disability' includes HIV, MS and certain forms of cancer within its definition.
* Employers should check that requirements, conditions or provisions do not have a discriminatory impact or alternatively, if there is, that there is justification.

Employers have a specific legal duty not to discriminate against employees on the grounds of their sex, marital status, race, transsexuality, disability, sexual orientation or religion. Additionally, there are other forms of discrimination, like those based on age, which currently are not specifically outlawed by statute, but where nevertheless it has been possible for employees to challenge discriminatory practices. Legislation outlawing age discrimination is effective from 1 October 2006. For an employer to be liable there must be unlawful discrimination. For example, the fact that an employer treats employees badly will not give rise to a discrimination claim unless the treatment is on the grounds of one of the subjects of specific statutory protection.

Discrimination can be:

* *direct* – when an individual is treated less favourably on the grounds of sex, transsexuality, religion, belief, sexual orientation, race or disability,
* *indirect* – where there is a provision, criterion or practice which would be to the detriment of a considerably larger proportion of women or of a particular racial group, which is not justifiable and which is to their detriment. It does not matter that the employer did not have lawful grounds for justifying discrimination on the date when it first occurred, provided that a case of lawful justification was made when the tribunal heard the case; or
* *by way of victimisation* – it is unlawful to victimise an employee because a discrimination claim has been made (*Sex Discrimination Act 1975, s 4*; *Race Relations Act 1976, s 2*).

Sexual or racial harassment also comes within the definition of discrimination and is unlawful, and employers are liable for acts of harassment carried out by their employees if they take no action (or ineffective action) to counter it (*Bracebridge Engineering v Darby [1990] IRLR 3*). The *Employment Equality (Sex Discrimination) Regulations 2005* (*SI 2005/2467*) define harassment as 'unwanted conduct, on grounds of sex or of a sexual nature'. The definition means that there is no requirement to show how a comparator of the opposite sex would have been treated. Employers should note that they can be held to be responsible for harassment that takes place outside of the employee's contractual hours (eg at after work social events) as these have been held to be 'extensions' of the workplace. They can also be liable in claims of negligence if the failure to protect an employee against victimisation and harassment results in physical or psychiatric injury.

A claim based on discrimination must be made by the employee within three months of the discriminatory act.

10.23   Categories of Discrimination

There are a number of categories of discrimination. These are discrimination on the grounds of:

- *sex* – it is unlawful for an employer to discriminate on the grounds of a person's sex or marital status (*Sex Discrimination Act 1975* as amended);
- *race* – it is unlawful for an employer to discriminate against employees or applicants for employment on racial grounds which include colour, race, nationality, ethnic or national origins (*Race Relations Act 1976*);
- *sexual orientation* – under the *Employment Equality (Sexual Orientation) Regulations 2003* (*SI 2003/1661*) it is be unlawful to discriminate against workers on the grounds of their sexual orientation;
- *religion* – the *Employment Equality (Religion or Belief) Regulations 2003* (*SI 2002/1899*) make discrimination unlawful if on the grounds of religion or belief;
- *transsexuality* – discrimination is prohibited on the grounds of gender reassignment (*Sex Discrimination Act 1975* as amended by the *Sex Discrimination (Gender Reassignment) Regulations 1999* (*SI 1999/1102*);
- *disability* – treating disabled persons less favourably than the non-disabled, where the employee's disability is the reason for the less favourable treatment, is unlawful (*Disability Discrimination Act 1995*); and
- *age* – although currently there is no legislation prohibiting discrimination on the grounds of age, there is a voluntary, non-statutory code of practice which recommends that employers do not discriminate on age grounds.

The *Employment Equality (Age) Regulations 2006* come into force on 1 October 2006. These follow the model of sex and race discrimination legislation by defining discrimination as direct or indirect and outlawing less favourable treatment based on age. However, according to a recent House of Lords ruling, setting an upper age limit for the right to claim unfair dismissal or redundancy is not indirectly discriminatory against men. An ACAS guide, *Age and the Workplace*, gives advice to employers on how to ensure compliance with the new law.

10.24   The Commissions

The Equal Opportunities Commission ('EOC') and the Commission for Racial Equality ('CRE') are statutory bodies set up under *section 53* of the *Sex*

Discrimination Act 1975 and *section 43* of the *Race Relations Act 1976*. They may give assistance to help appellants if the case is of some complexity or raises a question of principle.

If they believe unlawful discriminatory acts have been practised, the Commissions can conduct formal investigations for any purpose connected with their duties. Following such investigations, they may make recommendations and may issue a non-discrimination notice (ie require the employer to end the discrimination and to introduce policies and practices aimed at achieving this). In cases of persistent discrimination, the Commissions can apply to the county court for an injunction to restrain the employer.

Under the *Disability Rights Commission Act 1999*, a Disability Rights Commission has powers similar to those of the EOC and CRE.

The EOC, CRE and the Disability Rights Commission have a short leaflet, *Equal Opportunities is Your Business Too*, which advises small firms on general good practice in relation to equal opportunities (for information on obtaining copies see the CRE website at www.cre.gov.uk).

Under the *Equalities Act 2006* a new Commission for Equality and Human Rights replacing the EOC, CRE and DRC will come into force from a date announced by the Secretary of State. The single Commission will create a single channel for all discrimination claims.

10.25   Compensation

There is no upper-limit compensation in discrimination cases. Compensation is assessed by taking the sum which the successful applicant would have earned in his/her employment, deducting from that the amount he/she would or should have earned elsewhere, and then discounting the net sum by a percentage to reflect the chance that he/she might have left her employer anyway (*MOD v Wheeler [1998] IRLR 23*). Employees taking discrimination claims may also have grounds for personal injury claims where the discrimination has affected their physical or mental health but such claims have to be taken in conjunction with the discrimination claim itself. Claims can also be taken for aggravated damages, representing not the employee's financial loss, but to take account of the employer's attitude in the way that the claim is conducted or defended. As a guide these could be in the region of £5,000, although in one recent case the Court of Appeal awarded £20,000 in a case where an employer had done nothing to prevent the discrimination and had indeed promoted the harasser.

Compensation can also reflect injury to feelings. As a guide, in a case of serious discrimination this could be in the region of £25,000 but are unlikely ever to be set at less than £500, if awarded. Claims do not die with the applicant. They can continue to be pursued by the representatives of a dead employee.

10.26   Guides and Codes

The Equal Opportunities Commission has published *Dealing with Sexual Harassment at Work* (2002) which offers advice to employers and trade unions about preventing sexual harassment in the workplace (for information on obtaining copies see the EOC website at www.eoc.org.uk).

The Commission for Racial Equality has published guidelines on racial harassment. These define the harassment as 'unwanted conduct of a racial nature, or other conduct based on race'. *Racial Harassment at Work: What employers can do about it* is available from the CRE (for information on obtaining copies see the CRE website at www.cre.gov.uk).

The advisory service ACAS has also published two guides on harassment and bullying at work: *Bullying and Harassment at Work – Guidance for Employees* and *Bullying and Harassment at Work – a Guide for Managers and Employers* (for information on obtaining copies see the ACAS website at www.acas.org.uk).

The Employers' Forum on Disability has issued a guide, *Solutions at Work: Practical Guides to Managing Disability*, which answers a range of employers' questions on disability and takes managers through a selection of practical adjustments they can implement to recruit and retain disabled workers. (The guide is available from the EFD. Tel: 020 7089 2480.)

10.27 Payment Rights

> **At a Glance**
> * Every employee must be given, by the first pay date, an itemised pay statement.
> * There is an obligation to pay a statutory minimum wage.
> * Women have the right to be paid equally when they work on like work with men, when their work has been rated as equivalent to men's or where their work is of equal value.
> * To succeed in a claim for equal pay the employee needs to find a 'comparable' employee of the opposite sex who is being paid more.
> * It would be good practice for employers to audit pay to ensure that there are no differences based on sex. If differences emerge they must be justified under the material difference/material factor defences.

Pay in return for work is a basic element in the employment contract. Pay rights are normally based on the contract but there is statutory regulation of pay as it affects equal pay, guarantee pay, minimum pay and medical suspension pay. Additionally, employers have to provide an employee with a pay slip (*ERA 1996, s 8*) and to make no deductions from pay, other than those provided for by law (*ERA 1996, Pt II*).

Wages include fees, bonuses, commission, holiday pay, sick pay and maternity pay. Claims for notice pay or pay in lieu do not fall into the definition of wages, neither do claims regarding non-payment of car allowances. Where the employer provides a bonus that is purely discretionary this does not create a contractual entitlement. Employers cannot make deductions from wages unless the deduction is by statutory power (like income tax and National Insurance contributions) or there is a term agreed in writing in the employee's contract preceding the deduction.

If pay is determined through appraisal, it is important that employees know the criteria used and how the appraisal is carried out. They should also understand which core elements of their work are the subject of appraisal, for example the extent to which productivity, attendance, sickness, competence and so on are used to determine pay. It is important that pay systems and methods of determining pay are transparent, as otherwise they are vulnerable to equal pay claims.

10.28 Minimum Pay

The *National Minimum Wage Act 1998* imposes a national minimum, set at £5.05 an hour, for all workers aged 22 and over, effective from 1 October 2005. A lower rate of £4.25 an hour, effective from 1 October 2004, applies to those aged 18 to 21. Young people aged 16 and 17 (other than apprentices) have a minimum rate of £3.00 an hour.

The minimum applies to a broad category of worker, including agency and homeworkers as well as employees. There are a few exclusions, for instance, for people working on fishing vessels who are paid by share of profits, people employed in voluntary organisations, prisoners and schoolchildren.

The Act requires employers to keep records in relation to each worker, sufficient to show that they have been paid at least the national minimum. Workers have the right to see the records kept about them if they have reasonable grounds for believing that the minimum has not been paid. A written request for records requires these to be produced within 14 days.

The Inland Revenue is charged with enforcing the national minimum wage and has powers to demand records, enter premises and interview the employer. It can also serve enforcement notices on employers.

10.29 Equal Pay

Under the *Equal Pay Act 1970* employers are required not to discriminate on the grounds of sex in terms of pay or pay benefits offered, including:

- pension and survivors' benefits;
- sick pay;
- redundancy pay;
- and benefits like travel concessions and mortgage concessions.

Section 1 of the *Equal Pay Act 1970* implies an equality clause into every contract of employment where such a clause does not already exist. It also provides that women should be paid equally when they work on 'like work' with men, when their work has been rated as equivalent to men's, or where their work is of 'equal value'. Employees can use a questionnaire procedure to obtain information about comparable pay, to enable them to decide whether there may be grounds for an equal pay claim.

Employment Law

'Like work' is defined as being work which is 'the same or broadly similar' to that of a comparator of the opposite sex. It has been used by part-time workers comparing themselves with full-time workers and employees comparing their pay with that of their predecessors. The jobs being compared do not need to be identical, but broadly comparable. Where there are differences the tribunal will examine the frequency with which these occur.

A woman is also entitled to equal pay if her work 'in terms of the demands made on her' (eg under such headings as effort, skill and decision-making) is of 'equal value' to that of a man in the same employment (*Equal Pay Act 1970, s 1(2)(c)*).

10.30   *The 'Comparable' Employee*

To succeed in a claim, a woman (or man) needs to find a 'comparable' employee of the opposite sex who is paid more. Any employee can be chosen and the fact that another employee of the same sex as the 'comparable' employee is working with and paid at the same rate as the employee making the equal value claim does not act as a bar to the claim (*Pickstone v Freemans plc [1988] IRLR 357*).

The comparable employee must be employed either at the same workplace, or if at a different establishment, must be employed on the same terms and conditions as comparable workers in the applicant's own workplace or on such terms which would have been applied had there been comparable employees in that workplace (*British Coal v Smith and Others [1994] ICR 810*). There are circumstances where employees working for different employers can nevertheless make comparisons across each employer. This would be the case where there was a common source with central responsibility for their terms and conditions.

The choice of comparator is solely in the hands of the employee. An employer cannot impose a different comparator to defeat an equal pay claim. However, once the comparator has been chosen the applicant may only claim the same pay as the comparator. For instance, if the applicant has longer service than the comparator she cannot claim his rate of pay and an addition in recognition of her longer service.

10.31   *Employer's Defence*

There are two defences to an equal pay claim.

- Where the employee claims under '*like work*', the employer can allege that the pay disparity is due to a 'material difference' between the jobs. This has to be a real difference, significant and relevant, and can include merit pay additions, payments to reflect unsocial hours and so on. Paying a male employee extra to reflect his additional training and advisory role would come within this defence (*Baker and Others v Rochdale Health Authority [1994] IRLB 502*).
- Where an employee is claiming that the job is of '*equal value*' the employer can claim that there is a 'material factor' (such as a difference in pay which reflects the comparable employee's experience, even if not superior qualifications)

which is the reason for the pay difference. In such cases the employer does not need to provide a justification for the pay difference unless the material factor itself is tainted by sex discrimination.

Where the parties are in a 'adversarial relationship', for example where the employee is pursuing an equal pay claim which the employer opposes, the employer can legitimately take 'honest and reasonable' steps to get the other side to withdraw, including writing to employees in an attempt to get them to withdraw the claim, even if threats for future employment are part of the written approach (*St Helens MBC v Derbyshire and others A2/2004/1988; A/2004/1850*).

10.32   Maternity and Parental Leave

At a Glance
* All pregnant employees have the right to time off with pay to attend antenatal appointments.
* A woman pregnant or on maternity leave has the absolute statutory right not to be dismissed for pregnancy-related reasons.
* Every employee who is pregnant has the right to maternity leave together with the right to return to work at the end of it.
* The minimum amount of maternity leave is 26 weeks (ordinary). Women with at least a year's service have longer leave.
* Employees who meet the service qualifying conditions have the right to be paid at least statutory maternity pay while on maternity leave.
* Employees have the right to parental leave, to request flexible working and to time off to care for dependants.
* The partners of pregnant women have the right to two weeks' statutory paternity leave paid at £108.85 a week (2006/07) for those that meet the qualifying conditions.
* Adoptive parents also have the right to parental leave together with a right to maternity and paternity leave.

10.33   Pregnant Employees

A number of rights are afforded to women who are expecting or have recently given birth to a child. These include the right to:

* time off to get to and attend ante-natal appointments and classes (*ERA 1996, s 55*);
* assessment of risks she may be exposed to in order to ensure that she is not exposed to those risks (*Management of Health and Safety at Work (Amendment) Regulations 1994 (SI 1994/2865)*);
* not be suspended from work on maternity grounds (*Suspension from Work (on Maternity Grounds) Order 1994 (SI 1994/2930)*);

- not be refused employment because she is pregnant or on maternity leave (*Dekker v Stichting VJV-Centrum Plus [1992] ICR 325*); and
- not be dismissed because of her pregnancy or for any pregnancy-related reason for the whole of the period of her pregnancy and for the time that she is on maternity leave.

10.34   Maternity Leave

Under *section 71* of *ERA 1996*, every employee who is pregnant has the right to maternity leave together with the right to return to work at the end of it. The length of the leave is dependent on how long she has worked for her employer.

There are three levels of maternity leave:

- *ordinary* – a lower level, which is not dependent on service – this gives all employees the right to 26 weeks' maternity leave;
- *additional* – a higher level, provided the employee has worked for at least 26 weeks by the fourteenth week before the baby is due – this gives the employee the right to an additional 26 weeks' leave which runs on from the end of ordinary maternity leave; and
- *compulsory* – a compulsory maternity leave period of two weeks from the date of the baby's birth. A woman may not work during that period and an employer who permits her to do so may be liable in criminal penalties.

Maternity leave can start anytime between the eleventh week before the baby is due and the week it is born. However, if a woman is off sick for a pregnancy-related matter any time in the final four weeks before the week the baby is due, her employer can require her to begin the leave from that date.

During the period of ordinary leave, a woman is entitled to benefit from all of her contractual terms save those covering remuneration (*ERA 1996, s 71*). This means that she will continue to accrue rights to conditions like holidays, pension credits, service-related benefits, company cars and any other perks. She will even be entitled to a discretionary bonus, paid mainly or exclusively as an incentive for future work or loyalty. She also has the right to have her period of leave counted towards any service-related benefits.

Beyond the period of ordinary leave, an employee has the right to benefit from her employer's implied obligation of trust and confidence and to any contractual terms relating to notice, redundancy compensation, and disciplinary or grievance procedures (*Maternity and Parental Leave etc Regulations 1999* (*SI 1999 No 3312*), *Reg 17(1)*). The employee is also bound by obligations in relation to notice, confidentiality and any non-competition clauses.

At present a woman who is entitled to ordinary leave need do nothing at the end of her leave other than present herself for work. She is not obliged to give advance notice of her return date. However, if she wishes to return before the end of the ordinary leave, then she has to give at least 28 days' notice.

Employers have a legal duty to calculate their employee's return to work date (dependent on the employee's service) and give the employee that information in writing. This should normally be done within 28 days of the employee having given notice of her pregnancy and intention to take maternity leave.

10.35 Maternity Pay

All employees who at the beginning of the fourteenth week before the week that their baby is due:

- have worked for at least 26 weeks continuously; and
- have earned at least £84 a week (2006/07),

have the right to Statutory Maternity Pay ('SMP'), regardless of whether or not they intend to return to work.

SMP is payable for a maximum of 26 weeks and is set at the following rate:

- six weeks' pay at 90 per cent of average earnings; plus
- twenty weeks at a flat rate of £108.85 a week (2006/07).

Women earning less than £84 a week but more than £30 a week have the right to maternity pay calculated at 90 per cent of their previous earnings.

To gain her entitlement to SMP a woman must have complied with the notification rules. She must have given her employer 28 days' notice in writing of her intention to stop work and claim SMP. She must also produce a copy of her maternity certificate and have stopped work. Once she has returned to work, entitlement to SMP ends. The only exception to this rule is where she falls sick after a return to work but within the period of ordinary maternity leave. In this case she can revert back to SMP.

Employees who have no entitlement to SMP because they do not have the minimum 26 weeks' continuous service with the same employer, may be entitled to Maternity Allowance ('MA'). This is fixed at £108.85 a week (2005/07) for up to 26 weeks and is payable provided that in the 66 weeks before the week the baby is due the employee has worked for at least 26 weeks (even if they are not continuous) and was earning at least £84 a week. Women who are self-employed or unemployed have the right to the same level of MA.

Employers may reclaim 92 per cent of each payment of SMP. Small employers, defined as those whose National Insurance contributions do not exceed £40,000, can recover 100 per cent of SMP and an additional 4.5 per cent in compensation for employers' National Insurance costs.

The *Work and Families Act 2006* comes into force in April 2007 and will increase the period of statutory maternity pay from six to nine months and then there will be a further increase taking the total amount of leave to 12 months by the end of the current Parliament. The Act will also:

- give fathers the right to longer paternity leave, from the current two weeks to up to three months, but only if the child's mother forgoes some of her maternity leave; and
- give all carers the right to request flexible working, not just those who are the parents of young children.

10.36   Paternity and Parental Leave

All partners of pregnant women, including adoptive partners and same sex partners, have the right to up to two weeks' paternity leave to care for their new child or support the mother. The leave is paid at a flat rate, the maximum being £108.85 a week. The leave must be taken within the first eight weeks of the baby's birth and must be taken in one block to the maximum of two weeks' leave.

To implement the EU Parental Leave Directive, the Government introduced *sections 7* to *9* of the *Employment Relations Act 1999* and the accompanying *Maternity and Parental Leave etc Regulations 1999* (*SI 1999/3312*) which give UK workers, both men and women, the right to up to three months' parental leave to be taken anytime up to the child's fifth birthday.

The main rules for statutory parental leave are as follows:

*   the maximum amount of leave, which can be taken, is 13 weeks;
*   leave can be taken in blocks of no less than a week, and if the employee chooses to take less than a week it still counts as one of the 13 weeks;
*   employees must give at least 21 days' notice of intention to take the leave;
*   a maximum of four weeks can be taken in any one year;
*   the employer can postpone the taking of leave by up to six months where the business would be unduly disrupted, but cannot exercise this right in respect of a request for leave immediately after the child is born;
*   there is no provision that the leave should be paid; and
*   there is no requirement on the employer to keep records.

If a child is disabled, the right to up to 18 weeks' parental leave can be exercised anytime until the child is 18 years old, subject to the rest of the above rules.

10.37   Adoptive Parents

The *Maternity and Parental Leave etc Regulations 1999* (*SI 1999/3312*) extend to adoptive parents. The rules, which enable the parents to exercise the leave, are as for parental leave save that the right to the leave applies for the first five years after the adoption or until such time as the child reaches the age of 18, rather than the first five years of the child's life. In the case of an adoptive couple one parent will have the right to up to 26 weeks' ordinary adoption leave, followed by up to 26 weeks' additional adoption leave. Additional adoption leave is dependent on the employee having worked for their employer for at least 26 weeks by the week they have been told they will be matched. Statutory Adoption Pay (SAP) is paid at the standard rate of SMP £108.35 a week (2006/07) for 26 weeks. If earnings are less than £108.35, employees are entitled to 90 per cent of their average earnings. An adoptive parent earning less than £84 a week has no right to SAP.

10.38   Leave for Urgent Family Reasons

The *Employment Relations Act 1999* amends *ERA 1996* by inserting a new *section 57A*, which gives employees the right to take unpaid time off in cases of family emergencies involving parents, children, spouse or co-habitee or anyone who looks to the employee for assistance. A family emergency is defined as sickness, accident, criminal injury, death, funerals, absence of the carer for a family member and serious problems at the child's school. The right to take unpaid leave for death in the family only applies in relation to the death of a dependant.

A 'dependant' is defined as the employee's husband, wife, child, parent or someone who lives in the same household as the employee but not as a tenant, or a person who reasonably relies on the employee for assistance if ill, injured or assaulted. The amount of time off which must be given is defined solely as 'reasonable' time off. There is no statutory right to payment and the employee must tell the employer how long the absence will be, unless this is impossible at the time.

10.38A Flexible Working

Parents who have worked for their employer for at least 26 weeks under a contract of employment have the right to request to work flexibly, making the request in writing if required. The request can be made anytime up to two weeks before their child's sixth birthday. Employers have a duty to consider the request seriously and to respond to the employee by arranging a meeting to discuss the request. The employee has the right to bring a companion to the meeting provided that the employer also employs the companion. The employer can refuse the request if the employee has not followed the procedures or where there are sound business reasons for turning down the request. Any agreed change becomes a permanent change to the employee's terms and conditions. A tribunal can award up to eight weeks' pay (at no more than £290 a week (2006)) if an employer unreasonably turns down the request and up to two weeks' pay if there was no meeting.

10.39 Checklist

✓ Pregnant employees – Request MAT1 form to confirm pregnancy.

✓ Parental leave – Reclaim SMP through NI system. Qualifying employees must have at least a year's service and must give notice.

10.40 Sickness

At a Glance
* SSP is payable to eligible employees for up to 28 weeks.
* Dismissal for reasons of sickness can amount to a fair dismissal but the employer should normally have given warnings and consulted both with a doctor and with the employee.

Employment Law

10.41 Statutory Sick Pay ('SSP')

Statutory Sick Pay ('SSP') is payable to eligible employees for up to 28 weeks of absence from work in any one period of illness, although there is a procedure for 'linking' periods of illness provided that the break between them is never more than eight weeks. If illnesses are linked in this way the linking cannot extend beyond a three-year period.

SSP is paid at a flat rate of £70.05 (2006/07) provided gross weekly earnings are at least £84 a week (2006/07). The employee cannot claim for the first three days of sickness – these are 'waiting days'.

SSP is not payable to:

- employees over State pension age;
- employees who are sick while taking part in a strike;
- employees in legal custody;
- young people on youth training schemes if their employment status is not that of an employee; or
- employees whose 'linked' periods of illness exceed 28 weeks over a period of three years.

Eligible employees become entitled to SSP once they have been sick through illness for at least four days in a row and this period of absence includes three qualifying days. They must also have complied with the agreed notification procedures. The daily rate of SSP is the weekly rate divided by the number of qualifying days in the week.

Notification of absence through illness can be required by the end of the first day of illness, but if the employer does not specify a date, the employee has seven days before he/she needs to notify the employer in writing of his/her sickness and weekly thereafter. A medical practitioner's certificate cannot be required before the end of seven days of illness.

Employers are obliged to keep records of sickness absence and SSP payments and these must be held for at least three years. The records must include a note of the agreed qualifying days for SSP.

10.42 Dismissal

Dismissal for reasons of sickness may come within one of the definitions of fair dismissal.

An employer seeking to dismiss for reasons of sickness will normally be required to have:

- given warnings;
- consulted a doctor about the nature of the illness; and
- consulted the employee to see if there are alternatives to dismissal.

Matters which the employer can take into account can include:

- the length of sickness absence compared to periods of good health;
- the employer's need for the particular employee's work;

- the impact of the absence on the rest of the workforce; and
- the extent of consultation (*Lynock v Cereal Packaging Ltd [1988] ICR 670*).

Where an employee has persistent absences, albeit for genuine sickness reasons, an employer may fairly dismiss in the following circumstances:

- there are persistent absences for unconnected medical reasons;
- all those reasons are genuine in themselves;
- the absences have been frequent;
- they have occurred over a significant period of time; and
- a proper procedure, including giving warnings, has occurred.

10.43   Checklist

> ✓   Employees are eligible for SSP from their first day of work, provided they do not come within an excluded category.
>
> ✓   Establish a sickness absence procedure and ensure that all action in relation to sickness is in compliance with the policy.
>
> ✓   Ensure that there are warnings and that there has been consultation before any action to dismiss on the grounds of sickness.

10.44   Discipline and Grievances

> **At a Glance**
> * Employers must have a statutory dispute procedure that sets down minimum procedures for dealing with disciplinary and grievance matters.
> * An ACAS code of practice gives practical advice on how to draw up disciplinary rules.
> * A worker has the right to be accompanied by a companion of choice whenever asked to attend a formal disciplinary or grievance hearing.

10.45   Statement of Rules or Grievance

Section 1 of *ERA 1996* specifies that in workplaces where, when the individual starts work, there are already 20 or more employees, a statement must be given (or access to one provided) specifying any disciplinary rules or grievance procedures. The *Employment Act 2002* places a legal requirement on all employers to have a statutory dispute resolution procedure. As a minimum employees must be given a written statement of the charges against them, the right to a meeting and a right to an appeal.

Employment Law

The ACAS Code of Practice *Disciplinary and Grievance Procedures* (2004) gives practical advice on how to draw up disciplinary rules. It provides guidance on how the new rights to be accompanied to disciplinary or grievance hearings should operate and also on the appropriate procedures to use and the rights of the companion who may accompany the worker to the hearing. (For information on obtaining copies see the ACAS website at www.acas.org.uk.)

Workers usually must use internal grievance procedures before lodging a tribunal claim.

10.46   Disciplinary Procedure

It is important that employers have and follow an established disciplinary procedure. Adherence to the procedure will offer a strong defence to an unfair dismissal claim. *Schedule 2* of the *Employment Act 2002* sets out three steps that must be contained within the procedure. The procedure should begin without delay and the timing and location of the meetings should be reasonable to give the worker the opportunity to explain their case.

10.47   Disciplinary Hearing

It is important that the disciplinary hearing is free from bias. In particular, wherever possible, the person taking the disciplinary hearing should not have had any previous involvement in the events leading up to the hearing. Employers should take care before dismissing employees without a hearing even in cases where the employee faces criminal charges.

Section 10 of the *Employment Relations Act 1999* gives workers a legal right to be accompanied by a fellow worker or trade unionist (regardless of whether or not the union is recognised) in disciplinary and grievance hearings (defined in the *Employment Relations Act 1999, s 13(4)* and *13(5)* respectively).

If a trade unionist is chosen, that individual could be a lay member from the worker's own workplace or from another workplace with a different employer. The choice is entirely left to the worker. A full-time union official may also act as the companion. The companion will have the right to make a statement at the hearing and to confer with the worker. The companion will have legal protection from dismissal or victimisation if connected with acting as a representative. If employed by another employer the protection will extend to any action taken by that other employer on the grounds that the worker has acted as a companion. Where the companion is a lay trade unionist, the union will have to have certified in writing his/her competence to act as a companion.

The advisory service ACAS's Code of Practice *Disciplinary and Grievance Procedures* (see **10.45** above) gives advice on the certification of companions who are union officials and advises that it would normally be appropriate, where a union has recognition, for its officers to act as the companion, rather than officials from another unrecognised union.

10.48   Checklist

✓ All employers should have a procedure to cover disciplinary and grievance procedures.

✓ These must include, as a minimum, the right to:

- a written statement of charges,
- a meeting, and
- an appeal.

✓ Check that there is no risk of bias in the disciplinary procedure.

✓ Inform any employee facing a disciplinary or grievance procedure of the right to be accompanied.

10.49   Redundancy and Dismissal

At a Glance

* Where 20 or more redundancies are anticipated, the employer must notify the union (if recognised) or otherwise employee representatives and commence consultation in good time.

* The decision to make redundancies is one for the employer to make. There is no obligation to show that there is an economic justification for that decision.

* Within this consultation there is a legal obligation to consider alternatives to redundancy.

* Employers who fail to consult may be liable to pay a protective award to each employee.

* Selection criteria must not discriminate.

* Employees with two or more years' service who are selected for redundancy have the right to redundancy pay.

* The maximum statutory redundancy pay is £8,700 (2006).

* Employees have legal rights not to be dismissed unfairly or wrongfully.

* The employment contract will usually state the length of notice required to terminate the agreement.

* Definitions of dismissal:
   ○ constructive – employee terminates employment but alleges that the employer's conduct gave no alternative,
   ○ wrongful – dismissal in breach of contract,
   ○ unfair – any dismissal not for a fair reason.

* Non-renewal of a fixed term contract is also a dismissal.

* Employees have statutory protection against unfair dismissal provided they have one year's service with the same employer and are below retirement age.

* Compensation consists of:
  ○ basic award – calculated in a similar way to redundancy pay,
  ○ compensatory award – takes account of past/future loss of earnings and benefits subject to £58,400 (2006) maximum,
  ○ additional award – in cases where reinstatement has been refused.

10.50 Declaring Redundancies

When faced with the need to reduce staffing numbers or to radically reorganise the way that work is undertaken, employers have to comply with the legal rules on redundancy.

An employee targeted for redundancy acquires certain statutory rights including:

- the right to be consulted and/or for the employer to consult with a recognised union or with employee representatives elected for the purpose of consultation, over the proposed redundancy; and
- for employees with at least two years' continuous service to be paid redundancy pay.

There are specific statutory requirements for notice, both to the individual and the workplace representatives with whom consultation is to take place. The individual worker is entitled to at least the notice which it would take to lawfully terminate the contract. This most commonly is one week for every year of service. (For more information on rights to notice see **10.53–10.57** below.)

Under *section 188* of the *Trade Union and Labour Relations (Consolidation) Act 1992 (TULRCA 1992)*, as amended by *regulation 3* of the *Collective Redundancies and Transfer of Undertakings (Protection of Employment) (Amendment) Regulations 1995 (SI 1995/2587)*, employers should notify recognised trade unions or employee representatives if 20 or more redundancies are to take place within a 90-day period. The DTI must also be notified. A minimum period of consultation of at least 30 days (90 days if more than 100 employees are affected) must be allowed, regardless of the size of the employer (*De Grasse v Stockwell Tools Ltd [1992] IRLR 269*).

Where fewer than 21 redundancies are proposed, so that the statutory obligation to consult does not apply, employers should still consult with individual employees. However, a failure to do so will not necessarily make the redundancy selection unfair.

In the course of the consultation, workplace representatives should be provided with information which explains the method of calculating any non-statutory redundancy payments (*Trade Union Reform and Employment Rights Act 1993, s 34*).

If an employer refuses or fails to consult, the trade union or employee representative body can apply, within a three-month period, to a tribunal to ask for a protective award which will be granted unless it can be shown that there were special circumstances making it not reasonably practicable to consult. Whilst the law provides the employer with this defence of 'special circumstances', it is narrowly defined. For instance, the fact that a company is in receivership and needs to shed staff does not automatically amount to 'special circumstances'.

It is useful to agree a redundancy procedure in advance. If there is a recognised union the procedure will normally be agreed with the union. The procedure can set out what the selection criteria will be and how consultation will take place. It can also include details of the redundancy pay arrangements and the extent to which these improve upon the statutory minimum. It is useful if the procedure also deals with issues like time off to look for alternative work and entitlement to pay in lieu of notice, in cases where employees have the opportunity for alternative work with a new employer.

10.51   Selection for Redundancy

Employers are obliged to adopt criteria for selection for redundancy which do not discriminate on the grounds of sex, transsexuality, race, disability, trade union membership, sexual orientation and religion. In general a procedure which automatically selected part-time workers first would be considered discriminatory. However, there may be circumstances were employers can objectively justify such selection (*Kachelmann v Bankhaus Hermann Lampe [2001] IRLR 49*).

Women, during pregnancy and while on maternity leave, have the absolute right not to be selected for redundancy on the grounds of their pregnancy. In cases involving disabled employees, there may be a legal obligation to give priority to such an employee where there is alternative work.

Note that it is unlawful to select an employee for redundancy because of their trade union duties or activities.

10.52   Payments

Employees selected for redundancy have a statutory right to redundancy pay. The right is to a number of 'weeks' pay', depending on age and service. The 'weeks' pay' is subject to a maximum, currently £290 a week (2006) and the calculation is based on the employee's gross, not net, pay. This means that employees with higher earnings do not have these taken into account in the calculation of statutory redundancy pay.

Eligibility for redundancy pay is based on the employee's length of service, with a minimum of two weeks' pay after two years of continuous employment. The amount of the redundancy payment is calculated with reference to the period that the employee has been continuously employed, ending with the date of dismissal. The employee is then entitled to:

(*a*) one and a half week's pay for every year of employment which consists wholly of weeks in which the employee was not below the age of 41;

(b) one week's pay for every year of employment (not falling within (a) above) which consists wholly of weeks in which the employee was not below the age of 22; and

(c) half a week's pay for every year of employment not falling within either (a) or (b) above.

The total maximum number of years which can be taken into account is 20, giving a total maximum payment of £8,700 (2006).

Employees over the age of 64 have their amount payable reduced by one-twelfth for every month where his/her age exceeds 64.

Employers have to give the employee a written statement saying how redundancy pay has been calculated (*ERA 1996, s 165*), and are also obliged to give employee representatives information on how the calculation has been made.

10.53 Dismissal (Unfair, Constructive and Wrongful)

Employees have legal rights not to be dismissed unfairly or wrongfully and can pursue claims for reinstatement or compensation/damages in situations where a dismissal has occurred in breach of the legal rules.

The employment contract will usually state the length of notice required to terminate the agreement. The notice must at least be equal to that provided for in *section 86* of *ERA 1996*, which is a week for every year of service (with one week only up to the first two years and an overall maximum of twelve weeks). Where the contract does not specify the length of notice the tribunals can imply a right to 'reasonable' notice.

10.54 Constructive Dismissal

A constructive dismissal occurs when the employee terminates employment but alleges that the employer's conduct gave no alternative but to resign. The effect is that the employer has breached the contract. The breach must, however, be fundamental before a claim of constructive dismissal can be advanced, but a continuing series of breaches of contract can amount to a constructive dismissal. A dismissal can still be constructive even in cases where the employee alleges that the employer's actions had been cumulative or persistent, amounting to a breach of implied terms, even when the 'last straw' incident did not amount to a breach of contract and even where there is a gap in time between the previous incident of employer conduct and the last incident, provided that all together they amounted to a fundamental breach of contract. Demoting an employee where there are grounds for dismissal does not amount to a constructive dismissal even where there is nothing in the contract which gives the employer the right to demote.

10.55 Wrongful Dismissal

A dismissal is wrongful if it occurs by a breach of the contract (eg without the necessary contractual notice). A dismissal in breach of a contractual disciplinary procedure will also amount to a wrongful dismissal. A claim for wrongful dismissal has usually been dealt with in the civil courts, but may now also be dealt with by employment tribunals.

Wrongful dismissal claims, unlike those on unfair dismissal (see **10.56** below) are not limited to any overall maximum compensatory award and, therefore, pose a particular risk where senior, highly paid staff are involved.

10.56 'Fair'/'Unfair' Dismissal

Section 94 of *ERA 1996* protects eligible employees (see **10.57** below) from unfair dismissal. The legislation starts from the assumption that all dismissals are potentially unfair unless they fall within the range of what are known as 'fair' dismissals.

Some dismissals are automatically unfair – these are where the dismissal:

- is pregnancy related;
- is related to health and safety;
- is of a protected Sunday worker;
- relates to the exercise of rights under the *Working Time Regulations 1998* (*SI 1998/1833*);
- is connected with a business transfer;
- arises after the employee has blown the whistle on employer malpractice;
- is on the grounds of trade union membership;
- occurs because an individual has attempted to enforce a 'relevant statutory right', ie:
  ○ those conferred by *ERA 1996* which are enforceable by an employment tribunal,
  ○ minimum period of notice, or
  ○ union activities and time off for them;
- is connected with the fact that the employee would be covered by the national minimum wage;
- is of a pension fund trustee dismissed for reasons related to that role; or
- is on the grounds that the employee is an employee representative or a candidate in an election for being an employee representative.

A dismissal is fair if it relates to the employee's:

- capability or qualifications;
- conduct;
- redundancy;
- failure to comply with legislation like the *Health and Safety at Work etc. Act 1974*;

or if it is 'for some other substantial reason' (such as a business reorganisation, provided that there were sound business reasons for making the change).

10.57   Eligibility

To qualify for the right to pursue an unfair dismissal case under *section 108* of *ERA 1996*, an employee has to have one year's continuous service with the same or an associated employer, regardless of the number of hours worked in the week.

There is no service requirement where an employee claims unfair dismissal for reasons of:

- trade union membership or non-membership (*TULRCA 1992, s 152*);
- 'pregnancy-related reasons'; or
- certain other circumstances – 'automatically unfair dismissals'.

An employee who has passed 'normal retirement age' (ie the age at which employees normally retire, or if there is none, 65 years) cannot bring an unfair dismissal claim (*ERA 1996, s 109*).

10.58   Compensation and Other Remedies

If an employee succeeds at a tribunal, it may order his/her reinstatement or re-engagement. The difference between the two is that under reinstatement the employee returns to their own job with credit for all previous service. Under re-engagement the order is merely to provide the employee with new employment. However, both types of order are relatively rare. At present, fewer than 1 per cent of all tribunal awards end with reinstatement or re-engagement.

Most tribunal hearings where the employee succeeds result in an award of compensation. This consists of three elements, a basic award, a compensatory award and an additional award.

The basic award is calculated on the employee's length of service, with a maximum £8,700 (2006). It takes account of up to 20 years' of the employee's service and is limited to annually announced weekly maximums. The current weekly maximum is £290 (2006). (The minimum cannot be calculated at less than the rate of the statutory national minimum wage.) The rates are then adjusted for the number of years of continuous employment by a weekly rate reckoned backwards as follows:

(*a*) one and a half week's pay for each year of employment in which the employee was not below the age of 41;

(*b*) one week's pay for each year of employment not falling within (*a*) in which the employee was not below the age of 22; and

(*c*) half a week's pay for each such year of employment not falling within either (*a*) or (*b*).

The cash amount is reduced by one-twelfth for each month by which the employee's age exceeds 64.

Redundancy awards are deductible from the basic award.

The compensatory award is calculated on loss sustained, including loss of current and future wages. It is currently subject to an overall maximum of

£58,400 (2006). The award may be based on loss sustained, to include expenses incurred, loss of wages (current and future), loss of pension rights, values for the loss of a company car, loss of other benefits in kind including where share options lost on termination increase in value and loss of accrued statutory protection. The employee has a duty to mitigate (lessen) the loss caused by the dismissal.

An additional award of between 26 and 52 weeks' pay will be made where an employee has sought and won a reinstatement order but the employer has refused to comply.

10.59   Checklist

✓   When proposing redundancies.

  • If there are likely to be 21 or more redundancies consultation must take place.
  • Establish the selection criteria.

✓   Redundancy pay.

  • All redundant employees with two or more years' service qualify.
  • Employees must be given a written statement saying how redundancy pay has been calculated.

✓   Dismissal.

  • If employees have one or more years' service they can only be dismissed for a 'fair' reason.
  • Check if dismissal is for 'automatically unfair reason', for which there is no minimum service.

10.60   Transfer of Undertakings

At a Glance
* Contracts of employment existing at the time of the transfer are automatically transferred.
* Terms and conditions are protected without any time limit.
* The transfer has to be 'relevant' from one person to another, by sale or some other disposition, effected by two or more transactions.
* The transfer has to be of a 'going concern'.
* Usually tangible assets (property or employees) will transfer but their absence does not mean that there is not a relevant transfer.
* A dismissal for reasons of a transfer is automatically unfair.

10.61   Introduction

Where a business transfers from one employer to another there are specific legal rules which must be followed in relation to affected employees.

The *Transfer of Undertakings (Protection of Employment) Regulations 1981 ('TUPE') (SI 1981/1794)*, amended as a consequence of the *Transfer of Undertakings (Protection of Employees) Regulations 2006*, guarantee to employees' continuous employment rights when a trade or business is transferred by sale or other disposition.

TUPE has three principal aims:

- to protect existing employment rights;
- to oblige employers to consult over transfers; and
- to protect employees against dismissal.

Recognised trade unions, or employee representatives elected for the purpose, have rights to information and consultation before the transfer takes place. If it is believed that the transfer will result in measures to be taken in relation to employees, consultation must take place.

TUPE protects employees, including casual or temporary workers and trainees, but does not cover those working as 'self-employed' persons under a contract to offer their services.

10.62   What is a Transfer?

The types of transfer to which *TUPE* applies depend upon their classification as a 'relevant transfer' (*SI 1981/1794, reg 3*), defined as:

- from one person to another of an undertaking situated in the UK;
- effected by sale or some other disposition; and
- which may be effected by two or more transactions.

To decide on whether TUPE applies the tribunals look at two issues:

- whether a given activity or service constitutes an economic entity capable of being transferred; and
- whether that entity retains its identity after the transfer.

A 'service provision change', when a contract moves from one contractor to another, amounts to a relevant transfer. The only circumstances where it will not are in cases where the contract is for 'professional business services'. Employees transferred under TUPE have a free-standing right to claim constructive dismiss. The DTI has published guidance for employers, *A guide to the 2006 TUPE regulations for employees, employers and representatives*, which can be downloaded at www.dti.gov.uk/er/individual/tupeguide2006regs.pdf.

The transfer must be of a going concern, not a mere transfer of the assets of the business. Transfers of franchises and leases, therefore, also come within the definition.

10.63   Effect on Transferor and Transferee

Contracts of employment existing at the time of the transfer (which can include a period of time over which the transfer took place) are automatically transferred by the mere fact of the transfer of the undertaking regardless of the contrary intentions of the old and new employer (*Rotsart de Hertaing v J Benoidt [1997] IRLR 127*). However, the *TUPE Regulations 2006*, effective from 6 April 2006, in addition to making it clear that TUPE does apply in cases involving the transfer of services from the public to the private sector (a 'service provision change'), allow changes to terms and conditions to be agreed, if for an economic, technical, or organisational (ETO) reason which involves changes in the workforce. Where part of a business transfers, those employees identified as working at its premises and assigned to work at the premises being transferred are 'relevant employees' for the purpose of the transfer (see *Securicor Guarding Ltd and Others v Fraser Security Services [1996] IRLR 552* and *Buchanan-Smith v Schleicher & Co International [1996] IRLR 547*).

The transferee is usually liable for any pre-transfer unfair dismissal. The transferee will also be liable for any failure of the transferor to consult over the transfer prior to it taking place.

Following a relevant transfer, the transferee assumes the obligations of the transferor in respect of:

- terms and conditions of employment;
- claims regarding the payment of arrears;
- outstanding legal claims (eg any discrimination claims before employment tribunals);
- outstanding personal injury claims;
- disciplinary records; and
- contractual requirements concerning confidentiality, the status of patents etc.

In calculating entitlement to financial benefits, which are service-based, the new employer has to take account of the employee's service with the old employer as well as any subsequent service with the new employer, according to a ruling from the European Court of Justice.

10.64   Effect on Employment Contracts

All contracts of employment or employment relationships existing at the date of the transfer are automatically transferred to the new employer (*D'Urso v Ercole Marelli Elettromeccanica Generale SpA [1992] IRLR 136*). Continuity of employment and length of service also transfer.

Terms and conditions of employment should remain the same, with the new employer accepting the obligations of the old. There is no time limit after which this protection would no longer apply save in the circumstances detailed above, where there is a change to terms and conditions for an ETO reason. Employees do not, however, acquire rights that they would not previously have had from their old employer. Those employed 'immediately before' the transfer are deemed to be in the same position as they would have held had it not been for the transfer itself. They are obliged to continue to work under existing terms, including any terms giving them the right to benefit from profit-related pay. However, they have no right to benefit from terms offered by their previous employer to remaining employees after the transfer has taken place. Pension rights do not automatically transfer, although those transferred under *TUPE* retain an absolute right to any early retirement benefits they had accrued with their old employer.

10.65 Employees Refusing to Transfer

An employee has the right to object to a transfer and cannot be forced to go to the new employer. However, in such circumstances, the normal rule is that the employment contract terminates, but the employee is not treated as having been dismissed by his former employer (*Newns v British Airways [1992] IRLR 574* and the *Trade Union Reform and Employment Rights Act 1993, s 33(4A)*). There is an exception to this rule, in cases where employees object to the transfer because it would or could involve a substantial change to their working conditions, to their detriment.

10.66 Dismissal

If the new employer, following a transfer, dismisses transferred employees this is automatically unfair unless connected with an economic, technical or organisational ('ETO') change and in all the circumstances the decision to dismiss was reasonable (*SI 1981/1794, reg 8(2)*). However, once a tribunal finds that the dismissal is due to an impending transfer, it cannot go on to find that it is also for an ETO reason. Employees whose terms and conditions are changed to their detriment can now take constructive dismissal claims, even where the change does not amount to a breach of contract.

10.67 Checklist

> ✓ If transfers come within the definition of a relevant transfer, employers must consult the union if recognised or otherwise with workplace representatives elected for the purpose of consultation.
>
> ✓ The new employer must:
>
> - maintain transferred employees' existing terms and conditions;
> - accept transfer of any outstanding legal liabilities; and
> - not dismiss a transferred employee unless for an ETO reason.

10.68   Dispute Resolution

At a Glance
* ACAS has a general duty to promote the improvement of industrial relations.
* The CAC carries the main responsibility for the legal procedures covering trade union recognition.
* Most employment rights are pursued through employment tribunals and must be submitted within a specified time period. There is a right of appeal to the Employment Appeal Tribunal.

10.69   Introduction

Employers and employees can use the services of the Advisory Conciliation and Arbitration Service ('ACAS') and the Central Arbitration Committee ('CAC') to conciliate or arbitrate.

10.70   Advisory, Conciliation and Arbitration Service ('ACAS')

ACAS was established under *section 1* of the *Employment Protection Act 1975* (now *TULRCA 1992, ss 247–253*). It has a general duty to promote the improvement of industrial relations and also issues Codes of Practice and other guidance documents, which, although not legally binding, give advice on good practice and are taken account of by employment tribunals. A leaflet, *The Role of ACAS*, explains how the service operates. (See the ACAS website at www.acas.org.uk)

ACAS can conciliate in industrial disputes and on matters which are, or could be, subject to tribunal procedures. Either party can refer the dispute to ACAS, which may charge for its services but must give notice in advance if it intends to do so.

If a case is referred to it, the ACAS officer should bring the parties together and should explain and give guidance on the issues, seeking common ground. He/she must act without bias. If there is no prospect of success, he/she should withdraw and leave the decision to the employment tribunal. ACAS can make available a system of binding arbitration as an alternative to taking an employment tribunal claim for unfair dismissal.

10.71   Central Arbitration Committee ('CAC')

The CAC was established under *section 10* of the *Employment Protection Act 1975* (now *TULRCA 1992, s 259*). It carries the main responsibility for the legal procedures covering trade union recognition and can make awards of recognition where a union has demonstrated majority support. It can arbitrate in trade disputes at the request of either or both parties, although its arbitration is not legally binding. The CAC also has responsibility for hearing complaints regarding information disclosure. At the request of one or more parties, and with the consent of all parties, ACAS may refer all or any of the matters to which the dispute relates for settlement to the arbitration of the CAC. (See the CAC website at www.cac.gov.uk)

10.72 Employment Tribunals

Most employment protection rights can be pursued by employees through employment tribunals, with a right of appeal to the EAT and from there to the Court of Appeal and the House of Lords. In Northern Ireland, appeals go direct from the tribunals to the Court of Appeal. In Scotland, they go from the EAT to the Court of Session.

As a consequence of changes introduced through the *Employment Act 2002* workers must show that they have exhausted any internal grievance or disciplinary procedures before presenting their claim at a tribunal, and may also be obliged to go through a period of conciliation prior to any hearing. The Act introduced a fixed 'short' or 'standard' period of consultation prior to any claim being heard by a tribunal. Last minute settlements immediately prior to tribunal hearings can no longer be concluded with the assistance of ACAS. Certain cases, where the parties consent, where the case will not proceed to a full hearing, or where the only point of issue is one of law, can be heard by the chairperson alone.

Most claims to tribunals must be submitted within specified time limits and the employee's failure to do this is likely to make the claim invalid unless there are good grounds, acceptable to the tribunals. Tribunals have a broad discretion to add or substitute a party even if the time limit has expired. Tribunals may extend the time limit where it was not reasonably practicable for a claim to be presented in time.

10.73 Appeals

Either party can appeal from a decision of an employment tribunal, but the right to appeal is limited to those cases where it is submitted that the tribunal made an error in interpreting the law or, in very rare cases, that it made a mistake in interpreting the facts and that this was of such gravity that no reasonable tribunal assessing the facts before it could have come to the decision made. In general, applicants cannot present new evidence on appeal, in respect of a claim, which was not made at the initial tribunal hearing.

Appeals must be submitted within 42 days of the employment tribunal decision.

10.74   Other Relevant Legislation

In addition to the legal rules outlined above, employers should be aware of the existence of other legislation which may impact on employment rights. Of particular importance is the *Human Rights Act 1998.* This places obligations on, in particular, the public sector (and on sections of previously public sectors) to apply basic principles of human rights law, such as the right to privacy or the right to organise. Guidance documents are available from the Home Office at www.homeoffice.gov.uk/hract.

Appendix 1

Useful Websites on Employment Issues

Advisory, Conciliation and Arbitration Service (ACAS)	www.acas.gov.uk
Age Positive	www.agepositive.gov.uk
Central Arbitration Committee (CAC)	www.cac.gov.uk
Commission for Racial Equality (CRE)	www.cre.gov.uk
Disability Rights Commission (DRC)	www.drc-gb.org
Department for Trade and Industry (DTI)	www.dti.gov.uk/employment/index.html
Equal Opportunities Commission (EOC)	www.eoc.org.uk
Information Commissioner	www.informationcommission.gov.uk
Employment Tribunals Service (ETS)	www.employmenttribunals.gov.uk

11

Financial Reporting

11 Financial Reporting

11.1 Accounting Standards

At a Glance

* In recent years accounting standards in the UK have been developed by the Accounting Standards Board (ASB) under the auspices of the Financial Reporting Council (FRC), and a detailed consultation programme has been undertaken for each new standard.
* From 1 January 2005, listed groups are required to adopt international accounting standards in place of UK standards, and most other companies have the option of doing this in both individual and group accounts.
* The ASB has begun a programme to converge UK accounting standards with their international equivalents and this is likely to result in significant changes to the role of the ASB.
* Accounting standards apply to all accounts that are required to show a true and fair view, although they need not be applied to immaterial items.
* Each accounting standard is effective from the date specified in the standard, although early adoption is usually encouraged.
* Accounting standards should generally be regarded as applying to all transactions, unless an individual standard requires a different approach.
* Care is required over the early adoption of accounting treatments proposed in ASB Discussion Papers or FREDs, especially where they represent the updating of an existing accounting standard.
* Directors are generally required to state whether the accounts have been prepared in accordance with applicable accounting standards.
* Additional disclosures must be given if the company departs from applicable accounting standards when preparing its annual accounts.
* The Urgent Issues Task Force (UITF) considers interpretational issues arising from existing accounting and company law requirements.
* The Financial Reporting Review Panel (FRRP) enquires into accounts that appear to depart from the requirements of company law, accounting standards and UITF Abstracts.

> * Certain smaller entities are permitted to adopt the Financial Reporting Standard for Smaller Entities (FRSSE) in place of other accounting standards.
> * Statements of Recommended Practice (SORPs) set out recommended accounting practice for specialised sectors or industries.

11.2   The Present Regime

Accounting standards are developed in the UK by the Accounting Standards Board ('ASB') under the auspices of the Financial Reporting Council ('FRC'). Both bodies were established in 1990, together with the Financial Reporting Review Panel ('FRRP' – see **11.16** below) and the Urgent Issues Task Force ('UITF' – see **11.15** below). The structure of these bodies can be summarised as follows.

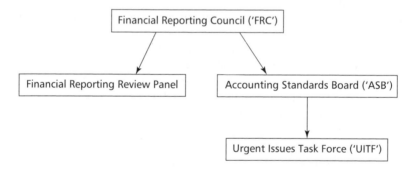

Prior to 1990, standards were developed by the Accounting Standards Committee ('ASC'). At its first meeting, the ASB formally adopted all existing accounting standards (22 at the time) developed by the ASC, but many of these have now been revised or superseded by new standards issued by the ASB. Standards issued by the ASC were described as Statements of Standard Accounting Practice ('SSAPs') and those issued by the ASB are described as Financial Reporting Standards ('FRSs'). Some of the present accounting standards are therefore in the form of SSAPs whilst others are FRSs, but all have the same status for practical purposes. The FRC's original remit has recently been widened to give it a more active role in relation to corporate governance and new responsibilities for the development of auditing standards and general oversight of the regulation of the accountancy and actuarial professions. As a result, the Auditing Practices Board, the Professional Oversight Board, the Accountancy Investigation and Discipline Board and the Board for Actuarial Standards also come under the umbrella of the FRC in the same way as the ASB and FRRP.

11.3   Development of Accounting Standards

Historically potential topics for accounting standards have been identified by the ASB from its own research and also from external sources, and ASB staff have then undertaken a programme of consultation and research, considering conceptual issues, existing practice in the UK, any existing pronouncements (both in the UK and abroad), and the practical implications of introducing new requirements in the UK. A Discussion Paper has usually been prepared setting out the main issues and inviting comments on the ASB's initial proposals. Following this initial consultation, a Financial Reporting Exposure Draft ('FRED') has been published to give those who are interested a chance to comment on the proposals and to enable the ASB to assess the likely level of acceptance before finalising the requirements. However, the current programme of international harmonisation means that accounting requirements are now being developed internationally rather than at a local level, although the ASB is generally continuing the exposure of proposed new or amended accounting standards as FREDs before implementation in the UK.

11.4　Adoption of International Standards

For accounting periods beginning on or after 1 January 2005, listed companies are required by an EU regulation to prepare group accounts in accordance with international accounting standards (IASs) adopted by the EU rather the UK accounting standards. UK company law has been amended to implement this requirement and also to give all companies other than charitable companies the option of preparing both individual and group accounts in accordance with IASs from the same date. Those most likely to take advantage of the IAS option are stand-alone listed companies, to make them more comparable with listed groups, and subsidiaries of listed companies, to avoid having to prepare two sets of figures each year (one based on IASs for consolidation purposes and another using UK standards for statutory accounts purposes). However, it is expected that many companies will continue to prepare their accounts in accordance with UK accounting standards in the immediate future at least. Charitable companies are currently excluded from the IAS regime on the basis that IASs have been drafted with profit-making entities in mind and are therefore not considered appropriate for the charity sector at present. A decision to adopt IASs will generally not be reversible, although a company is permitted to revert to the adoption of UK standards where:

- the company ceases to be listed;
- the company's parent ceases to be listed; or
- the company becomes a subsidiary of a parent that does not prepare IAS accounts.

Where appropriate, the fact that the accounts have been prepared in accordance with IASs must be disclosed in the notes to the accounts.

11.5　*Continuing Legal Requirements*

When a company is required or chooses to prepare IAS accounts, the provisions of *CA 1985* on the form and content of statutory accounts no longer apply.

However, this does not mean that all accounting provisions in the legislation can be ignored. In particular, the provisions that continue to apply even where IAS accounts are prepared include:

- the requirement to prepare and file annual accounts;
- where relevant, the requirement to prepare group accounts;
- disclosure requirements in respect of directors' remuneration and employee numbers and costs;
- disclosure requirements on the remuneration received by the auditors and their associates;
- disclosure requirements in respect of subsidiaries and other undertakings in which the reporting entity holds a significant investment; and
- the requirement to prepare a directors' report.

11.6 *Impact for Groups*

The option of adopting IASs operates independently for group and individual accounts. There is consequently nothing to prevent a parent company from preparing group accounts on the basis of IASs and individual accounts on the basis of UK standards (or vice versa), although to do so would inevitably involve a considerable amount of additional work. Directors of parent companies are expected to ensure consistency in the adoption of IASs within the group, unless there are good reasons against this, and subsidiaries will generally be expected to prepare their accounts on the basis used by the parent for its own individual accounts, although there is a specific exception where the parent prepares both IAS group and IAS individual accounts.

11.7 UK Convergence with IASs

In March 2004, the ASB issued a Discussion Paper *UK Accounting Standards: A Strategy for Convergence with IFRS* setting out its detailed plans for achieving the convergence of UK accounting standards with IASs. The Discussion Paper outlined the ASB's overall strategy and also set out specific proposals on the development or revision of individual accounting standards in the next few years. It seems likely that most companies will continue to adopt UK accounting standards for the immediate future at least, but the ASB is clear in its own mind that, in the medium to long term, there can be no case for maintaining two wholly different sets of accounting standards in the UK. This would create additional burdens for those preparing accounts, undermine the credibility of financial reporting in the UK and hamper comparability. The Board also takes the view that convergence in the form of broadly equivalent requirements will generally not be sufficient – the only way to prevent different interpretations arising in similar circumstances is for UK standards and international standards to be expressed in the same words.

The ASB initially planned to adopt a phased approach to convergence, but is now reconsidering this approach in the light of comments received from respondents and particular concerns over the latest international proposals on accounting for business combinations. These have highlighted the complexity of adopting a phased approach when there are clear inter-relationships between standards, some of which have been converged whilst others are still awaiting convergence. As a result, the ASB set out proposals for a revised convergence strategy in a short paper issued in January 2006 in advance of discussion at a public meeting in London later in the month. The ASB is considering changing to a 'big bang' approach to convergence, where it will continue to expose and finalise new UK accounting standards based on IFRSs but these will be given a common future implementation date rather than being implemented as they are finalised. The current expectation is that all of the new converged standards would come into effect for accounting periods beginning on or after 1 January 2009. Early adoption may be permitted in certain specific cases, but the inter-relationships between standards will generally preclude this.

11.8   Possibility of a Two-tier UK Regime

The second part of the ASB's January 2006 paper (see **11.7** above) considers which accounting standards should apply to which entities. This outlines recent progress in the IASB's plans to develop a new series of standards for entities that do not have public accountability. These are still being referred to as SME standards although the IASB does not currently intend to set financial thresholds for their use as is the case under the present UK small company reporting regime. The ASB is seeking views on whether full IFRSs (or EU-adopted IFRSs) would be appropriate for a wider group of entities – for instance, stand-alone listed companies, those of a similar size to listed entities and those with a significant element of public interest. For companies below this level, a two-tier regime could be developed involving:

- the continuation of a specific financial reporting regime for smaller entities, based either on the IASB's SME standards or, if these are found to be more appropriate to slightly larger entities, an updated FRSSE based on the underlying principles of IFRSs; and
- a separate financial regime for the vast number of entities that are not listed (or regarded as equivalent to listed or of significant public interest) but do not qualify as small – this regime is likely to be based on full IFRSs but with appropriate exemptions or adjustments to ensure that the cost of compliance does not significantly outweigh the related benefits.

Separate consideration will need to be given to the standards that should apply to public benefit entities, balancing the need for public accountability with cost/benefit issues. The EU has already specified that, for listed groups, national authorities such as the ASB should not impose requirements that are additional to those set out in IASs. The ASB also confirmed in its initial Discussion Paper (see **11.7** above) that it does not plan to introduce new UK standards that are more demanding or restrictive than the equivalent international standards, but where current UK requirements are already more demanding, these will generally be retained if it seems that the relevant international standard will eventually be improved.

In the latest consultation document on convergence, published in May 2006, the ASB suggests that:

- the scope of the Financial Reporting Standard for Smaller Entities (FRSSE) could be widened to encompass companies that qualify as medium-sized to introduce simplified accounting requirements for an additional 30,000 companies – the EC is also in the process of increasing the maximum financial thresholds for small and medium-sized companies once again, so there would be scope for an even greater impact if equivalent changes are made to UK law in due course;
- all quoted companies and other entities with public accountability should be required to adopted IFRSs, regardless of the level of their turnover and of whether they prepare individual or group accounts; and
- all subsidiaries of companies preparing IFRS group accounts should be required to adopt IFRSs, but with reduced disclosure requirements.

The ASB estimates that this would leave around 7,000 companies that do not qualify as small or medium-sized under UK company law, but do not meet the public accountability criteria and are not subsidiaries of listed or similar companies. No firm proposals have been put forward for these companies at present, but operating a separate financial reporting regime for a relatively small number of companies may not be practicable. One alternative might be to apply the IASB's proposed 'SME' standard to these entities, although they would clearly not qualify as SMEs under UK legislation.

11.9   Changes to the Role of the ASB

In March 2005, the ASB published an Exposure Draft of a Policy Statement setting out the Board's views on its future role. With the introduction of the IAS framework in the UK and the ASB's published plans to converge UK accounting practice with international requirements (see **11.7** above), much of the detailed work on the development of accounting standards will in future be undertaken by the International Accounting Standards Board (IASB) and the future role of the ASB therefore needs to be reassessed. The Exposure Draft 'Accounting Standard-Setting in a Changing Environment: The Role of the Accounting Standards Board' promotes the view that the ASB will continue to have a significant role in the development of IASs through participation in debates on the key issues and by responding to IASB consultations. It will also act as a link between the IASB and interested parties in the UK by maintaining a two-way dialogue and ensuring that the views and concerns of UK parties are relayed to the IASB. The other main activities of the ASB in future are expected to include:

- implementation of the UK convergence project;
- improving communication between companies and their investors; and
- influencing European policy on accounting standards.

11.10   Scope and Application of Accounting Standards

UK accounting standards apply to all accounts that are required to show a true and fair view of the profit or loss for the financial period and of the state of affairs of an entity at its balance sheet date. Consequently they apply not only to companies and groups, but also to unincorporated entities if these are required to prepare accounts that show a true and fair view. However, the requirements of accounting standards need not be applied to items that are considered immaterial in the context of the accounts as a whole. They also do not override any exemption from disclosure that is available by law. In its guidance, the ASB emphasises that, when applying UK accounting standards, preparers of accounts should follow the spirit and reasoning behind the requirements as explained in the standards themselves and in the ASB's *Statement of Principles for Financial Reporting.* Similarly, IASs are intended to be applied to all general purpose financial statements that are intended to present fairly the financial position, financial performance and cashflows of an entity.

11.11   Effective Date of Accounting Standards

Each accounting standard is effective from a specific date set out in the standard. The date chosen will take into account the fact that companies may need time to put detailed procedures into place in order to comply with the new accounting requirements. However, in most cases the effective date set is the latest date by which compliance must be achieved, and early adoption of new accounting standards is usually encouraged. However, the fact that a standard has been adopted early may need to be disclosed and there may be a prohibition on the early adoption of certain standards (for instance, where related company law requirements are not effective for earlier accounting periods). The question sometimes arises as to whether new requirements apply to all transactions or only to those arising after the effective date of the standard. The ASB's general view is that the requirements of UK accounting standards should be regarded as applying to all transactions, regardless of when they took place, unless a particular accounting standard specifies a different approach. Care is also required over the early adoption of accounting treatments proposed in Discussion Papers and FREDs. If the subject matter of a Discussion Paper or FRED is not covered by an existing accounting standard, the exposure document may be regarded as indicative of best practice and it may therefore be acceptable to adopt the accounting treatment proposed, bearing in mind that the final FRS may impose slightly different requirements. If the subject matter of the Discussion Paper or FRED is already covered in an accounting standard, the existing standard remains in force until it is replaced and accounts must therefore be prepared in accordance with the existing standard, even if it is expected that the standard will be superseded by new requirements. In these circumstances, it may be appropriate to explain the effect of the new proposals in a note to the accounts.

11.12   First-time Adoption of IASs

The IASB published IFRS 1 *First-time Adoption of International Financial Reporting Standards* in June 2003. With a small number of specific exceptions (which include accounting for past acquisitions), this standard requires a reporting entity to comply with all current IASB standards when it first prepares its accounts in accordance with international standards. The accounts must also explain how the transition to international standards has affected the entity's financial position, financial performance and cashflows. The stated aim is to provide investors with transparent information that is comparable over all periods presented, but in a way that keeps costs to an acceptable level. A company that is required to prepare accounts in accordance with IASs, or which chooses to do so (see **11.4** above), will therefore need to prepare comparative figures for the previous year, including an opening balance sheet for that year, on the same basis. This will be a major undertaking for any company in the year of transition to IASs. APB Bulletin 2005/3 *Guidance for Auditors on First-time Application of IFRSs in the United Kingdom and the Republic of Ireland* also provides guidance on a number of additional issues that may arise where accounts are prepared under IFRSs for the first time. These include:

- difficulties in identifying all relevant differences between the old and new financial reporting frameworks;
- significant changes to financial reporting systems and controls, which may increase the risk of error and the possibility of fraud or aggressive earnings management;
- additional going concern issues, particularly if new accounting requirements have implications for the company's borrowing powers or cause debt covenants to be breached;
- the potential impact of changes in accounting treatments on the amount of profits that the company has available for distribution; and
- the potential tax effects of the changes in accounting requirements.

The Bulletin can be downloaded from the APB website at www.frc.org.uk/apb/publications.

11.13   Disclosure of Compliance with Accounting Standards

In the case of Companies Act accounts (see **3.16** above), *paragraph 36A* of *Schedule 4* to the *Companies Act 1985* (*CA 1985*) requires the directors to state whether the company's accounts have been prepared in accordance with applicable accounting standards. There is an exemption from the disclosure requirement (but not from the requirement to follow applicable standards) for companies that qualify as small or medium-sized under the legislation. If there has been a departure from applicable accounting standards, particulars must be given, together with the reasons for the departure. The ASB's *Foreword to Accounting Standards* and FRS 18 *Accounting Policies* also require disclosure of the financial effect of a material departure from accounting standards. Where IAS accounts are prepared, *CA 1985* requires this fact to be stated in the accounts and IAS 1

Presentation of Financial Statements requires the notes to the accounts to include a clear statement on compliance with all requirements of IASs. The financial statements cannot be described as complying with international standards unless they comply with all relevant requirements.

11.14 Applicable Accounting Standards

Section 256 of *CA 1985* defines accounting standards as 'statements of standard accounting practice issued by such body or bodies as may be prescribed by regulations'. Applicable accounting standards are those that are relevant to the company's circumstances and to the accounts. For the purposes of UK company law, FRSs and SSAPs constitute 'accounting standards'. Where IAS accounts are prepared, accounting standards are IASs that have been adopted by the EU.

11.15 Role of the UITF

The role of the Urgent Issues Task Force ('UITF') is to help the ASB to fulfil its aim of responding promptly on urgent matters as they arise. The UITF considers issues that are covered by an existing accounting standard or a provision in company law but where conflicting or unacceptable interpretations have developed, or seem likely to develop. Having considered the issue and reached a conclusion, the UITF issues its consensus in the form of an Abstract, which usually becomes effective shortly after publication. Once it is in force, a UITF Abstract has the same authority, scope and application as an accounting standard and therefore forms part of standard accounting practice. However, the role of the Urgent Issues Task Force is also expected to change as a result of the convergence of UK accounting standards with international requirements (see **11.7** above). In future, any necessary interpretation of international standards will generally be dealt with by the International Financial Reporting Interpretations Committee (IFRIC) and will usually then be issued as a UITF Abstract for UK accounting purposes. However, where it seems that IFRIC will be unable to issue guidance in time to meet UK needs, the UITF may consider issuing its own non-mandatory guidance.

11.16 Role of the FRRP

The Financial Reporting Review Panel ('FRRP') enquires into accounts that appear to depart from the requirements of company law, accounting standards and UITF Abstracts, including the requirement for accounts to show a true and fair view in accordance with the relevant financial framework adopted. To date, reviews have concentrated on the accounts of public companies and larger private companies, but technically all companies come within the remit of the FRRP, unless they qualify as small or medium-sized under *CA 1985*. Historically, the FRRP has not reviewed accounts on a routine basis but has acted on matters drawn to its attention, either directly or indirectly. Qualified audit reports, press comment and referrals by individuals or companies could all result in an enquiry. Where revision of the accounts was considered necessary, the FRRP usually tried to reach voluntary arrangement with the directors, but it could seek a court order for revision of the accounts under *section 245B* of *CA 1985* if it was unable to reach a satisfactory agreement with the directors.

The various post-Enron reviews undertaken in the UK resulted in recommendations that the FRRP should develop a more proactive element to its work, that the Financial Services Authority should have a greater role in the enforcement process and that the Government should explore the scope for opening legal gateways to enable relevant information to be passed between the Inland Revenue and the FSA, FRRP and DTI to help in the identification of high-risk accounts. These changes were eventually introduced by the *Companies Act (Audit, Investigations and Community Enterprise) Act 2004.* In particular, the Secretary of State is now empowered to appoint a body or bodies to keep the periodic accounts and reports of listed companies under review and, where relevant, inform the Financial Services Authority of any conclusions reached. This provision is effective from 1 January 2005 and the FRRP has already begun to adopt a process of risk-based selection of accounts for review and to cover all published information issued by listed companies, including interim reports and preliminary announcements. The Panel announced in December 2005 that its monitoring activity for 2006/07 would continue to focus on the following industry sectors identified in the risk monitoring process for the previous period, but that selection would be widened to include some companies providing services to these sectors and that its specific issues reviews would include pensions disclosures:

- automobile;
- pharmaceutical;
- retail;
- transport; and
- utilities.

The FRRP also carried out reviews on a number of interim reports in 2005, focusing on companies whose accounts would be subject to significant change as a result of the adoption of IASs. Brief details of the results of this exercise are given at **11.126** below).

Other provisions in the *Companies Act (Audit, Investigations and Community Enterprise) Act 2004* allow the Inland Revenue to disclose relevant information to facilitate the investigation of company accounts by the FRRP, enable the FRRP to require a company and any officer, employee or auditor to provide information relevant to an investigation of the company's accounts for compliance with the requirements of *CA 1985* and establish gateways to enable the FRRP to disclose certain information to bodies such as the DTI, Treasury, Bank of England, FSA and Inland Revenue to assist them in carrying out their legal functions. These provisions came into effect on 6 April 2005. Directors' reports will also come within the remit of the FRRP for accounting periods beginning on or after 1 April 2006. In conjunction with the recent changes, the FRRP published a revised version of its Operating Procedures in April 2005. This confirms the Panel's intention to encourage directors to make additional information available on a voluntary basis as far as possible and only to use its new powers to require the provision of information as a last resort.

11.17 Current UK Accounting Standards and UITF Abstracts

As at 30 June 2006, the following accounting standards and UITF Abstracts were in issue:

SSAP 4	Accounting for Government Grants
SSAP 5	Accounting for Value Added Tax
SSAP 9	Stocks and Long-term Contracts
SSAP 13	Accounting for Research and Development
SSAP 19	Accounting for Investment Properties
SSAP 20	Foreign Currency Translation (superseded by FRS 23 for listed entities and others adopting FRS 26)
SSAP 21	Accounting for Leases and Hire Purchase Contracts
SSAP 25	Segmental Reporting
FRS 1	Cash Flow Statements
FRS 2	Accounting for Subsidiary Undertakings (updated December 2004)
FRS 3	Reporting Financial Performance
FRS 4	Capital Instruments (as amended by FRS 25)
FRS 5	Reporting the Substance of Transactions
FRS 6	Acquisitions and Mergers
FRS 7	Fair Values in Acquisition Accounting
FRS 8	Related Party Disclosures
FRS 9	Associates and Joint Ventures
FRS 10	Goodwill and Intangible Assets
FRS 11	Impairment of Fixed Assets and Goodwill
FRS 12	Provisions, Contingent Liabilities and Contingent Assets
FRS 13	Derivatives and Other Financial Instruments: Disclosures (superseded for most entities by FRS 25 and then FRS 29)
FRS 15	Tangible Fixed Assets
FRS 16	Current Tax
FRS 17	Retirement Benefits
FRS 18	Accounting Policies
FRS 19	Deferred Tax
FRS 20	Share-based Payment (applies to listed companies from 1 January 2005 and to other entities from 1 January 2006)
FRS 21	Events After the Balance Sheet Date
FRS 22	Earnings per Share
FRS 23	The Effects of Changes in Foreign Exchange Rates (applies only to entities adopting FRS 26)
FRS 24	Financial Reporting in Hyperinflationary Economies (applies only to entities adopting FRS 26)
FRS 25	Financial Instruments: Disclosure and Presentation (the disclosure requirements of FRS 25 are superseded by FRS 29 for accounting periods beginning on or after 1 January

	2007 and the standard is renamed 'Financial Instruments: Presentation')
FRS 26	Financial Instruments: Measurement (applies to listed companies from 1 January 2005 and to other entities adopting fair value accounting from 1 January 2006)
FRS 27	Life Assurance
FRS 28	Corresponding Amounts
FRS 29	Financial Instruments: Disclosures (applies from 1 January 2007 to entities adopting FRS 26)
UITF Abstract 4	Presentation of Long-term Debtors in Current Assets
UITF Abstract 5	Transfers from Current Assets to Fixed Assets
UITF Abstract 9	Accounting for Operations in Hyper-inflationary Economies (superseded by FRS 24 for entities adopting FRS 26)
UITF Abstract 11	Capital Instruments: Issuer Call Options (superseded by FRS 26 for entities adopting that standard)
UITF Abstract 15	Disclosure of Substantial Acquisitions
UITF Abstract 17	Employee Share Schemes (updated December 2004)
UITF Abstract 19	Tax on Gains and Losses on Foreign Currency Borrowings that Hedge an Investment in a Foreign Enterprise (amended by FRS 23 for entities adopting that standard, but continues to apply in its original form to other entities)
UITF Abstract 21	Accounting Issues Arising from the proposed Introduction of the Euro
UITF Abstract 22	The Acquisition of a Lloyd's Business
UITF Abstract 23	Application of the Transitional Rules in FRS 15
UITF Abstract 24	Accounting for Start-up Costs
UITF Abstract 25	National Insurance Contributions on Share Option Gains
UITF Abstract 26	Barter Transactions for Advertising
UITF Abstract 27	Revisions to Estimates of the Useful Economic Life of Goodwill and Intangible Assets
UITF Abstract 28	Operating Lease Incentives
UITF Abstract 29	Website Development Costs
UITF Abstract 30	Date of Award to Employees of Shares or Rights to Shares (superseded by FRS 20)
UITF Abstract 31	Exchange of Businesses and Non-monetary Assets for an Interest in a Subsidiary, Joint Venture or Associate
UITF Abstract 32	Employee Benefit Trusts and Other Intermediate Payment Arrangements
UITF Abstract 34	Accounting for Pre-contract Costs
UITF Abstract 35	Death-in-service and Incapacity Benefits
UITF Abstract 36	Contracts for Sales of Capacity
UITF Abstract 38	Accounting for ESOP Trusts
UITF Abstract 39	Members' Shares in Co-operative Entities and Similar Instruments
UITF Abstract 40	Revenue Recognition and Service Contracts
UITF Abstract 41	Scope of FRS 20
UITF Abstract 42	Reassessment of Embedded Derivatives

11.18   Current International Accounting Standards

The following international accounting standards and related statements by the International Financial Reporting Interpretations Committee were in issue at 30 June 2006:

IFRS 1	First-time Adoption of International Financial Reporting Standards
IFRS 2	Share-based Payment
IFRS 3	Business Combinations
IFRS 4	Insurance Contracts
IFRS 5	Non-current Assets Held for Sale and Discontinued Operations
IFRS 6	Exploration for, and Evaluation of, Mineral Resources
IFRS 7	Financial Instruments: Disclosures
IAS 1	Presentation of Financial Statements
IAS 2	Inventories
IAS 7	Cash Flow Statements
IAS 8	Accounting Policies, Changes in Accounting Estimates and Errors
IAS 10	Events After the Balance Sheet Date
IAS 11	Construction Contracts
IAS 12	Income Taxes
IAS 14	Segment Reporting
IAS 16	Property, Plant and Equipment
IAS 17	Leases
IAS 18	Revenue
IAS 19	Employee Benefits
IAS 20	Accounting for Government Grants and Disclosure of Government Assistance
IAS 21	The Effects of Changes in Foreign Exchange Rates
IAS 23	Borrowing Costs
IAS 24	Related Party Disclosures
IAS 26	Accounting and Reporting by Retirement Benefit Plans
IAS 27	Consolidated and Separate Financial Statements
IAS 28	Investments in Associates
IAS 29	Financial Reporting in Hyperinflationary Economies
IAS 30	Disclosures in the Financial Statements of Banks and Similar Financial Institutions
IAS 31	Interests in Joint Ventures
IAS 32	Financial Instruments: Disclosure and Presentation
IAS 33	Earnings per Share
IAS 34	Interim Financial Reporting
IAS 36	Impairment of Assets
IAS 37	Provisions, Contingent Liabilities and Contingent Assets
IAS 38	Intangible Assets
IAS 39	Financial Instruments: Recognition and Measurement
IAS 40	Investment Property
IAS 41	Agriculture
SIC 7	Introduction of the Euro

SIC 10   Government Assistance – No Specific Relation to Operating Activities

SIC 12   Consolidation – Special Purpose Entities

SIC 13   Jointly Controlled Entities – Non-monetary Contributions by Venturers

SIC 15   Operating Leases – Incentives

SIC 21   Income Taxes – Recovery of Revalued Non-depreciable Assets

SIC 25   Income Taxes – Changes in the Tax Status of an Enterprise or its Shareholders

SIC 27   Evaluating the Substance of Transactions Involving the Legal Form of a Lease

SIC 29   Disclosure – Service Concession Arrangements

SIC 31   Revenue – Barter Transactions Involving Advertising Services

SIC 32   Intangible Assets – Web Site Costs

IFRIC 1   Changes in Existing Decommissioning, Restoration and Similar Liabilities

IFRIC 2   Members' Shares in Co-operative Entities and Similar Instruments

IFRIC 4   Determining Whether an Arrangement Contains a Lease

IFRIC 5   Rights to Interests Arising from Decommissioning, Restoration and Environmental Rehabilitation Funds

IFRIC 6   Liabilities Arising from Participating in a Specific Market – Waste Electrical and Electronic Equipment

IFRIC 7   Applying the Restatement Approach under IAS 29 *Financial Reporting in Hyperinflationary Economies*

IFRIC 8   Scope of IFRS 2

IFRIC 9   Reassessment of Embedded Derivatives

11.19   Financial Reporting Standard for Smaller Entities ('FRSSE')

A Financial Reporting Standard for Smaller Entities ('FRSSE') was first published in November 1997 and came into immediate effect. The FRSSE has been updated on a number of occasions since it was first published. The latest version was issued in April 2005 and is effective for accounting periods beginning on or after 1 January 2005. The FRSSE may be adopted in financial statements that are intended to give a true and fair view of the financial performance and financial position of companies that qualify as small under *CA 1985* and of other entities that would qualify if they were incorporated under *CA 1985*. For accounting periods beginning on or after 1 January 2005, the FRSSE is only relevant to small companies if they prepare Companies Act accounts (see **3.16** above). If the FRSSE is adopted, this fact must be stated in the accounts. The contents of the FRSSE are based on other UK accounting standards, but definitions and accounting requirements are set out in a more straightforward manner, and more complex issues that are not expected to arise in smaller entities are excluded from the FRSSE. The document is reviewed on an annual basis so that its requirements are kept up to date with developments in accounting practice. An appendix to the FRSSE links its requirements with those in accounting standards, and where issues arise that are not specifically covered in the FRSSE, those preparing the accounts are required to have regard to other standards and UITF Abstracts as a means of establishing current practice. The FRSSE includes a specific additional require-ment for the accounts to disclose any personal guarantees given by the directors in respect of company borrowings.

The ASB published an Exposure Draft of proposed amendments to the FRSSE in April 2006. Comments on the proposals were invited by 31 July 2006 and a revised FRSSE is likely to apply for accounting periods beginning on or after 1 January 2007. The most significant changes are:

- a proposal to incorporate the key principles of FRS 20 'Share-based Payment' into the FRSSE without amendment or simplification;
- the incorporation of the consensus paragraphs from UITF Abstract 40 'Service contracts and revenue recognition' into the body of the FRSSE (these are currently included in Appendix III); and
- excluding from the scope of the FRSSE any smaller entities that choose to adopt fair value accounting.

To keep the document to a manageable size, the ASB also proposes removing the appendices which set out the derivation of FRSSE requirements and sum-marise the simplifications applied, although this material will continue to be freely available on the ASB website.

11.20   'One-stop Shop' Document

The version of the FRSSE published in April 2005 takes the form of a 'one-stop shop' document, encompassing all of the accounting requirements that apply to small companies. Company law requirements are distinguished from other aspects of the FRSSE by being set out in small capitals in the text, and reflect the provisions that apply for accounting periods beginning on or after 1 January 2005. Only the most common balance sheet format from *CA 1985* (Format 1) is included in the document but companies applying the FRSSE continue to have the option of adopting the alternative balance sheet format if they wish. However, in the case of the profit and loss account, only Formats 1 and 2 from *CA 1985* are now available to companies applying the FRSSE. The ASB emphasises that smaller unincorporated entities adopting the FRSSE are not bound by the com-pany law requirements set out in the document, but notes that they should have regard to the accounting principles, presentation and disclosure requirements set out in company law (or other equivalent legislation) that are considered necessary for the presentation of a true and fair view.

11.21   IASB Proposals for SMEs

In June 2004, the International Accounting Standards Board (IASB) published a discussion paper 'Preliminary Views on Accounting Standards for Small and Medium-sized Entities' outlining its initial thoughts on this issue and inviting comments before the next stage in the development process. Given the ASB's programme to converge UK accounting standards with international requirements (see **11.7** above), this could eventually impact on smaller entities in the UK. The IASB's initial proposals differ significantly from the small company financial reporting regime that has developed in the UK in recent years. The IASB proposes that its SME pronouncements would apply to entities that do not have public accountability rather than to entities that meet a certain size criteria. The Discussion Paper suggests that an entity would be regarded as having public accountability if there is a high degree of outside interest from non-management investors or other stakeholders, or if the entity has an essential public service responsibility because of the nature of its operations. Furthermore, every entity will be regarded as having public accountability until it has informed each of its owners (including any not otherwise entitled to vote) of the intention to adopt SME standards and none of them objects to this. Adoption of the SME standards would have to be disclosed in the accounts and also in any auditors' report.

The IASB initially planned a complete series of SME standards rather than a stand-alone document like the FRSSE, with the suggested objectives of the SME standards including a focus on the needs of users of SME accounts and reducing the financial reporting burden for relevant businesses, whilst still allowing an easy transition to IFRSs as and when necessary. The Discussion Paper suggested that any modifications would be most likely to relate to disclosure and presentation issues, and that there should be a rebuttable presumption that no changes would be made to recognition and measurement principles. Whilst the approach appears to be broadly similar to that adopted in developing the FRSSE, the UK simplifications for small companies do currently encompass certain recognition and measurement issues as well as disclosure and presentation points – for instance, by excluding from the FRSSE detailed recognition and measurement requirements relating to transactions that arise only rarely in SMEs. However, in the light of responses to the Discussion Paper, the IASB has made certain changes to its original plans. In particular, it has agreed that measurement and recognition simplifications should be considered as well as disclosure and presentation issues and is also giving consideration to the development of a single, stand-alone IFRS rather than a series of SME standards. The ASB has recently confirmed that it intends to continue with a separate financial reporting regime for smaller entities but it is expected to wait until the IASB proposals are finalised before deciding whether to adopt these or to develop a revised FRSSE based on the underlying principles of international requirements (see **11.8** above).

11.22   Statements of Recommended Practice ('SORPs')

Statements of Recommended Practice ('SORPs') set out recommended UK accounting practice for specialised sectors or industries. They are developed by bodies representing the appropriate sector or industry and are supplementary to accounting standards, legislation and other regulations affecting the business. Bodies wishing to develop a SORP are expected to meet criteria laid down by the ASB and to develop the SORP in accordance with the ASB's Code of Practice. The ASB will review the proposed SORP and, where appropriate, issue a 'negative assurance' statement for publication in the document, confirming that:

- the SORP does not appear to contain any fundamental points of principle that are unacceptable in the context of current UK accounting practice; and
- the SORP does not conflict with a UK accounting standard or with the ASB's plans for future accounting standards.

The contents of a SORP do not override the requirements of accounting standards, UITF Abstracts or relevant legislation. The ASB Code of Practice specifically notes that the fact that a SORP has not been updated does not exempt relevant entities from complying with more recent accounting standards and UITF Abstracts. If new standards and Abstracts conflict with the provisions of a SORP, those provisions cease to have effect. FRS 18 *Accounting Policies* requires specific disclosures to be given in the accounts when an entity comes within the scope of a SORP.

11.23   Further Information

For further information on current developments and copies of accounting standards and other documents discussed above, see the ASB website at www.frc.org.uk/asb and the IASB website at www.iasb.org.

11.24   **True and Fair View**

At a Glance
- *CA 1985* requires Companies Act accounts to show a true and fair view.
- The interpretation of what constitutes a true and fair view will vary over time, based largely on the requirements of the accounting standards in force at the time.
- The ASB *Foreword to Accounting Standards* considers the status of UK accounting standards in the context of UK company law.
- In certain exceptional circumstances, directors preparing Companies Act accounts are required to depart from the specific accounting requirements of *CA 1985* – this is commonly referred to as the use of the true and fair override.
- Specific disclosures must be given in the accounts whenever the true and fair override is used.
- Different requirements apply where IAS accounts are prepared.

11.25   Requirement for Companies Act Accounts to Show a True and Fair

Where Companies Act individual accounts are prepared, *section 226A(2) of CA 1985* requires the company's balance sheet to give a true and fair view of the state of affairs of the company at the end of the financial period and the profit and loss account to give a true and fair view of the profit or loss for the financial period then ended. A similar requirement for Companies Act group accounts is set out in *section 227A(2) of CA 1985*. Where compliance with the provisions of *Schedule 4 to CA 1985* (or, in the case of group accounts, *Schedule 4A*) and other relevant provisions of the legislation is not sufficient for the accounts to give a true and fair view, the additional information necessary to achieve a true and fair view must be given in the accounts or the notes to the accounts. The true and fair view requirement applies to the accounts of all companies, regardless of their size.

11.26   What Constitutes a True and Fair View?

Although the concept of the true and fair view lies at the heart of financial reporting in the UK, there is no clear definition, in the legislation or elsewhere, of what constitutes a true and fair view. This is essentially a question of judgement and, as a legal concept, it can only be interpreted by the court. It is a dynamic concept and the interpretation of what constitutes a true and fair view will vary over time, based largely on the accounting standards in force at any given date. New accounting standards are developed, and existing standards revised, to take account of changes in business practice and in the general economic climate, and an accounting treatment that was accepted as giving a true and fair view ten years ago will not necessarily achieve such a view today.

11.27   Impact of UK Accounting Standards

The interpretation of 'true and fair' will usually be governed by generally accepted accounting practice and, in particular, the requirements of UK accounting standards. Each accounting standard states that it applies to all financial statements that are required to show a true and fair view. The *Foreword to Accounting Standards*, issued in 1993 by the ASB, considers the status of accounting standards in the context of UK company law, and an appendix to the document sets out an Opinion by Miss Mary Arden QC (now the Honourable Mrs Justice Arden) on the true and fair requirement. This includes detailed consideration of the relationship between accounting standards and the legal requirement for company accounts to show a true and fair view. The main points set out in the Opinion are:

- although the true and fair requirement is a question of law and must therefore be interpreted by the court, this cannot be done without evidence of the practice and views of accountants – the more authoritative the practices and views, the more ready the court will be to follow them;
- the *Companies Act 1989* amended *CA 1985* to give statutory recognition to accounting standards;

- *CA 1985* requires disclosure of non-compliance with accounting standards rather than compliance with them – the court is therefore likely to infer that accounts will usually follow accounting standards in meeting the true and fair requirement and that any departure from accounting standards needs to be explained and disclosed in the accounts;
- once an accounting standard has been issued, the court is likely to hold that compliance with the standard will be necessary for accounts to show a true and fair view – this view is likely to be strengthened by the extent to which the standard is subsequently accepted in practice;
- the converse will not necessarily apply, and a lack of support for an accounting standard will not automatically lead the court to conclude that a true and fair view can be achieved without compliance with the standard;
- the fact that a departure from an accounting standard is disclosed in accordance with the requirements of *CA 1985* does not necessarily mean that the departure is permitted under the legislation.

It is advisable to read the full Opinion in any case where departure from an accounting standard is being contemplated (for information on obtaining copies see the ASB website at www.frc.org.uk/asb).

11.28 True and Fair Override

If, in special circumstances, compliance with the provisions of *Schedule 4* to *CA 1985* (or, in the case of group accounts, *Schedule 4A*) or with other provisions in the legislation would be inconsistent with the requirement for Companies Act accounts to show a true and fair view, *sections 226A(5)* and *227A(5)* of *CA 1985* require the directors to depart from the requirements of the Act and make specific disclosure of this in the accounts. This is commonly referred to as the 'true and fair override'. A departure from the requirements of *CA 1985* might arise in one of two ways. Firstly, some accounting standards specifically require departure from the requirements of the legislation in order to achieve a true and fair view – examples include the non-depreciation of investment properties under SSAP 19 *Accounting for Investment Properties*, the treatment of certain exchange gains and losses under SSAP 20 *Foreign Currency Translation*, and the non-amortisation of certain categories of goodwill under FRS 10 *Goodwill and Intangible Assets*. Secondly, in very rare and exceptional circumstances, it may be necessary to depart from the requirements of accounting standards in order to achieve a true and fair view – the legislation requires accounts to be prepared in accordance with the applicable standards and a departure from these will therefore constitute a departure from the requirements of *CA 1985*.

11.29 Disclosing use of the True and Fair Override

Where the directors depart from the requirements of the Act under *section 226A(5)* or *227A(5)* of *CA 1985*, the accounts must disclose:

- particulars of the departure;

- the reasons for the departure; and
- the effect of the departure.

FRS 18 *Accounting Policies* deals with these disclosure requirements in more detail and requires the following information to be given:

- a clear and unambiguous statement that there has been a departure from the requirements of company law, accounting standards or UITF Abstracts, as appropriate, and that the departure is necessary in order to achieve a true and fair view;
- a statement of the treatment that company law, accounting standards or UITF Abstracts would normally require and a description of the treatment actually adopted; and
- a description of how the position shown in the financial statements is different as a result of the departure – this should include quantification of the effect except where this is already evident in the financial statements themselves, or where the effect cannot be quantified (in which case the circumstances must be explained).

FRS 18 requires this information to be given in the note to the accounts on compliance with applicable accounting standards (see **11.13** above), or to be cross-referenced to this note. If the departure continues in future years, the disclosures must be given each year, with comparatives. If the departure applies only to the figures for the previous year, the disclosures must still be given in respect of those figures. For information on obtaining copies of FRS 18 see the ASB website at www.frc.org.uk/asb.

11.30   Different Requirements for IAS Accounts

Similar but slightly different requirements apply where a company is required or chooses to prepare IAS accounts individual and/or group accounts (see **3.16–3.17** above). The legislation does not set out any specific requirements on the form or content of IAS accounts, although it does include a requirement for the auditors to express an opinion on whether or not the accounts show a true and fair view in accordance with the relevant financial reporting framework applied in their preparation. Two documents have been published on this issue since the IAS framework was introduced into UK company law for accounting periods beginning on or after 1 January 2005. In August 2005, the Financial Reporting Council (FRC) published a paper 'The implications of new accounting and auditing standards for the true and fair view and auditors' responsibilities'. This sets out a detailed analysis and interpretation of the new framework of accounting and auditing standards and concludes that:

- the concept of the true and fair view remains a cornerstone of financial reporting and auditing in the UK;
- there has been no substantive change in the objectives of an audit and the nature of auditors' responsibilities; and

- the need for professional judgement remains central to the work of preparers and auditors of accounts in the UK.

This paper is available from the FRC website at www.frc.org.uk/. Prior to this, in June 2005, the Financial Reporting Review Panel (FRRP) published an opinion by Freshfields Bruckhaus Deringer on the effect of the IAS Regulation on the requirement under *CA 1985* for accounts to show a true and fair view. The key points highlighted in this opinion are:

- the true and fair override no longer applies to companies who prepare their accounts in accordance with IASs;
- for companies preparing IAS accounts, references to the 'true and fair view' in the legislation are references to the requirement under IASs for accounts to achieve a fair presentation;
- the application of IASs, together with additional disclosure where necessary, is presumed to result in financial statements that achieve a fair presentation;
- IAS 1 *Presentation of Financial Statements* acknowledges that it may be necessary to depart from strict compliance with a requirement of a standard or related interpretation in order to achieve a fair presentation, but only in very rare circumstances, and where such a departure is required, certain additional disclosures must be given, including the nature of the departure and the reasons for it.

The opinion is available from the FRRP website at www.frc.org.uk/frrp/.

11.31   Materiality

> **At a Glance**
> * An item is generally regarded as material to the financial statements if its misstatement or omission might reasonably be expected to influence the decisions or assessments made by a user of the financial statements.
> * Materiality will not usually be relevant in the context of the preparation of accounting records.
> * Certain disclosures must always be given in annual accounts, regardless of whether the item in question is material.
> * The requirements of accounting standards should generally be applied to all material transactions, regardless of when they took place.
> * Key factors in assessing the materiality of an item include its size, its nature and the surrounding circumstances.
> * In making the assessment, information should be viewed from a user's perspective.
> * Both the quantitative and the qualitative aspects of an item or transaction should be taken into account when assessing its materiality.

11.32   Nature of Materiality

In the case of UK accounting practice, paragraph 3.29 of the ASB's *Statement of Principles for Financial Reporting* describes materiality as a threshold quality in that it provides a cut-off point for establishing whether an item needs to be considered in detail in relation to the accounts. The document goes on to explain that:

> 'An item of information is material to the financial statements if its misstatement or omission might reasonably be expected to influence the economic decisions of users of those financial statements, including their assessments of management's stewardship.
>
> Whether information is material or not will depend on the size and nature of the item in question judged in the particular circumstances of the case.'

The *Statement of Principles* also emphasises that the inclusion of immaterial information can impair the understandability of the other information provided. Immaterial information should therefore be excluded. Materiality is different to the qualitative characteristics of financial information that are discussed in the *Statement of Principles* (ie relevance, reliability, comparability and understandability), because these represent the characteristics that information must have if it is to be useful to a user of the accounts. The materiality of an item should be considered before its other qualities are assessed, because:

* if the information is not material, it cannot be useful to a user of the accounts and therefore does not need to be considered further;
* if the information is material, it will be useful to a user of the accounts, and its qualitative characteristics will therefore need to be assessed.

For information on obtaining copies of the *Statement of Principles* see the ASB website at www.frc.org.uk/asb.

In the case of IAS accounts, a similar position is set out in the IASB's *Framework for the Preparation and Presentation of Financial Statements* and in paragraph 11 of IAS 1 *Presentation of Financial Statements*, which states that:

> 'Omissions or misstatements of items are material if they could, individually or collectively, influence the economic decisions of users taken on the basis of the financial statements. Materiality depends on the size and nature of the omission or misstatement judged in the surrounding circumstances. The size or nature of the item, or a combination of both, could be the determining factor.'

11.33   Influence on the Decisions of Users

The main issue to be considered in establishing whether an item is material or not is whether a user of the accounts may make a different decision or assessment if the relevant detail or information is made available to him. This definition of materiality is emphasised in:

* the ASB *Statement of Principles* [paragraph 3.30];
* FRS 8 *Related Party Transactions* [paragraph 20];
* the UK and Ireland version of International Standard on Auditing 320 (ISA 320) *Audit Materiality* [paragraph 3];

- the IASB's *Framework for the Preparation and Presentation of Financial Statements* [paragraphs 29 and 30]; and
- IAS 1 *Presentation of Financial Statements* [paragraph 11].

A similar approach is taken in the guidance published in January 2006 by the DTI's Operating and Financial Review Working Group on Materiality (see **11.95** below).

A wide range of users of accounts is identified in the *Statement of Principles*, including:

- existing investors, taking decisions on whether to increase, hold or sell their investments;
- potential investors, deciding whether or not to invest in the entity;
- employees and prospective employees, assessing the ability of the entity to provide secure employment opportunities, remuneration and retirement benefits;
- lenders, taking decisions on whether to maintain, increase or decrease the level of financing provided to the entity;
- suppliers and customers, taking decisions on whether to trade with the entity; and
- the general public, assessing the contribution of the entity to the local economy.

11.34 Accounting Records

The ICAEW Statement 'The Interpretation of Materiality in Financial Reporting' emphasises that the concept of materiality will not usually apply in the context of the preparation and maintenance of accounting records, as accuracy and precision are essential in this case. However, where items are recorded on the basis of best estimates or market values, or where costs and expenses need to be allocated between different activities, a degree of subjectivity will often come into play and materiality may consequently become a relevant issue.

11.35 Cases Where Materiality Does Not Apply

Certain disclosures have to be given in annual accounts, regardless of whether the item is material in the context of the accounts as a whole, or in relation to other items or totals within the accounts. For instance, in the case of companies, the detailed disclosures in respect of directors' emoluments and the remuneration of the auditors must always be given, even though some of the amounts involved may not be considered material in the context of the accounts as a whole. Similarly, *CA 1985* does not permit disclosures to be omitted from the directors' report on the grounds that the amounts involved are not material.

11.36 Requirements of UK Accounting Standards

Under UK accounting practice, paragraph 13 of the *Foreword to Accounting Standards* states that accounting standards need not be applied to immaterial items and this is repeated in the introductory note to each accounting standard. The Foreword also emphasises that the requirements of accounting standards should generally be applied to all material transactions, irrespective of the date of the transaction. Many accounting standards refer to material items in one context or another. For example, accounting standards may require:

- disclosure of material items – for instance, exceptional items under the requirements of FRS 3 *Reporting Financial Performance*;
- disclosure of material differences where items are calculated under different methods – for instance, the disclosure of historical cost profits or losses under FRS 3 *Reporting Financial Performance*;
- disclosure of material events or conditions – for instance, the sale or termination of an operation under FRS 3 *Reporting Financial Performance*;
- the application of a specific accounting treatment to material items – for instance, adjusting the accounts for certain material post balance sheet events under FRS 21 *Events after the Balance Sheet Date*; and
- the application of a specific accounting treatment where material events or transactions occur – for instance, accounting for transactions on the basis of their economic substance under FRS 5 *Reporting the Substance of Transactions*.

CA 1985 also states that amounts which are not material in the context of a provision of *Schedule 4* may be disregarded for the purposes of that provision.

11.37 Assessing Materiality

The materiality of an item (or an error) will therefore usually need to be assessed in a variety of ways:

- in relation to the accounts as a whole;
- in relation to the total (or totals) in which it is (or should be) included;
- in relation to the individual profit and loss account heading or balance sheet heading in which it is (or should be) included;
- in relation to other related items in the profit and loss account and balance sheet;
- in relation to the corresponding figure (or figures) for the previous year.

11.38 Key Factors to Consider

The materiality of an individual item cannot be assessed in isolation. There are three key factors, all of which are important to the assessment:

- the size of the item;
- the nature of the item;
- the surrounding circumstances.

For instance, it is not possible to say whether an item (or an error) of £35,000 is material without also knowing its nature and the reasons why it arose. Knowing the size alone is not sufficient. It is also not possible to deal with the question of materiality on a purely mathematical basis – the final assessment will often be subjective and will invariably require the exercise of professional judgement. Whilst percentage guidelines may be helpful as part of the assessment process (for instance, whether an item represents (say) 5 per cent or more of the profit for the year, or (say) 10 per cent or more of a particular balance sheet or profit and loss account heading), they should not be used as the sole means of assessing whether or not an item is material for accounting purposes.

11.39   Nature of an Item

The following points should usually be taken into account when considering the nature of an individual item or error:

- the event or transaction that gave rise to it;
- the legality of the event or transaction and its likely consequences;
- the identity of any other parties, and their relationship to the reporting entity;
- the relevant profit and loss account or balance sheet heading;
- any other related disclosure requirements, either in *CA 1985* or in accounting standards.

11.40   User's Perspective

In assessing the materiality of an item or error, it is also important to consider both the context of the item in the accounts and the way in which a reader of the accounts may use the information provided in the accounts. For instance, a user will rarely make decisions on the basis of accounting information for one year only – he/she is more likely to:

- compare the latest information with the details for previous years, identify any trends and use this information to make projections and forecasts for future years;
- compare the latest information with equivalent information in respect of similar entities.

The impact that the information may have on decisions made by the user is of primary importance when assessing materiality. It is therefore important to view the information (or potential lack of it) from the user's perspective.

11.41   Qualitative Aspects of Transactions

The Financial Reporting Review Panel ('FRRP' – see **11.16** above) criticised the 1995 group accounts of RMC Group plc for failing to disclose an expense that the Panel considered to be material. The issue related to restrictive trade practices fines and related legal costs totalling just under £5 million which were paid by a subsidiary during 1995. The matter originally arose in 1988 and details of the legal action had been given in the group accounts each year. The 1994 accounts disclosed the matter as a contingent liability. The 1995 accounts of the subsidiary disclosed the payment of the fines, but no mention of them was made in the group accounts. The group profits for the year were £173 million, and the costs of £5 million were presumably not considered to be material in the context of the group results. The Panel took the view that the nature and circumstances of the fines were such that they should have been drawn to the attention of users of the group accounts. Their decision was based on guidance in the ICAEW Statement 'The Interpretation of Materiality in Financial Reporting' and the ASB *Statement of Principles for Financial Reporting* (in its draft form at that stage). The Panel has therefore emphasised that qualitative aspects of significant transactions need to be considered as well as quantitative ones. This applies equally in the case of IAS accounts, even though this case arose in the context of UK accounting practice.

11.42   Other Issues to Consider

Other issues that may affect the assessment of whether an item or error is material include:

- whether there is already an element of estimation or approximation in the calculation of the item – for instance, the valuation of long-term contracts will usually involve an assessment of the expected outcome, whereas the amount due to a creditor can often be calculated with a reasonable degree of precision;
- whether the inclusion or exclusion of an item, or correction or non-correction of an error, has the effect of:
  - reversing a trend,
  - turning a profit into a loss, or vice versa,
  - changing the margin of solvency shown in the balance sheet,
  - altering the degree of compliance with debt covenants – these are considered to be 'critical points' and may indicate that it is appropriate to use a lower materiality level than might otherwise be the case;
- an item that is small in the context of the accounts may nevertheless be material, depending on the circumstances – for instance, where a particular item of income or expenditure would normally be large, the fact that it is small in the current year may be relevant to a user of the accounts;
- as well as considering the materiality of individual items, it will usually be necessary to consider similar items in aggregate as well, as the total may be material, even if the individual components are not.

11.43   Exclusion of Immaterial Items

The consideration of materiality is equally important in establishing whether certain details need not be shown separately in the accounts. For instance, reporting in detail on items that are not material, and which are therefore not useful to a user of the accounts, may result in information that is relevant and useful becoming obscured. However, as explained above, certain information must always be disclosed to meet the requirements of *CA 1985*, even though it may not appear to be material in the context of the accounts.

11.44   Statement of Directors' Responsibilities

At a Glance
* Audited accounts that are required to show a true and fair view should include a formal statement of the directors' responsibilities in respect of the accounts.
* If the directors do not make such a statement, the auditors must include a description of the directors' responsibilities in their audit report.
* The statement should cover the requirements for the directors to:
  * prepare accounts that show a true and fair view;
  * select suitable accounting policies and apply them consistently;
  * make judgements and estimates that are prudent and reasonable;
  * state whether applicable accounting standards have been followed;
  * prepare accounts on a going concern basis unless this is inappropriate;
  * keep proper accounting records;
  * safeguard the assets of the company;
  * take reasonable steps to prevent fraud and other irregularities; and
  * where relevant, take responsibility for the maintenance and integrity of corporate and financial information included on the company's website.
* In the case of small and medium-sized companies, no reference needs to be made to the adoption of applicable accounting standards.
* A different statement of directors' responsibilities is required where the company is exempt from having its annual accounts audited.
* The wording of the statement may need to be adapted in the case of specialised businesses and unincorporated entities.

11.45   Requirement to Include a Statement of Responsibilities in the Annual Accounts

The inclusion of a formal statement of directors' responsibilities in respect of the accounts is addressed in the UK and Ireland version of International Standard on Auditing 700 (ISA 700) *The Auditor's Report on Financial Statements* (copies are available from the APB website at www.frc.org.uk/apb/publications). This standard applies in all cases where audited accounts are required to show a true and fair view. Auditors are required to refer in their report to a description of the responsibilities of the directors in respect of the accounts and to distinguish the responsibilities of the auditors from those of the directors. If a statement of the directors' responsibilities is not given in the annual report and accounts, or if the statement given is not considered adequate, the auditors are required to include an appropriate description of the directors' responsibilities within their audit report. In the case of listed companies, the Financial Services Authority ('FSA') requires the directors to include in the annual report a narrative statement on how it has applied the principles set out in the *Combined*

Code, together with details of, and reasons for, any areas of non-compliance. *Provision C.1.1* of the *Combined Code* recommends that the directors explain their responsibility for preparing the accounts, and that there is also a statement by the auditors clarifying their reporting responsibilities. The purpose of both statements is to help shareholders understand the respective roles and responsibilities of the directors and the auditors.

11.46 Presentation of the Statement

It is always preferable for the directors to make a separate statement of their responsibilities for the accounts rather than leaving this to be dealt with by the auditors. The *Combined Code* previously recommended that the directors' statement was given 'next to' the statement of the auditors' responsibilities (which usually forms part of the audit report). The wording of the present *Combined Code* is more flexible and removes any confusion over the location of the statement. It has often been given above or below the auditors' report, or on the immediately preceding page, but it is also acceptable for the statement to be given within the directors' report or in a separate corporate governance report.

11.47 Content of the Statement

The following matters should be covered in the directors' statement:

- the requirement under company law for directors to prepare annual accounts giving a true and fair view of the profit or loss for the year and of the state of affairs of the company (and, where relevant, the group) at the end of the year;
- in preparing those accounts, the requirement for the directors to:
  - select suitable accounting policies,
  - apply those accounting policies on a consistent basis,
  - make judgements and estimates that are prudent and reasonable,
  - state whether applicable accounting standards have been followed, subject to any material departures disclosed and explained in the accounts, and
  - prepare the accounts on a going concern basis unless it is not appropriate to presume that the company will continue in business;
- the requirement for the directors to:
  - keep proper accounting records,
  - safeguard the assets of the company, and
  - take reasonable steps to prevent and detect fraud and other irregularities;
- where the annual accounts and reports are published on the internet, the fact that the directors are responsible for the maintenance and integrity of any corporate and financial information included on the company's website.

11.48 Small and Medium-sized Companies

Small and medium-sized companies are not required to state whether their accounts have been prepared in accordance with applicable accounting standards.

It would therefore be inappropriate for a comment on this to be included in the directors' responsibilities statement in the accounts of small and medium-sized companies. The statement on compliance with applicable accounting standards is therefore only required where the company does not qualify as small or medium-sized under *CA 1985*.

11.49 Example Wording

The latest example wording for a statement of directors' responsibilities in respect of the accounts is given in Appendix 4 to APB Bulletin 2005/4 *Auditors' Report on Financial Statements in Great Britain and Northern Ireland* (copies are available from the APB website at www.frc.org.uk/apb/publications). This gives the following suggested wording for a non-publicly traded company:

'Example: Statement of directors' responsibilities for the accounts

The directors are responsible for preparing the Annual Report and the financial statements in accordance with applicable law and United Kingdom Generally Accepted Accounting Practice.

Company law requires the directors to prepare financial statements for each financial year which give a true and fair view of the state of affairs of the company and of the profit or loss of the company for that period. In preparing these financial statements, the directors are required to:

(a) select suitable accounting policies and then apply them consistently;
(b) make judgements and estimates that are reasonable and prudent;
(c) state whether applicable accounting standards have been followed, subject to any material departures disclosed and explained in the financial statements;[*]
(d) prepare the financial statements on the going concern basis unless it is inappropriate to presume that the company will continue in business.

The directors are responsible for keeping proper accounting records that disclose with reasonable accuracy at any time the financial position of the company and enable them to ensure that the financial statements comply with the Companies Act 1985. They are also responsible for safeguarding the assets of the company and hence for taking reasonable steps for the prevention and detection of fraud and other irregularities.

The directors are responsible for the maintenance and integrity of the corporate and financial information included on the company's website. Legislation in the United Kingdom governing the preparation and dissemination of financial statements may differ from legislation in other jurisdictions.'[†]

* Not required for companies that qualify as small or medium-sized under CA 1985.

† Required only where the financial statements are published on the internet.

The Bulletin notes that the responsibilities of the directors of a publicly traded company will be dependent on the particular regulatory environment in which it operates and may vary depending on the rules of the market to which the securities are admitted to trading. It also notes that directors preparing IAS accounts may need to take legal advice on what should be included in the statement of their responsibilities.

The directors of most companies choose to make the statement in terms of their general responsibilities, as set out above. It is equally acceptable for the statement to be made in more positive terms, for instance by stating that the directors are of the opinion that appropriate accounting policies have been adopted and applied consistently.

11.50   Impact of Audit Exemption

Where a small company is exempt from an audit under *section 249A* of *CA 1985*, a different statement of directors' responsibilities is required. The legislation specifies the content of the statement and requires it to be given on the balance sheet, above the signature of director(s). Full details are given at **1.17 DIRECTORS' STATEMENT**.

11.51   Specialised Businesses and Unincorporated Entities

ISA 700 (see **11.42** above) applies to all audit reports on accounts that are required to show a true and fair view. The wording of the statement of directors' responsibilities may need to be amended to reflect the specific requirements applying to specialised businesses (eg banks and insurance companies). In the case of unincorporated entities (such as charities and pension funds) the responsibilities of the directors, managers or trustees may not be so clearly defined and may vary quite considerably between apparently similar entities. Care must be taken to ensure that the statement given in the annual accounts properly reflects the responsibilities actually in place under the relevant constitution or trust deed.

11.52   Form and Content of Companies Act Individual Accounts

At a Glance
* Where Companies Act accounts are prepared, *CA 1985* offers a choice of four formats for the profit and loss account and two formats for the balance sheet – once a format has been chosen, it must be used consistently from year to year unless there are good reasons for making a change.
* *CA 1985* requires or permits some adaptation of the formats in certain circumstances.
* Certain additional items must be shown in the profit and loss account.

* Additional information or analyses must be given in the notes to the accounts.
* Accounting standards generally require more detailed disclosures to be given in the notes to the accounts – some add new items to the standard formats or require additional statements to be included in the accounts.
* The ASB has issued proposals for replacing the profit and loss account and statement of total recognised gains and losses with a single performance statement.
* Comparative figures must be given for each item in the profit and loss account and balance sheet, and most disclosures in the notes to the accounts.
* *CA 1985* and UK accounting standards prescribe the principles to be adopted when preparing accounts.
* *CA 1985* generally prohibits the off-setting of assets and liabilities, and of income and expenditure.
* UK accounting standards require accounts to reflect the substance of transactions undertaken by the company (where this differs from their legal form).
* Fair value accounting may be adopted for certain assets and liabilities.

11.53 Preparation of Companies Act Individual Accounts

For accounting periods beginning on or after 1 January 2005, most companies have the option of preparing either Companies Act individual accounts or IAS individual accounts (see **3.16** above). Where IAS accounts are prepared, the detailed provisions of *CA 1985* on the form and content of accounts no longer apply and the company must comply instead with the detailed requirements of all relevant international accounting standards. Where Companies Act accounts are prepared, the detailed provisions of *CA 1985* continue to apply, as do the requirements of all relevant UK accounting standards. The following paragraphs summarise the main requirements in respect of Companies Act individual accounts.

11.54 Prescribed Formats

Paragraph 1(1) of *Schedule 4* to *CA 1985* requires a company to use one of the prescribed formats set out in the legislation for the profit and loss account and for the balance sheet. The legislation provides a choice of four formats for the profit and loss account and two formats for the balance sheet – these are all set out in *paragraph 8* of *Schedule 4* to *CA 1985*. The directors can chose which format to adopt in each case, but once a format has been selected, the legislation requires it to be used consistently year by year unless there are good reasons for changing to another format. If a format is changed (for instance, where a change in activity makes an alternative profit and loss account format more appropriate to the company's business), details of the change must be disclosed in the accounts and the reason for the change must be explained. The formats do not generally indicate where sub-totals should be drawn and the directors are therefore free to decide on this themselves, subject to the additional disclosure requirements of accounting standards (see **11.56** below). Small companies adopting the FRSSE are now restricted to the use of two profit and loss account formats rather than the four set out in the legislation (see **11.19–11.20** above).

11.55   Structure of the Formats

The formats are set out in the legislation using a hierarchy of:

- letters and Arabic numbers for the profit and loss account; and
- letters, Roman numbers and Arabic numbers for the balance sheet.

The letters and numbers given in the formats do not have to be reproduced in the accounts – they are provided so that other sections of the legislation can refer to the headings by category. Individual headings and sub-headings set out in the formats should normally appear in the annual accounts in the order prescribed in the legislation, although *paragraph 33(3)* of *Schedule 4* to *CA 1985* requires the directors to adapt or rearrange the items identified by Arabic numbers if the special nature of the company's business requires this. Items may be shown in greater detail than the formats require and additional items may be added, provided that they are not already shown elsewhere in the formats (in other words, this provision cannot be used to change the location of an item that is already in the formats). Headings identified by Arabic numbers may be combined in the accounts if the individual amounts are not material. They may also be combined on the face of the profit and loss account or balance sheet if this facilitates assessment of the company's financial performance or financial position, but in this case the individual components must be shown separately in the notes to the accounts.

11.56   Additional Profit and Loss Account Disclosures

In addition to the details set out in the standard profit and loss account formats, *paragraph 3(6)* of Schedule 4 to *CA 1985* requires every profit and loss account to show the profit or loss on ordinary activities before taxation. For accounting periods beginning before 1 January 2005, there was also a requirement under *CA 1985* for dividends paid and proposed, and transfers to or from reserves, to be shown in the profit and loss account. This requirement was removed by the *Companies Act 1985 (International Accounting Standards and Other Accounting Amendments) Regulations 2004 (SI 2004/2947)* for accounting periods beginning on or after 1 January 2005, and replaced by a new *paragraph 35A* of *Schedule 4* which requires the following information to be given in the notes to the accounts:

- amounts set aside or withdrawn from reserves;
- the aggregate amount of dividends paid in the year, other than those for which a liability existed at the previous balance sheet date;

- the aggregate amount of dividends that the company is liable to pay at the balance sheet date; and
- the aggregate amount of dividends proposed before the date of approval of the accounts and not included in the above disclosures.

This change enables companies to comply with FRS 21 *Events After the Balance Sheet Date* which also came into effect on 1 January 2005. FRS 21 does not permit a proposed dividend which is still subject to shareholder approval to be included in the balance sheet, on the basis that it does not meet the accounting definition of a liability at the balance sheet date. The change also removed the requirement for dividends paid during the year to be reported in the profit and loss account, and so allows them to be accounted for as transactions with shareholders, as required by FRS 25 *Financial Instruments: Disclosure and Presentation*.

11.57   Notes to the Accounts

The profit and loss account and balance sheet formats require additional information or analyses to be given for certain items. These disclosures are usually given in the notes to the accounts, together with other detailed disclosures required by the other paragraphs of *Schedule 4* to *CA 1985*. Further disclosure requirements are set out in:

- *Schedule 5* to *CA 1985*, which requires the accounts to include detailed information on related undertakings, such as subsidiaries, associates and joint ventures; and
- *Schedule 6* to *CA 1985*, which requires the accounts to give detailed information on emoluments, benefits in kind, incentives, share options and compensation for loss of office paid to or received by the company's directors, and also pension arrangements made by the company for the benefit of the directors (see **23.31 DIRECTORS' REMUNERATION**).

11.58   Requirements of Accounting Standards

Accounting standards also require additional disclosures to support figures shown in the profit and loss account and balance sheet. The additional details are usually required to be given in the notes to the accounts, except in the case of FRS 3 *Reporting Financial Performance* which requires:

- the separate disclosure of 'operating profit' on the face of the profit and loss account;
- all figures from turnover through to operating profit to be analysed into amounts relating to continuing, discontinued and newly acquired operations – as a minimum, the figures for turnover and operating profit must be analysed in this way on the face of the profit and loss account;
- separate disclosure on the face of the profit and loss account of:
  - profits and losses on the sale or termination of operations,
  - costs of a fundamental reorganisation or restructuring that has a material effect on the nature and focus of operations, and

○ profits or losses on the disposal of fixed assets (other than marginal adjustments to depreciation charged in previous years).

FRS 3 also requires annual accounts to include a statement of total recognised gains and losses, to draw together all gains and losses recognised during the financial period, and to include a reconciliation of movements in shareholders' funds. The same standard also deals with the definition and disclosure of exceptional items and extraordinary items (although the latter are now very rare, as a result of the stringent definitions in FRS 3). FRS 1 *Cash Flow Statements* requires the presentation of a cashflow statement in the format specified in the standard. FRS 22 *Earnings per Share* sets out detailed requirements on the calculation and disclosure of earnings per share – the standard applies to all companies whose shares are publicly traded (or about to become publicly traded) and to any company which chooses to disclose earnings per share on a voluntary basis. For information on obtaining copies of accounting standards see the ASB website at www.frc.org.uk/asb.

11.59   Expected Future Developments

In December 2000, the ASB issued FRED 22 *Revision of FRS 3: Reporting Financial Performance* which proposes some significant changes to present disclosure requirements (for information on obtaining copies see the ASB website at www.frc.org.uk/asb). The proposals represent an agreed international approach to reporting financial performance and replace the present profit and loss account and statement of total recognised gains and losses with a single performance statement showing all the gains and losses recognised during a financial period. The proposed performance statement is divided into three sections:

• operating;
• financial and treasury;
• other gains and losses.

The proposals have since been taken forward as a joint ASB/IASB project and the IASB published an Exposure Draft of proposed amendments to IAS 1 *Presentation of Financial Statements* in March 2006. The proposals include a requirement for companies to present income and expenses separately from changes in equity arising from transactions with owners, and the option for entities to present income and expenses in a single performance statement or in two statements (ie with certain income and expenses shown in a Statement of Recognised Income and Expense and all other items shown in the income statement). This approach is very similar to that already required in the UK under FRS 3 *Reporting Financial Performance*. The ASB has therefore decided not to propose amendments to UK accounting practice at present. A second stage of the project will consider the presentation and aggregation of information in the performance statement and other elements of the financial statements, and the ASB hopes that this will build on the proposals developed in FRED 22 and its subsequent joint project with the IASB.

11.60   Comparative Figures

Under *paragraph 4* of *Schedule 4* to *CA 1985*, comparative figures must be given for each item in the profit and loss account and balance sheet and for most of the additional information that has to be disclosed in the notes to the accounts. If an item appears in the previous year, but not in the current year, the heading and comparative amount must still be given in the profit and loss account or balance sheet. However, if there is no amount to be shown under a particular heading in either the current or the previous year, the heading should not appear in the accounts. Where any figure reported in the accounts is not directly comparable with the equivalent amount for the previous year, the corresponding figure for the previous period may be adjusted and the notes to the accounts must give details of any adjustment made or of any non-comparability that has not been adjusted. FRS 28 *Corresponding Amounts* also sets out requirements on the disclosure of corresponding amounts in financial statements. The standard requires corresponding amounts to be given for every item in the primary financial statements (currently the profit and loss account, statement of total recognised gains and losses, balance sheet and cashflow statement) and requires a corresponding amount to be adjusted if it is not directly comparable with the amount shown for the current year, unless an accounting standard or UITF Abstract requires or permits an alternative treatment. This allows scope for individual accounting standards to specify that comparatives need not be adjusted in certain circumstances – for instance, on the introduction of new accounting requirements where the restatement of comparatives on a consistent basis is considered to be too onerous and would outweigh the related benefits. Details of any adjustment made to comparative figures, and the reason for it, must be given in the notes to the accounts. The same requirements generally apply to information disclosed in the notes to the accounts, although FRS 28 sets out specific exemptions from the disclosure of comparative information for the following:

- movements in fixed assets during the year;
- transfers to or from reserves and provisions;
- the accounting treatment of acquisitions; and
- details of shareholdings in subsidiary undertakings and significant investments in other undertakings, including associates and joint ventures.

This retains most of the disclosure exemptions previously set out in *CA 1985* but which were removed by the *Companies Act 1985 (Investment Companies and Accounting and Audit Amendments) Regulations 2005* (*SI 2005/2280*). The main exception is that *CA 1985* previously included a further exemption relating to the disclosure of comparative information on loans and other transactions involving directors and other officers. The ASB has taken the view that corresponding amounts for these disclosures are readily available and that disclosure would enhance the usefulness of financial statements and so has not included an equivalent exemption in FRS 28.

11.61   Accounting Principles

Paragraphs 10–13 of *Schedule 4* to *CA 1985* require company accounts to be based on the principles of going concern, consistency, accruals and prudence. These principles apply to all companies, regardless of size, and are considered to have such general acceptance that there is no requirement to refer to the fact that they have been followed when preparing the accounts – a company is presumed to have observed them unless its accounts state otherwise. The directors are only permitted to depart from the accounting principles where there are special reasons for doing so and the accounts must disclose particulars of the departure, the reasons for it and the financial effect. Detailed guidance on the principles that should be followed when preparing annual accounts, including practical interpretation of the *CA 1985* requirements, can be found in the ASB's *Statement of Principles for Financial Reporting* and in FRS 18 *Accounting Policies*. Brief details are set out below.

11.62   *Going Concern*

CA 1985 does not provide any detailed guidance on going concern. FRS 18 describes the going concern basis as the hypothesis that the entity is to continue in operational existence for the foreseeable future. When preparing accounts, the standard requires the directors to assess whether there are any significant doubts about the entity's ability to continue as a going concern and requires financial statements to be prepared on a going concern basis unless:

* the entity is being liquidated or has ceased trading;
* the directors intend to liquidate the entity or to cease trading; or
* the directors have no realistic alternative but to liquidate the entity or to cease trading.

In these circumstances the entity should prepare the financial statements on a different basis. Additional disclosures may need to be given in the notes to the accounts where uncertainties affect the assessment of going concern. Detailed guidance on the factors that directors should take into account when assessing going concern can be found in the UK and Ireland version of International Standard on Auditing 570 (ISA 570) *Going Concern* (available from the APB website at www.frc.org.uk/apb/publications) and in the Joint Working Group Guidance *Going Concern and Financial Reporting* (see also **6 CORPORATE GOVERNANCE**).

11.63   *Consistency*

Accounting policies provide a framework within which assets, liabilities, income and expenditure are recognised, measured and presented in financial statements, and they help to improve the comparability of financial information. Both *CA 1985* and FRS 18 require accounting policies to be applied consistently within an accounting period and from one financial year to the next. However, situations will inevitably arise from time to time which make it necessary for an entity to change one or more of its accounting policies. For instance, a new accounting standard may have been introduced which requires a different accounting treatment to the one previously adopted, or the nature or scale of activities may have changed so that an existing accounting policy is no longer acceptable. FRS 18 requires accounting policies to be regularly reviewed, and sets out specific accounting and disclosure requirements that apply whenever an accounting policy is changed.

11.64   *Accruals*

CA 1985 requires all income and charges relating to the financial year to be taken into account, regardless of the date of receipt or payment. FRS 18 also requires adoption of the accruals method of accounting, which it describes as requiring:

> '... the non-cash effects of transactions and other events to be reflected, as far as is possible, in the financial statements for the accounting period in which they occur and not, for example, in the period in which any cash involved is received or paid'.

Provision must therefore be made for all expenses and losses relating to the year in question, and for income and profits relating to that year, subject to the requirement for prudence (see **11.65** below).

11.65   *Prudence*

CA 1985 requires the amount of any item in the accounts to be determined on a prudent basis. In particular, only profits realised at the balance sheet date should be included in the profit and loss account, and all losses or liabilities which have arisen (or are likely to arise) in respect of the current financial year or any previous financial year must be taken into account. This includes any liabilities or losses that only become apparent between the balance sheet date and the date on which the accounts are formally approved and signed by the directors. FRS 18 does not deal with prudence as such, but emphasises the need for financial information to be reliable and also the legal requirement that only realised profits are to be included in the accounts. The standard notes that profits should be treated as realised for accounting purposes only when they have been realised in the form of cash or of other assets, the ultimate cash realisation of which can be assessed with reasonable certainty. In the section on reliability, FRS 18 makes the following points:

- under conditions of uncertainty, financial information is reliable if it has been prudently prepared (ie a degree of caution has been applied in exercising judgement and making necessary estimates);
- it is not necessary to exercise prudence where there is no uncertainty; and
- it is not appropriate to use prudence as a reason for creating hidden reserves or excessive provisions, deliberately understating assets or gains, or deliberately overstating liabilities or losses.

11.66   Offsetting

Paragraph 5 of *Schedule 4* to *CA 1985* generally prohibits the offsetting of assets and liabilities when calculating figures for disclosure in the balance sheet, and of income and expenses when calculating figures for disclosure in the profit and loss account. *Paragraph 14* of *Schedule 4* to *CA 1985* also emphasises the requirement to consider separately the individual components of assets and liabilities when calculating aggregate amounts. This means, for instance, that a potential overstatement of the value of one investment cannot be ignored on the basis that it is compensated for by an understatement in the value of a different investment.

11.67   Substance Over Form

Under FRS 5 *Reporting the Substance of Transactions*, accounts are required to reflect the commercial substance of the transactions entered into by the reporting entity rather than their legal form (where this is different). The commercial substance of a transaction is not always easily identifiable, especially where:

- the principal benefits of an asset are in some way separated from legal ownership;
- the transaction involves options or conditions that are not commercially realistic (for instance, where the terms of an option mean that it is virtually certain not to be exercised); and
- the overall commercial effect of a series of transactions is different from the apparent effect of the individual transactions.

When assessing the substance of a transaction, the standard requires greater emphasis to be given to the aspects of the transaction that are likely to have a practical commercial effect. Where an overall commercial effect is achieved by a series of transactions, the standard requires the series to be considered as a whole rather than as individual transactions. FRS 5 is deliberately conceptual rather than factual in nature to prevent transactions being structured so as to circumvent prescribed rules (for information on obtaining copies see the ASB website at www.frc.org.uk/asb).

Also, for accounting periods beginning on or after 1 January 2005, *Companies Act 1985 (International Accounting Standards and Other Accounting Amendments) Regulations 2004 (SI 2004/2947)* insert a new *paragraph 5A* into *Schedule 4* to the *Companies Act 1985*, which requires the directors to have regard to the substance of the reported transaction or arrangement, in accordance with generally accepted accounting principles, when determining how items are presented in the profit and loss account and balance sheet. Similar amendments are made to *Schedule 8*, *Schedule 9* and *Schedule 9A* so that the new provision also applies to small companies preparing shorter form accounts and to banks and insurance companies.

11.68   Fair Value Accounting

The 4th and 7th EC Company Law Directives, which form the basis of the *CA 1985* requirements on individual and consolidated accounts, were recently amended by the EU Fair Value Directive to allow certain financial instruments to be included in the balance sheet at fair value, and changes in that fair value to be reflected in the profit and loss account. In the UK, fair value accounting has been made optional rather than mandatory and can be applied to both individual and consolidated accounts. It has been introduced by the *Companies Act 1985 (International Accounting Standards and Other Accounting Amendments) Regulations 2004* (*SI 2004/2947*) which insert the following new paragraphs into *Schedule 4* to *CA 1985*:

(i) *paragraphs 34A to 34F* which set out detailed provisions on the adoption of fair value accounting; and

(ii) *paragraphs 45A to 45D* which deal with the additional disclosures that must be given in the accounts when fair value accounting has been adopted.

Similar amendments have been made to *Schedule 8, Schedule 9* and *Schedule 9A* to *CA 1985*, so that fair value accounting is available to all companies, including small companies preparing shorter form accounts, and banks and insurance companies. In effect, the new provisions allow certain investments to be marked to market and also facilitate the use of hedge accounting in specific circumstances. Prior to these changes, financial instruments were usually accounted for at cost, which in the case of derivatives is often nil. Even if advantage was taken of the alternative accounting rules, any changes in value had to be dealt with through the revaluation reserve rather than the profit and loss account. Under the new legislation, most financial instruments (including derivatives) may be included in the accounts at fair value provided that this can be determined reliably on the basis set out in the legislation. However, fair value accounting cannot be applied in the case of financial liabilities unless they are derivatives or are held as part of a trading portfolio. FRS 25 *Financial Instruments: Disclosure and Presentation* and FRS 26 *Financial Instruments: Measurement* set out the detailed UK framework for the adoption of fair value accounting, together with FRS 23 *The Effects of Changes in Foreign Exchange Rates* and FRS 24 *Financial Reporting in Hyperinflationary Economies* where relevant. The presentation requirements of FRS 25 apply for accounting periods beginning on or after 1 January 2005 and the disclosure requirements apply no later than the accounting period in which FRS 26 is adopted. FRS 26 applies for accounting periods beginning on or after 1 January 2005 for listed companies and for accounting periods beginning on or after 1 January 2006 for any other entity which adopts fair value accounting (voluntary adoption from 1 January 2005 is also acceptable in this case). The new legislation also permits fair value accounting to be applied to investment property and to living animals and plants, where such treatment is permitted under international accounting standards. Under UK accounting practice, investment property must be accounted for in accordance with SSAP 19 *Accounting for Investment Properties*. There are currently no UK accounting standards dealing specifically with living animals and plants, although the ASB is considering the implementation in the UK of IAS 41 *Agriculture.*

11.69 Form and Content of Companies Act Group Accounts

At a Glance

* Companies Act group accounts must be prepared in the form of consolidated accounts and must generally include the accounts of the parent company and all its subsidiaries.
* A parent company that is required to prepare group accounts need not publish its own profit and loss account.
* *CA 1985* and FRS 2 *Accounting for Subsidiary Undertakings* set out detailed rules on what constitutes a subsidiary undertaking.
* In certain circumstances, a subsidiary undertaking is permitted or required to be excluded from the consolidated accounts.
* The assets, liabilities, profits, losses and cashflows of certain other entities ('quasi-subsidiaries') may also need to be included in the group accounts, even if these entities do not meet the legal definition of a subsidiary undertaking.
* The results of associates and joint ventures should normally be included in group accounts using the equity method of accounting.
* *CA 1985* and UK accounting standards include detailed rules on the preparation of consolidated accounts and on accounting for acquisitions and mergers.
* Companies Act group accounts must follow one of the *CA 1985* formats for the profit and loss account and balance sheet, as amended by the legislation to cater specifically for a group situation.
* Group accounts are subject to the same true and fair requirement as individual company accounts.
* *CA 1985* requires certain additional items to be shown in the profit and loss account.
* Directors must ensure that the financial year of each subsidiary undertaking coincides with that of the parent unless there are good reasons against this.

11.70 Preparation of Companies Act Group Accounts

For accounting periods beginning on or after 1 January 2005, most parent companies have the option of preparing either Companies Act group accounts or IAS group accounts (see **3.17** above). Where IAS group accounts are prepared, the detailed provisions of *CA 1985* on the form and content of accounts no longer apply and the parent must comply instead with the detailed requirements of all relevant international accounting standards. Where Companies Act group accounts are prepared, the detailed provisions of *CA 1985* continue to apply, as do the requirements of all relevant UK accounting standards. The following paragraphs summarise the main requirements in respect of Companies Act group accounts.

11.71 Consolidated Accounts

Under *sections 227A(1)* and *229(1)* of *CA 1985*, Companies Act group accounts must be prepared in the form of consolidated accounts and must include the accounts of the parent company and all its subsidiary undertakings. The only exception to this rule is where a subsidiary undertaking is required or permitted by the legislation, or by accounting standards, to be excluded from the consolidation. Other detailed rules on the form and content of group accounts are set out in *Schedule 4A* to *CA 1985*. The requirements of accounting standards, particularly FRS 2 *Accounting for Subsidiary Undertakings*, must also be taken into account (for information on obtaining copies see the ASB website at www.frc.org.uk/asb).

11.72 Parent Company Profit and Loss Account

Under *section 230(3)* of *CA 1985*, a parent company which is required to prepare group accounts need not publish its own profit and loss account as part of those accounts, provided that:

- the group accounts state that this exemption applies; and
- the notes to the parent company's individual balance sheet (which must be published as part of the group accounts) show the company's profit or loss for the year, calculated in accordance with the accounting requirements of *CA 1985*.

The exemption relates only to publication of the parent company's profit and loss account – the company must therefore still prepare a full profit and loss account in the format required by the legislation, and this must be formally approved by the directors. However, where the parent prepares Companies Act individual accounts, *section 230(4)* grants exemption from some of the supplementary disclosures that would otherwise need to be given in the notes to the accounts. The exemption from publication of the parent's profit and loss account continues to apply where IAS accounts are prepared, but the disclosure exemptions are not relevant in this case.

11.73 Definition of Subsidiary Undertaking

The detailed rules on what constitutes a subsidiary undertaking are set out in *section 258* of *CA 1985* and in FRS 2 (see **11.71** above). Certain changes were made to these definitions for accounting periods beginning on or after 1 January 2005. In particular, the existence of a participating interest is no longer required and it is the power to exercise dominant influence, or the actual exercise of such influence, that determines whether an entity is a subsidiary. The focus of the definitions is the ability of the parent to control the subsidiary. Although *CA 1985* uses terms such as 'exercises a dominant influence' and 'managed on a unified basis', it does not expand on these. FRS 2 gives detailed guidance on how these terms should be interpreted for practical purposes. *Schedule 10A* to *CA 1985* provides guidance on the interpretation of voting rights for the purpose of establishing whether an entity is a subsidiary undertaking.

11.74 Exclusion of a Subsidiary from the Group Accounts

Section 229 of *CA 1985* permits a subsidiary undertaking to be excluded from the consolidation if:

- severe long-term restrictions hinder the parent's ability to exercise its rights over the assets and management of the entity; or
- the interest is held exclusively for resale.

FRS 2 (see **11.71** above) includes detailed guidance on the conditions that should be met for exclusion to be justified on these grounds, but where the conditions are met the standard requires exclusion rather than permitting it. FRS 2 also prescribes the accounting treatment to be adopted in each case: a subsidiary excluded on the grounds of long-term restrictions should be accounted for as a fixed asset investment and an interest held exclusively for resale should be accounted for as a current asset investment. For accounting periods beginning before 1 January 2005, both *CA 1985* and FRS 2 required a subsidiary to be excluded from the consolidation where its activities were so different from the rest of the group that its inclusion in the consolidation would be incompatible with the true and fair view, but both the legislation and the accounting standard have been amended so that exclusion on these grounds is no longer required or permitted for accounting periods beginning on or after 1 January 2005. *CA 1985* also permits a subsidiary to be excluded from the consolidation in two other situations:

- where inclusion would not be material for the purpose of achieving a true and fair view (if two or more subsidiaries are involved, materiality must be assessed on an aggregate basis) – FRS 2 makes no reference to this as accounting standards are only intended to apply to material items;
- where the necessary information cannot be obtained without undue expense or delay – FRS 2 does not permit exclusion on these grounds.

In any case where a subsidiary is excluded from the consolidation, both *CA 1985* and FRS 2 require detailed disclosures to be given in the accounts.

11.75 Quasi-subsidiaries

An undertaking may in effect be controlled by another entity, and generate benefits for that entity, without meeting the definition of a subsidiary undertaking set out in *CA 1985* or FRS 2 (see **11.71** above). Such an undertaking is described as a 'quasi-subsidiary' in FRS 5 *Reporting the Substance of Transactions* and the standard generally requires the assets, liabilities, profits, losses and cashflows of the quasi-subsidiary to be included in the group accounts of the 'parent' in order to reflect the true substance of the arrangements (for information on obtaining copies see the ASB website at www.frc.org.uk/asb). Consideration of whether an entity meets the definition of a 'quasi-subsidiary' must take into account:

- who gains the benefit from the entity's net assets;
- who bears the inherent risks relating to the net assets; and
- who directs the operating and financial policies of the entity.

Risk is defined in the standard as including the potential to gain as well as the possible exposure to loss, and the ability to prevent others from gaining access to benefits or from directing the entity's policies are equally relevant to the assessment. For accounting periods beginning on or after 1 January 2005, the changes to the definition of a subsidiary made by the *Companies Act (International Accounting Standards and Other Accounting Amendments) Regulations 2004 (SI 2004/2947)* are likely to mean that certain entities that were previously included in consolidated accounts as quasi-subsidiaries will in future be accounted for as subsidiaries.

11.76   Associates and Joint Ventures

It has become common practice for companies and groups to carry out part of their business activities through entities that are not subsidiary undertakings but over which the investor nevertheless has a considerable degree of influence. An associate is defined as an entity, other than a subsidiary, in which the investor has a participating interest and over whose operating and financial policies the investor exercises significant influence. *Section 260(1)* of *CA 1985* defines a participating interest as an interest held on a long-term basis for the purpose of securing a contribution to activities through the exercise of control or influence. FRS 9 *Associates and Joint Ventures* gives detailed guidance on the practical application of this definition and of the term 'significant influence' (for information on obtaining copies see the ASB website at www.frc.org.uk/asb). A shareholding of 20 per cent or more will usually constitute a participating interest, although it is possible to rebut this presumption in certain cases. Although it would be inappropriate to consolidate fully the results, assets and liabilities of an associate into the group accounts, it is also accepted that it would be misleading to ignore the nature of the relationship and account for the associate in the same way as other investments (for instance, by simply reflecting any dividends received as income in the profit and loss account). Both *CA 1985* and FRS 9 therefore require the results of associates to be included in group accounts using the equity method of accounting. Under this method, the investing group's share of the profit or loss of the associate is included in the profit and loss account, and its share of the underlying net assets of the associate is included in the group balance sheet.

FRS 9 also includes detailed guidance on the definition of a joint venture and requires such an entity to be accounted for using the gross equity method of accounting. This is broadly the same as the equity method of accounting but with two additional disclosure requirements:

- the investor's share of the turnover of the joint venture must be shown in the consolidated profit and loss account; and
- the investor's share of the gross assets and liabilities of the joint venture should be shown in the consolidated balance sheet.

Care is needed in the presentation of these figures to ensure they are not confused with those of the group, or do not appear to be included as part of the totals for the group. Further disclosures must be given where a major part of the business is conducted through joint ventures.

11.77   Consolidation Rules

Both *CA 1985* and FRS 2 (see **11.71** above) set out detailed rules on the preparation of consolidated accounts, the main points being that:

- uniform accounting policies should be used throughout the group to determine the amounts to be included in the group accounts – where (in exceptional circumstances) this is not possible, full details of the differences must be disclosed in the accounts;
- where assets held by any group undertakings include profits or losses arising from intra-group transactions (for instance, where items in stock have been purchased from another group company at more than cost price), the full amount of the profit or loss must be eliminated when preparing the consolidated accounts;
- amounts due to and from undertakings included in the consolidation, and income and expenditure relating to transactions between them, must be eliminated from the consolidated accounts; and
- the amount of capital and reserves attributable to shares held by any minority interests, and the profit or loss on ordinary activities (and any extraordinary items) attributable to them, must be shown separately in the consolidated accounts – *Schedule 4A* to *CA 1985* amends the balance sheet and profit and loss account formats to provide additional headings for these disclosures.

There are also detailed rules in the legislation, and in particular in accounting standards, on accounting for acquisitions and mergers and for any goodwill that arises on consolidation.

11.78   Acquisitions and Mergers

There are currently two permitted methods of accounting for the combination of existing businesses – acquisition accounting and merger accounting. Merger accounting can only be used when the stringent criteria set out in *CA 1985* and

FRS 6 *Acquisitions and Mergers* are met. Most business combinations are therefore accounted for as acquisitions. Under this method of accounting, the assets and liabilities of the acquired entity are brought into the group accounts at fair value as at the date of acquisition, and the results of the entity are included in the group accounts only from the date of acquisition. FRS 7 *Fair Values in Acquisition Accounting* sets out rules on how the fair value of each type of asset and liability should be established. Any difference between the purchase consideration and the aggregate fair value of the assets and liabilities acquired constitutes purchased goodwill. For information on obtaining copies of the above accounting standards see the ASB website at www.frc.org.uk/asb.

11.79 Goodwill

Goodwill is a means of recognising that the value of a business as a whole is often more than the aggregate value of the underlying assets and liabilities. Neither *CA 1985* nor FRS 10 *Goodwill and Intangible Assets* permits internally-generated goodwill to be recognised on the balance sheet. Goodwill is therefore only recognised for accounting purposes when it is purchased as part of a business acquisition. When a company buys an unincorporated business, any goodwill acquired will be recognised on the company's own balance sheet along with the other business assets and liabilities acquired. When a company acquires a business by buying shares in another company, any goodwill acquired is recorded only when the accounts of the company and its new subsidiary are consolidated to form group accounts. Goodwill arising in a company's own accounts and goodwill arising on consolidation must be accounted for in accordance with FRS 10. The standard requires purchased goodwill to be capitalised as an asset and amortised over its useful economic life. There is a rebuttable presumption that the useful economic life of goodwill is no more than 20 years. If it can be demonstrated that the expected life of the goodwill is indefinite, the asset should not be amortised but a detailed impairment review must be carried out each year. This treatment will require use of the true and fair override, as *CA 1985* requires all goodwill to be amortised. Annual impairment reviews must also be carried if the goodwill is amortised over a period of more than 20 years. FRS 10 sets out separate requirements on accounting for negative goodwill, which arises when the purchase consideration is less than the aggregate fair value of the assets and liabilities acquired. For information on obtaining copies of FRS 10 see the ASB website at www.frc.org.uk/asb.

11.80 Prescribed Formats

Paragraph 1(1) of *Schedule 4A* to *CA 1985* states that Companies Act group accounts must comply, as far as is practicable, with the requirements of *Schedule 4* to *CA 1985* as if the undertakings included in the consolidated accounts were a single entity. The accounts must therefore follow one of the prescribed formats for the balance sheet and profit and loss account in the same way as Companies Act individual accounts. However, *paragraphs 17* and *21* of *Schedule 4A* specifically amend the formats to:

- include appropriate headings for the disclosure of minority interests; and
- analyse income from participating interests, and investments in participating interests, into those relating to associated undertakings and those relating to other participating interests.

All of the format rules for individual accounts apply in exactly the same way to consolidated accounts (see **11.55** above). For the purpose of the rules on adapting or combining headings, the profit and loss account headings in respect of minority interests are treated as if they had been assigned an Arabic number and the balance sheet headings as if they had been assigned a letter.

11.81   True and Fair View

Companies Act group accounts are required by *section 227A(2)* of *CA 1985* to show a true and fair view of the state of affairs of the group undertakings as a whole at the end of the financial period, and of their profit or loss for the year then ended, so far as concerns the members of the parent company. Where compliance with *Schedule 4A* to *CA 1985* and with other requirements set out in the legislation is not sufficient to achieve a true and fair view, additional information must be given. If, in special circumstances, compliance with the provisions of *Schedule 4A* to *CA 1985* or with other provisions in the legislation would be inconsistent with the requirement for the accounts to show a true and fair view, the directors must depart from the requirements of *CA 1985* and make specific disclosure of this in the accounts. This is considered in more detail at **11.28–11.29** above – the same principles apply for group accounts as for individual accounts.

11.82   Additional Profit and Loss Account Disclosures

In addition to the disclosures required by the standard formats, a group profit and loss account must show the profit or loss on ordinary activities before taxation. The notes to the accounts must include the new *CA 1985* disclosures in respect of dividends and transfers to and from reserves (see **11.56** above), although the dividend details will relate only to dividends paid or proposed to be paid by the parent company to its own shareholders. Similarly, the disclosure requirements in respect of directors' emoluments and benefits relate only to the directors of the parent company, although the amounts shown must include all amounts paid to or received by those directors, including any remuneration for their services as a director of one or more of the subsidiaries. The additional disclosures required by accounting standards apply to group accounts in the same way as to individual accounts, as do the rules on disclosure of comparative figures and the prohibition on offsetting (see **11.59–11.68** above).

11.83 Accounting Date of Subsidiary Undertakings

Under *section 223(5)* of *CA 1985*, the directors of a parent company must ensure that the financial year of each subsidiary undertaking coincides with that of the parent unless, in their opinion, there are good reasons against this. In this case, *paragraph 2(2)* of *Schedule 4A* to *CA 1985* requires Companies Act group accounts to include:

- the latest accounts of the subsidiary undertaking, provided that these are for a period ending not more than three months before the financial year-end of the parent company; or
- interim accounts for the subsidiary made up to the financial year-end of the parent company.

FRS 2 *Accounting for Subsidiary Undertakings* (see **11.71** above) sets out more stringent rules, requiring the accounts of all subsidiary undertakings included in the consolidated accounts to be for the same accounting period and made up to the same accounting date as the accounts of the parent, as far as is practicable. Where a subsidiary has a different financial year-end, interim accounts should therefore be prepared for consolidation purposes. Only if this is not practicable should the latest accounts of the subsidiary be used, and even then adjustments must be made to reflect any changes in the intervening period if these have a material effect on the group accounts. The standard also requires additional disclosure in the notes to the accounts when a subsidiary prepares its accounts to a different accounting date, or for a different accounting period, from that of the parent company.

11.84 Directors' Report

At a Glance
* Directors are required to prepare a report for each financial year – where the company is required to prepare group accounts, the directors' report must also provide information for the group as a whole.
* The detailed contents of the directors' report are prescribed in *CA 1985*.
* The auditors are specifically required to consider whether the information presented in the directors' report is consistent with the annual accounts.
* The report must include a fair review of the development of the business during the year and the position at the end of the year.
* The ASB has issued a non-mandatory Reporting Statement 'Operating and Financial Review' to provide a framework for the discussion of a company's performance and financial position.
* Detailed disclosures must be given on directors' interests in shares and share options.

> * Extensive disclosures on political donations and expenditure are required as a result of the *Political Parties, Elections and Referendums Act 2000.*
> * Where the company's accounts are subject to audit, the directors' report must include formal confirmation that the directors have disclosed all relevant information to the auditors.

11.85   Requirement to Prepare a Directors' Report

Under *section 234* of *CA 1985*, the directors are required to prepare a report for each financial year. The detailed contents of the report are specified partly in *sections 234ZZA and 234ZZB* of and partly in *Schedule 7* to *CA 1985*. A number of changes have been made to the detailed disclosure requirements for accounting periods beginning on or after 1 April 2005. In particular, the requirements in respect of the business review are much more prescriptive than under the previous legislation. The changes were introduced by the *Companies Act 1985 (Operating and Financial Review and Directors' Report etc.) Regulations 2005 (SI 2005/1011)*, which also included a statutory requirement for quoted companies to prepare an Operating and Financial Review (OFR) for accounting periods beginning on or after 1 April 2005. However, this element of the new legislation was subsequently repealed before it came fully into effect, although the preparation of an OFR continues to be encouraged by the ASB (see **11.89** below). The report must be approved by the board and signed on their behalf by a director or by the company secretary. Where the company is required to prepare group accounts under *CA 1985*, the directors' report must also provide the required information for the group as whole – however, disclosure requirements in respect of the directors relate only to the directors of the parent company. The rules on laying and delivering the annual accounts also apply to the directors' report (see **3.28** LAYING AND DELIVERING ACCOUNTS). There are penalties for failing to comply with the requirement to prepare a directors' report, or for failing to meet the content requirements, although it is a defence for a director to demonstrate that he/she took all reasonable steps to achieve compliance.

The draft Company Law Reform Bill published in May 2006 proposes the introduction of a new liability for directors in respect of false or misleading statements made in the directors' report or the directors' remuneration report (see **23.42–23.53**), and in any information derived from those reports that is included in a summary financial statement (see **11.99**). Under the new provisions, a director will be liable to compensate the company for any loss suffered by it as a result of any untrue or misleading statement made in such a report, or of the omission of anything which the legislation requires to be included, if he/she knew the statement to be untrue or misleading, or was reckless as to whether it was untrue or misleading, or he/she knew the omission to be a dishonest concealment of a material fact.

11.86 Principal Contents

The directors' report must include the following information each year:

(*a*) a fair review of the development of the business during the year and the position at the end of the year and a description of the principal risks and uncertainties facing the company (or group);

(*b*) the amount (if any) recommended to be paid as dividend;

(*c*) the amount that the directors propose to take to reserves;

(*d*) the principal activities of the company (or the group) during the year;

(*e*) an indication of likely future developments in the business;

(*f*) an indication of any research and development activities;

(*g*) an indication of the existence of any branches outside the UK;

(*h*) details of any important events since the end of the financial year;

(*j*) details of any substantial difference between the market values and balance sheet values of interests in land held by the company (or the group);

(*k*) the names of all who served as directors at any time during the year;

(*l*) the interests held by each director (including any held by his immediate family) in the shares or debentures of the company, or of any other body corporate in the same group – the following details must be given:

    (i) interests held at the end of the financial year, and

    (ii) for each director with interests at the end of the year, interests at the beginning of the year or at the date of appointment if this took place during the year;

(*m*) the number or amount of any rights to subscribe for shares or debentures in the company, or any other body corporate in the same group, which were granted to or exercised by each director (or his immediate family) during the year;

(*n*) where the company (or group) has made any donation to a registered party or to any other EU political organisation or incurred any EU political expenditure and the aggregate of all such donations and expenditure exceeded £200, the directors' report must include:

    (i) the name of the registered party or other political organisation to whom a donation was made,

    (ii) the total amount donated to each party or organisation during the financial year,

    (iii) the total amount of any other EU political expenditure during the financial year;

(*o*) if the company (or group) has made any contribution to a non-EU political party, the directors' report must state the amount of the contribution or, where relevant, the total amount of the contributions made during the financial year;

(*p*) if the company (or group) has given more than £200 for charitable purposes, the directors' report must state the amount given during the financial year for each charitable purpose;

(*q*) where the average number of employees exceeds 250:

    (i) a statement on the company's policy on employment, training, career development and promotion of disabled persons, and

(ii) a statement on action taken during the year to introduce, maintain or develop arrangements to provide relevant information to employees, consult them on a regular basis, encourage employee involvement in the company's performance and achieve an awareness amongst employees of financial and economic factors affecting the company's performance; and

(r) the company's policy and practice on the payment of creditors – this only needs to be given by a company that:

(i) was a public company at any time during the year, or

(ii) did not qualify as small or medium-sized, and was a member of a group headed by a public company at any time during the year.

(s) unless the information is not material for an assessment of the company's (or group's) assets, liabilities, financial position and results, an indication of:

(i) the company's (or group's) financial risk management objectives and policies, including the policy for hedging if hedge accounting is used, and

(ii) the company's (or group's) exposure to price risk, credit risk, liquidity risk and cashflow risk;

(t) if the company has provided a qualifying third party indemnity for the benefit of a director of the company or of an associated company during the year, or if such a provision is in force at the time of approval of the report, a statement of that fact [*CA 1985, s 309C*].

Wholly-owned subsidiaries of a company incorporated in Great Britain are exempt from the disclosures under (*n*), (*o*) and (*p*) above, on the basis that the information will be included in the group accounts.

Paragraphs 7 and *8* of *Schedule 7* to *CA 1985* also require various disclosures in respect of transactions involving the company's shares. In the case of listed company, FSA Listing Rule 9.8.6R also requires disclosure of significant shareholdings in the company at a date not more than one month prior to the date of the notice of the Annual General Meeting. The draft Company Law Reform Bill published in May 2006 proposes adding a new Part 7 to *Schedule 7 to CA 1985*, which will require certain additional disclosures to be given in the directors' reports of companies whose shares are publicly traded on a regulated market. The proposed disclosures include details of the company's capital structure, information on significant shareholdings, any special rights with regard to control of the company, any restrictions on voting rights or the transfer of securities, rules on the appointment or replacement of directors, and details of the directors' powers, including any relating to the issuing or buying back of shares by the company. The Bill notes that these amendments will apply to directors' reports for financial years beginning on or after 20 May 2006.

11.87   Consistency with the Accounts

The information given in the directors' report must be consistent with any related information given or included in the annual accounts. The auditors are specifically required to consider whether the directors' report is consistent with the accounts and to include an opinion on this in their report on the accounts. This is a new reporting responsibility which applies for accounting periods beginning on or after 1 April 2005 – previously, auditors were only required to report on any unresolved inconsistencies identified as a result of their review of the directors' report. The work that auditors need to undertake and the latest guidance on reporting are considered in more detail at **1.78** above.

11.88   Fair Review of the Business

For accounting periods beginning on or after 1 April 2005, the requirement for the directors' report to include a business review is much more prescriptive than under the previous legislation. The report must include a balanced and comprehensive review of the business and details of the principal risks and uncertainties that it faces. In particular, the review must include:

- explanations of amounts included in the financial statements for the year;
- analysis using key financial performance indicators; and
- where appropriate, analysis using other key performance indicators (KPIs), particularly on environmental and employee issues.

Where a parent company prepares group accounts, the review should cover the company and the subsidiary undertakings included in the consolidation. Small companies are exempt from the requirement to include a business review in the directors' report and medium-sized companies are exempt from the requirement to disclose non-financial KPIs, although they are still expected to provide relevant financial indicators. Companies within the size criteria which do not generally qualify for SME exemptions because they are part of an ineligible group are granted the same directors' report exemptions as other smaller companies. Following the repeal of the legislation that would have introduced a statutory OFR requirement for quoted companies, the DTI issued additional guidance on the new requirements for an enhanced business review to be included in the directors' report, together with an invitation to comment on whether any aspects of the business review requirements need further clarification or amendment. The DTI guidance also refers specifically to the following documents as useful points of reference for directors when preparing their report:

- the ASB Reporting Statement *Operating and Financial Review* (see **11.89–11.93** below);
- guidance on reporting on employee matters published by Accounting for People;
- guidance on environmental reporting published by DEFRA (see **11.94** below); and
- guidance published by the DTI Materiality Working Group (see **11.95** below).

The draft Company Law Reform Bill published in May 2006 includes certain additional requirements on the content of the business review which will apply in the case of a quoted company. In effect, these reintroduce into the legislation some of the requirements originally included in the provisions on the preparation of a statutory OFR. The draft legislation provides that, to the extent necessary for an understanding of the development, performance or position of the company's business, the business review of a quoted company should include:

- the main trends and factors likely to affect the future development, performance and position of the company's business; and
- information on environmental matters (including the impact of the company's business on the environment), the company's employees, and social and community issues – these disclosures should include details of the company's policies and their effectiveness.

If the review does not include information on any of the matters specified in the legislation, it will have to state which items have been excluded.

The draft Bill also proposes the reintroduction of a provision stating that information about impending developments or matters in the course of negotiation need not be disclosed if disclosure would, in the opinion of the directors, be seriously prejudicial to the interests of the company. This was also previously included in the provisions on the statutory OFR but will in future apply to all business reviews included as part of the directors' report.

11.89 ASB Reporting Statement *Operating and Financial Review*

The ASB issued a non-mandatory Statement *Operating and Financial Review* in July 1993 to provide a framework for the discussion, within the annual report, of the main factors underlying a company's financial performance and financial position. A revised version of the Statement was published in January 2003 and provided a broader framework for the discussion of business performance than its 1993 predecessor. The revised Statement set out the principles that directors should follow when preparing an OFR and detailed guidance on their practical application. The document was intended primarily for listed companies and other larger organisations, but the ASB emphasised that the principles were relevant to all entities. The 2003 Statement was initially superseded by Reporting Standard 1 (RS 1) *Operating and Financial Review* published by the ASB in May 2005 in preparation for the introduction of statutory OFRs for quoted companies, but when the statutory OFR legislation was repealed, RS 1 was replaced by a new ASB Reporting Statement *Operating and Financial Review*. This was issued in January 2006 and sets out the latest best practice guidance on the preparation of an OFR or detailed business review. The document has two main sections – the first sets out the principles that directors should apply when preparing an OFR and the second provides a disclosure framework. Separate 'Implementation Guidance' shows how some of the recommended disclosures might be handled in practice. Although the document gives an indication of topics and issues that may need to be covered in the business review, neither the Statement nor the related 'Implementation Guidance' is intended to be exhaustive and directors may need to consider including other matters, depending on the particular circumstances of the company or group. Where relevant, companies are encouraged to disclose the fact that they have complied with the ASB Statement, but there is no requirement to do so, given its non-mandatory status.

11.90 *Presentation of an OFR Analysis*

The OFR analysis should be presented through the eyes of the directors and should focus on issues of concern to members, but recognising that the information may also be of interest to other stakeholders. The report should have a forward-looking orientation, as the objective is to help shareholders understand and assess the company's strategies and the potential for these to succeed. In particular, it should cover:

- the development and performance of the business during the year;
- the position of the business at the end of the year;
- the main trends and factors underlying the above; and
- the main trends and factors likely to affect the business's future development, performance and financial position.

The directors should discuss the issues that have affected performance of the business during the period and those that are expected to affect its future performance and financial position. In particular, the discussion should comment on the impact of any significant events occurring after the balance sheet date and on any predictive comments included in previous reviews that were not borne out by events. The ASB also notes that directors may want to include a statement that, even though it is provided in good faith, forward-looking information should be treated with caution in view of the surrounding uncertainties.

11.91 *Other Key Principles*

The OFR should:

- complement and supplement the details provided in the financial statements;
- be written in a clear and readily understandable style;
- be comprehensive and understandable;
- be balanced and neutral, dealing even-handedly with both positive and negative issues; and
- be comparable over successive periods and, if appropriate, with other entities in the same industry or sector.

The ASB also emphasises that the objective of the OFR is quality rather than quantity, and that the inclusion of too much information can result in significant issues becoming obscured. As under the previous guidance, the review should highlight any adjustments that have been made to information derived from the financial statements and provide a reconciliation of the figures.

11.92 *Detailed Disclosures*

As under the previous guidance, directors are encouraged to discuss the resources available to the business, and especially any that are not reflected in the balance sheet, together with:

- the risks and uncertainties facing the business, and how these are managed;
- significant relationships likely to influence performance and business value;
- the company's capital structure, cashflows, liquidity and treasury policies; and
- any receipts from, and returns to, shareholders.

The discussion should include a description of the environment in which the business operates, including its main markets, its competitive position and any significant features of the relevant regulatory, economic and social environment. The OFR should also explain the longer-term objectives of the business, including those in relevant non-financial areas, and the directors' strategies for achieving these.

11.93 *Key Performance Indicators*

There is a particular emphasis on the disclosure of the key performance indicators (KPIs), both financial and non-financial, that the directors consider to be the most effective and critical in managing the business and measuring delivery of the company's strategies. The Implementation Guidance sets out examples of KPIs that might be used and the issues that the directors need to consider in each case. DEFRA has subsequently published more detailed guidance on reporting on environmental issues (see **11.94** below). The ASB also recommends that the following details should be given for each KPI shown in the OFR, to help users understand and evaluate the information provided:

- the definition, purpose and calculation method used;
- the source of underlying data and, where relevant, an explanation of any assumptions made;
- quantification of, or commentary on, future targets; and
- where available, the corresponding amount for the previous year.

Any changes to key performance indicators, or to the calculation methods used, from the previous year should also be highlighted and any significant changes in the underlying accounting policies adopted in the financial statements should be explained.

11.94 DEFRA Guidance on Environmental Reporting

In January 2006, the Department for Environment, Food and Rural Affairs (DEFRA) published new guidance on environmental reporting in *Environmental Key Performance Indicators: Reporting Guidelines for UK Business*. This defines which KPIs are likely to be most relevant to each business sector and suggests how companies can use these to manage their environmental performance. The document recommends that the directors' report discusses the impacts of the business on the environment and of the environment on the business, the policies adopted for managing these, and the company's actual performance in doing so. The report identifies 22 environmental KPIs that are considered to be significant to UK businesses, and companies are generally encouraged to report on up to five of them, concentrating on those that are most significant to their particular circumstances. The guidance looks at the underlying principles of environmental reporting, including the need for transparency, accountability and credibility, and the need for KPIs to be quantitative, relevant and comparable, so that the performance of an entity can be assessed over time and in relation to its competitors. Businesses are encouraged to present KPIs in absolute terms for the reporting period and also in relation to a normalising factor, such as turnover or production output. Each KPI reported should be accompanied by a general narrative explaining its purpose and impacts, the calculation methods used and any relevant assumptions made. Progress against targets should also be discussed, regardless of whether this reflects improvements or setbacks, with information on how any problem areas are being tackled. The guidelines also highlight the importance of reporting on any fines and associated costs incurred in respect of environmental issues, regardless of the amount and materiality of these, together with the number of any related prosecutions. The guidance can be downloaded from the DEFRA website at http://www.defra.gov.uk/environment/business/envrp/guidelines.htm.

11.95　DTI's 'Practical Guidance for Directors'

In December 2002, as part of the project to introduce a statutory OFR, the DTI established a separate working group to develop broad principles and practical guidance for directors on how to establish whether an item is sufficiently material to be included in the OFR. The group issued an initial guidance document in May 2004, in conjunction with draft regulations on the statutory OFR. An updated version of the guidance was expected to be issued once the OFR regulations had been finalised. However, following the repeal of the statutory OFR provisions, the DTI reissued the original guidance document in January 2006 without further amendment. As a result, the document continues to refer to the draft OFR regulations, even though the guidance is now intended to assist directors in the preparation of an enhanced business review for the directors' report or a voluntary OFR. Part I of the guidance covers the need for directors to understand the objectives of an enhanced business review or OFR and to:

- take a broad view, which includes exploring and understanding the agendas of all the stakeholders that are likely to influence the company's performance, either directly or indirectly;
- act collectively in making good faith, honest judgements on what should and need not be reported and on how the information is presented;
- identify any areas where access to additional skills and knowledge is required (eg environmental, social and community issues); and
- achieve an appropriate balance between historic review and the trends and factors most likely to affect future performance.

Whether an individual item is disclosed or not will depend not only on its nature and size but also on the effect that it may have in the particular circumstances of the business and on how it may be viewed in conjunction with other information about the company or group. For each area, the guidance explains the underlying principles and then illustrates them with practical examples of issues that may arise in a specific type of business and the sort of disclosure that the directors might make in these circumstances. Part II of the guidance highlights the importance of establishing a sound process to provide evidence that the directors have taken their reporting responsibilities seriously. In particular, the process should be properly planned, recorded and communicated and should have a clear timetable which allows for appropriate consultation, both within the organisation and externally where necessary. The guidance also recommends a major internal review of the process every three to five years, linked to the company's strategic planning cycle. The process should conclude with a formal sign-off by the board as a whole, not only on the inclusion or exclusion of individual items, but also that the information given provides a thorough and balanced picture, and that nothing of significance has been overlooked.

11.96   Likely Future Developments

CA 1985 requires the directors to give an indication of the likely future developments of the company and its subsidiaries. The legislation provides no detailed guidance on the form that this statement should take or the type of issue that should be covered and directors are, therefore, free to decide how best to present the information. This aspect of the directors' report can be a particular problem area for directors of listed companies, as they need to ensure that their comments cannot later be deemed to constitute a profit forecast. The DTI guidance on the preparation of an enhanced business review emphasises that directors will need to consider disclosing information on trends and factors likely to affect the future development, performance or financial position of the business where this is necessary to give the balanced and comprehensive analysis required by the legislation. The ASB recommends that an OFR or enhanced business review should have a forward-looking orientation, but notes that directors may want to include a statement that, whilst provided in good faith, forward-looking information should be treated with caution in view of the surrounding uncertainties. Also, in September 2003, the Institute of Chartered Accountants in England and Wales (ICAEW) published guidance on the preparation and publication of prospective financial information (PFI). Whilst most PFI will be published in order to comply with listing and other regulatory requirements, the guidance includes a separate section on voluntary PFI, which includes relevant disclosures in an OFR or directors' report. The document *Prospective Financial Information: Guidance for UK Directors* is available from the ICAEW website at http://icaew.co.uk/pfi.

11.97   Directors' Share Interests

The disclosure requirements on directors' share interests set out in *paragraphs 2, 2A* and *2B* of *Schedule 7* to *CA 1985* are extremely complex, particularly as the wording or meaning is not always clear. Interpretations and opinions consequently vary on precisely what needs to be included in the disclosures. For the purposes of the disclosures, the term 'director' includes shadow directors, and an interest in shares or debentures is given the very broad definition set out in *paragraph 1* of *Schedule 13* to *CA 1985*, so that any interest of any kind whatsoever in relevant shares or debentures constitutes a disclosable interest. A director's interests are also deemed to include any interests held by his/her immediate family, which in this context means the director's spouse, infant children and infant step-children – it does not include parents, brothers, sisters or children over the age of 18. However, if any members of the director's immediate family are also directors of the company, their interests are separately disclosable and are therefore not deemed to be interests of the director. Where a director of a wholly-owned subsidiary is also a director of its holding company and his/her interests will therefore be disclosed in the directors' report for the holding company, the information does not need to be given by the subsidiary, although in this case it is usual to explain where the details can be found.

It should also be noted that, in the case of a listed company, FSA Listing Rule 9.8.6R requires the following additional disclosures to be given:

- an analysis of each director's interests at the end of the financial year between beneficial and non-beneficial holdings; and
- details of any changes in those interests between the end of the financial year and one month prior to the date of the notice of the annual general meeting (or a statement that there have been no changes).

11.98   Political Donations

The *Political Parties, Elections and Referendums Act 2000* came into effect on 16 February 2001. In the context of political donations by companies it broadly requires:

- prior shareholder approval for political expenditure within the EU and for aggregate donations to EU political organisations of more than £5,000 by a company and its subsidiaries in any twelve-month period;
- disclosure of the detailed names and amounts where the aggregate amount of political expenditure and political donations in the EU by a company or group exceeds £200; and
- disclosure of the aggregate amount paid or donated to non-EU political parties (in this case there is no *de minimis* amount).

Where a payment or donation is to be made by a subsidiary, prior approval must also be obtained from the shareholders of the holding company. Wholly-owned subsidiaries of UK holding companies are exempt from the disclosure requirements, on the basis that the details will be given in the holding company's accounts. If these requirements are not followed, the directors will be personally liable to make good the amount paid or donated and to pay damages for any loss suffered by the company. In the case of non-compliance by a subsidiary, the directors of the holding company will also be personally liable.

11.99   Summary Financial Statements

At a Glance

* Subject to certain conditions, companies are permitted to issue a summary financial statement to their shareholders in place of the full annual accounts and reports.
* Each shareholder retains the right to receive a copy of the full annual accounts and reports.
* The company must undertake a formal process of consultation with those entitled to receive the accounts before it can take advantage of the option to issue a summary financial statement.
* The minimum content of a summary financial statement is prescribed in *CA 1985*.
* A summary financial statement must also include certain statements to clarify its status, together with a special report from the auditors.
* Research has shown that companies see both advantages and disadvantages in preparing a summary financial statement, but shareholders are more likely to read a summary document than the full accounts and reports.
* There are two practical approaches to preparing a summary financial statement.
* Many companies include more than the minimum contents in a summary financial statement.

11.100   Background

Legislation permitting listed companies to issue a summary financial statement to their shareholders in place of the full annual report and accounts was first introduced in the *Companies Act 1989*. The timing of the legislation coincided with the significant increase in the number of individual shareholders as a result of the Government's privatisation programme. In 1995, a number of changes were made to the administrative process to try to encourage a greater take-up of the option, but the number of companies who issue summary financial statements remains comparatively low. For accounting periods beginning on or after 1 January 2005, the *Companies Act 1985 (International Accounting Standards and Other Accounting Amendments) Regulations 2004 (SI 2004/2947)* extend the option to prepare summary financial statements to all companies, subject to certain conditions set out in the related regulations. The basic provisions on summary financial statements are set out in *section 251* of *CA 1985*. The detailed requirements on the form and content of summary financial statements, and the conditions under which they may be issued, are set out in the *Companies (Summary Financial Statement) Regulations 1995 (SI 1995/2092*, as updated by subsequent SIs).

11.101   Prohibition on Summary Financial Statements

Under *SI 1995/2092*, a company is not permitted to issue summary financial statements if the memorandum and articles of association prohibit this (for instance, by specifying that copies of the full annual accounts and reports should be sent to members and others entitled to receive them). If the issuing of summary financial statements is permitted by the memorandum and articles of association but is prohibited by an instrument governing any debentures that are in issue, the company will have to issue the full report and accounts to the debenture-holders but should be able to take advantage of the option to issue summary financial statements to the members and other persons entitled to receive accounts. The regulations have been updated by the *Companies (Summary Financial Statement) (Amendment) Regulations 2005* (*SI 2005/2281*) to cater specifically for companies who are required or choose to prepare their annual accounts in accordance with international accounting standards (IASs) and for the extension to all companies of the option to issue a summary financial statement. As a result, the regulations now specify that a company can only issue a summary financial statement if its full accounts have been audited.

11.102   Right to Receive Full Accounts

Even if a company takes advantage of the option to prepare a summary financial statement, each shareholder and other person entitled to receive the accounts retains the right to receive a copy of the full annual accounts and report in respect of any financial year. The company cannot issue summary financial statements in place of the full accounts and report without first ascertaining that the entitled individual is happy to receive them. Also, a company cannot send out summary financial statements in place of full accounts unless:

- the period for laying and delivering accounts for that year has not yet expired;
- the summary financial statement has been approved by the board; and
- the full accounts, on which the summary financial statement is based, have been signed by a director on behalf of the board.

11.103   Consultation with Entitled Persons

Regulation 5 of *SI 1995/2092* permits a company to give an entitled person notice that, in future, he/she will be sent a summary financial statement for each financial year in place of the full accounts and report, unless they notify the company in writing that they wish to receive the full documents. The notice issued by the company must:

- state that the summary financial statement for a financial year will contain a summary of the company or group's profit and loss account, balance sheet and (where relevant) directors' remuneration report for that year, and may include additional information derived from the directors' report for that year;

- be accompanied by a printed card or form enabling each entitled person to notify their wish to receive the full accounts by marking a box on the card or form – the company is responsible for paying the return postage, except where the contact address for the entitled person is outside the EC;
- specify the date by which the card or form must be returned – this must be at least 21 days after the service of the notice and not less than 28 days before the first date on which copies of the full accounts and reports for the next financial year are sent out to entitled persons;
- include a prominent statement to the effect that a summary financial statement will not contain sufficient information to allow as full an understanding of the results and state of affairs of the company or group as the full documents would, and that members and other entitled persons have the right to obtain a copy of the full accounts and reports, free of charge; and
- state that the summary financial statement will include a statement from the auditors on whether:
  - the summary financial statement is consistent with the full accounts and (in the case of a quoted company) the directors' remuneration report for the relevant financial year, and where information derived from the directors' report is included in the summary financial statement, with that report;
  - the summary financial statement complies with the requirements of *section 251* of *CA 1985* and the related Regulations, and
  - their report on the full accounts was qualified or unqualified.

11.104   Alternative Consultation Method

As an alternative, *regulation 6* of *SI 1995/2092* allows a company to send an entitled person both the full accounts and reports and a summary financial statement for a financial year, and at the same time give notice that, in future, only the summary financial statement will be sent out unless the company receives notification of their wish to receive the full documents. This notice must also be accompanied by a prepaid reply card or form enabling the entitled person to indicate their wish to receive the full documents by marking a box on the card or form. Again, the company is not responsible for the return postage if the contact address for the entitled person is outside the EC.

11.105   Form and Content of Summary Financial Statements

The summary financial statement must be derived from the company's annual accounts and reports. Where the underlying accounts are Companies Act accounts (see **3.16** above), the following minimum content of the statement is specified in *Schedule 1* to *SI 1995/2092*:

- a summary profit and loss account, including;
  - turnover,
  - income from shares in group undertakings and participating interests,

- o other interest receivable and similar income, and interest payable and similar charges,
  - o profit or loss on ordinary activities before taxation,
  - o tax on profit or loss on ordinary activities,
  - o profit or loss on ordinary activities after tax,
  - o extraordinary income and charges, after tax,
  - o profit or loss for the financial year,
- the following details in respect of dividends:
  - o the aggregate of dividends paid in the year, other than those for which a liability existed at the previous balance sheet date;
  - o the aggregate amount of dividends that the company is liable to pay at the balance sheet date; and
  - o the aggregate amount of dividends proposed before the date of approval of the accounts and not included in the above disclosures;
- in the case of an unquoted company, the whole of (or a summary of) the note to the accounts setting out the details of aggregate directors' remuneration required by *CA 1985, Sch 6, para 1(1)*;
- in the case of a quoted company, either the whole of the directors' remuneration report or, as a minimum:
  - o the aggregate information on directors' remuneration required by *CA 1985, Sch 6, para 1(1)*,
  - o the statement of the company's policy on directors' remuneration for future years, and
  - o the performance graph summarising shareholder return;
- a summary balance sheet, showing a single amount for each item that is assigned a letter in the *CA 1985* standard formats.

Where the underlying accounts are IAS accounts, a new *Schedule 3A* to the Regulations requires the summary financial statement to include, as a minimum:

- the whole of (or a summary of) the note to the accounts setting out the details of aggregate directors' remuneration required by *CA 1985, Sch 6, para 1(1)*;
- in the case of a quoted company, a statement of the company's policy on directors' remuneration and the performance graph summarising shareholder return;
- a summary profit and loss account showing each of the headings and subtotals required under IASs or, where the directors consider it appropriate, a combination of such headings and sub-totals where they are of similar nature;
- the information concerning dividends recognised and proposed given in the full accounts and reports;
- a summary balance sheet showing each of the headings and sub-totals required under IASs or, where the directors consider it appropriate, a combination of such headings and sub-totals where they are of similar nature.

In both cases, comparative figures must be given for each item and, where the company is required to prepare group accounts, consolidated figures must be presented. In practice, most companies who issue summary financial statements include more than the minimum information – in particular, summarised cashflow information and corporate governance reporting is usually included. *SI 1995/2092* also includes separate requirements for banking and insurance companies and groups.

11.106   Other Statements to be Included

The summary financial statement must be signed by a director on behalf of the board and the name of the signing director must be stated. The document must also include:

- a clear statement that it is only a summary of the information given in the company's annual accounts and (where relevant) directors' remuneration report;
- a statement on whether or not it contains additional information derived from the directors' report and, if it includes such information, the fact that it does not include the full text of the directors' report;
- a formal statement, in a prominent position, that the summary does not contain sufficient information to allow as full an understanding of the results and state of affairs of the company or group as the full documents would, and that members and other entitled persons have the right to obtain a copy of the full accounts and reports, free of charge;
- a clear statement of how members and other entitled persons can obtain the full accounts and reports for the current year, and how they can elect to receive these in future years in place of the summary financial statement;
- a report from the auditors on whether:
  - ○ the summary financial statement is consistent with the full accounts and reports for the relevant financial year,
  - ○ the summary financial statement complies with the requirements of *section 251* of *CA 1985* and the related Regulations, and
  - ○ the auditor's report on the full accounts and, where relevant, the auditable part of the directors' remuneration report was qualified or unqualified – if it was qualified, the report must be set out in full, together with any additional information needed to understand the qualification (eg a particular note to the accounts);
  - ○ for accounting periods beginning on or after 1 April 2005, the auditors' opinion on consistency between the directors' report and the accounts was qualified or unqualified – where the opinion was qualified, the qualification must be set out in full, together with any additional material needed for the qualification to be understood; and
  - ○ the auditors' report on the full accounts contained a statement under *section 237(2)* or *section 237(3)* of *CA 1985* (see **1.59–1.60** above) – if such a statement was included, the auditors' report on the full accounts must be set out in the summary financial statements.

There is no requirement for the company to send a prepaid reply card or form to entitled persons after the initial consultation, even though they retain the right to request copies of the full accounts and reports each year.

11.107   The Purpose of Summary Financial Statements

The provisions allowing companies to prepare and issue summary financial state-ments were introduced to recognise the fact that the needs of shareholders and other users of the accounts can vary quite significantly. The disclosures required by accounting standards and companies' legislation are becoming increasingly complex, and whilst the information now required may be highly relevant to technically sophisticated users of accounts, it is evident that many private share-holders are confused by the volume of detail given in a full set of accounts. In some cases, the level of detailed disclosures can actually obscure the key infor-mation that private shareholders require from the accounts. The main aims of the summary financial statement are to remove most of the more complex disclo-sures and concentrate on the key issues that are of relevance to individual share-holders, and to enable companies to present this key information in a user-friendly manner, for instance by making appropriate use of charts and graphs.

11.108   Perceived Advantages and Disadvantages

A working party established by the Institute of Chartered Accountants in England and Wales ('ICAEW') reported in 1996 on the results of research amongst companies (see below) on why they decided to produce or not to prepare a summary financial statement, and amongst shareholders (see **11.109** below) on the relative merits to them of full accounts and a summary financial statement ('Summary Financial Statements: The Way Forward', ICAEW, July 1996). The main reasons given for not making use of summary financial statements were:

- potentially higher production costs, especially in the first year, and no sig-nificant cost savings anticipated in subsequent years;
- the additional administrative burden;
- that the use of a summary financial statement would run counter to the pre-sent philosophy of providing fuller information to shareholders.

The main advantages reported by companies who had issued summary finan-cial statements were:

- better communication with shareholders;
- actual cost savings.

The point on actual cost savings is particularly interesting. Whilst the majority of companies who decided to prepare summary financial statements did so pri-marily to improve communication with their shareholders, nearly all of them found that the exercise also achieved some cost savings. It may be that com-panies not currently using summary financial statements are being unnecessarily pessimistic in their assessment of the costs and the additional administrative effort required. It should be emphasised that most of the research referred to in the report was undertaken before the changes introduced by *SI 1995/2092*, which simplified the consultation process with shareholders and may already have helped to alleviate some of the concerns over costs and administration.

11.109   Views of Shareholders

The ICAEW report (see **11.108** above) also summarised the results of a survey to assess the reactions of shareholders to summary financial statements. This indicated a high degree of enthusiasm for summary financial statements amongst shareholders. The key conclusions from the research were:

- shareholders were more likely to read some or all of the summary financial statement than to open and read the full accounts – a summarised document is therefore helpful in improving communication with shareholders;
- where a summary financial statement was made available, a very high proportion of shareholders (in the order of 90 per cent) opted to receive the summary rather than the full annual report and accounts;
- the summarised results, chairman's statement and overall business review were the most widely read parts of the document;
- other financial information, the report by the auditors and any additional details (eg on corporate governance issues) were generally not widely read by shareholders; and
- there was a clear preference for a short document rather than a longer one.

A further point highlighted by the research was that very few companies had carried out any direct consultation with shareholders to try to identify their specific needs and ensure that these were being satisfied, despite the fact that the research amongst companies had indicated that shareholder pressure would encourage them to consider preparing a summary financial statement.

11.110   A Practical Approach to Producing Summary Financial Statements

There are essentially two approaches to the preparation of a summary financial statement:

- the production of two completely separate and free-standing documents – the summary financial statement and the full annual report and accounts; and
- the production of a summary financial statement and a supplementary document containing additional information – in this case, the summary financial statement and the supplementary document together constitute the full annual report and accounts.

The second approach is by far the more common in practice. Failure to consider this method of preparation may be one of the factors that explains why companies not preparing summary financial statements quote potentially higher costs (or no anticipated cost savings) as one of the reasons against using them, whilst those preparing summary financial statements have achieved actual cost savings. A potential disadvantage of the second approach is that analysts and other technically minded users of the accounts may find it irritating to have to refer to two documents. However, this can usually be overcome by careful planning of the contents of each part of the document and clear cross-referencing.

11.111   Usual Contents of Summary Financial Statements

There is a broad consensus amongst companies who do prepare summary financial statements on the basic contents of the document. These invariably go beyond the minimum contents laid down in Regulations and usually comprise:

- financial highlights;
- chairman's statement;
- an operational review of the business, which often makes extensive use of colour photographs and other illustrations;
- the summarised profit and loss account and balance sheet;
- summarised cashflow information;
- information on directors' remuneration; and
- financial calendar.

Corporate governance issues are also usually referred to in the summary financial statement, but the level of detail given varies. Despite the preference for short documents highlighted in the shareholder research, summary financial statements these days are often substantial documents, with many being between 20 and 40 pages in length.

11.112   Interim Reports

At a Glance
* The FSA *Listing Rules* require listed companies to issue an interim statement each year, giving details of their results for the first half of the financial year.
* The FSA *Listing Rules* require the interim statement to be notified within 90 days of the period end – the ASB Statement 'Interim Reports' recommends that it is issued within 60 days of the period end.
* There is no formal requirement for the auditors to review or report on the interim statement but directors often arrange for this to be done as a separate engagement.
* FSA requirements on the minimum contents of an interim statement are now broadly consistent with the recommendations set out in the ASB Statement 'Interim Reports'.
* A management commentary on the results for the first half of the year should be included in the interim statement.
* The interim statement should be prepared on the basis of the company's normal accounting policies and should take account of any change in accounting policy that is to be implemented in the accounts for the full financial year.
* Earnings per share should be calculated and disclosed in the same way as in the annual accounts.
* The ASB Statement includes detailed guidance on the measurement and recognition of income and expenditure in the interim statement.

> * Comparative figures should cover both the corresponding interim report and the last full financial year.
> * An interim statement must include the formal statements that have to be given in non-statutory accounts.
> * In February 2006, the Financial Reporting Review Panel issued a short report on the results of its review of the interim reports of companies affected by the transition to IASs.

11.113   Requirement to Prepare an Interim Report

The FSA *Listing Rules* require listed companies to issue an interim statement each year, giving details of their results for the first half of the financial year (see **18.36** below). Other companies are free to issue interim statements on a voluntary basis if they wish, although few choose to do so. The FSA requirements on the minimum content of an interim statement have now been brought broadly into line with the recommendations set out in the ASB Statement 'Interim Reports' (see **11.116** below).

Companies may issue information on a more regular basis, for instance quarterly. Where this approach is adopted, the reports for the first and third quarters tend to be less detailed than those produced for the half-year.

Where a listed company changes its accounting reference date and the change results in an accounting period of 14 months or more, the FSA *Listing Rules* require publication of a second interim report covering either the period to the previous accounting reference date or a period ending not more than six months before the new accounting reference date.

11.114   Impact of IAS Accounts

The ASB Statement *Interim Reports* was developed in the context of accounts and reports prepared under the requirements of *CA 1985* and so does not take account of the requirement for listed groups to adopt international accounting standards (IASs) from 1 January 2005 (see **3.17** above). Such companies must continue to comply with the requirements of the FSA *Listing Rules* on the preparation of interim reports. At present, these are broadly consistent with the recommendations set out in the ASB Statement. Companies adopting international standards must also comply with IAS 34 *Interim Financial Reporting*. This sets out basic requirements on the preparation and content of an interim financial report but does not provide the same degree of detailed guidance as the ASB's non-mandatory Statement.

11.115   Purpose of Interim Reports

For listed companies, interim reports form an important part of the process of communicating with shareholders and with the financial market as a whole, enabling readers to monitor the progress and development of the business and assess the impact of recent events. The reaction of the financial markets to information given in interim reports can be significant and many companies provide more than the minimum details required.

11.116   Timing and Distribution of Interim Reports

Interim reports are issued to all shareholders. The ASB Statement *Interim Reports* recommends that the interim report should be issued within 60 days of the period-end (for information on obtaining copies see the ASB website at www.frc.org.uk/asb). However, the *Listing Rules* currently allow a slightly longer timescale for the preparation of the interim report, requiring it to be notified within 90 days of the period-end.

11.117   Review by the Auditors

There is currently no formal requirement for auditors to review or report on interim reports before they are published. The ASB Statement *Interim Reports* (see **11.116** above) recommends disclosure of the extent to which the information given in the interim report has been audited or reviewed. APB Bulletin 1999/04 *Review of Interim Financial Information* sets out guidance on the procedures that should be undertaken where auditors are asked to review an interim report, although it notes that the directors (or, where relevant, the Audit Committee – see **1.137** AUDIT COMMITTEES) may ask the auditors to carry out specific agreed procedures as an alternative to this. Where an interim report is reviewed in accordance with the APB guidance, the FSA *Listing Rules* require the auditors' review report to be published as part of the interim report. The latest guidance on the wording of the review report can be found in APB Bulletin 2001/02 *Revisions to the Wording of Auditors' Reports on Financial Statements and the Interim Review Report*. Because the recommended review work is limited in scope, and does not constitute an audit, the auditors will normally report in terms of 'negative assurance' – in other words, they report that nothing has come to their attention to indicate that material modification is required to the information presented in the report. APB Bulletin 1999/04 recommends that, where the scope of the work agreed between the directors and auditors is less than that set out in the Bulletin, the directors should describe the interim report as 'neither audited nor reviewed'. APB Bulletins can be downloaded from the APB website at www.frc.org.uk/apb/publications.

11.118   Contents of an Interim Report

The ASB published its Statement *Interim Reports* (see **11.116** above) in September 1997 in response to issues raised in the Cadbury Report. The objective of the Statement is to improve the timeliness, quality, relevance and consistency of information published in the form of interim reports. The ASB Statement is non-mandatory but it sets out best practice for companies that are required to publish an interim report, and all listed companies are encouraged to follow its recommendations. Many companies were already providing much of the information recommended in the ASB Statement, but it is helpful to have formal guidance on the contents of an interim report, and in particular on the principles to be followed in dealing with some of the potentially difficult issues that can arise. The principles set out in the guidance are equally relevant to reports produced on a more regular basis. Companies preparing IAS accounts must also take into account the requirements of IAS 34 *Interim Financial Reporting*. The recommended contents for an interim report are:

- a balanced narrative commentary on the main factors influencing performance during the period and the financial position at the period end;
- a summarised profit and loss account, showing:
  - turnover,
  - operating profit or loss,
  - net interest payable/receivable,
  - profit or loss on ordinary activities before tax,
  - tax on profit or loss on ordinary activities,
  - profit or loss on ordinary activities after tax,
  - minority interests,
  - profit or loss for the period;
- details of dividends paid and proposed;
- a statement of total recognised gains and losses;
- a summarised balance sheet, showing:
  - fixed assets,
  - current assets:
    - stocks,
    - debtors,
    - cash at bank and in hand,
    - other,
  - creditors: amounts falling due within one year,
  - net current assets/liabilities,
  - total assets less current liabilities,
  - creditors: amounts falling due after more than one year,
  - provisions for liabilities and charges,
  - capital and reserves,
  - minority interests;
- a summarised cashflow statement, showing:
  - net cash inflow/outflow from operating activities,
  - returns on investments and servicing of finance,
  - taxation,
  - capital expenditure and financial investment,
  - acquisitions and disposals,
  - equity dividends paid,
  - management of liquid resources,
  - financing,
  - increase/decrease in cash.

11.119　Other Disclosures

The ASB Statement *Interim Reports* (see **11.116** above) recommends the following additional disclosures:

- where relevant, amounts relating to associates and joint ventures should be shown separately in the summarised profit and loss account;
- turnover and operating profit in respect of any acquisitions or discontinued operations should be shown separately on the face of the summarised profit and loss account – for this purpose, operations are to be regarded as discontinued if the sale or termination was completed in the interim period, or by the earlier of the date of approval of the interim report or three months after the end of the interim period;
- segmental analyses of turnover and profit or loss before interest should be given, using the same business and geographical classifications as in the annual accounts;
- any exceptional items occurring in the interim period should be disclosed, including items required to be shown separately in the profit and loss account under FRS 3 *Reporting Financial Performance* (ie profits and losses on the sale or termination of an operation, costs of a fundamental reorganisation or restructuring, and profits and losses on the disposal of fixed assets);
- reconciliations of operating profit to operating cashflow and the movement of cash to the movement in net debt should be given; and
- the following should be clearly stated:
  - the period covered by the interim report,
  - the date on which the interim report was formally approved by the board of directors, and
  - the extent to which the information in the interim report has been audited or reviewed.

The results of operations that are in the process of discontinuing, or which are expected to be classified as discontinued in the accounts for the full financial year, may be shown separately in the notes to the interim report.

11.120　Management Commentary

Because the interim report is intended to update shareholders and other interested parties on the company's performance since the latest annual accounts, the management commentary should focus on recent events, activities and circumstances. The commentary should therefore discuss the financial information shown in the interim profit and loss account, statement of total recognised gains and losses, balance sheet and cashflow statement in the context of events since the previous financial year-end. It is important that the review does not concentrate solely on performance in the period, as shown in the profit and loss account, but also considers related issues such as working capital, liquidity and net debt. Significant trends and events mentioned in the commentary should be supported by the figures shown in the primary statements or by additional disclosures in the notes. Additional information should be given where this is necessary for an understanding of the significant items in the primary statement (for instance, additional information about company borrowings may need to be given if this is a significant issue).

The ASB Statement *Interim Reports* (see **11.116** above) recommends that the management commentary on the interim figures explains the reasons for significant movements in key indicators and gives a balanced view of the perceived trends within the business, so that readers of the report can understand the main factors influencing the company's performance during the period under review and its position at the end of that period. The report should therefore discuss both positive and negative aspects of the interim period. Where the business is seasonal, it will be particularly important to provide sufficient information for readers to understand the interim results in the context of the full financial year. The commentary should also draw attention to any events and changes occurring during the interim period that are likely to have a significant impact in the second part of the year, even though they may not have affected the company's performance in the period under review. Where relevant it should also cover significant changes in fixed assets and investments, capital structure, financing, commitments and contingencies.

The management commentary included in an interim report is not intended to be as detailed as an operating and financial review presented as part of the annual accounts and reports. However, the guidance in the ASB Reporting Statement *Operating and Financial Review* may be useful in helping to identify key issues that should be discussed in the interim report (see **11.89–11.93** above – for information on obtaining copies see the ASB website at www.frc.org.uk/asb).

11.121 Accounting Policies

Interim reports should be prepared using the company's normal accounting policies and should include a statement that the policies are the same as those disclosed in the last published accounts, or explain any differences. Where it is known that a change in accounting policy is to be made in the accounts for the full financial year, the interim report should normally be prepared on the basis of the new policy, all relevant comparative figures should be restated and the cumulative effect on opening reserves should be disclosed. If the interim figures are not presented on the basis of the new accounting policy, the estimated financial effect of the change in policy should be disclosed. Any other prior period adjustments (eg to correct fundamental errors) should be reflected in the interim report in the same way as changes in accounting policy.

11.122 Earnings Per Share

Basic earnings per share should be calculated from the interim results and disclosed in the interim report in the same way as in the full annual accounts. If the company adopts a policy of disclosing additional calculations of earnings per share in its annual accounts, the same details should be given in the interim report.

11.123   Basis of Presentation of Financial Information

One particular issue that arises in the case of an interim report is whether the interim period is treated as part of an annual reporting cycle or as a discrete accounting period, distinct from the annual cycle. The ASB Statement *Interim Reports* (see **11.116** above) recommends that the latter method is used so that the measurement and recognition of income and expenditure is consistent with the annual accounts. Specific guidance is given in the Statement on accounting for items such as bonuses, profit-sharing arrangements and volume discounts that will normally only be calculated at the end of the financial year. The treatment depends on whether there is an obligation at the end of the interim period to transfer economic benefits as a result of past events. For instance, if a profit-related bonus is to be paid at the end of the year, it will be appropriate to recognise a proportion of this in the interim period, based on the profit earned to date, if past practice shows that the company has a constructive obligation to make the payment. A genuinely discretionary bonus paid at the end of the year would not be recognised in the interim figures. However, the ASB Statement also notes that it will sometimes be necessary to look at the expected income or expense for the full year in order to calculate the amount to be recognised in the interim period. The most obvious example here is taxation and considerable guidance is given on this. The likely effective tax rate for the full year should be calculated, expressed as a percentage of the expected results for the full year, and this percentage should be applied to the interim profit or loss to calculate the interim tax charge. More detailed calculations may be needed where different tax jurisdictions are involved or where different tax rates apply to material categories of income. Other points to note in relation to the presentation of financial information in interim reports are:

- the results of foreign group entities should be translated in line with the company's usual accounting policy;
- asset revaluations will not usually be required for interim report purposes, although certain disclosures are recommended; and
- materiality should be assessed in relation to the interim period rather than the expected results and financial position at the end of the financial year.

11.124   Comparative Figures

Comparative figures for the summarised profit and loss account, statement of total recognised gains and losses and summarised cashflow statement should cover the corresponding interim period in the previous year and also the last full financial year. This is to help provide a meaningful view of the company's performance to date, especially where the business is seasonal. In the case of the balance sheet, the critical comparative figures are those for the last full financial year, although those for the corresponding interim period may also be given.

11.125   Statutory Disclosure

Where an interim report contains information for a full financial year of the company or information as at the company's normal financial year-end (for instance, comparative profit and loss account information for the previous financial year, and comparative balance sheet information as at the end of the last financial year), the interim report will constitute 'non-statutory accounts' under *section 240* of *CA 1985* and must include the statements required by that section. This is considered in more detail at **3.83 NON-STATUTORY ACCOUNTS.**

11.126   FRRP Review of Interim Reports

The remit of the Financial Reporting Review Panel (FRRP) has been widened to include reviews of all financial information published by companies that come within the scope of its activities, including interim reports and preliminary announcements (see **11.16** above). The Panel announced in December 2004 that one of the key elements of its proactivity work programme for 2005/06 would be a review of interim reports prepared by listed groups who would be adopting international accounting standards (IASs) for the first time, and in February 2006 it published a short report on its work to date in this area. UK listed companies were not required to comply with IAS 34 *Interim Financial Reporting* in the period under review and the report notes that few opted to do so voluntarily. The FRRP review therefore concentrated on compliance with the requirements of the UK *Listing Rules* on the form and content of an interim report. A total of 70 interim reports were reviewed and the Panel raised issues on 16 of these. Three of these cases were still ongoing at the time that the report was published. Two cases involved complex or controversial issues and so required the appointment of Panel groups, but the other 14 were dealt with by written requests to the companies concerned to provide additional information. No formal press announcements had been made by the FRRP as a result of the reviews completed by the time of the report, and there had been no requirement for companies to restate their published results, although the Panel notes that a number had agreed to make improved disclosures in the future. Issues highlighted in the reviews have included the following:

- *Income statement:* The format of this part of the interim report is less prescriptive under IASs and the FRRP noted that some companies were using sub-totals such as 'trading profit' or 'operating profit' but were excluding certain items that the Panel expected to be included. In some cases, companies also failed to provide separate details of material amounts of overseas tax and tax relating to associates, and gave a net figure for finance income and costs rather than the separate amounts.
- *Cashflow statement:* Certain items in the cashflow statement were misclassified between investing and financing activities and the definition of cash equivalents was not always sufficiently precise, leading to uncertainty over which items had been included.

- *Statement of Changes in Equity:* This should have two separate elements – a Statement of Recognised Income and Expense and a Statement of Changes in Equity – and the Panel noted some confusion over the allocation of items between the two. Particular problems were identified with the treatment of actuarial gains and losses on defined benefit retirement schemes and credits relating to share options.
- *Accounting policies:* The Panel noted that most new accounting policies arising from the adoption of IASs were described clearly and comprehensively, but there were cases where the accounting policy was not clear or did not appear to cover all aspects of the business or where inappropriate wordings from UK GAAP had been retained. However, the Panel was satisfied that the main problem was over the description of the policies actually adopted rather than over the policies themselves.
- *True and fair override:* The true and fair override now applies only where accounts are prepared under the form and content requirements of the *Companies Act 1985* (see **11.30** above). The Panel emphasised that, in the rare circumstances where a departure from a standard was considered necessary in IAS accounts, the accounts should make clear that this was a departure under the provisions of IAS 1 *Presentation of Financial Information* rather than a true and fair override under company law.

The Panel also noted the omission in some cases of certain aspects of the statement in respect of the auditors' report on the last financial statements and emphasised that an interim report prepared under IASs continues to constitute non-statutory accounts (see **3.83** and **11.125** above).

11.127   Preliminary Announcements

At a Glance
* The FSA *Listing Rules* require listed companies to make a preliminary announcement of their annual results and dividends within 120 days of the year-end.
* The ASB Statement *Preliminary Announcements* encourages companies to make their preliminary announcement within 60 days of the year-end and to issue their accounts and reports as soon as practicable thereafter.
* The audit of the underlying accounts should be substantially complete before the preliminary announcement is issued – the Auditing Practices Board has issued guidance on when an audit should be regarded as 'substantially complete'.
* The FSA requires directors to obtain agreement from the auditors before the preliminary announcement is issued and to give details in the announcement of any qualification of the auditors' report.
* Preliminary announcements tend to be issued only to institutional investors and financial analysts, but the ASB Statement encourages

companies to make them more widely available to maintain parity between shareholders.
* FSA requirements on the minimum contents of a preliminary announcement are now broadly consistent with the recommendations set out in the ASB Statement.
* The management commentary should discuss the results for the second half of the year as well as the company's overall performance and financial position.
* The preliminary announcement should be prepared on the basis of the company's normal accounting policies – any changes in accounting policy should be explained and the financial effect should be disclosed.
* Earnings per share should be calculated and disclosed in the same way as in the annual accounts.
* Comparative figures should cover the last full financial year – companies are also encouraged to disclose the figures for the second half of the year, with comparatives.
* A preliminary announcement must include the formal statements that have to be given in non-statutory accounts.

11.128 Requirement to Prepare a Preliminary Announcement

The FSA *Listing Rules* require listed companies to notify a preliminary statement of annual results and dividends immediately after it has been approved by the board. Under the current *Listing Rules*, the preliminary announcement must be notified within 120 days of the end of the accounting period, although an extension of this deadline may be granted in exceptional circumstances. The minimum contents required by the *Listing Rules* are broadly in line with those set out in the ASB Statement *Preliminary Announcements* (for information on obtaining copies see the ASB website at www.frc.org.uk/asb). Technically, this document is non-mandatory but it sets out best practice on the form and content of preliminary announcements and listed companies are therefore encouraged to follow its recommendations. In many ways, interim reports and preliminary announcements are very similar in nature. Both communicate new information on the company's performance and financial position and, in each case, the reaction of the financial markets to the information given can be significant.

11.129 Impact of IAS Accounts

The ASB Statement *Preliminary Announcements* was developed in the context of accounts and reports prepared under the requirements of *CA 1985* and so does not take account of the requirement for listed groups to adopt international accounting standards (IASs) from 1 January 2005. Such companies must continue to comply with the requirements of the UK *Listing Rules* on the preparation of a preliminary announcement. At present, these are broadly consistent with the recommendations set out in the ASB Statement. No international accounting standards or other pronouncements deal specifically with the preparation and content of a preliminary announcement.

11.130   Timing of Preliminary Announcement

The ASB Statement *Preliminary Announcements* (see **11.128** above) encourages companies to issue their preliminary announcement within 60 days of the financial year-end, and to issue the full report and accounts (and, where relevant, the summary financial statement) as soon as practicable thereafter, although it acknowledges that individual circumstances may make it impractical for some companies to achieve this target. The FSA has therefore set a longer deadline of 120 days from the end of the accounting period. The ASB Statement also considers the need for the figures in the preliminary announcement to be reliable and the impact that this might have on the timing of publication. It recommends that:

- the audit of the draft financial statements should be substantially complete at the date of the announcement;
- all the figures in the preliminary announcement should agree with the draft financial statements on which the audit is substantially complete; and
- any non-financial information or commentary included in the preliminary announcement should be consistent with the draft financial statements and with the figures set out in the preliminary announcement.

Companies are encouraged to make their preliminary announcement as soon as the main figures have been agreed by the auditors, rather than waiting for the audit to be fully completed. This recognises that, in practice, it will usually take time to finalise the detailed notes to the financial statements and the other reports published with them, but this will not affect the reliability of the principal figures. APB Bulletin 2004/1 *The Auditors' Association with Preliminary Announcements* provides guidance on when the audit should be regarded as being substantially complete (copies can be downloaded from the APB website at www.frc.org.uk/apb/publication). To prevent any misunderstanding, the ASB Statement recommends that the preliminary announcement should state that the audit report on the full financial statements has not yet been signed, if that is the case.

11.131   Need to Obtain Auditors' Agreement

It is important that the information released in the preliminary announcement is reliable and the FSA therefore requires the directors to obtain agreement from the auditors before the preliminary announcement is approved for issue. APB Bulletin 2004/1 *The Auditors' Association with Preliminary Announcements* (see **11.130** above) recommends that the role of the auditors in respect of the preliminary announcement is set out in writing (this is usually dealt with by including an appropriate paragraph in the audit engagement letter) and that the auditors issue a formal letter to the directors confirming their agreement to publication of the preliminary announcement. If the audit report on the financial statements is likely to be qualified, the FSA requires the preliminary announcement to include details of the nature of the qualification.

In February 2003, the APB wrote to the auditors of listed companies to alert them to the fact that shareholders can sometimes be misled by the way in which pro-forma information is included in unaudited announcements of interim and annual results in addition to the statutory figures. In the APB's view, pro-forma information is most likely to misinform when it is given greater prominence than statutory information, where its purpose is not explained and when it is not reconciled to the statutory information. Before agreeing to the release of a preliminary announcement, auditors are therefore recommended to consider whether:

- appropriate prominence has been given to the statutory figures;
- any pro-forma information states clearly why it has been prepared;
- any pro-forma information is reconciled to the statutory figures; and
- any pro-forma information is not misleading in the form or context in which it is presented.

This guidance has now been incorporated in APB Bulletin 2004/1.

11.132   Distribution of Preliminary Announcement

Interim reports are issued to all shareholders, but preliminary announcements tend to be issued only to financial analysts and institutional shareholders. The ASB Statement *Preliminary Announcements* (see **11.128** above) emphasises that all shareholders should be treated equally and encourages companies to make better use of technology (for instance, by making preliminary announcements available on the internet) and to give all shareholders the option of receiving a copy of the preliminary announcement as soon as it is issued (for instance, by establishing a pre-registration scheme or publishing an address or telephone number from which copies can be obtained).

The draft Company Law Reform Bill published in May 2006 reflects the recommendation made in the recent company law review that all quoted companies should make their preliminary announcement available on a website.

11.133   Contents of a Preliminary Announcement

The FSA *Listing Rules* specify that a preliminary announcement must contain, as a minimum, a profit and loss account, balance sheet and cashflow statement, together with any significant information necessary to enable the company's results and financial position to be properly assessed. The ASB Statement *Preliminary Announcements* (see **11.128** above) recommends the following contents for a preliminary announcement:

- a balanced narrative commentary on the main factors influencing performance during the period and the financial position at the period end;
- a summarised profit and loss account, showing:
  - turnover,
  - operating profit or loss,
  - net interest payable/receivable,
  - profit or loss on ordinary activities before tax,
  - tax on profit or loss on ordinary activities,
  - profit or loss on ordinary activities after tax,
  - minority interests,
  - profit or loss for the period;
- details of dividends paid and proposed;
- a statement of total recognised gains and losses;
- a summarised balance sheet, showing:
  - fixed assets,
  - current assets:
    - stocks,
    - debtors,
    - cash at bank and in hand,
    - other,
  - creditors: amounts falling due within one year,
  - net current assets/liabilities,
  - total assets less current liabilities,
  - creditors: amounts falling due after more than one year,
  - provisions for liabilities and charges,
  - capital and reserves,
  - minority interests;
- a summarised cashflow statement, showing:
  - net cash inflow/outflow from operating activities,
  - returns on investments and servicing of finance,
  - taxation,
  - capital expenditure and financial investment,
  - acquisitions and disposals,
  - equity dividends paid,
  - management of liquid resources,
  - financing,
  - increase/decrease in cash.

A reconciliation of movements in shareholders' funds only needs to be included when there are additional movements to be explained (ie movements other than those shown in the statement of total recognised gains and losses).

11.134 Other Disclosures

The ASB Statement *Preliminary Announcements* (see **11.128** above) recommends the following additional disclosures:

- where significant, amounts relating to associates and joint ventures should be shown separately in the summarised profit and loss account;
- turnover and operating profit in respect of any acquisitions or discontinued operations should be shown separately on the face of the summarised profit and loss account in accordance with the requirements of FRS 3 *Reporting Financial Performance*;
- where significant, the segmental analyses of turnover and profit or loss before interest to be given in the full report and accounts should also be disclosed in the preliminary announcement;
- sufficient information should be given for readers to understand any significant changes in the effective tax rate from the previous year – in some cases, the tax charge may need to be analysed into its main components;
- any exceptional items should be disclosed, either or the face of the profit and loss account or in the notes, in accordance with FRS 3 *Reporting Financial Performance*;
- reconciliations of operating profit to operating cashflow and the movement of cash to the movement in net debt should be given; and
- the preliminary announcement should state the period covered and the date on which it was formally approved by the board of directors.

11.135 Management Commentary

The aim of the management commentary in a preliminary announcement is to enable shareholders and other interested parties to understand the main factors that have influenced the company's performance during the financial year and its financial position at the year-end. As well as commenting on the year as a whole, the ASB Statement *Preliminary Announcements* (see **11.128** above) recommends that management discuss and explain in particular the salient features of the second half of the year (ie the period not covered by the interim report). These represent new information for shareholders, but are often subsumed into the details of the full year without specific comment. It is also important that the review does not concentrate solely on performance in the period, as shown in the profit and loss account, but also considers related issues such as working capital, liquidity and net debt. Significant trends and events mentioned in the commentary should be supported by the figures shown in the primary statements or by additional disclosures in the notes. Additional information should be given where this is necessary for an understanding of the significant items in the primary statement. The information given in the preliminary announcement should be succinct, consistent with the details to be given in the full report and accounts, and comparable with reports previously published.

The report should discuss both positive and negative aspects of the financial year and should include adequate information on any seasonal activity, so that the impact of this can be fully appreciated. The commentary should also draw attention to any events and changes occurring during the current financial year that are likely to have a significant impact in the following year, even though they may not have affected the company's performance in the period under review. Where relevant it should also cover significant changes in fixed assets and investments, capital structure, financing, commitments and contingencies.

The management commentary included in a preliminary announcement is not intended to be as detailed as an operating and financial review presented as part of the annual accounts and reports. However, the guidance in the ASB Reporting Statement *Operating and Financial Review* may be useful in helping to identify key issues that should be discussed in the preliminary announcement (see **11.89–11.93** above – for information on obtaining copies see the ASB website at www.frc.org.uk/asb).

11.136   Accounting Policies

The accounting policies used in preparing the preliminary announcements should be consistent with those in the full accounts, and the preliminary announcement should include a statement that the policies are the same as those disclosed in the last published accounts, or explain any differences. If there has been a change in accounting policy, the preliminary announcement should be prepared on the new accounting policy, all relevant comparative figures should be restated on the basis of the new policy and the cumulative effect on opening reserves should be disclosed. If any other prior period adjustments are necessary (eg to correct fundamental errors), these should be reflected in the preliminary announcement in the same way as changes in accounting policy.

11.137   Earnings Per Share

Basic earnings per share should be calculated and disclosed in the preliminary announcement in the same way as in the full annual accounts. If the company adopts a policy of disclosing additional calculations of earnings per share in its annual accounts, the same details should be given in the preliminary announcement.

11.138   Comparative Figures

Comparative figures for the summarised profit and loss account, statement of total recognised gains and losses, summarised balance sheet and summarised cashflow statement should cover the last full financial year. The ASB Statement *Preliminary Announcements* (see **11.128** above) also recommends that the preliminary announcement should set out information on the second half of the year, together with comparatives for the equivalent period in the previous year, to support the management commentary and facilitate an understanding of the company's current performance.

11.139   Statutory Disclosure

A preliminary announcement contains information for the current and previous financial years of the company and also information as at the company's current and previous financial year-end. It therefore constitutes 'non-statutory accounts' under *section 240* of *CA 1985* and must include the statements required by that section. This is considered in more detail at **3.83 NON-STATUTORY ACCOUNTS**.

11.140   Reporting on the Internet

At a Glance

* Many companies now use a website to disseminate financial informa-tion, but concern has been expressed over the lack of any formal require-ments or guidance on this form of financial reporting.
* The Government has proposed that listed companies should be required to publish their annual accounts and reports on a website.
* A Discussion Paper published by the International Accounting Standards Committee (IASC) in 1999 set out suggested contents for a Code of Conduct on internet reporting.
* Further guidance was issued in August 2002 by the International Feder-ation of Accountants (IFAC).
* *CA 1985* now permits companies to distribute their annual accounts and reports electronically.
* Auditing Standards specify the steps that auditors should take when accounts are to be made available on a website or distributed electronically.
* The Institute of Chartered Secretaries and Administrators (ICSA) has also issued guidance on communicating electronically with shareholders.

11.141   Impact of the Internet

In November 1999, the International Accounting Standards Committee ('IASC') published a Discussion Paper *Business Reporting on the Internet*, which sets out the results of academic research undertaken for the IASC on the technological opportunities for electronic reporting of financial information and current prac-tice on using the internet for business reporting (for information on obtaining copies see the IASB website at www.iasb.org.uk). The research shows that nearly 80 per cent of listed companies with websites make use of them to disseminate financial information. However, this form of reporting goes beyond the trad-itional reporting boundaries and there is concern that regulators and accounting standard setters are not keeping pace with the technological changes. Business reporting on the internet is seen as a valuable tool in developing investor rela-tions, but a major problem at present is the lack of any formal guidance on this form of reporting. Consequently, users have no guarantee on the quality of the information presented or on its comparability with the information published by other businesses. There is particular concern that companies often fail to distin-guish information that has been audited from that which is unaudited.

There is also a wide variety in the level of information provided. Some websites include only brief summary reports, some allow downloading of elec-tronic versions of the printed financial statements and others present the full financial statements for on-screen viewing. Where the website includes only extracts of the full financial report, there is concern that users may be given a misleading impression. Many sites simply present financial information as if it were in printed form, which can make it cumbersome and inflexible. A small number of more advanced sites allow users to manipulate the underlying data to suit their own purposes, and this is expected to become more widespread as technology continues to develop.

Following the recent company law review, the draft Company Law Reform Bill published in May 2006 reflects the proposal that all quoted companies should be required to publish their annual accounts and reports on a website as soon as practicable after they have been approved and the audit report signed, and within four months of the financial year end at the latest.

11.142   Suggested IASC Code of Conduct

The Discussion Paper concluded that a Code of Conduct should be developed for internet reporting to deal with issues of immediate concern and, in the longer term, that standards should be developed to deal with reporting under develop-ing technologies. The paper sets out the recommended content of the Code of Conduct and, although this is not a formal document, companies which are already making use of the internet for financial reporting may find it helpful to bear in mind the points raised. The recommendations include the following.

- *Consistency.* Financial information published on the internet should be con-sistent with similar information published in another medium (eg in printed form). If documents provided online do not include the full information from the original format, this fact should be stated and a point of contact provided for obtaining the missing information. If any information provided on the internet is additional to that provided in another form, this fact should also be stated.
- *Multiple online files.* Where financial reports are divided into separate docu-ments for online presentation, the complete set should be listed together on the website and there should be appropriate cross-referencing between documents.
- *Boundaries of financial statements.* The boundaries of the complete set of financial statements should be clearly recognisable so that a user knows when he/she has moved out of this area.

- *Other financial information.* Where an entity includes on its website financial information or similar data that is not derived from its financial statements (eg forecasts, environmental information, social responsibility information), this information should not be presented in a manner which suggests that it conforms to an IASC or similar reporting standard.
- *Excerpts.* If a website includes only excerpts from a complete set of financial statements (eg just an income statement or a balance sheet, without the related notes), it should be clearly identified as an excerpt and details should be provided of how the full copy can be obtained.
- *Historical summaries.* If a historical financial summary is published on the website, the underlying accounting principles should be clearly identified. In particular, it should be clear whether the figures are those originally reported or whether they have been restated to be consistent with the requirements of new reporting standards.
- *Supplementary information.* Supplementary information that would not otherwise be widely available (eg data for analysts' briefings, press releases, other investor relations material) should be provided online for the benefit of all shareholders.
- *Auditors' report.* It should be clear which information is subject to an audit opinion, and any qualification in the auditors' report should be clearly noted. If information is provided in more than one language, but only the primary language financial statements were audited, this fact should be stated in the translated versions.
- *Stability.* All pages should be identifiable and recreatable to enable users to bookmark them and return to the data in future.
- *Archiving.* Once financial information has been made available online, it should be archived and should not be removed from the site. Archived information should be clearly identified as such to avoid confusion with more recent material.
- *Dating.* All pages should show clearly the date of origin and the date of the last amendment.
- *Downloads.* Key data should be provided in a format that can be downloaded for offline analysis. As a minimum, the statutory filings made by the entity in its primary jurisdictions should be downloadable.
- *Notification of updates.* Users should be informed of significant changes to the website, either through an e-mail notification service or by providing a date order listing of changes.
- *Currency conversions.* If the website offers a facility for changing the reporting currency on the basis of period-end or average exchange rates, this 'convenience translation' should be clearly identified for what it is and should state that it does not conform to the translation requirements of accounting standards.
- *Responsibility.* Users have a right to presume that the entity is taking legal responsibility for the accuracy and completeness of the financial information provided on its website. If this is not the case, this fact should be clearly stated. Any data on the site that was created outside the company should be clearly identified and its source noted.

- *Security.* All reasonable precautions should be taken to prevent unauthorised alteration of the data. The Discussion Paper proposes that, once a Code of Conduct is developed, websites providing financial information should be required to state their compliance with the Code, or specify any departures.
- *Other recommendations.* Other recommendations in the Discussion Paper include:
  - listed companies should prepare their websites in such a way that business reporting information for investors is clearly distinguished from promotional and other material;
  - auditors of listed companies should be responsible for ensuring that audited and unaudited information on the website is clearly distinguished; and
  - auditors of listed companies should ensure that the company conforms fully to the Code of Conduct where it claims to do so, or that any deviations are noted in the audit report.

11.143   Subsequent Guidance from IFAC

In August 2002, the International Federation of Accountants (IFAC) published *Financial Reporting on the Internet*. This has been developed by IFAC staff in the course of work on other projects and builds on the IASC discussion paper. The paper has not been formally approved by IFAC and consequently does not have the status of a formal IFAC document. It is intended to stimulate discussion and provide guidance to companies currently using the internet to report financial information. It considers issues under the following headings.

- *Internet Reporting Policy – Matters of principle.* This summarises management's responsibility for considering:
  - the type of information to be provided,
  - the involvement of the auditor,
  - the format in which the information will be provided, and
  - when the information will be provided.
- *Internet Reporting Policy – Practical issues.* This covers:
  - the need to distinguish clearly between audited and unaudited information,
  - the need to distinguish between information intended to supplement the financial information (eg press and analysts briefings) and promotional or marketing information,
  - the use and maintenance of hyperlinks to third party internet sites (eg financial analysts),
  - the inclusion of third party analyses and information on a company website,
  - the frequency of changes to financial information provided on a website.
- *Internet Reporting Policy – Control issues.* This covers:
  - controls over the approval of information provided on a website,
  - the security of financial information provided on a website,
  - the need to state clearly how users can obtain further information in either electronic or written form.

- *Management's responsibilities for content.* This includes guidance on:
  - ensuring the consistency of financial information to be provided on a website;
  - the need to establish retention policies for website material;
  - dealing with changes in accounting policy.
- *Timeliness.* This discusses the need for website information to be clearly dated and the need to ensure that any requirements on the release of price sensitive information are complied with.
- *Content – Financial information.* This deals with publication of the auditors' report, interim financial reporting, and the disclosure of aggregated, disaggregated or additional financial information on a website.
- *Security.* This emphasises management's responsibility for preventing the corruption or distortion of financial information on a website by employees (either accidentally or intentionally) or by third parties. As well as ensuring that changes are properly authorised, the controls and procedures should enable all changes to be detected and monitored.
- *Other issues.* Other issues covered in the paper include the translation of financial information into other languages, the provision of information in a format that can be downloaded and procedures to inform interested parties of changes to the website.

The paper can be downloaded free of charge from the Bookstore (under the 'Other' category) on the IFAC website at http://www.ifac.org/Store/.

11.144   Satisfying Legal Requirements by Electronic Means

The *Companies Act 1985 (Electronic Communications) Order 2000 (SI 2000/3373)* came into force on 22 December 2000 and clarifies that references to sending accounts and reports to those entitled to receive them include:

- sending copies by electronic communication to the address notified to the company for that purpose by the person entitled to receive the documents; or
- where the company and the person entitled to receive the accounts so agree, publishing the documents on a website, notifying the person in the manner agreed that they have been published in this way and providing him/her with both the address of the website and details of where and how the documents may be accessed on the website.

Further information on this is given at **3.31** USE OF ELECTRONIC COMMUNICATION.

11.145   Audit Considerations

Initial guidance on the additional audit considerations that arise when financial information is made available electronically was set out in APB Bulletin 2001/1 *The Electronic Publication of Auditors' Reports*. This emphasised that the directors are responsible for ensuring that financial information made available on a website is not tampered with or amended. APB Bulletin 2005/4 *Auditors' Reports on Financial Statements in Great Britain and Northern Ireland* now recommends that an additional paragraph is included at the end of the statement of directors' responsibilities where the company's financial statements are published on a website (see **11.49** above). Bulletin 2001/1 also provided guidance on the work that auditors should do when financial statements were published on a website or distributed to shareholders by electronic means, and on the adjustments that should be made to the wording of the auditors' report when published electronically. This has now been superseded by Appendix 1 to the UK and Ireland version of ISA 720 *Other Information in Documents also Containing Audited Financial Statements*. This covers:

- the work that auditors should carry out to check information that is presented electronically;
- issues relating to the wording of the audit report in order to identify which information has been audited, reviewed or read (as appropriate);
- the need to identify the accounting and auditing standards that have been applied; and
- the need to limit the auditors' association with any other information distributed with the annual report.

Copies of APB Bulletins and the UK and Ireland versions of ISAs can be downloaded from the APB website at www.frc.org.uk/apb/publications.

11.146　ICSA Guidance on Electronic Communications

The Institute of Chartered Secretaries and Administrators ('ICSA') has also issued *Electronic Communications with Shareholders: A Guide to Best Practice*. This sets out 25 points of recommended best practice, together with detailed guidance for directors and employees on issues such as:

- points to consider before offering the facility to shareholders;
- what to do if electronic communication fails;
- keeping records to establish proof of sending;
- separate identification of statutory and audited material on the website; and
- security issues, including systems to check that statutory and audited information made available on a website has not been tampered with.

Further details can be found on the ICSA website (www.icsa.org.uk) and copies of the full text can be obtained from ICSA, 16 Park Crescent, London W1B 1AH.

Appendix 1

Useful Websites on Financial Reporting Issues

Financial Reporting Council	www.frc.org.uk
Accounting Standards Board	www.frc.org.uk/asb
International Accounting Standards Board	www.iasb.org
Financial Reporting Review Panel	www.frc.org.uk/frrp
Auditing Practices Board	www.frc.org.uk/apb
Institute of Chartered Accountants in England and Wales	www.icaew.co.uk
Institute of Chartered Accountants of Scotland	www.icas.org.uk
Institute of Chartered Accountants in Ireland	www.icai.ie
Association of Chartered Certified Accountants	www.acca.co.uk
Chartered Institute of Public Finance and Accountancy	www.cipfa.org.uk

Appendix 2

Checklist for the Preparation of a Summary Financial Statement

A company can issue a summary financial statement to its shareholders if the answer to **all** of the following questions is 'Yes':

- Do the company's Articles of Association allow it to distribute a summary financial statement in place of the full accounts and reports? (see **11.101** above)
- Have the company's full accounts been audited? (see **11.101** above)
- Has the company consulted shareholders about its proposal to issue a summary financial statement and given them the option to request a copy of the full accounts and reports instead? (see **11.103** and **11.104** above)

If the company's full accounts are Companies Act accounts (see **3.16–3.17** above), the summary financial statement should include the following minimum information (consolidated figures must be given if the company is required to prepare group accounts).

☐ A summary profit and loss account, including;
- turnover;
- income from shares in group undertakings and participating interests;
- other interest receivable and similar income, and interest payable and similar charges;
- profit or loss on ordinary activities before taxation;
- tax on profit or loss on ordinary activities;
- profit or loss on ordinary activities after tax;
- extraordinary income and charges, after tax; and
- profit or loss for the financial year.

☐ The following details in respect of dividends:
- the aggregate of dividends paid in the year, other than those for which a liability existed at the previous balance sheet date;
- the aggregate amount of dividends that the company is liable to pay at the balance sheet date; and
- the aggregate amount of dividends proposed before the date of approval of the accounts and not included in the above disclosures.

☐ In the case of an unquoted company, the whole of (or a summary of) the note to the accounts setting out the details of aggregate information on directors' remuneration required by *CA 1985, Sch 6, para 1(1)*.

☐ In the case of a quoted company, either the whole of the directors' remuneration report or, as a minimum:

- the aggregate information on directors' remuneration required by *CA 1985, Sch 6, para 1(1)*;
- the statement of the company's policy on directors' remuneration for future years; and
- the performance graph summarising shareholder return.

☐ A summary balance sheet, showing a single amount for each item that is assigned a letter in the *CA 1985* standard balance sheet formats.

If the company's full accounts are IAS accounts (see **3.16–3.17** above), the summary financial statement should include the following minimum information (consolidated figures must be given if the company is required to prepare group accounts).

☐ the whole of (or a summary of) the note to the accounts setting out the details of aggregate directors' remuneration required by *CA 1985, Sch 6, para 1(1)*;

☐ in the case of a quoted company, a statement of the company's policy on directors' remuneration and the performance graph summarising shareholder return;

☐ a summary profit and loss account showing each of the headings and sub-totals required under IASs or, where the directors consider it appropriate, a combination of such headings and sub-totals where they are of similar nature;

☐ the following details in respect of dividends:

- the aggregate of dividends paid in the year, other than those for which a liability existed at the previous balance sheet date;
- the aggregate amount of dividends that the company is liable to pay at the balance sheet date; and
- the aggregate amount of dividends proposed before the date of approval of the accounts and not included in the above disclosures;

☐ a summary balance sheet showing each of the headings and sub-totals required under IASs or, where the directors consider it appropriate, a combination of such headings and sub-totals where they are of similar nature.

Irrespective of whether the underlying accounts are Companies Act accounts or IAS accounts, the summary financial statement must include the following.

☐ Comparative figures for each item presented.

☐ The signature of a director on behalf of the board, and the name of that director.

☐ A clear statement that the document is only a summary of the information given in the company's annual accounts and (where relevant) the directors' remuneration report.

☐ A statement on whether or not the summary financial statement contains additional information derived from the directors' report and, if it includes such information, the fact that it does not include the full text of the directors' report;

☐ A formal statement, in a prominent position, that the summary does not contain sufficient information to allow as full an understanding of the results and state of affairs of the company or group as the full documents would, and that members and other entitled persons have the right to obtain a copy of the full accounts and reports, free of charge.

☐ A clear statement of how members and other entitled persons can obtain the full accounts and reports for the current year, and how they can elect to receive these in future years in place of the summary financial statement.

☐ A report from the auditors on whether:
- the summary financial statement is consistent with the full accounts and reports for the relevant financial year;
- the summary financial statement complies with the requirements of *section 251* of *CA 1985* and the related Regulations;
- their report on the full accounts and (where relevant) the auditable part of the directors' remuneration report was qualified or unqualified – if it was qualified, the report must be set out in full, together with any additional information needed to understand the qualification;
- their opinion on consistency between the directors' report and the accounts was qualified or unqualified – where the opinion was qualified, the qualification must be set out in full, together with any additional material needed for the qualification to be understood; and
- their report on the full accounts contained a statement under *section 237(2)* or *section 237(3)* of *CA 1985* (see **1.59–1.60** above) – if such a statement was included, the auditors' report on the full accounts must be set out in the summary financial statements.

☐ Where the summary financial statement is to be made available to a wider group than entitled persons (for instance, through publication on a website), the statement in respect of non-statutory accounts required by *section 240(3)* of *CA 1985* (see **3.84** above) – *section 251(7)* of *CA 1985* includes an exemption from this disclosure if the summary financial statement is provided only to entitled persons.

Companies are free to give additional information in the summary financial statement if they wish.

NB: Separate requirements apply to banking and insurance companies.

Fraud

 Fraud

12.1 Understanding Fraud

At a Glance
* Fraud encompasses the use of deception to obtain unjust or illegal financial gain, and intentional misrepresentations affecting the financial statements.
* The nature of fraud usually depends on the type of business, the reason for the fraud and who is perpetrating it.
* The view that fraud is a victimless crime is rapidly losing ground.
* Recent terrorist attacks and accounting scandals have heightened the general awareness of fraud and the damage that it can cause to the economy.
* A principal theme is the need for a major change in business culture and attitudes.
* Fraud may involve an individual or a group of people, and may involve management, employees or third parties (or a combination of these).
* The two key factors that encourage fraud are motive and opportunity.
* Accounting manipulation is usually driven by business pressures, whereas other forms of fraud are usually driven by personal pressures.
* Unidentified or temporary weaknesses in systems and controls can increase the inherent risk of fraud.
* The internet creates increasing opportunities for high speed and high frequency fraud.
* Increased regulation is likely to be imposed as a result of the recent accounting scandals.
* The primary role of the Fraud Advisory Panel is to raise awareness of the social and economic damage caused by fraud.
* Useful information can be found on websites dedicated to the issue of fraud.

12.2   What is Fraud?

There is no single definition of fraud. Auditing Standards describe fraud as comprising:

- the use of deception to obtain unjust or illegal financial advantage; and
- intentional misrepresentations affecting the financial statements.

Fraud may involve physical theft or misappropriation of cash or goods, recording transactions with no substance (such as payments to fictitious employees or suppliers) and falsifying or altering accounting and other records to cover up theft or misappropriation. It also includes the manipulation or distortion of data, either for tangible gain (for instance to increase the payments under bonus or commission schemes) or simply to present the details in a more favourable light (for instance, to meet targets, show improved results or enhance share performance).

The nature of fraud often depends on the type of business, the reason for the fraud and who is perpetrating it. Certain businesses, particularly those involving access to high levels of cash or movable goods, are particularly vulnerable to fraud involving personal gain for the fraudster. In this context, the more common types of fraud include:

- the theft of cash or stock;
- the submission of false expense claims; and
- purchasing frauds involving false invoices or fictitious suppliers.

Financial information will usually be misstated in these cases, but primarily to cover up the fraudulent activity rather than as an end in itself. Fraud involving the intentional misrepresentation of financial information is more likely to be driven by the need to meet or exceed performance targets, either for a business segment or for the business as a whole and is much more likely to involve those in more senior positions within the business.

The Fraud Bill, which is expected to come into effect in the summer of 2006, will create a statutory offence of fraud which will be committed when a person dishonestly carries out one of the following acts with the intent of making a gain, causing loss or exposing another person to the risk of loss:

- makes a false representation;
- wrongfully fails to disclose information; or
- secretly abuses a position of trust.

12.3   New and Emerging Areas of Fraud

The growth of e-commerce and the wide availability of the internet have created a number of new avenues for fraudsters to explore. Recent years have seen a worrying growth in cybercrime, including activities such as cyberlaundering, cyberextortion, advanced fee frauds, the sale of stolen or counterfeit goods through the internet, credit card fraud, computer hacking, phishing, cybersquatting and other e-mail and internet scams. Many e-commerce transactions proceed without human intervention by the service provider and automated transactions should therefore be subject to particularly careful scrutiny. Identity theft, where the fraudster uses the identity of an individual or a company to open bank accounts and/or obtain payments, credit or goods and services, is also facilitated by use of the internet. The Fraud Advisory Panel has published a number of useful guides and reports on these and other issues, all of which are available free of charge from its website (see **12.11** below).

12.4   A Low Profile Issue?

Fraud has tended to be given a relatively low profile within the business community. Concerns over the impact of adverse publicity have resulted in many companies being reluctant to report and follow up any frauds that are identified and it is therefore difficult to estimate the true cost of fraud, although the report *The Economic Cost of Fraud* produced for the Home Office by National Economic Research Associates (NERA) towards the end of 2000, suggested that it could be in the order of £14 billion per annum. However, the view that fraud is a victimless crime is rapidly losing ground as everyone becomes more aware of the impact that serious fraud can have on the general public in terms of business failures (and thus reduced employment opportunities), loss of (or reductions in) pensions and savings, higher insurance premiums, higher banking costs and, potentially, higher taxes.

12.5   Impact of Recent Events

The terrorist attacks in New York and Washington in September 2001 and various accounting scandals that have come to light in recent years, especially those at Enron and Worldcom, have all served to heighten the general awareness of fraud and the damage that it can cause to the business economy. There has been an increased focus on the use of fraud and money laundering to secure funds to support terrorist activity, and on the need for tighter legislation and controls to prevent this. Similarly, the various accounting scandals have highlighted how quickly share prices and the investment markets can collapse when business confidence is destroyed. Whilst these are large, high profile businesses, the issue of fraud, the damage it can cause and the need to prevent it, are equally relevant in a smaller, owner-managed company.

12.6   Need for Culture Change

One of the principal themes emerging from recent events is the need for a major change in business culture and attitudes. Various initiatives have been developed in recent years, including the *Combined Code* (and its predecessor Codes), to try to create a business culture of transparency, integrity and accountability. This is something that must come from the top of an organisation – it will only happen if the board is prepared to recognise the issue and take appropriate action, setting a strong example at board level. In particular, it is important to encourage a climate of openness and trust, where all employees accept the responsibility for upholding high standards and feel confident in reporting any concerns to management. The Government has also expressed concern that awards of large share options packages to senior executives might be creating 'perverse incentives' rather than encouraging the achievement of performance targets. Both the *Combined Code* and the regulations for quoted companies on the directors' remuneration report require the disclosure of detailed information on the use of share options and other long-term incentive schemes (see **6.27** DIRECTORS' REMUNERATION and **23.31** DIRECTORS' REMUNERATION) to enable shareholders and others to assess the potential impact of these arrangements.

12.7 Who Perpetrates Fraud?

Fraud on a company may involve a single individual or a group of individuals, and may be committed by management, employees or third parties. In many cases, a degree of collusion will be needed in order to perpetrate the fraud. Employee or management fraud intended to achieve personal gain will often be committed with third party help, and those committing fraud from outside the organisation will often need internal assistance. For instance, many purchasing frauds require collusion between a supplier and an employee involved with purchase transactions. The two key factors that encourage fraud are motive and opportunity. The motive for fraud can be very wide-ranging. Accounting manipulation is usually driven by business pressures, such as the need to:

- achieve or exceed budgets and targets;
- maintain or improve the share price;
- secure additional funding; and
- support weak or failing ventures.

The demands on senior management are not only internal and there is particular concern that the attitude of financial analysts and commentators is fuelling the development of an aggressive attitude to earnings management within the business community. Unrealistic reporting deadlines can also put undue pressure on senior management. Other types of fraud are more likely to be driven by personal pressures, such as those arising from excessive greed, an attempt to resolve personal financial difficulties, general career dissatisfaction or a desire for revenge. Businesses can also become the victims of various types of cybercrime, usually perpetrated by third parties who have no direct connection with the company (see **12.3** above).

12.8 Nature of Fraud

Accounting manipulations that amount to fraud might include:

- the creation of false sales;
- the deliberate overstatement of assets;
- the deliberate suppression of liabilities;

- failure to take account of the substance of all elements of a transaction (ie recognising only those elements that help to achieve the required overstatement or understatement of income, expenses, assets or liabilities);
- delaying or advancing income or expenditure;
- manipulation of pricing agreements; and
- inappropriate use of reserves.

In the case of other types of fraud, the opportunity is usually greatest where there are limited deterrents or little chance of the fraud being discovered. Many of those who commit this type of fraud are opportunists, and unidentified, or even temporary, weaknesses in systems and controls can make the company especially vulnerable. For instance, new business activities, changes to management information systems, changes in management, the prolonged absence of key individuals and weakened controls as a result of reduced staffing levels can all increase the inherent risk of fraud. There can also be particular problems in areas where management are heavily reliant on specialist expertise. For instance, if the management team has only limited computer expertise, they may in effect place heavy reliance on relatively junior employees in areas where there is enormous scope for manipulation.

It is usually inevitable that what begins as a small fraud will grow, particularly where accounts manipulation is involved, either as an end in itself or to cover up a fraud of a different type. If income for the current year has been inflated in order to show the required level of performance, further inflation is going to be needed in the next accounting period in order to maintain the 'growth'.

12.9   Internet Fraud

Fraud is now more organised than ever before and the internet has opened up increasing opportunities for high speed and high frequency frauds. Relatively common internet frauds include identity fraud, credit card fraud and the theft of confidential data (see also **12.3** above). Particular care is needed when developing websites, as poor programming and website design can result in relatively easy but unauthorised access being given to data, which can then be corrupted or used for fraudulent purposes. Also, encryption techniques will sometimes not be as sound as they appear and may therefore not give the required degree of physical security over data.

12.10   Reaction to Recent Accounting Scandals

The reaction to the recent accounting scandals is likely to result in an increased regulatory cost for business generally. The UK Government commissioned reviews of financial reporting, auditing and the roles of non-executive directors and audit committees, and these led to the introduction of a revised *Combined Code* for accounting periods beginning on or after 1 November 2003 (see **6.6–6.7** above) and changes to the regulation of the audit and accountancy profession (see **1.30–1.33** above).

12.11   The Fraud Advisory Panel

The Fraud Advisory Panel was established in 1996, on the initiative of the Institute of Chartered Accountants in England and Wales (ICAEW), and it acts as a focal point for the generation and exchange of ideas and information aimed at fighting fraud in its various forms. The members of the Panel are drawn from the legal and accountancy professions, industry and commerce, the academic world, the police and a range of government and quasi-governmental bodies. The work of the Panel is directed by a Steering Group and is carried out by a series of working parties. The Panel's primary role is to raise awareness of the social and economic damage caused by fraud, and in particular to:

- develop proposals to reform the law and public policy on fraud;
- develop proposals to enhance the investigation and prosecution of fraud;
- advise business on fraud prevention, detection and reporting;
- assist in improving fraud related education and training in business and the professions; and
- establish a more accurate picture of the extent, causes and nature of fraud.

The reports and guidance material produced by the Panel to date include:

- *Fraud Bill: Guidance for Industry* (April 2006)
- *Fighting Fraud: A Guide for SMEs* (2nd Edition – February 2006)
- *Sample Fraud Policy Statements* (February 2006)
- *Protecting Your IT Systems: A Guide for SMEs* (September 2005)
- *Have You Been Scammed? Identifying Internet and Email Scams* (July 2004)
- *Cybercrime and the Proceeds of Crime Act* (March 2004)
- *Identity Theft: Do You Know the Signs?* (July 2003)
- *Cybercrime: What Every SME Should Know* (2002)

These are all available free of charge from the Panel's website at www.fraudadvisorypanel.org. Membership of the Panel is open to individuals and corporate bodies that share its values. Further information can be obtained from The Fraud Advisory Panel, Chartered Accountants' Hall PO Box 433, Moorgate Place, London, EC2P 2BJ (*tel*: 020 7920 8721; *fax*: 020 7920 8545, website: www.fraudadvisorypanel.org).

12.12   Other Information

The Fraud Advisory Panel's website (www.fraudadvisorypanel.org) includes a useful list of other websites dealing with fraud, as does the website for the Centre for Fraud Management Studies (CFMS), based at the Liverpool Business School, Liverpool John Moores University (http://cwis.livjm.ac.uk/bus/fraud/). This site also gives information on the Centre's fraud management courses and current studies and research into fraud issues.

12.13   Responsibility for Fraud Prevention and Detection

At a Glance

* Company directors have a collective responsibility for taking reasonable steps to prevent and detect fraud and other irregularities.
* An internal audit function can help management to identify and assess fraud risk and develop appropriate systems and controls.
* External auditors are required to plan their work so that they have a reasonable expectation of detecting material errors and misstatements arising from fraud, but do not have a responsibility to detect all fraud or error that may exist within a business.
* The role of the audit committee is to provide assurance that the board's collective responsibility for financial matters and internal control is being properly discharged.

12.14   Collective Responsibility of Directors

The directors have joint and several responsibility for safeguarding the assets of the company, and must therefore take reasonable steps to prevent and detect fraud and other irregularities. This is specifically referred to in the statement of the directors' responsibilities that must be published as part of the annual accounts (see **12 FINANCIAL REPORTING**). Although it may be helpful for management purposes to allocate the management of security issues to a specific director or other senior individual within the organisation, the directors always retain collective responsibility for the prevention and detection of fraud.

12.15   Role of Internal Audit

Internal auditors are not responsible for designing and implementing systems, nor for the prevention and detection of fraud. However, the work of an internal audit function can help management to identify and assess potential risks within the business, and to develop appropriate systems and controls to reduce these risks to an acceptable level. This includes the inherent risk of fraud. The internal audit function provides a useful source of information for management on what is actually happening within the organisation. Its remit is generally much wider than the prevention and detection of fraud, and includes providing assurance on issues such as the completeness and accuracy of the company's accounting and other records, and the overall efficiency of the operations. However, by focusing its efforts on the effectiveness of the company's system of internal control, reporting any weaknesses and concerns and recommending appropriate changes to policies, procedures and controls, an internal audit function can help the directors to demonstrate that they are paying due attention to their responsibility for safeguarding the company's assets. Internal auditors can also be commissioned to undertake special assignments to assist management in the development of the business. These might include occasional more detailed forensic checks on accounting and other operational controls designed to limit the opportunity for fraud. Further information on establishing and operating an internal audit function is given in **1 AUDIT**.

12.16   Role of External Auditors

For many years there has been a commonly held, and misconceived, view that the detection of fraud is an important aspect of the role of the external auditors. The auditing profession has made considerable efforts in recent years to explain the role and responsibilities of external auditors, and the nature of an audit, in an attempt to eliminate this 'expectations gap'. External auditors are appointed to express an independent opinion on the annual financial statements. Their work is therefore directed towards identifying any potentially material misstatements in the accounts, including any that arise as a result of fraud and other irregularities. Auditors are required by professional auditing standards to plan their work so that they have a reasonable expectation of detecting material errors and misstatements arising from fraud.

In carrying out their work, the external auditors will review the company's systems and controls, carry out certain test checks, and report to management any weaknesses and concerns that they identify, but the external audit should not be relied upon to detect all fraud and irregularities that may exist within the organisation. The auditors will usually emphasise this in their report to management on significant issues that have come to their attention during the audit (see **1 AUDIT**). If the company does not have an internal audit function, the directors might consider arranging for the external auditors to carry out occasional more detailed forensic checks on the systems and controls as a separate exercise.

If the external auditors do detect, or have reason to suspect, fraud during the course of their work, they will normally report this to the directors. However, separate arrangements may apply where the auditors suspect that directors are involved in the fraud, in the case of regulated businesses and where money laundering is suspected. If the company has an audit committee, the auditors may report through that committee if they have reason to believe that executive directors may be involved in the fraud.

12.17   Role of the Audit Committee

The precise role of the audit committee must be tailored to the needs of the individual company, but broadly the role of an audit committee is to provide assurance that the board's collective responsibility for financial matters and internal control is being properly discharged. The audit committee's responsibilities will usually include reviewing the results of the work of the external auditors and, where relevant, the internal auditors, and ensuring that points brought to the attention of management are being properly followed up and actioned.

Under the present *Combined Code*, the specific responsibilities of the audit committee include:

- reviewing the company's internal financial controls and, unless addressed by a separate risk committee of independent directors or by the board itself, the company's internal control and risk management systems;
- reviewing the arrangements by which staff may, in confidence, raise concerns about possible improprieties in matters of financial reporting or other issues, with the objective of ensuring that arrangements are in place for proportionate and independent investigation and appropriate follow-up action.

The existence of an audit committee can help to demonstrate a climate of discipline and control within the business and can provide a useful forum, independent of the executive management team, for the finance director, external auditors and head of internal audit to raise issues of concern where necessary. Further information is given in **1** AUDIT.

12.18 Minimising the Risk of Fraud

At a Glance
- * Fraud risk should be managed in a way that reduces it to an acceptable level.
- * Rigorous personnel procedures, for both permanent and temporary staff, can help to reduce the risk of fraud.
- * The likelihood of fraud arising should be assessed for each area of the company's activities (including those that are peripheral to the main business), and the controls to prevent each fraud risk should be identified.
- * Steps should be taken to correct any missing or weak controls.
- * The importance of management attitude and the general ethos of the organisation cannot be overemphasised.
- * Biometrics can now be used to improve the security of access controls.
- * All businesses should be aware of the risks of becoming inadvertently involved in money laundering.

12.19 Managing the Risk

Fraud is one of the many inevitable risks that any business faces. The risk of fraud arising can never be wholly eliminated, but it can be managed and reduced to an acceptable level by taking practical, common sense precautions and making use of cost-effective accounting and operational controls. Careful planning should enable appropriate controls to be introduced without disrupting the efficient operation of the business. However, the potential benefit of reducing risk to an acceptable level must always be balanced against the cost of doing so. If the directors decide not to take steps to reduce a potential risk, on the basis that the ongoing cost of doing so is too great, it is important that they do so with a clear understanding of the possible consequences.

12.20   Personnel Procedures

Rigorous personnel procedures can help to reduce the risk of fraud. It is particularly important to take up references for all potential new employees and to follow these up thoroughly. For instance, organisations frequently fail to confirm the qualifications and experience of prospective employees, follow up any apparent gaps in the previous employment record or investigate further any issues that may be referred to, however obliquely, in references from former employers.

Consideration should also be given to introducing the same procedures for temporary staff, particularly where they are to work in areas of the business that could be particularly susceptible to fraud. If temporary staff will have the same access to company records and assets as permanent employees, there is little justification for less rigorous personnel checks. Where the business makes regular use of temporary staff through employment agencies, it may be appropriate to check that the agency has adequate procedures in place on this.

If certain services are contracted out to other organisations (for instance, cleaning or maintenance services) it will usually be sensible to confirm that the main contractor carries out thorough checks on their employees and that proper records are maintained of who is working at each location at any given time. This is especially important when the individuals have regular access to the company's premises at times when management and staff are not usually present. Contracts of service for employees should normally provide for immediate suspension on the suspicion of fraud, to help prevent further loss and to preserve security over company records and assets. Similar arrangements may be appropriate for temporary staff and for contracted services.

12.21   Review and Assessment of Activities

The initial step in minimising the risk of fraud is to identify all the company's activities and assess the likelihood of fraud arising in each area. This review should encompass all those activities that are peripheral to the main business but which may nevertheless provide scope for material fraud. In many ways these activities often represent a higher risk as they can easily be overlooked and are frequently not subjected to the same degree of scrutiny as the key aspects of the business. For instance, peripheral activities might include the disposal of fixed assets, or the management of the company's car fleet. It is important to recognise that giving one person access both to company assets and to the related accounting or operational records significantly increases the opportunity for fraud. Hence the frequent emphasis by auditors on the need for segregation of duties wherever practicable. If at all possible, the following five aspects of a transaction should be fully segregated:

- initiation;
- authorisation;

- execution;
- custody of any related assets; and
- recording in the accounting records.

If segregation is not possible (for example, due to the small size of the organisation and the limited number of staff available) compensating checks and controls should be introduced. Business operations in remote locations will also usually present a higher risk of fraud – a higher degree of autonomy may be necessary for a remote operation to function efficiently, but this will usually bring with it an increased risk of abuse.

12.22   E-commerce and IT Issues

Businesses should also undertake a careful review and assessment of the potential exposure to the additional risks arising from cybercrime and other e-commerce and IT issues. Both internal and external risks should be considered, including those arising from:

- the actions of management and employees;
- viruses, bots and other malware;
- computer hacking;
- extortion and denial of service attacks; and
- the use of unprotected wireless networks.

Businesses should also consider the need to ensure compliance with any relevant legal and other requirements – for instance, security standards set out in the Payment Card Industry (PCI) rules and the obligation under the *Data Protection Act 1998* to protect any personal information entrusted to them.

12.23   Assessment of Controls

Having identified the fraud risks, the next step is to identify the controls that are already in place to prevent fraud wherever a potential risk arises. This should highlight any areas where:

- there is an absence of appropriate controls;
- controls are weak; or
- there is a lack of appropriate management information.

Steps can then be taken to introduce new or enhanced controls and to improve the flow of information. In some cases, the analysis may reveal an excess of controls in a particular area, which might enable some rationalisation and provide scope for additional controls in weaker areas. It is important to remember that a control that is effective in preventing errors will not necessarily be effective in preventing fraud (eg a determined fraudster can easily forge an authorisation signature). It is also essential to confirm that the controls identified do actually operate in practice.

12.24   Management Attitude

The importance of management attitude and the general ethos of the organisation cannot be overemphasised. Fraud is much less likely to be perpetrated in a culture that is honest and open. It is essential that the directors make their views on the unacceptability of fraud and dishonesty explicit and that they lead by example, by setting out clear rules (and not bending them) and ensuring that all business practices are honest and above board. Employees should be left in no doubt as to the consequences of involvement in fraud. Management can impress this on their staff by:

- having a clear company policy on fraud, publicising this within the organisation and drawing it to the attention of third parties, such as customers and suppliers;
- including fraud awareness in staff induction programmes;
- incorporating on-going fraud awareness training into staff development programmes and emphasising that all employees have a responsibility for the prevention and detection of fraud;
- having a confidential 'whistle-blowing' procedure (see **12.29** below);
- developing a fraud response plan, to make it clear that action will be taken promptly and effectively if fraud is identified (see **12.34** below); and
- following up all allegations of fraud sensitively but thoroughly, and being prepared to take action against any perpetrators of fraud who are identified.

Implementing an effective system of internal control, and monitoring it regularly, helps to ensure that transactions are recorded accurately and that company assets are safeguarded. It also demonstrates to the employees that the directors take their responsibilities in this area seriously. A relaxed management attitude towards procedures and controls sends the opposite message. Rewarding staff for appropriate attention to control and compliance issues, as well as for financial performance, can also help to highlight the importance of these issues to the business as a whole.

12.25   Biometrics

A relatively recent development is the increasing use of biometrics to help protect a business against fraud – for instance, the use of techniques such as facial recognition, finger print recognition and iris recognition gives a much higher level of access security than a system of passwords.

12.26   Money Laundering

Certain businesses, in particular those in the financial services sector, are subject to stringent legal requirements in respect of the identification and reporting of money laundering and it is essential that such businesses have procedures and controls in place to ensure that they fulfil their duties in this area. However, any business could potentially be an unwitting party to money laundering and it is therefore advisable to ensure that management and staff are aware of the need to question unusual and potentially dubious transactions and know who to inform in such circumstances. New regulations on money laundering were introduced under the *Proceeds of Crime Act 2002* in an attempt to make criminal activity less profitable. The definition of money laundering under the new legislation is much broader and encompasses acquiring, possessing, dealing with or concealing the proceeds of any activity that constitutes a criminal offence in the UK. Certain professionals, including accountants and solicitors, have a duty to report any knowledge or suspicions of money laundering by their clients to the Serious Organised Crime Agency (SOCA). New rules also apply to any business that deals in goods and accepts in cash the equivalent of 15,000 euros (approximately £10,000) or more for any single transaction. Such businesses must register with HM Customs & Excise and put anti money laundering systems in place or stop accepting large payments in cash and insist on payment by methods such as credit card or cheque.

12.27   Detection of Fraud

> **At a Glance**
> * All managers and staff should be aware of the potential warning signs of fraud.
> * A clear, straightforward procedure for 'whistle-blowing' by employees can be of significant help in the detection of fraud.
> * Any business areas performing differently from expectations should be investigated.
> * The use of management override of internal controls should be carefully monitored.
> * Any seemingly unusual behaviour by employees should be investigated.
> * Any apparently unusual transactions should always be investigated.
> * The company should maintain its own fraud record and analyse the information for any particular patterns.

12.28   Awareness of Warning Signs

Many frauds come to light by accident or as the result of a tip-off. However, putting procedures in place to detect fraud can help to ensure that any irregularities come to light at an early stage and that any loss is minimised. They can also act as a useful deterrent. It may be helpful to allocate the management of security issues, including the prevention and detection of fraud, to a specific individual within the organisation. However, all members of the management team, and preferably all employees, need to be aware of the potential warning signs of fraud and to be constantly alert for them. Experience has shown that when fraud is detected, the warning signs have often been apparent for some time but have either not been noticed by management or have been noted but not acted upon.

Fraud

A strong system of internal controls should help to ensure that any irregularities are highlighted. However, regular monitoring is important, both to check that the controls are actually operating as intended (for instance, staff may be tempted to take short cuts to save time) and to ensure that controls are kept up-to-date as the business develops (for instance, new activities may not be adequately covered by existing controls, or organisational changes may have inadvertently resulted in a control lapsing). It is also important to consider whether management can override the controls and, if so, how often this is done in practice. An internal audit function can provide valuable assistance on these points. Taking prompt and appropriate action on weaknesses in systems and controls highlighted by the auditors (both external and internal) helps to demonstrate management's commitment to operating an effective system of internal control.

12.29 Whistle-blowing Procedures

The company should develop and publicise a clear, straightforward system for 'whistle-blowing' by employees. This will only operate satisfactorily if there is a climate of openness, honesty and trust and if employees feel confident that they will not suffer personally as a result of raising their concerns. Options to consider include reporting:

- through the line manager – although such a system will need to provide for cases where the employee suspects the line manager of being implicated in the fraud;
- directly to an identified member of senior management;
- directly to an identified member of the audit committee; or
- through a confidential fraud telephone hotline (which may be either internal or external).

It is generally inadvisable to use e-mail for this purpose. Whatever method best suits the company's circumstances, it is important that employees see that their concerns are taken seriously and are properly followed up, and that confidentiality is maintained. Where suspected fraud is reported in good faith, the employee will usually be protected under the *Public Interest Disclosure Act 1998*. The effective operation of the 'whistle-blowing' procedures should be regularly reviewed.

12.30 Business Areas Performing Unexpectedly

Directors should ensure that regular checks are carried out, using performance indicators relevant to the business, to identify any areas that are performing differently from expectations. For example, where a business area regularly performs better than expected, it is possible that the results are being manipulated, whilst a business that is consistently falling below expectations could potentially be the subject of cash or purchasing frauds. Wherever possible, financial information should be reviewed in conjunction with non-financial data as this may help to highlight any inconsistencies (for instance, it should be possible to review payroll totals in conjunction with independently prepared details of employee numbers). The most useful performance indicators will depend on the nature of the business, but those in common use include:

- gross margin – significant fluctuations could indicate manipulation of sales figures, purchasing fraud or theft of stock;
- stock turnover – significant fluctuations could indicate theft of stock, or purchasing fraud;
- debtors: sales ratio (average debtor days) – significant fluctuations could indicate manipulation of sales figures, or teeming and lading of cash received;
- age analysis of debtors – increase in old balances could indicate cash fraud;
- creditors: purchases ratio (average creditor days) – significant fluctuations could indicate purchasing fraud;
- average pay per employee – significant increase could indicate payments to fictitious employees.

Unusual trends or fluctuations should be thoroughly investigated, and apparently plausible explanations should always be corroborated. It is also worth remembering that too much consistency might in itself be suspicious. It has been known for a business unit to perform exactly in line with budget each year – on further investigation, it transpired that the unit had in fact performed consistently above budget and that management and staff had colluded to divide the excess profits between them.

12.31   Opportunity for Management Override

Directors should be constantly aware of situations where line managers and senior employees may have the opportunity to override internal controls, or to arrange for figures to be presented in a more positive light. This can be a particular problem where an autocratic individual occupies a senior post, or in the case of remote operations, where local management may need a higher level of autonomy for the operation to function efficiently. These situations should be subject to careful monitoring and, in the case of other locations, regular visits should be made to check on what is actually happening in practice. An internal audit function can be very useful in this situation. The setting of performance targets and the operation of incentive schemes are well accepted methods of managing businesses. However, both require careful monitoring and review on a regular basis. The setting of over-ambitious targets can encourage manipulation of the figures to show the desired result, and this can be a particular problem where employee earnings are directly affected by the financial performance of the business (for instance, through bonus schemes, profit sharing schemes, sales commission or earn out arrangements).

12.32   Staff Issues

Low staff morale can generate a higher risk of fraud, and a high level of staff turnover could be indicative of general management problems and potential fraud. Disaffected staff may be tempted to cut corners or not operate controls properly, or may be tempted to take advantage of systems' weaknesses as revenge for lack of job satisfaction or to redress the feeling that they are not being adequately rewarded for their efforts. Independent debriefing of leavers can sometimes highlight the existence of fraudulent activity or concerns over dishonest business practices that would not otherwise have come to light. Any seemingly unusual behaviour by employees should be investigated. Some examples are detailed below.

- A reluctance to take regular holidays may be due to the need to conceal an ongoing fraud. Fraud can often come to light during a sudden and unexpected absence of the person perpetrating it. Some organisations have a rule that staff must take at least two consecutive weeks' holiday each year – both for the physical well-being of the employee and to reduce the opportunity for long-term fraud to go undetected.
- Regular late-working by individual employees, whether paid or unpaid, should always be investigated and monitored – it may result from a need to cover up fraudulent activities in the absence of other members of staff. There are numerous examples of apparently diligent, long-standing employees working long hours, seemingly for the benefit of the company, but in fact to conceal their fraudulent activity. A trusted employee can be in a powerful position, especially if management have become relaxed about monitoring their activities.
- A refusal to change jobs or accept a promotion, or the consistent failure by a manager to delegate certain activities, may all be due to the need to conceal an ongoing fraud.
- An apparent discrepancy between an employee's earnings and their lifestyle is a common indicator of fraud.

12.33   Unusual Transactions

Management should always investigate apparently unusual transactions – for instance, an individual transaction that cannot immediately be explained or which seems to lack commercial substance or sense, or an unexpected quantity of a particular type of transaction, such as an abnormally high level of sales credit notes or an unusually large number of outstanding items on the bank reconciliation (especially if they seem to have been outstanding for some time). Frequent or regular systems breakdowns may also be a warning signal – they can provide a useful opportunity to conceal transactions or manipulate financial information. Businesses undertaking automated e-commerce transactions should also ensure that these are subject to careful scrutiny, with particular attention to the following issues:

- is the transaction or activity normal for this customer?
- does the transaction make sense from a commercial/personal point of view?
- has the pattern of transactions changed?
- if the transaction is with an overseas entity, is there a good business reason for this?

12.34   Collating Information on Fraud

An issue that is often overlooked is the potential benefit of a company maintaining its own record of suspected and actual fraud, and analysing this to see if any particular patterns emerge. This may be helpful in the ongoing development and monitoring of the company's response to fraud.

12.35   Developing a Fraud Response Plan

> **At a Glance**
> * A fraud response plan sets out company policy on fraud and the action to be taken when fraud is suspected.
> * The plan should explain who will lead the investigation and the detailed procedures that will be followed.
> * The fraud response plan should be regularly reviewed to ensure that it is kept up-to-date.

12.36   Benefits of a Fraud Response Plan

A fraud response plan should include the general company policy on fraud and should also set out the action to be taken when fraud is suspected. Having a detailed fraud response plan in place helps to ensure that everyone is clear about the action that needs to be taken if and when fraud is identified or suspected. Thinking about the issues in advance helps management to ensure that all the relevant aspects are covered. It is much more difficult to react promptly and effectively without a plan to follow. In particular, a detailed document setting out the policies and procedures to be followed in the case of fraud has the following benefits:

- it demonstrates that management is in control of the situation;
- it can help to minimise the risk of further loss once the fraud has been detected;
- it should improve the chance of recovering the loss already incurred, or of maximising the amount recovered; and
- it can help the company to minimise the potential adverse commercial effect (for instance, where supplier or customer accounts are affected).

It also provides a clear statement to employees that the directors are not prepared to condone fraud and will take appropriate action against anyone found to be involved in fraudulent activity. The Fraud Advisory Panel publishes model fraud policy statements that companies can adapt to their own circumstance (see **12.11** above).

12.37 Contents of the Plan

The plan should include the following.

- A clear statement of company policy on fraud, and in particular who should be contacted when there is any suspicion of fraud.
- Details of who will take responsibility for leading any investigation of suspected fraud.
- Relevant legal and personnel procedures. As noted above, it will usually be helpful to ensure that employment contracts provide for any employee suspected of fraud to be suspended immediately and either isolated or removed from the premises. The company should adopt a consistent policy for staff throughout the organisation – employees can be given the wrong message if (say) management are treated more leniently than other members of staff.
- Specific procedures for securing the company's assets and records when fraud is suspected, both to prevent further loss and to ensure that potential evidence is not destroyed – for instance, the procedures might include changing locks, security passes and computer passwords. Particular care is needed in these days of advanced computer technology – it has been known for a suspended employee to delete vital information by accessing the company's records from a remote computer terminal.
- Procedures for carrying out a detailed investigation into the suspected fraud – this may be done internally or may require specialist assistance. In particular, the gathering of supporting evidence will usually require expert knowledge to ensure that it is sufficiently reliable for use in a prosecution.
- Procedures for making contact with the police, the company's insurers or the business regulators (where relevant).
- Procedures for making internal reports on the issue (eg to the audit committee or main board).
- The company's policy on seeking the recovery of funds.
- Procedures for dealing with any publicity issues that might arise from the fraud.

It is also important that the directors should be seen to act immediately to enhance controls over the business area that was the subject of the fraudulent activity.

12.38 Regular Review

The fraud response plan should be subject to regular review to ensure that it takes account of any recent changes, for instance:

- new developments within the business; and
- changes resulting from the development of new technologies and any new external reporting requirements.

Appendix 1

Useful Websites on Fraud and Related Issues

Fraud Advisory Panel	www.fraudadvisorypanel.org
Centre for Fraud Management Studies	cwis.livjm.ac.uk/bus/fraud
ICAEW Audit and Assurance Faculty	www.icaew.co.uk/aafac
Institute of Internal Auditors (UK and Ireland)	www.iia.org.uk
Institute of Directors	www.iod.com
Business Link	www.businesslink.gov.uk
Department of Trade and Industry	www.dti.gov.uk
European Anti-fraud Office	http://europa.eu.int/comm/ dgs/olaf/
ACPO Fraud Prevention	www.uk-fraud.info/
Crimestoppers	www.crimestoppers.org.uk
National Hi-tech Crime Unit	www.nhtcu.org/
Serious Fraud Office	www.sfo.gov.uk
Serious Organised Crime Agency	www.soca.gov.uk

Fraud

Appendix 2

Checklist – Prevention and Detection of Fraud

This checklist summarises some of the key issues that need to be considered when dealing with the prevention and detection of fraud. It should not be regarded as comprehensive – other issues may need to be taken into account, depending on the particular circumstances of the business.

☐ Are all directors made fully aware of their collective responsibility for the prevention and detection of fraud?

☐ Do the directors encourage a business culture that is open and honest, and lead by example?

☐ Has the company developed a clear policy on fraud and is this:

- widely publicised amongst employees?
- drawn to the attention of third parties (eg customers and suppliers)?

☐ Do the company's personnel procedures ensure that:

- the stated qualifications and experience of new employees are verified;
- any apparent gaps in the employment record of new employees are investigated;
- references are taken up for all new employees;
- any points raised in employee references are followed up;
- the same procedures are applied for temporary as well as permanent staff;
- where agency staff are used, the company understands the level of checking that has been carried out by the agency;
- where a service is contracted out to a third party, the company understands the level of checking carried out by the contractor, especially where individuals will be given access to the company's premises outside normal working hours;
- all employment contracts and other service contracts provide for immediate suspension on the suspicion of fraud;
- all employees are required to take at least two consecutive weeks' holiday each year;
- regular late-working by employees is monitored and investigated;
- an independent debriefing interview is held with all leavers?

☐ Is fraud awareness included in staff induction programmes?

☐ Is on-going fraud awareness training incorporated into staff development programmes?

☐ Does the company have a confidential 'whistle-blowing' procedure?

☐ Is the effectiveness of the 'whistle-blowing' procedure subject to regular review?

☐ Are staff rewarded for appropriate attention to compliance and control issues as well as for financial performance?

☐ Has the company assessed the likelihood of fraud arising:

- in each principal area of the business;
- in each peripheral area of the business (eg disposal of fixed assets, management of company car scheme)?

☐ Has the company identified and assessed the controls that operate to prevent fraud in each case where a potential risk arises and taken steps to:

- introduce new controls where gaps are evident;
- strengthen potentially weak controls;
- ensure the proper flow of relevant management information;
- rationalise any areas where excessive bureaucracy has been identified?

☐ Has the company confirmed that the identified controls are actually operating in practice?

☐ Do the company's procedures ensure that, as far as practicable, the following aspects of each business transaction are segregated:

- initiation;
- authorisation;
- execution;
- custody of related assets; and
- recording in the accounting records?

☐ Are procedures and controls regularly reviewed and updated to take account of developments in the business?

☐ Are procedures and controls regularly reviewed and updated to take account of technological developments and the potential impact on the business of cybercrime and related fraud issues?

☐ If the company is subject to legal requirements in respect of money laundering, have appropriate procedures and controls been put in place?

☐ Are all directors and staff aware of the issues relating to money laundering, and the risk of the company becoming inadvertently involved?

☐ Have procedures been put into place to detect and prevent inadvertent involvement in money laundering activities?

☐ Are all directors and staff made aware of the potential warning signs of fraud?

☐   Is the use of management override of controls monitored and reviewed?

☐   Have appropriate performance indicators been identified for each aspect of the business?

☐   Are all variations from expected performance, and any unusual trends, thoroughly investigated and explanations corroborated?

☐   Is the use of incentive schemes and performance targets monitored and reviewed, to confirm that it is not encouraging manipulation of the underlying figures?

☐   Are regular control visits made to remote business locations?

☐   Do the company's procedures ensure that all unusual transactions are investigated?

☐   Do the directors collate information on actual and suspected fraud within the business and review this for any particular patterns?

☐   Does the company have an up-to-date fraud response plan setting out:

- the company policy on fraud;
- who will lead any investigation into suspected fraud;
- the detailed procedures that will be followed, covering in particular:
  ○ suspension and isolation/removal of relevant individuals,
  ○ protection of the company's records and assets,
  ○ gathering of reliable evidence,
  ○ contact with relevant third parties (eg police, insurers, regulators), and
  ○ internal reporting?
- the company's policy on seeking recovery of funds?
- procedures for dealing with any related publicity issues?

13

Health and Safety

Health and Safety

13 Health and Safety

13.1 Employee Safety and Welfare

> **At a Glance**
> * The *Health and Safety at Work etc. Act 1974* requires employers to ensure the health, safety and welfare of their employees.
> * Employers must ensure that work activities do not expose people other than employees (for example members of the public) to health and safety risks.
> * Employers must protect the mental, as well as physical, welfare of employees.
> * Every employer with five or more employees must prepare a written health and safety policy.
> * Recognised trade unions have the right to appoint safety representatives, which the employer must consult on a range of health and safety issues.
> * Employees must take reasonable care for the health and safety of themselves and others at work.
> * Employers must not charge employees for any item of safety equipment or protective clothing required by law.

The main piece of legislation covering health and safety and applying to virtually all workers and workplaces is the *Health and Safety at Work etc. Act 1974* (*HSWA 1974*). This sets out the general principles for protecting the health and safety of employees and others affected by work activity. *HSWA 1974* lays down broad general duties and acts as a framework, with more detailed health and safety regulations and Approved Codes of Practice ('ACoPs') being made under the main Act.

The *Health and Safety at Work etc. Act 1974*:

* imposes duties on employers and employees;
* outlines the role of the Health and Safety Commission ('HSC'), the Health and Safety Executive ('HSE' – the HSC's enforcement arm) and its medical arm – the Employment Medical Advisory Service ('EMAS');

- sets out enforcement provisions (including powers to issue improvement and prohibition notices); and
- details the penalties for non-compliance.

In partnership with Lexis Nexis UK, the HSE's website, www.hsedirect.com, assists employers in meeting their health and safety responsibilities. This provides instant access to a huge source of material containing the full text of Acts, regulations and Approved Codes of Practice and HSE guidance on the legislation, on workplaces, substances and processes. It also contains EU directives, news, case summaries, HSE press releases, HSE forms, links to other sites and selected material from Lexis Nexus UK. As well as being available on the internet, it is available in CD-Rom format.

13.2   Employers' Duties

Section 2 of *HSWA 1974* requires every employer to ensure, so far as is reasonably practicable (see **13.3** below), the health, safety and welfare of all employees. In particular, employers must, so far as is reasonably practicable:

- provide and maintain plant and systems of work so that they are safe and without risks to health;
- make arrangements for ensuring that articles and substances are used, handled, stored and transported safely and without risks to health;
- provide the necessary information, instruction, training and supervision to ensure the health and safety at work of employees;
- maintain any place of work under the employer's control in a safe condition and without risks to health, including safe access and egress; and
- provide and maintain a working environment without risks to health and with adequate facilities and welfare arrangements.

13.3   *So Far as is Reasonably Practicable*

The duties under *section 2* of *HSWA 1974* are qualified by the phrase 'so far as is reasonably practicable'. This has been interpreted in the courts as meaning that the costs of carrying out the health and safety measures must not be grossly disproportionate to the benefits to be obtained from doing them. Technical means and financial considerations can be taken into account.

In *R v Nelson Group Services (Maintenance) Ltd [1999] IRLR 646*, the Court of Appeal held that the fact that an employee carrying out work had done the work carelessly or failed to take a precaution that should have been taken, does not of itself preclude the employer from establishing a defence of reasonable practicability. This is a question of fact depending on the circumstances of each case. The employer must show that everything reasonably practicable has been done to ensure that a person doing the work has the necessary skill and instruction, safe systems of work have been laid down, adequate supervision is given and safe plant and equipment has been provided.

13.4   *Safe System of Work*

Section 2 of *HSWA 1974* does not go into detail about what constitutes a safe system of work. The HSE advocates that clear procedures should be adopted to maintain safe systems. For serious hazards a written 'permit to work' system should be adopted. It suggests that employers, when analysing safe systems, should consider the following.

Checklist

☐ Who is in charge of the job?

☐ Do the responsibilities overlap with someone else's?

☐ Is there anything which is not someone's responsibility?

☐ Has anyone checked that the equipment, tools or machines are right for the job?

☐ Are safe ways of doing the job already in place?

☐ Could the job interfere with the health and safety of others?

☐ Are safe working procedures laid down for the job? Is there any HSE guidance on the subject?

☐ Have people been trained and instructed concerning the dangers and limitations of the equipment?

☐ If the job cannot be finished today, can it be left in a safe state?

☐ Are clear instructions left for the next shift?

☐ Are the production people aware of what maintenance staff are doing and vice versa?

☐ What might go wrong?

Health and Safety

13.5   *Safety Policies*

Section 2 of *HSWA 1974* also requires every employer with five or more employees to prepare a written health and safety policy. This should detail the hazards present at the workplace, and the organisation and arrangements in force for carrying out the policy. It must be revised 'as often as may be appropriate' and brought to the notice of employees (*HSWA 1974, s 2(3)*).

It should set out the employer's aims and objectives for improving health and safety and how these will be met, and it should state the arrangements for monitoring the effectiveness of the policy. It should also set out all those persons in the organisation with health and safety responsibilities.

An Introduction to Health and Safety – Health and Safety in Small Business is a free basic guide for small businesses, including two ready-made self-assessment forms for a risk assessment and a health and safety policy. It is available from:

HSE Books
PO Box 1999
Sudbury
Suffolk
CO10 2WA
Tel: 01787 881165
Fax: 01787 313995
Online: www.hsebooks.co.uk

13.6 *Stress and Harassment*

Employers must protect the mental as well as physical welfare of employees. In the first case to demonstrate this, *Walker v Northumberland County Council [1995] IRLR 35*, the court held that as part of the general duty of care to provide a safe workplace, an employer had to take reasonable steps to avoid exposing employees to a health-endangering workload. The employee, however, must still establish that his medical condition arose out of the employer's breach of duty and that the psychiatric damage was reasonably foreseeable. In this case, despite being aware of an earlier nervous breakdown suffered by one of its employees, and an increase in his volume of work, the Council failed to ensure that promised back-up assistance was available. In these circumstances, the judge felt able to conclude that the employer was in breach of its duty and was liable in damages. The employee was later awarded damages for stress of £175,000.

Since Walker, there have been many compensation awards in connection with stress made both in the courts and in out-of-court settlements. The Court of Appeal case, *Sutherland v Hatton [2002] IRLR 263*, overturned compensation awards for three out of four claimants, and in doing so set out guidelines for how County Courts should decide future stress compensation cases. These include the following.

- There must have been reasonably foreseeable signs of stress.
- No occupation should be regarded as intrinsically dangerous to mental health.
- Employers providing a confidential advice service, with referral to counselling and treatment services, are unlikely to be found liable.
- Employers are usually entitled to assume that employees can withstand the normal pressures of the job, unless they are aware of a particular problem or vulnerability, and can take what they are told by employees at face value, without making searching enquiries, unless there is good reason to think otherwise.
- There must be psychiatric injury resulting from the stress.

In *Young v The Post Office [2002] IRLR 660*, the Court of Appeal confirmed that the employers were in breach of their duty of care when they failed to ensure that the arrangements made for an employee returning to work after a nervous breakdown were carried through. The employee had subsequently suffered a recurrence of his psychiatric illness within seven weeks of returning to work.

The employer had argued that it was up to the employee to speak out if he felt under stress, but this was rejected by the court.

In *Pratley v Surrey County Council [2003] IRLR 794*, a Court of Appeal case, it was held that the employers had not breached their duty of care to an employee who suffered depressive illness as a result of the employer's failure to introduce a promised system to reduce her workload. This had occurred when the employee had returned to work from holiday. Although the failure to introduce the system had caused the depressive illness, the court said that the employers could not have reasonably foreseen that an immediate collapse would occur. A distinction was made between the risk of psychiatric injury as a result of continuing work overload, and a risk of collapse in the short term.

A Court of Appeal case, *Bonser v RJB Mining (UK) Ltd [2004] IRLR 164*, found that a claim for damages for psychiatric illness caused by stress at work had not reached the high threshold set in *Hatton v Sutherland*.

The Court of Appeal, overturning a High Court case, said that the employer could not have reasonably foreseen that if they did not reduce the claimant's workload she would have a nervous breakdown. The claimant had to establish not simply that it was reasonably foreseeable that overwork would lead to stress, but that it would lead to a breakdown in the stressed employee's health.

In this case, the claimant's conduct and complaints were not sufficient to put her employers on notice that she was vulnerable to imminent risk of health. The only visible sign was that she had been tearful on one occasion.

Barber's case against Somerset County Council (one of the cases heard alongside *Hatton v Sutherland*) was successfully appealed in the House of Lords. The judges in the case, overturning the Court of Appeal decision, said that the employers were liable for the teacher's psychiatric illness which had been caused by stress and pressure of work.

The House of Lords held that in deciding whether an employer was in breach of the duty of care owed to an employee with regard to psychiatric illness caused by stress at work, the case of *Stokes v Guest Keen and Nettleford (Bolts and Nuts) Ltd [1968] 1 WLR 1776* should be referred to: 'the overall test is still the conduct of the reasonable employer taking positive thought for the safety of his workers in the light of what he knows or ought to know'.

The judges said that the *Sutherland* guidelines should be seen as practical guidance, but not as having statutory force, and that the particular facts of each case needed to be considered.

The Court of Appeal ruled on six stress cases in *Hartman v South Essex Mental Health and Community Care NHS Trust [2005] IRLR 293*, clarifying the law following the *Barber v Somerset County Council* and *Sutherland v Hatton* cases.

The overall test remains the conduct of the reasonable and prudent employer taking positive thought for his workers' safety in light of what he ought to know. Employers are liable for psychiatric injury caused by work-related stress which arose from a breach of duty, which was reasonably foreseeable. In deciding whether the injury was reasonably foreseeable, confidential information disclosed to the occupational health department must not be attributed to employer knowledge.

In *Hone v Six Continents Retail Ltd [2006] IRLR 49*, the Court of Appeal found against the employers, who had appealed against a decision by a county court judge that it was reasonably foreseeable that an employee would suffer psychiatric injury if he continued to work long hours without adequate support. The Court of Appeal confirmed that the employers were liable for the psychiatric injury which had been sustained as a result of occupational stress.

Mr Hone was a licensed house manager at a pub run by Six Continents. He had complained of regularly working 90 hours a week, and his employers had agreed to appoint an assistant manager, following a meeting at which he had mentioned working long hours and tiredness. However, only occasional support was provided, and he later collapsed at work after suffering giddiness and chest pain, and did not return to his job. He claimed damages for psychiatric injury caused by stress, which in turn was caused by working excessive hours. The county court judge agreed and awarded him damages of £21,840.

The Court of Appeal found that the county court judge had not erred in holding that it was reasonably foreseeable that the manager would suffer psychiatric injury if he continued to work long hours without adequate support and that, in failing to provide that support, the employers were liable for the injury which the claimant sustained as a result of stress at work.

Reference was also made to the clear and workable test set out in *Sutherland v Hatton* in determining whether psychiatric injury to an employee was reasonably foreseeable: 'To trigger a duty to take steps, the indications of impending harm to health arising from stress at work must be plain enough for any reasonable employer to realise that he should do something about it.'

The introduction of an Approved Code of Practice on stress was put on hold to allow the development of clear, agreed standards of management practice against which an employer's performance in managing stress can be measured. The Health and Safety Executive (HSE) then issued a new set of Management Standards to help employers work with their employees to manage the risks from work-related stress.

The Standards are based on a continuous improvement model featuring a benchmarking tool to help managers gauge stress levels, compare themselves with other organisations, and work with employees to identify solutions.

They are not new Regulations. Along with the toolkit, the Standards help large organisations meet their existing duty of care and their duty to assess the risk of work-related stress. The standards define the characteristics of an organisation where stress is managed effectively.

The Standards and advice on how to use them are available at www.hse. gov.uk/stress.

A HSE guidance leaflet, *Making the Management Standards Work: How to apply the standards in your workplace*, outlines the stress management standards.

The guidance complements the risk assessment approach outlined in the HSE's current guidance for managers about work-related stress *Tackling work-related stress – A managers' guide to improving and maintaining employee health and well-being* (HSG218).

The guidance, *Tackling Work-related Stress: a Manager's Guide to Improving and Maintaining Employee Health and Well Being* (HSG218) is aimed at managers in organisations employing more than 50 people and is available from HSE Books.

The *Protection from Harassment Act 1997* was used for the first time in 2005 in an employment law case, taken by a hospital employee who was being bullied and harassed by his manager. Under the Act behaviour amounting to harassment includes knowingly causing alarm or distress, and it must occur on more than one occasion. The Act allows civil cases, as well as criminal ones, to be taken to claim for damages.

In *Majrowski v Guy's and St Thomas's NHS Trust [2005] IRLR 340* the court held that the employer can be held vicariously liable where one employee harasses another employee, or another person, as long as there is an employment connection.

In *First Global Locums Ltd and Others v Cosias [2005] IRLR 873*, the *Protection from Harassment Act 1997* was again used in an employment situation.

13.7   *Duties to Non-employees*

Section 3 of *HSWA 1974* obliges employers to conduct undertakings in such a way as to ensure that persons other than their employees (eg members of the public and persons employed by others) are not exposed to risks to their health or safety.

The level of the duty in relation to contractors will vary – from doing little more than warning the contractor of potential dangers and coordinating operations where an employer subcontracts part of its undertaking to a contractor that operates a comprehensive system of supervision and instruction, to taking the same precautions for the contractors' workers as for its own employees where the contractor is providing workers totally under the employer's instruction and control.

Three elements have to be provided in order to establish a *prima facie* liability under *section 3* of *HSWA 1974*:

- that the defendant was an employer within the meaning of *HSWA 1974*;
- that the activity or state of affairs which gave rise to the complaint fell within the ambit of the defendant's conduct of the undertaking; and
- that there was a risk to the health and safety of persons, other than employees, who were affected by the conduct of that aspect of the undertaking.

(*RMC Roadstone Products Ltd v Jester [1994] IRLR 330*.)

If these three elements are proved, conviction will follow unless the defendant can satisfy the court on the balance of probabilities that it did all that was reasonably practicable to comply with the duty imposed.

Health and Safety

Viasystems (Tyneside) Ltd v Thermal Transfer (Northern) Ltd [2005] IRLR 983 involved damage caused to a factory by a workman who was employed through a series of subcontracts to fit air conditioning.

The Court of Appeal considered whether there could be dual vicarious liability, and decided that this was legally permissible. It found that the second and third defendants were both vicariously liable for the negligence of a workman which caused extensive damage to the claimants' factory. The worker in question was employed by the third defendants, who had contracted to supply his labour to the second defendants for the purposes of carrying out work at the premises.

The court said that the long-standing assumption that liability must rest on one employer or the other made little sense in a modern context.

13.8   *Consultation with Safety Representatives*

Section 2(4) of *HSWA 1974* makes provision for regulations to be made giving recognised trade unions the right to appoint safety representatives. A trade union is recognised for the purposes of these regulations where the employer recognises the union for any collective bargaining purposes.

Section 2(6) of *HSWA 1974* states that every employer must consult such safety representatives appointed 'with a view to the making and maintenance of arrangements which will enable him and his employees to co-operate effectively in promoting and developing measures to ensure the health and safety at work of the employees, and in checking the effectiveness of such measures'. Where requested (by two or more safety representatives) the employer must set up a safety committee.

The *Safety Representatives and Safety Committees Regulations 1977* (*SI 1977/500*), as amended, set out in detail the functions of safety representatives and safety committees and employers' duties to consult with safety representatives.

The *Health and Safety (Consultation with Employees) Regulations 1996* (*SI 1996/1513*) give non-union employees the same rights to consultation that union safety representatives have, but are more limited – for instance, there is not the right to carry out inspections of the workplace. They apply where there is no union, or the union is not recognised in a workplace, or with regard to a particular group of workers.

13.9   Duties of Owners and Occupiers

Section 4 of *HSWA 1974* states the general duties of owners, occupiers and others who have control of premises and sets out requirements concerning places of work. Such persons must ensure that premises and plant and machinery under their control may be used without risks to health and safety.

13.10   Employees' Duties

Section 7 of *HSWA 1974* sets out that every employee must take reasonable care for the health and safety of himself and other people at work. If there is a legal requirement on an employer to do certain things for reasons of health and safety, then the employee must co-operate with the employer to enable the employer to fulfil his legal duty.

Section 8 of *HSWA 1974* prohibits interference by anyone with anything provided in the interests of health and safety at work.

13.11 Approved Codes of Practice ('ACoPs')

Codes of Practice do not have the same legal force as the health and safety regulations themselves, but they are considered 'admissible evidence' in criminal proceedings for contravention of a provision for which an associated Code of Practice is in force. They often set out the requirements in more detail than the regulations. Failing to follow a Code of Practice is not an offence in itself, but an employer will need to demonstrate that equally effective methods have been adopted to signal compliance with the law.

13.12 Guidance Notes

Guidance notes are prepared by the HSE on various health and safety topics in the following subject areas:

- medical;
- environmental hygiene;
- chemical safety;
- plant and machinery;
- general.

While guidance notes do not have any legal force, if an employer does not warn employees of dangers referred to in the notes, then the employee may be able to prove negligence in a civil claim for damages. Guidance notes are useful documents because they set out safe procedures to be followed when using certain substances or items of equipment. (For information on obtaining copies of HSE publications see **13.5** above.)

13.13 Risk Assessment and Management

At a Glance
* Employers must carry out a 'suitable and sufficient' risk assessment, which must be recorded where there are five or more people employed.
* Employers must implement preventative and protective measures.
* There must be adequate arrangements for the effective planning, organisation, control and monitoring of health and safety measures.
* Health surveillance is required where an identifiable and detectable condition related to the work is likely to occur, and surveillance is likely to increase the protection of employees.
* Competent staff must be appointed to assist with health and safety.

Health and Safety

* Procedures for serious and imminent risk, specifying the circumstances under which employees can stop work, must be established.
* Employees must be provided with comprehensive and relevant health and safety information.
* Employers in shared workplaces must co-operate and co-ordinate health and safety measures.
* Temporary workers must be provided with information on the necessary skills needed to carry out work safely.
* Employers must assess the risks to the health and safety of new and expectant mothers.
* Employers must protect the health and safety of young workers.

The *Management of Health and Safety at Work Regulations 1999* (*SI 1999/3242*) came into force in December 1999, replacing the 1992 Regulations and incorporating other earlier amending regulations concerning new and expectant mothers and young workers.

The Regulations were amended to allow employees and employers to claim damages for breaches of the Regulations. Employees can now claim damages from their employer in a civil action, where they suffer injury or illness as a result of the employer breaching the Regulations. Employers can bring actions against employees for breach of their duties under the Regulations.

As a result of the *Management of Health and Safety at Work (Amendment) Regulations 2006* (*SI 2006/438*), which came into force on 6 April 2006, *regulation 22* of the *Management of Health and Safety at Work Regulations 1999* has been amended to exclude the right of third parties to seek damages from employees in breach of their duties under these Regulations. The effect of this amendment is to extend the same protection to employees regarding third party liability, as already applies to employers.

These Regulations clarify what employers must do to comply with their duties under *HSWA 1974*. The main requirements are for employers to:

* carry out risk assessments;
* make and record arrangements for implementing the health and safety measures identified as being necessary by the risk assessment;
* appoint competent people to help implement the health and safety arrangements;
* establish emergency procedures;
* provide understandable information and adequate training to employees; and
* co-ordinate on health and safety measures with other employers sharing the same workplace.

13.14   Risk Assessments

A central requirement of the Regulations is the carrying out of a 'suitable and sufficient' risk assessment (*SI 1999/3242, reg 3*), in order to decide what health and safety measures are needed, where there are five or more people employed. This should 'involve management, whether or not advisors or consultants assist', although, according to the Approved Code of Practice, specialist advice may be necessary.

The definition of 'suitable and sufficient' is further explained in the Code of Practice, which gives guidance on compliance with *SI 1999/3242*. This indicates that the level of detail in the risk assessment should be determined by the risks and that there is no need to evaluate those that are trivial. The risk assessment must be recorded where there are five or more people employed.

A free leaflet, *Five Steps to Risk Assessment*, providing simple and practical guidance, has been produced by the HSE. The five steps which should be followed are as follows.

Checklist

☐ look for the hazards;

☐ consider who may be harmed;

☐ consider how would they be harmed;

☐ evaluate the risks and decide whether or not more precautions should be taken; and

☐ record the findings and revise it as necessary.

The leaflet contains a list of useful publications and a basic form for conducting risk assessments which employers can use or adapt for their own circumstances. (For information on obtaining copies of HSE publications see **13.5** above.)

13.15 Preventative and Protective Measures

Employers must implement any preventative and protective measures on the basis of the following principles (*SI 1992/3242, reg 4*):

- avoiding risks;
- evaluating risks that cannot be avoided;
- combating risks at source;
- adapting the work to the individual, particularly with regard to workplace design, the choice of work equipment and working and production methods, with a view to alleviating monotonous work and work at a predetermined work-rate;
- adapting to technical progress;
- replacing the dangerous with safe or safer alternatives;
- developing a coherent overall prevention policy covering technology, work organisation, working conditions, social relationships, and the working environment;

Health and Safety

- giving priority to collective over individual protective measures; and
- giving appropriate instructions to employees.

13.16   Health and Safety Arrangements

Regulation 5 of *SI 1999/3242* requires employers to ensure that adequate arrangements are in place regarding 'effective planning, organisation, control, monitoring and review of protective and preventative measures'.

These arrangements, as in the case of the risk assessment, must be in writing where there are five or more employees. Employers already have to produce a written safety policy under *section 2(3)* of *HSWA 1974* (see **13.5** above).

13.17   Serious and Imminent Danger

Procedures for serious and imminent risk, including specifying the circumstances in which employees can stop work or take other remedial action, must be established (*SI 1999/3242, reg 8*).

Also, a sufficient number of competent personnel, who have sufficient training and experience, must be nominated to implement the procedures. Again, these procedures must normally be written down.

Employers must arrange any necessary contacts with external services, particularly with regard to first-aid, emergency medical care and rescue work (*SI 1999/3242, reg 9*).

13.18   Health Surveillance

Regulation 6 of *SI 1999/3242* requires employers to carry out health surveillance 'as is appropriate having regard to' the risks to the health and safety of employees as revealed by the risk assessment.

Health surveillance should be carried out according to the Approved Code of Practice where:

- there is an identifiable condition related to the work;
- the condition is detectable;
- it is likely that the condition could occur; and
- surveillance is likely to further protection of the health of the employees to be covered.

The HSE publication, *Health Surveillance at Work* HSG61, describes what is meant by health surveillance and how this differs from other means of monitoring employee health, runs through the principles of carrying out effective health surveillance programmes and outlines good practice (for information on obtaining copies of HSE publications see **13.5** above).

13.19   Competent Staff

Under *regulation 7* of *SI 1999/3242* employers are required to appoint competent staff to assist in ensuring that the protective and preventative measures identified as necessary by the assessment are established. Competent employees should be appointed in preference to external sources for health and safety advice and assistance.

13.20 Training and Information

Regulation 10 of *SI 1999/3242* states that employees must be provided with specific 'comprehensible and relevant' information. *Your Health and Safety: A Guide for Workers,* which covers what employers must tell employees, is available from HSE Books (see **13.5** above).

Employers and the self-employed sharing the same workplace must co-operate and co-ordinate safety measures (*SI 1999/3242, reg 11*) in order to ensure that health and safety legislation is complied with, and that all employees on the site are informed of the risks to health and safety from all the work activities taking place.

In addition, *SI 1999/3242, reg 12* requires employers to ensure that any contract workers are provided with information about the risks and the health and safety measures taken.

Regulation 13 of *SI 1999/3242* requires employers to provide health and safety training, during working hours, for new recruits and where there are new or increased risks. This may be where, for example, new equipment has been introduced, or there is a change in work organisation. They must also take account of workers' capabilities.

13.21 Temporary Workers

The Regulations also require employers to provide information on the necessary occupational qualifications or skills needed to carry out the work safely (and to carry out any necessary health surveillance) to workers on fixed-term contracts (*SI 1999/3242, reg 15*).

13.22 New and Expectant Mothers

Where the workforce includes women of childbearing age, the employer must also assess how any hazards might specifically affect the health and safety of new or expectant mothers (*SI 1992/3242, reg 16*). Where a woman has provided written notification of her condition, the employer must arrange to alter her working conditions or working hours where the risks cannot be controlled by other means. This may mean suspending that woman from work on full pay for as long as necessary to avoid the risks. New or expectant mothers may also be suspended from night work where they have a signed certificate from a registered medical practitioner or midwife stating that this is necessary.

In *Hardman v Mallon [2002] IRLR 516*, the Employment Appeal Tribunal held that a failure to carry out a risk assessment in respect of a pregnant woman, as required by the *Management Regulations* (*SI 1999/3242*), is sex discrimination.

Guidance to help employers ensure that pregnant women are provided with a safe and healthy workplace has been published by the HSE. This outlines that employers must carry out a proper risk assessment to identify potential hazards to pregnant workers. *New and Expectant Mothers at Work, a Guide for Employers* is strongly supported by the Equal Opportunities Commission (EOC) and the baby charity, Tommy's. It gives detailed advice on the possible chemical, physical and biological risks to new and expectant mothers, and is available from HSE Books, price £9.50.

The *Employment Rights Act 1996* requires that any alternative work offered under the Regulations must be suitable and appropriate and on terms and conditions no less favourable than her normal terms and conditions.

13.23   Young Workers

Employers have to protect young workers from risks to their health and safety arising from lack of experience or maturity (*SI 1999/3242, reg 19*) and must not employ a young person for work:

- which is beyond their physical or psychological capacity;
- which involves harmful exposure to radiation or toxins or carcinogens which chronically affect human health;
- which involves the risk of accidents which may not be recognised or avoided by young people by virtue of their inexperience; or
- where there is a risk to health from extreme cold or heat, noise or vibration.

In addition, the *Children (Protection at Work) Regulations 1998* (*SI 1998/276*) control the working time of children aged 14 and 15.

Young People at Work: A Guide for Employers explains employers' duties to protect the health and safety of young people at work and offers specific guidance on risks young people are likely to encounter (for information on obtaining copies of HSE publications see **13.5** above).

13.24   Approved Code of Practice

Copies of *Management of Health and Safety at Work: Approved Code of Practice* are available from HSE Books (see **13.5** above).

13.25   **Workplace Safety**
13.26   Workplace (Health, Safety and Welfare) Regulations 1992

The *Workplace (Health, Safety and Welfare) Regulations 1992* (*SI 1992/3004*) apply to virtually all fixed workplaces and lay down a wide range of requirements relating to the structure and organisation of the workplace, repair, maintenance, housekeeping, and facilities for staff.

13.27 Employers' Duties and Industry-specific Legislation

Under the Regulations, employers must ensure that workplaces comply with the requirements set out in the following paragraphs. The HSE produces a free leaflet entitled *Workplace Health, Safety and Welfare: A Short Guide for Managers* summarising the legal requirements and providing practical advice on general workplace health and safety (further relevant HSE publications are noted in italics – for information on obtaining copies see **13.5** above).

- **Health**
  - Ventilation – *General Ventilation in the Workplace: Guidance for Employers*
  - Temperature – *Thermal Comfort in the Workplace: Guidance for Employers; Heat stress in the workplace: What you need to know as an employer.*
  - Lighting – *Lighting at Work*
  - Cleanliness and waste materials
  - Room dimensions and space
  - Workstations and seating – *Seating at Work*
- **Safety**
  - Workplace equipment, devices and systems
  - Floors and traffic routes
  - Falls or falling objects
  - Transparent surfaces
  - Windows, skylights and ventilators
  - Safe cleaning of windows and skylights
  - Organisation of traffic routes – *Workplace Transport Safety: An Employer's Guide*
  - Doors and gates
  - Escalators and moving walkways
- **Welfare**
  - Sanitary conveniences
  - Washing facilities
  - Drinking water
  - Accommodation for clothing
  - Facilities for changing clothes
  - Facilities for rest and to eat meals

In February 2006, MPs voted in favour of a total ban on smoking in all enclosed public spaces in England. The ban is expected to take effect in summer 2007. In Scotland, the *Smoking, Health and Social Care (Scotland) Act*, which bans smoking in enclosed public places such as workplaces, pubs and restaurants, came into effect in March 2006. In Northern Ireland, a ban came into force in April 2006. The Welsh Assembly has also agreed to a ban in principle.

Work at height

Regulations applying to all work at height where there is a risk of a fall liable to cause personal injury came into force in April 2005. The new Regulations remove the old division between low and high falls, abolishing the 'two-metre rule'. Falls from any height must be prevented.

The Regulations do not ban ladders, as has been rumoured in some industries, but they do require that they are only used when all other safer alternatives for work at height have been ruled out, and they must be used sensibly. A risk assessment must show that the task is low risk and of short duration, or that there are site features that mean other equipment is not appropriate. If so, then ladders can be used.

There are also regulations which apply in particular types of workplaces and industries, such as construction sites, the railway industry, the offshore industry, the nuclear industry, mines and quarries. For more information on these, visit the Health and Safety Executive website at www.hse.gov.uk.

13.28   Fire Precautions Legislation

At a Glance
* Employers must carry out an assessment of the risk of fire and take steps to deal with any fire risks in the workplace.
* A fire certificate is required if there are more than 20 people employed in the premises, or there are more than 10 people working elsewhere than on the ground floor.
* A fire alarm system and a protected means of escape must also be provided in premises with a fire certificate.
* All employees should receive fire instructions at least once, and preferably twice a year.

The main legislation concerning fire safety in workplaces is the *Fire Precautions Act 1971,* the *Fire Precautions (Workplace) Regulations 1997* (*SI 1997/1840*) and the *Management of Health and Safety at Work Regulations 1999* (*SI 1999/ 3242*). In addition, the *Building Regulations 1991* (*SI 1991/2768*) apply to buildings being built and to major alterations to existing buildings.

13.29   *Fire Certificates*

Under the *Fire Precautions Act 1971*, certain types of premises are 'designated' and require a fire certificate. This includes most types of workplace – offices, shops and railway premises, factories, hotels and hostels have all been designated. These require a fire certificate where more than 20 people are working in the premises, or where there are more than ten people working elsewhere than on the ground floor. This applies whether or not there are different employers.

The fire certificate covers escape routes, location of fire fighting equipment, fire safety signs, testing and maintenance of equipment, fire drills, training and limits on the number of occupants.

13.30   *Fire Precautions (Workplace) Regulations 1997*

The *Fire Precautions (Workplace) Regulations 1997* (*SI 1997/1840*) require employers and those in control of workplaces to determine and provide the necessary measures, having regard to the specific circumstances of the workplace, needed to meet the risks of fire.

Checklist

Employers must:

☐ ensure the workplace is equipped with appropriate firefighting equipment, fire detectors and alarms and that any non-automatic firefighting equipment is readily accessible, easy to use and indicated by signs (*SI 1997/1840, reg 4*);

☐ take measures for firefighting, nominate and train employees to implement those measures, and arrange contacts with external emergency services (*SI 1997/1840, reg 4*);

☐ keep emergency routes and exits clear and ensure that they lead as directly as possible to a place of safety (*SI 1997/1840, reg 5*);

☐ have a suitable system of maintenance for fire precautions in relations to the workplace, equipment and devices (*SI 1997/1840, reg 4*).

The *Fire Precautions (Workplace) Regulations 1997* were amended in order to remove the so-called 'civil liability exclusion' to allow employees to claim damages from their employer where they have suffered injury or illness as a result of their employer breaching the regulations. Employers can bring actions against employees for breach of their duties under the Regulations.

Regulatory Reform Order

Fire safety legislation, which is currently spread over 120 Acts, will be simplified, rationalised and consolidated, using a regulatory reform order. One simple risk-based fire regime, applying to all buildings which the public might use (except for private dwellings) will be created in order to remove the confusion caused by current overlapping regimes.

The *Regulatory Reform (Fire Safety) Order* will take effect on 1 October 2006, not in April 2006 as had previously been announced. A series of guides will also be published to assist those preparing fire risk assessments. More information on these is available at www.firesafetyguides.odpm.gov.uk.

The main effect of the changes will be a move towards greater emphasis on fire prevention in all non-domestic premises, including the voluntary sector and self-employed people with premises separate from their homes. Fire certificates will be abolished and will cease to have legal status. The *Fire Safety Order* will apply in England and Wales. Northern Ireland and Scotland will have their own laws.

Responsibility for complying with the *Fire Safety Order* will rest with the 'responsible person'. In a workplace, this is the employer and any other person

Health and Safety

who may have control of any part of the premises, eg the occupier or owner. In all other premises the person or people in control of the premises will be responsible.

If there is more than one responsible person in any type of premises, all must take all reasonable steps to work with each other.

The responsible person will have to carry out a fire risk assessment which must focus on the safety in case of fire of all 'relevant persons'. It should pay particular attention to those at special risk, such as the disabled and those with special needs, and must include consideration of any dangerous substances likely to be on the premises.

The fire risk assessment will help to identify risks that can be removed or reduced, and to decide the nature and extent of the general fire precautions needed to protect people against the fire risks that remain. If five or more people are employed, the significant findings of the assessment must be recorded. The new rules will be enforced by the local fire and rescue service authority who will carry out regular inspections, with top priority going to those premises presenting most risk to the community.

As *Finance Director's Handbook* went to press, the *Regulatory Reform Order* was not yet in force. For the latest information on fire safety law, visit the Office of the Deputy Prime Minister website at www.odpm.gov.uk and follow the links to fire safety law.

13.31   *Regulations Covering Electricity and Gas at Work*

The *Electricity at Work Regulations 1989* (*SI 1989/635*) are concerned with the prevention of danger from electric shock and burn, electrical explosion or arcing, or from fire or explosion. The *Gas Safety (Installation and Use) Regulations 1998* (*SI 1998/2451*) contain requirements relating to gas fittings, meters and regulators, installation pipework, gas appliances, maintenance and miscellaneous provisions.

13.32   The Control of Noise at Work Regulations 2005

At a Glance

Employers must:

* Assess the risks to their employees from noise at work.
* Take action to reduce the noise exposure that produces those risks.
* Provide their employees with hearing protection if they cannot reduce the noise exposure enough through other methods (making hearing protection available on request at 80 dB and ensuring it is worn at 85 dB).
* Make sure the legal limits on noise exposure (87 dB daily or weekly exposure or peak sound pressure of 140 dB taking account of hearing protection) are not exceeded.
* Provide employees with information, instruction and training.
* Carry out health surveillance where there is a risk to health.

The main provisions of the Regulations are as follows.

Regulation 4 sets out:

- lower exposure action values – the lower of the two levels of daily or weekly personal noise exposure or of peak sound pressure which, if reached, or exceeded, require specified action to be taken to reduce risk;
- upper exposure action values – the higher of the two levels of daily or weekly personal exposure or of peak sound pressure, which if reached or exceeded, require specified action to be taken to reduce risk;
- exposure limit values – the level of daily or weekly personal noise exposure or of peak sound pressure, which must not be exceeded; and
- peak sound pressure – the maximum sound pressure to which an employee is exposed:

The lower exposure action values are:

- a daily or weekly personal noise exposure of 80 dB (A);
- a peak sound pressure of 135 dB (C).

The upper exposure action values are:

- a daily or weekly personal noise exposure of 85 dB (A);
- a peak sound pressure of 137 dB (C).

The exposure limit values are:

- a daily or weekly personal noise exposure of 87 dB (A);
- a peak sound pressure of 140 dB (C).

Where the exposure of an employee to noise varies markedly from day to day, the employer may use the weekly personal noise exposure instead.

In applying the exposure limit values – but not the lower and upper exposure action values – account must be taken of any personal hearing protection provided.

Regulation 5 requires a suitable and sufficient assessment of the risk to health and safety created by exposure to noise at the workplace, where the work is liable to expose any employees to noise at or above a lower exposure action value. This should identify the measures that need to be taken to comply with the Regulations.

The employer must assess whether any employees are likely to be exposed to noise at, or above, a lower exposure action value, an upper exposure action value or an exposure limit value.

Regulation 6 requires the elimination of exposure to noise at work, or where this is not reasonably practicable, reduced to as low a level as is reasonably practicable. If an employee is likely to be exposed to noise at or above the upper exposure action value, exposure must be reduced to as low a level as reasonably practicable, through a programme of organisational and technical measures – not personal hearing protectors.

The employer must ensure that employees are not exposed to noise above an exposure limit value. If an exposure limit value is exceeded, the employer must immediately reduce exposure to noise below the exposure limit value, identify the reason, and modify organisational and technical measures to prevent it being exceeded again.

Noise in rest facilities, where these are provided, must be reduced to a level suitable for their purposes and conditions of use.

Regulation 7 outlines the requirements regarding hearing protection. Where employees are likely to be exposed to noise at or above a lower exposure action value, personal hearing protection must be available to these employees on request. Personal hearing protection must be provided where an employee is likely to be exposed to noise below an upper exposure action value, where the employer is unable to reduce the levels of noise by other means.

If there is likely to be exposure at or above an upper exposure action value in any area of the workplace, this must be designated a hearing protection zone, demarcated and identified by a sign indicating that ear protection must be worn.

Regulation 8 requires that equipment is fully and properly used, and is maintained in an efficient state, in efficient working order, and in good repair.

Employees must make full and proper use of personal hearing protectors provided by the employer, and report any defects in control measures or personal hearing protectors.

Regulation 9 requires that health surveillance, including hearing testing, should be carried out where a risk assessment indicates that there is a risk to the health of employees who are, or are liable to be, exposed to noise.

Regulation 10 deals with information, instruction and training where employees are exposed to noise likely to be at or above a lower exposure action value.

The HSE has produced new guidance, *Noise at Work – Guidance for Employers on the Control of Noise at Work Regulations 2005*, which is available free from the HSE.

Vibration

Regulations controlling the risks from vibration at work came into force in July 2005 as a result of the *European Physical Agents (Vibration) Directive (Directive 2002/44)*, which deals with the control of diseases caused by vibration at work from equipment, vehicles and machines.

The *Control of Vibration at Work Regulations 2005* require employers to take action to prevent their employees from developing diseases caused by exposure to vibration at work from equipment, vehicles and machines.

Two types of vibration hazard are covered by the Regulations:

- Hand-arm vibration, which affects people who use hand-held or hand-guided power tools and those workers holding materials that vibrate when fed into machines. Long-term exposure to high levels of hand-arm vibration can lead to a range of disabling conditions including vibration white finger, permanent loss of feeling in the fingers and painful joints in the hands, wrists and arms; and
- Whole-body vibration, which occurs when people are sitting or standing on industrial machines or moving vehicles which transmit vibration and shocks into the operator. Long-term exposure to high levels of whole-body vibration is associated with low back pain.

The Regulations specify daily levels of vibration exposure where employers are required to take action to control risks (the exposure action values); and where they must prevent further daily exposure (the exposure limit values).

13.33   Manual Handling Operations Regulations 1992

At a Glance
* Manual handling includes carrying, lifting, pushing, pulling and holding loads.
* Loads include people and animals.
* The first priority is to avoid the need for manual handling operations.
* If manual handling operations that carry a risk of injury are carried out, a risk assessment must be carried out, and the risks reduced as far as reasonably practicable.
* Workers carrying out manual handling with risk of injury must be provided with training and information about the weight of the load.

The *Manual Handling Operations Regulations 1992* (*SI 1992/2793*) put the emphasis on the need for employers to assess the risk of injury from the manual handling of loads and establish a clear hierarchy of prevention and control measures:

* manual handling should be avoided where reasonably practicable;
* where it is not reasonably practicable to avoid the need for manual handling, a suitable and sufficient assessment of manual handling operations must be carried out;
* where it is not reasonably practicable for manual handling operations to be avoided and there is risk of injury, employers must take appropriate steps to reduce the risk of injury to the lowest level reasonably practicable.

Where risk of injury remains, the employer must take appropriate steps (such as training) to provide employees with general indications, and, where reasonably practicable, precise information, on the weight of the load, and the heaviest side of any load where the centre of gravity is not positioned centrally.

In *Swain v Denso Martin Ltd, The Times, 24 April 2000*, the Court of Appeal ruled that the fact that an employer had failed to carry out a risk assessment did not mean that he was not under a duty to take steps to give information about the weight of a load where there was a risk of injury.

In *Sussex Ambulance NHS Trust v King [2002] EWCA Civ 953*, the Court of Appeal allowed an appeal by Sussex Ambulance Trust against an order giving judgment against them for £34,000 for injuries sustained by one of their ambulance technicians when carrying a patient downstairs. The judges took into account the difficulties the ambulance service had reconciling its duties towards a patient with their duties towards their employees.

Health and Safety

In a 2002 Court of Appeal case, *O'Neill v DSG Retail Ltd, Times Law Reports, 9 September 2002,* it was held that an employer required to take appropriate steps to reduce a risk of injury to the lowest level reasonably practicable, must in assessing the risk, consider the particular task, the context of where it is performed and the employee required to perform it.

And the High Court ruled in a case involving East Sussex County Council *[2003] EWHC 167 (Admin)* that a manual handling policy that simply bans all manual lifting is unlikely to be lawful.

Copies of *Manual Handling: Guidance on Regulations* (L23) are available from HSE Books (see **13.5** above).

13.34 Control of Substances Hazardous to Health Regulations 2002 and Other Regulations Controlling Hazardous Substances

At a Glance
* Employers must carry out an assessment of the risks to health from exposure to any hazardous substance in the workplace.
* Hazardous substances should be eliminated from the workplace where reasonably practicable, or safer substitutes used.
* If hazardous substances are used, or arise, control measures should be used to prevent or control the risk.
* Personal protective clothing or equipment should only be used as a last resort, if no other method of control is appropriate.
* Adequate control relies on compliance with workplace exposure limits.
* The Regulations apply to both chemical and biological agents, whether or not exposure to such biological agents is deliberate, such as for laboratory workers, or incidental, for sewage workers, cleaners and farmers.
* In certain circumstances, employers must draw up detailed procedures for dealing with accidents, incidents and emergencies that involve hazardous substances.

Under the Regulations, employers must carry out an assessment of the risks to health from exposure to any hazardous substances in the workplace (*SI 2002/2677, reg 6*).

If there are risks to health, the employer must work through a hierarchy of prevention and control measures (*SI 2002/2677, reg 7*):

* elimination; or (where this is not practicable)
* substitution with a less hazardous substance, or the same substance in a less hazardous form; then
* use of control measures (eg local exhaust ventilation); and (if no other method of control is possible)
* provision of personal protective clothing.

Workplace exposure limits

Adequate control relies on complying with workplace exposure limits (WELs), which have now replaced maximum exposure limits (MELs) and Occupational Exposure Standards (OESs). All MELs, and most OESs, are transferred into the new system as WELs and retain their previous numerical values.

Existing requirements to follow good practice have been clarified and brought together by the introduction of eight principles in the *Control of Substances Hazardous to Health (Amendment) Regulations 2004*, which came into effect in April 2005.

These are:

- design and operate processes and activities to minimise emission, release and spread of substances hazardous to health;
- take into account all relevant routes of exposure – inhalation, skin absorption and ingestion – when developing control measures;
- control exposure by measures that are proportionate to the health risk;
- choose the most effective and reliable control options which minimise the escape and spread of substances hazardous to health;
- where adequate control of exposure cannot be achieved by other means, provide, in combination with other control measures, suitable personal protective equipment;
- check and review regularly all elements of control measures for their continuing effectiveness;
- inform and train all employees on the hazards and risks from the substances with which they work and the use of control measures developed to minimise the risks; and
- ensure that the introduction of control measures does not increase the overall risk to health and safety.

In certain circumstances, employers must draw up detailed procedures for dealing with accidents, incidents and emergencies that involve hazardous substances.

Dugmore v Swansea NHS Trust and Morriston NHS Trust [2003] IRLR 164 showed that employers have an absolute duty to adequately control exposure to substances hazardous to health, where this cannot be prevented. The qualification of reasonable practicability applies only to prevention, and not to the secondary duty of control.

And in *Coxall v Goodyear [2002] IRLR 742*, which was heard in the Court of Appeal, it was found that an employer's failure to follow its doctor's advice to move, or dismiss, an asthmatic employee from a job causing harm was a breach of duty.

Code of Practice L5 *Control of Substances Hazardous to Health Regulations 2002 (Fifth Edition) Approved Code of Practice and Guidance* has been published by the HSE and is available from HSE Books.

Other guidance includes *COSHH Essentials: Easy steps to control chemicals, Control of Substances Hazardous to Health* and *COSHH – A Brief Guide to the Regulations* which sets out in simple step-by-step approach eight basic steps employers must take to control exposure to hazardous substances to prevent ill health. The guide can be ordered from HSE Books.

There are also a number of more specific regulations covering hazardous substances. For example, the *Chemicals (Hazard Information and Packaging for Supply) Regulations 2002* contain the requirements concerning labelling and preparing safety data sheets, the *Control of Major Accident Hazard Regulations 1999* cover workplaces using, storing and producing large quantities of hazardous substances, and there are regulations covering asbestos, lead, legionnaires' disease, explosives and the transport of dangerous substances, for example. For more information on these, visit the Health and Safety Executive website at www.hse.gov.uk.

13.35 Plant, Machinery and Equipment

13.36 Provision and Use of Work Equipment Regulations 1998

The *Provision and Use of Work Equipment Regulations 1998* (*SI 1998/2306*) govern the selection and operation of machinery, tools and equipment, and aim to ensure the safe provision and safe use of work equipment in all industry sectors.

The definition of 'work equipment' covers machinery, appliances, apparatus, tools and any assembly of components which function as a whole. 'Use' covers starting, stopping, modifying, programming, setting, transporting, maintaining, servicing and cleaning.

Checklist

Under the Regulations employers must comply with the following general requirements:

☐ ensure that work equipment is constructed or adapted so as to be suitable for the task for which it will be used (*SI 1998/2306, reg 4*);

☐ take into account the working conditions and hazards when selecting equipment (*SI 1998/2306, reg 4*);

☐ ensure that work equipment is maintained in an efficient state, in efficient working order and in good repair and keep any maintenance logs on machinery (*SI 1998/2306, reg 5*);

☐ where the safety of work equipment depends on the installation conditions, ensure that it is inspected after installation and before being put into service for the first time, or after assembly at a new site or in a new location (*SI 1998/2306, reg 6*);

☐ where there are specific risks involved, ensure that use is restricted to those given the task of using it – repair, modification, servicing and maintenance work must be carried out by those designated to perform such work and who have received adequate training (*SI 1998/2306, reg 7*);

☐ ensure that appropriate information, instruction and training is given to employees and any supervisors or managers who are responsible for work equipment used at work (*SI 1998/2306, regs 8, 9*); and

☐ ensure that work equipment complies with any relevant EU Directives (*SI 1998/2306, reg 10*).

Employers must also ensure that the work equipment complies with the more specific requirements outlined in *SI 1998/2306, regs 11–24*. These concern:

- dangerous parts of machinery (*SI 1998/2306, reg 11*);
- protection against specified hazards (*SI 1998/2306, reg 12*);
- high or very low temperatures (*SI 1998/2306, reg 13*);
- control systems and devices (*SI 1998/2306, regs 14–18*);
- isolation from sources of energy (*SI 1998/2306, reg 19*);
- stability (*SI 1998/2306, reg 20*);
- lighting (*SI 1998/2306, reg 21*);
- maintenance operations (*SI 1998/2306, reg 22*);
- markings (*SI 1998/2306, reg 23*); and
- warnings (*SI 1998/2306, reg 24*).

In *Junttan Oy v Bristol Magistrates Court [2002] EWHC (Admin) 566; [2002] 2 CMLF 37*, a company argued that the magistrates court had no jurisdiction to hear the case because the HSE had breached a European Machinery Directive by instigating proceedings under the *Health and Safety at Work etc. Act 1974,* where the maximum penalty for a breach is a fine of up to £20,000, rather than the *Supply of Machinery (Safety) Regulations 1992 (SI 1992/3073)*, which implemented the Directive, where the maximum penalty for a breach is £5,000.

The HSE admitted that it had failed to follow the procedure under article 7 of the machinery directive for withdrawing dangerous machinery from the market and reporting it to the European Commission, but the High Court said that this was not a bar on prosecution. The judge said that it could not have been intended that article 7 should prevent a prosecution where a manufacturer of machinery may have committed a criminal offence, and he ruled that it had no relevance to enforcement action involving criminal proceedings.

However, he said that the HSE should have prosecuted under the regulations, which provided for a specific statutory offence rather than using section 6 of the Act, even though the penalties were lower.

Simple Guide to the Provision and Use of Work Equipment Regulations 1998 (INDG291) is available from HSE Books (see **13.5** above).

Health and Safety

13.37 Lifting Operations and Lifting Equipment Regulations 1998

Under the *Lifting Operations and Lifting Equipment Regulations 1998* (*SI 1998/2307*), dutyholders have the choice to have their lifting equipment thoroughly examined by a competent person at the intervals set out in the Regulations – six months for equipment for lifting people and accessories (eg hooks and eyebolts) and twelve months for other lifting equipment. Alternatively, an examination scheme can be drawn up and intervals set for thorough examination based on a risk assessment.

Simple Guide to the Lifting Operations and Lifting Equipment Regulations *1998* (INDG290) is available from HSE books (see **13.5** above).

13.38 Personal Protective Equipment

The *Personal Protective Equipment at Work Regulations 1992* (*SI 1992/2966*) lay down the type and standard of personal protective equipment ('PPE') to be used when risks cannot be otherwise avoided.

The Regulations state that PPE means 'all equipment (including clothing affording protection against the weather) which is intended to be worn or held by a person at work which protects him against one or more risks to health and safety, and any addition or accessory designed to meet that objective'. This includes weatherproof clothing and safety footwear, but excludes ordinary working clothes which do not protect the health and safety of the user.

Checklist

Employers must:

☐ ensure that suitable PPE is provided to employees where risks to health and safety have not been adequately controlled by other means (the guidance makes it clear that PPE is a 'last resort') (*SI 1992/2966, reg 4*);

☐ ensure that where more than one type of PPE is necessary, the equipment is compatible (*SI 1992/2966, reg 5*);

☐ carry out an assessment before choosing PPE to ensure it is suitable (*SI 1992/2966, regs 6, 7*);

☐ provide safe storage facilities for PPE (*SI 1992/2966, reg 8*);

☐ provide information, instruction and training about the risks the PPE will avoid or limit, and how the PPE should be used and any action the employee must take to ensure that it remains in good repair and efficient working order (*SI 1992/2966, reg 9*); and

☐ ensure that PPE is being used properly by employees (*SI 1992/2966, reg 10*).

Regulation 10 of SI 1992/2966 says that employees must use the PPE as trained to do so, and must report any loss or defect (*SI 1992/2966, reg 11*). By virtue of *section 9 of HSWA 1974* no charge can be made to the worker for the provision of PPE which is only to be used at work.

In *Fytche v Wincanton Logistics plc [2004] IRLR 817*, a tanker driver had been issued with safety boots with steel toecaps to protect his feet from heavy objects falling on them. His tanker became stuck in snow, and as he dug it free, one boot leaked through a tiny hole. He suffered frostbite and part of his toe had to be amputated as a result.

He claimed that because the boots had steel toecaps, they were personal protective equipment and the hole meant that the employers were in breach of their duty under the Regulations to keep such equipment in good repair. However, his claim was rejected in the county court, High Court and Court of Appeal, on the grounds that the Regulations only require the employer to maintain or repair so as to guard against the risk for which it was supplied.

The House of Lords agreed. It held that the duty to keep PPE efficient and in good repair was not an absolute duty. It was held that the duty only related to the purpose of protecting against the relevant risk, and not to any other risks which might arise. One of the judges said that the implications of a decision which went the other way would have meant that employers could be held liable for risks that could not reasonably have been foreseen.

A free HSE leaflet entitled *A Short Guide to the Personal Protective Equipment at Work Regulations 1992* sets out the requirements in relation to employees and the self-employed and gives advice on assessing suitable PPE, training and maintenance (for information on obtaining copies of HSE publications see **13.5** above).

13.39   Display Screen Equipment

The *Health and Safety (Display Screen Equipment) Regulations 1992* ('*VDU Regulations*') (*SI 1992/2792*) require employers to analyse workstations used by users or operators to assess the health and safety risks inherent in use, and to reduce the risks to the lowest extent reasonably practicable. A display screen equipment user is defined as 'an employee who habitually uses display screen equipment as a significant part of his normal work'. The workstation definition applies to the furniture used in connection with the visual display unit ('VDU') as well as to the equipment itself.

The Regulations define display screen equipment (DSE) as 'any alphanumeric or graphic display screen regardless of the display process involved'. A European Court of Justice case, *Dietrich v Westdeutscher Rundfunk (OJ C 302, 21 October 2000)* involved a film cutter and ruled that the term 'graphic display screen' had to be interpreted to include screens displaying film recordings.

13.40   *Daily Work Routines*

The employer must plan work activities so that 'daily work on display screen equipment is periodically interrupted by such breaks or changes of activity as reduce their workload at that equipment' (*SI 1992/2792, reg 4*).

13.41   *Eyesight Tests*

Regulation 5 of *SI 1992/2792* obliges employers to provide users who so request it with an appropriate eye and eyesight test (which includes a test of vision and examination of the eye by a registered ophthalmic optician or a registered medical practitioner) before starting VDU work, at regular intervals, and if they experience visual difficulties attributable to the work.

If normal corrective appliances cannot be used, and 'special corrective appliances' (ie lenses prescribed specifically for VDU work) are necessary, the cost of the eye tests and any lenses prescribed for VDU work must be met by the employer.

13.42   *Training Requirements*

Regulation 6 of *SI 1992/2792* covers the provision of training and says that employers must provide health and safety training, and retraining where the workstation is substantially modified. Under *regulation 7* of *SI 1992/2792*, users must be provided with adequate information on all aspects of safety and health relating to their workstation and measures taken to comply with the *VDU Regulations*.

13.43   *Guidance for Conducting Risk Assessments*

The guidance *Working with VDUs* was revised by the HSE and takes account of minor changes in the law that came into effect as a result of the *Health and Safety (Miscellaneous Amendments) Regulations 2002* (*SI 2002/2174*). Other HSE guidance, *The Law on VDUs – an Easy Guide* was also revised.

13.44   **Working Hours**

At a Glance
* The maximum working week is 48 hours unless a worker has voluntarily 'opted out' and agreed in writing to work more than this.
* The maximum a night worker can work is eight hours' night work.
* Night workers are entitled to a free health assessment.
* Workers are entitled to:
    ○ a daily rest period of 11 hours;
    ○ a day off each week; and
    ○ a rest break of at least 20 minutes, if working more than six hours.
* Workers are also entitled to a minimum of four weeks' paid annual leave.
* There are a number of excluded sectors and groups of workers.

The majority of workers are legally entitled to a maximum working week, paid holidays, and to breaks and rest periods, as a result of the *Working Time*

Regulations 1998 (*SI 1998/1833*) which came into force on 1 October 1998. Most UK employees have the right to:

- a maximum working week of not more than 48 hours, including overtime;
- a maximum of eight hours' night work;
- a daily rest period of eleven hours;
- a day off per week;
- a rest break if working more than six hours; and
- paid annual leave of four weeks.

Apart from certain groups of workers who are specifically excluded, the Regulations apply to all workers with the exception of the genuinely self-employed. Freelancers, temporary and agency staff are all covered.

13.45　Excluded Sectors and Workers

The *Working Time (Amendment) Regulations 2003* (*SI 2003/1684*) implemented the Horizontal Amending Directive in August 2003 and affect employment sectors previously excluded from the 1998 Working Time Directive.

　　Working time measures were extended to all non-mobile workers in road, sea, inland waterways and lake transport; all workers in the railway and offshore sectors, and to all workers in aviation who are not covered by the sectoral Aviation Directive. The Regulations applied to junior doctors from 1 August 2004.

　　Mobile workers in road transport have more limited protection. Those who are subject to European Drivers' hours rules 3820/85 are entitled to four weeks' paid holiday, and those working nights are entitled to a health assessment. Mobile workers not covered by these rules are entitled to an average 48 hours a week, four weeks' paid holiday, health assessments for night workers and adequate rest.

13.46　Unmeasured Working Time

The regulations on the maximum working week, the length of night work, and daily rest, weekly rest and rest breaks for adult workers do not apply to workers whose working time is not measured or predetermined, or where the worker can determine it himself or herself (*SI 1998/1833, reg 20*). Additional hours which a worker chooses to do without being required to by the employer do not count as working time.

13.47　The Maximum Working Week

The maximum working week, including overtime, is set at 48 hours per week (ie seven days) when averaged over a 17-week reference period (*SI 1998/1833, reg 4*).

　　Employers must take all reasonable steps, in keeping with the need to protect the health and safety of workers, to ensure that the 48-hour limit is complied with (*SI 1998/1833, reg 4(2)*). They must also keep records for two years to show that the limits on the maximum working week are being complied with for all workers (*SI 1998/1833, reg 9*).

Health and Safety

Regulation 5A limits the working time of young workers to eight hours a day and 40 hours a week. Employers are required to ensure that these limits are complied with.

13.48 Opting-out

Workers may agree to opt out of the maximum working week, in which case this must be agreed with the employer in writing (*SI 1998/1833, reg 4(2)*). This opt-out is voluntary.

Checklist

If workers do opt out of the maximum working week, the employer must:

☐ keep up-to-date records of workers who have opted out;

☐ permit HSE or local authority inspectors to inspect the records on request; and

☐ provide an inspector with any information they may request regarding any such workers.

Even when individuals choose to work more than 48 hours, however, there is an absolute limit of 78 hours per week and 13 hours per day. This is because the Regulations also provide for a minimum of eleven hours rest period per day and an additional 24-hour break per week (see **13.53–13.54** below).

13.49 Calculating Working Time

There are no clear guidelines on how to calculate the 48 hours, which cover periods when an employee is actually working, and may or may not include lunch breaks.

The definition of what is included in working time is very important for the Regulations. The worker must be working, at the employer's disposal and carrying out an activity or duties. This may include time for which the worker is not paid or is outside the contract.

In *Landeshauptstadt Kiel v Jaeger [2003] IRLR 804*, the European Court of Justice held that the time spent by a hospital doctor on call, where presence in the hospital is required, is working time, for the purposes of the Regulations. The decisive factor was said to be that they are required to be present at a place determined by the employer, and be available to the employer.

There is a proposal from the European Commission that time spent on-call should not count as working time, even if the employee is required to be at their workplace.

However, in *Dellas v Premier Ministre [2006] IRLR 225*, the European Court of Justice (ECJ) ruled that on-call time at the employer's premises must be taken into account in its entirety in the calculation of the maximum daily and weekly working time.

13.50   Night Work

A night worker is defined as a worker who works at least three hours per day during night time on the majority of days or 'as a normal course' (*SI 1998/1833, reg 6*). Night time is a period of at least seven hours, including the period between midnight and 5am, as laid down in an agreement or contract, or in the absence of such an agreement the period between 11pm and 6am (*SI 1998/1833, reg 6*).

A night worker must not normally work more than eight hours in each 24-hour period when averaged over any 17-week reference period (*SI 1998/1833, reg 6(3)*).

Although the provisions on the length of night work can be altered or excluded by a collective or workforce agreement (see **13.60** below), compensatory rest must be made available.

Employers must also ensure that night workers whose work involves special hazards or heavy physical or mental strain do not work more than eight hours in any 24-hour period (*SI 1998/1833, reg 6(7)*). Such work includes that identified in a collective or workforce agreement which takes account of the specific effects and hazards of night work, or as is recognised in a risk assessment made by the employer under *regulation 3* of *SI 1999/3242* as involving a significant risk to the health or safety of workers.

Regulation 6A requires employers to ensure that no young worker works between 10pm and 6am, unless they are contracted to work after 10pm, in which case they should not work between 11pm and 7am. There are a number of exceptions to this, relating to particular occupations and particular circumstances, which include working in hospitals, cultural, artistic, sporting or advertising activities. There are also exceptions in the case of young workers employed in areas such as agriculture, retail trading, catering, and the hospitality industry.

13.51   *Health Assessment and Transfer of Workers to Day Work*

Employers must not assign adult workers to night work, or young workers to work between 10pm and 6am, unless they have ensured the worker has the opportunity of a free health assessment before taking up the assignment, or such a health assessment had previously been done and the employer believes it still to be valid (*SI 1998/1833, reg 7*). Night workers must also have the opportunity of free health assessments at appropriate regular intervals. Assessments can be provided by an occupational health doctor or a GP. The employer must meet the cost of an assessment and the worker must not lose wages for any time lost.

The health and capacities assessment for adolescent workers (16 and 17 year olds) will need to consider physical and psychological abilities to undertake the night work to which they are assigned.

If a doctor advises an employer that a worker is suffering from health problems that he/she considers to be caused by night work, and it is possible to transfer the worker to work which is suited to him/her that is not night work, the employer must transfer the worker to daytime work (*SI 1998/1833, reg 7(6)*). However, there is no absolute protection for workers other than pregnant women and disabled people if there is no suitable work to transfer to.

13.52   Record Keeping

Employers must keep records for two years to show that the regulations on the length of night work for all night workers and those exposed to particular danger, and on health assessments are being complied with for all workers (*SI 1998/1833, reg 9*).

Rest
13.53   Daily Rest

Adult workers are entitled to at least eleven consecutive hours, and young workers (16 and 17 year olds) to at least twelve consecutive hours, rest period in each 24-hour period (*SI 1998/1833, reg 10*). With regard to young workers, the rest period can be interrupted in the case of activities involving periods of work that are split up over the day or of short duration (*SI 1998/1833, reg 10(3)*).

13.54   Weekly Rest

Adult workers are entitled to an uninterrupted rest period of at least 24 hours in each seven-day period (*SI 1998/1833, reg 11*). The employer can decide that this is taken as two uninterrupted rest periods of at least 24 hours in each 14-day period, or one uninterrupted rest period of at least 48 hours in each 14-day period (*SI 1998/1833, reg 11(2)*).

Young workers are entitled to at least 48 hours in each seven-day period (*SI 1998/1833, reg 11(3)*). This may be interrupted 'in the case of activities involving periods of work that are split up over the day or are of short duration, and may be reduced where justified by technical or *organisational* reasons, but not to less than 36 consecutive hours'.

The seven-day, or 14-day, period starts at midnight between Sunday and Monday, unless otherwise specified in an agreement or contract. The minimum rest period for an adult worker must not include any part of the daily rest period, except where this is justified by objective or technical reasons or reasons concerning the organisation of work.

13.55   Rest Breaks

Workers are entitled to a rest break where they work more than six hours in a day (*SI 1998/1833, reg 12*). The length of the rest break and the way in which it is taken are to be determined by a collective or workforce agreement. However, the rest break must be an uninterrupted period of at least 20 minutes and away from the workstation if the worker has one.

Young workers are entitled to a rest break of at least 30 minutes, which should be consecutive if possible, where the daily working time is more than four and a half hours (*SI 1998/1833, reg 12(4)*). Again, the break should be away from the workstation if there is one. If a young worker is employed by more than one employer on any day, the total number of hours worked is added together for the purposes of determining whether he/she is entitled to a break.

13.56 *Special Cases*

The regulations on the length of night work, and daily rest, weekly rest and rest breaks for adult workers do not apply to workers:

- whose work and home are distant from one another, or whose different places of work are distant from one another;
- who are engaged in security or surveillance work requiring a permanent presence in order to protect property and people;
- whose work involves the need for continuity of service or production, for instance services relating to the reception, treatment or care provided by hospitals;
- in jobs where there is a foreseeable surge of activity (eg in tourism); and
- whose work is affected by unusual and unforeseeable circumstances beyond the control of the employer, exceptional events, whose consequences could not have been avoided, or an accident or the imminent risk of an accident.

In addition, the working week of these workers is determined as an average over 26 weeks instead of 17 weeks.

However, where workers are required to work during rest periods or rest breaks, the employer must give the worker an equivalent period of compensatory rest. In exceptional cases where this is not possible, the employer must give the worker appropriate protection to safeguard his/her health and safety.

In *Pfeiffer v Deutsches Rotes Kreuz [2005] IRLR 137*, an ECJ case involving German Red Cross rescue workers, it was held that the activities of these emergency workers fall within the scope of the Directive.

In addition, the Court held that individual contracts of employment incorporating a collective agreement allowing working hours to be extended beyond the 48-hour maximum working week were not sufficient to allow a valid opt-out of the 48-hour maximum working week. The Court said that a worker's consent must be given not only individually, but also expressly and freely.

13.57 *Shift Workers*

The regulations on the daily and weekly rest periods do not apply to shift workers when they change shifts and cannot take the rest periods between the end

Health and Safety

of one shift and the start of the next one. Similarly, they do not apply to workers whose work is split up over the day (eg cleaners). Shift work is defined as including the need for workers to work at different times over a given period of days or weeks (*SI 1998/1833, reg 22*).

However, if workers lose out on their rest periods, because of moving straight from one shift to another, they must be given an equivalent period of compensatory rest. In exceptional cases, where this is not possible, the employer must provide protection to safeguard the worker's health and safety.

13.58   Holidays

Workers are entitled to four weeks' annual leave. The leave year begins on the date provided for in an agreement or contract or, where it is not specified, on the date on which employment begins. Where a worker starts work later than the date on which the first leave year begins, he/she is entitled to an amount of leave proportional to the amount of the leave year remaining.

Leave may be taken in instalments, but it may only be taken in that leave year, and it may not be replaced by payment in lieu except where the worker's employment is terminated.

As a result of the *Working Time (Amendment) Regulations 2001 (SI 2001/3256)* the limitation on entitlement to annual leave to workers who have been continuously employed for thirteen weeks has been revoked. Instead, the extent to which a worker is able to exercise their entitlement to leave during the course of their first year of employment is limited to the amount accrued at that time. Accrual is at the rate of one-twelfth of the annual entitlement at the beginning of each month.

Cases on holidays in recent years include the following:

In *Davies and Others v M J Wyatt (Decorators) Ltd [2000] IRLR 759*, the EAT ruled that employers cannot unilaterally reduce employees' hourly rates of pay to fund holiday pay to which employees are entitled under the *Working Time Regulations 1998* (*SI 1998/1833*), unless there has been a consensual agreement.

In *Byrne Brothers (Formwork) Ltd v Baird and Others [2002] IRLR 96*, the EAT ruled in favour of 'labour-only subcontractors' who were not entitled to holiday pay under the terms of their subcontractors agreement with the company. It held that labour-only subcontractors in the construction industry were workers within the meaning of *regulation 2(1)* of the *Working Time Regulations 1998*. The workers worked exclusively for the company on one site for a significant and indefinite period, under the close direction of the company and were paid on a time basis. They were therefore entitled to holiday pay.

Commissioners of Inland Revenue v Ainsworth [2005] IRLR 465 overruled *Kigass Aero Components Ltd v Brown*, and ruled that workers on long-term sick leave are no longer entitled to sick pay and are not entitled to the annual four weeks' holiday pay set out in the *Working Time Regulations*.

In *Leisure Leagues UK Ltd v Maconnachie [2002] IRLR 600*, the EAT confirmed that when calculating the daily rate of pay for the purpose of calculating accrued holiday entitlement, annual salary is divided by the number of working days in the year, rather than calendar days.

In *Hill v Chapell [2003] IRLR*, the EAT held that where a worker's employment is terminated during the course of a leave year, and at this point, proportionately more leave has been taken than the worker is entitled to, the employer cannot recover any excess holiday pay unless a relevant agreement has been made under *regulation 14(4)* of the *Working Time Regulations*. In this case, an agreement had not been entered into.

In *Commissioners of Inland Revenue and Others v Post Office Ltd [2003] IRLR 199*, the EAT held that subpostmistresses were not 'workers' for the purposes of the *Working Time Regulations*. The contracts between the Post Office and the applicants were not ones where the individual 'undertakes to do or perform personally any work' within the relevant statutory definitions of 'worker', since they could choose whether or not to do the work themselves.

The fact that in order to qualify for 'holiday substitution allowance', a subpostmaster or postmistress had certified that they gave on average not less than 18 hours' personal service each week, did not amount to an undertaking personally to do the work. In addition, they did not fall into the definition of a 'worker' because they are carrying out a business undertaking, and the Post Office is a client of that business undertaking.

In *Addison and Another t/a Brayton News v Ashby [2003] IRLR 211*, the EAT held that a 15-year-old paper boy who was of compulsory school age, was not a 'worker' within the meaning of *regulation 2(1)* of the *Working Time Regulations*, and was therefore not entitled to paid annual leave under *regulation 13*.

Merino Gomez v Continental Industrias del Caucho SA [2004] IRLR 407 is a European Court of Justice case which looked at the right to take paid annual leave during a period other than during maternity leave. The case makes it clear that this is the case where the dates of annual holiday are fixed in advance by a collective agreement coinciding with the worker's maternity leave.

In *Bamsey and Others v Albon Engineering and Manufacturing plc*, the Court of Appeal looked at the rate of pay for annual leave where regular overtime is carried out. The court held that the workers were only entitled to holiday pay calculated on the basis of their contractual 39 hour basic working week, even though they regularly worked substantial amounts of overtime, which they were contractually obliged to do, but the employers were not obliged to provide.

There have also been a number of cases involving holiday pay being included in a 'rolled-up' basic rate. The DTI has now changed its guidance in this area. Following a European Court of Justice (ECJ) Judgment on 16 March 2006, Rolled Up Holiday Pay (RHP) is considered unlawful and employers should renegotiate contracts involving RHP for existing employees/workers as soon as possible so that payment for statutory annual leave is made at the time when the leave is taken. Where an employer has already given RHP in relation to work undertaken, and the payments have been made in a transparent and comprehensible manner, they can be set off against any future leave payments made at the proper time.

Health and Safety

13.59   *When Leave can be Taken*

Employees can take leave when they want by giving notice to the employer when leave will be taken and, when leave is for part of a day only, for how long (*SI 1998/1833, reg 15*). The notice must be given at least twice as many days in advance of the first day of leave as the number of days or part-days to which it relates.

The employer, however, can require leave to be taken or not taken on particular days by giving notice before the relevant date (*SI 1998/1833, reg 15(2)*).

13.60   Collective and Workforce Agreements

Negotiations about the *Working Time Regulations 1998* (*SI 1998/1833*) are by a process of collective agreement between employers and recognised trade unions, or by 'workforce agreements' where there are no recognised trade unions.

The terms of a collective agreement become part of the individual worker's contract of employment and thus are legally enforceable by that individual so that any improvements negotiated through the collective agreement will apply to individual workers.

Collective or workforce agreements may modify or exclude the regulations on the length of night work and daily rest, weekly rest and rest breaks for adults (*SI 1998/1833, reg 23*). They can also alter the reference period for calculating the average working week from 17 weeks up to a maximum of 52 weeks.

Checklist

The Regulations state that a workforce agreement:

☐   must be in writing and must specify the date of operation of the agreement;

☐   must not last for more than five years;

☐   applies to all relevant members of the workforce, or part of the workforce;

☐   must be given to all the workers covered by the agreement, together with any necessary guidance, before it is signed; and

☐   must be signed by representatives of the workforce, or part of the workforce.

However, if the workforce has 20 or fewer workers, the majority of the workforce can sign the agreement rather than the representatives. These workplace agreements cannot include workers whose terms and conditions are decided by collective agreement.

13.61   Protection Against Discrimination

The *Employment Rights Act 1996* has been amended by the *Working Time Regulations 1998* (*SI 1998/1833*) so that workers cannot be victimised if they refuse to do something contrary to the Regulations or to forego their rights provided in the Regulations. If a worker is dismissed on such grounds this is automatically regarded as unfair dismissal.

13.62   Accidents and Injuries at Work
13.63   Health and Safety (First-aid) Regulations 1981

The *Health and Safety (First-aid) Regulations 1981* (*SI 1981/917*) provide that employers are under a general duty to make adequate and appropriate first-aid provision for employees if they are injured or become ill at work (*SI 1981/917, reg 3*). This includes providing first-aid equipment and people for administering first-aid.

An employer should make an assessment of first-aid needs appropriate to the circumstances of each workplace (this should be reviewed from time to time). In deciding how much first-aid provision is necessary, in terms of both equipment and personnel, the employer should have regard to:

- workplace hazards and risks;
- the size of the organisation;
- the organisation's history of accidents;
- the nature and distribution of the workforce;
- the remoteness of the site from emergency medical services;
- the needs of travelling, remote and lone workers;
- employees working on shared or multi-occupied sites; and
- annual leave and other absences of first-aiders and appointed persons.

Copies of the Approved Code of Practice *First-aid at Work* and the guidance booklet *First-aid Training and Qualifications for the Purposes of the Health and Safety (First-aid) Regulations 1981* are available from HSE Books (see **13.5** above).

13.64   Accident/Injury Reporting

The *Reporting of Injuries, Diseases and Dangerous Occurrences Regulations 1995* (*RIDDOR 1995*) (*SI 1995/3163*) require that certain events relating to accidents and ill-health at work must be recorded, notified and reported by a 'responsible person' to the enforcing authority, which may be the HSE or the local authority environmental health department.

There is a facility to report all cases to a single point, the Incident Contact Centre ('ICC'). This means that employers do not need to be concerned about which office and which enforcing authority should be reported to.

Health and Safety

Postal reports should be sent to: Incident Contact Centre, Caerphilly Business Park, Caerphilly, CF83 3GG. Internet reports can be made at www.riddor.gov.uk or www.hse.gov.uk. Telephone reports can be made to 0845 300 9923, faxed reports to 0845 300 9924 and e-mailed reports to riddor@natbrit.com.

Railway and mines incident-reporting operate under separate existing arrangements.

Under *RIDDOR 1995*, 'responsible persons' (normally employers) must notify enforcing authorities by the quickest means possible of the following:

- the death of a person as a result of an accident arising out of or in connection with work;
- a major injury suffered as a result of an accident arising out of or in connection with work;
- an injury suffered by a person not at work (eg a visitor, customer, client, passenger or bystander) as a result of an accident arising out of or in connection with work;
- a major injury suffered by a person not at work, as a result of an accident arising out of or in connection with work at a hospital;
- a dangerous occurrence.

13.65   Record-keeping Requirements

Regulation 7 of *SI 1995/3163* outlines the record-keeping requirements imposed on the employer. Records on reportable events must be kept for three years at the usual place of business.

Railway and mines incident-reporting operate under separate existing arrangements.

13.66   *Accidents and Injuries*

There is a new Accident Book which was produced in order to improve health and safety and data protection compliance. The *HSE Accident Book* is available price £4.75 from HSE Books.

Checklist

The accident book must contain the following information:

- ☐ full name, address and occupation of the injured person;
- ☐ date and time of the accident;
- ☐ place where the accident happened;
- ☐ cause and nature of the injury; and
- ☐ name, address and occupation of the person giving the notice, if other than the injured person.

The HSE has published new guidance on how to investigate accidents and incidents, including near misses.

Copies of investigating accidents and incidents – a workbook for employers, unions, safety representatives and safety professionals (HSE Ref. HSG245) is available from HSE Books.

13.67 Enforcement of Health and Safety Legislation

At a Glance

* Health and safety laws are enforced by Health and Safety Executive (HSE) inspectors, or environmental health officers in local authorities, depending on the type of workplace.
* Improvement notices require action to be taken to improve health and safety within a given time.
* Prohibition notices are served where there is an imminent danger of personal injury.
* Prosecutions can be taken against companies and individual directors and other officers.
* Prosecutions for health and safety offences can result in fines, and prison sentences in certain cases.

13.68 Health and Safety Executive ('HSE')

The Health and Safety Executive ('HSE') is the main operational arm of the Health and Safety Commission ('HSC') and has the day-to-day responsibility for the enforcement of health and safety legislation. It is divided into several inspectorates. The HSE also provides advice, guidance and information for employers on how to comply with health and safety law.

The HSC's enforcement policy statement sets out specific criteria for deciding whether to investigate and prosecute breaches of health and safety law.

The policy applies to all Britain's enforcing authorities, including the Health and Safety Executive (HSE) and all local authorities in England, Scotland and Wales. It makes clear to inspectors, employers, workers and the public what standards they should expect when it comes to enforcing health and safety in the workplace.

The policy states that a prosecution should normally take place in any one of a number of circumstances, including:

* when a workplace death is caused by a breach of the law;
* if there has been reckless disregard of health and safety requirements;
* if the offender's standard of health and safety management is far below what is required.

Decisions on whether to investigate a workplace incident must take account of a number of factors, including:

- the severity and scale of potential, as well as actual, harm;
- the offender's previous health and safety record;
- the wider relevance of the incident, including the public concern it causes.

The policy also requires all Britain's enforcing authorities and their inspectors to:

- ensure they consider the role of the management chain, and individual directors and managers, in any possible offences, and take enforcement action against them if the evidence shows this is justified;
- notify the director of an offending organisation each time the enforcing authority issues an improvement notice, prohibition notice or takes a prosecution against that organisation;
- publicise annually the names of all organisations and individuals convicted of health and safety offences over the previous twelve months, as well as similar information regarding all improvement and prohibition notices issued over the same period;
- publicise the decision-making process so that everyone can understand how the enforcement policy works in practice. The enforcement policy statement is on the web at www.gov.uk/pubns/hsc15.pdf. Copies of the HSC's Enforcement Policy Statement (HSC15) are available from HSE Books.

13.69   Environmental Health Officers and Inspectors ('EHOs')

Environmental health officers ('EHOs') located in local authority environmental health departments are responsible for enforcing health and safety law in offices, shops and warehouse-type premises and in some cultural establishments and residential accommodation.

HSE and environmental health inspectors have the power to:

- enter premises;
- inspect and investigate;
- take measurements, samples and photographs;
- require an area or machine to be left undisturbed;
- seize, render harmless or destroy dangerous items;
- obtain information; and
- take statements.

They also have the power to issue improvement and prohibition notices and can bring prosecutions against any person contravening a relevant statutory provision.

13.70   Company Officers

Although prosecutions can be taken against a company, *section 37* of *HSWA 1974* allows prosecutions of directors, managers, company secretaries or similar company officers. This applies where an offence alleged against the company is considered to have been committed with the 'consent or connivance of, or to have been attributable to any neglect on the part of' any of those company officers.

The Government announced a range of measures to increase the penalties awarded to companies and their directors when safety standards are breached in *Revitalising Health and Safety*, a health and safety strategy document published in 2000.

This included 'naming and shaming' companies and individuals convicted of health and safety breaches in an annual report published by the HSE, aimed at increasing publicity about successful prosecutions.

The first report was published in November 2000 and the sixth report was published in 2005. The web only publication can be accessed at: www.hse.gov.uk/enforce/off0405/index.htm.

Checklist

HSE guidance on health and safety responsibilities for company directors and board members of public sector organisations, *Directors' Responsibilities for Health and Safety*, states that boards must:

☐ accept joint responsibility and leadership for their organisations' health and safety performance and ensure that the organisation has a clear health and safety policy which explains how it intends to deliver its health and safety objectives;

☐ appoint one board member to champion health and safety issues;

☐ ensure that individual members of the board recognise their personal liabilities and responsibilities under health and safety law;

☐ consult staff fully (via trade union representatives where appropriate) on all health and safety issues as required by health and safety law; and

☐ keep informed about all health and safety issues affecting the organisation and its performance.

By following the guidance, directors will normally be doing enough to comply with the law.

Although every company must have a health and safety policy by law, it is not currently UK law for companies to include health and safety in their annual reports. HSE guidance on annual reporting sets out the minimum standards for what annual reports should say about health and safety. This includes:

☐ outlining the company's health and safety policy;

☐ significant risks faced by employees/others and the strategies and systems in place for controlling those risks;

☐ the company's health and safety goals/targets, which should be measurable and relate to the health and safety policy;

☐ details of progress towards achieving goals/targets;

☐ plans for the forthcoming period; and

☐ arrangements for consulting employees and involving safety reps.

The report should also include data on the company's health and safety performance, including:

☐ the number of injuries, illnesses and dangerous occurrences, reportable under the *Reporting of Injuries, Diseases and Dangerous Occurrences Regulations 1995* (RIDDOR);

☐ details of any fatalities and remedial action taken;

☐ the number of physical or mental work-induced health problems reported for the first time during that period;

☐ the number of employee days lost through work-related illness or injury;

☐ the number of health and safety enforcement or prohibition notices served on the company, with brief details;

☐ the number and nature of health and safety convictions for the period in question, including fines imposed and remedial action taken; and

☐ the total cost to the company of work-related injuries and illness suffered by staff over the reporting period.

The penalty for breaching health and safety law is normally a fine but in some cases a prison sentence may be used.

Employers can also be imprisoned if they are found guilty of manslaughter in the case of a workplace death, and in theory a company can be found guilty of manslaughter. However, the current law of corporate manslaughter has generally proved difficult to use in practice and the law in this area is to be reformed.

The Government outlined the need for reform in its introduction to the draft *Corporate Manslaughter Bill*, which was published in March 2005, admitting that there was 'public concern that the law is not delivering justice, a feeling that has been underlined by the lack of success of corporate manslaughter prosecutions following a number of public disasters'.

Announcing the Bill, the then Home Secretary Charles Clarke said: 'This Government is committed to delivering a criminal justice system that commands the confidence of the public. A fundamental part of this is providing offences that are clear and effective. The current laws on corporate manslaughter are neither, as a number of unsuccessful prosecutions over the years stand testament.'

The key problem with existing law is the need to show that a single individual at the very top of a company is personally guilty of manslaughter before the company can be prosecuted. This has become known as the 'identification' principle. It requires that a 'directing mind' – i.e. someone who could be said to embody the company in his or her actions and decisions – has to be identified, and to be shown to be guilty of manslaughter. If this cannot be shown, a company escapes liability.

What this has meant in practice is that only very small companies have been able to be convicted of the offence of corporate manslaughter, while a number of high profile cases against large companies, including P&O European Ferries and Great Western Trains, for example, have all failed. It has become very clear that the law is failing to operate flexibly to reflect the reality of decision making in large organisations with complex management structures and lines of control, and is not providing proper accountability or justice for victims.

The final Bill is now awaited. More information is available on the Home Office website at www.homeoffice.gov.uk.

Recent manslaughter prosecutions include the following.

Construction company proprietor Wayne Davies of A & E Buildings, based in Knighton, Powys, was recently sentenced to an 18-month custodial sentence for manslaughter in January 2006, following a prosecution brought by the Crown Prosecution Service (CPS). The case, heard at Hereford Crown Court, followed a joint investigation between the police and the Health and Safety Executive (HSE) into the death of Mark Jones.

Mr Jones was killed as a result of injuries he received when he fell from a 'homemade' basket, suspended from the forks of a telehandler owned by Davies, while installing a barn roof on a farm. The telehandler tipped over, throwing Mr Jones, along with another employee who was seriously injured, around 25 feet to the ground.

Davies failed in both his duty to ensure the safety of his employees and in his responsibility to provide safe and suitable means of working at height. He was found guilty of a breach of the *Health and Safety at Work etc. Act 1974, section 2(1)* for failing to ensure the safety of employees in the time before the incident.

In addition he also pleaded guilty to a single charge of providing a telehandler and equipment that was not properly maintained, breaching *regulation 5* of the *Provision and Use of Work Equipment Regulations 1998 (SI 1998/2306)*.

In March 2006, company director Mark Connor, of MAC Machinery Services, was found guilty on four counts of manslaughter following the deaths of four rail workers at Tebay, Cumbria, in February 2004. The men were hit by a runaway trailer, owned by the company. Newcastle Crown Court heard that Connolly had been 'grossly negligent' when he had deliberately disconnected the hydraulic brakes on two wagons, because it was cheaper than carrying out proper repairs, and that he had 'scant regard' for railway safety.

13.71 Safety Representatives and Employee Consultation

The *Safety Representatives and Safety Committees Regulations 1977 (SI 1977/500)* introduced the right for recognised trade unions to appoint safety representatives.

They set out the functions of safety representatives and safety committees and employer's obligations to consult safety representatives. Only recognised trade unions can appoint safety representatives.

The employer must be notified in writing, by or on behalf of the union, of the names of the appointed safety representatives. The Regulations recommend that a safety representative should have been employed by the employer for two years, or have had at least two years' experience in similar employment, where reasonably practicable.

The number of safety representatives who can be appointed depends on the size of the workforce and workplace, whether there are different sites, the variety of different occupations, the operation of shift systems and the type of risks of work activity.

13.72   Employers' Duties

The *Safety Representatives and Safety Committees Regulations 1977* (*SI 1977/500*) place certain duties upon employers. These include:

- consulting with safety representatives;
- providing facilities and assistance to safety representatives;
- making information available to safety representatives.

13.73   Representatives' Rights and Functions

Each safety representative has a right to 'such time off with pay during the employee's working hours as shall be necessary' in order to carry out his functions and for training.

The safety representatives' functions are to:

- investigate potential hazards and dangerous occurrences and examine the causes of accidents;
- investigate members' complaints;
- make representations to the employer;
- carry out inspections at least every three months and after a notifiable accident, dangerous occurrence or after a notifiable disease has been contracted; and
- consult with and receive information from HSE inspectors and other enforcement officers on behalf of members and attend meetings of the safety committee.

Most employment tribunal cases have concerned time off for training. In an Employment Appeal Tribunal (EAT) case, *Duthie v Bath and North East Somerset Council EAT/0561/02*, it was confirmed that safety representatives have a right to training that is 'reasonable in all the circumstances', rather than what the employer considers to be necessary.

Section 28 of the *Trade Union Reform and Employment Rights Act 1993* introduced legal protection for safety representatives and other employees who take action or raise concerns about health and safety at work.

'The Brown Book' (*Safety Representatives and Safety Committees* (L87)), which contains the *Safety Representatives and Safety Committees Regulations 1977* (*SI 1997/500*), the Approved Code of Practice and guidance, is available from HSE Books (see **13.5** above).

13.74 *Health and Safety (Consultation with Employees) Regulations 1996*

The *Health and Safety (Consultation with Employees) Regulations 1996* (*SI 1996/1513*) effectively top up the consultation arrangements under the *Safety Representatives and Safety Committees Regulations 1977* (*SI 1977/500*).

There is a duty on employers to consult any employees who are not members of a group covered by trade union safety representatives on health and safety matters. Employers have the choice of consulting their employees directly or through elected representatives. The employer must provide the necessary information to enable the employees or representatives to participate fully and effectively in the consultation. In the case of representatives, this information must also be sufficient to enable them to carry out their functions under the Regulations. These include representing the group of employees in consultations with HSE inspectors and making representations to the employer on:

- potential hazards and dangerous occurrences at the workplace which affect or could affect the group of employees he represents; and
- general matters affecting the health and safety of those employees.

Where the employer consults representatives, it must ensure that each of them is provided with reasonable training in respect of those representatives' functions under the Regulations, for which the employer must pay. It must also allow each representative such time off with pay as is necessary to enable him/her to undergo such training or to perform his/her functions under the Regulations and must allow similar time off to a candidate for election as a representative in order to perform his/her functions as a candidate.

The Regulations amend the *Employment Rights Act 1996* so as to protect an employee who takes part in consultation with an employer under the Regulations, or who takes part in an election for representatives, from unfair dismissal or from suffering a detriment as a result.

A Consultation Document seeking views on how to encourage, improve and increase worker involvement in health and safety risk management has been issued by the HSE. This may result in amendments to the law on consultation with employees.

13.75 Public Interest Disclosure Act 1998

The *Public Interest Disclosure Act 1998,* which amended the *Employment Rights Act 1996*, gives workers legal protection if they raise issues of serious concern about their workplace, including safety concerns, with their employer. Workers have protection against victimisation or dismissal if they 'blow the whistle' and can take their case to an employment tribunal.

The protection given by the law to workers who take action about health and safety issues is wider than the previous protection. The new law extends protection to all workers, and to raising concerns about environmental issues.

A dismissal of any worker making a protected disclosure is automatically unfair, regardless of the length of service.

A former train driver and safety representative, Laurie Holden, was awarded compensation of £55,000, including a payment for aggravated damages and injury to feelings, after he won an unfair dismissal case against train company Connex. He had resigned from Connex after suffering stress and complaining that he was victimised for blowing the whistle about signals passed at danger and other safety issues.

Appendix 1

Useful Websites on Health and Safety Issues

Health and Safety Executive	www.hse.gov.uk
Department of Trade and Industry	www.dti.gov.uk
Office of the Deputy Prime Minister	www.odpm.gov.uk
Home Office	www.homeoffice.gov.uk

Health and Safety

Insurance

Insurance

14.1 General Principles

> **At a Glance**
> * Arranging appropriate insurance cover is one method of protecting the company against potential risks that could have a significant impact on the business.
> * Insurance can provide cover against liabilities, loss or damage to assets and loss of profits.
> * Every employer must hold employers' liability insurance, and certain other types of cover (eg professional indemnity insurance) are required for specific businesses or activities.
> * A registered insurance broker or other independent adviser can help assess insurance needs and identify suitable policies.
> * All insurance contracts are undertaken on the principle of utmost good faith – the insured is therefore responsible for making full declaration of any circumstances that might influence the insurer's decision on whether to accept the transfer of risk.

14.2 Risk Management

Risk management is the process of:

* identifying the risks that potentially threaten the business;
* assessing the likelihood of each risk actually crystallising in practice and the expected impact on the business if it does crystallise;
* wherever possible, establishing procedures to reduce risk to an acceptable level; and
* deciding to what extent the company should seek protection against any remaining risks.

Arranging appropriate insurance cover is one method of protecting the company against potential risks that could have a significant impact on the business. In each case, the benefit of taking out insurance against the potential risk should be weighed against the cost of doing so.

14.3   Types of Insurance

Broadly, insurance may be arranged to give protection against:

- liabilities arising under specific legislation or common law;
- loss or damage to the company's assets (including intangible assets, such as goodwill, patents and trade marks, and personnel); and
- loss of profits.

Every employer is required by law to hold employers' liability insurance and every business must arrange at least third party insurance cover for each road vehicle that it operates. Other insurance is generally voluntary, although certain specialised businesses and activities may be required to arrange specific additional cover (eg professional indemnity insurance).

14.4   Insurance Brokers

Unless appropriate expertise is available within the organisation, it will usually be advisable to use the services of a registered insurance broker or other independent adviser to help assess insurance needs, identify suitable policies and arrange the agreed level of cover at a reasonable cost. The broker or adviser will receive either an agreed fee or commission from the insurer, which will be included in the cost of the insurance policy.

14.5   Issues to Consider

Whilst the cost of the insurance cover – and comparison of this with the benefit obtained – will be a key issue, it is not the only factor that needs to be taken into account in identifying a suitable insurer and insurance policy. Other relevant issues include:

- any exclusions to the proposed policy;
- any warranties that the company will be expected to fulfil;
- any excess that will remain payable by the company in the event of a claim;
- any discounts offered for lack of claims under the policy; and
- the manner in which claims will be settled by the insurer.

The Institute of Directors has published a number of helpful guides to insurance, including one on keeping insurance costs to a minimum, which deals with issues such as:

- arranging cover in good time and as a package covering all of the entity's insurance needs;
- providing evidence of risk management processes and business continuity planning;

- having a good health and safety record;
- considering different payment methods; and
- where relevant, making use of specialist insurers with a better understanding of the related risks.

The guides are available free of charge from the publications section of the Institute of Directors' website at www.iod.com.

14.6   Utmost Good Faith

All insurance contracts are undertaken on the principle of utmost good faith. This means that the insured person or entity is responsible for making full disclosure to the insurer of any circumstances that could influence the professional judgement of a prudent insurer in deciding whether to accept the transfer of risk and/or in setting the premium payable for the transfer of that risk. Once a policy has been taken out, the insured also has a responsibility to inform the insurer of any changes during the period of insurance that could be relevant or material to the contract.

14.7   **Compulsory Cover**

At a Glance
- * Every employer must be insured against legal liability for the death, bodily injury or illness of employees arising out of and in the course of their employment.
- * Employers' liability insurance must be provided by an authorised insurer approved by the DTI.
- * The minimum level of cover for employers' liability insurance is £5 million for any one occurrence.
- * A copy of the employers' liability insurance certificate must be displayed in a prominent place at each business location.
- * Documentation in respect of employers' liability insurance should be retained indefinitely as claims can often arise some time after the event.
- * Every road vehicle owned by the company must, as a minimum, be insured against liability to any third party for death or bodily injury and for damage to property.
- * The company should check that employees who use their own vehicle for company business are specifically covered for business use under their own vehicle insurance policies.

Insurance

14.8   Employers' Liability Insurance

Under the *Employers' Liability (Compulsory Insurance) Act 1969,* every employer carrying on business in the UK must be insured against legal liability for the death, bodily injury or illness of employees arising out of and in the course of their employment under a contract of service or an apprenticeship. There are only limited exceptions to the requirement – for instance, where the owner of a business is the only employee or where only close family members are employed in an unincorporated business. The insurance must be provided by an authorised UK insurer approved by the DTI or by an authorised EU insurer which has notified the DTI of its wish to provide insurance in the UK. The policy protects the employer against claims for damages brought by an employee and should cover:

- negligence of the employer in failing to use reasonable skill and care in:
  - providing suitable and safe plant,
  - providing a safe system of work,
  - providing a safe place of work, and
  - engaging suitable and competent employees;
- breach of statutory regulations by the employer (eg health and safety); and
- negligence of other employees of the employer.

Under the legislation, an employer must be insured for at least £5 million for any one occurrence, although in practice insurers will often provide a higher level of cover than this. The requirement for this insurance covers employees working in Great Britain, Northern Ireland, the Channel Isles and the Isle of Man, but the cover should extend to employees travelling on business or working temporarily in other countries. A copy of the certificate confirming that the required insurance cover is in place must be displayed in a prominent place at each business location. Claims under employers' liability insurance will sometimes be made some time after the event and possibly after the individual has ceased to be employed by the company (for instance, where ill-health caused by exposure to toxic substances only becomes apparent at a later stage). It is therefore advisable for the company to retain all documentation relating to employers' liability cover, even though individual policies may have expired some time ago.

14.9   Motor Insurance

Under the *Road Traffic Act 1988,* every vehicle used on the road must be insured against liability to any third party for death or bodily injury and damage to property. This is usually referred to as 'third party only' insurance. Any business that uses road vehicles must arrange this minimum level of cover for each vehicle. Third party insurance cover will normally include the cost of any legal fees incurred in defending a claim. In practice, many companies will wish to consider additional cover under one of the following forms of insurance:

- *third party, fire and theft* – this extends the minimum third party cover to include fire damage to, and theft or attempted theft of, the insured vehicle;
- *comprehensive* – this extends the cover to include any accidental damage to the insured vehicle and may include additional specific cover (eg in the case of unauthorised use of the vehicle).

The insurer may place restrictions on the vehicle being used by young or inexperienced drivers.

14.10   *Use of Employee's Own Car*

An employee who uses his/her own vehicle to carry out company business will be covered against claims from third parties under their own motor insurance policy if this specifically includes business use of the vehicle. If business use is not included under the employee's vehicle insurance policy, the employer may be vicariously liable for any claims by third parties. It is therefore advisable to require employees to demonstrate that they have the appropriate level of cover before allowing them to use their own vehicles on company business, and to ensure that this is maintained in future years, or to take out contingent third party cover to indemnify the company against any vicarious claims.

14.11   Voluntary Cover

At a Glance
* Most businesses will want to arrange insurance cover against damage to, or loss of, assets that are of high value and/or critical to the business.
* Any exclusions under an individual policy should be carefully reviewed so that additional arrangements can be put in place where necessary.
* Buildings are usually insured on the basis of the cost of reinstating the building, including related site clearance costs and professional fees.
* If average applies to a policy, it is important to appreciate that the settlement value of any claim will be reduced accordingly.
* Policies for plant and equipment may be based on full replacement cost or on depreciated asset values.
* In the case of stock, it is important to clarify when responsibility for insurance cover transfers between the buyer and the seller.
* Business interruption insurance provides compensation for the financial effects of disruption to the business as a result of events covered by other insurance.
* Digital risk insurance can provide additional protection for a business that is heavily dependent on electronic data.
* Public liability insurance provides cover against legal liability for the death or bodily injury of a third party, or damage to the property of a third party, as a result of the company's activities.
* Product liability insurance provides cover against legal liability for the death or bodily injury of a third party, or damage to the property of a third party, as a result of using a product sold, serviced or repaired by the company.
* Professional indemnity insurance provides cover against legal liability arising from a failure to exercise due skill and care in carrying out a professional contract, resulting in loss to the other party.
* *CA 1985* permits a company to take out certain insurance cover on behalf of directors and officers.
* A company may wish to insure against the potential risks to the business arising from the death, incapacity or ill-health of key individuals.

Insurance

14.12   Insurance of Assets

Most businesses will wish to arrange some level of insurance cover against damage to, or loss of, assets that are of high value and/or critical to the business, including in particular:

- buildings;
- plant and other equipment;
- stock;
- goods in transit; and
- money.

A variety of different policies will usually be available, under which the insurer will usually pay the estimated value of the asset in the event of loss, and in the case of damage will have the option of either meeting the cost of repair or replacing the damaged asset. The policy may cover all risks or may be restricted to certain specific risks, such as fire and special perils (eg explosions). An 'all risks' policy will generally cover fire, special risks and accidental damage, although the insurer will often make a number of specific exclusions which should be carefully reviewed so that additional arrangements can be put in place if this is considered necessary in the company's particular circumstances.

14.13   *Buildings*

In the case of property, it is usually advisable to insure on the basis of the cost of reinstatement of the building, including any related site clearance costs, professional fees and local authority costs. If average applies to the policy, so that (say) only 80 per cent of the total value at risk is insured, it is important to appreciate that the settlement value of any claim will be reduced by 20 per cent, even if the claim is for less than the total value insured, and this will leave the company to meet the balance of the costs, which could be substantial. In the case of leased property, the lessor may include specific insurance requirements in the terms of the lease and the company will need to ensure that it meets any obligations that it has accepted in signing the lease. It is also important to keep the insurance arrangements under regular review to ensure that the values used are up to date. Another option here is to arrange the insurance cover on a 'day one basis' so that the reinstatement value declared when the policy begins is adjusted for a specific inflation provision included in the policy.

14.14   *Plant and Other Equipment*

Most insurance policies will provide cover for plant and equipment based on the value of the asset at the time of loss or damage. Alternatively, insurance cover may be arranged on a new-for-old basis, so that the full cost of replacement is insured rather than the depreciated value of the asset. Particular care is needed over insurance arrangements for computer equipment, especially where this is critical to the business operations. Cover should include any repairs not covered by other maintenance arrangements and also the loss or corruption of data.

14.15 *Stock and Goods in Transit*

Stock will usually need to be insured against theft and against damage as a result of fire or flood. Factors to consider in arranging insurance cover for stock include:

- assessment of the maximum stock level that is likely to be held;
- when the company becomes responsible for stock items delivered by suppliers – for instance, should the company be arranging cover for goods in transit or is the supplier responsible for this; and
- when the company ceases to be responsible for goods that it has sold to customers – again, who is responsible for insuring the assets whilst they are in transit.

Insurance cover should normally be based on the maximum expected level of stock, but where actual stock levels are expected to be lower than this for much of the time, it should be possible to arrange for the insurer to take this into account in setting the related premium. Once again, the value insured should be kept under regular review and updated as necessary.

14.16 *Money*

Depending on the company's circumstances, insurance arrangements for money may need to cover:

- cash held on the premises (both during and after normal business hours);
- cash, cheques and other non-negotiable instruments during transit; and
- personal injury to employees transporting cash.

The policy should provide protection against theft by company employee as well as external loss.

14.17 Business Interruption

Business interruption insurance is designed to provide compensation for the financial effects of disruption to the normal operation of the business, as a result of events that are covered by other insurance. For instance, buildings insurance may cover the cost of rebuilding the company's operating premises after a fire but the company will not receive any compensation for the loss of business income whilst the rebuilding work is in progress unless it has also arranged business interruption insurance. The detailed contents of policies vary and should be designed as far as possible to suit the particular circumstances of the company. It will usually be advisable to cover the following at least:

- consequential loss of profits;
- book debts, to cover situations where the underlying debtor records are destroyed; and

Insurance

- computer damage, where this results in loss of income or in the business incurring additional costs in order to maintain some level of operation.

The cover will be subject to a maximum indemnity period to prevent a business claiming indefinitely under the policy. Claims will therefore be accepted from the date the damage occurs to the date when normal business resumes, or to the end of the maximum indemnity period, whichever is the earlier. The maximum indemnity period will need to be agreed when the policy is arranged, based on the particular circumstances of the company. It advisable to base the assessment on a major catastrophe, such as an extensive fire, and to take account of all other relevant factors, which might include:

- the length of time that is likely to be needed to clear debris, obtain any local authority consents and carry out the repair or rebuilding of property;
- expected delivery times for essential plant and equipment, and any periods needed for commissioning or testing;
- any ongoing commitments under lease or rental agreements; and
- the time that may be needed to rebuild the customer base.

It is also advisable to ensure that the policy allows claims to be made, and paid, throughout the indemnity period and not just at the end of it. The insurers will usually require each claim submitted to be reviewed and certified by an independent accountant.

14.18   Wider Cover for Business Interruption

Business interruption insurance will usually cover loss of income as a result of damage to insured property and equipment owned or used by the insured. Some companies may wish to extend the normal cover to include events such as:

- damage to other property in the area, which prevents access to the company's business premises and equipment;
- damage to the premises or equipment of suppliers and/or customers, which has an adverse impact on the company due to lack of supplies or reduced demand;
- events which result in disruption to the business without causing physical damage (eg bomb threats); and
- serious disruption to utility supplies.

Whether this level of cover is considered necessary will depend on the circumstances of the company and the likelihood of such an event happening in practice.

14.19   Digital Risk Insurance

With the increasing use of IT and the development of e-commerce, electronically-held data can now represent a significant business asset. Digital risk insurance can be taken out to provide protection against occurrences such as the accidental loss of electronic data, the deliberate or malicious destruction of electronic data, the impact of computer crime on the business (for instance, as a result of hacking or phishing attacks) and the failure of critical electronic systems (eg interactive websites).

14.20   Public Liability

Public liability insurance provides protection against legal liability for the death or bodily injury of a third party, or damage to the property of a third party, as a result of the company's activities. The policy should also provide cover for the costs incurred by the injured party as a result of the accident or event. Policies will usually include territorial restrictions and it is important to review these and confirm that the coverage is sufficiently wide to meet the company's needs. In the UK, policies will usually be arranged on the loss occurring basis, which means that claims will be met in respect of death, injury or damage caused during the period of indemnity, regardless of when the claim is actually made. The precise terms of the policy should be reviewed to confirm they provide adequate cover for all relevant aspects of the company's business.

14.21   Product Liability

In many ways, product liability insurance is similar to public liability insurance and is designed to protect the company against legal liability for death or bodily injury caused to a third party, or damage caused to the property or equipment of a third party, as a result of using a product manufactured, sold, serviced or repaired by the company. Not all businesses will need to carry product liability insurance. Once again, the precise terms of the policy, and any territorial restrictions, should be carefully reviewed to ensure coverage is sufficiently wide for the company's needs. Depending on the nature of the business, companies may want to extend the normal cover to include liability arising from defective designs, specifications or instructions and the potential costs of product recalls.

14.22   Professional Indemnity

Professional indemnity insurance provides protection against liability arising from failure to exercise due skill and care in carrying out a professional contract, resulting in a loss to the other party. Practising accountants, solicitors and architects are usually required by their professional bodies to carry such insurance, but many other professionals are now seeking similar protection in view of the generally more litigious climate. However, the increase in professional negligence claims has inevitably resulted in higher premiums for this type of insurance and, in some cases, difficulty in obtaining the required level of cover. Only the unintentional failure to exercise due skill and care will be covered by the policy – no protection will be given in the case of fraudulent or dishonest conduct. All claims made during the period of indemnity are normally covered, regardless of when the act of negligence arose. The insured is therefore required

Insurance

to make full disclosure of circumstances and events that might give rise to a claim as soon as they are identified, and to make similar declarations at each renewal date.

14.23 Directors and Officers

The duties of directors are considered in more detail in **8 DIRECTORS' DUTIES**. Claims may be brought against directors in the event of negligence, default, breach of duty or breach of trust in relation to the company. The *Companies Act 1985* permits (but does not require) a company to indemnify directors against proceedings brought by third parties. Actions brought by the company and its associates are specifically excluded from these provisions. The indemnity can generally cover both legal costs and the financial costs of an adverse judgement, but it cannot cover:

- the legal costs of an unsuccessful defence of criminal proceedings;
- fines imposed in criminal proceedings;
- penalties imposed by regulatory bodies; or
- certain applications under *CA 1985* where the court refuses to grant relief to the director.

Companies who provide such an indemnity must disclose this fact in the directors' report (see **11.86** above) and shareholders have the right to inspect any indemnification agreement. Similarly, a company is permitted (but not required) to pay a director's defence costs as they are incurred, although if the defence is unsuccessful, the director will be required to repay any costs that are not covered by an indemnity as discussed above. A company is also permitted to take out insurance against such liability on behalf of the directors and officers. The company will therefore usually want to arrange insurance cover:

- for any costs incurred in defending actions where it has indemnified the directors (as explained above); and
- to protect the directors in circumstances where the company cannot indemnify them.

However, no protection will be provided against claims involving dishonesty, fraudulent conduct or the obtaining of personal profit by illegal means.

14.24 Key Person Insurance

Where the success of a company is heavily dependent on individual directors or other employees, the company may want to insure against the potential risks to the business arising from the death, incapacity or ill-health of those individuals. Potential risks might include:

- disruption of the business due to loss of personal skill and experience;
- loss of business income (eg through loss of personal contacts);

- loss of confidence in the business, both in terms of key relationships (eg bankers, investors) and in general terms; and
- costs incurred in recruiting a suitable replacement.

It should be possible to take out key person insurance against these and similar risks, if the company can demonstrate the importance of the individual to the business, and if the period of cover is reasonable. The level of cover will usually be linked to the individual's remuneration. The cover may be taken out on a regular basis, or to provide additional protection at certain times (for instance, when a number of key individuals are travelling together or when the business needs to be sure that it can maintain its present income levels in order to repay borrowings on time). Key person insurance is designed to protect the company, rather than to provide any benefit for the individual affected.

14.25   Employee Benefits

As a separate arrangement, many companies include private health insurance and/or personal accident insurance in the benefits offered to employees as part of their remuneration package. Private health insurance can enable individuals to receive treatment more promptly or at a time that suits both them and the business. Personal accident cover is usually provided under a group scheme and is designed to pay benefits in the event of death, incapacity or serious disability. Other similar types of insurance include critical illness cover, which provides a cash lump sum for individuals in the event of a serious illness, and income protection insurance, which is designed to pay an individual's salary in a period when they are incapacitated.

Insurance

Appendix 1

Useful Websites on Insurance Issues

Association of British Insurers	www.abi.org.uk
British Association of Insurance Brokers	www.biba.org.uk
Institute of Directors	www.iod.com
Business Link	www.businesslink.gov.uk
ICAEW Finance and Management Faculty	www.icaew.co.uk/fmfac

Intangibles

Intangibles

15 Intangibles

15.1 Nature of Intangible Assets

> **At a Glance**
> * Intangible assets are defined as non-financial fixed assets that do not have a physical substance, but are identifiable and are controlled by an entity through custody or legal rights.
> * The capitalisation of internally developed brands and publishing titles is not permitted under FRS 10 *Goodwill and Intangible Assets*, but purchased brands and titles can be capitalised if their fair value can be established.
> * The ASB Reporting Statement *Operating and Financial Review* encourages discussion of the strengths and resources of a business, including any intangible assets that are not shown on the balance sheet.

15.2 Definition of an Intangible Asset

Under UK accounting practice, intangible assets are defined in FRS 10 *Goodwill and Intangible Assets* as:

> '…non-financial fixed assets that do not have physical substance but are identifiable and are controlled by the entity through custody or legal rights'.

For information on obtaining copies of FRS 10 see the Accounting Standards Board ('ASB') website at www.frc.org.uk/asb.

An identifiable asset is defined in companies' legislation as one that can be disposed of separately without the disposal of a business of the entity. An asset that can only be disposed of as part of the revenue-earning capacity to which it contributes is indistinguishable from the goodwill relating to that activity and should therefore be accounted for as goodwill (see **15.29–15.31** below). Slightly different definitions apply under IASs.

15.3 Examples of an Intangible Asset

Examples of intangible assets include:

* patents;
* trade marks;

Intangibles

- copyright;
- licences and quotas; and
- franchises.

Other types of technical or intellectual property may also qualify as intangible assets, depending on whether they can be separately disposed of. Wider forms of intangible asset, such as the personal skills that have been developed by a group of employees, or a customer or client list, will not meet the accounting definition of an intangible asset, because the entity that holds them at any point in time is not considered to have sufficient control over the potential benefits that they represent to be able to recognise them as assets for accounting purposes.

15.4   Control of an Intangible Asset

Control of an intangible asset is usually secured through some form of legal right. For instance, a patent or trademark can be registered to prevent others gaining access to the asset or being able to use or copy it. A licence or franchise will allow the holder access to the benefits of a particular asset, usually for a fixed period of time. Control is more difficult to demonstrate in the absence of legal rights to the asset, but as the FRS 10 definition suggests (see **15.2** above), control may be achieved through custody – for instance, by maintaining secrecy over specific technical knowledge developed within a business.

15.5   Valuation of Brands and Titles

A particular market developed some years ago in the valuation of brands and publishing titles and some companies tried to capitalise these items as intangible assets in their accounts on the grounds that they had the right to the benefits represented by the asset that they had developed and could sell this if a suitable opportunity arose. However, this accounting treatment for brands and titles is not permitted under FRS 10, which became effective for accounting periods ending on or after 23 December 1998 (see **15.2** above). Under the standard, an internally developed intangible asset can only be capitalised if it has a readily ascertainable market value. The guidance in the standard concludes that there is no readily ascertainable market value for assets such as brands and publishing titles because each one is intrinsically unique. For the same reason, replacement cost is difficult to establish. Internally developed brands and titles should therefore not be capitalised as assets. However, where a brand or title is purchased separately it can be capitalised at cost. Where a brand or title is acquired as part of a business, it may be capitalised separately if its fair value can be established. The standard notes that techniques have been developed for estimating the value of intangibles such as brands and titles (eg based on indicators of value such as multiples of turnover) and that these may be used to establish fair value at the time of acquisition. The end result, therefore, is that a company that has developed a brand will not be able to account for this as an intangible asset, but a company that has purchased a brand will usually be able to do so. However, where capitalisation is being considered, careful attention should be given to all of the surrounding issues raised in the accounting standard, as a number of FRRP cases (see **11.16** above) have highlighted inappropriate application of the requirements. IASs allow certain internally generated assets to be recognised if they meet relevant criteria, but specifically exclude items such as internally generated brands and titles from this accounting treatment.

15.6   Discussion in Operating and Financial Review

The non-mandatory ASB Reporting Statement *Operating and Financial Review* ('OFR') published in January 2006 (see **11.89** to **11.93** above) encourages discussion of the strengths and resources of the business that are not reflected in the balance sheet, including brands and similar intangible items.

15.7   Accounting for Intangible Assets

At a Glance
* Under UK accounting practice both *CA 1985* and FRS 10 *Goodwill and Intangible Assets* set out rules on the capitalisation of intangibles.
* FRS 10 includes separate requirements on initial recognition for intangibles that are developed internally, those that are acquired as part of a business and those that are purchased separately.
* An intangible asset may be revalued if it has a readily ascertainable market value (as defined in the standard), provided that all other capitalised intangible assets in the same class are revalued at the same time.
* Intangible assets that have been capitalised should be amortised over their expected useful economic lives, with the amortisation charged to the profit and loss account on a systematic basis.
* An intangible asset that is regarded as having an indefinite useful economic life should not be amortised.
* There is a rebuttable presumption that the useful economic life of an intangible asset should be no more than 20 years.
* Useful economic lives should be reviewed at the end of each accounting period and revised where necessary.
* A residual value should only be assigned to an intangible asset if it can be measured reliably.
* Intangible assets that are amortised over a period of more than 20 years, and those which are not amortised, must be reviewed annually for impairment.
* The ASB has proposed changes to the present accounting requirements as part of its project to converge UK accounting practice with international requirements.
* Slightly different requirements apply under IASs.

Intangibles

15.8   Capitalisation of Intangible Assets

Under the *Companies Act 1985*, a company's balance sheet may only include amounts in respect of concessions, patents, licences, trade marks and similar rights if:

- the assets were acquired for valuable consideration and are not required to be shown under goodwill; or
- the assets were created by the company itself.

FRS 10 *Goodwill and Intangible Assets* provides the first definitive guidance on accounting for intangible assets. The standard includes a definition of intangible assets (see **15.2** above) and guidance on applying this definition in practice. The standard also notes that software development costs that are directly attributable to bringing a computer system or other computer-related equipment into working order should be treated as part of the cost of the related hardware. Certain intangible assets (such as research and development costs and oil and gas exploration and development costs) are excluded from FRS 10 on the basis that they are covered by more specific accounting requirements.

15.9   Initial Recognition

FRS 10 (see **15.2** above) sets out separate requirements on initial recognition for intangible assets that are purchased externally and those that are developed internally. Purchased intangible assets are classified further into those acquired as part of a business and those purchased separately. The following requirements apply:

- an internally developed intangible asset should only be capitalised if it has a readily ascertainable market value;
- an intangible asset purchased separately from a business should be capitalised at cost; and
- an intangible asset acquired as part of a business should be capitalised separately from goodwill if its value can be measured reliably at the time of initial recognition – in other cases the value of the intangible asset should be subsumed within the amount attributed to goodwill.

Readily ascertainable market value is defined in FRS 10 as a value established by reference to a market where:

- the asset belongs to a homogeneous population of assets that are equivalent in all material respects; and
- an active market, evidenced by frequent transactions, exists for that population of assets.

The guidance suggests that certain operating licences, franchises and quotas might meet these conditions, but a brand, publishing title or patent would not usually do so as each of these is inevitably unique, even though other similar assets may exist and may be traded from time to time.

15.10   Valuing an Intangible Asset Acquired as Part of a Business

An intangible asset acquired as part of a business should initially be recorded at fair value, but where the asset does not have a readily ascertainable market value, the fair value should be restricted to an amount that does not create or increase any negative goodwill arising on the acquisition (see **15.29–15.31** below). Fair value should be established in accordance with FRS 7 *Fair Values in Acquisition Accounting* (for information on obtaining copies see the ASB website at www.frc.org.uk/asb). This requires fair value to be based on replacement cost, which in most cases will be the estimated market value of the asset. The standard also considers fair value in the context of unique intangible assets, such as brands, for which replacement cost or market values may be difficult to determine. In some cases techniques have been developed for estimating the value of such assets for the purpose of sale and purchase agreements, and the guidance in the standard notes that it may be appropriate to use these to establish fair value for accounts recognition purposes in the case of an acquisition.

15.11   Revaluation of Intangible Assets

Where an intangible asset has a readily ascertainable market value, as defined in the standard, it may be revalued to market value, provided that all other capitalised intangible assets of the same class are revalued at the same time. The standard defines a class of intangible assets as 'a category of intangible assets having a similar nature, function or use in the business of the entity' and suggests that licences, quotas, patents, copyrights, franchises and trade marks are examples of such classes. The guidance also notes that further subdivision may be appropriate in certain cases – for instance, where an entity holds licences with different functions within the business. Intangible assets used in different segments of the business may also be treated as separate classes of intangible assets. The standard does not specify a frequency of revaluation, but states that, once an intangible asset has been revalued, the valuation should be updated sufficiently often to ensure that the carrying value of the asset does not differ materially from its market value at the balance sheet date. Where an intangible asset has been revalued, the amortisation charge should be based on the revalued amount and the remaining useful economic life of the asset. Amortisation charged before the revaluation took place should not be written back in the profit and loss account.

15.12   Amortisation

The *Companies Act 1985* requires any items capitalised as intangible fixed assets to be amortised over their expected useful economic lives in the same way as any other fixed assets. Under FRS 10 (see **15.2** above), an intangible asset that is regarded as having a limited useful economic life must be amortised on a systematic basis over that life, but an intangible asset that is regarded

Intangibles

as having an indefinite useful economic life should not be amortised. Amortisation should be charged to the profit and loss account for the year, on a systematic basis over the useful economic life of the asset, using a method that reflects the expected pattern of depletion of the asset. A straight-line method should be used unless another method can be shown to be more appropriate. For instance, where a licence covers production of a finite quantity of a particular product rather than unlimited production over a period of time, it may be more appropriate to base amortisation on the quantity produced rather than the period of the licence. However, the ASB has proposed an amendment to FRS 10 to clarify that there are unlikely to be circumstances that would support an amortisation method that is less conservative than straight line.

15.13   *Determining Useful Economic Life*

FRS 10 (see **15.2** above) defines the useful economic life of an intangible asset as 'the period over which the entity expects to derive economic benefit from that asset'. There is a rebuttable presumption that the useful economic life of an intangible asset should be no more than 20 years, and this presumption can only be rebutted if:

- the durability of the intangible asset can be demonstrated and justifies a life of more than 20 years; and
- the intangible asset is capable of continued measurement so that annual impairment reviews can be carried out.

The standard notes that the useful economic lives of intangible assets will often be uncertain, but this does not justify an assumption that the life of a particular intangible asset is 20 years, or that its life is indefinite. Conversely, uncertainty should not be used to justify the adoption of an unrealistically short life. A prudent but realistic estimate of the useful economic life must be made for each intangible asset. The standard also notes that an asset will not be capable of continued measurement where the cost of carrying out the measurement is unjustifiably high – for instance, where the amounts involved are not sufficiently material to justify the detailed procedures needed to carry out an annual impairment review.

15.14   *Legal Rights Granted for a Finite Period*

Legal factors may also influence the useful economic life of an intangible asset, in that they may restrict the period during which the reporting entity has access to the economic benefits associated with the asset. The useful economic life of an intangible asset is therefore the shorter of:

- the period over which the future benefits are expected to arise; and
- the period over which the reporting entity is expected to have control of those benefits.

Where access to the benefits is granted for a finite period, the useful economic life of the asset will usually be limited to that period. The life of the asset should only be extended beyond this period if, and to the extent that, the legal rights over the asset are renewable and renewal is assured. The standard gives the following additional guidance on when the renewal of rights may be regarded as being assured:

- if the value of the intangible asset does not reduce as the initial expiry date approaches, or where the value reduces only by an amount reflecting the cost of renewal of the rights;
- where there is evidence that the rights will be renewed (eg on the basis of past experience); and
- where there is no evidence that the entity has breached any conditions under the terms of the original rights which might otherwise prevent the rights being renewed.

Any costs that are expected to recur each time the legal rights are renewed should be excluded from the amount treated as having a longer life.

15.15   *Review of Economic Lives*

The useful economic lives of intangible assets should be reviewed at the end of each accounting period and revised where necessary. Where the useful economic life of an intangible asset is adjusted, the carrying value of the asset should be amortised over its revised remaining useful economic life. If the revision extends the life of the asset to a period of more than 20 years from the date of its acquisition, the additional requirements of FRS 10 (see **15.2** above) on annual impairment reviews automatically come into effect.

15.16   Residual Value

A residual value should only be assigned to an intangible asset if it can be measured reliably. The residual value of an intangible asset will generally only be significant and capable of reliable measurement where the entity has a legal or contractual right to receive a certain sum at the end of the period during which it has use of the asset, or where there is a readily ascertainable market value for the residual asset.

15.17   Requirement for Impairment Reviews

Impairment is defined as 'a reduction in the recoverable amount of a fixed asset or goodwill below its carrying value' and recoverable amount is the higher of:

- *net realisable value* – the amount at which an asset could be disposed of, less any direct selling costs; and
- *value in use* – the present value of the future cashflows obtainable as a result of an asset's continued use, including those resulting from its ultimate disposal.

Intangibles

Intangible assets that are amortised over a period of 20 years or less must be reviewed for impairment at the end of the first full financial year following acquisition and in other periods if events or changes in circumstances indicate that the carrying value of an asset may not be fully recoverable. Intangible assets that are amortised over a period of more than 20 years, or are not amortised, should be reviewed for impairment at the end of each accounting period.

Impairment reviews should generally be carried out in accordance with the requirements of FRS 11 *Impairment of Fixed Assets and Goodwill* although a more straightforward approach may be used in the first year for an asset purchased as part of a business acquisition. The accounting treatment of any impairment losses suffered, and any future reversals of those losses, is also covered in FRS 11 (for information on obtaining copies see the ASB website at www.frc.org.uk/asb). However, in the case of intangible assets, most reversals will be the result of the internal generation of intangible asset value and should therefore not be recognised in the accounts.

15.18   ASB Proposals for Change

The ASB published the following Exposure Drafts in July 2005:

- FRED 36 *Business Combinations and Amendment to FRS 2 Accounting for Subsidiary Undertakings*;
- FRED 37 *Intangible Assets*; and
- FRED 38 *Impairment of Assets*.

These form a package of proposed new standards arising from the completion of the IASB's project on accounting for business combinations and are based on IASB proposals for the revision of IFRS 3 *Business Combinations* and IAS 27 *Consolidated and Separate Financial Statements*, together with the existing requirements of IAS 38 *Intangible Assets*. The ASB has clear reservations about certain aspects of these proposals and considers that some of the changes would not represent an improvement in UK accounting practice. The proposals would

- require an intangible asset to be recognised when it is separable (i.e. it is separate from the entity and can be transferred or disposed of either on its own or together with a related contract asset or liability) or when it arises from contractual or legal rights, regardless of whether those rights are separable – this would result in more intangible assets being recognised than under current UK practice;
- require internally generated intangible assets arising from development activities to be recognised where relevant criteria are met; and
- require website development costs to be accounted for as internally generated intangible assets rather than as tangible fixed assets.

At the time of publication, the ASB put forward a number of options on the timing of adoption of these standards for respondents to consider. These could have resulted in full or partial implementation of the changes for accounting periods beginning on or after 1 January 2007. However, the ASB is currently in the process of a more fundamental reconsideration of its convergence programme (see **11.7** above) and so implementation of the above changes seems likely to be deferred until a later date.

15.19   Accounting under IASs

Companies preparing IAS accounts (see **3.16** and **3.17** above) are required to comply with IAS 38 *Intangible Assets* in place of the accounting requirements of *CA 1985* and FRS 10. The main differences under IAS 38 are that:

- an intangible asset is identifiable when it is separable from the entity or it arises from contractual or other legal rights – there is no requirement for the asset to be capable of separate disposal in the second case;
- an internally generated intangible asset can be recognised if it meets relevant criteria, which are similar to those in SSAP 13 on the recognition of development costs – however, items such as brands and titles are excluded from this treatment;
- there is no rebuttable presumption that the useful economic life of an intangible asset is not more than 20 years; and
- an impairment review is only required for an asset with a finite life if there is an indication that impairment has occurred, but annual reviews are required for an asset with an indefinite life.

15.20   Intellectual Property Protection

> **At a Glance**
> * Intellectual property enables businesses and individuals to protect the rights that they hold in their own inventions, creations and ideas and to sell them in the same way as other assets.
> * Intellectual property protection gives the holder the exclusive right to benefit from the property and to control the access to it, and use of it, by other parties.
> * Patents are used to protect inventions, including new and improved processes, and must be formally registered in order to take effect.
> * Trade marks are used to distinguish the products or services of different businesses but are not protected unless they have been registered.
> * Design rights and copyright are granted automatically as soon as there is a record of the material that has been created.
> * Use of protected rights can be granted to others by licence.
> * The existence of intellectual property rights should be given as much publicity as possible to reduce the risk of the rights being abused.

15.21   What is Intellectual Property?

Intellectual property (sometimes referred to as 'IP') enables individuals and businesses to protect the rights that they hold in their own inventions, creations and ideas and to sell them in the same way as physical assets. In most cases, the right of the individual or business has to be registered in order for the protection to take effect, but in certain cases it is available automatically. Also, some rights may be capable of protection under more than one form of intellectual property.

15.22   Forms of Intellectual Property

There are four main types of intellectual property – patents, trade marks, designs and copyright – although protection can be afforded to a much wider range of private property rights, including plant varieties, performance rights and trade secrets. The benefit of intellectual property protection is that it gives the holder the exclusive right to benefit from the property and to control the access to it, or use of it, by other parties. Use of intellectual property without the appropriate permission usually amounts to infringement and could therefore be the subject of legal action, although in many cases this will only be used as a last resort. Rights are usually given for a specific territory, so registration may be needed in more than one country.

15.23   Patents

Patents are used to protect inventions, including new and improved products and processes that are capable of industrial application. Patents must be formally registered in order to take effect and applications in respect of UK rights should be made to the UK Patent Office (The Patent Office, Concept House, Cardiff Road, Newport, South Wales NP10 8QQ; *tel:* 08459 500 505). A patent valid in the UK can also be obtained from the European Patent Office, but the application must be cleared by the UK Patent Office for security reasons. A patent lasts for a finite period (20 years in the UK) and gives the inventor or creator of a product or process the right to prevent others from making, using or selling that product or process without permission. Permission to make, use or sell the product or process can be granted by licence to third parties if the holder of the patent so chooses. The holder can also sell the patent to a third party, in which case he will sacrifice all rights over the product or process unless other formal arrangements have been made with the new owner (eg through an appropriate licence). Patents should be applied for as soon as possible – protection will not be granted for any rights that have already been disclosed to the public. Independent advice on more complex issues in respect of patents (eg the patenting of computer software) can be obtained from a patent agent through the Chartered Institute of Patent Agents (The Staple Inn Buildings, High Holborn, London WC1V 7PZ; *tel:* 020 7405 9450).

15.24   Trade Marks

Trade marks are signs used to distinguish the products or services of one business from those supplied by another party. They can include words, logos, slogans, shapes and colours and are usually protected so that they can be used as marketing tools. A trade mark is not protected unless it has been registered with the UK Patents Office (see **15.21** above) or the Office for Harmonisation in the Internal Market.

15.25   Design Rights and Copyright

Design rights and copyright differ from other forms of intellectual property in that they are granted automatically to the creator as soon as there is a record (in whatever form) of the material that has been created. There is consequently no requirement to register the right to achieve the protection offered. However, it is usually advisable to take steps to prove that the material was original to the creator. Design right is not a monopoly right but a right to prevent deliberate copying. Additional protection can be obtained by registering a design with the UK Patents Office (see **15.23** above). This gives the holder the exclusive right to make, import, sell or hire out any item to which the design has been applied, or to grant permission to others to use the design on agreed terms.

15.26   Granting Use to Others

The use of protected rights can be granted to others by licence. In the case of copyright, this is often done through collecting societies, who make the detailed arrangements and therefore avoid the need for the copyright holder to arrange individual licences for each user. However, in the case of patents, trademarks and registered design rights, where the owner is more likely to want to exercise close control, individual licence agreements will need to be made with each potential user on terms acceptable to both parties.

15.27   Preventing Unauthorised Use

The existence of intellectual property rights over a product, process, trademark, design or copyright material should be publicised as much as possible, to reduce the chance of other parties using it without permission on the grounds that it was not evident that it was intellectual property. In the case of particularly significant rights, the owner may want to arrange insurance to cover the cost of potential actions to enforce the rights that he holds.

15.28   Further Information

A Government-backed website is now available at www.intellectual-property. gov.uk which draws together basic information on intellectual property and is regularly updated for current developments. It also provides links to other relevant sites, including those for the UK Patents Office and the Chartered Institute of Patent Agents.

Intangibles

15.29 Goodwill

> **At a Glance**
> * Under UK accounting practice purchased goodwill is defined as the difference between the cost of an acquired entity and the aggregate of the fair values of that entity's identifiable assets and liabilities.
> * Internally generated goodwill cannot be recognised on the balance sheet.
> * Positive purchased goodwill should be capitalised as an asset on the balance sheet – any negative goodwill should be shown separately below the heading for positive goodwill.
> * The fair values of the identifiable assets and liabilities acquired should be established in accordance with FRS 7 *Fair Values in Acquisition Accounting*.
> * Goodwill should be amortised on a systematic basis over its expected useful economic life, with the amortisation charged to the profit and loss account.
> * Goodwill that is considered to have an indefinite useful economic life should not be amortised.
> * There is a rebuttable presumption that the useful economic life of goodwill is no more than 20 years.
> * The useful economic life of goodwill should be reviewed at the end of each accounting period and revised where necessary.
> * Goodwill that is amortised over a period of more than 20 years, and goodwill that is not amortised, must be reviewed annually for impairment.
> * FRS 10 specifies how and when any negative goodwill should be recognised in the profit and loss account.
> * The ASB has proposed changes to the present accounting requirements as part of its project to converge UK accounting practice with international requirements.
> * Slightly different requirements apply under IASs.

15.30 Nature of Goodwill

Under UK accounting practice, FRS 10 *Goodwill and Intangible Assets* (see **15.2** above) defines purchased goodwill as:

> '... the difference between the cost of an acquired entity and the aggregate of the fair values of that entity's identifiable assets and liabilities'.

Positive goodwill arises where the cost of acquisition exceeds the aggregate fair values of the identifiable assets and liabilities of the business acquired – in other words, where the value of the business as a whole is considered to be more than the aggregate of the values of its component parts and the purchaser is therefore prepared to pay more than the value of the individual assets and liabilities that make up the business. Negative goodwill arises in the converse situation – where the value of the business is considered to be less than the value of the component parts and the aggregate fair values of the identifiable assets and liabilities are therefore more than the cost of acquisition. Negative goodwill is expected to arise only rarely.

15.31   Recognition of Goodwill

Neither the *Companies Act 1985* nor FRS 10 (see **15.2** above) permit internally generated goodwill to be recognised on the balance sheet. Goodwill is therefore only recognised for accounting purposes when the business to which it relates is purchased by another party. Under FRS 10:

- positive purchased goodwill should be capitalised and classified as an asset on the balance sheet;
- any negative goodwill that arises on an acquisition should be recognised in the accounts and shown separately on the face of the balance sheet immediately below the goodwill heading – a sub-total of the net amount of positive and negative goodwill should also be given.

Purchased goodwill arising on a single transaction should not be divided into positive and negative components.

15.32   Value of Purchased Goodwill

When a business is acquired, the value of the purchased goodwill is established by comparing the fair values of the various assets and liabilities at the time of acquisition with the fair value of the consideration given by the purchaser. Any excess of the consideration over the fair values of the net assets represents the value of the purchased goodwill. Where an intangible asset is acquired as part of the transaction, it should normally be capitalised separately. However, if its value cannot be measured reliably, it should be subsumed within the amount of the purchase price attributed to goodwill. Where an acquisition appears to give rise to negative goodwill, the fair values of the assets acquired should be tested for impairment and the fair values of the liabilities acquired should be reviewed carefully to confirm that they have not been understated and that no items have been overlooked. FRS 7 *Fair Values in Acquisition Accounting* provides detailed guidance on establishing the fair values of individual assets and liabilities at the time of acquisition and the fair value of the purchase consideration (which will not necessarily be in the form of cash) (for information on obtaining copies see the ASB website at www.frc.org.uk/asb).

15.33   Amortisation

The following amortisation requirements apply under FRS 10 (see **15.2** above):

- where purchased goodwill is regarded as having a limited useful economic life, it should be amortised on a systematic basis over that life – the amortisation should be charged in the profit and loss account for the year;

Intangibles

- where purchased goodwill is considered to have an indefinite useful economic life, it should not be amortised.

The *Companies Act 1985* requires goodwill to be amortised systematically over a finite period, and an entity following the requirements of FRS 10 in respect of goodwill that is considered to have indefinite life will therefore need to adopt the true and fair override and make appropriate disclosures in the accounts (see **11 FINANCIAL REPORTING**). No residual value should be attributed to purchased goodwill. Amortisation must be charged on a systematic basis over the useful economic life of the goodwill, using a method that reflects the expected pattern of depletion. A straight-line method should be used unless another method can be shown to be more appropriate. However, an amortisation method that is less conservative than the straight-line method is unlikely to be justifiable.

15.34   *Determining the Useful Economic Life of Goodwill*

FRS 10 defines the useful economic life of purchased goodwill as 'the period over which the value of the underlying business acquired is expected to exceed the values of its identifiable net assets'. The assessment will need to take into account the useful economic lives of any intangible assets not recognised separately because their values cannot be measured reliably. There is a rebuttable presumption that the useful economic life of goodwill should be no more than 20 years, and this presumption can only be rebutted if:

- the durability of the acquired business can be demonstrated and justifies a life of more than 20 years; and
- the goodwill is capable of continued measurement so that annual impairment reviews can be carried out.

The guidance in the standard emphasises that it is inappropriate to assume that the premium of an acquired business over its net asset value can be maintained indefinitely. In practice, purchased goodwill will usually be replaced by internally generated goodwill over time and, because internally generated goodwill should not be recognised for accounting purposes, it is important that the write-off period for the purchased goodwill is sufficiently short to allow it to be eliminated from the accounts before it is fully replaced with internally generated goodwill.

The useful economic life of goodwill will often be uncertain, but this does not justify an assumption that it has a life of 20 years, or that its life is indefinite. Conversely, uncertainty should not be used to justify the adoption of an unrealistically short life. A prudent but realistic estimate of the useful economic life must be made in each case where goodwill arises.

15.35   *Durability and Continued Measurement*

The guidance in FRS 10 (see **15.2** above) emphasises that the durability of a business will vary depending on various factors, including:

- the nature of the business;
- the stability of the industry in which it operates;

- the typical lifespan of the products to which the goodwill relates;
- the extent to which the acquisition overcomes market entry barriers that will continue to exist; and
- the expected impact of competition in future years.

In practice, these are factors that will also need to be considered when determining the useful economic life of goodwill. The standard also notes that goodwill will not be capable of continued measurement where the cost of carrying out the measurement is unjustifiably high – for instance, where the acquired business is merged with an existing business to such an extent that the acquired goodwill cannot be separately identified and reviewed in future years.

15.36   *Review of Economic Life*

The useful economic life of purchased goodwill should be reviewed at the end of each accounting period and revised where necessary. Where the useful economic life is adjusted, the carrying value of the goodwill should be amortised over its revised remaining useful economic life. If the revision extends the life of the goodwill to a period of more than 20 years from the date of its acquisition, the additional requirements of FRS 10 (see **15.2** above) on annual impairment reviews automatically come into effect.

15.37   Impairment Reviews

Impairment is defined as 'a reduction in the recoverable amount of a fixed asset or goodwill below its carrying value' and recoverable amount is the higher of:

- *net realisable value* – the amount at which an asset could be disposed of, less any direct selling costs; and
- *value in use* – the present value of the future cashflows obtainable as a result of an asset's continued use, including those resulting from its ultimate disposal.

Goodwill that is amortised over a period of 20 years or less should be reviewed for impairment at the end of the first full financial year following acquisition and in other periods if events or changes in circumstances indicate that its carrying value may not be fully recoverable. Goodwill that is amortised over a period of more than 20 years, or is not amortised, should be reviewed for impairment at the end of each accounting period. Impairment reviews should generally be carried out in accordance with the requirements of FRS 11 *Impairment of Fixed Assets and Goodwill* although in most cases a more straightforward approach can be used in the first year following an acquisition (for information on obtaining copies see the ASB website at www.frc.org.uk/asb). The guidance in FRS 10 emphasises that:

- the recognition of an impairment loss must be justified by reference to expected future cashflows, in the same way as the absence of an impairment loss;
- the fact that the value of the goodwill may not be capable of continued measurement in future does not necessarily justify writing off the entire balance at the time of the first year impairment review.

Impairment losses, and any subsequent reversals, should be accounted for in accordance with FRS 11. Most reversals will be the result of the internal generation of goodwill and should therefore not be recognised in the accounts.

15.38   Accounting for Negative Goodwill

Under UK accounting practice, negative goodwill up to the fair values of the non-monetary assets acquired should be recognised in the profit and loss account in the period in which those assets are recovered (ie through depreciation or on sale of the assets). Any negative goodwill in excess of the fair values of the non-monetary assets acquired should be recognised in the profit and loss account in the periods expected to benefit.

15.39   ASB Proposals for Change

The ASB published the following Exposure Drafts in July 2005:

- FRED 36 *Business Combinations and Amendment to FRS 2 Accounting for Subsidiary Undertakings*;
- FRED 37 *Intangible Assets*; and
- FRED 38 *Impairment of Assets*.

These form a package of proposed new standards arising from the completion of the IASB's project on accounting for business combinations and are based on IASB proposals for the revision of IFRS 3 *Business Combinations* and IAS 27 *Consolidated and Separate Financial Statements*, together with the existing requirements of IAS 38 *Intangible Assets*. The ASB has clear reservations about certain aspects of these proposals and considers that some of the changes would not represent an improvement in UK accounting practice. In particular, the proposals would

- change the accounting treatment of goodwill by requiring it to be measured at cost less impairment losses, with no provision for regular amortisation;
- change the accounting treatment of negative goodwill by requiring this to be applied initially to reduce any related positive goodwill to zero, and any remaining excess to be recognised as a gain on acquisition; and
- require goodwill to be recognised in full, regardless of the level of interest acquired by the parent entity.

Proposed changes to the accounting treatment of intangible assets, which would in some cases impact on the amount of goodwill recognised in respect of an acquisition, are summarised at **15.18** above. At the time of publication, the ASB put forward a number of options on the timing of adoption of these standards for respondents to consider. These could have resulted in full or partial implementation of the changes for accounting periods beginning on or after 1 January 2007. However, the ASB is currently in the process of a more fundamental reconsideration of its convergence programme (see **11.7** above) and so implementation of the above changes seems likely to be deferred until a later date.

15.40   Accounting under IASs

Companies preparing IAS accounts (see **3.16** and **3.17** above) are required to comply with IFRS 3 *Business Combinations* and IAS 38 *Intangible Assets* in place of the accounting requirements of *CA 1985* and FRS 10. The main differences are:

- IFRS 3 is more stringent on the identification and separate recognition of intangible assets at the time of acquisition, rather than allowing items to be subsumed within the value of goodwill;
- the period in which adjustments can be made to provisional fair values is generally shorter under IFRS 3 than under FRS 7, and the accounting treatment of any changes differs between the two standards;
- IFRS 3 requires goodwill to be reviewed annually for impairment and does not allow amortisation – consequently there is no rebuttable assumption that the useful economic life of goodwill does not exceed 20 years;
- IFRS 3 requires any negative goodwill to be offset against any related positive goodwill, with any excess taken to the profit and loss account in the year of acquisition; and
- different accounting requirements apply under FRS 2 and IFRS 3 where an acquisition takes place in stages rather than as a single transaction.

Appendix 1

Useful Websites on Intangibles

UK Intellectual Property	www.intellectual-property.gov.uk
Intellectual Property Institute	www.ip-institute.org.uk
UK Patent Office	www.patent.gov.uk
European Patent Office	www.european-patent-office.org
World Intellectual Property Organisation	www.wipo.int
Chartered Institute of Patent Agents	www.cipa.org.uk
Accounting Standards Board	www.frc.org.uk/asb
International Accounting Standards Board	www.iasb.org
Financial Reporting Review Panel	www.frc.org.uk/frrp

Investor Relations

16 Investor Relations

16.1 Shareholder Engagement

> **At a Glance**
> * There is a growing demand for shareholders to develop a closer relationship with the boards of the companies in which they invest.
> * The distinction between governance and management must be maintained – in particular, good investor relations should not result in shareholders becoming management by proxy.
> * All shareholders must be treated equally.
> * The *Combined Code* encourages constructive use of the AGM, and changes are to be made to company law with the same objective in mind.
> * There is a significant degree of common interest between individual shareholders and institutional shareholders.
> * The *Combined Code* encourages the development of a constructive relationship between the company and its institutional investors.
> * Institutional investors are encouraged to make full use of their voting rights, and directors are advised to keep up-to-date with the voting guidelines issued by the various representative bodies.
> * The Institutional Shareholders' Committee has developed guidelines on the level of contact between companies and their institutional investors.
> * Institutional investor organisations carry out detailed analyses of compliance with the *Combined Code* and other corporate governance issues.
> * Quoted companies are now required to disclose information on total shareholder return and compare this with an appropriate market index.

16.2 The Growth of Shareholder Activism

There is a growing demand for shareholders to develop a closer relationship with the boards of the companies in which they invest. This has been fuelled in particular by concerns over the issue of directors' remuneration and also by recent accounting scandals that have come to light in the USA. Shareholders have three primary concerns:

- preservation of their rights as owners of the business;
- minimising the risk associated with their investment; and
- enhancing the long-term value of that investment.

Currently, shareholder voting is the principal means by which shareholders exercise their rights but shareholder activism is becoming a much broader issue and one of which companies need to be increasingly aware. There was a sharp increase in shareholder activism in the UK in 2003 and 2004, particularly in respect of directors' remuneration and compensation packages, and the implementation of the current version of the *Combined Code* with effect from 1 November 2003 has prompted more detailed consideration of corporate governance issues in general.

16.3 Relationship Between Board and Shareholders

It is essential to recognise the distinction between governance and management in this context. Good investor relations are an important means of achieving accountability and transparency through improved disclosure on key issues and better communication of business strategy, but they should not result in shareholders seeking to become management by proxy. The *Cadbury Report* summarised the relationship between the board and the company's shareholders as follows:

- the shareholders, as owners of the company, elect the directors to run the business on their behalf, and hold them accountable for its progress and development;
- the directors report to the shareholders on their stewardship of the company and its assets; and
- the shareholders appoint external auditors to provide an independent check on the company's financial statements.

The Cadbury Committee considered suggestions on how the accountability of directors to shareholders might be strengthened but concluded that shareholders should continue to make their views known to the board through direct communication and through attendance at annual general meetings. The Committee also noted that shareholder organisations set up to represent shareholder interests generally might provide an opportunity for individual shareholders to act collectively if they wish. Whilst shareholders cannot be involved in the detailed direction and management of their company, they are entitled to insist on a high standard of corporate governance, evidenced by compliance with the *Combined Code.*

16.4 Combined Code Principles on Shareholder Relations

Section D of the *Combined Code* identifies two principles in respect of the company's relations with its shareholders:

- there should be a dialogue with shareholders based on the mutual understanding of objectives – the board as a whole is responsible for ensuring that this dialogue takes place; and

- the board should use the AGM to communicate with private investors and encourage their participation.

The current version places greater emphasis on the collective responsibility of the board in the area of shareholder relations than the original Code. The supporting principles also note that, whilst recognising most shareholder contact will be with the chief executive and finance director, the chairman and where appropriate other directors (including the senior independent director) should maintain sufficient contact with shareholders to understand their issues and concerns, using whichever methods are most practical and efficient. The best practice provisions include the following recommendations:

- the chairman should discuss governance and strategy with major shareholders and should ensure that the views of shareholders are communicated to the board as a whole;
- non-executive directors should be offered the opportunity to attend meetings with major shareholders and should expect to attend if requested by the shareholders;
- the senior independent director should attend sufficient meetings with a range of major shareholders to listen to their views and develop a balanced understanding of their issues and concerns; and
- the board should disclose in the annual report the steps taken to ensure that the members of the board, and the non-executive directors in particular, develop an understanding of the views of major shareholders about the company (eg through direct face-to-face contact, analysts' or brokers' meetings, surveys of shareholder opinion etc).

16.5   Equal Treatment of All Shareholders

The *Cadbury Report* raised a number of issues on communication with shareholders, and with institutional shareholders in particular. The fact that institutional shareholders usually have more access than individual shareholders to the boards of their investee companies, does not in any way reduce the company's obligation to treat all shareholders equally. This is one of the underlying principles of the FSA's continuing obligations for listed companies and a prime tenet of company law. The directors of listed companies must therefore take steps to ensure that any significant statements concerning the company are made publicly so that they are equally available to all shareholders. This is considered in more detail in the section below on inside information (see **16.18** below).

16.6   Constructive Use of the AGM

The AGM provides the main opportunity each year for shareholders to raise issues and concerns with the directors of the company. The *Combined Code* includes four best practice provisions on constructive use of the AGM:

- companies should count all proxy votes and, except where a poll is called, should indicate the level of proxies lodged on each resolution, the balance

for and against the resolution and the number of abstentions, after the resolution has been dealt with on a show of hands;
- separate resolutions should be proposed on each substantially separate issue,
and in particular a resolution should be proposed on the annual report and
accounts;
- the chairman of the board should arrange for the chairmen of the audit, remuneration and nomination committees to be available to answer questions at
the AGM and for all directors to attend; and
- companies should arrange for the notice of the AGM and related papers to be
sent to shareholders at least 20 working days before the meeting.

For accounting periods ending on or after 31 December 2002, the *Directors'
Remuneration Report Regulations 2002* (*SI 2002/1986*) also require a formal resolution to be put to the shareholders of a quoted company on the company's annual
remuneration report (see **23.43 DIRECTORS' REMUNERATION: QUOTED COMPANIES**).

16.7   Government Proposals for Change

The Government White Paper *Modernising Company Law* issued in July 2002
includes a number of measures designed to improve the quality of shareholder
input at the AGM and in particular to give shareholders adequate opportunity
to raise matters of concern. The proposals include:

- changes to the timing of the AGM;
- a requirement for annual accounts and reports to be distributed more quickly
after the year end;
- a requirement for quoted companies to publish both their preliminary
announcement and their annual accounts and reports on a website;
- new provisions on the circulation of members' resolutions and statements;
and
- greater powers for proxies at meetings and new requirements on the conduct
and results of polls.

These proposals are explained in more detail at **6.47 GOVERNMENT PROPOSALS TO
IMPROVE AGMS** and are now included in the draft Company Law Reform Bill
published in May 2006.

16.8   Institutional Investors

The *Cadbury Report* noted that institutional shareholders hold the majority of
shares in listed companies, but emphasised that in many cases they hold them on
behalf of individuals (eg as members of pension schemes or beneficiaries of insurance policies) and that there is a significant degree of common interest between
individual shareholders and institutional shareholders. In particular, both have
the same interest in standards of financial reporting and corporate governance.

Since the publication of the *Cadbury Report* there has in fact been a rapid
growth of active private investors. This is attributed to a variety of factors,

Investor Relations

including the interest generated by the growth of the dot.com industry (despite its subsequent problems), technological development (the internet has made it much easier to buy and sell shares) and the substantial growth of journalism on personal financial issues. However, there is no doubt that institutional investors continue to represent a very significant proportion of shareholders and are in a unique position to develop closer links with the companies in which they invest.

16.9 Developing a Constructive Relationship

The *Cadbury Report* drew attention to three key issues that were considered to be critical to the development of a constructive relationship between companies and their shareholders:

- the need for institutional investors to encourage regular contact at senior executive level to exchange views and information on strategy, performance, board membership and quality of management;
- the need for institutional investors to make positive use of their voting rights and to exercise their votes on a regular basis; and
- the need for institutional investors to take a positive interest in the composition of boards and the appointment of non-executive directors with appropriate experience and independence.

These have now been developed further in the *Combined Code*, which identifies three principles in relation to institutional investors:

- institutional shareholders should be ready, where practicable, to enter into a dialogue with companies based on the mutual understanding of objectives;
- when evaluating governance arrangements, and in particular those relating to board structure and composition, institutional shareholders should give due weight to all relevant factors drawn to their attention; and
- institutional shareholders have a responsibility to make considered use of their votes.

16.10 Shareholder Voting

Institutional investors are actively encouraged by their umbrella organisations to exercise all of their voting rights and to oppose the creation or continuation of equity shares that do not carry full voting rights. The best practice guidance in the *Combined Code* includes three provisions on shareholder voting:

- institutional shareholders should take steps to ensure that their voting intentions are being translated into practice;
- on request, institutional shareholders should make available to their clients information on the proportion of resolutions on which votes were cast and non-discretionary proxies lodged; and
- major shareholders should attend AGMs wherever practicable, and company registrars should facilitate this.

The *Combined Code* does not include any specific recommendations on the disclosure of compliance with the principles or provisions relating to institutional shareholders, but the Hampel Committee did indicate their hope that these shareholders would disclose to the relevant companies, and possibly also to the public as a whole, the extent to which they are following them.

16.11   Institutional Shareholders' Committee ('ISC')

The Institutional Shareholders' Committee (ISC) represents the interests and concerns of institutional investors, with representatives from:

- the Association of British Insurers (ABI);
- the National Association of Pension Funds (NAPF);
- the Association of Investment Trust Companies (AITC); and
- the Investment Management Association (IMA).

The ISC has issued guidance to institutional investors covering issues such as:

- communication with boards;
- the use of voting rights;
- board composition;
- directors' remuneration; and
- takeover bids.

On the subject of shareholder voting, the guidelines note that institutional investors should support boards by positive use of their voting rights unless they have good reason for doing otherwise. Where an institutional investor considers it appropriate to vote against a particular proposal, the issue should be raised with the board in good time to allow for the problem to be considered and, if possible, a satisfactory solution found. If a solution proves impossible, it may be appropriate for a spokesperson to attend the meeting to explain why the proposal is being opposed. A poll should also be demanded in such cases, to ensure that the vote is properly recorded.

16.12   ISC Statement of Principles

The ISC published a *Statement of Principles* in October 2003. These represented the first comprehensive statement of best practice governing the responsibilities of institutional shareholders and investment managers in relation to the companies in which they invest. They aimed to secure value for the ultimate beneficiaries (ie pension scheme members and individual savers) through consistent monitoring of the performance of those companies, backed up by direct engagement where appropriate. A revised Statement was published in October 2005, following a review of the impact of the original document, although no significant changes to the existing principles were found to be needed. The principles make it clear that if companies persistently fail to respond to concerns, ISC members will vote against the Board at general meetings. The principles set out best practice for institutional shareholders and investment managers, under which they will:

- maintain and publish statements of their policies in respect of active engagement with the companies in which they invest;
- monitor the performance of and maintain an appropriate dialogue with those companies;
- intervene where necessary;
- evaluate the impact of their policies; and
- in the case of investment managers, report back to the clients on whose behalf they invest.

The associations making up the ISC encourage all their members to adopt and comply with the principles. The Government has previously consulted on possible legislation to underpin the obligations of institutional investors to promote their beneficiaries' interests through shareholder activism. However, it has now indicated that it welcomes the ISC's development of an approach based on best practice. The ISC intends to review the Statement again in 2007.

16.13   Voting Guidelines

Voting guidelines are regularly issued to institutional investors by organisations such as NAPF, ABI and Pensions Investment Research Consultants (PIRC), based on their assessment of the key current issues. Issues that have received most focus in recent times include:

- directors' remuneration (including incentive schemes, service contracts and notice periods);
- the independence of non-executive directors; and
- issues relating to the external audit (eg the level of non-audit services provided by the auditors, connections between the directors and auditors, reappointment or changes in the appointment of auditors, and the role and constitution of the audit committee).

Directors are well advised to keep track of the current issues being raised by these organisations so that they can be forewarned of any difficulties that are likely to arise at the AGM. Relevant information can usually be found on their websites and in some cases will be circulated to larger listed companies in advance of the publication date for their annual reports and accounts.

16.14   Dialogue with Companies

The revised Code includes just one supporting principle on dialogue with companies, which notes that institutional shareholders should apply the principles set out in the *The Responsibilities of Institutional Shareholders and Agents: Statement of Principles* published by the ISC (see **16.12** above) and which should be reflected in fund manager contracts. The principles are intended to ensure that shareholders derive value from their investments by encouraging institutional shareholders and agents to identify problems at an early stage to minimise any loss of shareholder value, and to deal promptly and effectively with any concerns over under-performance. The ISC guidance includes the following points:

- institutional shareholders and agents should review annual report and accounts, other circulars and general meeting resolutions (either directly or through contracted research providers), as well as attending meetings where appropriate, to determine if and when it is necessary to enter into an active dialogue with the investee company's board and senior management;
- as part of this monitoring process, institutional shareholders and agents should satisfy themselves that effective board and committee structures are in place and that independent directors are providing adequate oversight;
- institutional shareholders and agents should exercise their votes and, where necessary, intervene objectively and in an informed way – where it would make intervention more effective, they should engage with other shareholders;
- if boards do not respond constructively, institutional shareholders and agents should decide on a case by case basis whether to escalate their action by:
  - holding additional meetings with management to discuss their concerns,
  - expressing concern through the company's advisers,
  - meeting with the chairman, the senior independent director, or all the independent directors,
  - making a public statement in advance of the AGM (or EGM),
  - submitting resolutions at shareholders' meetings, or
  - requisitioning an EGM (possibly to change the board).

The guidance identifies the following issues as those which might prompt active shareholder intervention if the company's position gives rise to particular concerns:

- company strategy;
- operational performance;
- acquisition/disposal strategy;
- failure by independent directors to hold executive management properly to account;
- failure of internal controls;
- inadequate succession planning;
- unjustifiable failure to comply with the *Combined Code*;
- inappropriate remuneration levels, incentive packages and/or compensation packages; and
- approach to corporate social responsibility.

16.15   Level and Extent of Contact

Previously, it was generally accepted that the chairman should be the main channel of communication with institutional investors on matters of concern, and a direct approach to the senior independent director was seen as a last resort and an indication that something was seriously amiss. However, both the present *Combined Code* and the latest ISC guidance suggest a greater level of direct contact between institutional shareholders and the independent directors, and with the senior independent director in particular. Views have been divided on whether the institutional investors should have more regular contact with the independent non-executives in general. One school of thought says that the independent directors are regarded as representing the interests of all shareholders in board decisions and that they should therefore listen regularly to the concerns of shareholders, as well as to company management, customers and suppliers. The opposing view maintains that the independent directors are not shareholder representatives as such (although it is acknowledged that they do have a particular role to play in matters that might give rise to conflicts of interest between the executive directors and the shareholders – for instance, remuneration issues, succession planning and audit matters) and that it is essential for them to be able to exercise their independent judgement, uninfluenced by particular groups of investors. There is also concern that companies need to maintain good relationships will all shareholders, not just with their institutional investors. However, following its initial assessment of the impact of the present *Combined Code*, the FRC specifically noted that investors are reporting improved dialogue with companies (see **6.8** above).

16.16   Evaluation of Governance Disclosures

The institutional investor organisations referred to above (NAPF, ABI, PIRC etc) carry out detailed analyses of compliance with the *Combined Code* and of issues such as the level of directors' remuneration and the use of share option and other long-term incentive schemes. The analyses are then made available to institutional shareholders so that relevant issues can be raised with individual companies where appropriate. The *Combined Code* includes the following supporting principles on the evaluation of corporate governance disclosures:

- institutional shareholders should consider carefully the explanations given for departures from the *Combined Code* and make reasoned judgements in each case;
- if they do not accept the company's position, institutional shareholders should give an explanation to the company in writing and be prepared to enter into a dialogue;
- a box-ticking approach to assessing corporate governance should be avoided; and
- when assessing corporate governance, institutional shareholders should bear in mind the size and complexity of the company and the nature of the risks and challenges that it faces.

The preamble to the *Combined Code* also highlights the importance of the evaluation of governance being carried out with common sense in order to promote partnership and trust, based on mutual understanding. Governance should not be evaluated in a mechanistic way and departures from the *Combined Code* should not automatically be treated as breaches without considering the company's explanations.

16.17 Board Performance Measures

One of the issues raised in the Higgs Review (see **6.17 THE HIGGS REVIEW**) was whether more should be done to review and report on board performance. This subject has been addressed to some extent in the *Directors' Remuneration Report Regulations 2002* (*SI 2002/1986*) which require quoted companies to provide information on total shareholder return over a five year period and compare this with a general market index (see **23.43 DIRECTORS' REMUNERATION: QUOTED COMPANIES**).

16.18 Inside Information

At a Glance
* Information that is at variance with the generally held view of a company's status within the market can have a significant effect on its share price.
* The *UK Listing Rules* and *Disclosure Rules* require certain inside information to be announced to the market as a whole without delay.
* Detailed guidance is given in the Disclosure Rules, which form part of the *FSA Handbook*.
* The *Listing Rules* specify certain matters that must always be announced on the grounds that they will usually be price sensitive.
* There is no set formula or threshold for identifying inside information that is disclosable.
* The fact that it is possible for the public to obtain certain information does not necessarily mean that the information is deemed to be public knowledge.
* The board should define company policy and procedures for identifying and disseminating inside information.
* Certain information is exempt from disclosure, or may be disclosed in confidence to a specific group of recipients.
* It is advisable to define clearly who is responsible for making formal announcements to the Regulatory Information Services and for dealing with analysts, investors and the press.
* All announcements must give a balanced and understandable assessment of the company's position and prospects.
* If a breach of confidence arises, the directors should immediately make either a full or a holding announcement.
* If inadvertent selective disclosure is made, the same information must be announced immediately to the market as a whole.

* Particular care is needed where inside information is to be presented at the AGM.
* A consistent 'no comment' policy is usually the best way to handle market rumours.
* Companies are encouraged to co-operate with analysts but should not release inside information when dealing with their questions.
* Where a company is listed in more than one jurisdiction, information should be released simultaneously wherever possible.
* The ICAEW has issued guidance on the publication of prospective financial information.

16.19   The Importance of Price Sensitive Information

Stock markets need a flow of relevant and timely information in order to function well. Information on the performance of a listed company, and its future prospects, is of particular interest as this will form the basis of most investment decisions. Information that is at variance with the generally held view of a company's status within the market can have a particularly significant effect on its share price and is therefore said to be 'price sensitive'. Under the *UK Listing Rules*, inside information which might be price sensitive must be announced to the market as a whole without delay and must not be given to anyone else before it has been notified in this way. The detailed requirements on disclosure, together with supplementary guidance, are now set out in the *Disclosure Rules* which form part of the *FSA Handbook*.

16.20   Underlying Principles of the Listing Rules and Disclosure Rules

Two significant principles underlie all of the continuing obligations set out in the *UK Listing Rules* and *Disclosure Rules*:

* all relevant information must be disclosed on a timely basis; and
* all shareholders must be treated equally.

These principles are designed to protect investors, in that they ensure that the market operates in an orderly manner and that all users have simultaneous access to the same relevant information. The *Disclosure Rules* elaborate on how these principles are to be achieved through the actions of listed companies. They form part of the *FSA Handbook* which is available on the website of the Financial Services Authority (FSA), which is now the UK Listing Authority (UKLA), at www.fsa.gov.uk/pages/Doing/UKLA/. The UKLA also operates a helpdesk (*tel:* 020 7943 0333) which is open from 8.00am to 6.00pm each business day.

16.21   General Disclosure Obligation

Under *Disclosure Rule DR2.2*, a listed company must notify a Regulatory Information Service without delay of any information that meets the definition of inside information set out in the *FSA Handbook*. Key aspects of this definition include the fact that the information is of a precise nature (ie it indicates circumstances or events that exist or are expected to arise) and is not generally available, but if it were generally available would be likely to have a significant effect on the price of the entity's shares or other securities as a result of a reasonable investor using it as part of the basis of his/her investment decision. The guidance in the *Disclosure Rules* notes that information is likely to be considered relevant to the decisions of a reasonable investor if it affects:

- the company's assets and liabilities;
- the performance or expected performance of the business;
- the financial position or condition of the business;
- major new developments in the company's business; or
- information previously disclosed to the market.

16.22   Matters that Must be Announced

The *UK Listing Rules* require certain matters to be announced to the market on the grounds that they will usually be price sensitive. These include major acquisitions and disposals (ie those above the size criteria specified in the *Listing Rules*), fundamental changes in the scale or direction of a business, profit warnings and transactions with related parties. Information on dividends and changes in the composition of the board must also be announced as a matter of course.

16.23   What Constitutes Inside Information?

Companies often have difficulty in deciding what they are required to announce and when, although the UKLA generally advises them to err on the side of caution in cases of doubt. Precisely what constitutes inside information that is price sensitive will vary between companies, depending on a variety of factors such as size, recent developments and the sector(s) in which the business operates. There is no set formula for identifying inside information and no set threshold, in terms of percentage price movement, that determines price sensitivity. The UKLA guidance recommends that the following factors are taken into account.

- Is the information specific and precise? The more specific and precise it is, the more likely it is to be price sensitive.
- What effect might the information or event have on potential determinants of the company's share price such as future reported earnings per share, pre-tax profits or borrowings? The greater the impact on share price, the more likely the information is to be price sensitive.

The company's professional advisers should normally be consulted on these issues and it may also be appropriate to contact the UKLA helpdesk, especially if a situation arises that is not specifically dealt with in the guidance material. In particular, professional advisers should have an understanding of the market expectations built into the company's share price and therefore be able to advise on the likely impact of the new information.

16.24 When is Information Public Knowledge?

Certain potentially price sensitive information, such as a change in UK interest rates, will be public knowledge and so does not need to be announced to the markets unless it has an unusual or unexpected impact on the company. However, the mere fact that it is possible for information to be obtained by the public is not necessarily enough for it to be considered public knowledge. For instance, information that is only available on payment of a fee is not generally regarded as being readily available and thus public knowledge. Similarly, information that is not generally publicised, or known to be available, may not be deemed to be public knowledge.

16.25 Identification of Inside Information

The board is responsible for defining the company's overall policy on the control and dissemination of inside information. Each company should have a consistent procedure for determining what information is price sensitive and for releasing that information to the market. It is often helpful to develop, in conjunction with the company's professional advisers, a 'sensitivity list' setting out the types of information that are likely to be price sensitive for the company – this should facilitate the assessment of price sensitivity as each element of new information emerges. The list should be subject to regular review so that the relevant factors are kept up-to-date. The company should also have clear procedures for keeping price sensitive information confidential until the moment of announcement.

16.26 Exemptions from Disclosure

Disclosure Rule DR2.5 specifically exempts a company from disclosing inside information about impending developments or matters in the course of negotiation, and lists the individuals and organisations to whom the company can selectively disclose such information in order to facilitate those developments or negotiations. These exemptions enable a company to maintain confidential discussions in respect of mergers and acquisitions, or issues such as new product development, and to pass relevant information in confidence to:

- its own advisers, and the advisers of any other persons involved or potentially involved in the development or matter in question;
- persons with whom the company is negotiating (or intends to negotiate) any commercial, financial or investment transaction – this includes prospective underwriters or placees of the company's securities;

- representatives of the company's employees, or trades unions acting on their behalf;
- government departments, and a range of statutory and regulatory bodies; and
- in certain circumstances, major shareholders, lenders and credit-rating agencies provided that they are bound by a duty of confidentiality.

To qualify for the exemption, the company must be satisfied that the recipients of the information are aware that they must not deal in the company's securities until the information has been made available to the public. The company can only delay announcing the information if it is able to keep it confidential within the permitted group of recipients – if it appears that the information has leaked, regardless of who was responsible for this, the company must make an announcement without delay. The board may find it helpful to agree a draft announcement in advance, for use if such circumstances should arise. However, the guidance in *Disclosure Rule DR2.5.4* emphasises that this exemption cannot be used to delay public disclosure of financial difficulties or a deterioration in the company's financial condition, although the fact or substance of any negotiations to try to deal with such a situation would usually be covered. The fact that public disclosure of the company's financial situation may jeopardise subsequent negotiations cannot generally be used to justify a delay in making a public announcement.

16.27   Defining Communication Responsibility

The dissemination of information is usually easier to control if the responsibility is restricted to a small number of defined individuals, and the risk of making unauthorised or careless disclosure should be reduced. It is therefore advisable to define clearly who is responsible for making any formal announcements to the Regulatory Information Services and who is responsible for communicating with analysts, institutional investors and the press. Providing this information to the analysts, investors and the press, together with an explanation of the company's policy on communication, can help to reduce pressure to reveal information prematurely. It should be made clear to all other employees that they are prohibited from communicating information to anyone outside the company.

16.28   Making an Announcement

Companies must take all reasonable care in the production of any statement, forecast or announcement made through the Regulatory Information Services, to ensure that it is not misleading, false or deceptive and does not omit anything likely to affect the import of the announcement. *Principle D1* of the *Combined Code* also requires the board to present a balanced and understandable assessment of the company's position and prospects. This applies to all price sensitive reporting, not just to documents such as the annual reports and accounts, preliminary announcements and interim reports. All announcements must therefore deal even-handedly with both bad news and good news and both should be presented with equal prominence. Similarly, the presentation of financial information should not be adjusted in a way that makes it appear more favourable than it really is. *Disclosure Rule DR2.3* deals specifically with the publication of information on the internet and in particular requires:

- inside information made available on a company website to be notified to a Regulatory Information Service before or at the same time as publication on the website;
- inside information notified to a Regulatory Information Service to be made available promptly on the company website and to remain available for a period of at least one year after publication.

16.29 Action Where a Breach of Confidence is Identified

If a company has reason to believe a breach of confidence has occurred (or is likely to occur) the directors should, as a minimum, issue a holding announcement to the effect that the company expects, in the near future, to release information which may be price sensitive. A short delay in the issue of information is considered acceptable if it is necessary to clarify the situation but a holding announcement should only be used where a company and its professional advisers think there is a danger of information leaking out when the facts are not yet in a position to be confirmed. A holding announcement should give an outline of the subject matter, the reasons why a full announcement cannot be made, and an undertaking to announce further details as soon as possible. In extreme circumstances, the directors may need to ask the UKLA to suspend the listing of the company's shares until a full announcement can be made, although it should be remembered that suspended companies are still obliged to meet their continuing obligations – suspension does not, therefore, relieve the company of the obligation to disclose relevant information as soon as it becomes available.

16.30 Inadvertent Selective Disclosure

If price sensitive information is inadvertently disclosed on a selective basis (eg to an individual analyst or journalist), the company must take immediate steps to ensure that a full announcement is made, so that all users of the market have access to the same information. This should be done as soon as the company becomes aware that selective disclosure has already been made.

16.31 Potential Problems at the AGM

Particular care should be taken over presentations at the AGM, especially if there is to be comment on the company's trading performance in the early part of the current financial year. If price sensitive information is likely to be raised at the AGM, arrangements should be made for the same information to be notified to a Regulatory Information Service, so that any announcement at the AGM is made no earlier than the time at which the information is released to the market.

16.32   Dealing with Rumours

A 'no comment' policy is usually the best approach when handling rumours, especially those that have been circulated to try to generate a premature release of information. Such a policy must be used consistently, regardless of whether the company is simply exempt from the requirement to make an announcement at that time (eg because a matter is in the course of negotiation) or whether there is no price sensitive information to be announced. Any inconsistency in approach might result in third parties inferring whether or not the release of price sensitive information is imminent and this might constitute inadvertent selective disclosure.

16.33   Dealing with Analysts

The UKLA encourages companies to co-operate with analysts wherever possible, as they play a significant and constructive role in the efficient operation of the market. However, it is advisable for each company to have a clear policy about the extent to which the questions raised by analysts will be answered. Questions should not be answered if the answers, either individually or cumulatively, would amount to the release of price sensitive information. However, the fact that information is unpublished does not necessarily make it price sensitive, and any information that is not price sensitive (either on its own or in conjunction with other information) may be used in answering questions raised by analysts.

16.34   Global Announcements

Companies that are listed in more than one jurisdiction should try to co-ordinate the release of announcements in all countries so that all investors have access to the information at the same time. Also, where the requirements of another jurisdiction go beyond those of the UKLA, the same level of information must be released in London as in that other jurisdiction. However, the general obligation that price sensitive information is announced without delay still stands in these circumstances, and companies should therefore not delay an announcement on the grounds that another market to which the information must also be released is not open.

16.35   ICAEW Guidance on Prospective Financial Reporting

In September 2003, the Institute of Chartered Accountants in England and Wales (ICAEW) published new guidance for directors on the publication of prospective financial information. This consolidates current best practice in market reporting, particularly where changes in expectations, profit forecasts, profit warnings and estimates of future funding requirements are involved. There are currently no financial reporting standards or other statements of best or recommended practice in the UK to help directors prepare prospective financial information and it is hoped that formalisation of the issues will:

- increase investor confidence in the reliability and quality of prospective financial information as a sound basis for their investment decisions;
- provide a set of benchmarks that directors, investors, analysts and commentators can use to assess the quality of such information and promote continuing improvement;
- help directors to address legal risks in the current liability environment as well as risks of damage to reputation; and
- reinforce directors' efforts to prevent or correct unrealistic market expectations and reduce the pressures that may lead to aggressive earnings management.

The guidance can be downloaded from the ICAEW website at www.icaew. co.uk/pfi or obtained from the ICAEW, Chartered Accountants Hall, Moorgate Place, London, EC2P 2BJ.

16.36 Corporate Ethics and Corporate Social Responsibility ('CSR')

At a Glance
- Corporate ethics and corporate social responsibility are becoming increasingly high profile issues.
- Corporate ethics should focus on internal issues that are within the company's control and over which it can exercise real influence.
- Ethical behaviour can only be achieved in a corporate culture where honesty and integrity are considered to be paramount.
- The specific ethical matters needing consideration, and the potential problem areas, will vary depending on the nature and scale of the company's operations.
- The benefits of ethical conduct may be difficult to measure, especially in the short term, but high ethical standards are increasingly seen as an asset and unethical behaviour as a liability.
- Increased bureaucracy and controls are likely to be imposed if companies are not prepared to act voluntarily and demonstrate their commitment to corporate ethics.
- An ethical code should establish the corporate culture that the board wishes to create and set down the standards of behaviour that the company expects.
- Ethical issues should be incorporated into the company's ongoing training programme.
- Many companies find it helpful to require employees to sign an annual declaration that they have read, understood and applied the company's ethical code in their work.

* Regular checks should be made on compliance with the company's ethical code and stringent action taken in respect of any violations.
* Companies should also consider developing a formal policy on corporate social responsibility issues.
* The ABI has issued disclosure guidelines to encourage companies to discuss corporate social responsibility matters in the annual report.
* DEFRA has published detailed guidance on reporting on environmental issues.
* The Global Reporting Initiative (GRI) has also developed guidelines on sustainability reporting.

16.37   Increase in Ethical Awareness

Corporate ethics and corporate social responsibility have developed an increasingly high profile, especially in the light of the scandals at Enron and Worldcom. In the past, it may have been tempting for directors to regard business ethics as well intentioned but as of little practical value in the real world. However, ethical perspectives are coming more and more to the forefront of social thought, and the public – and in particular potential employees, investors and customers – are generally better informed and more ethically conscious than they were even ten years ago.

16.38   Responsible Action

A business that operates in an ethical way should be directly and indirectly sensitive and responsive to the reasonable needs of its various stakeholders, including employees, customers, suppliers, the local community, the environment and society in general. Even company law recognises that the fiduciary duties and responsibilities of directors extend beyond their responsibility to the shareholders. Under the draft statement of directors' duties set out in the Company Law Reform Bill, published in May 2006, a director must act in good faith, and in the way that he/she considers will be most likely to promote the success of the company for the benefit of the members as a whole. In fulfilling this overriding duty, a director must also have regard to certain other factors, including:

* the likely long-term consequences of any decisions;
* the interests of the company's employees;
* the need to foster business relationships with suppliers, customers and others;
* the impact of the company's operations on the environment and the local community;
* the desirability of maintaining a reputation for high standards of business conduct; and
* the need to act fairly between members.

16.39   Internal or External Focus?

Corporate ethics and corporate social responsibility are sometimes seen as involving an outward-focused social vision for improvement – for instance, broad ideals set out in corporate codes and mission statements. In fact, they are much more about internal issues that are within the company's control and over which it can exercise real influence. The general public is becoming increasingly sceptical about codes and statements which do not appear to have any noticeable impact on the company's day to day activities and which perhaps represent good intentions rather than an actual commitment to change. Corporate ethics and social responsibility should be based on the broad principles of integrity and fairness, and should focus on issues such as product and service quality, customer satisfaction, fair business dealing, sound employment practices, transparency and accountability, and the responsibilities of the business to the local community and the environment. Acting in an ethically responsibly manner means acting thoughtfully and weighing up the benefits and harm that each particular course of action might bring in the longer term. Unethical conduct is often focused on short-term advantages without considering the mid- and long-term consequences.

16.40   Complex Issues

Corporate ethics is not a straightforward subject and many of the surrounding issues can be complex. The specific ethical matters needing consideration in any business will vary depending on the nature and scale of its operations, but they might include:

- the sourcing of goods and services from low-wage countries;
- the use of child labour in developing countries;
- equity in pay and conditions;
- protecting the environment; and
- ethical trading, and in particular the acceptability of making 'commission' payments.

Many of these issues will need to be considered in context of local conditions in the century concerned and the impact on the lifestyle of the individuals involved.

16.41   Corporate Culture

Every company has a corporate culture – the unwritten rules that are understood, accepted and followed by everyone and which establish how the company is run on a day to day basis. In some companies, a specific corporate culture will have been created by management, whilst in others the culture may simply have evolved over time, without much attention being paid to whether or not it is right for the business. Every company should therefore examine its corporate culture from time to time and should consider whether any aspects have become outdated.

More traditional, long-established companies may find it more difficult to accept that their corporate culture has become out of step with the views of today's society and that change is needed. Ethical behaviour can only be achieved in a corporate culture where honesty and integrity are considered to be paramount. Recent accounting scandals have raised numerous questions about the adoption of aggressive accounting techniques, the manipulation of profits and the use of off balance sheet financing and other financial engineering techniques to create a more favourable impression of the business. Directors need to give serious consideration to the following questions.

- What kind of organisation do we want this to be?
- Which values really matter to us?
- How do the directors articulate and reinforce these to other managers and staff?
- How do the directors react to the pressures arising from market expectations?
- How does this impact on other managers and staff?

16.42   Potential Problem Areas

Potential problem areas will vary depending on the nature and scale of the company's operations, but some of the more common issues include the following.

- *Incentive schemes.* Whilst incentive schemes can be a useful motivation tool, they also bring inherent dangers – it is now well recognised that the payment of large executive bonuses, especially in the form of share options or based on profits, can encourage managers to take whatever action they deem necessary to maintain profit levels or keep the share price up. They can also encourage individuals to focus on short-term results rather than longer term issues such as the company's credibility and reputation. Reward schemes need to be designed around the company's longer term aims and to reward genuine performance (which may be more difficult to measure) rather than short-term achievements.
- *Market pressures.* Financial analysts tend to be preoccupied with immediate results and steadily rising earnings, but there are very few businesses that can achieve these over an extended period of time. Many executives feel compelled to feed the market's hunger for rapid growth and this can divert their energies away from managing the business towards managing the market's expectations of the company. Market demands can also result in over-optimistic predictions of growth and a reluctance to make a public acknowledgement of problems and weaknesses, although it is inevitable that difficulties will be encountered in any business from time to time.
- *Business survival.* Executives will sometimes feel compelled to adopt practices that they would otherwise consider unacceptable because it seems necessary to ensure the survival of the business and/or to protect their own careers – commercial demands therefore prevail over the guidance of their own consciences.

- *Commission payments.* Demands for 'commission' payments for favours done in business dealings can be a particular problem when dealing with officials and individuals in developing countries. Gaining an unlawful advantage by means of corruption is never legitimate under any circumstances and businesses are generally advised to publicise the fact that they do not tolerate this, even when it might be commercially advantageous and would probably go undetected. There may be circumstances where a business sees less of a moral dilemma in making a payment in order to speed up a process that is legal and will be carried out in due course, although this undoubtedly puts those who can afford to pay at an advantage and could therefore be considered contrary to fair trading. It is for each business to decide what is acceptable and what is not, but once this decision has been made, no compromise of the company's agreed standards should be permitted.
- *Gifts.* Gifts and hospitality from customers, suppliers and other business contacts may also give rise to problems. It is advisable to develop guidelines for both the giving and receiving of such items, usually with a requirement for disclosure of any significant gifts or hospitality offered.

It is also important that mechanisms are in place to allow appropriate consultation and discussion within the company in situations where it may be difficult to reach a judgement on whether a particular course of action is ethical or not.

16.43   Benefits of Ethical Conduct

The benefits of ethical conduct can be difficult to measure, especially in the short term. The disadvantages, in terms of lost business and additional costs, are likely to be more readily apparent, especially in the early stages. However, commercial success is usually interpreted these days as more than financial results and corporate reputation is now regarded as a valuable asset, albeit one which takes time to build. High ethical standards are increasingly recognised as an asset and unethical behaviour is seen as a liability. A strong corporate image can also bring competitive advantage and can help to attract investors, customers and potential employees. The benefits of high ethical standards include:

- attracting high quality employees – an ethically sound and socially responsible business is generally seen as a more attractive employer, especially as many employees today look at more than just remuneration when applying for a position;
- greater job satisfaction for employees – research has shown that there is a direct correlation between ethical conduct and job satisfaction and that employees generally have a greater sense of belonging, and are more committed and innovative, in an environment in which ethical conduct has strong support from senior management;
- reduced likelihood of friction with campaigners and protest groups, which can divert a considerable amount of management time;

- reduced internal friction – employee morale tends to fall if the company becomes the focus of public criticism or if colleagues are seen, or thought, to be advancing their own careers in an unethical way; and
- good relationships with the local community improve company credibility and reputation and can help to generate valuable public support for company expansion programmes.

Whilst some may have felt in the past that businesses acting in a socially responsible manner would not survive in a cut-throat, competitive, profit-focused market, research has in fact shown that such companies are usually more profitable in the long term. Although financial costs may be incurred in developing and maintaining ethical awareness programmes, these appear to be significantly outweighed by the subsequent benefits gained.

16.44   Avoiding Further Regulation

Businesses frequently complain about the extent and complexity of laws and regulations and the administrative overload that this can create. However, commercial freedom goes hand in hand with responsibility and the increased public awareness of, and demand for, ethical and socially responsible behaviour is likely to lead to increased bureaucracy and controls if companies are not prepared to act voluntarily. Company directors need to accept the rapidly changing environment and be pro-active in championing ethical standards rather than trying to defend positions that may have been acceptable in the past but are no longer considered to be so. Whilst individual corporate action may seem to have only a marginal affect, a positive example set and made plain for all to see may encourage others to follow suit and begin an upward trend. Positive change has to begin somewhere.

16.45   Developing an Ethical Code

An ethical code should be more than a list of rules or instructions that must be followed – it should establish the corporate culture that the board wishes to create, and set down the standards of behaviour that the company expects when commercial decisions have to be taken under time or financial constraints. In particular, it should make clear that management is not indifferent to the way in which business goals are achieved. Directors might begin by considering the following questions.

- Does every employee understand what is expected of him/her?
- Is every employee encouraged to behave responsibly?
- Does the business have values that should never be sacrificed in pursuit of profit, and are these communicated effectively across the organisation?
- Is there a well-understood framework for making decisions on ethical issues – and does this apply to all levels within the business?
- Are employees encouraged to discuss any ethical dilemmas that they encounter – and is it clear who they should approach in these circumstances?

- How does the company respond in such a situation?
- Is it evident that the company expects and rewards ethical behaviour?

An ethical code can be established and operated in any size of organisation and, once developed and communicated, it should be regarded as binding on all directors and employees.

Once finalised, the code is usually made available to the public as well as internally.

16.46   Contents of an Ethical Code

Ethical codes can cover a broad range of issues, which generally include:

- the legal obligations of employees;
- employee conduct;
- insider dealing;
- honesty and integrity – including the transparency of company policy and actions;
- equity and fairness – including the treatment of stakeholders such as customers, suppliers, employees and their families, the local community and shareholders (especially any minority shareholders);
- stakeholder rights – including the confidentiality of information;
- product or service standards; and
- the exercise of corporate and managerial power.

To be effective, the code must reflect the specific circumstances of the company and should not attempt to set standards which cannot reasonably be expected to be applied in practice. It is important that a company's ethical code addresses any issues that are particular sensitive, or that imply particular vulnerability, in the context of its activities. For instance, a company that has an extensive business involvement in developing countries may be more susceptible to requests for bribes or 'commission' payments and its ethical code must make clear what is and is not considered to be acceptable behaviour. Similarly, the approach to research and experimentation will be highly relevant to some businesses, but of no relevance whatsoever in others. It should also be remembered that a commitment to comply with legal requirements may not be sufficient to achieve ethical conduct when dealing with countries that offer little in the way of legislation on issues such as child labour, child protection, product safety and environmental protection. What is legal will not necessarily be ethical.

16.47   Independent Review

Commissioning an independent review of the company's proposed ethical code can help to ensure that it deals with the underlying issues on a broad basis and takes into account all relevant interests and opinions, particularly where complex issues are involved. Whilst the final decision on the content of the code rests with management, an independent review can also help to ensure that any differences of opinion have been fully explored and resolved through sound argument rather than through the use of executive and managerial power.

16.48 Implementation and Training

Effective training and good internal communication are key elements in the process of implementing an ethical code. Encouraging ethical conduct involves developing good habits and ethical issues should therefore be incorporated into the company's ongoing training programme and not considered to be a one-off training issue. This also makes it easier to implement changes to the company's code where necessary. Case studies can be a valuable tool in encouraging a debate on specific ethical problems and can help to emphasise the fact that the underlying issues will often be complex and require careful consideration. Such discussions can also help to develop greater understanding between colleagues and to dispel the attitude that 'everybody does it'. It is important that the internal communication programme covers all directors and employees, and that at least one individual is identified who can be approached in confidence with queries on ethical issues.

16.49 Annual Employee Sign-off

Many companies find it helpful to require employees to sign an annual declaration that they have read, understood and applied the company's ethical code in their work. This highlights the importance of the code and helps to keep ethical goals and standards at the forefront of the mind. Similarly, incorporating compliance with the code into the employee appraisal process and reward programme helps to demonstrate management's commitment to the underlying principles, although it is not always easy to find appropriate criteria by which to measure or evaluate ethical conduct.

16.50 Dealing with Violation of the Code

Regular checks should be made on compliance with the company's ethical code. For instance, this might be incorporated into internal audit work or might be dealt with as a separate exercise by the officer with overall responsibility for ethical issues. Any potential violation of the ethical code must be investigated and stringent action taken where appropriate, so that all employees are given the clear message that management considers this to be a serious matter. Directors may also wish to implement whistle-blowing or similar confidential procedures to ensure that potential violations are highlighted at an early stage (see **12.27** above). Under the *Combined Code*, the audit committee's responsibilities include reviewing the arrangements by which staff may, in confidence, raise concerns about possible improprieties in matters of financial reporting or other issues, and ensuring that arrangements are in place for proportionate and independent investigation and appropriate follow-up action.

16.51　Reporting on Corporate Social Responsibility

There is an increasing interest in the approach of individual companies to corporate social responsibility. Society has generally moved from a willingness to take good corporate behaviour on trust to wanting to see it demonstrated and explained. The ASB's Reporting *Statement Operating and Financial Review* recognises that company performance is now defined in much broader terms than financial performance and, in particular, that performance reporting might incorporate non-financial measures such as those relating to corporate social responsibility issues (see **11.89 ASB REPORTING STATEMENT 'OPERATING AND FINANCIAL REVIEW'**).

16.52　Developing an Appropriate Policy

Companies should therefore be thinking about developing a policy on corporate social responsibility issues as well as developing and publishing an ethical code. Points to consider include the following.

Checklist

✓　Does the company's corporate governance framework include accountability for managing corporate social responsibility issues?

✓　Do the company's performance reporting processes cover corporate social responsibility issues?

✓　Is there a formal mechanism for identifying stakeholder concerns and for providing them with feedback on progress?

✓　Are the company's expectations on corporate social responsibility issues communicated to suppliers and other business partners?

16.53　Disclosures on Corporate Ethics and CSR

The Association of British Insurers (ABI) has produced disclosure guidelines to help institutional investors discuss these issues with the companies in which they invest. The guidelines note that investors are anxious to avoid unnecessary prescriptive requirements or the imposition of costly measures, but hope that shareholder value will be enhanced by the early identification and management of risks arising from social, environmental and ethical matters. Shareholders with a specific interest in ethical investment may look for more extensive disclosures and some companies may wish to give additional information to attract investment from specific investors. The guidelines recommend the following disclosures.

The annual report should include a statement on whether the board:

- takes regular account of the significance of social, environmental and ethical (SEE) matters to the business of the company;
- takes account of SEE matters in the training of directors;
- has identified and assessed the significant risks to the company's short- and long-term value arising from SEE matters, as well as the opportunities to enhance value that may arise from an appropriate response;
- has received adequate information to make this assessment; and
- has ensured that the company has in place effective systems for managing significant risks, including where relevant performance management systems and appropriate remuneration incentives.

With regard to policies, procedures and verification, the annual report should:

- include information on SEE-related risks and opportunities that may significantly affect the company's short- and long-term value, and how they might impact on the business;
- describe the company's policies and procedures for managing risks to short- and long-term value arising from SEE matters – if the company has no such policies and procedures, the board should give reasons for their absence;
- include information about the extent to which the company has complied with its policies and procedures for managing risks arising from SEE matters; and
- describe the procedures for verification of SEE disclosures.

It is hoped that the guidelines will help to develop best practice in the area of managing and reporting on corporate social responsibility issues. They are intended to be relevant to all companies, regardless of size, although it is acknowledged that smaller companies in particular may need time to achieve full compliance. Where appropriate, the ABI notes that a statement in the annual report on the intent to comply would be helpful.

16.54   DEFRA Guidance on Environmental Reporting

DEFRA published new guidance on environmental reporting in January 2006, in conjunction with the introduction of more specific requirements on the content of the business review that forms part of the annual directors' report. Further details can be found at **11.94** above.

16.55   Global Reporting Initiative (GRI)

The Global Reporting Initiative has also developed guidance that is designed to achieve comparability in sustainability reporting. The first *Sustainability Reporting Guidelines* were published in 2000 and a revised version (G2) was issued in 2002. A further revision is currently in progress and a consultation draft was issued for comment in January 2006. The new guidelines (G3) are expected to be finalised by October 2006 and will then replace the G2 version. The guidelines include recommendations on:

- reporting principles;
- the issues that should be reported on;
- ensuring the quality of reported information;
- management approach to sustainability issues;
- performance indicators in respect of sustainability issues;
- the frequency and method of reporting; and
- assurance issues.

Full details are available on the GRI website at www.globalreporting.org.

16.56   DTI Guidance

The DTI has set up a website to support its policy of assisting the development of greater contact between business and society. The site contains a number of case studies showing the benefits that can be obtained by adhering to good practice in the area of corporate social responsibility. There is also information on the action being taken by the Government to facilitate the development of corporate social responsibility. The site can be found at www.societyandbusiness.gov.uk.

Appendix 1

Useful Websites on Investor Relations Issues

Association of British Insurers	www.abi.org.uk
National Association of Pensions Funds	www.napf.co.uk
Association of Investment Trust Companies	www.aitc.co.uk
Investment Management Association	www.investmentuk.org
Institutional Voting Information Service	www.ivis.co.uk
Institute of Chartered Accountants in England and Wales	www.icaew.co.uk
Chartered Institute of Personnel and Development	www.cipd.co.uk
DEFRA	www.defra.gov.uk
Global Reporting Initiative (GRI)	www.globalreporting.org
Government Gateway to Corporate Social Responsibility	www.societyandbusiness.gov.uk

17

IT

 IT

17.1 IT Strategy

At a Glance

* As a business develops and expands, it becomes increasingly important for the directors to agree an overall IT strategy.
* A major issue to consider is the potential impact on the business of systems or network failures, especially where there is heavy reliance on electronic communication.
* Software requirements should be analysed in detail and decisions taken on whether to develop bespoke software or make use of standard software packages.
* Staff training and the development of clear operations manuals should be considered as part of the IT strategy.
* Appropriate attention should be paid to legal requirements on the retention of accounting and other records and the need to ensure that they remain accessible for the specified period of time.

17.2 Importance of Developing an IT Strategy

Computer equipment is now readily available and for the most part reasonably priced. In a small business it may be relatively straightforward to control what is purchased, but as a business develops into various departments and units, often with some degree of autonomy and budgetary control, it becomes increasingly important for the directors to agree an overall IT strategy to deal, in particular, with:

- value for money in the purchase of computer hardware, software and related products;
- the need for equipment and software to be compatible throughout the organisation;
- making the most of any opportunities for networks and interfaces that will improve the speed of processing and the quality of management information; and

- achieving maximum benefit for the business from the investment in computers and related products.

Once a strategy has been established, clear guidelines should be issued to staff on the purchase of computers and related assets, and on the authorisation procedures that will be applied. Both the strategy and the guidelines will need to be kept under regular review, given that computer technology is such a fast-moving field.

17.3   Impact of Downtime

A major issue in considering any IT strategy will be the potential impact on the business of downtime if the systems or networks should fail. There will almost always be some impact on the processing and availability of accounting and other management information, but wider issues may also come into play, especially if the business relies heavily on telecommunications – for instance, where a significant element of business comes via the internet or extensive reliance is placed on e-mail. The impact will vary, depending on the nature and size of the business, but it is important that the potential risks are identified and procedures put into place to reduce the risk to an acceptable level and to limit the potential impact on the business.

Issues to consider might include:

- paying due attention to the quality of systems, components and after-sales service when considering new purchases;
- if the business makes significant use of networks, having a small number of stand-alone computers that are protected from the impact of serious network failures;
- using stand-alone equipment to test new systems or run large programs so that any problems encountered do not cause the entire network to crash;
- weighing up the costs and benefits of relevant maintenance agreements – for instance, to ensure on-site repair or replacement within an acceptable period of time; and
- establishing a programme for the regular review, upgrading and/or replacement of equipment to allow the business to take advantage of the latest technology and improvements in the speed and quality of processing.

17.4   Software

The approach to software will again depend mainly on the nature and size of the business. The strategy needs to analyse the software requirements and establish in each case whether appropriate software should be:

- developed in house by company staff;
- developed in house by contract programmers;
- developed by a suitable software house; or
- purchased in the form of standard software packages.

The development of bespoke software should provide an end product better suited to the individual needs of the business, but at a price. The success of bespoke software also depends heavily on the quality of the planning process and in particular the preparation of a clear, detailed and comprehensive specification for the work. Standard software packages will usually be much more cost effective but, inevitably, it is rare to find one that meets the precise needs of every user. Other factors affecting the choice might include:

- the availability of suitable in-house expertise;
- how quickly the program is required;
- how critical the program will be to the business – for instance, how regularly it will be used and whether it forms an integral part of the operations or simply provides supporting information; and
- the extent to which regular updating or maintenance facilities will be required – for instance, payroll software will need to be updated promptly for PAYE and National Insurance changes as they occur.

Where standard software packages are used, it is important to ensure that the business obtains the appropriate licences to enable the software to be used on the required number of machines. Procedures will also need to be put into place to control the use of software and ensure that the conditions set out in the licence agreements are complied with.

17.5   Staff Training

Staff training in the use of IT is a significant issue and one that should be considered as part of the IT strategy. The development of appropriate IT skills is important, both to minimize the risk of a serious systems failure or other computer-related disruption being caused by basic user errors, and also to ensure that the business obtains maximum benefit from its investment in computer technology – this will not happen unless staff have a thorough understanding of the systems to which they have access and learn to use them in the most efficient and effective way. Training needs should therefore be analysed and appropriate skills training offered, either in house or with external training providers. The provision of skills training should also be supported by the availability of clear user and operations manuals.

17.6   Retention of Records

The legal requirements on the retention of accounting and other records are considered in **3 COMPANY LAW**. Where records are maintained in non-legible form, such as computer files, it is important that due attention is paid to their retention and that they remain accessible for the required period of time. This is an issue that can easily be overlooked when computer hardware and software is upgraded or replaced and it is appropriate to include it within the IT strategy, to ensure that the necessary controls are in place.

17.7   IT Strategy Checklist

The checklist in Appendix 2 at the end of this chapter summarises some of the key issues that need to be considered when developing an IT strategy. It should not be regarded as comprehensive – other issues may need to be taken into account, depending on the particular circumstances of the business.

17.8   Security Issues

At a Glance

* IT security issues to consider include the physical security of equipment, access and processing controls, and protection against viruses and other systems invasions.
* Procedures should be established to identify who holds portable IT equipment at any point in time, clarify who is responsible for its security and ensure that confidential material is not held on such equipment.
* Access to systems and electronic information should be controlled by an effective system of user identification and passwords.
* With the increasing use of real-time processing, a strong system of output controls, reasonableness checks and exception reporting is needed to confirm the completeness and accuracy of processing.
* Up-to-date virus protection software should be used to check all disks, e-mail attachments and downloads from the internet, to minimise the risk of serious disruption as a result of virus infection.
* Firewalls should be used to prevent unauthorised access to systems and the unauthorised transfer of data.
* Additional procedures and controls will be needed in larger businesses with a substantial in-house IT department.

17.9   Different Aspects of Security

The issue of security in the context of IT equipment can be broken down into a number of different aspects:

* physical security of equipment;
* access controls – to ensure that only authorised users can access the system;
* processing controls – to ensure that processing is accurate and complete;
* virus protection;
* the use of mobile devices (eg laptops, PDAs);
* software asset management;
* controls over the disposal of IT equipment; and
* additional issues that apply in larger businesses with substantial IT departments.

Companies should also consider the need to develop and communicate clear policies on the personal use of e-mail and internet facilities by employees. If the company plans to monitor such usage, all employees must be made aware of the reasons for this and the extent to which monitoring will take place. In developing such policies, care must be taken to avoid any infringement of human rights, and appropriate controls must be established over access to and use of any information obtained as a result of the monitoring process.

17.10   Physical Security

The need for physical security over buildings and ways of achieving this are considered in **22 PROPERTY**. PCs, printers, laptops, scanners, computer chips and other computer-related equipment are very vulnerable to theft as they are usually readily moveable, usable and saleable. It is advisable to mark all such equipment with the business name and/or postcode, both to make it less attractive to would-be thieves and also to increase the possibility of return if it should be stolen. Particular care should be taken over laptops and similar equipment that may be removed from the business premises on a regular basis. Controls should be introduced to identify who holds the equipment at any particular point in time and staff should be made aware of their responsibility for the security of the equipment whilst it is in their possession. Insurance policies should be regularly checked to ensure that any specific requirements on the physical security of assets are complied with and that the level of cover is not jeopardised. Regular back-ups, and controls to prevent confidential information being retained on readily portable equipment, should help to minimise the risk of serious loss or disruption to the business in the event of theft.

17.11   Access Controls

Access to computer systems and information stored electronically is usually controlled by a system of user identification and passwords. Passwords should not be shared and should be changed regularly. There should also be a system in place to ensure that user details and passwords are deleted promptly from the system when employees leave the company. It is preferable for users to have one password for access to the system and a different password for transaction processing. Different levels of access controls can also be used to prevent general access to higher level and confidential information. The correct use of the password procedure, and any other access controls, should be reviewed on a regular basis. In particular, the system should be set up to report any password infringements and any changes to standing data on the system, for follow up at an appropriate management level. Automatic logging-off after a specified period of inactivity can also help to prevent unauthorised users gaining access through unattended equipment.

17.12   Processing Controls

Traditionally, processing controls were applied by developing various controls over the information input to the computer system and checking these against the eventual output details to confirm the completeness and accuracy of processing.

However, with the increasing use of real-time processing, there is only limited opportunity, if any, to establish suitable input controls. Businesses therefore face an increased risk of error, either accidental or fraudulent, and must place more reliance on output controls to confirm the completeness, accuracy and reasonableness of processing. It is good practice for the system to maintain a log of users and operators, and of the activities carried out, so that any problems identified can be traced back to their source. In some cases, it may still be appropriate to use control totals (eg document/record counts, sequence checks, hash totals) to confirm the accuracy of processing.

Consideration should also be given to the use of range checks and reasonableness checks within computer programs (eg the automatic checking of amounts against established standards), and the production of exception reports (eg all transactions above or below sensible parameters) to help minimise the risk of loss from sizeable unauthorised transactions. These controls will not work effectively unless the exception reports are reviewed promptly and any unusual items properly investigated. It will also be important to ensure that the system provides an adequate audit trail for each transaction to enable any queries to be properly followed up.

17.13   Virus Protection

A virus is a piece of software written specifically to have an adverse effect on the way in which a computer works – some viruses are classed as benign (eg they simply display a message without causing any damage to the underlying computer system) but others, classified as malignant, can cause serious damage by corrupting and/or destroying files and systems. Some malignant viruses, such as the Melissa virus, do not cause damage as such but replicate themselves at great speed and create significant disruption by causing a system to become overloaded. There are three principal ways in which a computer system can be infected with a virus.

- *Download from the internet.* It is possible to download a virus from the internet, usually by downloading infected software. However, reputable software companies are very aware of the issues, and of the potential impact on their reputation if they should prove to be the source of a virus. They therefore operate stringent controls, and provided software is only downloaded from reputable sites there should be only a minimal risk of infection.
- *E-mail attachment.* Another way in which a virus commonly spreads is through an infected attachment to an e-mail – in this case the virus is activated by opening the attachment. At present a virus must be 'executed' in order to work – it must therefore be part of another program or macro. A plain text file or plain e-mail cannot carry a virus and opening an e-mail alone will not activate a virus present in an attachment – it is the opening of the attachment that causes the problem.
- *Floppy disks.* A virus can also be transferred between computers through the use of floppy disks – in this case, simply inserting and reading the disk can activate the virus.

It is therefore essential to operate some form of virus protection, and to ensure that this is updated regularly (preferable weekly or even daily) to ensure that the protection is effective against new viruses that have only just come to light. Virus protection software can be used to check all floppy disks, all e-mail attachments and all downloads from the internet. Even with protection in place it is important to have policies and procedures to minimise the risk of any problems. These might include:

- ensuring that all staff are aware of the issues and why it is essential for the business to have policies and procedures to minimise the risk – many companies now make failure to comply with such policies and procedures a disciplinary offence;
- prohibiting the download of software from anything other than reputable sites and in particular the download and use of pirate software;
- operating a stringent policy on the opening of e-mail attachments – it should be made clear to all staff that an unexpected attachment should not be opened, even if the sender is apparently known to them, without checking first that it is genuine;
- a policy on the use of e-mail for personal purposes can also help to control the risk of infection by reducing the level of e-mail traffic.

Firewalls can be used as an additional form of protection to prevent unauthorised access to a network or server, and to prevent the unauthorised transfer of material.

17.14   Use of Mobile Devices

Additional security issues arise these days as a result of the widespread use of mobile devices such as laptops and PDAs. As well as taking measures to achieve physical security for any such company assets (see **17.10** above), appropriate steps should also be taken to secure the considerable amount of confidential data that may be removed from the company's premises by these means. For instance, encryption techniques may be used to ensure that any data held on a portable device that is lost or stolen cannot be easily accessed by third parties. Similar issues arise where a company operates a policy of homeworking, with the result that employees may hold confidential company data on their own computers. The insurance cover for mobile devices and equipment used by homeworkers should also be checked. Clear policies should be established on all of these issues and it is usually advisable to get employees to sign an acknowledgement that they have read these and agree to abide by them.

17.15   Software Asset Management

All directors and employees should be made aware of the copyright issues applying to software and the various forms of software piracy that can arise. The use of illegal software can arise as a result of downloads from illegal websites, the unauthorised copying of software or using more copies of a software program than is permitted under the licences held by the company. There is also a risk of hardware being purchased with illegal copies of software already installed. Steps to prevent these problems and to monitor the business's use of software might include:

- establishing a clear policy on the purchase of both hardware and software and ensuring that this is clearly communicated to all employees;
- carrying out regular reviews of the company's software needs, to identify any programs that are no longer used or software that is not operating satisfactorily;
- preparing an inventory of software assets;
- carrying out a regular audit to compare the amount of software in use with the related purchases or licences held by the company; and
- monitoring compliance with the company's policies to guard against the acquisition and use of illegal software.

The British Software Alliance (www.bsa.org.uk) provides free basic auditing tools for use in software asset management, as well as details of specialists who can help with this process.

17.16   Controls Over the Disposal of IT Equipment

Companies should also establish clear policies for the disposal of old or surplus IT equipment and for ensuring that any confidential data is irretrievably deleted before disposal. This is not as straightforward a process as it may seem as it will usually involve more than the simple deletion of files. Files that have simply been deleted from the computer will generally remain accessible to those with specialist IT knowledge even though they are no longer evident to regular users.

17.17   Additional Issues for Substantial IT Departments

Larger businesses which operate a substantial in-house IT department to develop and operate more complex computer systems will need to consider additional security issues, including:

- the need for appropriate segregation of duties between the IT and user departments, and within the IT department, so that the functions of operations and programming are properly separated;
- the need to develop written standards for the development, implementation, programming and operation of computer programs;
- appropriate procedures to ensure that all amendments to existing programs are properly authorised, controlled and tested before implementation, and that such changes are clearly recorded for future reference;
- the need to maintain a log of who has accessed the system and computer programs – the log should be regularly reviewed at an appropriate level;
- the need to control access to the IT facility, particularly outside normal business hours.

17.18   Disaster Recovery Planning

At a Glance
* Policies and procedures should be established for regular back-ups of computer files, and regular checks made to ensure that they are being followed in practice.
* Back-up copies of significant files should be kept in a secure, off-site location.
* Arrangements should be made, and tested, for access to an alternative processing site.
* Every business should develop a clear, written plan of the action to be taken in the event of a major disaster.

IT

17.19   Back-up Procedures

Every business hopes that a disaster will never occur but most people are aware of the need to take regular back-ups of computer files to ensure that the system can be restored promptly and with minimum disruption to the ongoing business activities. As well as establishing policies and procedures for regular back-ups, it is important to check that these are actually followed in practice – it is easy for staff to become complacent, and for procedures to lapse.

17.20   Storage of Back-up Copies

It is particularly important that back-up copies of all significant computer files are kept in a secure, off-site location so that they are protected and available for use in the event of serious disruption to the main business premises. Arrangements should also be made, and tested, for access to an alternative processing site so that the back-up copies can be used to restore the systems as soon as possible if re-entry to the company's own premises, or access to the necessary equipment, is restricted for any length of time.

17.21   Preparation of a Disaster Recovery Plan

Every company should develop a clear, written plan for the action that will be taken in the event of a major disaster, such as a serious fire or flood, to limit disruption to the business. It will be much easier to cope with the initial recovery period successfully if these issues have been thought through in advance and there are clear lines of responsibility and a defined action plan to be followed. Issues to consider include:

* division of actions and responsibilities between the management team;
* detailed arrangements for maintaining the business activities as far as possible;
* detailed arrangements for restoring critical systems within a given timescale;

- detailed arrangements for continuing the processing of information and for ensuring the continuation of appropriate authorisation procedures and controls;
- detailed arrangements for restoring ancillary systems as soon as is practicable;
- steps that need to be taken now, and also on an ongoing basis, to enable the agreed recovery plan to be put into immediate action should the need arise.

A copy of the plan should be retained in a secure location away from the company's premises.

Appendix 1

Useful Websites on IT Issues

Business Software Alliance	www.bsa.org.uk
ICAEW IT Faculty	www.icaew.co.uk/itfac
Institute of Directors	www.iod.com
Business Link	www.businesslink.gov.uk
Association of British Insurers	www.abi.org.uk
British Association of Insurance Brokers	www.biba.org.uk
Get Safe Online	www.getsafeonline.com
DTI Information Security	www.dti.gov.uk/sectors/infosec/index.html

IT

Appendix 2

IT Strategy Checklist

This checklist summarises some of the key issues that need to be considered when developing an IT strategy. It should not be regarded as comprehensive – other issues may need to be taken into account, depending on the particular circumstances of the business.

☐ Does the company have clear policies and procedures to achieve value for money in the purchase of:

- computer hardware;
- computer software;
- other related products?

☐ Does the company have policies and procedures to ensure that computer equipment and software acquired throughout the organisation is fully compatible?

☐ Does the company have procedures to ensure that it makes maximum use of networks and interfaces to speed up processing and provide better management information?

☐ Does the company have procedures to ensure that it takes advantage of new developments as they arise?

☐ Does the company have procedures to ensure that it receives the maximum benefit from its investment in IT?

☐ Does the company have policies and procedures to reduce the potential impact of systems downtime on the business – for instance:

- clear policies on quality of product and after-sale service;
- stand-alone computers that can continue to be used if the network fails;
- stand-alone computers to test new systems and programs;
- appropriate arrangements for prompt on-site repair or replacement;
- a programme for the regular review and upgrading or replacement of equipment?

☐ Has the company properly considered the advantages and disadvantages of using:

- bespoke software;
- standard software packages?

☐ Do staff receive appropriate IT training:

- to minimise the risk of serious problems arising as a result of user errors;
- to maximise the benefits of the company's investment in IT?

☐ Is the need for additional or updated training reviewed on an ongoing basis?

☐ Does the company have procedures to ensure that accounting and other records remain accessible when hardware or software is changed or upgraded?

☐ Does the company have appropriate procedures to:

- ensure the physical security of all IT equipment;
- restrict unauthorised internal access to the systems;
- ensure that all computer processing is accurate and complete;
- protect the systems and networks from attack by viruses;
- prevent unauthorised external access to the systems and networks, and the unauthorised transfer of data?

☐ Does the company have clear policies to secure the confidentiality of data held on mobile devices used by directors and employees, or equipment used by homeworkers?

☐ Have appropriate insurance arrangements been made for mobile devices used by directors and employees, and any equipment used by homeworkers?

☐ Has the company established appropriate software asset management procedures to ensure that:

- all directors and employees are made aware of software copyright issues and the various forms of software piracy that can arise;
- the company has a clear policy on the use of software and communicates this to all directors and employees;
- the company's software needs and usage are subject to regular review;
- an up-to-date inventory of software is maintained and compared on a regular basis with the software actually in use;
- compliance with the company's policies on software is regularly monitored?

☐ Has the company established appropriate controls to ensure that all confidential data is irretrievably deleted from all old or surplus IT equipment prior to disposal?

☐ If systems and software are developed in-house, does the company have:

- appropriate segregation of duties between the IT and user departments;
- written standards for the work of the IT department;

- appropriate controls over amendments to systems and programs;
- a detailed log of who has accessed systems and programs;
- appropriate controls over the IT function, especially out of normal working hours?

☐ Does the company have policies and procedures to ensure the regular back-up of computer files?

☐ Are back-up files stored in a secure, off-site location?

☐ Has the company made, and tested, alternative processing arrangements?

☐ Has the company prepared a clear, written disaster recovery plan?

☐ Is a copy of the disaster recovery plan stored in a secure offsite location?

Listing Requirements

18 Listing Requirements

18.1   The Decision to Seek Public Investment

> **At a Glance**
> * A private company cannot offer its shares to the public, but a public company may do so.
> * Applying for listing is a complex and costly step and is usually only undertaken where a substantial amount of capital needs to be raised.
> * A higher level of accountability is imposed on the directors of listed companies.
> * The Financial Services Authority (FSA) is the UK Listing Authority (ULKA).
> * Specific legal requirements are laid down on the content of documents issued to public investors.
> * The admission of securities to listing and their admission to trading are now distinct parts of the listing process.
> * Any securities for which listing is sought must be freely transferable.
> * The *Prospectus Regulations 2005* (*SI 2005/1433*) define what constitutes an offer to the public.
> * A company may be able to offer shares to the public by means of an offer for subscription or a private placing.
> * A minimum market capitalisation is specified for a listed company.

18.2   Private and Public Companies

A UK company can be formed and registered as a private company or as a public company. Specific additional requirements apply to a public company under company law – for instance, the nominal value of its allotted share capital must be not less than £50,000 and there are specific requirements on the extent to which the allotted shares must be paid up. Other provisions in company law also make certain distinctions between the two types of company. A private company can re-register as a public company, and vice versa. The vast majority of UK companies are private companies and as a result are prohibited by company law from offering their shares to the public. Many are nevertheless substantial businesses. Similarly, many of the companies registered as public companies have not applied for their shares to be listed or traded on an alternative exchange.

18.3   Higher Degree of Accountability

The requirements for achieving and maintaining a listing are complex and expensive. Listing is therefore a major step and is unlikely to be an attractive option unless a substantial amount of capital needs to be raised. Companies can also apply to have their debt securities listed and traded on the London Stock Exchange (LSE), or on other exchanges, regardless of whether their shares are also listed. Once a company's securities have been listed, a higher level of accountability is imposed on the directors and they can expect regular comment on the company's performance and financial position from analysts and in the financial press. The directors will also be subject to certain restrictions on their personal share dealings because they will generally be regarded as possessing unpublished price sensitive information (see **18.24** below and **16.18** INSIDE INFORMATION).

18.4   UK Listing Authority

The Financial Services Authority (FSA) is the UK Listing Authority (UKLA), having taken over this role from the LSE in 2000. A company wishing to have its shares listed on the LSE must comply with the UKLA's and LSE's initial requirements to achieve listing and admission to trading, and also accept the continuing obligations laid down by the UKLA to ensure the proper operation of the market. To achieve a full listing of shares, either a prospectus (where shares are being offered to the public for the first time) or listing particulars (for subsequent public offers) must be issued in accordance with *Part VI* of the *Financial Services and Markets Act 2000* (*FSMA 2000*) and the *Prospectus Regulations 2005* (*SI 2005/ 1433*), which implement the requirements of the EU Prospectus Directive in the UK. Under the legislation and the related FSA Prospectus Rules, a prospectus must be issued when an offer of transferable securities is made to the public or such securities are admitted to trading on a regulated market, except where an appropriate exemption applies. Separate requirements apply under Part VI of FSMA to offers of unlisted securities on trading markets such as the Alternative Investment Market (AIM) (see **18.11** below). AIM is now an exchange regulated market (as opposed to a regulated market) and so does not come within the scope of the EU *Prospectus Directive*.

18.5   Documents Issued to Public Investors

The basic contents of documents issued to public investors under UK legislation are prescribed by the EU *Prospectus Directive*. These require documents to include the information that is considered necessary to enable investors and their advisors to make an informed assessment of the assets, liabilities, financial position, profits, losses and prospects of the issuer and of the rights attaching to the shares. The detailed requirements for obtaining a full listing and for admission to trading on AIM are broadly similar, but are more onerous for full listing and therefore more expensive. Additional requirements laid down by the LSE must also be complied with. Corporate governance, and detailed reporting on the various issues it encompasses, has also become increasingly demanding for listed companies in recent years (see **6 CORPORATE GOVERNANCE**).

18.6   Admission to Listing and to Trading

The admission of securities to listing and their admission to trading are now technically distinct parts of the listing process – the former is controlled by the FSA and the latter by the LSE (or other exchange where appropriate). Application for admission to listing and trading must be made through a sponsor and, under *section 75* of *FSMA 2000*, requires the consent of the company. All companies whose shares are publicly traded are also subject to regulation by the Panel on Takeovers and Mergers. This is a non-statutory body which aims to ensure fair and equal treatment for all shareholders.

18.7   Shares to be Freely Transferable

It is a requirement of the UK *Listing Rules* that the transfer of fully paid shares is not restricted in any way under the company's articles of association, and the FSA will only grant an exemption from this requirement in exceptional circumstances. Any pre-emption rights of existing equity shareholders must therefore be removed before a company's shares can be offered to the public.

18.8   What is 'the Public'?

Under the EU *Prospectus Directive* offers to fewer than 100 people per EEA state are not regarded as offers to the public and offers of securities that are not transferable are not deemed to be offers to the public. There is also an exemption for offers that are made only to qualified investors (as identified on a register maintained by the FSA) on the basis that these individuals are sufficiently knowledgeable to understand the potential risks involved.

18.9   Offers for Subscription and Private Placings

Shares may also be offered to the public without a formal prospectus or listing particulars by making use of an offer for subscription or a private placing (for instance, to a single investor, such as a venture capital company, or to a small group of investors), provided that the conditions for exemption are met. There are certain prohibitions on placing securities for which listing is not being sought, essentially because it may be difficult to buy or sell such securities, or to ascertain their market value. An offer for subscription may or may not be underwritten – underwriting ensures that the issuer will receive the full amount of funding required, but the underwriters will need to be paid a commission for accepting the risk. Private placings and offers for subscription will usually be 'financial promotions' under the provisions of *FSMA 2000* and will therefore be subject to some degree of formality and regulation, to ensure that investors are given sufficient information to support their decision to invest and have some level of assurance on its quality and accuracy. Under *FSMA 2000*, an offer document will generally need to be issued or approved by an authorised person, although exemption may be available if the offer is restricted to business and professional investors. There is an overriding requirement under *FSMA 2000* that documents should not be misleading or incomplete.

18.10   Minimum Capitalisation

The minimum capitalisation required for a full listing is £700,000 but it is relatively rare for companies with a capitalisation less than £10 million to seek such a listing. The total costs of listing are typically between 5 per cent and 15 per cent of the amount raised, depending both on the level of funding sought and also on whether the company uses:

- an offer for sale (which is the most expensive method);
- an offer for subscription; or
- a private placing.

18.11   Applying for Admission to the Alternative Investment Market (AIM)

At a Glance
* The Alternative Investment Market (AIM) provides a second tier market for small, young and growing companies.
* The requirements are less stringent than for full listing but certain conditions must nevertheless be met.
* The company must appoint a nominated advisor and a nominated broker.
* After two years, the company can move to a full listing or can remain within AIM.

18.12   Objectives of AIM

The Alternative Investment Market (AIM) was launched in 1995 as a second tier market administered by the LSE and intended for smaller companies. The objectives of AIM are to allow small, young and growing companies to raise capital from the public and also to provide a market on which their shares may be traded. Many of the companies that apply for admission to AIM will not be eligible for full listing, usually because their market capitalisation is too low, their trading record too short or the proposed number of shareholders is too small. Others may decide that full listing is not appropriate for them for other reasons. In theory, the costs of admission to AIM should be lower than those of a full listing, although this is not always borne out in practice.

18.13 Conditions for Admission

Companies of any type may apply for admission to AIM and there are no minimum requirements on the length of the company's trading record, the number or percentage of shares that must be in public hands after admission, or the company's market capitalisation. However, the company must:

- be incorporated as a public company (either in the UK or elsewhere), and have shares that are freely transferable;
- appoint and retain a nominated adviser and a nominated broker;
- publish audited accounts that are prepared in accordance with UK generally accepted accounting practice, US generally accepted accounting practice or International Accounting Standards;
- publish an AIM admission document containing the information specified by the LSE and *FSMA 2000*;
- adopt a code of conduct for directors equivalent to the Model Code for AIM companies (which generally prohibits directors from trading in the company's shares whilst in possession of unpublished price sensitive information); and
- agree to comply with certain continuing obligations after admission.

If the company's trading record is less than two years, all directors and employees holding 1 per cent or more of the class of shares to be admitted to AIM must agree not to sell any shares for at least one year after admission. This is to reassure new investors that the existing management is committed to the future success of the company.

18.14 Nominated Advisor and Nominated Broker

The company's nominated adviser, who must be approved to act in that capacity by the LSE and authorised to do so under *FSMA 2000*, has primary responsibility for effecting the company's admission to AIM, although the directors are responsible for ensuring compliance with the relevant rules. The nominated broker must be a member of the LSE. In addition to these nominated advisors, the company will need professional help and advice from its solicitors and accountants.

18.15 Moving to Full Listing

After a period of trading on AIM, a company can apply for admission to the Main Market (i.e. full listing) if this seems appropriate to its circumstances at the time. However, there is no compulsion to seek a full listing and the company's shares can continue to be traded on AIM if this is considered to be more appropriate.

18.16   Applying for a Full Listing

> **At a Glance**
> * The detailed conditions for a full listing are set out in the UK *Listing Rules* and *Prospectus Rules*.
> * Special arrangements apply for innovative high growth companies.
> * The company must prepare a detailed prospectus or listing particulars and obtain prior approval from the UKLA before publication.
> * There are also stringent rules on advertisements in connection with listing applications.
> * The UK Listing Authority (UKLA) is given wide powers in respect of the listing of company securities.

18.17   Conditions for Full Listing

Significant changes were made to the regime for admission to the Main Market with effect from 1 July 2005 as a result of the implementation of the EU *Prospectus Directive*. The requirements for listing are now set out in three sets of rules issued by the FSA:

* the *Prospectus Rules*;
* the *Listing Rules*; and
* the *Disclosure Rules*.

These form part of the FSA *Handbook*, which replaces the former UKLA *Sourcebook* from 1 July 2005. A summary of the contents of each set of rules is given in Appendix 2 to this Chapter. A up-to-date version of the FSA *Handbook* is available on the FSA website at www.fsa.gov.uk/handbook/.

The principal requirements for admission to full listing are:

* the company must be incorporated as a public company;
* the expected market value of the equity securities for which listing is sought must be at least £700,000 (although the UKLA has authority to allow a lower value provided that it is satisfied on the marketability of the shares);
* the securities for which listing is sought must be freely transferable;
* the company must have published or filed accounts for three years (although exceptions may be made in certain circumstances);
* the latest audited accounts must be made up to a date not more than six months before the date of publication of the prospectus or listing particulars;
* at least 25 per cent of the class of shares for which listing is sought must be in public hands by the time dealing commences;
* the company must at all times be capable of carrying on its business independently of any controlling shareholder; and
* the company must accept the continuing obligations of the UKLA and any continuing requirements of the exchange on which its shares will be traded.

It is also possible for a company to seek a listing without simultaneously offering securities to the public (for instance, where its shares are already widely held by investors and it has no requirement for additional capital). This is comparatively rare in practice, but is a method sometimes used by foreign companies whose shares are already listed on other markets.

18.18 Prospectus or Listing Particulars

The company must prepare a detailed prospectus or listing particulars, as appropriate, and obtain prior approval from the UKLA before publication. The document must also be registered at Companies House before publication and must include a statement that this obligation has been fulfilled. *Section 80* of *FSMA 2000* sets out the general duty on disclosure and summarises the details that must be given, but the precise requirements are set out in the UK *Prospectus Rules*.

Derogations from the specified contents of the prospectus or listing particulars may be authorised by the UKLA in exceptional circumstances (for instance, where it is agreed that information should be omitted in the public interest, where disclosure would be seriously detrimental to the issuer, or where the information is of minor importance and will not affect the assessments made by investors). Supplementary listing particulars may need to be issued if there is a significant change in circumstances, or a significant new matter arises, after the preparation of the original document but before dealing in the securities commences.

18.19 Advertisements

FSMA 2000 also sets out provisions on advertisements in connection with listing applications. These cover items such as mini prospectuses (which are essentially summary versions of the main prospectus) and advertising through the media. Certain advertisements are prohibited from publication unless they have been authorised by a competent authority.

18.20 UKLA Powers

The UKLA is given specific authority to:

- refuse an application for listing;
- require an issuer to publish information that it considers appropriate in order to protect investors and maintain the smooth operation of the market;
- conduct investigations into circumstances suggesting a breach of the UK *Listing Rules*, *Prospectus Rules* or *Disclosure Rules* or an offence under the relevant legislation;
- impose financial penalties and/or publish censure statements for a breach of the UK *Listing Rules*, *Prospectus Rules* or *Disclosure Rules*;
- dispense with, or modify, the application of the *Listing Rules*, *Prospectus Rules* or *Disclosure Rules* where it considers this appropriate (subject to the requirements of the underlying EU Directives and related legislation);

Listing Requirements

- suspend the listing of any securities and impose conditions for the lifting of the suspension; and
- cancel the listing of securities.

18.21 Continuing Obligations

At a Glance
* The continuing obligations of a listed company are set out in the UK *Listing Rules.*
* There is an overriding requirement that all inside information that may be price sensitive must be notified to a Regulatory Information Service without delay.
* Specific requirements apply if the Regulatory Information Services are not open for business when information needs to be notified.
* Any changes to the company's securities must be notified to the market.
* Major interests in the company's shares must also be notified to the market.
* The company must ensure equal treatment between shareholders, and between holders of any debt securities.
* The company must take steps to enable all shareholders to exercise their rights.
* Special requirements apply where the company has a controlling shareholder.
* Extensive information about the company's directors must be given to investors and potential investors.
* The directors must comply with the provisions of the Model Code (or a company equivalent) when dealing in the company's shares.
* The UK *Listing Rules* set out detailed requirements on financial reporting by a listed company.
* Detailed rules on company transactions ensure that shareholders are informed of significant transactions and, where appropriate, have the opportunity to vote on the issue.
* The *Listing Rules* include specific requirements on dealing with treasury shares.
* The UKLA has the power to impose a range of sanctions for breach of the continuing obligations.

18.22 UK Listing Rules and Related Guidance

The continuing obligations of a listed company are set out primarily in the UK *Listing Rules*, but reference will also need to be made to the *Disclosure Rules*.

The principal continuing obligations are summarised below, but reference should be made to the UK *Listing Rules* and *Disclosure Rules* for the precise requirements. Separate requirements apply to specialised entities, which include:

- property companies;
- investment companies;
- public sector issuers;
- venture capital trusts; and
- oversea companies.

Separate obligations also apply where only debt securities are listed.

18.23   General Disclosure Obligation

There is an overriding requirement that all inside information which may be price sensitive must be notified to a Regulatory Information Service without delay (see **16.18 INSIDE INFORMATION**). Directors also have an ongoing obligation to take all reasonable care that any published statement, forecast or other information is not misleading, false or deceptive, and that it does not omit any information that is likely to affect its import.

18.24   Release of Information Outside Normal Hours

Companies should not provide information to a Regulatory Information Service outside normal working hours and simultaneously release it to the media, even with the proviso that it is under an embargo until it has been published by the Regulatory Information Service. The *Disclosure Rules* also include provisions on the release of information on company websites. These emphasise that:

- inside information must not be published on the company's website as an alternative to notification to a Regulatory Information Service;
- inside information must be notified to a Regulatory Information Service before, or simultaneously with, publication on the company's website;
- information announced through a Regulatory Information Service should also be made available on the company's website by the close of the business day following the day of the announcement, and should remain available on the website for a period of one year.

18.25   Capital

Matters that a listed company must notify to a Regulatory Information Service without delay include:

- any proposed alteration to the capital structure of the company, including the structure of any listed debt securities;
- any new issue of debt securities;
- any changes in the rights attaching to securities;
- details of the drawing or redemption of listed securities;

- the basis of allotment of listed securities offered generally to the public and of open offers to subscribers;
- any extension of the time granted for the currency of temporary documents of title;
- the effect of any issue of further securities on the terms of the exercise of rights under options, warrants and convertible securities; and
- the results of any new issues of listed securities (subject to certain exceptions).

When further securities are issued in the same class as listed securities, an application for their listing must be made not more than one month after allotment. The UKLA must be informed in writing if the proportion of any class of listed equity shares in public hands falls below 25 per cent of the total issued share capital of that class (although the UKLA may agree a lower threshold in certain circumstances). Listed securities must also be admitted to trading at all times, and the UKLA must be informed immediately in writing of their admission, cancellation, suspension or readmission. Specific requirements apply under the *Listing Rules* where the company proposes to purchase some of its own shares.

18.26 Major Interests in Shares

A listed company is also required to notify a Regulatory Information Service without delay of:

- any information disclosed to it under *CA 1985, ss 198–208* (major interests in the share capital of the company); and
- any information obtained by the company pursuant to *CA 1985, s 212* where it is apparent that the existence of, or a reduction or increase in, a major interest in the company's share capital should have been notified under *CA 1985, ss 198–208* but has not been disclosed.

A company that is not subject to the requirements of *CA 1985* is required to give the equivalent information.

18.27 Rights of the Holders of Listed Securities

The company must ensure equality of treatment for all shareholders who are in the same position and for all holders of a class of debt securities. If the company proposes to issue equity shares for cash, it must first offer them to existing equity shareholders and to holders of other equity securities in proportion to their existing holdings. Slightly amended arrangements apply in the case of a rights issue or open offer. However, if the shareholders agree formally to disapply their statutory pre-emption rights under *section 89(1)* of *CA 1985*, general offers of equity shares for cash will be permitted. Special requirements on share issues also apply to a listed company that is a subsidiary company or a holding company.

18.28   Communication with Shareholders

A listed company must ensure that appropriate facilities and information are available in each State in which its securities are listed to enable shareholders to exercise their rights. In particular the company must:

- inform shareholders of all meetings that they are entitled to attend;
- enable them to exercise their voting rights where appropriate; and
- publish and distribute notices and circulars on:
  - the allocation and payment of dividends and interest,
  - details of any issue of new securities, and
  - the redemption or repayment of securities.

The company is also required to appoint a registrar and, where appropriate, a paying agent in the UK, unless the company provides financial services and performs these roles itself. Proxy forms must be sent out with notices of meetings and must comply with the requirements of the UK *Listing Rules*. If a circular is issued to the holders of a particular class of security, a copy or a summary of the contents must be issued to holders of all other listed securities, unless the information is irrelevant to them. Documents must be distributed by first class mail (or equivalent) in the UK and other EU Member States, and by airmail (or equivalent) to shareholders based in other countries. Two copies of circulars, notices, reports and other announcements must be sent to the UKLA at the same time as they are issued, and two copies of resolutions passed by the company (other than those relating to ordinary business at the AGM) must be forwarded to the UKLA without delay after the meeting. The UKLA will make these items available for public inspection through its Document Viewing Facility. The company must also notify a Regulatory Information Service that the document has been made available for inspection, or provide a Regulatory Information Service with the full text of the document.

18.29   Controlling Shareholder

A company with a controlling shareholder must be capable at all times of carrying on business independently of that shareholder, and all transactions between the company and the shareholder must be at arm's length and on a normal commercial basis.

18.30   Directors

The directors of a listed company must make a formal statement that they accept responsibility for the information contained in a prospectus or listing particulars, and for compliance with the UK *Listing Rules, Prospectus Rules* and *Disclosure Rules*. Extensive details about each director, and other members of senior management, must be included in the prospectus or listing particulars, and full details of any new directors must be notified to a Regulatory Information Service when they are appointed. The information to be notified includes:

- other directorships in quoted companies in the last five years;
- any unspent convictions relating to indictable offences;
- any personal bankruptcies or individual voluntary arrangements;
- any receiverships, compulsory liquidations, voluntary liquidations or voluntary arrangements involving a company in which the individual was an executive director at the time or in the preceding twelve months;
- details of any similar matters in respect of a partnership in which the individual was a partner;
- any public criticism of the individual by statutory or regulatory authorities (including designated professional bodies); and
- whether the individual has been disqualified by the court from acting as a company director or in the management or conduct of affairs of any company.

Negative statements should be given where appropriate. All changes involving the board must be notified to a Regulatory Information Service, including any changes to the significant functions or executive responsibilities of an individual director.

18.31 Share Dealings

The company must notify a Regulatory Information Service without delay of:

- any dealings in the company's shares by directors (and persons connected with them) notified to the company under *CA 1985, ss 324–328*; and
- any grant of options to a director or a person connected with him/her.

18.32 *Compliance with the Model Code*

The Model Code is appended to Rule LR9 of the UK *Listing Rules* and is designed to ensure that directors and certain other relevant employees, and persons connected with them, do not deal in the company's securities when they may be in possession of unpublished price sensitive information. Listed companies must require their directors and other relevant employees to comply with a Code on share dealings that is no less exacting than the Model Code and are free to impose more stringent requirements if they wish. The company's list of relevant employees for this purpose may change, depending on what is happening in the company – for instance, there may be a small group of people who are permanently on the list and a larger group who are added or deleted depending on the nature of any unpublished price sensitive information at a particular point in time.

Directors and relevant employees must not deal in the company's shares without receiving clearance to do so from the Chairman or another designated director. Clearance cannot be given if there is any unpublished price sensitive information, even if the director or employee is not aware of that information. The company must keep a written record of all requests for clearance to deal, and of the responses given to those requests. If permission to deal is granted, it is recommended that only a short period is allowed for the dealing to take place (eg 24 hours) and that there is a requirement to reconfirm the clearance if there is any delay beyond this.

18.33   *Exceptions in Limited Circumstances*

The Model Code identifies dealings which are not subject to the Code and which can therefore take place at any time without prior clearance. In certain circumstances, grants of share options may be permitted during a prohibited period and the exercise of options during such a period may also be allowed in limited circumstances, but sale of the resulting securities will generally not be permitted. Permission to sell, but not to buy, may also be given in exceptional circumstances – the Model Code gives as an example a pressing personal financial commitment that cannot otherwise be satisfied. Directors may also be given permission to acquire qualification shares in certain circumstances.

18.34   *Breaches of the Code*

Any failure to comply with the Model Code (or the company's equivalent) must be notified to the UKLA as soon as possible. The UKLA will also contact the company if it becomes aware of an unnotified breach, to request an explanation. The UKLA may take disciplinary action and may require notification of the circumstances of the breach to the Regulatory Information Service.

18.35   Financial Information

The annual reports and accounts of a listed company must be published as soon as possible after approval and within six months of the end of the financial year at the latest. A preliminary announcement of results must be notified to a Regulatory Information Service without delay once it has been approved and within 120 days of the end of the financial period at the latest (see **11.128 PRELIMINARY ANNOUNCEMENTS**). Failure to submit the preliminary announcement on time will result in suspension of the company's securities. The annual accounts must be audited, consolidated (where relevant) and must give a true and fair view, and the corporate governance disclosures required under the UK *Listing Rules* must be given in the annual report. Details of directors' shareholdings in the annual report must be analysed between beneficial and non-beneficial holdings, and the information must also be updated to within one month of the date of the notice of the AGM. Any change of accounting reference date must be notified to a Regulatory Information Service without delay.

18.36   *Interim Reporting*

An interim report giving details of the company's performance and financial position for the first half of the financial year must be notified to the Regulatory

Information Service without delay after approval and within 90 days of period end at the latest. The content of the interim report is specified in the UK Listing Regulations (see **11.112 INTERIM REPORTS**). A second interim report may be required if the company changes its accounting reference date. Failure to submit the interim report on time will result in suspension of the company's securities. If the figures in the report have been audited or reviewed in line with current guidance from the Auditing Practices Board, the auditors' report must be included in the published statement.

18.37   Listed Company Transactions

The rules on listed company transactions set out in the UK *Listing Rules* are designed to ensure that shareholders are informed of significant transactions and, where appropriate, have the opportunity to vote on the issue. Transactions in the ordinary course of the company's activities are generally covered by the exemptions set out in the *Listing Rules*. Four classes of transaction are identified, determined by a series of percentage ratios – the larger the transaction, the more extensive the required disclosures and the greater the need for shareholder approval. The four classes and the related disclosure and approval requirements are as follows.

Size	Percentage ratios	Announcement	Circular	Shareholder approval
Class 3	Less than 5%	Yes*	No	No
Class 2	5%–24.99%	Yes	No	No
Class 1	25%–99.99%	Yes	Yes	Yes
Reverse take-over	100% or more	Yes	Yes	Yes

Only if the transaction is an acquisition and the consideration includes the issue of securities for which listing will be sought, or if the company releases any details to the public.

The percentage ratios cover:

- gross assets of the subject as a percentage of the gross assets of the listed company;
- profits attributable to the subject as a percentage of the profits of the listed company;
- turnover of the subject as a percentage of the turnover of the listed company;
- consideration for the transaction as a percentage of the market capitalisation of the listed company; and
- gross capital of the subject as a percentage of the gross capital of the listed company.

The *Listing Rules* specify how the ratios should be calculated and which figures should be used in each case. The UKLA may agree to substitute alternative calculations where appropriate – for instance, where using the standard calculations produces an anomalous result due to comparing profits with losses, or where the sphere of activity of the listed company makes the standard calculations inappropriate. If the listed company has published a half-year balance sheet, these asset figures must be used for classification purposes, even if the interim balance sheet has not been audited or reviewed.

18.38   *Notification of Transactions*

The detailed contents of the announcement and circular (where relevant) for each type of transaction are set out in the UK *Listing Rules*. The company must notify a Regulatory Information Service as soon as the terms of the transaction have been agreed and must keep the UKLA updated with any significant changes. Announcements do not usually have to be reviewed by the UKLA before publication, but circulars issued to shareholders must normally be submitted for prior review (only circulars that are regarded as being routine in nature are exempt from this general requirement).

18.39   *Related Party Transactions*

A transaction that involves a related party (eg a transaction between the company or its subsidiary and a director or substantial shareholder or their associate) will usually require both an announcement and a circular to shareholders seeking their approval. Very small transactions are generally exempt from these requirements, although details must be provided in writing to the UKLA before the transaction takes place, together with:

- confirmation from an acceptable independent advisor that the terms of the transaction are fair and reasonable; and
- an undertaking to give details of the transaction in next annual report and accounts.

The definition of a related party for these purposes is complex and companies should therefore consult their professional advisers and the UKLA to clarify the precise requirements in each case.

18.40   Treasury Shares

Company law currently allows companies to purchase their own shares in specific circumstances, but requires those shares to be treated as cancelled on purchase. Since 1 December 2003, the *Companies (Acquisition of Own Shares) (Treasury Shares) Regulations 2003 (SI 2003/1116)* have enabled certain companies to hold their own shares in treasury and to sell them for cash or transfer them to an employee share scheme. These provisions apply only to qualifying shares, which are defined as those:

- included in the UK Official List, or officially listed in another EEA state; or
- traded on the Alternative Investment Market or on a regulated market in another EEA state.

There are limits on the aggregate nominal value of shares that can be held as treasury shares and specific rules on dealing with the shares. In particular, a company cannot exercise any rights in respect of treasury shares, and no dividend or other distribution can be paid in respect of them. The legislation also specifies to what extent the proceeds from the sale of treasury shares can be treated as realised profits. Initial requirements on accounting for treasury shares were set out in UITF Abstract 37 *Purchases and Sales of Own Shares* but this has been superseded by FRS 25 *Financial Instruments: Disclosure and Presentation* for accounting periods beginning on or after 1 January 2005. Under FRS 25, any own shares acquired by an entity must be deducted from equity. No gain or loss should be recognised in the profit and loss account on the purchase, sale, issue or cancellation of own shares and any consideration paid or received should be recognised directly in equity. The same treatment applies regardless of whether the shares are held by the entity or by another member of the consolidated group. (For information on obtaining copies of FRS 25, see the ASB website at www.frc.org.uk/asb.) The *Listing Rules* also include specific requirements on dealing with treasury shares, including in particular:

- a prohibition on sales or transfers out of treasury during a prohibited period (eg a close period or when the company is in possession of price sensitive information); and
- a requirement to disclose information on sales and transfers into and out of treasury, and any cancellations, to a Regulatory Information Service.

18.41   Breaches

Any breaches of the continuing obligations should be notified immediately to the appropriate section of the UKLA. Companies will be contacted by the UKLA where the Authority becomes aware of an unnotified breach. In both cases, the UKLA will want to discuss why the breach occurred, what corrective action may be needed and what steps should be taken to prevent similar breaches arising in future. The UKLA has the power to impose a range of sanctions for breach of the continuing obligations.

Appendix 1

Useful Websites on Listing Requirements

FSA *Handbook*	www.fsa.gov.uk/handbook/
Financial Services Authority	www.fsa.gov.uk
London Stock Exchange	www.londonstockexchange.com
Panel on Takeovers and Mergers	www.thetakeoverpanel.org.uk
Institute of Directors	www.iod.com

Listing Requirements

Appendix 2

Summary of Contents of UK Listing Rules, Prospectus Rules and Disclosure Rules

Listing Rules

LR 1	Preliminary
LR 2	Requirements for listing
LR 3	Listing applications
LR 4	Listing particulars for professional securities market and certain other securities
LR 5	Suspending, cancelling and restoring listing
LR 6	Additional requirements for listing for equity securities
LR 7	Listing principles
LR 8	Sponsors
LR 9	Continuing obligations
LR 10	Significant transactions
LR 11	Related party transactions
LR 12	Dealing in own securities and treasury shares
LR 13	Contents of circulars
LR 14	Secondary listing of overseas companies
LR 15	Investment entities
LR 16	Venture capital trusts
LR 17	Debt and specialist securities
LR 18	Certificates representing certain securities
LR 19	Securitised derivatives
LR App 1	Relevant definitions
LR App 2	Fees and financial penalty income
LR App 3	List of Regulatory Information Services
LR transchedule	Transitional provisions

Prospectus Rules

PR 1	Preliminary
PR 2	Drawing up the prospectus
PR 3	Approval and publication of prospectus
PR 4	Use of languages and third country issuers
PR 5	Other provisions
PR App 1	Relevant definitions
PR App 2	Fees
PR App 3	Schedules and Building Blocks and Table of Combinations of Schedules and Building Blocks

Disclosure Rules

19

Management Accounting

19 Management Accounting

19.1 Comparison with Financial Accounts

At a Glance
* Management accounts are detailed internal accounts prepared on a regular basis throughout the financial year to enable management to review business activity and profitability.
* There are no formal requirements on the basis of preparation of management accounts, although it is advisable for them to follow the company's normal accounting policies where practicable.
* The need for accuracy and completeness must be balanced against the need for prompt preparation to enable timely decisions to be taken.
* The management accounts should be reconciled to the financial accounts at the end of the financial year.

19.2 Financial Accounts

Financial accounts are the detailed financial statements that every company must present to the members and file with the Registrar each year. They will usually cover a period of twelve months, unless the company has changed its accounting reference date, and will usually comprise:

* a profit and loss account;
* a statement of total recognised gains and losses;
* a cashflow statement;
* a balance sheet; and
* detailed notes to the accounts.

Financial accounts must show a true and fair view and must be prepared in accordance with applicable accounting standards. They must also be audited by an independent registered auditor, unless the company meets the *Companies Act 1985* criteria for audit exemption. These issues are considered in more detail in **1 AUDIT** and **11 FINANCIAL REPORTING**.

19.3   Management Accounts

Management accounts are internal accounts, prepared on a sufficiently regular basis to enable directors and other senior managers to review business activity and profitability during the course of the financial period and to respond promptly to any problems and opportunities that may be highlighted by the figures.

19.4   Basis of Preparation of Management Accounts

There is no requirement for management accounts to show a true and fair view or to comply with accounting standards, although it is sensible for them to follow the company's normal accounting policies as far as is practicable to avoid unnecessary differences between the two sets of accounts. The objective of management accounts is to provide regular and prompt feedback on the company's current performance. The need for accuracy and completeness must therefore be weighed against the need to produce the information in time for management to take appropriate decisions. Although management accounts should be prepared as accurately as possible, they will not usually include the detailed adjustments that are made in finalising a set of financial accounts (eg to account for year-end accruals and prepayments) and, in particular, they will not usually reflect items such as current tax, deferred tax and dividends. An element of accuracy in the detailed figures is therefore sacrificed in order to prepare management accounts on timely basis.

19.5   Reconciliation with Financial Accounts

Although the management accounts may not be prepared on the same basis as the financial accounts, it is important that the results shown in the two sets of accounts at the end of the financial year are reconciled. This should help to demonstrate that there are no serious errors and omissions in the financial accounts and will also help directors to understand how the details shown in the financial accounts relate to the information that they have been using to manage the company during the financial year, and thus to have confidence in the financial accounts for which they are ultimately responsible. Such a reconciliation can also help to identify items that could usefully be brought into the management accounts to refine and improve internal reporting in subsequent years.

19.6   Budgets and Forecasts

At a Glance
* The regular review of management accounts is most useful when the details for the period can be compared with a related budget as well as with the equivalent details for the previous year.

* The budget should be demanding but achievable, and should be developed with appropriate input from individual departments or functions.
* A detailed timetable for the budget preparation process can help to ensure that the process is well co-ordinated.
* Budget assumptions should be established at an early stage and should be set out in writing to help ensure consistency between different departments and functions.
* The preparation of an annual budget provides a good opportunity for a critical review of company overheads.
* Proposed capital projects should be analysed in detail so that the impact on the profit and loss account, and on the cashflow forecast, can be properly assessed.
* The annual budget should be appropriately phased to facilitate proper comparison with actual results.
* The annual budget should encompass balance sheet and cashflow details as well as profit and loss account information.

19.7   Value of Budgets and Forecasts

The regular review of management accounts is most useful when the details for the period can be compared with a related budget as well as with the equivalent details for the previous year. Realistic budgets, prompt monthly reporting of actual results and a regularly updated forecast of the results for the full financial year provide the foundations for strong financial management of a business. The budget should be demanding but achievable, and it is important that all relevant individuals have an input to the detail, so that they are encouraged to take ownership of the end result and accept responsibility for helping to achieve the target that has been set.

19.8   Preparing a Budget

Good co-ordination of the budgeting process is essential, especially in a larger organisation where individual departments may appear to be relatively autonomous. Appropriate input from individual departments or functions will be important but preparation of a budget for the company as a whole will require more than simply aggregating the contributions provided by each individual unit. It is helpful to have a timetable for the process, so that everyone involved understands when information is required, and at what level of detail, and can plan the preparation of their element accordingly. In a small organisation, the preparation of the budget will usually be handled by the directors and senior managers. In a larger organisation, the first stage may be to ask each unit to prepare their element of the budget and then for a small working group to consider the aggregation of this initial input, make any necessary central adjustments and discuss with the units any amendment needed to their input

Management Accounting

as a result. The final budget should be formally considered and approved by the directors.

19.9   Budget Assumptions

Preparation of a budget will always involve making a number of assumptions – for instance:

- the price increases that can be achieved and when these can be brought into effect;
- the expected level of sales of existing goods and services;
- whether any new products or services are to be introduced during the year and, if so:
  - when they are likely to be available,
  - what level of initial interest they are likely to attract, and
  - whether any specific marketing initiatives or purchase incentives are likely to be needed;
- expected increases in regular costs, including for instance:
  - wages and salaries,
  - materials and other purchases,
  - overheads (eg rent, power, telephone), and
  - impact of fluctuations in exchange rates;
- changes in cost levels expected in the current year – for instance:
  - cost of new marketing initiatives,
  - costs of opening new sites, or closing existing sites,
  - recruitment of, or reductions in, staff and when these will take place,
  - research and development initiatives, and
  - costs arising from legislative changes (eg health and safety, environmental issues).

It is important that the main elements of the budget assumptions are established at an early stage and are set out in writing, especially where the budget input comes from a number of different departments or units. Setting out clear guidelines at the outset will help to ensure that departmental budgets are prepared on a consistent basis and that the assumptions made are consistent between departments.

19.10   Liaison Between Units

Where a number of different units or departments are involved in preparing initial budget information, it is important for there to be good liaison between them. For instance, an understanding of the sales budget will be critical for those preparing the budget for direct costs. In a smaller organisation, where the number of people involved in the budgeting process is likely to be limited, information will usually flow freely between those who are involved. In a larger organisation, more careful planning will usually be needed – for instance, the timetable will probably need to allow for the sales budget to be prepared at an early stage in the process because other departments will need to have this information in order to prepare their own contribution.

19.11   Overheads

Preparation of the annual budget provides an opportunity for the company's overheads to be carefully reviewed. The temptation to budget simply for an inflationary increase over the costs for the previous year should be avoided. A zero-based budgeting approach (in effect starting with a blank sheet of paper) can often be the most helpful way of focusing attention on how various activities are currently being carried out and whether this is in fact the most cost-effective approach. For instance, such a review may indicate that it would be beneficial to sub-contract certain activities to a third party rather than trying to execute and manage them in house. All overhead costs should be budgeted in detail, supported by relevant calculations and workings. In particular, large round-sum allowances should not be accepted.

19.12   Capital Expenditure

Capital expenditure should be budgeted for in the same level of detail as other costs. Even though the full cost of assets will not usually be charged in the profit and loss account in the year of acquisition, there will be an ongoing charge for depreciation over the estimated life of the asset, and the cashflow impact of the expenditure will need to be reflected in the cashflow forecast that should form part of the overall budget (see **2.7 NEED FOR CASHFLOW FORECASTS**). Proposed capital projects should be analysed in detail, giving both the timing and amount of the individual elements of the expenditure. It is also important to ensure that any related costs are also reflected in the budget – for instance, the cost of software to operate proposed new computer equipment, or additional insurance costs that may be incurred as a result of the purchase of new equipment. Similarly, the capital expenditure plans should reflect the projections made elsewhere in the budget – for instance, if the sales and production budgets assume a significant increase in production, will the company's present plant and equipment be able to achieve this, or are additional or replacement items of equipment likely to be needed? The capital budget should also explore the various methods of financing the new assets – for instance, whether some form of leasing would be more cost effective than outright purchase.

19.13   Phasing the Budget

Monthly management reporting can only be truly effective if the annual budget is properly phased – calendarising a budget by dividing the overall totals by twelve will not produce meaningful monthly analyses to help the directors manage the business, because the real issues behind the variances shown in the monthly reports will be masked by seasonal fluctuations and other similar factors. Each item in the budget must therefore be budgeted on a month-by-month basis rather than just for the year as a whole. This information will also be needed to prepare meaningful cashflow forecasts (see **2.7 NEED FOR CASHFLOW FORECASTS**).

19.14   Balance Sheet and Cashflow

The emphasis in the budgeting process tends to be on the profit and loss account, because the company's turnover and profitability will often be seen as key indicators of the success of the business. However, as explained in **2 CASH-FLOW MANAGEMENT**, the management of working capital can also be a critical factor and it is therefore equally as important to include balance sheet and cashflow information in the budget. Actual performance should be compared against these elements of the budget as part of the regular monthly monitoring process, so that appropriate management action can be taken to improve these areas when required.

19.15   Management Accounts and Reporting

At a Glance
* Management accounts are usually prepared monthly, although quarterly reporting may be considered adequate in a smaller business.
* Management accounts should usually be available within two weeks of the end of the relevant month or quarter.
* There is no standard format for management accounts – the structure should be designed to provide the information that the directors and senior managers need to manage the business effectively.
* Management accounts should incorporate comparisons with the budget for the current year and with the equivalent period in the previous year, with variances presented in both figures and percentages.
* A short written commentary can help to focus attention on the key issues arising.
* It can be helpful to include an updated forecast for the full year as part of the regular management reporting process, but this should not replace the original budget in the detailed summaries.

19.16   Timetable for Preparation

The regularity with which management accounts are prepared will depend on the particular circumstances of the business. For many companies, directors and senior managers will need information to be available on a monthly basis, but smaller businesses may find quarterly reporting adequate. Whatever schedule is agreed for the preparation of management accounts, it is important to set a timetable for their preparation. This will help to demonstrate to the staff concerned the importance that the directors and senior managers attach to the prompt availability of the information. The detailed timetable should usually allow for the management accounts to be available within two weeks of the end of the relevant month (or quarter). It can be useful to schedule a regular meeting at which the management accounts will be reviewed and discussed by the directors and senior managers, and appropriate action agreed. This can act as a good incentive for the information to be prepared on time. Information on specific elements of the detailed financial information (eg sales figures, aged debtor details) may need to be circulated daily or weekly to those with particular responsibility in the relevant area.

19.17   Format of Management Accounts

There is no standard format for management accounts. The structure should be designed to provide the information that the directors and senior managers need in order to manage the business successfully. The format of the balance sheet will probably be similar to that given in the financial accounts but the profit and loss account will need to give considerably more detail than the standard *Companies Act 1985* format. For a manufacturing business, the management accounts profit and loss account might show:

- sales;
- cost of sales:
  - direct labour costs,
  - materials,
  - factory costs (eg rent, power, hire and leasing charges),
  - other direct production costs (including depreciation of equipment) etc;
- gross profit;
- selling and distribution costs:
  - relevant staff costs,
  - advertising,
  - motor expenses (including depreciation of relevant cars) etc;
- administrative costs:
  - relevant staff costs,
  - telephone,
  - printing, postage and stationery,
  - legal and professional charges,
  - depreciation of computers and office equipment etc;
- operating profit;
- interest paid and received;
- net profit.

The structure of the management accounts should give sufficient detail for directors and senior managers to gain a good understanding of the company's performance and financial position, but the information should be summarised in such a way that critical figures and comparisons do not become obscured. Depending on the nature of the business, other supporting details may need to be included in the reporting package (eg employee numbers, tenders submitted and accepted). Where appropriate, use should be made of graphic presentation methods to highlight trends and other comparisons.

19.18   Comparisons

The management accounts should incorporate comparisons with the budget for the current year and with the actual figures for the same period in the previous year, together with details of the variances in both figures and percentages. An appropriate layout might be as in the following example.

Example

Budget for current year	Budget for year to date	Actual year to date	Variance from budget to date	Variance from budget to date	Actual for previous year to date	Variance from previous year	Variance from previous year
£	£	£	£	%	£	£	%

19.19   Commentary

It will usually be helpful for the directors and senior managers to receive a brief written commentary on the information shown in the management accounts, as well as the detailed figures. This should be prepared by finance staff, in conjunction with other employees where additional information is needed. The commentary should give a brief explanation of the main variances from the budget and the previous year, together with other relevant details that may not be apparent from the figures (for instance, a small overall variance in one expense category may be the combination of two significant but compensating variances which should be brought to the attention of the directors and senior managers). This will help to focus the attention of directors and senior managers on the key issues and help in their review and understanding of the figures. However, they should not rely solely on the detail provided in the commentary and should be prepared (and encouraged) to ask questions on other items.

19.20   Balance Sheet and Cashflow

The regular management accounts presented to directors and senior managers should incorporate detailed balance sheet and cashflow information, including appropriate comparison of the actual position with that originally forecast. This information is an important factor in the effective management of the company's working capital (considered in more detail in **2 CASHFLOW MANAGEMENT**).

19.21   Updated Forecast

It will usually be helpful for management purposes for an updated forecast for the year to be included in the regular reporting. The forecast may not need to be updated every month – in some cases a quarterly update will suffice. The forecast should be based on the actual figures to date and the expected outcome for the remainder of the year, and should be supported by a brief commentary. The expected outcome will be based on the original budget for the remainder of the year, adjusted for the effects of any action taken by management in response to the actual results achieved to date and any other changes that are known to be needed (eg to reflect the loss of business with a major customer). The inclusion of an up-to-date forecast enables the directors and senior managers to review the expected result for the year alongside details of the original budget. The original budget should not be replaced with the latest forecast, as management will then lose sight of the original target and will be unable to put the actual results to date and the forecast into context with this. The aim should still be to achieve the budget wherever possible, by taking action to counter any problems that have arisen to date, and it is therefore important that the original budget continues to form part of the reporting process.

19.22   Ratio Analysis

At a Glance
* It will often be helpful to incorporate a number of performance ratios into the management reporting package.
* The directors and senior managers should agree in advance on the most relevant ratios for the business, adding appropriate new information as the business expands and develops.
* Management may also find it helpful to consider certain investment ratios as part of the regular reporting package.

19.23   Performance Ratios

Ratio analysis is an important management tool and it will usually be helpful to incorporate a number of performance ratios into the monthly management reporting package. Not all ratios will be meaningful in the context of a particular business and the directors and senior managers should therefore agree in advance on what information would be most appropriate, and then be prepared to adapt and refine this as the business develops or activities and circumstances change. Performance ratios to consider include the following.

* *Return on capital employed:* Sometimes called 'return on investment', or 'return on operating assets', this ratio expresses profit as a percentage of the amount invested in the business. There are different definitions of what

Management Accounting

constitutes capital employed, investment or operating assets in this context – the important issue is to agree on a definition and use it consistently to calculate this ratio within the business.

- *Gross profit margin:* This expresses gross profit as a percentage of sales. Separate ratios may need to be calculated for each main activity or sales category for the ratio analysis to be meaningful.
- *Stock turnover:* This expresses stock as a percentage of cost of sales. The ratio is often multiplied by 365 to indicate how many days it takes to convert stock into sales. It may be necessary to analyse the ratio by main stock category to identify where any problems are occurring.
- *Debtor ratio:* This usually expresses debtors as a percentage of annual sales, multiplied by 365 to indicate how many days' sales have yet to be converted into cash. Different methods of calculation can be used for monthly reporting purposes. A realistic target should be set for debtor days and actual performance monitored closely against this. A very small increase in debtor days can have a significant adverse impact on the company's cashflow.
- *Creditor ratio:* This usually expresses creditors as a percentage of purchases and expenses, multiplied by 365 to indicate the average period of credit that the company is taking from suppliers. Different methods of calculation can be used for monthly reporting purposes. Once again, small changes in the ratio can have a significant impact on the company's cashflow.
- *Liquidity ratio:* The current ratio expresses current assets as a percentage of creditors due within one year (excluding borrowings), and is used to indicate the company's ability to meet its short-term commitments as they fall due. A ratio of 1 or less will indicate that the company has liquidity problems, especially as it will usually take time for some of the current assets (eg stock) to be converted into cash. Liquidity can also be assessed by the quick ratio, which expresses current assets other than stock as a percentage of creditors due within one year (again excluding borrowings). This ratio compares the total of liquid and near liquid assets with short-term liabilities, and the aim should once again be for a ratio of more than 1. A ratio below 1 will usually indicate the need for extended credit, additional borrowings or a further injection of cash.
- *Employee ratios:* Some businesses, particularly those in the service sector, may find ratios such as sales (or fee income) per employee, profit per employee and professional staff to support staff helpful in managing staff levels and profitability.
- *Gearing ratio:* This expresses net borrowings as a percentage of shareholders' funds. Borrowings will usually include preference shares, debentures, loans, overdrafts and other financing liabilities – in other words, any liability that gives rise to an interest commitment, regardless of whether this is fixed or variable. Net borrowings is the total of these items less cash and other liquid resources. The ratio indicates the extent to which the company's operations are being financed by borrowings rather than investment from the shareholders. A high gearing ratio will usually indicate that the company has a substantial commitment in terms of interest and could be seriously affected by

increases in interest rates, unless measures have been taken to prevent this – for instance, through the use of fixed-rate borrowings or the purchase of an interest rate cap.

- *Interest cover:* This compares profit before interest with interest payable and is a measure of the company's ability to meet any increase in interest costs. The aim should usually be to have interest cover of between 4 and 5 (ie profit before interest is at least four times higher than the interest cost).

19.24   Investment Ratios

Although not as directly relevant to the management of company performance, management may also find it useful to consider certain investment ratios as part of the monthly reporting process. Once again, what is relevant will depend on the particular circumstances of the company, but measures to consider include the following.

- *Gross dividend yield:* This compares the annual dividend per share with the current market price of each share and indicates the return that each share-holder is currently receiving on his/her investment.
- *Gross percentage dividend:* This compares the annual dividend per share with the nominal value of each share. It is only useful for comparing the company's dividend payments year by year.
- *Dividend cover:* This compares the company's earnings (the profit after tax which is attributable to the ordinary shareholders) with the total paid to those shareholders in dividends for the year. It indicates the likelihood of the company being able to maintain current dividend levels in future years. Where dividend cover is close to 1, the company has used all of (and possibly more than) its earnings for the year to pay dividends to the ordinary shareholders.
- *Earnings per share:* This relates the company's earnings to the average number of shares in issue during the period and is regarded as a measure of the true growth of the company. Listed companies are required to disclose basic (and, where appropriate, diluted) earnings per share on the face of the profit and loss account and, under UK accounting practice, FRS 22 *Earnings per Share* sets out detailed requirements on how these figures should be calculated (for information on obtaining copies see the Accounting Standards Board website at www.frc.org.uk/asb). Entities preparing IAS accounts (see **3.16–3.17**) must comply instead with the equivalent requirements in IAS 33 *Earnings per share.*
- *Price-earnings ratio:* This compares the current market price of the company's shares with earnings per share. A high ratio may indicate that the market expects earnings to increase in the future, but the calculation might also be affected by other issues such as an increase in the share price in anticipation of a takeover.

Appendix 1

Useful Websites on Management Accounting Issues

Chartered Institute of Management Accountants	www.cimaglobal.com.
ICAEW Finance and Management Faculty	www.icaew.co.uk/fmfac
Association of Chartered Certified Accountants	www.accaglobal.com
Business Link	www.businesslink.gov.uk
Institute of Directors	www.iod.com
Institute of Internal Auditors	www.iia.org.uk

Payroll

20 Payroll

20.1 Payroll Administration

> **At a Glance**
> * A business that employs staff has onerous responsibilities in respect of PAYE and National Insurance.
> * A small company with few employees may find it more cost effective to outsource the payroll function, although responsibility for compliance with the various regulations will always remain with the employer.
> * Payroll records must be retained for at least three years from the end of the tax year to which they relate.
> * Controls need to be established to ensure the accuracy and completeness of payroll processing.

20.2 Setting up a Payroll System

The decision by any business to employ staff brings with it a number of additional duties and responsibilities, both in terms of compliance with employment and other relevant legislation and in terms of the administration of a payroll system. Staff will need to be paid on time, either each week or each month, and the employer has onerous duties under the regulations for PAYE and National Insurance. It is therefore vital that the payroll function operates smoothly and provides the necessary information on time and in a readily usable format.

20.3 Outsourcing

A major issue to consider is whether the company should run the payroll function in house or whether the work should be contracted out to a specialist. A small company with few employees may find it more cost effective to contract out the work rather than devoting time to training staff to deal with it in house. A large company with a substantial number of employees may find it equally productive to outsource the payroll function, given the volume of transactions and specialist knowledge needed, especially as the complexity of the issues that need to be dealt with will often increase with a larger workforce. The extent to which the preparation of the payroll is outsourced can also vary. In some cases, the third party will look after all aspects of the company's payroll function, whilst in other cases the role will be more that of a processing bureau for the payroll itself, with most of the detailed supporting work carried out by the company in house. Many businesses still deal with all aspects of payroll in house. Whatever approach is taken to the detailed administrative work, responsibility for compliance with the various regulations remains with the employer.

20.4   Records

An employer is required by the regulations to maintain detailed payroll records, which must be retained for at least three years from the end of the tax year to which they relate, although a retention period of at least six years is usually recommended.

20.5   Controls

Regardless of whether the payroll is prepared in house or externally, appropriate controls should be introduced to ensure that:

- payments are only made to those actually employed by the company;
- employees are only paid for the hours actually worked or contracted for;
- the correct rates of pay are applied; and
- all deductions and other calculations are properly carried out.

Directors and managers may find it particularly helpful to use exception reports to monitor payroll costs, especially where the number of employees makes detailed checking impractical. For instance, a monthly report highlighting gross pay, net pay, deductions and rebates above reasonable parameters can be useful in focusing attention on those areas where errors or irregularities may have occurred.

20.6   PAYE

At a Glance
* The PAYE system requires each employer to calculate the income tax due on the remuneration paid to each employee and to account for this to HM Revenue and Customs.
* The onus is on the employer to establish whether any individual working for the business is employed or self-employed – this is a complex issue and will usually depend on the terms of the contract under which the individual is working.

* The IR35 legislation, introduced in April 2000, changed the tax treatment of individuals who provide personal services through an intermediary company.
* A new employer should provide appropriate details to HM Revenue and Customs to enable a PAYE scheme to be registered for the business.
* PAYE deducted from payments to employees must generally be paid to HM Revenue and Customs by the 19th of the following month, although smaller businesses may be permitted to account quarterly.
* HM Revenue and Customs specifies the detailed PAYE records that must be kept and the details that must be provided to each employee.
* Appropriate HM Revenue and Customs forms must be completed for new employees and leavers.
* Detailed year-end returns must be submitted to HM Revenue and Customs by 19 May each year.
* By 31 May each year, every employee must be provided with a form P60 summarising their income, PAYE and National Insurance details for the previous tax year.
* A form P11D must be completed for every director and for every employee who earns at least £8,500 a year (including expenses and benefits).
* An employer may seek a dispensation from HM Revenue and Customs not to report certain benefits on forms P11D – this can save a considerable amount of administrative time.
* HM Revenue and Customs carries out regular PAYE audits to confirm that employers are complying with the relevant regulations.
* Regular PAYE 'health-checks' can help to identify potential problems at an early stage.

20.7   PAYE System

The 'Pay As You Earn' ('PAYE') system requires each employer to calculate the income tax due on the remuneration paid to each employee, deduct this from the gross remuneration paid each week or month and pay the amount deducted over to HM Revenue and Customs, together with any National Insurance Contributions payable by the employer and the employee (see **20.22–20.25** below). An employer who fails to account properly for PAYE could be held liable for the tax due and not paid over to HM Revenue and Customs and will not necessarily have recourse to the employee for reimbursement. Part-time and casual employees are generally subject to the same PAYE requirements as full-time employees. Care must also be taken where relevant to ensure that the company complies with the requirements of the Construction Industry Scheme (CIS). This is designed to prevent tax evasion by contractors and sub-contractors within the construction industry, but the scope of the scheme is wider than the title implies because any business whose average annual expenditure on construction operations over a period of 3 years exceeds £1 million will generally be deemed to be a contractor and so will come within the scope of the scheme. Separate rules apply for businesses that have been in existence for less than 3 years.

20.8   Employed or Self-employed

The onus is on the employer to establish whether any individual working for the business is employed, in which case PAYE tax must be deducted from any payments to that individual and accounted for to HM Revenue and Customs, or self-employed in which case the individual has full responsibility for his/her own tax affairs. Whether someone is employed or self-employed is a complex issue and will depend on the terms of the contract under which the individual is working for the company. Neither the company nor the individual can simply decide that the worker is self-employed without considering the details of the arrangement and referring to HM Revenue and Customs guidance on this subject. Relevant factors will usually include:

- who controls when, how and where the work is carried out;
- whether the individual must do the work personally or can hire someone else to do it;
- whether the individual works set hours or a given number of hours each week or month;
- whether the individual is paid by the hour, week or month, and whether he/she receives overtime; and
- who provides any equipment that the individual needs to carry out the work.

In any case where there is doubt over the correct treatment, the company's PAYE district should be contacted for guidance or professional advice should be taken. An employer who incorrectly treats an individual as self-employed rather than employed could be held liable for any PAYE not deducted, without necessarily having recourse to the individual for reimbursement.

20.9   IR 35 and Personal Service Companies

New legislation came into effect from 6 April 2000 which changes the tax treatment of individuals who provide personal services to a client through an intermediary company. Where the individual works under the direction, supervision or control of the client, so that he/she is to all intents and purposes an employee of the client, the intermediary is required to account for PAYE and National Insurance on all income relating to that contract, subject to the deduction of any allowable business expenses actually incurred (ie those that would normally be allowable in the case of an employee) and a 5 per cent deduction to cover the administration expenses of the intermediary. Once again, this can be a complex area to deal with in practice, and professional advice should be sought where necessary.

20.10   New Employer

A new employer should contact HM Revenue and Customs New Employers' Helpline (*tel:* 0845 60 70 143) as soon as possible to notify them that the company is about to set up a payroll. They will usually ask for the following information:

- company name and registered office;
- details of the company's activities;
- names, addresses and National Insurance numbers of the directors;
- the date on which the first employees started (or will start) employment;
- how many employees the company expects to have;
- the date of the first payment to employees; and
- if the company's payroll is to be outsourced, details of who will be running it.

Once registered for PAYE, the company will receive a New Employer's Starter Pack with various guides and forms to help with the establishment and maintenance of the payroll records and the detailed tables that will be needed if PAYE and National Insurance Contributions are to be calculated manually. The company will also be allocated a PAYE reference number which should be quoted in all correspondence with the tax office.

20.11   Payment to HM Revenue and Customs

PAYE deducted from payments to employees should normally be paid over to HM Revenue and Customs by the 19th of the month following that in which the wages or salaries are paid to the company's employees (ie PAYE deducted from salaries paid at the end of June must be paid to HM Revenue and Customs by 19 July). The company will be given a PAYE payment reference and will be sent a book of payment slips for each tax year although electronic payment is encouraged. Interest and penalties can be charged for late payment of the amounts due. Smaller businesses, whose total payments for PAYE, National Insurance and other relevant deductions are expected to average less than £1,500 per month, can arrange to make payments quarterly rather than monthly by contacting their HM Revenue and Customs Accounts Office.

20.12   Records

The company can either maintain manual payroll records, or can use a suitable computer program for this. Manual records are usually only used these days if the company has a small number of employees. Whichever system is adopted, the company is responsible for accounting for PAYE as soon as a payment is made to an employee. The company will need to know the tax code of each employee and details of any employment income that they have received during the year from another employer (see **20.13** below). If the calculations are carried out manually, the amount of PAYE due for each employee will need to be calculated from the tables provided by HM Revenue and Customs and the details recorded on a P11 deductions working sheet for that employee. If a computerised payroll system is used, the calculations will be carried out automatically on the basis of the employee information input and a computerised version of the P11 deductions working sheet should be produced. Each employee must be provided with a payslip showing the gross pay for the week or month, the amounts deducted for PAYE and National Insurance, any other deductions and the amount of net pay. The payslip should also show totals for the year to date. The basic calculations may be complicated by the need to account for items such as the repayment of student loans, which are dealt with through the PAYE system, or where payments such as Statutory Sick Pay ('SSP') (see **10.41 STATUTORY SICK PAY**) or Statutory Maternity Pay ('SMP') (see **10.35 MATERNITY PAY**) apply.

20.13   New Employees

A new employee should be asked to provide parts 2 and 3 of form P45 from his/her previous employer. This will show the individual's current tax code and the total income received and PAYE deducted to date in the current tax year, all of which should be used to complete a new P11 deductions working sheet for that employee (or, where relevant, be input into the computer system) in accordance with HM Revenue and Customs guidance. The company should retain part 2 of the form to support the entries made in its payroll records and forward part 3 immediately to the relevant tax office. If the new employee does not have a form P45, the company should complete form P46 and ask the employee to sign the appropriate declaration. A copy of the form should be sent to the tax office and the company should deduct PAYE from payments to the employee as directed on the form until it receives further communication from the tax office.

20.14   Leavers

When an employee leaves, the company should complete a four-part form P45 using the latest details on the P11 deductions working sheet for that employee. Part 1 must be sent to the tax office, parts 1A, 2 and 3 should be given to the employee, and part 4 should be retained with the company's payroll records.

20.15   Year-end Returns

Towards the end of each tax year, HM Revenue and Customs will issue the company with form P35 – Employer's Annual Return for completion. The company will need to obtain and complete a three-part form P14/P60 for each employee (these can be completed manually or by computer) showing the total paid and total PAYE and National Insurance deducted during the tax year. A separate form must be completed for any employee for whom there is no P14 (for instance, because the amounts paid to the employee were below the income tax and National Insurance thresholds). When all the P14/P60 forms have been completed, the totals should be transferred to form P35. As well as including various declarations, this form requires the total PAYE and National Insurance for the year for all employees to be reconciled with the amounts paid by the company to HM Revenue and Customs during the course of the year. Any amounts identified on the form as still outstanding must be paid to HM Revenue and Customs by 19 April following the end of the tax year. Interest and penalties can be charged for late payment. The completed P35 and P14 forms should be submitted to HM Revenue and Customs by 19 May each year – once again penalties can be charged for late submission. A copy of the relevant form P14 (in this case given the reference P60) must be given to each employee by 31 May following the end of the tax year.

20.16   Electronic Filing of Year-end Returns

Electronic filing of year-end employer returns is compulsory with effect from the following tax years:

- 2004/05 for employers with 250 or more employees;
- 2005/06 for employers with between 50 and 249 employees;
- 2009/10 for employers with fewer than 50 employees.

Electronic filing means filing using the internet service for PAYE or Electronic Data Interchange (EDI) – it does not include filing by magnetic media. In order to meet the new requirements, employers will therefore need to file forms P35 and P14 electronically using software that meets the HM Revenue and Customs standard. There is no requirement to file other forms (eg P11D, P45, P46) electronically at this stage. The Inland Revenue is trying to encourage smaller businesses (ie those with less than 50 employees and/or pensioners) to move towards electronic filing by offering the following cash incentives for early adoption:

- £250 for 2005/06
- £250 for 2006/07
- £100 for 2007/08
- £75 for 2008/09

20.17   Forms P11D (or P9D)

An employer must complete form P11D for every director and for every employee who earns £8,500 a year or more (including any expenses and benefits). This form records all the benefits and expenses provided on behalf of that director and employee. Form P9D will need to be completed for any employee earning less than £8,500 who is provided with certain benefits. The taxation of benefits provided and expenses paid to employees is a complex area and reference should be made to the detailed guidance issued by HM Revenue and Customs. Professional advice should be sought in areas of doubt. The completed forms must be submitted to HM Revenue and Customs by 6 July each year, together with form P11D(b) which summarises any Class 1A National Insurance that is due on the benefits (see **20.22–20.25** below). Forms P11D can now be submitted electronically by making appropriate arrangements through HM Revenue and Customs website at www.hmrc.gov.uk. A copy of form P11D (or P9D as appropriate) must also be given to the relevant employee by 6 July each year.

20.18   HM Revenue and Customs

An employer may seek a dispensation from HM Revenue and Customs not to report certain benefits and expenses payments on forms P11D. HM Revenue and Customs will issue a dispensation notice if they are satisfied that:

- the employees would be able to obtain a deduction for the expenses or benefits in arriving at their personal tax liability; and
- payment of the expenses or benefits is properly controlled by the company.

Having a dispensation in place can save the employer a considerable amount of administrative time in collating information and processing P11D forms. A dispensation can be arranged by obtaining HM Revenue and Customs document P11DX *How to cut down on your paperwork: Dispensations* (see HM Revenue and Customs website at www.hmrc.gov.uk) and completing the application form included with this, or by providing the relevant tax office with details of the employees for which dispensation is sought, the types of expenses and benefit payments to be covered and the company's system for controlling and authorising payments. Expenses and benefits should continue to be reported on forms P11D until the employer has received formal written notification from HM Revenue and Customs that a dispensation has been approved.

20.19   PAYE Audits

HM Revenue and Customs carries out regular PAYE audits to confirm that an employer is operating PAYE and National Insurance on all employee earnings and complying with the relevant regulations. The stated aim is to review each large and medium-sized employer at least once every five years. The PAYE auditor is entitled to review any records relating to the calculation and payment of employee earnings, the deduction of tax under the PAYE system and the calculation of National Insurance. Most audits will reveal some errors and discrepancies and HM Revenue and Customs will then seek a settlement of any outstanding PAYE and National Insurance. Their initial proposals may include extrapolation of the results of the period reviewed to cover the previous six tax years, and earlier periods if they suspect that there has been a deliberate understatement. Agreement of the amount due may therefore require some careful negotiation and professional advice should be sought where necessary. Penalties may also be charged, depending on the seriousness of the errors and omissions.

20.20   PAYE 'Health Checks'

The issues that arise from the operation of PAYE can be complex and wide-ranging and penalties for failing to comply with the regulations can be severe.

It can therefore be helpful to arrange regular 'health checks' of the PAYE system by someone with the appropriate specialist knowledge, so that any aspects that might give rise to problems in the event of a PAYE audit are identified at an early stage. This should allow potential difficulties to be resolved promptly and prevent serious underpayments going undetected for any length of time.

20.21   National Insurance

At a Glance
* There are various classes of National Insurance contributions covering employers, employees, self-employed individuals and those who wish to make voluntary contributions.
* Employer and employee contributions must be calculated weekly or monthly, depending on how the employee is paid.
* The total of employer and employee contributions must be paid over to HM Revenue and Customs by the employer with the PAYE payment for the relevant month.
* Total employer and employee National Insurance Contributions for the year must be entered on the employer's year-end return, and the relevant details for each employee must be shown on their form P60.
* An employer may also be liable to pay Class 1A National Insurance Contributions on certain benefits paid to employees – these contributions must be calculated in conjunction with the preparation of forms P11D and must be paid to HM Revenue and Customs by 19 July each year.

20.22   Categories of National Insurance

Class 1 National Insurance Contributions are payable by both employers and employees, in each case based on the earnings of the employee. Employers are also liable to pay Class 1A contributions on the taxable value of most benefits provided to an employee. Other classes of National Insurance (Classes 2, 3 and 4) apply to self-employed individuals and those who wish to make voluntary contributions. An individual may be liable (or entitled) to pay more than one class of contribution, but there are maximum levels for overall contributions and relief is also given where contributions are payable under certain combinations of the various classes. The rules on deemed employment under the National Insurance regulations can be complex, but in general, an individual who is an employee for the purposes of income tax and employment protection law will also be an employee for National Insurance purposes. Detailed guidance on the calculation and payment of National Insurance Contributions will be issued to new employers at the same time as the related PAYE information (see **20.10** above).

Payroll

20.23 Calculation and Records

A lower earnings limit applies (the primary threshold – currently £97 per week), below which no National Insurance Contributions are payable by either the employee or the employer. An employee is liable to pay National Insurance at the set rate (currently 11 per cent for most employees) on all earnings above the primary threshold up to the Upper Earnings Limit ('UEL') and at 1 per cent on earnings above the UEL. An employer is required to pay National Insurance at the set rate (currently 12.8 per cent) on all earnings of the employee above the secondary threshold – this was previously slightly higher than the primary threshold, but the two were brought into line for the 2002/03 tax year onwards. The relevant National Insurance Contributions must be calculated weekly or monthly, depending on how the employee is paid, and recorded on the P11D deductions working sheet also used for PAYE purposes (see **20.12** above). The calculation can be carried out manually using tables provided by HM Revenue and Customs or, where the payroll is computerised, by the relevant computer program. Separate rules apply for calculating National Insurance Contributions for directors.

20.24 Payment to HM Revenue and Customs

The total of employer and employee National Insurance Contributions for each month must be paid to the Inland Revenue along with the PAYE due for that month either electronically or using the standard payslip provided (see **20.11** above).

20.25 Year-end Returns

The total of employee and employer National Insurance Contributions for each employee must be entered on the year-end P14/P60 return for that employee and transferred to form P35 – Employer's Annual Return (see **20.15** above). The P35 form requires the total National Insurance for the year in respect of all employees to be reconciled with the amount paid to HM Revenue and Customs during the course of the year, and any amounts still outstanding must be paid by 19 April. Interest and penalties can be charged for late payment. Towards the end of the tax year, HM Revenue and Customs will also issue the employer with form P11D(b). This should be completed in conjunction with the P11D forms for employees (see **20.17** above) to show the total of any Class 1A National Insurance Contributions due by the employer on benefits provided to employees. These contributions should be paid to HM Revenue and Customs by 19 July following the end of the tax year, either electronically or using the special payslip provided. Form P11D(b) must be submitted, with the P11D forms, by 6 July following the end of the tax year.

Appendix 1

Useful Websites on Payroll Matters

HM Revenue and Customs	www.hmrc.gov.uk
ICAEW Tax Faculty	www.icaew.co.uk/taxfac
Business Link	www.businesslink.gov.uk
Institute of Directors	www.iod.com

Pensions

21 Pensions

21.1 Types of Pension Scheme

At a Glance

* The provision of good retirement benefits is often seen as an important element of the remuneration package offered to employees and the action of a responsible employer.
* Employees are increasingly being encouraged to contract out of the secondary State pension scheme and to make their own alternative provision.
* Under a defined benefit scheme, the benefits payable on retirement are fixed, either as an amount or as a proportion of salary – this is advantageous for the scheme member but the cost to the employer can fluctuate significantly over time.
* Under a defined contribution scheme, the benefits payable on retirement depend on the amount accumulated in respect of each scheme member – the employer has the benefit of a fixed cost but the employee bears the risk of the fund being insufficient to provide the level of retirement benefits hoped for.
* Directors may want to consider other options that share the risks and costs of pension provision more equitably between employer and employee.
* Any individual (and their employer) can contribute to a personal pension, provided that he/she is not already a member of an occupational pension scheme.
* From April 2001, certain individuals who are members of an occupational pension scheme can also contribute to a personal or stakeholder pension.
* All employers with five or more employees must generally give them access to a stakeholder pension scheme, unless they have made alternative pension provision.
* A Small Self Administered Scheme ('SSAS') generally has fewer than 12 members and is subject to special HMRC rules.

21.2   Retirement Provision

Although most employees will qualify for State pension benefits on retirement, many people will want to make additional provision to ensure that they can maintain their lifestyle after retirement and perhaps to give themselves the option of retiring before the normal retirement age. The provision of good retirement benefits is therefore often seen as an important element of the remuneration package offered to employees and potential employees and the action of a responsible employer. Generous tax benefits are also available on contributions by employers and employees to pension schemes approved by HMRC.

21.3   State Pensions

Most employees will qualify for basic State pension on retirement, although the amount that they receive will depend on whether they have a full National Insurance Contributions record, the details for which are very complex. In addition to basic pension, the State Second Pension (previously the State Earnings Related Pension Scheme or SERPS) enables employees to build up a further pension entitlement. Employees can choose to remain within the State Second Pension scheme, or to contract out of this and participate instead in an occupational pension scheme offered by their employer or make other personal pension arrangements. There is expected to be an increasing encouragement for employees to contract out of the additional State scheme and make alternative pension provision in order to reduce the potential burden on government resources of present demographic trends (ie reducing birth rates and longer life expectancy). Many employers already offer their employees access to an occupational pension scheme, which may operate on the basis of defined benefits or defined contributions, or to a group pension personal pension plan. At the time of writing, state pension arrangements are undergoing a major review and consideration is being given to the introduction of a planned national pensions savings scheme based on an employee contribution of 4 per cent of salary, a Government contribution of 1 per cent in the form of tax relief and an employer contribution of 3 per cent of salary. Involvement in the scheme would be automatic, with each employee having the option of opting out if they wish. This contrasts with the present approach where employees are generally given the opportunity to opt in to pension arrangements if they wish. This change could result in a significant increase in employer costs in respect of pensions, given that many employees currently choose not to take advantage of some of the pension benefits offered to them through defined contribution or stakeholder schemes.

21.4   Defined Benefit Schemes

A defined benefit retirement scheme is one under which the benefits payable on retirement are fixed, either as an amount or as a proportion of salary. Where benefits are defined in relation to salary they are usually based on the individual's final salary or his/her average salary for (say) the last three years before retirement.

This is advantageous for the member, as he/she is assured of receiving a pension of a known amount. However, the employer has a commitment to ensure that sufficient funds are invested to enable the scheme to meet the guaranteed pension payments. The cost to the employer is consequently very dependent on a variety of factors and can fluctuate significantly over time. The cost of operating a defined benefit scheme has generally increased in recent years as a result of high salary levels, changes in life expectancy and the poor performance of the underlying investment markets. The nature of defined benefit schemes also means that they are more tightly regulated than defined contribution schemes and the accounting implications are much more complex. Defined benefit schemes are therefore generally becoming less popular with employers. Contributions to the scheme will often be paid by both the employer and the employee, but the level of the employees' contribution will usually be fixed and it is therefore the employer contribution that varies to make good any deficit in funding or, where permitted, to absorb any surplus that arises.

FRS 17 *Retirement Benefits* was published in November 2000 and became fully effective for accounting periods beginning on or after 1 January 2005 for companies adopting UK accounting practice (see **21.21**). FRS 17 introduced significant changes to the way in which defined benefit retirement schemes are accounted for and has had a significant impact on the profit and loss accounts and balance sheets of many companies. The standard specifies how scheme assets and scheme liabilities should be measured and generally requires the surplus or deficit in the scheme to be recognised as an asset or liability on the balance sheet. The depressed state of the equity market in recent years has resulted in many pension schemes showing a deficit in funding and the new accounting requirements have introduced the related liabilities onto company balance sheets. In some cases, there have been consequences for the company's ability to comply with existing loan covenants or the availability of sufficient distributable reserves to maintain dividend payments. Companies preparing IAS accounts have faced similar issues in complying the requirements of IAS 19 *Employee Benefits* which is in fact much wider in scope than the UK standard. FRS 17 has received a certain degree of criticism and has in some cases been quoted as the cause of companies deciding to close their defined benefit schemes and replace them with defined contribution schemes. However, the accounting standard is not the root cause of the problem – the new requirements are simply forcing directors to recognise that defined benefit retirement schemes can leave a business exposed to significant risks and that these need to be managed in the same way as other business risks.

21.5   Defined Contribution Schemes

In the case of a defined contribution scheme (sometimes referred to as a 'money purchase scheme'), a fixed amount is contributed each year in respect of each member of the scheme, usually divided between the employer and employee and set as a proportion of the employee's salary. The amount contributed in respect of each individual member is accumulated in a separate account, and the pension payable to that employee will depend on the value of that fund at the date of his/her retirement. The employer therefore has the benefit of a fixed cost, but the employee bears the risk of the fund being insufficient to provide the level of pension that he/she hoped for at the time of retirement. The scheme funds may be invested in a variety of ways – in some schemes, the individual members may participate in decisions on how their particular fund is dealt with, in others this will be entirely at the discretion of the pension scheme trustees. A defined contribution scheme may be established as:

- an employer-sponsored occupational pension scheme approved by HMRC; or
- a group personal pension arrangement, under which an individual pension plan is arranged for each employee.

In the case of a group personal pension arrangement, it is not compulsory for the employer to make contributions to the scheme.

21.6   Other Options

The two basic forms of pension scheme discussed above leave the risks associated with the provision of retirement benefits primarily with the employer (in the case of defined benefit schemes) or with the employee (in the case of defined contribution schemes). Some companies may feel that neither of these is entirely appropriate for them and may therefore wish to explore other options that share the risks and costs of pension provision more equitably between employer and employee. Other options that may be worth considering are considered briefly below, in a broadly reducing order of risk to the employer.

21.7   Shared Risk Final Salary Scheme

A shared risk final salary schemes preserves the advantages of a defined benefit scheme in that the retirement benefits continue to be based on the employee's final salary, but there is a greater sharing of the associated risk between the employer and the employee. This sharing can be achieved by one or more of the following:

- making both the employer and employee contributions variable, depending on the results of the regular actuarial valuation;
- giving scheme members the option of paying a higher contribution in order to maintain benefits at the current level, or continuing at the current contribution level and accepting the resulting reduction in benefits; or
- providing guaranteed benefits at a relatively low level, with additional benefits granted on a discretionary basis if funding levels, or company performance, permit.

21.8   Career Average Salary Scheme

Under a career average salary scheme, retirement benefits are accrued each year in relation to the employee's salary for that year and the annual benefit is then revalued each year, up to retirement, in line with an appropriate index. Breaking the link between retirement benefits and the employee's final salary removes the impact of salary inflation during the employment period. The employee's pension on retirement is the aggregate of the revalued benefit calculated for each year of employment.

21.9   Hybrid Schemes

Hybrid schemes usually provide the employee with a mixture of defined benefit and money purchase benefits. For instance, a hybrid scheme might provide money purchase benefits up to a certain age (say 40) and then defined benefits for subsequent years of employment. This type of scheme can be advantageous to younger employees, who may want to transfer the money purchase benefits if their employment changes, but also gives older employees the security of defined benefits as they approach retirement age. Alternatively, a hybrid scheme may provide defined benefits on salary up to a specified level, and then money purchase benefits in respect of any salary above this. This can be particularly helpful in giving lower-paid employees the security of fixed retirement benefits whilst transferring some of the associated risk to those on higher salaries.

21.10   Cash Schemes

An employer can commit to providing a guaranteed lump sum to the employee at retirement, usually based on a proportion of final salary for each year of service, as in the case of a standard defined benefit scheme. The risk up to the date of retirement therefore continues to be borne by the employer, but the risk after retirement is transferred to the employee, who can retain part of the lump sum and use the balance to purchase an annuity.

21.11   Insured Schemes

An insured pension scheme is one under which the scheme trustees enter into an agreement with a life assurance company and pay appropriate premiums to secure the required benefits for the members and meet the costs of administering the scheme. This approach is more straightforward administratively and is therefore often favoured by smaller companies. In the case of a defined contribution scheme, a series of insurance policies may be needed to match the separate funds for the individual members.

21.12   Personal Pensions

Any individual can contribute to a personal pension, provided that he/she is not already a member of an occupational pension scheme. The individual makes contributions into an account with a personal pension provider, who invests the money on their behalf. Employers can also contribute to the personal pension plan of an employee. There are limits on the amount that an individual can contribute to a personal pension in each tax year, based on their earnings in that period and on their age. The percentage of earnings that can be contributed increases as the individual gets closer to retirement. From April 2001, members of an occupational pension scheme who earn less than £30,000 per annum, and who are not controlling directors, are allowed to contribute up to £3,600 each year to an additional personal or stakeholder pension.

21.13   Stakeholder Pensions

A stakeholder pension is a particular type of personal pension which became available from 6 April 2001 to encourage more people, especially those who are not high earners, to plan for their retirement. With effect from October 2001, the *Welfare Reform and Pensions Act 1999* and the *Stakeholder Pension Schemes Regulations 2000 (SI 2000/1403)* require all employers with five or more employees to give their employees access to a stakeholder pension scheme, although there is no requirement for an employer to offer such access to employees earning less that the lower earnings limit. However, an employer who operates an occupational pension scheme is exempt from the stakeholder requirement if the current scheme is open to all employees who:

- are aged over 18 and are more than five years younger than the normal retirement age under the scheme; and
- have completed one year's service with the company.

Where an existing scheme does not meet the requirements for exemption, it may be possible to make some modifications so that the employer qualifies for exemption, although the full cost of doing so will need to be carefully considered. The only commitment required from the employer is to provide the required level of access to the pension scheme – individual employees remain free to decide whether or not to join and the employer is not currently required to make any contributions to the scheme (although this may be introduced at some point in the future).

An employer is also exempt from the requirement to provide access to a stakeholder pension where a group personal pension arrangement is in place and:

- it is a term of the employment contract that all employees aged 18 or over who have completed three months' service and whose earnings are at least equivalent to the lower earnings limit have a right to join the scheme;
- the employer will pay contributions of at least 3 per cent of the employee's basic pay (or a lower amount equivalent to the contributions that the employee is willing to make);
- the employer offers a payroll deduction facility to members of the scheme; and
- the scheme does not impose any penalties on members who transfer out or stop making contributions.

Checklist

Any employer with five or more employees who is not covered by one of these exemptions must:

✓ consult with employees or their representative organisations about the choice of scheme;

✓ nominate a stakeholder scheme;

✓ provide employees or their representative organisations with contact details for the nominated scheme;

✓ allow representatives of the nominated scheme reasonable access to the employees; and

✓ enable employees to make contributions to the nominated scheme by deduction from their pay, and forward these contributions to the scheme within 19 days of the end of the month in which they were deducted.

21.14   Small Self Administered Schemes ('SSASs')

A Small Self Administered Scheme ('SSAS') generally has fewer than twelve members and is subject to special HMRC rules. The scheme is almost invariably a defined contribution scheme and benefits from:

• a higher permitted level of self-investment in the employer company than for other approved schemes; and
• reduced regulation, particularly where all the members of the scheme are also trustees and decisions require unanimous agreement.

21.15   Pension Scheme Administration

At a Glance
* The *Pensions Act 2004* is now the main legislation governing the control and management of occupational pension schemes.
* The Pensions Regulator supervises the regulation of all occupational pension schemes.
* Most pension schemes are set up as trusts and established under a formal trust deed – the trustees must therefore comply with trust law as well as the more specific requirements of pensions legislation.
* Pensions legislation also gives the sponsoring employer certain duties and responsibilities.
* Most defined benefit schemes are subject to a minimum funding requirement.

* Pension scheme trustees generally have a duty to obtain audited financial statements within seven months of the end of the scheme financial year.
* The form and content of pension scheme accounts is specified in various regulations under the *Pensions Act 1995* and also in the SORP *Financial Reports of Pension Schemes.*
* Certain schemes are exempt from the requirement to appoint scheme auditors, although some of them may still require an audit under the terms of their trust deed.
* Regulations under the *Pensions Act 1995* set out the procedures that must be followed when appointing auditors and when there is a change of auditor.
* The HM Revenue and Customs Pension Schemes Office is responsible for approving pension schemes for tax purposes, and for withdrawing approval where necessary.

21.16   Pension Act 2004

The *Pensions Act 2004* is now the main legislation governing the management and control of occupational pension schemes. The Act is primarily enabling legislation and detailed requirements are set out in related regulations and Codes of Practice developed under the Act. A number of these are still in the course of development. Certain regulations established under the *Pensions Act 1995* also remain in force, including in particular the following regulations governing financial reporting and auditing requirements.

* the *Occupational Pension Schemes (Disclosure of Information) Regulations 1996 (SI 1996/1655)*;
* the *Occupational Pension Schemes (Scheme Administration) Regulations 1996 (SI 1996/1715* as amended by subsequent SIs); and
* the *Occupational Pension Schemes (Requirement to Obtain Audited Accounts and a Statement from the Auditor) Regulations 1996 (SI 1996/1975* as amended by subsequent SIs).

21.17   The Pensions Regulator

The *Pensions Act 2004* also established the position of the Pensions Regulator, to take on the functions previously carried out by the Occupational Pensions Regulatory Authority, but with considerably wider powers and responsibilities. The main objectives of the Regulator are to protect the interests of occupational pension scheme members, limit the situations in which compensation from the Pension Protection Fund might be required, and improve the administration of pension schemes. The Regulator's powers include:

* collecting data on individual schemes through regular returns, reports of breaches and other notifiable events – the Regulator also has the power to demand certain documents or information relevant to its work;

- taking action to protect the security of members' benefits where necessary – this might include:
  - issuing improvement notices to individuals or companies, requiring action to be taken within a specific time limit,
  - taking steps to recover unpaid contributions from employers,
  - issuing a freezing order to temporarily halt the winding-up of a scheme, so that any concerns can be investigated,
  - the disqualification of trustees,
  - the imposition of fines for breaches of the requirements and prosecution in the courts in the case of certain offences;
- where there is reason to believe that an employer is deliberately trying to avoid its pension obligation and relying on the Pension Protection Fund to meet the liabilities, issuing contribution notices, financial support directions and/or restoration orders.

21.18   Pension Scheme Trustees

Most pension schemes are set up as trusts and are established under a formal trust deed, which gives the scheme trustees responsibility for stewardship and custody of the scheme assets. Most pension schemes must therefore comply with general trust law as well as with the more specific requirements of pensions legislation, and the duties of the pension scheme trustees will usually include:

- observing the terms of the trust;
- acting at all times in the best interests of the beneficiaries of the trust;
- acting impartially between any different classes of beneficiary;
- acting prudently and making appropriate use of any particular skills and experience that they have;
- not profiting from the trust (other than as members of the scheme);
- exercising investment powers in accordance with the legislation;
- appointing professional advisers;
- maintaining specified bank accounts, books and records;
- obtaining audited financial statements and appropriate reports from the actuary.

A trustee of the pension scheme who is also a director of the sponsoring company must take particular care not be influenced by his dual capacity. The legislation also includes specific provisions on the appointment of member-nominated trustees. Certain individuals are disqualified from acting as a trustee, including individuals with a conviction for an offence involving dishonesty or deception, undischarged bankrupts and those disqualified from appointment as a company director. *The Pensions Act 2004* also introduces new requirements on the knowledge and understanding that trustees will be expected to have in order to fulfil their role effectively, although there is a special dispensation for new trustees to give them a period of six months in which to undertake appropriate training. It is also important for such knowledge and skills to be kept up to date and both individual trustees and the board as a whole are recommended to keep appropriate records of the training undertaken. The Pensions Regulator (see **21.17** above) provides a number of guidance documents for pension scheme trustees to help them to understand their duties and responsibilities (for information on obtaining copies see the Pensions Regulator's website at www.thepensionsregulator.gov.uk).

21.19   Sponsoring Employer

The sponsoring employer is also given a number of duties and responsibilities under the legislation, including:

- paying employer contributions in accordance with a defined schedule;
- paying employee contributions over to the scheme within 19 days of the end of the month in which they are deducted from employees' pay;
- where the employer operates the pensions payroll on behalf of the scheme, paying into a separate bank account any benefits which have not been paid to members within two days;
- a duty to disclose to the trustees or managers the occurrence of any event relating to the employer which could reasonably be considered to be of material significance to the exercise of their functions;
- a duty to disclose to the trustees or managers any information reasonably required for the proper performance of their duties or those of the professional advisers to the scheme.

Under the regulations, the power to make payments to employers may only be exercised by the trustees.

21.20   Statutory Funding Objective

Under the *Pensions Act 2004*, a new Statutory Funding Objective has been introduced to replace the previous Minimum Funding Requirement, which gave rise to a number of concerns when it was initially implemented and which the Government now considers has not fulfilled its purpose. The new objective is that a defined benefit scheme has sufficient assets to meets its current and future liabilities, calculated on an actuarial basis. The calculation of scheme liabilities must be based on prudent economic and actuarial assumptions and carried out with actuarial advice, using an accrued benefits funding method. Any change from the method or assumptions used in the previous calculation must be justified by a change of legal, demographic or economic circumstances. Each scheme must prepare a Statement of Funding Principles setting out how the Statutory Funding Objective will be met. Detailed requirements are set out Code of Practice 3, which also emphasises the need for trustees to have a proper understanding of the funding decisions they make and the implications for the scheme. The *Occupational Pension Schemes (Scheme Funding) Regulations 2005* set out the information that should be covered in the Statement of Funding Principles. This includes information on:

- any funding objectives provided in the scheme rules, or which the trustees have adopted, in addition to the statutory funding objective;
- any arrangements for a person other than the employer or a member to contribute;

Pensions

- any power to make payments to the employer out of the scheme and when such power may be exercised;
- any discretionary power to provide benefits for any members and the extent to which this is taken into account in funding;
- how often the trustees obtain actuarial valuations.

If an actuarial valuation shows that a scheme is not in a position to meet its liabilities, the trustees must put a recovery plan into place and send a copy to the Pensions Regulator. The recovery plan must specify the period over which the shortfall in funding is to be eliminated so that the Statutory Funding Objective can be met. The Code of Practice notes that the aim should be for the shortfall to be eliminated as quickly as the employer can reasonably afford.

21.21   Financial Reporting

Under current legislation, pension scheme trustees have a duty to obtain audited financial statements within seven months of the end of the scheme financial year. Auditors have a duty to report to the Pensions Regulator (see **21.17** above) any breach of this provision by the trustees.

Checklist

The annual report should comprise the following:

✓ a trustees' report, providing information on the management of the scheme and developments during the scheme year;

✓ an investment report, reviewing investment policy and the performance of the scheme during the year;

✓ a compliance statement, giving additional disclosures about the scheme required by the legislation and any other voluntary disclosures which are not sufficiently material to require inclusion in the trustees' report;

✓ financial statements giving a true and fair view of the financial transactions of the scheme during the year and of the disposition of its net assets at the end of the year; and

✓ actuarial statements – these vary depending on the nature of the scheme but will usually include an opinion from the actuary on the security of accrued rights and prospective rights, and on compliance with the minimum funding requirement.

The form and content of the financial statements are specified in various regulations under the *Pensions Act 1995* and the trustees are also required to state whether they have been prepared in accordance with the Statement of

Recommended Practice ('SORP') 'Financial Reports of Pension Schemes', issued by the Pensions Research and Accountants Group ('PRAG') under the Accounting Standards Board ('ASB') Code of Practice for the development of SORPs (see **11.22 STATEMENT OF RECOMMENDED PRACTICE (SORPS)**). A revised version of this SORP was published in November 2002 and applies for scheme years beginning on or after 1 January 2003.

21.22   Audit

Section 47 of the *Pensions Act 1995* requires the trustees or managers of every occupational pension scheme to appoint suitably qualified auditors. The scope of the auditors' work and the format and content of their report varies depending on the nature of the scheme. The following are exempt from the legal requirement to appoint scheme auditors:

- superannuation funds and unfunded schemes;
- money purchase SSASs where all members are trustees and all decisions require unanimous agreement;
- non-approved schemes;
- schemes with less than two members;
- schemes providing only death benefits and no accrued rights;
- ear-marked money purchase schemes where all benefits are secured by insurance or annuity contracts and are specifically allocated to individual members, and where all members are trustees and all decisions are by unanimous agreement; and
- certain specifically named schemes and public service schemes.

However, the trust deed for such schemes may still require an audit, even though the scheme is exempt from this requirement under the regulations. Also, certain earmarked funds that are exempt from the full audit requirement must still appoint auditors under the legislation to report on the contributions made to the scheme. Where the appointment of auditors is required by law, the regulations lay down specific appointment procedures that must be followed. The trustees are required to send a Notice of Appointment to the auditors specifying:

- the date on which the appointment is to take effect;
- to whom the auditors are to report; and
- from whom the auditors will take instructions.

Guidance issued by the Auditing Practices Board ('APB') recommends that the Notice should also:

- state the date of the scheme year end and specify which scheme years are to be subject to audit; and
- be clear as to the name of the scheme to which the auditor is being appointed – where the appointment covers a number of schemes, there should be a separate letter for each scheme or a schedule detailing all the schemes covered.

The appointment does not become effective until the auditors have formally acknowledged receipt of the Notice of Appointment, which they are required to do within one month. They should also formally document the terms of their engagement in a letter to the trustees, to help prevent any misunderstandings over the scope of their work and the respective responsibilities of the scheme auditors, trustees and managers. If an auditor ceases to hold office for any reason, the trustees are required to make a new appointment within three months. Auditors who are invited to accept appointment after this deadline are required to report to the Pensions Regulator (see **21.17** above) the breach of duty by the trustees. Auditors who resign or are removed are required to make a statement of any circumstances connected with their resignation or removal which, in their opinion, significantly affect the interests of the members, prospective members or beneficiaries of the scheme, or to state that there are no such circumstances. A copy of the statement must be included in the annual report, except where it is simply a declaration that there are no circumstances to report.

21.23 Taxation

The HM Revenue and Customs Pension Schemes Office ('PSO') is responsible for approving pension schemes for tax purposes, and for withdrawing that approval where necessary. Almost all schemes are approved under HMRC's discretionary powers rather than under the restricted conditions set out in the *Income and Corporation Taxes Act 1988*. Approval of a scheme means that employer and employee contributions to that scheme are deductible for tax purposes. Changes to an approved scheme must be notified to the PSO and approval of the scheme will automatically lapse if the alteration is not considered to be acceptable. An exempt approved scheme is exempt from UK income tax on investment income and capital gains arising on its investments.

21.24 Accounting for Pensions and Other Retirement Benefits

At a Glance
* FRS 17 *Retirement Benefits* is effective for accounting periods beginning on or after 1 January 2005.
* Companies preparing IAS accounts must comply with the requirements of IAS 19 *Employee Benefits*, rather than those of FRS 17.
* In the case of a defined contribution scheme, the contributions payable by the employer for each accounting period are charged to the profit and loss account.
* In the case of a defined benefit scheme, the annual cost to the employer is more difficult to quantify and requires regular actuarial calculations to be carried out.

* FRS 17 requires scheme assets to be measured at fair value and scheme liabilities to be measured on an actuarial basis, using the projected unit method of valuation.
* Actuarial assumptions should be mutually compatible and should achieve the best estimate of the future cashflows that will arise.
* Scheme liabilities should be discounted at the current rate of return on a high quality bond of equivalent currency and term.
* The surplus or deficit in the scheme should generally be recognised as a separate item on the face of the balance sheet.
* FRS 17 specifies how the change in the net defined asset or liability each year should be reflected in the profit and loss account and statement of total recognised gains and losses.
* Detailed disclosures must be given in the notes to the accounts.
* Special requirements may apply where more than one employer participates in a defined benefit scheme (eg where a single scheme operates for a group of companies).

21.25   FRS 17 Retirement Benefits

Under UK accounting practice, companies must comply with FRS 17 *Retirement Benefits* which is fully effective for accounting periods beginning on or after 1 January 2005. If the standard is not adopted early, detailed additional disclosures must be given in the accounts in the intervening years. The standard deals with how an employer should account for the costs and liabilities that arise from the provision of retirement benefits to employees, and the requirements cover all retirement benefits that an employer is committed to making, regardless of whether the commitment is statutory, contractual or implicit and wherever the commitment arises (ie in the UK or abroad).

The standard is complex and only an outline of the requirements is given here. For information on obtaining copies of FRS 17 see the ASB website at www.frc.org.uk/asb.

Companies preparing IAS accounts must comply with IAS 19 *Employee Benefits* rather than FRS 17. The international standard is wider in scope than FRS 17, but generally imposes similar requirements on accounting for retirement benefits. The main differences are:

* there is more flexibility in the accounting treatment of actuarial gains and losses under IAS 19;
* different requirements apply to group pension schemes under IAS 19; and
* IAS 19 does not allow defined benefit pension assets and liabilities to be shown net of any related deferred tax.

21.26   Accounting for a Defined Contribution Scheme

Accounting for a defined contribution scheme is relatively straightforward. The cost to the employer is equal to the contributions payable to the scheme for the accounting period and the charge to the profit and loss account each year will therefore represent the contributions payable by the employer in respect of that accounting period. This figure must be calculated on an accruals basis and the amount charged may therefore not be the same as the amount actually paid over to the scheme during the period. The standard specifies that the cost must be recognised in arriving at operating profit in the profit and loss account and the accounts must include the following disclosures:

- the nature of the scheme (ie the fact that it is a defined contribution scheme);
- the cost for the period; and
- any outstanding or prepaid contributions at the balance sheet date.

21.27 Difficulties with Defined Benefit Schemes

Under a defined benefit scheme, the employer will usually have a commitment to ensure that there are sufficient funds in the scheme to pay the appropriate benefits and may be required to make good any potential deficit in the funding of the scheme. In the case of a defined benefit scheme, therefore, the full extent of the employer's commitment is more difficult to quantify and to account for. Actuarial calculations must be carried out on a regular basis to establish the overall funding level of the scheme and to assess the level of contributions required to maintain adequate funding of the scheme. One of the particular problems is the very long-term nature of such schemes and the fact that a number of assumptions about future events will need to be made in order to carry out the calculations. Most of the detailed requirements of FRS 17 (see **21.25** above) therefore deal with accounting for defined benefit retirement schemes.

21.28 Actuarial Valuations

Actuarial valuations provide the actuary's best estimate of the cost to the employer of providing the promised retirement benefits to employees. In carrying out a valuation, a number of assumptions about future events will need to be made and the decisions taken here can have a very significant effect on the level of contributions required. The main assumptions will cover issues such as:

- future pay increases;
- future rates of inflation;
- increases in pension payments;
- changes to the number of employees in the scheme;
- the age profile of employees; and
- expected earnings from scheme investments.

Once decisions have been reached on these factors, the actuary will assess how the scheme should be funded to ensure that adequate resources are available to meet the pension commitments as they fall due. The aim is to ensure that present and future contributions to the scheme will be sufficient to secure payment of the agreed benefits to employees as they retire.

21.29 Valuation Methods

Various actuarial methods can be used to determine the liabilities of a defined benefit scheme and thus the level of contributions needed to achieve and maintain adequate funding. The two principal categories of actuarial valuation methods are:

- *accrued benefits methods* – these are based on the principle that the obligation to provide retirement benefits to an employee will be greater as that employee gets closer to retirement; and
- *prospective benefits methods* – these are based on the principle that the obligation to provide retirement benefits to an employee accumulates evenly throughout the period of that individual's employment.

FRS 17 (see **21.25** above) requires scheme liabilities to be measured using the projected unit method. This is an accrued benefits valuation method under which allowance is made for projected earnings. Further guidance on this method is given in Guidance Note 26 (GN26) *Pension Fund Terminology* issued by the Faculty and Institute of Actuaries (for information on obtaining copies see the Faculty and Institute of Actuaries website at www.actuaries.org.uk).

21.30 Measurement of Scheme Assets and Liabilities

Under FRS 17 (see **21.25** above) scheme assets should be measured at their fair value at the company's balance sheet date. Scheme assets include current assets as well as investments, and any current liabilities (such as accrued expenses) should be deducted. The standard includes specific guidance on establishing fair value for each category of pension scheme asset. Scheme liabilities comprise liabilities in respect of:

- benefits promised under the formal terms of the scheme; and
- any constructive obligations for further benefits where a public statement or past practice by the employer has created a valid expectation in the employees that these benefits will be granted.

These liabilities should be measured on an actuarial basis using the projected unit method (see **21.29** above).

21.31 Actuarial Assumptions

Actuarial assumptions underlying the valuation of scheme liabilities should be mutually compatible (ie they must reflect the underlying economic factors on a consistent basis), and they should lead to the best estimate of the future cashflows that will arise. The directors (or equivalent) have ultimate responsibility for the assumptions, but they should be set on advice given by an actuary. Any assumptions that are affected by economic conditions should reflect market expectations at the balance sheet date. The assumptions should also reflect expected future events that will affect the cost of the benefits to which the employer is committed (either legally or constructively) at the balance sheet date. Depending on the nature of the scheme these will usually include:

- expected cost of living increases;
- salary increases (where the pension is to be based on final salary); and
- expected early retirement (where the scheme gives this right to employees).

Expected future redundancies should not be reflected in the assumptions as the employer is not committed to making them. When the employer does become committed to making redundancies, the impact on the scheme should be treated as a settlement or curtailment. Also, it should not be assumed that benefits will be reduced below those currently promised (eg on the grounds that the employer will curtail the scheme at some point in the future).

21.32   Discounting of Scheme Liabilities

Scheme liabilities should be discounted at a rate reflecting the time value of money and the characteristics of the liability. This should be assumed to be the current rate of return on a high quality (AA) corporate bond of equivalent currency and term to the scheme liabilities. The FRS 17 guidance (see **21.25** above) notes that, if no suitable corporate bond can be identified, the rate of return on appropriate government bonds, together with a margin for assumed credit risk spreads (from the global bond markets), may provide an acceptable alternative.

21.33   Frequency of Valuations

Full actuarial valuations by a professionally qualified actuary should be obtained at intervals not exceeding three years. The actuary should review the valuation at each balance sheet date and update it to reflect current conditions – for instance, the fair values of scheme assets and financial assumptions such as the discount rate may need to be adjusted each year.

21.34   Balance Sheet Recognition of Surplus or Deficit

The surplus or deficit in a defined benefit scheme is the excess or shortfall of the value of the scheme assets over or below the present value of the scheme liabilities. The employer should recognise:

- a liability to the extent that it reflects a legal or constructive obligation to make good the deficit; and
- an asset to the extent that this can be recovered through reduced contributions or through refunds from the scheme.

A legal obligation to make good a deficit in the scheme may arise under the terms of the trust deed. A constructive obligation may arise if the employer has in the past acted to make good similar deficits. A scheme surplus will give rise to an asset for the employer to the extent that the employer has control over its use as a result of past events. Under most schemes, the employer's obligation will be to pay contributions at the level recommended by the actuary to keep the scheme fully funded. There will not usually be any requirement to generate a surplus in the scheme. Where a surplus does arise, it is therefore unlikely that the employer could be required to continue to make contributions to maintain the surplus. Also, the decision on whether the surplus should be used to improve scheme benefits will usually rest with the employer. In most cases, therefore, control over the use of a surplus will rest with the employer. FRS 17 (see **21.25** above) gives detailed guidance on determining the amount that can be recovered from reduced contributions, reflecting refunds from the scheme in the accounts of the employer and accounting for a surplus that is used to improve benefits.

21.35   Balance Sheet Presentation

Any unpaid pension contributions at the balance sheet date should be shown within creditors due within one year. The defined benefit asset or liability, net of any related deferred tax, should be shown separately on the face of the balance sheet as follows:

- in a balance sheet prepared under Format 1 of *Schedule 4* to the *Companies Act 1985*, after item J (Accruals and deferred income) but before item K (Capital and reserves);
- in a balance sheet prepared under Format 2 of *Schedule 4* to the *Companies Act 1985*, an asset should be shown after item D (Prepayments and accrued income) in the 'Assets' section and a liability should be shown after item D (Accruals and deferred income) in the 'Liabilities' section.

Appendix I to FRS 17 (see **21.25** above) gives an example layout for this disclosure. Where an employer has more than one scheme, the total of any defined benefit assets and the total of any defined benefit liabilities should be shown separately on the face of the balance sheet.

21.36   Performance Statements

FRS 17 (see **21.25** above) requires the change in the net defined benefit asset or liability (other than changes arising from contributions to the scheme) to be analysed into its detailed components and prescribes how each component should be reflected in the performance statements (ie the profit and loss account and statement of total recognised gains and losses). Broadly:

- current service cost should be taken into account in arriving at operating profit;
- the net of interest cost and the expected return on assets should be shown as other finance costs, adjacent to interest on the profit and loss account;
- actuarial gains and losses should be recognised in the statement of total recognised gains and losses.

The standard also includes detailed requirements on accounting for past service costs (which arise when an employer commits to providing a higher level of benefit than previously promised), settlements, curtailments and death-in-service and incapacity benefits. It also deals with accounting for any tax effects arising from pension costs and commitments.

21.37   Disclosure

FRS 17 (see **21.25** above) prescribes very detailed disclosures to be given in the accounts, the principal items being:

- the nature of the scheme (ie the fact that it is a defined benefit scheme);
- the date of the most recent full actuarial valuation on which amounts in the financial statements are based;
- contributions made in respect of the accounting period and any agreed contribution rates for future years;
- each of the main financial assumptions used at the beginning of the period and at the balance sheet date;
- a note showing the fair value of scheme assets, the present value of scheme liabilities, the resulting surplus or deficit and an analysis of the movement in the surplus or deficit during the period;
- where the defined benefit asset or liability in the balance sheet differs from the scheme surplus or deficit shown in the note, an explanation of the difference;
- a five-year summary of the difference between expected and actual returns on assets, experience gains and losses arising on scheme liabilities and total actuarial gains or losses – this disclosure is to highlight trends, which will generally be more relevant than gains or losses in one period.

The analysis of reserves in the notes to the financial statements should distinguish the amount relating to the defined benefit asset or liability, net of related deferred tax.

In May 2006, the ASB published proposals to amend the disclosure requirements of FRS 17 to take account of recent changes in pensions legislation and to address concerns that the information currently provided in respect of defined benefit retirement schemes does not enable accounts users to assess fully the risks arising for the employer. There are two distinct aspects to the Exposure Draft 'Proposed Amendment to FRS 17 *Retirement Benefits* and Reporting Statement *Retirement Benefits – Disclosures*'. Firstly, the ASB proposes replacing the disclosure requirements in FRS 17 with those set out in the recently updated IAS 19 *Employee Benefits.* The second element of the proposals comprises a draft ASB Reporting Statement *Retirement Benefits – Disclosures.* This sets out six principles that companies should take into account when disclosing information on retirement benefits in the annual accounts and recommends a number of additional disclosures, some of which are currently required under FRS 17 but would not form part of the revised standard. Once finalised, the Statement would be non-mandatory but would represent best practice for any entity operating a defined benefit retirement scheme. The recommendations are intended to help accounts users to assess the risks and rewards arising from such a scheme, but provide companies with a degree of flexibility in how they present the relevant information. The ASB plans to bring the changes into effect for accounting periods ending on or after 31 December 2006. However, it considers that all of the proposed disclosures deal with information that companies already need to prepare for management or regulatory purposes and so should not result in significant additional work or costs.

21.38 Entities with More Than One Defined Benefit Scheme

Where an employer has more than one defined benefit scheme, the required disclosures may be given in total, separately or in such groupings as are felt to be most useful (for instance, by geographical location, or where schemes are subject to significantly different risks). Where the disclosures are given in total, the assumptions should be given in the form of weighted averages or relatively narrow ranges, with separate disclosure of any items outside the range.

21.39 Multi-employer Schemes

In some cases, more than one employer may participate in the same retirement scheme. For instance, this situation is relatively common in groups of companies, where a single retirement scheme is operated for the whole group and each subsidiary participates in the scheme in respect of its own employees. If the scheme is a defined contribution scheme, the multi-employer aspect does not give rise to any particular accounting issues. Where more than one employer participates in a defined benefit scheme, the general requirement under FRS 17 (see **21.25** above) is that each employer should account for the scheme as a defined benefit scheme. However, the standard recognises that this may not be appropriate or practical in every case and two specific exceptions to this general rule are therefore permitted:

- where the employer's contributions are set in relation to the current service period only (ie they are not affected by any surplus or deficit in the scheme relating to the past service of its own employees or any other members of the scheme), the scheme should be accounted for as a defined contribution scheme – this treatment should only be adopted where there is clear evidence that the employer cannot be required to pay additional contributions relating to past service, including the existence of a third party which accepts the obligation to fund the pension payments if the scheme's assets should prove to be insufficient;
- where the employer's contributions are affected by a surplus or deficit in the scheme but the employer is unable to identify its share of the underlying assets and liabilities in the scheme on a consistent and reasonable basis, the employer should account for the scheme as a defined contribution scheme but should disclose:
  - the fact that the scheme is a defined benefit scheme but the employer is unable to identify its share of the underlying assets and liabilities, and

○ any available information on the surplus or deficit in the scheme and the implications for the employer.

In the case of a group scheme, the second exception only enables the individual subsidiaries (and, where appropriate, the parent company in its own individual accounts) to account for the scheme as a defined contribution scheme. The scheme must still be accounted for as defined benefit scheme in the group accounts, as it does not constitute a multi-employer scheme at this level and the impracticality of identifying individual shares of the underlying assets and liabilities is no longer relevant.

21.40   ASB Pensions Research Project

In October 2005, the Accounting Standards Board (ASB) announced that it was undertaking a research project into accounting for pension costs. The implementation of FRS 17 (see **21.25** above) has given rise to comments on a number of issues and the legal and regulatory environment for company pension schemes has changed significantly since the standard was originally published. In particular, a number of the changes introduced by the *Pensions Act 2004* may have an impact on relevant financial reporting issues. There are also certain differences at present between FRS 17 and the related international accounting standard, which is also likely to be reviewed in the relatively near future. The ASB's project is intended to assist the development of future UK and international accounting standards and will consider the fundamental principles of pensions accounting. It will also cover financial reporting by pension schemes. The issues considered will include:

- how the relationship between an employer and a pension scheme can best be reflected in the employer's financial statements;
- how an employer's liability in respect of pensions should be quantified, including:
  ○ the most appropriate actuarial method to use,
  ○ whether the employer's liability should reflect future salary increases, and
  ○ what discount rate should be used to translate future cash flows into a realistic present value;
- whether (and, if so, how) the expected return on assets should be reflected in the employer's financial statements;
- the impact on financial reporting of recent regulatory developments; and
- whether the disclosures currently required are still appropriate.

The ASB expects to publish the results of the project during the course of 2006.

Appendix 1

Useful Websites on Pensions Issues

The Pensions Regulator	www.thepensionsregulator.gov.uk
The Pension Service	www.thepensionservice.gov.uk
Department for Work and Pensions	www.dwp.gov.uk
Pension Advisory Service	www.stakeholderhelpline.org.uk
The Pension Trust	www.thepensiontrust.org.uk
Occupational Pensioners Alliance	www.opalliance.org.uk
Business Link	www.businesslink.gov.uk
Institute of Directors	www.iod.com
Faculty and Institute of Actuaries	www.actuaries.org.uk
Accounting Standards Board	www.frc.org.uk/asb
Pension Research and Accountants Group	www.prag.org.uk
HM Revenue and Customs	www.hmrc.gov.uk
Chartered Institute of Management Accountants	www.cimaglobal.com

22

Property

Property

Property

22.1 Freehold Property

> **At a Glance**
> * It is usually advisable to involve the company's legal advisers and tax advisers at an early stage when the purchase or sale of freehold property is being considered.
> * A sale and leaseback transaction may be used to release funds tied up in freehold property.
> * The accounting treatment of a sale and leaseback transaction will depend on the detailed terms of the agreement.

22.2 Benefits of Freehold Property

Freehold interest in property is a long-term interest – the business is the owner of the property and is generally free to retain it or to decide if and when to sell it. The main advantages of a freehold interest are:

* freedom to make additions and alterations, subject to appropriate planning consent;
* the potential for the asset to increase in value; and
* the availability of an asset that can be offered as security for borrowing purposes.

The principal drawbacks are the need to finance the original purchase and the ongoing commitment to repair and maintain the property to protect its value. The purchase and sale of freehold property will generally require professional assistance from the company's legal advisers. The tax implications, particularly in the case of a property sale, also need careful consideration and it is worth taking appropriate professional advice at an early stage rather than waiting until the negotiations are nearing completion.

22.3   Sale and Leaseback Transactions

Sale and leaseback transactions are sometimes used to release funds tied up in freehold property. Basically, the company sells the property to a third party and then leases it back at a commercial rent, thus releasing capital into the business in exchange for a regular financial commitment in respect of the rent. The agreement may involve the outright sale of the property, but will often include a commitment or option for the company to repurchase it at some point in the future. The sale price may be the market value of the property or some other agreed value and, where a repurchase option is included, the repurchase price may be fixed, may vary with the period of the leaseback arrangement, or may be based on market value at the time of repurchase. Under FRS 5 *Reporting the Substance of Transactions*, the accounting treatment adopted for a sale and leaseback transaction will depend on the detailed terms of the agreement (for information on obtaining copies see the Accounting Standards Board ('ASB') website at www.frc.org.uk/asb). If the substance of the transaction is that of a secured loan (for instance, where the sale price is lower than market value, or it is highly likely that an option to repurchase will be exercised), the property will remain on the company's balance sheet and the 'borrowing' undertaken will be shown as a liability.

22.4   Leasehold Property

At a Glance

* An interest in leasehold property may be short term or long term – any lease running for less than 50 years is regarded as a short-term lease.
* Professional advice should usually be sought to ensure that the terms of a lease agreement are not unduly disadvantageous to the business or likely to give rise to problems during the course of the lease.
* A break clause is an important element of any lease agreement.
* A business tenant should also try to ensure that a lease agreement includes the right to assign or sublet the lease to another tenant.
* Lease incentives may be offered by a lessor to encourage the lessee to enter into a lease agreement.
* Specific requirements on the renewal of lease agreements are set out in the *Landlord and Tenant Act 1954*.
* A property lease will usually meet the definition of an operating lease – therefore, the lessee should normally charge the rental payments over the period of the lease and the lessor should normally recognise the rental income over that period.
* For accounting purposes, lease incentives should generally be treated as part of the rental payments under the lease.

22.5   Benefits of Leasehold Property

An interest in leasehold property may be short term or long term. Any lease running for less than 50 years is regarded as a short-term lease. The main advantages of taking a leasehold interest in a property are:

- the cost in spread over the period of the lease in the form of rental payments (although some lease agreements may provide for an initial premium to be paid in addition to the ongoing rental);
- depending on the terms of the lease, the landlord may be responsible for major repair work.

The principal disadvantages of leasehold are:

- there may be restrictions on the way in which the property can be used (these are usually the result of local planning restrictions);
- the landlord may place restrictions on the extent to which the property can be altered to suit the purposes of the business;
- the landlord may be able to terminate the lease at the end of the agreement, although considerable protection is available to a business tenant who has satisfied all of his obligations under the original lease (see **22.8** below).

22.6   Principal Elements of a Lease Agreement

Lease agreements are generally long and complex documents, and professional advice will usually be needed to ensure that the terms of the lease are not unduly disadvantageous to the business or likely to give rise to problems during the lease term. The agreement should specify the rent payable and will normally provide for a rent review at regular intervals, together with details of the method by which any increases in rent will be calculated. A break clause is an important element of the agreement, as it will provide an opportunity to exit from the lease if the business should wish to leave the premises before the original agreement expires. A business tenant should also try to ensure that the agreement includes the right to assign or sublet the lease to another tenant, to help avoid a situation where the company remains committed to considerable financial outlay in respect of a property that it no longer needs. The lease should also state clearly:

- who is responsible for insuring the property and any conditions relating to insurance cover (eg the minimum amount of cover required);
- who is responsible for repairing and maintaining the property during the lease term;
- whether the tenant needs to obtain the landlord's consent before making any alterations or improvements to the property – where the agreement provides for prior consent, the *Landlord and Tenant Act 1927* prevents the landlord from withholding this unreasonably.

If the tenant is responsible for repairs and maintenance, the lease agreement will usually give the landlord the right to enter and inspect the premises at least annually. Where the landlord is responsible for repairs and maintenance, the tenant will usually be required to serve an appropriate notice on the landlord in order to bring the obligation into effect.

22.7   Lease Incentives

A lessor will sometimes offer an incentive to encourage a lessee to enter into a lease agreement. Such incentives include:

- a cash payment to the lessee at the beginning of the lease;
- reimbursement or assumption of costs relating to the termination of an existing lease;
- reimbursement or assumption of relocation costs;
- an initial rent-free period, or an initial period at a reduced rental;
- a payment to meet the cost of fitting out the premises to suit the lessee's business.

Current accounting practice requires such incentives to be treated as part of the rental payments under the lease (see **22.9** below).

22.8   Renewal of Lease Agreements

The *Landlord and Tenant Act 1954* generally gives business tenants the right to renew a property lease at the end of their tenancy. Under the legislation, the landlord is able to serve the tenant with a notice of termination of the lease, expiring no earlier than the date on which the lease itself expires. The notice must be set out in a prescribed form, must explain the grounds on which the landlord intends to oppose renewal of the tenancy and must be issued not more than twelve months, and not less than six months, before the end of the lease term. Case law has held that inaccurate notices served by a landlord (for instance, where errors have been made in the name of the landlord or the tenant) are invalid. Under the legislation, the only reasons for opposing renewal of a tenancy are:

- the tenant has failed to:
  - pay rent on time,
  - comply with obligations to repair the property,
  - comply with other significant obligations under the lease;
- the landlord has offered the tenant alternative accommodation;
- where part of the premises are currently sub-let, the landlord could achieve a better return by letting the property as a whole;
- the landlord proposes to demolish or rebuild the property; or
- the landlord intends to occupy the premises.

The tenant must respond to the notice within two months by issuing a counter-notice stating whether or not he is prepared to give up possession of the leased property. Failure to issue the counternotice in time results in the tenant losing his right to apply to the court for a renewed tenancy. If renewal negotiations are not completed within the two-month period, the tenant should make an application to the court for a renewed tenancy – this must be done within the next two months (ie no later than four months after the date of the landlord's notice) in order to protect the tenant's right to renewal. In cases where the landlord is contesting renewal because he intends to demolish or rebuild the property, the court will expect to see clear evidence that he is committed to doing so and has a reasonable prospect of obtaining necessary planning consents. Where the court upholds the landlord's application on any of the last three grounds noted above, the tenant may be entitled to compensation for any improvements made to the property during his tenancy.

22.9   Accounting Issues

A property lease will usually meet the definition of an operating lease. The lessee will therefore charge the rental payments to the profit and loss account over the period of the lease, and the lessor will account for the property as a fixed asset and recognise the rental income over the period of the lease. The Urgent Issues Task Force ('UITF') reconsidered the accounting treatment of lease incentives from the perspective of both the lessor and the lessee and issued UITF Abstract 28 *Operating Lease Incentives* in February 2001 (for information on obtaining copies see the ASB website at www.frc.org.uk/asb). Under the Abstract:

- all incentives for the agreement of a new or renewed operating lease should be recognised as an integral part of the net payment agreed for the use of the asset, irrespective of the nature or form of the incentive or the timing of the payments;
- a lessee should recognise the aggregate benefit of incentives as a reduction of the rental expense and should allocate the benefit over the shorter of the lease term and a period ending on the date from which the prevailing market rental is expected to be payable – the allocation should be on a straight-line basis unless another systematic basis is more representative of the time pattern of the lessee's benefit from the use of the leased asset; and
- a lessor should recognise the aggregate cost of incentives as a reduction of rental income and should allocate this cost over the lease term or a shorter period ending on the date from which the prevailing market rental is expected to be payable – the allocation should be on a straight-line basis unless another systematic basis is more representative of the time pattern in which the benefit from the leased asset is receivable.

Where a lessor provides incentives for the lease of building that is accounted for as an investment property, the value attributed to the property in the balance sheet should not include any amount that is reported as a separate asset (eg as accrued rent receivable).

Property

22.10   Security

At a Glance

* Good security arrangements will often be a requirement under the company's insurance policies and may help to reduce the related insurance premiums.
* The level of compliance with any detailed insurance requirements should be kept under regular review.
* Buildings should be subject to regular maintenance checks to identify and repair any potentially weakened areas.
* Alarm systems can be an effective way of improving the physical security of premises but quality, proper installation and regular maintenance, together with appropriate staff training, are usually essential to effective operation.
* Electronic surveillance systems can be useful in monitoring particularly vulnerable areas, but good controls over, and regular maintenance of, the system are essential.
* Appropriate security policies and procedures can help to improve staff awareness of the underlying issues.
* Particular care should be taken over the disposal of combustible waste and the retention of combustible or hazardous goods on site.
* Precautions should be taken to prevent serious and costly damage during adverse weather conditions.

22.11   Extent of Security Arrangements

The extent of the security arrangements that a business needs to put into place will depend on a number of issues, including:

* the nature of the business and any specific security risks arising from this – for instance, the level of cash and valuable, moveable assets held on the premises (PCs, printers, laptops and computer chips are particularly vulnerable to theft);
* the ease of access to the property from roads, footpaths, open spaces, staircases, flat roofs or adjoining premises – for instance, theft will generally be easier if vehicles can be driven up to or into the premises; and
* the likelihood of a break-in outside business hours attracting attention – for instance, premises in remote locations, such as isolated industrial estates, are often more vulnerable.

Good security measures will often be a requirement under the company's insurance policies and compliance with any detailed provisions should be kept under regular review to ensure that insurance cover is maintained at the required level. Crime can represent a significant cost for business, both in terms of the loss of valuable assets and business information, and the amount of management time needed to deal with it. Insurance companies and the local police crime prevention unit are usually happy to advise on security issues, and evidence of a good security policy may be helpful in controlling the level of related insurance costs. Buildings occupied by several companies tend to be more hazardous and may therefore be more costly to insure than a single-occupancy building.

22.12 Physical Security of Premises

Issues to consider in respect of the physical security of business premises include:

- *Visibility:* Clear views of expensive equipment from outside the property can make it an attractive target – swivel blinds help to obscure the view (provided they are actually used).
- *Doors:* Doors and doorframes should be of good, solid construction and frames should be fixed securely to the surrounding structure. Further protection (eg lining with sheet metal) may be needed in particularly vulnerable locations. Any glass panels should be fitted with toughened or laminated security glass, covered with anti-shatter film or protected by grilles or shutters.
- *Locks:* Premises should usually be secured by insurance-approved five- or seven-lever mortice locks, fitted by an approved installer (eg a member of the Master Locksmiths' Association). Fire doors are often one of the weakest parts of the building and the local fire authority should be able to advise on appropriate security measures. Generally, there should be no problem in fire doors having the same quality locks as other doors, or being protected by security grilles/gates, provided that there is a system to ensure that these are opened whenever the premises are occupied.
- *Windows:* Toughened or laminated glass should be used for windows and skylights, especially where these are easily accessible. Another option is to use steel bars or security grilles, although these may make the building look less attractive to visitors. Some grilles can be folded back when the building is occupied, but the effectiveness then depends on each grille being put into place when the room or building becomes unoccupied.
- *Lighting:* Exterior floodlighting can be a strong deterrent to intruders. Lighting can be controlled by time switches or activated when movement is detected.
- *Patrols:* Smaller businesses may find it worthwhile to join with other local businesses to form a watch scheme or to employ a regular patrol or security service. Larger companies may make similar arrangements individually.

The building should also be subject to regular maintenance checks and arrangements should be made for any necessary repairs to be carried out promptly, to prevent access being obtained through potentially weakened parts of the property.

22.13 Use of Alarm Systems

The installation of an alarm system can be an effective way of improving the security of premises. Such systems vary in complexity and price, but quality is usually important if the system is to work well. Many insurance companies require alarm systems to comply with European Norm EN50131 (which superseded British Standard BS4737 from 1 October 2005) and require the installation and maintenance to be carried out by a company approved by the National Approval Council for Security Systems ('NACOSS'), now part of the National Security Inspectorate. Keyholders for the premises will need to be identified and notified to the police or security monitoring firm to ensure a prompt response if the alarm is activated. A major drawback with alarm systems is that they are prone of false alarms, especially if they have been incorrectly installed or are not properly maintained, or if users do not fully understand how to operate them. The police will quickly withdraw their support if there are too many false alarms, so it is important to ensure that an alarm system is properly installed and maintained and that all staff authorised to set or deactivate the alarm are properly trained. Other relevant issues include:

- security over the alarm code itself – this should never be kept on the premises, or disclosed to unauthorised persons;
- security over any special code to abort a false alarm;
- procedures to deal with faults in the alarm system, or in the telephone connection that alerts the police or security monitoring firm.

Any operating problems or faults should be reported to the insurers immediately. Failure to do this could invalidate the insurance cover on the property. Smoke screens can be used in conjunction with alarm systems to disorientate any intruders and restrict their opportunity steal from the premises if they manage to gain access.

22.14   Electronic Surveillance Systems

The installation of basic electronic surveillance equipment (eg a camera, monitor and recorder) can help to monitor activity in particularly vulnerable areas of a property, such as around external doors and in car parks. Evidence suggests that a visible camera acts as a strong deterrent to would-be thieves. However, the system will only be effective if it is properly controlled and maintained – for instance, if there is an established system for changing the recording tape, and if any images recorded are clear and usable.

22.15   Company Procedures and Policies

The introduction of appropriate security policies and procedures can be helpful in improving staff awareness of the importance of this matter. Possible ideas include:

- a system to ensure that there is always at least one company representative in the reception area to the premises;
- the use of visitor badges to identify genuine visitors (including those carrying out repairs or maintenance work) and an encouragement to staff to challenge

other unknown individuals on the premises – larger organisations, where staff do not necessarily know one another, may need to use some form staff identity badge as well;
- consideration of the use of restricted entry systems to the premises, or to particular parts of the building (eg individual floors);
- having a named person to be responsible for checking that the premises and any surrounding area are secure at the end of each working day;
- ensuring that keys are only held by named individuals and that all keys to safes, secure locations and external doors are removed from the premises when closed – keyholders should also understand the potential risk from leaving keys lying around (it needs only a few minutes to take an impression);
- postcoding or name-marking valuable pieces of equipment – this makes them less attractive to would-be thieves and improves the chance of return if they should be stolen; and
- restricting the amount of cash kept on the premises outside business hours and using a good quality safe (anchored to the floor if necessary) for any that does need to be retained.

22.16   Protection Against Fire and Arson

Arson is the main cause of serious fires in business premises. As well as taking normal security measures over entry to the premises, the company should have procedures to ensure that:

- all combustible waste is removed from the premises as soon as possible, and is retained securely in the interim period;
- all combustible materials and hazardous goods (eg flammable substances) are locked away separately when not in use, including at the end of each working day.

In some cases, it may be appropriate to consider installing fire-break walls and fire-resistant floors to help prevent the spread of fire throughout a building. Every building should have suitable types of fire protection equipment, properly positioned throughout the premises, and clear, regularly tested procedures for evacuation in the case of fire or any other emergency.

22.17   Protection Against Adverse Weather

Severe and costly damage to business premises can be caused during adverse weather conditions and by leaks from burst water pipes. Precautions to help prevent this include ensuring that:

- roofs, guttering and pipes are regularly inspected and any repairs or maintenance needed is carried out promptly;
- stock, machinery and any other contents that are susceptible to water damage are stored on upper floors if possible, or are at least raised off the ground to minimise damage in the event of a flood – businesses based in areas known to

be liable to flooding should obtain specialist advice on protecting the property and its contents;

- all water tanks and pipes are properly lagged, although the underside of water tanks should be left clear to allow heat to reach them;
- adequate heating is maintained throughout the building in colder weather – if the property is to be left unoccupied for a prolonged period of time, consideration should be given to draining the water system; and
- tall buildings, towers and chimneys should be protected against lightning in accordance with British Standard 6651 Protection of Structures Against Lightning.

Appendix 1

Useful Websites on Property Issues

Royal Institution of Chartered Surveyors	www.rics.org
Business Link	www.businesslink.gov.uk
Department for Constitutional Affairs	www.dca.gov.uk
Office of Public Sector Information (for online legislation)	www.opsi.gov.uk/legislation/
Landlord Zone	www.landlordzone.co.uk
National Security Inspectorate	www.nsi.org.uk
British Security Industry Association	www.bsia.co.uk
Crime Reduction	www.crimereduction.gov.uk

Property

23

Remuneration

23 Remuneration

23.1 Remuneration Planning

At a Glance
* Remuneration planning can be an important tool in attracting and retaining high quality staff.
* Employees are often unaware of the true value of the benefits included in their remuneration package, or of the cost to the employer.
* Recruitment bonuses ('golden hellos') are now common at all employment levels.
* Wider issues – such as working patterns, training and development, and career progression – may be equally important to many employees.
* A number of benefits can be offered at little or no cost to the employer.

23.2 Need for Remuneration Planning

Remuneration planning can be an important tool in attracting and retaining high quality staff. The complete remuneration package offered by an employer, including the various benefits that it encompasses in addition to basic salary, will be the deciding factor for many individuals in whether to stay with their existing employer or take up an opportunity offered elsewhere. Other devices, such as bonus schemes or share incentive schemes, may be used to help reward and retain key members of staff. Remuneration arrangements therefore need to be carefully planned and kept under constant review to enable the business to attract the right calibre staff whilst continuing to maintain control over the potential costs of doing so.

23.3 Communication with Employees

Research has indicated that, although the overall remuneration package is of considerable importance to employees, they are often unaware of the true value of benefits included in the package or of the cost to the employer. The average cost to employers is frequently more than 30 per cent of basic salary, whereas employees usually estimate the benefits that they receive to be worth around 20 per cent of salary. Businesses are therefore unlikely to gain full benefit from the remuneration packages that they offer unless the underlying facts are communicated more clearly to employees.

23.4   One-off Payments

As well as offering comprehensive remuneration packages to employees and potential employees, some businesses offer a recruitment bonus (or 'golden hello') to attract new staff. These usually take the form of a lump-sum payment either at the time of joining or as a guaranteed bonus at the end of the first year. Recruitment bonuses are now common at all levels – for instance, they are used both to attract experienced, skilled executives to the board and also to recruit high calibre graduates (with student loans to repay). At the other end of the employment cycle, termination payments (or 'golden handshakes') have been a familiar element of business life for many years, particularly at executive level. These may take the form of lump sum payments, additional pension contributions in the run-up to retirement or the gift of a company car.

23.5   Wider Issues

It is also important to remember that, for many staff these days, wider issues such as working patterns, opportunities for training and development, career progression, flexibility and management style can be equally as important as remuneration and benefits. Softer benefits such as flexible working, family-friendly policies and personal development programmes should therefore be taken into consideration as well.

23.6   Low-cost Benefits

There are a number of benefits that an employer may be able to offer employees at little or no cost to the business. For instance, corporate purchasing power will usually enable an employer to negotiate significant savings on products such as life assurance and medical insurance, or reduced membership fees for local facilities such as health clubs and sports associations. An employee who takes up the option of arranging insurance cover or joining the club or association is responsible for meeting the costs of doing so but benefits from the saving negotiated, without any direct cost to the employer.

23.7   Flexible Benefit Schemes

At a Glance
* Schemes that give each employee a degree of flexibility over the benefits they receive are particularly helpful to couples where both partners are working and might otherwise be offered similar benefits.

> * Flexible schemes often operate by allocating a system of points to each benefit and allowing employees to choose a mix of benefits to match the total points allocated to them.
> * Alternatively, employees may be allocated an initial benefits package with the flexibility to opt out of certain benefits in order to add a new benefit or 'trade up' to a higher level of an existing benefit.
> * The employer must decide whether the provision of retirement benefits is regarded as a separate benefit or included as part of the flexible benefits package.

23.8   Benefits of a Flexible Benefit Scheme

Although benefit schemes are seen as an important element of remuneration, it can be difficult, particularly with a large and diverse workforce, to establish which individual benefits are likely be most attractive to employees and therefore meet the objective of recruiting and retaining high quality staff. More and more employers are consequently providing benefit schemes that give employees a degree of flexibility over the benefits that they receive. Such a scheme is seen as particularly helpful by couples where both partners are working and may otherwise be offered the same or similar benefits by their employer. With a flexible benefit package, each employee can tailor the arrangements to his/her individual needs and can choose which benefits to take and which to disregard. Any proposals to introduce such a scheme will need careful consideration, particularly as regards:

- the benefits that employees would actually like to receive;
- the feasibility of offering a flexible scheme;
- the administrative issues that may arise; and
- a cost/benefit analysis.

In considering costs, it is important to remember that Class 1A National Insurance Contributions are now payable by an employer on most benefits provided to employees (see **20.22 CATEGORIES OF NATIONAL INSURANCE**).

23.9   Practical Application

Flexible schemes often operate by allocating a system of points to each benefit, usually based on the cost of that benefit to the employer. Employees may be allocated a set number of benefit points and can chose a mix of benefits to utilise these, or they may be allocated an initial benefit package with the flexibility to opt out of certain benefits and use those points to add a new benefit or 'trade up' to a higher level of an existing benefit – for instance, a better quality company car. The complexity of the scheme, and the range of benefits offered,

Remuneration

will usually depend on the size of the employer. Examples of benefits that are frequently offered in flexible benefit schemes include:

- risk benefits:
    - life assurance,
    - long-term disability insurance,
    - critical illness insurance,
    - private healthcare insurance,
    - private dental insurance;
- personal benefits:
    - additional holiday,
    - childcare or crèche facilities,
    - day care for other dependants (eg elderly relatives),
    - financial counselling,
    - sabbaticals or career breaks,
    - time off for voluntary work or community service activities;
- company cars;
- financial benefits:
    - season ticket loans,
    - general loans,
    - relocation packages for new joiners,
    - mortgage subsidies,
    - assistance with school fees.

Risk benefits referred to here differ from those mentioned at **23.6** above as in this case the company will meet the cost.

23.10   Retirement Benefits

The provision of retirement benefits is common in the UK and is one of the most substantial benefits offered to employees, although it may not always be seen as such, especially by younger members of staff who may find it difficult to think about planning for retirement. Whether the provision of retirement benefits is included in a flexible benefit package or remains as a separate issue is something for each employer to decide. Once again, there is the difficulty that a group pension scheme will usually try to cater for a wide variety of different needs and may not offer benefits to suit certain employees. However, many employers consider that they have some moral responsibility to ensure that employees make appropriate provision for their retirement and may not want to be seen as encouraging them to sacrifice long-term pension benefit for short-term gain in the form of other benefits. Depending on the particular nature of the pension scheme(s) offered, it may be possible to retain basic pension arrangements as a separate benefit, but allow for additional contributions to be made as part of the flexible benefits package.

23.11 Bonus and Other Incentive Schemes

At a Glance
* Bonus and incentive schemes are designed to enhance business performance by rewarding employees who perform well, as well as helping with the retention of high calibre individuals.
* Care should be taken over the wording of provisions on discretionary bonuses in contracts of employment.
* Care is also required over bonuses paid on the basis of operating profits achieving or exceeding a specified amount, as these may act as an incentive to manipulate or distort the reported figures.
* Incentive schemes usually extend over a longer period of time (eg three years) and are used to motivate individuals to meet specific targets that are challenging but achievable.
* Targets may relate to individual performance, the performance of a unit or team, or a combination of the two.
* The full financial implications of bonus and incentive schemes need to be carefully assessed.
* Listed companies in particular need to take account of the requirements of the *Combined Code* on the operation of long-term incentive schemes for directors.

23.12 Enhancing Company Performance

Bonus and other incentive schemes will usually be linked in some way with company or business unit performance. They are therefore designed to enhance business performance by rewarding employees who perform well, as well as to help with the retention of directors and staff, particularly those who are seen as critical to the success of the business. They show that the contribution that each individual makes to the business is valued and ensure that clear performance objectives are identified to maintain the focus of that individual. Bonus and incentive schemes may operate for a specific group of employees (eg directors and senior management) or more widely throughout an organisation.

23.13 Discretionary Bonus Schemes

Employment contracts often provide for the employee to be considered for an annual bonus payment at the discretion of the employer. There may be an additional provision that this is dependent on the performance of the individual or the performance of the business as a whole. This may not be sufficient to give the employer absolute discretion over the award each year. Case law has established that the employer must not exercise such discretion unreasonably or capriciously – for instance, by refusing to pay a bonus when it is evident that an employee has made a very considerable contribution to the overall profitability of the business. Particular care should therefore be taken over the wording of provisions on discretionary bonuses in contracts of employment.

23.14 Defined Bonus Schemes

In other cases, bonus scheme arrangements may be much more specific, so that a bonus is payable if (say) operating profit exceeds a given level and higher bonuses may be payable as profits increase. Particular care needs to be taken over such arrangements, especially when they are based on unit or department performance, as they can also act as an incentive for management and staff to manipulate or distort the figures reported in order to trigger the bonus payment. It is also important to define clearly what is meant by 'operating profit' (or whatever term is used in the bonus agreement).

23.15 Incentive Schemes

Incentive schemes are used to motivate directors and employees to meet specified targets which support the principal objectives of the business. Such schemes often extend over a period of time (for instance, a scheme may be based on performance over a three-year period) and may result in cash payments or the granting of shares or share options in the business (see **23.20–23.23** below), or a combination of the two, to those who achieve the agreed performance targets. Targets should be challenging but achievable. Separate schemes may need to be used for directors/senior managers and other employees, to reflect the different responsibilities that each group has within the business. An incentive scheme may be related to individual performance targets, or team/unit performance, or an element of both. It may also be linked to the financial performance of a business unit or of the business as a whole. Inevitably, there are advantages and disadvantages to each approach, and these must be weighed up in the context of the company's particular circumstances. Some schemes also involve a retention or 'lock-in' element, whereby all or part of the incentive is only payable if the director or employee remains with the company for a fixed period of time (eg a further year after the incentive has been earned). Factors such as company policies and values will also be relevant, as an incentive scheme that appears inconsistent with these is unlikely to achieve the required degree of motivation and encouragement.

23.16 Financial Implications

The full financial implications of bonus schemes and other incentive schemes need to be taken into account. For instance, payments in cash may qualify as pensionable earnings and the employer may therefore be committed to paying pension contributions on the amount of the bonus or incentive payment. For accounting purposes, bonus and other incentive scheme costs will usually need to be charged in the profit and loss account for the period in which the employee performs the services that are being paid for or rewarded. Appropriate provision should therefore be made in the accounts each year to reflect the amount of bonus or incentive scheme payment 'earned' in respect of that year, regardless of when this is actually paid. These will often need to be based on the best estimate of the expected liability at the balance sheet date, and in the case of long-term schemes will need to be adjusted at each balance sheet date for any changes in expectations until the final cost to the company is known.

23.17 Pensions Implications

Remuneration that relies heavily on bonus or similar payments (eg commission) can also be disadvantageous for an employee approaching retirement, particularly if the variable element reduces as retirement approaches. If he/she is a member of a defined benefit retirement scheme where pension benefits are paid on the basis of final salary, a sharp reduction in bonus or commission payments could have a significant impact of the level of pension received. One possible solution to this problem may be for the pension entitlement to be based on a variable accrual rate, depending on the ratio of actual remuneration to basic salary.

23.18 Listed Companies

In the case of listed companies, the *Combined Code* includes detailed recommendations on the operation of long-term incentive schemes for the benefit the directors, and on the detailed disclosures that should be given in the accounts where such schemes are used (see **6 CORPORATE GOVERNANCE**).

23.19 Share-based Remuneration

At a Glance
* Many employees now have a better understanding of the benefits of receiving part of their remuneration in the form of shares or share options.
* Employee share schemes must meet certain conditions in order to be approved by the HRMC – the receipt of shares or share options under unapproved schemes can have significant personal tax consequences for the individual.
* Employer's National Insurance Contributions are also payable on gains made by directors and employees on the exercise of share options under unapproved schemes.
* The accounting implications of employee share schemes need to be carefully considered. FRS 20 and IFRS 2 *Share-based Payment* generally require an appropriate expense to be recognised in the profit and loss account in the period in which the related services are received.
* From 1 December 2003, certain companies are allowed to purchase their own shares and hold them in treasury, sell them or transfer them to an employee share scheme.

Remuneration

23.20 Attraction of Share-based Remuneration

Despite the problems and commercial risks faced by dot.com businesses, the media attention focused on them, and in particular on the millionaire status of their owners, has encouraged employees to consider more carefully the potential benefits in receiving part of their remuneration in the form of shares or share options. The result is that many employees are now keen to join the new share-holding culture. Employee share schemes also offer potential tax advantages to employees, provided that the scheme has been approved by the Inland Revenue. Incentive schemes often provide for payment wholly or partly in shares or share options (see **23.12–23.18** above).

23.21 Approved Schemes

Employee share schemes must fulfil certain conditions in order to be approved by the HMRC – these cover issues such as the option exercise price, the period during which options can be exercised, the value of shares held by an individual and those eligible to participate in the scheme. Two new types of employee share scheme were introduced in the *Finance Act 2000*. All-employee share ownership plans ('AESOPs') are designed to offer all employees the opportunity to buy shares in the company or to receive shares without cost and free of tax. Similarly, the Enterprise Management Incentive ('EMI') provides a scheme to enable certain small companies to grant share options to no more than 15 employees. Gains on the exercise of these options are potentially chargeable to capital gains tax, but the gains will in effect be tax free if they are within the annual personal exemption (£8,800 for the 2006/07 tax year) and the employee does not have chargeable gains from other sources.

There can be significant personal tax implications for directors and employees who receive shares or shares options under share schemes that have not been approved by the HMRC.

23.22 National Insurance Implications for Unapproved Schemes

There are also National Insurance implications in the case of unapproved schemes, in that employer's National Insurance Contributions are payable on any gains made by directors and employees on the exercise of options granted after 5 April 1999 under such schemes. This can represent a considerable additional cost to the employer. It can also give rise to significant administrative problems as the employer will not always be in a position to know when the options have been exercised. Legislation is now in place which enables an employer to reach a formal agreement with the employee that the latter will bear some or all the National Insurance liability, but this inevitably reduces the potential value of the option to the employee. If the employer retains some or all of the National Insurance liability, UITF Abstract 25 *National Insurance Contributions on Share Option Gains* requires provision to be made in the accounts when the option is granted, on the basis that this is when the obligation to pay the contribution arises (for information on obtaining copies see the Accounting Standards Board ('ASB') website at www.frc.org.uk/asb). If the terms of the share option arrangement include a performance period, the provision should be allocated over the period from the date of the grant to the end of the performance period. The calculations should be based on the best estimate of the liability that has accrued at the balance sheet date and should be adjusted each year for any changes in circumstances and expectations. Where there is no performance period, the full amount of the provision must be charged immediately to the profit and loss account.

23.23   Accounting Implications

Under UK accounting practice, the requirements of FRS 20 *Share-based Payment* apply to listed companies for accounting periods beginning on or after 1 January 2005 and to other companies for accounting periods beginning on or after 1 January 2006. Earlier adoption is encouraged but should be disclosed in the accounts. Smaller companies adopting the FRSSE are likely to have to comply with similar requirements from 1 January 2007. In the case of IAS accounts, IFRS 2 *Share-based Payment* applies for accounting periods beginning on or after 1 January 2005. Both FRS 20 and IFRS 2 are based on the following principles:

- when an entity receives goods or services under a share-based payment transaction, it should recognise an expense (or, where appropriate, an asset);
- the expense or asset should be recognised over the period in which the services are rendered or when the goods are received; and
- the goods or services received under a share-based payment transaction should be measured at fair value.

The standards apply to all share-based payment transactions, including employee share option schemes, Save-As-You-Earn (SAYE) schemes and similar arrangements for employees, as well as any share-based transactions involving non-employee goods and services. The standards identify two main types of share-based payment:

- equity-settled share-based payments – where payment under the transaction is made in the form of equity instruments; and
- cash-settled share-based payments – where payment is made in cash or other assets, but the amount paid is based on the value of an equity instrument of the reporting entity.

Equity-settled transactions with employees should always be measured at the fair value of the equity instrument granted. Separate requirements apply to share-based payment transactions involving third parties. Prior to the introduction of FRS 20 and IFRS 2, it was usually possible under UK accounting practice to structure employee share schemes so that there was no charge to the profit and loss account for employee remuneration paid in the form of shares or share options. Consequently, the new accounting requirements will have a significant impact on the accounts of companies making use of employee share schemes. For information on obtaining copies of FRS 20 and IFRS 2, see the ASB website at www.frc.org.uk/asb and the IASB website at www.iasb.org.

23.24 Treasury Shares

Company law currently allows companies to purchase their own shares in specific circumstances, but requires those shares to be treated as cancelled on purchase. Since 1 December 2003 certain companies have been allowed to hold their own shares in treasury and to sell them for cash or transfer them to an employee share scheme, subject to certain conditions. These provisions apply only to qualifying shares, which are defined as those:

- included in the UK Official List, or officially listed in another EEA state; or
- traded on the Alternative Investment Market or on a regulated market in another EEA state.

Initial requirements on accounting for treasury shares were set out in UITF Abstract 37 *Purchases and Sales of Own Shares* but this has been superseded by FRS 25 *Financial Instruments: Disclosure and Presentation* for accounting periods beginning on or after 1 January 2005. Under FRS 25, any own shares acquired by an entity must be deducted from equity. No gain or loss should be recognised in the profit and loss account on the purchase, sale, issue or cancellation of own shares and any consideration paid or received should be recognised directly in equity. The same treatment applies regardless of whether the shares are held by the entity or by another member of the consolidated group. For information on obtaining copies of FRS 25, see the ASB website at www.frc.org.uk/asb. For companies preparing IAS accounts (see **3.16–3.17**), similar requirements apply under IAS 32 *Financial Instruments: Disclosure and Presentation*.

23.25 Company Cars

At a Glance
- Company car schemes have generally become less popular as a result of recent changes to the taxation system for this particular form of benefit.
- Employer's National Insurance Contributions are also payable on car and fuel benefits paid to directors and higher paid employees.
- From 6 April 2002, the taxable benefit in respect of a company car is based on the CO_2 emission of the vehicle.
- A further taxable benefit arises where a director or higher paid employee is provided with free private fuel in addition to a company car.
- From 2003/04 the fuel charge is based on the CO_2 emission of the vehicle in the same way as the car benefit.

23.26 Advantages of Flexibility

For many years, the provision of a company car was regarded as a key element in a remuneration package, but changes to the taxation system for this particular form of benefit in recent years mean that company car schemes have generally become less popular. Some employees will still see a car as an attractive option, but many companies now give employees the opportunity to opt out of the car scheme for a cash alternative, or to trade down to a smaller size of car, either for cash or as part of a flexible benefits package (see **23.8–23.10** above). As with most other benefits, employers are now liable to pay National Insurance Contributions on car and fuel benefits provided to directors and higher paid employees and this can represent a significant additional cost to the business.

23.27 Tax System for Company Cars

The tax system for company cars underwent a radical change with effect from 6 April 2002. The taxable benefit is still based on the list price of the car but the percentage of list value used depends on the carbon dioxide emission of the vehicle – the more environmentally-friendly the car is, the lower the taxable benefit will be. The percentage to be applied to list value ranges from 15 per cent for the lowest emission cars to 35 per cent for those at the top of the emission list. Diesel cars are subject to a surcharge of 3 per cent, although this has no impact on the upper limit of 35 per cent. Discounts can also be applied to reduce the charge for cars registered in 1998 or later which are battery electric, hybrid electric, or run on liquid petroleum gas or compressed natural gas. The level of business mileage undertaken during the tax year no longer plays any part in the calculations. The same figure applies for the calculation of employer's Class 1A National Insurance Contributions on the car benefit. Employers have to forward details of the carbon dioxide emissions of their company cars to the HMRC to enable them to issue appropriate PAYE codes for directors and employees with company cars.

23.28 *Carbon Dioxide Emissions*

For cars registered on or after 1 March 2001, the CO_2 g/km rating required for working out the car benefit charge is shown on the DVLA's new car registration form V5. Indicative CO_2 emissions figures for all new car models can also be found on the Vehicle Certification Agency website (www.vca.gov.uk). For cars registered earlier than this, the Society of Motor Manufacturers and Traders (SMMT), under an agreement with the HMRC, is providing a CO_2 emissions internet enquiry service (www.smmt.co.uk), with information for all cars first registered from January 1998 to 28 February 2001. This service should help employers to find out the CO_2 emissions figure for a particular make and model of car. Single enquiries are free of charge but a charge will be made for multiple enquiries and for those who require the whole database. Details of the costs are shown in the 'Fleet Contact Form' which can be accessed from the introduction page for the CO_2 database on the SMMT website.

23.29 Fuel Scale Charge

Where a director or an employee earning more than £8,500 a year is provided with a company car and also petrol for private use, the cash equivalent of the fuel benefit is also chargeable to tax. From 6 April 2003, the fuel scale charge is based on the level of CO_2 emissions of the car (see **23.26** above on the tax system for company cars). As with the basic car benefit, there will be a 3 per cent supplement for diesels and a discount for alternative fuelled cars. This means that, the same figures are now used to calculate tax and Class 1A National Insurance on both company car and private fuel benefits. In the case of the private fuel benefit, the percentage calculated is applied to a standard figure for the tax year – this figure has been set at £14,400 since 6 April 2003. Where an employee opts out of the free fuel during the tax year, the tax and Class 1A National Insurance liability will be reduced proportionately. However, if the employee opts back into the free fuel later in the tax year, a full year's tax and Class 1A National Insurance Contributions will become payable.

23.30   Directors' Remuneration: All Companies

At a Glance
* *CA 1985* requires detailed disclosures on directors' remuneration to be given in the notes to the accounts.
* Separate disclosure requirements apply for quoted and unquoted companies.
* Aggregate disclosures must be given in respect of emoluments, contributions to defined contribution retirement schemes, share options, amounts payable under long-term incentive schemes and the number of directors accruing benefits under defined benefit retirement schemes.
* Slightly reduced disclosure requirements apply in the case of small companies.
* Additional aggregate information must be given by quoted and AIM companies.
* Bonus payments that require shareholder approval should normally be included in emoluments in the year in which they are approved.
* Awards under long-term incentive schemes are similarly disclosable when the director becomes entitled to receive payment.
* All pension schemes must be classified as either defined contribution or defined benefit for disclosure purposes.
* The money value of any benefits in kind must be included in emoluments.
* Amounts paid to, or receivable by, a person connected with a director must be included in the disclosures.
* Particular difficulties can arise in groups of companies, especially if all directors' remuneration is paid by the holding company.

23.31   Disclosure Under the Companies Act 1985

A company's annual accounts must include detailed information on remuneration paid to, or receivable by, anyone who was a director during the year. The disclosure requirements cover all amounts receivable by the directors in respect of their services as directors of the company (and, where relevant, of its subsidiaries), regardless of who actually makes the payment. The legislation requires basic disclosures to be given by all companies, and then makes a clear distinction between quoted and unquoted companies in requiring more detailed information to be given. The requirements were broadly similar for accounting periods ending before 31 December 2002, although greater detail was required in the case of quoted companies, but the *Directors' Remuneration Report Regulations 2002 (SI 2002/1986)* introduced some significant changes to the disclosure requirements for quoted companies for accounting periods ending on or after 31 December 2002 (see **23.43** below). For these purposes, a quoted company is defined as a company whose equity share capital is:

- included in the Official List of the London Stock Exchange;
- officially listed in an EEA State; or
- admitted to dealing on the New York Stock Exchange or the Nasdaq exchange.

The basic disclosure requirements for all companies are considered below and the more detailed requirements for quoted and unquoted companies are covered in the remaining two sections of this chapter. The same disclosure requirements apply, irrespective of whether the company prepares Companies Act or IAS accounts (see **3.16** above).

23.32   Basic Disclosure for All Companies

The basic requirement is that every company must disclose in the notes to the accounts:

- the aggregate of the emoluments paid to, or receivable by, the directors in respect of their qualifying services (which include services as director of a subsidiary or in the management of the company or group);
- the aggregate value of any contributions paid by the company in respect of directors into a pension scheme where the benefits depend on the level of contributions paid (ie defined contribution schemes – see **21.5** DEFINED CONTRIBUTION SCHEMES);
- the number of directors who are accruing retirement benefits under money purchase schemes; and
- the number of directors who are accruing retirement benefits under defined benefit schemes.

The contributions made during the year to defined benefit retirement schemes do not have to be disclosed. Separate requirements apply to small companies, as explained at **23.34** below. Emoluments are defined in the *Companies Act 1985 (CA 1985)* as including salary, bonus, fees, benefits in kind, expense allowances (if these are chargeable to UK income tax) and amounts paid on acceptance of office as director. This list is not intended to be exhaustive and any other similar amounts paid to, or receivable by, directors will therefore be disclosable. Share options, pension contributions and amounts payable under long-term incentive schemes are specifically excluded from the definition of emoluments as they are subject to separate disclosure requirements.

23.33   Small Companies

A company that qualifies as small under *CA 1985* is only required to give the following details in respect of directors' emoluments in its accounts:

- the aggregate of the amounts that would otherwise be disclosable individually, i.e:
  - ○ emoluments paid to or receivable by the directors,
  - ○ money or assets received or receivable by the directors under long-term incentive schemes (other than shares and share options), and
  - ○ company contributions to money purchase pension schemes for the benefit of directors;
- the number of directors accruing retirement benefits under money purchase schemes; and
- the number of directors accruing retirement benefits under defined benefit pension schemes.

The exemption relates only to the emoluments disclosures – other disclosure requirements (eg compensation for loss of office) continue to apply.

23.34   Quoted and AIM Companies

In addition to the above aggregate information, quoted companies and those whose equity share capital is listed on the Alternative Investment Market (AIM) must disclose:

- the aggregate gains made by directors on the exercise of share options; and
- the aggregate of the amounts paid to, or receivable by, directors under long-term incentive schemes in respect of qualifying services and the net value of any assets (other than cash or share options) receivable by directors under such schemes.

23.35   Avoiding Duplication

If any of the required details are readily ascertainable from other information included with the accounts, such as a remuneration report (see **23.43 DIR-ECTORS' REMUNERATION: QUOTED COMPANIES**), they generally do not have to be disclosed again. The one exception is aggregate gains on the exercise of share options which must always be shown separately in the notes to the accounts of a quoted or AIM company. In practice, it is helpful for the notes to the accounts to include a cross-reference to where the detailed information on directors' remuneration can be found.

23.36   Bonus Payments

As explained at **23.16** above, provision should usually be made in the accounts for bonuses in the year in which they are earned. Where a bonus payment to directors requires approval by the shareholders before the directors are entitled to receive it, it is usual to treat the bonus as being receivable by the directors (and therefore disclosable within directors' emoluments) in the year in which shareholder approval is given, even though the bonus may have been charged to the profit and loss account in an earlier period.

23.37   Benefits in Kind

Emoluments specifically include the estimated money value of benefits in kind received by a director otherwise than in cash. The most common benefits in kind are:

- company car;
- free or subsidised accommodation;
- insurance for the benefit of the director (eg private health cover, indemnity insurance, personal accident cover);
- loans at preferential interest rates;
- relocation costs (unless the relocation is clearly for business purposes).

Some of these may also be disclosable in the annual accounts as loans or transactions with directors (see **8 DIRECTORS' DUTIES**). Share options are subject to separate disclosure requirements and are therefore specifically excluded from emoluments for disclosure purposes. The main difficulty with benefits in kind is establishing an appropriate and realistic money value for the benefit. In most cases, market value will provide the best estimate of money value.

23.38   Long-term Incentive Schemes

Under *CA 1985*, amounts payable under long-term incentive schemes are disclosable when they are paid to or receivable by the director. The director must therefore have the right to receive a sum before it becomes disclosable. Amounts should therefore normally be disclosed in the year in which the director becomes entitled to receive payment. In the case of a long-term incentive scheme, the director will not usually be entitled to receive payment until all the specified conditions have been met. Even though it will usually be necessary to accrue for the payments in each accounting year, these sums will not become disclosable until all the relevant conditions have been met and the director becomes entitled to receive payment. As with annual bonuses, this will not always match the actual timing of the payment. Complex schemes which extend over a number of years will sometimes include the provision of a guaranteed minimum payment to the directors once a specified target has been achieved. In this case, the guaranteed minimum payment will become disclosable in the year in which the target is achieved, as this is when the directors become entitled to the minimum payment. The *Combined Code* also includes a number of recommendations in respect of long-term incentive schemes for directors (see **6.30 PERFORMANCE-RELATED PAY**).

23.39 Pension Arrangements

For the purposes of the *CA 1985* disclosures referred to in paragraph **23.33** above, all pension schemes must be classified as either defined contribution or defined benefit schemes (see **21 PENSIONS**). Any death in service benefits are to be disregarded when classifying a pension scheme for disclosure purposes. A pension scheme under which a director will be entitled to receive both money purchase benefits and defined benefits is classified as a defined benefit scheme for disclosure purposes. Where a scheme provides for the director to receive money purchase benefits or defined benefits, whichever is the greater, the company is allowed to assume for disclosure purposes that the benefits will be whichever appears more likely at the end of the financial year in question.

23.40 Payments to and from Other Parties

Amounts paid to or receivable by a person connected with a director or a body corporate controlled by him are specifically included within the disclosure requirements. Disclosure therefore cannot be avoided by arranging for the payment to be made to a connected party. In the case of payments to a company owned by the director, the emoluments note to the accounts usually includes an explanation that some or all of the payments have been made through that company. Emoluments also include all relevant amounts in respect of a director's services paid by, or receivable from the company, the company's subsidiary undertakings and any other person, unless the director must in turn account to the company or any of its subsidiary undertakings for the amounts received.

23.41 Particular Problems in Groups of Companies

In some groups, all directors' remuneration is paid by the holding company. Recharges may be made to subsidiary undertakings to reflect the cost of the services of their directors, but this will not always be done. This can cause difficulties over the disclosure of directors' remuneration in the accounts of the holding company and the subsidiaries. Directors' remuneration in the accounts of the holding company will comprise:

- remuneration paid to directors of the holding company in respect of their services to the company and management of the company and group; and
- if any holding company directors are also directors of one or more of the subsidiaries, remuneration paid to them for their services in relation to these companies.

Remuneration paid to those who are directors of subsidiaries but who are not directors of the holding company is not disclosable in the accounts of the holding company. The same disclosure requirements apply in the holding company's accounts, regardless of whether some or all of the remuneration costs are recharged to the subsidiaries.

Where the holding company recharges the subsidiaries with the cost of remunerating their directors, each subsidiary should disclose as directors' remuneration the amount paid to the holding company in respect of directors' services to the company. If the holding company makes a global recharge to the subsidiaries to cover general management costs, including directors' remuneration, but the element for directors' remuneration cannot be separately identified, an appropriate apportionment should be made for disclosure purposes. Where the holding company does not recharge the subsidiaries with the costs of remunerating their directors, the costs borne by the holding company are still disclosable as directors' remuneration in the accounts of the subsidiary – it is not acceptable to simply disclose the fact that the directors have been remunerated by the holding company and not quantify the amount that they have received. However, it may be helpful to explain that this cost has been borne by the holding company and is not charged in the subsidiary's accounts.

Where directors of a subsidiary are also directors or employees of the holding company, it is sometimes argued that the holding company remunerates them only for their services to the holding company and that they receive no remuneration in respect of their services as directors of the subsidiary. The validity of this argument will usually depend on the amount of time that the director or employee devotes to the subsidiary company. If the time is relatively small it may be acceptable that he/she does not receive remuneration for services as a director of the subsidiary. In this case, a brief explanation should be included in the subsidiary's accounts.

23.42   Directors' Remuneration: Quoted Companies

At a Glance
* The detailed disclosure requirements for quoted companies were changed by the *Directors' Remuneration Report Regulations 2002* (*SI 2002/1986*) for accounting periods ending on or after 31 December 2002.
* For accounting periods ending on or after 31 December 2002, the directors of a quoted company are required to prepare a separate directors' remuneration report.
* Certain elements of the directors' remuneration report are subject to audit.
* The general meeting at which the annual reports and accounts are laid must include a resolution inviting the shareholders to approve the directors' remuneration report.
* The content of the directors' remuneration report is specified in the legislation and includes:
  ○ detailed information on the remuneration paid to each individual director, and the pension entitlements of directors,

> ○ a statement on the company's future remuneration policy,
> ○ an explanation of any performance-related elements of remuneration,
> ○ details of service contracts and any related compensation commitments, and
> ○ comparative information on shareholder return for the last five years.
> * In the case of listed companies, certain additional disclosures are required by the FSA *Listing Rules*.
> * The legislation also specifies which elements of the directors' remuneration report should be included in summary financial statements.

23.43   Additional Disclosures for Quoted Companies

As explained in **23.31** above, *CA 1985* sets out basic disclosure requirements on directors' emoluments and pensions that apply to all companies and then distinguishes between quoted and unquoted companies in respect of certain more detailed disclosures. The detailed requirements for quoted companies were changed by the *Directors' Remuneration Report Regulations 2002* (*SI 2002/1986*) for accounting periods ending on or after 31 December 2002. A quoted company is one whose equity share capital is listed in the UK or an EEA State, or dealt in on the New York or Nasdaq exchanges.

23.44   Directors' Remuneration Report

For accounting periods ending on or after 31 December 2002, the directors of a quoted company are required to prepare a directors' remuneration report containing the detailed information specified in a new *Schedule 7A* to *CA 1985*. Current directors and those who have served as director in the preceding five years are given a specific duty to disclose relevant information to the company to enable the report to be prepared. The report must be formally approved by the directors and must be signed on behalf of the board by a director or by the company secretary. A signed copy must be delivered to the registrar as part of the company's annual reports and accounts. The auditors are required to report on the auditable part of the report (which is defined as the part covering the detailed disclosures on remuneration received by the directors) and to include any missing information in their audit report, so far as they are reasonably able to do so.

23.45   Shareholder Approval

The general meeting at which the annual reports and accounts are laid must include a resolution enabling the shareholders to approve the directors' remuneration report, and details of the resolution must be set out in the notice of the meeting. However, the legislation notes that this requirement does not mean that the entitlement of any individual to the remuneration shown in the report is conditional on the resolution being passed.

23.46   Contents of the Remuneration Report

The legislation generally requires detailed information to be given in tabular form and in a way that links the information to each director by name. The detailed contents of the directors' remuneration report are divided into two elements – those that are subject to audit and those that are not.

23.47   *Contents Subject to Audit*

The following information must be disclosed and is also subject to audit:

- for each director who served during the financial year, the total amount of:
  - salary and/or fees,
  - bonuses,
  - expense allowances that are chargeable to UK income tax,
  - any compensation for loss of office and similar payments,
  - the estimated money value of any benefits in kind, and
  - the sum total of all these amounts, and the equivalent total for the previous financial year;
- the nature of any element of a remuneration package which is not cash;
- for each director who served during the financial year, the number of shares subject to a share option (distinguishing between those with different terms and conditions) at:
  - the beginning of the year, or the date of appointment if later,
  - the end of the year, or the date of ceasing to be a director if earlier;
- information on share options awarded, exercised and lapsed during the year, and any variations to terms and conditions;
- for each share option that was unexpired at any time during the year:
  - the price (if any) paid for its award,
  - the exercise prices,
  - the date from which the option can be exercised, and
  - the date on which the option expires;
- a summary of any performance criteria upon which the award or exercise of a share option is conditional, and any changes made in the year;
- for any share option exercised during the year, the market price at the time of exercise;
- for each share option that was unexpired at the end of the financial year:
  - the market price at the year-end date, and
  - the highest and lowest market price during the year;
- for each director who served during the financial year, details of interests in long-term incentive schemes, showing:
  - interests at the beginning of the year, or the date of appointment if later,
  - awards during the year, and
  - interests at the end of the year, or on ceasing to be a director if earlier;
- for each disclosed interest in long-term incentive schemes, the date by which the qualifying conditions have to be fulfilled and details of any variations in the terms and conditions made during the year;

Remuneration

- for each scheme interest that has vested during the year, details of any shares, the amount of any money and the value of any other assets that have become receivable as a result;
- for each director who served during the financial year and has rights under a defined benefit retirement scheme:
  - details of any changes during the year in their accrued benefits under the scheme,
  - the accrued benefits at the end of the year,
  - the transfer value of the accrued benefits, calculated as recommended by the Institute of Actuaries and Faculty of Actuaries (see **23.49** PENSION ENTITLEMENTS),
  - the equivalent transfer value at the end of the previous year and the difference between this and the current transfer value, after deducting any contributions made by the director in the current year;
- for each director who served during the financial year and has rights under a money purchase retirement scheme, details of the contributions paid or payable by the company during the year;
- details of certain excess retirement benefits paid to directors or former directors;
- details of any significant awards to former directors (eg compensation for loss of office, pensions);
- for each director who served during the financial year, the aggregate amount of any consideration (including any benefits in kind) paid to, or receivable by, a third party for making available the services of the individual as a director.

The legislation allows a limited degree of aggregation of the information on share options where the required details would otherwise result in a disclosure of excessive length. Compensation payments to directors may also require shareholder approval under *CA 1985*, although this is not usually necessary for genuine payments in respect of damages for breach of contract or for pensions in respect of past services. If significant non-cash items are included, the compensation payments may also require approval under the provisions on substantial property transactions in *section 320* of *CA 1985*. Payments to third parties for the services of a director arise most commonly where a substantial investor (eg a bank or venture capital company) has the right to appoint a director to the board of the investee company and payment for the services of this director is made to the investor rather than to the director himself.

23.48   *Contents Not Subject to Audit*

The following information is required to be disclosed, but is not subject to audit:

- the names of the members of any committee that considered directors' remuneration during the year and the names of any other individuals (whether directors or not) who provided advice or services to that committee, together with details of the nature of the advice or services;
- a statement of the company's policy on directors' remuneration for the forthcoming year and for subsequent financial years – this must include for each

individual who has served as a director between the end of the financial year under review and the date on which the annual reports and accounts are laid before the members:

- ○ a detailed summary of any performance conditions in respect of awards under share option or long-term incentive schemes,
- ○ an explanation of why these performance conditions were chosen,
- ○ a summary of the methods used in assessing whether the performance conditions are met, and why those methods were chosen,
- ○ if any performance condition involves comparison with external factors, a summary of the factors to be used and the identity of any companies or index used for comparison purposes;
- a description of, and explanation for, any significant changes to the terms and conditions of entitlement under share option or long-term incentive schemes;
- an explanation of why any entitlements under share option or long-term incentive schemes are not subject to performance conditions;
- the relative importance of elements of remuneration that are related to performance and those that are not;
- a summary of the company's policy on the duration of directors' service contracts and on notice periods and termination payments under those contracts;
- the following information on the contract of service, or contract for services, of each person who served as a director during the financial year:
  - ○ date of the contract, the unexpired term and any notice period,
  - ○ any provision for compensation on early termination, and
  - ○ sufficient information on any other provisions to enable a member to estimate the company's liability in the event of early termination of the contract;
- an explanation for any significant awards during the year to former directors (eg compensation for loss of office, pensions); and
- a line graph showing the total shareholder return for the last five years on:
  - ○ a holding of the class of equity shares whose public trading has resulted in the company meeting the definition of a quoted company, and
  - ○ a hypothetical holding of shares, based on a broad equity market index, together with the name of index and why it was chosen.

In the case of the share performance graph, there is no requirement to disclose information for periods before the new regulations came into effect – in the early years, therefore, information will be given for one to four years as appropriate. The legislation includes detailed guidance on calculating total shareholder return for this purpose.

23.49   Directors' Pension Entitlements

Defined benefit retirement schemes usually link pension entitlement to final salary or average salary over a fixed period (say the last three years). The *Greenbury Report* (see **6.5** above) suggested that, in these circumstance, the best measure of the pension entitlement earned by an individual director during the year was the present value of the additional entitlement earned as a result of the additional length of service, any increase in salary and any changes in the scheme, less any pension contributions made by the director during the period. The *Report* also recommended that any major changes compared with the previous year should be explained. These recommendations did not totally solve the problem, however, as there are two possible methods of calculating pension entitlement: the accrued benefit method and the transfer value method. A consultation exercise did not produce any clear consensus on which approach should be used for disclosure purposes – directors and companies were generally in favour of the accrued benefit method, whilst investors and their representatives generally preferred the transfer value method. The Faculty of Actuaries and the Institute of Actuaries therefore put forward recommendations proposing two separate disclosures for each director:

- the increase in his/her accrued pension entitlement, excluding any annual inflation adjustment made to all deferred pensions; and
- the transfer value of the increased benefit, disclosed either as a figure calculated on the basis of actuarial advice, or by giving sufficient information for shareholders to make a reasonable assessment of the value.

These recommendations were accepted by the FSA and were incorporated in the *Listing Rules,* together with a requirement to disclose the total accrued pension entitlement of each director at the end of the financial year. They have now also been included in the *Directors' Remuneration Report Regulations 2002.*

23.50   *Disclosure of Transfer Value*

Where a transfer value is disclosed, it should be calculated in accordance with *Actuarial Guidance Note 11* (GN 11) but should not include any deduction for underfunding. Companies may wish to make clear in the report that transfer values represent a liability of the company, not sums paid (or due) to the individual directors.

23.51   *Disclosure of Additional Information*

Where the company adopts the approach of providing additional information, this should normally include:

- the current age of the director;
- the normal retirement age of the director;
- any contributions paid or payable by the director during the year under the terms of the scheme;
- details of spouse and dependants' benefits;
- details of early retirement rights and options, and expectations of pension increases after retirement (whether guaranteed or not); and
- discretionary benefits for which allowance is made in transfer values on leaving, and any other relevant information which will significantly affect the value of benefits.

Voluntary contributions and benefits should not be included in any of these disclosures.

23.52   Disclosure Under FSA Listing Rules

Under the current FSA *Listing Rules*, certain additional disclosures are required in respect of directors' remuneration, in particular an explanation of, and justification for:

- any element of remuneration (other than basic salary) that is pensionable; and
- any service contracts which provide for, or imply, notice periods in excess of one year or which include provisions for compensation exceeding one year's salary and benefits.

23.53   Summary Financial Statements

The provisions of *CA 1985* on summary financial statements require, in the case of a quoted company, the inclusion of either the whole of the directors' remuneration report or, as a minimum:

- aggregate information on directors' remuneration (see **23.33** above);
- the statement of the company's policy on directors' remuneration for future years; and
- the performance graph summarizing shareholder return.

Further information on summary financial statements, which can now be prepared by all companies, subject to certain conditions, can be found at **11.99** above.

23.54   Directors' Remuneration: Unquoted Companies

At a Glance
- * Unquoted companies are generally required to give details of the number of directors who exercised share options during the year and who received shares under long-term incentive schemes during the year.
- * They must also disclose the aggregate of amounts payable under long-term incentive schemes during the year and the net value of any assets receivable by directors under such schemes.
- * Unquoted companies are also generally required to give details of the remuneration of the highest paid director, and additional information on compensation for loss of office and any excess retirement benefits paid to directors and former directors.
- * The accounts must also disclose the aggregate amount paid to, or receivable by, third parties for making available the services of any person as a director.

23.55   Additional Disclosures for Unquoted Companies

As explained in **23.31** above, *CA 1985* sets out basic disclosure requirements on directors' emoluments and pensions that apply to all companies and then distinguishes between quoted and unquoted companies in respect of certain more detailed disclosures. In the case of unquoted companies, the following details must be given in addition to those summarised in **23.33** above:

- the number of directors who exercised share options during the year;
- the number of directors who received shares during the year under long-term incentive schemes in respect of qualifying services; and
- the aggregate of the amounts paid to, or receivable by, directors under long-term incentive schemes in respect of qualifying services and the net value of any assets (other than cash, share options or shares) receivable by directors under such schemes.

The distinction made between quoted and unquoted companies avoids the need for unquoted companies to value shares granted to directors under long-term incentive schemes and to calculate gains made by directors on the exercise of share options. Companies that qualify as small need not give these additional disclosures, although the aggregate amount payable under long-term incentive schemes must be included in the overall emoluments disclosure (see **23.34** above).

23.56   Highest Paid Director

Where the aggregate of emoluments and amounts receivable by directors under long-term incentive schemes (other than shares and share options) exceeds £200,000, an unquoted company must give the following details:

- the amount, in total, that relates to the highest paid director;
- whether the highest paid director exercised any share options during the year;
- whether the highest paid director received any shares during the year in respect of qualifying services under a long-term incentive scheme;
- the amount of any company pension contributions to money purchase schemes for that director; and
- if retirement benefits may be payable to this director under a defined benefit scheme, his accrued pension at the end of the year and, where applicable, the amount of any accrued lump sum under the scheme.

The Act includes specific provisions on how accrued pensions and accrued lump sum entitlements should be calculated. Companies that qualify as small need not give these additional disclosures.

23.57   Compensation for Loss of Office

The aggregate compensation for loss of office paid to, or receivable by, directors and former directors must also be disclosed by all unquoted companies, regardless of size. Compensation for loss of office constitutes a separate category of payment to directors and should not be included in the figure for directors' emoluments for the period. Where compensation payments include non-cash benefits, these should be included in the disclosures at their estimated money value and the nature of the benefit must be disclosed. Compensation payments to directors may also require shareholder approval under *CA 1985*, although this is not usually required for genuine payments in respect of damages for breach of contract or for pensions in respect of past services. If significant non-cash items are included, the compensation payments may also require approval under the provisions on substantial property transactions in *section 320* of *CA 1985*. Where a retired director continues to have an involvement with the company in a part-time or consultancy capacity, any payments in excess of normal market rates for the work performed may well include an element of compensation for loss of office, in which case the details should be disclosed.

23.58   Excess Retirement Benefits

CA 1985 also requires disclosure of certain retirement benefits paid to directors and former directors that are in excess of the amount to which they became entitled on retirement (or on 31 March 1997, if later), although there is an exemption for general increases received by all members of a retirement scheme and for amounts that can be met without recourse to additional contributions.

23.59   Payments to Third Parties

The accounts of all unquoted companies must also disclose the aggregate amount paid to, or receivable by, third parties for making available the services of any person as a director of the company or otherwise in connection with the management of the affairs of the company or group. The most common example of this is an arrangement whereby a substantial investor in a company (eg a bank or venture capital company) has the right to appoint a director to the board of the investee company and payment for the services of this director is made to the investor rather than to the director himself.

Remuneration

Appendix 1

Useful Websites on Remuneration Issues

Chartered Institute of Personnel and Development	www.cipd.co.uk
Business Link	www.businesslink.gov.uk
Institute of Directors	www.iod.com
Department for Work and Pensions	www.dwp.gov.uk
HM Revenue and Customs	www.hmrc.gov.uk
ICAEW Tax Faculty	www.icaew.co.uk/taxfac
Chartered Institute of Taxation	www.tax.org.uk
Vehicle Certification Agency	www.vca.gov.uk
Society of Motor Manufacturers and Traders	www.smmt.co.uk
Accounting Standards Board	www.frc.org.uk/asb

Appendix 2

Directors' Remuneration Report Checklist

This checklist is based on the requirements of *Schedule 7A* of *CA 1985*, which apply for accounting periods ending on or after 31 December 2002, and the current FSA *Listing Rules*. For earlier periods, equivalent disclosures were recommended under the *Combined Code*. The second column indicates the origin of the disclosure requirement. Additional details may need to be given, depending on the specific circumstances of the company.

A   Contents subject to audit

The following information must be disclosed and is subject to audit:

☐   For each director who served during the financial year, and in tabular form, the total amount of:
Sch 7A, 6(1)–(2) & (4)
FSA LR 9.8.8(2)

- salary and/or fees;
- bonuses;
- expense allowances that are chargeable to UK income tax;
- any compensation for loss of office and similar payments;
- the estimated money value of any benefits in kind; and
- the sum total of all these amounts, and the equivalent total for the previous financial year.

☐   The nature of any element of a remuneration package which is not cash.
Sch 7A, 6(3)

☐   For each director who served during the financial year, and in tabular form, the number of shares subject to a share option (distinguishing between those with different terms and conditions) at:
Sch 7A, 7, 8(a)
FSA LR 9.8.8(2)

- the beginning of the year, or the date of appointment if later;
- the end of the year, or the date of ceasing to be a director if earlier.

☐   Information on share options awarded, exercised and lapsed during the year,
Sch 7A, 8(b) & (d)
FSA LR 9.8.8(2)

and any variations to terms and conditions of a share option.

☐ For each share option that was unexpired at any time during the year: *Sch 7A, 89(c)* *FSA LR 9.8.8(2)*

- the price (if any) paid for its award;
- the exercise prices;
- the date from which the option can be exercised; and
- the date on which the option expires.

☐ A summary of any performance criteria upon which the award or exercise of a share option is conditional, and any changes made in the year.   *Sch 7A, 8(e)* *FSA LR 9.8.8(2)*

☐ For any share option exercised during the year, the market price at the time of exercise.   *Sch 7A, 8(f)* *FSA LR 9.8.8(2)*

☐ For each share option that was unexpired at the end of the financial year: *Sch 7A, 8(g)* *FSA LR 9.8.8(2)*

- the market price at the year-end date; and
- the highest and lowest market price during the year.

☐ For each director who served during the financial year, details of interests in long-term incentive schemes, showing: *Sch 7A, 10, 11(a)–(c)* *FSA LR 9.8.8(3)–(6)*

- interests at the beginning of the year, or the date of appointment if later;
- awards during the year, showing whether they crystallise in the year or in subsequent years;
- the money value and number of shares, cash payments or other benefits received during the year; and
- interests at the end of the year, or on ceasing to be a director if earlier.

☐ For each disclosed interest in long-term incentive schemes, the date by which the qualifying conditions have to be fulfilled and details of any variations in the terms and conditions made during the year.   *Sch 7A, 11(1)(d)*

☐ If shares may become receivable in respect of an interest awarded during the year: *Sch 7A, 11(2)*

- the number of those shares;
- the market price of the shares at the time of the award; and

- details of any qualifying conditions relating to performance.

☐ For each scheme interest that has vested during the year, details of any shares, the amount of any money and the value of any other assets that have become receivable as a result.

Sch 7A, 11(1)(e)

☐ If shares have become receivable as a result of an interest vesting during the year:

Sch 7A, 11(3)

- the number of those shares;
- the date on which the interest was awarded;
- the market price of the shares at the time of the award;
- the market price of the shares when the interest vested; and
- details of any qualifying conditions relating to performance.

☐ For each director who served during the financial year and has rights under a defined benefit retirement scheme:

Sch 7A, 12(2)
FSA LR 9.8.8(12)

- details of any changes during the year in their accrued benefits under the scheme;
- the accrued benefits at the end of the year;
- the transfer value of the accrued benefits, calculated as recommended by the Institute of Actuaries and Faculty of Actuaries (see **23.49** above);
- the equivalent transfer value at the end of the previous year; and
- the difference between the opening transfer value and the current transfer value, after deducting any contributions made by the director in the current year.

☐ For each director who served during the financial year and has rights under a money purchase retirement scheme, details of the contributions paid or payable by the company during the year.

Sch 7A, 12(3)
FSA LR 9.8.8(11)

☐ Details of certain excess retirement benefits paid to directors or former directors (see **23.58** above).

Sch 7A, 13

☐ Details of any significant awards to former directors (eg compensation for loss of office, pensions).

Sch 7A, 14
FSA LR 9.8.8(2)

Remuneration

☐ For each director who served during the   *Sch 7A, 15*
financial year, the aggregate amount of any
consideration (including any benefits in kind)
paid to, or receivable by, a third party for
making available the services of the individual
as a director.

B   Contents not subject to audit

The following information is required to be disclosed, but is not subject to audit:

☐ The names of the members of any   *Sch 7A, 2(a)–(c)*
committee that considered directors'
remuneration during the year and the names
of any other individuals (whether directors
or not) who provided advice or services to
that committee, together with details of the
nature of the advice or services.

☐ A statement of the company's policy on   *Sch 7A, 3(1) &*
directors' remuneration for the forthcoming   *(2)(a)–(d)*
year and for subsequent financial years,   *FSA LR 9.8.8(1)*
drawing attention to any factors specific to
the company – this must include for each
individual who has served as a director
between the end of the financial year under
review and the date on which the annual
reports and accounts are laid before
the members:

- a detailed summary of any performance
  conditions in respect of awards under
  share option or long-term incentive schemes;
- an explanation of why these performance
  conditions were chosen;
- a summary of the methods used in
  assessing whether the performance
  conditions are met, and why those
  methods were chosen;
- if any performance condition involves
  comparison with external factors, a
  summary of the factors to be used and the
  identity of any companies or index used
  for comparison purposes.

☐ A description of, and explanation for, any   *Sch 7A, 3(2)(e)*
significant changes to the terms and   *FSA LR 9.8.8(10)*

conditions of entitlement under share
option or long-term incentive schemes.

☐ An explanation of why any entitlements   *Sch 7A, 3(2)(f)*
under share option or long-term incentive
schemes are not subject to performance
conditions.

☐ A statement of the company's policy on   *FSA LR 9.8.8(10)*
the granting of options or awards under
employee share schemes and other
long-term incentive schemes and an
explanation and justification of any
departure from, or change in, that policy
during the year.

☐ The relative importance of elements of   *Sch 7A, 3(3)*
remuneration that are related to performance
and those that are not.

☐ A summary of the company's policy on the   *Sch 7A, 3(4)*
duration of directors' service contracts and
on notice periods and termination payments
under those contracts.

☐ The following information on the contract of   *Sch 7A, 5(1)*
service, or contract for services, of each
person who served as a director during the
financial year:

- date of the contract, the unexpired term
  and any notice period;
- any provision for compensation on early
  termination; and
- sufficient information on any other
  provisions to enable a member to estimate
  the company's liability in the event of early
  termination of the contract.

☐ The unexpired term of any director's service   *FSA LR 9.8.8(9)*
contract of a director proposed for election or
re-election at the forthcoming AGM, or if any
such director does not have a service contract,
a statement of that fact.

☐ Details of any service contracts which provide   *FSA LR 9.8.8(8)*
for, or imply, notice periods in excess of one
year, or which include provisions for
predetermined compensation which include
provisions for predetermined compensation

Remuneration

which exceeds one year's salary and benefits, together with an explanation of the reasons.

☐ An explanation for any significant awards during the year to former directors (eg compensation for loss of office, pensions).

Sch 7A, 5(2)

☐ An explanation of, and justification for, any elements of remuneration other than basic salary that are pensionable; and

FSA LR 9.8.8(7)

☐ a line graph showing the total shareholder return for the last five years on:

Sch 7A, 4

- a holding of the class of equity shares whose public trading has resulted in the company meeting the definition of a quoted company; and
- a hypothetical holding of shares, based on a broad equity market index, together with the name of the index and why it was chosen.

24

Sources of Finance

24 Sources of Finance

24.1 The Search for Finance

> **At a Glance**
> * The business development giving rise to the need for additional funding will often indicate the most appropriate source of finance.
> * Grant funding should always be considered, but this is unlikely to meet the full cost of any project.
> * It is generally unwise to attempt to finance major purchases or business development from a bank overdraft.
> * Any application for finance will need to demonstrate the credit-worthiness and viability of the business to the potential financier.
> * Issues such as overall cost, flexibility and level of security required will all need to be taken into account in deciding on the best option.

24.2 Planning the Search

Sound business structures and operations need to be financed properly, and there will come a time in the life of every business when additional funds are needed, either to purchase fixed assets, to fund a particular initiative or development within the business or to enable the strategic plan for the business to be put into place. The business development giving rise to the need for funding will usually indicate the most appropriate source of finance and the term of the finance should generally be matched as far as possible with the life of the asset or project. Grant funding should always be considered, although this is unlikely to meet the full cost of any project, so the business will usually need to raise some funds from other sources as well. Some form of loan finance, including options such as leasing, will usually be the most appropriate method of funding asset purchases, whereas funding from other investors may be needed to finance the longer-term development of the business. It is generally unwise to attempt to finance major purchases or business development from a bank overdraft – the rate of interest will usually be unacceptably high and overdrafts are repayable on demand, so the bank would be able to withdraw the facility at any time if it was unsatisfied with the progress or management of the business.

24.3   Demonstrating Credit-worthiness

Any application for finance, be it for loan, investment or grant funding, will need to demonstrate the credit-worthiness and viability of the business to the potential financier. A lender will be looking for assurances that interest payments can be met and that the loan can be repaid when due. An investor will seek assurance that the business is properly managed and that there is a strong possibility of a good return on the investment (as well as repayment of the investment itself). Grant-making bodies will usually look for confirmation that the business is viable and also meets the criteria and objectives of the grant scheme. Most financiers will want to see a detailed business plan and cashflow projections, together with evidence of sound management and accounting practices. Further guidance on the preparation of business plans and cashflow forecasts is given in **25 STRATEGIC PLANNING** and **2 CASHFLOW MANAGEMENT**.

24.4   Carrying Out the Search

Checklist

Once the need for additional finance has been identified, the following steps should be taken:

✓   define precisely what funding is needed and why;

✓   establish which funding options are potentially available – in particular, check whether any grants might be available;

✓   explore which of these options are likely to be the most appropriate, taking professional advice if necessary;

✓   select a sample of potential financiers and contact them to discuss pricing and deal terms;

✓   select the most favourable option, based on issues such as overall cost, flexibility of the package, level of security required and any other issues of particular concern to the business; and

✓   check that the business plan and cashflow forecast can support the cost of the chosen option.

24.5   Borrowing

At a Glance
* Debt finance is usually seen as more accessible than investment finance, and generally requires a lower level of accountability.

* Banks are still seen as the most important source of debt finance for business, but it is always worth exploring other options and other finance providers.
* A bank term loan may be a good option, especially if the repayment period can be linked to the life of an asset or project.
* A commercial mortgage is usually most suitable for the purchase of property, but may not cover the full cost.
* For a new property, a build and finance deal may be available through the construction company.
* The Small Firms Loan Guarantee Scheme helps small businesses who are unable to obtain conventional loans because of a lack of security.
* Factoring or invoice discounting can be used to boost cashflow but is not a suitable means of raising finance for capital or longer-term projects.

24.6   Advantages and Disadvantages

Debt financing is often seen as more accessible than investment finance and as generally requiring a lower level of accountability. For instance, although a lender may require regular financial information from the borrower, it is likely that there will be less direct input into the management of the business than in the case of an equity investor. This can be attractive to entrepreneurs who do not want to relinquish a degree of control over the business. Banks are still seen as the most important source of finance for business and the importance of developing and maintaining a good relationship with the company's bankers should not be overlooked. However, when seeking additional finance it is always worth exploring other options and finance providers (including other banks), if only for comparison purposes. The choice of lender, particularly for more substantial borrowings, needs careful thought and research, taking into account issues such as:

* the level of service provided;
* the speed with which the loan can be arranged;
* security requirements, including any requests for personal guarantees (which should be avoided if at all possible);
* heavy redemption penalties;
* mandatory insurance policies;
* any other commitments demanded which might be disadvantageous (eg a requirement for business banking to be maintained with the same bank); and
* any hidden charges.

Interest rates will inevitably be an important issue as well, but should not be considered in isolation from the above.

24.7   Bank Loan

Although bank overdrafts are not usually suitable for financing asset purchases, a bank term loan may be a good option, especially if the repayment period can

Sources of Finance

be related to the life of the asset. The regular financial commitment is usually known in advance and the loan will not become repayable on demand unless clauses or covenants are breached. Interest rates may be fixed or variable, or capped for an agreed period of time. Security may be an issue with this form of finance, especially if it is used to fund the purchase of plant and equipment whose secondhand value may not be sufficient to cover the debt. In these circumstances, the bank will look for security on other assets and possibly through personal guarantees.

24.8 Commercial Mortgage Loan

A commercial mortgage is a loan secured against a specific asset and is usually most suitable for a property purchase, although mortgage loans may be available for the acquisition of substantial plant and equipment. Banks may only be prepared to offer a limited term on a commercial mortgage, and the potential repayment of the loan can therefore put quite a strain on the business. Also, a mortgage loan will not usually cover the full cost (for instance, it may be restricted to 70 per cent of the asset value) so that the business may need to fund a substantial element from other sources. As with term loans, interest rates may be fixed, variable or capped for an agreed period.

24.9 Build and Finance Arrangement

Where a new property is constructed, finance may be available through the construction company by means of a build and finance deal. Basically, this takes the form of a design and build contract, with the construction company selling the completed asset on to a property company and the business renting it from this company.

24.10 Small Firms Loan Guarantee Scheme

The Small Firms Loan Guarantee Scheme guarantees loans from banks and other financiers to small businesses who are unable to obtain a conventional loan because of a lack of security. A number of changes were made to the scheme with effect from 1 December 2005 and the Government hopes that more lenders will be encouraged to participate as a result. Loans of £5,000 to £250,000 can be made available under the scheme for periods of two to ten years. The Small Business Service (SBS) guarantees 75 per cent of the loan and a premium of 2 per cent per annum is payable to the SBS for the provision of this guarantee. The company must have annual turnover of no more than £5.6 million and have operated for less than five years. This is to help ensure that funding under the scheme is directed towards start-ups and young businesses. Some business activities or projects are specifically excluded from the scheme. Information can be obtained from the Small Business Service, 1 Victoria Street, London SW1H 0ET (*tel:* 020 7215 5363; *web:* www.sbs.gov.uk).

24.11   Factoring/Invoice Discounting

Factoring and invoice discounting is now an established means of financing a growing business. It is not a suitable way of raising finance for capital or long-term investment but it can be used to boost the cashflow of a business and therefore release additional working capital, or possibly to provide funds for an investment project that will generate increased sales. The finance raised by factoring or invoice discounting is based on debtors and is therefore linked strongly to sales, so it can have the advantage that the funding available grows along with the business. Some factoring companies have expanded their business so that they can now offer cash against a combination of debtors, stock, plant and buildings in certain circumstances, but they will usually look for additional reassurance on the viability of the business before agreeing to such an arrangement. Information on this form of finance is available from the Factors and Discounters Association (*tel:* 020 8332 9955; *web:* www.thefda.org.uk).

24.12   Leasing and Similar Arrangements

At a Glance
* Hire purchase is a well-established method of asset-based finance – it is usually readily available, easy to arrange and the cost to the business is clear from the outset.
* Leasing agreements can be complex legal documents and it is essential to check all the underlying details and ensure that the implications are fully understood before accepting the commitment.
* Leasing agreements come in two basic forms – finance leases and operating leases.
* A lessee under a finance lease will usually need to recognise the leased asset as a fixed asset and to reflect the outstanding liability to the lessor in the balance sheet.
* Operating leases can be particularly useful for acquiring assets that are subject to regular technological change.
* Contract hire is a common form of operating lease for motor vehicles.
* Certain manufacturers or dealers provide finance for the purchase of their own products – this is particularly common in the IT field and motor dealerships.
* A sale and leaseback arrangement can be used to release funds tied up in a major asset.

Sources of Finance

24.13   Decision to Use Asset-based Finance

Before deciding to use any form of asset-based financing, it is important to consider whether the acquisition of the asset will have both short-term and long-term benefits for the business, whether the additional commitment might put an unmanageable financial burden on business and whether the period of the lease or similar arrangement is appropriate for the asset in question. As with any form of loan finance, it is also important to prepare cashflow projections for the period of the lease to confirm that the business can meet the financial commitment required.

24.14   Hire Purchase

Hire purchase is a well-established method of asset-based finance. It will usually involve the payment of an initial deposit, with the balance of the asset cost, and interest on the borrowing, payable over a specified period of time. The finance company purchases the asset on behalf of the customer and remains the legal owner until the final instalment under the agreement has been paid. The financier can therefore reclaim the asset if the payments are not met. This form of finance is readily available and usually easy to arrange, and the financial commitment for the business is clear from the outset. The transaction is secured on the relevant asset and no additional commitments are usually required, especially as the borrowing is repaid over a relatively short timespan. An asset purchased under a hire purchase agreement will usually be accounted for in the same way as an asset acquired by outright purchase, with the total due to the finance company shown as a liability in the balance sheet.

24.15   Leasing

A lease is a contract between the lessor and lessee under which the lessor buys and owns the asset and hires it to the lessee for rental payments over a predetermined period. The lessor can sometimes claim capital allowances on the asset and, if so, will usually pass the benefit on to the lessee in the form of reduced rentals.

Once again the arrangement gives a degree of certainty over the financial commitment that the business is undertaking, but lease agreements can be complex legal documents and it is essential to check all the details and understand all aspects of the transaction before accepting the commitment. If there is any doubt over the meaning or practical effect of certain terms in the contract, it will usually be advisable to take professional advice. In many cases, the lease payments will be spread evenly over the term of the lease, but some arrangements involve a lump sum payment at either the beginning or the end of the contract. Leases come in two basic forms, although with the complexity of some arrangements these days, there can be a number of grey areas.

- *Finance lease:* Under a finance lease, the amount payable by the lessee will cover all or most of the cost of the asset, together with the financing charges raised by the lessor. The lessee will have the use of the asset for all or most of its useful life and to all intents and purposes will be treated as the owner of the asset, even though the lessor may hold legal title. The lessee will usually need to account for the asset as a fixed asset and reflect the outstanding commitment to the lessor as a liability in the balance sheet.

- *Operating lease:* An operating lease will not usually cover the full useful life of the asset and the amount paid by the lessee will often be substantially less than the full value of the asset. The asset will be returned to the lessor at the end of the lease and the lessor will assume any residual risk (eg that the realisable value of the asset is lower than anticipated). Operating leases can be particularly useful for acquiring assets that are subject to regular technological advances, as the lessee will have the opportunity to upgrade to a newer technology at the end of the lease. Contract hire is a particularly common form of operating lease, especially for motor vehicles. Many property leases will also be classified as operating leases. At present, operating leases are usually accounted for by charging the rentals on a straight-line or other more appropriate basis over the term of the lease, but changes put forward in the Accounting Standards Board ('ASB') Discussion Paper *Leases: Implementation of a New Approach* and a subsequent joint project with the IASB would make significant changes in this area and require certain assets and liabilities created by operating leases to be recognised on the balance sheet in the same way as those created by finance leases (for information on obtaining copies see the ASB website at www.frc.org.uk/asb).

Leasing is a competitive market and it is important to shop around, although where substantial and regular leasing arrangements are anticipated a good relationship with a financier can be helpful. Leasing arrangements are usually provided by the major banks, finance houses and certain manufacturers (see **24.16** below). Some leasing companies specialise in start-up or early-stage businesses. Members of the Finance and Leasing Association are expected to operate within an established code of conduct – full details can be obtained from the Association at 2nd Floor, Imperial House, 15–19 Kingsway, London WC2B 6UN (*tel:* 020 7836 6511; *web:* www.fla.org.uk).

24.16   Manufacturer/Dealer Leases

Certain manufacturers and dealers provide finance for the purchase of their own products – this is particularly common in the IT field and in motor dealerships. A manufacturer or dealer lease can be quite cost effective as it is intended to act as an additional incentive to buy the product. The main disadvantage is usually the restriction on choice.

24.17   Sale and Leaseback Arrangement

A sale and leaseback arrangement can be used to release funds that are tied up in a major asset, such as a property. The business sells the property to the financier and then leases it back at a commercial rental. The company benefits from an injection of cash and spreads the cost over the term of the leaseback arrangement. There is a potential disadvantage in that the business may lose a valuable asset, although the arrangement can often include a commitment or option to repurchase at some point in the future. The accounting treatment of a sale and repurchase transaction will depend on the detailed terms of the contract – if the substance of the transaction is that of a secured loan, the property will remain on the balance sheet together with the liability to the 'lender'.

24.18   Equity

At a Glance
* A business may be able to raise additional finance through the issue or sale of equity capital, although entrepreneurs often see a serious disadvantage in losing an element of control.
* Business angels are successful business people who are prepared to take an equity stake in a business – they may invest alone or as part of small group.
* The ideal candidate for a business angel is a business with a good product or service and a capable management team, but which needs help with strategic issues and finance in order to grow.
* Business angels will normally expect to realise their investment in four to seven years.
* Venture capital finance is designed to help a business grow, and a higher level of funding will usually be available from this source.
* Venture capitalists normally look for rapid growth rates and are therefore particularly interested in innovative projects that create a new market.
* As with business angels, it is important to consider the potential exit routes for the investor.
* Flotation on the Alternative Investment Market (AIM) or the London Stock Exchange might be possible where more substantial levels of capital are required.
* The procedures for flotation are complex, and appropriate professional advice should be sought at an early stage.
* The reporting requirements for, and other expectations of, quoted companies are considerably more stringent than those for private companies.
* The Government has introduced a number of measures aimed at bridging the finance gap experienced by small businesses.

24.19   Options for Raising Capital from Equity

It may be possible for a business to raise additional finance through the issue or sale of equity capital – this method is most likely to be used to fund the strategic growth and development of a business. A potential disadvantage of this route for many entrepreneurs will be the concept of losing an element of control over the business, as most investors taking an equity stake in a private company will expect to have some direct involvement in the business. For raising more substantial levels of capital, a flotation might be considered, either on the Alternative Investment Market or the full Stock Exchange.

24.20   Business Angels

Business angels are wealthy individuals, mainly successful business people in their own right, who are prepared to take an equity stake in a business, most commonly one based locally or in a sector in which they already have some experience. Business angels may invest alone or as part of a small group of investors and their motivations for doing so will often be diverse. They will usually expect to have a direct, hands-on approach to the investment, which some businesses may find intrusive but which can in fact be of tremendous help to a growing business. As well as extensive personal experience, a business angel will often provide access to a strong network of business contacts. There may also be less pressure to provide a quick return on this form of investment. Wider factors such as personal chemistry between the business angel and the existing management team are also of critical importance. Business angels usually invest primarily in start-ups and early-stage businesses and the cash investment that they provide allows the business to expand, develop or make other planned changes. Many businesses make the mistake of borrowing as much as they can first, often at prohibitive interest rates, and only looking for alternative sources of finance when they no longer constitute an attractive investment. The ideal candidate for a business angel is a business with a good product or service and a capable management team, but which needs help with strategic issues and additional capital in order to take the next step in growing the business. Potential investors will expect to examine information about the business, including business plans and projected cashflows, but their reviews will generally not be as detailed or as rigorous as those of (say) venture capitalists. Individual business angels will usually expect to invest up to £50,000, although a larger investment will be possible where a group of individuals is involved. They will normally expect to realise their investment in around 4 to 7 years, usually by means of a trade sale (eg to another business), a sale to existing shareholders or a sale to a third party. A company wishing to pursue this form of investment should contact the British Business Angels Association, New City Court, 20 St Thomas Street, London SE1 9RS (*tel:* 0207 089 2305; *fax:* 0207 089 2301; *web:* www.bbaa.org.uk).

24.21   Venture Capital

Venture capital finance is funding that is designed to grow a business, and a higher level of funding will usually be available than from most other sources. Certain venture capitalists specialise in funding businesses at a particular stage in their development, or in providing finance to particular business sectors, whilst others are more general in their approach. The principal stages in the life of a business, and the corresponding finance that may be sought from a venture capitalist, are:

- *Seed finance* – this is provided before a business has started up, to enable an initial business concept to be researched, assessed and, if appropriate, developed;
- *Start-up finance* – this is provided to companies that are in the process of being set up, or have been in business for a short time but have not sold their product or service commercially, to assist with development and initial marketing;
- *Early-stage finance* – this is provided to companies that have successfully completed the development stage, but require further funds to begin commercial production or sale;
- *Expansion finance (or development finance)* – this is provided to companies that are already breaking even or trading profitably, to assist with growth and expansion of the business;
- *Mezzanine finance (or bridge finance)* – this is made available to a privately owned company that is in the process of becoming publicly quoted;
- *Management buy-out finance* – this is provided to an existing management team to enable them to acquire the business in which they are currently working;
- *Management buy-in finance* – this is provided to a group of managers (or possibly to an individual manager) from outside the business to enable them to buy into the company.

A potential venture capital investor will carry out a detailed examination of the business to assess the potential risks and rewards before committing to the investment, and will assess the management team, to determine whether it has the skills and ability to take the business forward. As with business angels, a venture capitalist will often expect to have a direct involvement in the running of the business and will bring valuable experience and a network of business contacts. Venture capitalists will normally look for a rapid growth rate and are therefore particularly interested in innovative projects that create a new market, preferably with limited competition. Once an investment has been made, they will monitor performance very closely and some businesses may again see this as interference and loss of control. As with business angels, it is important to consider the potential exit routes for the investor, which will usually be one of the following:

- trade sale (eg to another company);
- repurchase of the investment by the company and/or its existing owner-managers (subject to *Companies Act 1985* requirements);
- sale to another investment institution; or
- flotation of the company.

Inevitably there will also be certain investments that fail. Businesses seeking venture capital finance should consult the British Venture Capitalist Association (*tel:* 020 7025 2950; *web:* www.bvca.co.uk) for further information.

24.22   Flotation

Raising equity capital from the public may also be an option for some companies – this can be done by placing shares through an issuing house, by entry to the Alternative Investment Market or by full listing on the London Stock Exchange. The procedures for any of these are complex and can take time to put into place. Appropriate professional advice will always be needed and should be sought at an early stage. In any case where shares are issued to the public, stringent legal requirements on the provision of detailed information to potential investors come into effect, and for entry to one of the principal markets, the rules of the relevant listing authority must also be followed. Only a public limited company ('plc') can issue shares to the public, and such a company must have a minimum share capital of £50,000. Companies coming to one of the public markets will usually be expected to have a minimum of a three-year trading history. It should also be remembered that the reporting requirements for, and other expectations of, quoted companies are much more onerous than those for privately owned companies. See **18 LISTING REQUIREMENTS**.

24.23   Possible Future Developments

In April 2003, the Government published a consultation paper *Bridging the finance gap: A consultation on improving access to growth capital for small businesses*. This explored the difficulties that small businesses encounter in accessing modest amounts of equity capital and the causes of this finance gap, which is felt to be particularly acute for potential high-growth small businesses. Only a small minority of businesses are able to raise equity of more than £250,000 from private sources (including business angels), but commercial venture capitalists are often reluctant to invest less than £1 million. Since this consultation, various tax measures have been introduced with the aim of making the Enterprise Investment Scheme and Venture Capital Trusts more attractive to investors, and new sources of risk capital for smaller enterprises have been introduced through the Regional Venture Capital Fund and Early Growth Funds. Further details are available from the Small Business Service (www.sbs.gov.uk).

24.24   **Grants and Other Government-backed Funding**

At a Glance
* Grants can provide an excellent source of finance, especially for new and developing businesses, but the process for obtaining a grant can be slow and any grant offered will usually meet only part of the overall funding requirement.
* The DTI is the main source of information on government sponsored grants.

Sources of Finance

> * There are specific steps that a business can take to help with the smooth progress of a grant application.
> * EU Structural Funds provide support for projects to encourage economic regeneration in depressed or declining areas.
> * The DTI's Grant for Research and Development helps individuals and small and medium-sized businesses to research and develop technologically innovative products and processes.
> * Enterprise Grants are available to small and medium-sized businesses based in designated Enterprise Grant Areas.
> * Regional Selective Assistance grants encourage businesses to locate or expand in particular areas of the country.

24.25   Advantages and Disadvantages

Grants can be an excellent source of finance, particularly for new and developing businesses, and have the advantage that they are generally not repayable and rarely involve any loss of control over, or outside involvement in, the business. The disadvantage is that the process for obtaining a grant can be time-consuming and comparatively slow, and that any grants offered will invariably only meet part of the overall funding requirement. Only the main grant schemes are summarised below – there are a wealth of others, some of which apply to specific sectors and regions. Keeping up to date with the latest information can be one of the biggest problems. The DTI is the main source of information on government-sponsored grants (*tel:* 020 7215 5000; *web:* www.dti.gov.uk), together with the local Business Link. The Business Link website (www.businesslink.gov.uk/) includes a Business Support Directory intended to help businesses identify suitable grants and other forms of assistance.

Alternatively, the Enterprise Advisory Service offers a searchable database at www.govgrantsglobal.com at an annual cost of £59 plus VAT.

24.26   Applying for Grants

There are specific steps that a business can take to help with the smooth progress of a grant application. In particular:

- an application is more likely to be successful if it concentrates on a clearly defined project (including the benefits to the local community) for which assistance is being sought, rather than on individual items of equipment that will be purchased;
- an application may be more successful if it is submitted as soon as possible after the grant scheme becomes available, when there should be plenty of funds to allocate – hence the importance of keeping up to date with developments;
- the objectives of the funding body should be checked and the application should make clear how the proposed project satisfies these;

- the project should not be started until the grant application has been considered and a response received – under most schemes an application will only be accepted if the project will not go ahead without the grant; and
- if matched funding is a requirement, ensure that this is in place before the application is submitted and that full details are provided to the grant-making body.

Where an application is being made for a substantial grant, or where specific technical expertise or personal knowledge of the application process would be helpful, it may be worth seeking professional assistance. Personal contact with the grant provider can also be helpful.

24.27   EU Structural Funds

EU Structural Funds provide the main programme of grant support and provide funds for projects that will encourage economic regeneration in areas where a decline of traditional industries has led to serious economic and social problems. There are currently four structural funds:

- *European Regional Development Fund ('ERDF')* – this aims to reduce regional imbalances and assist disadvantaged regions;
- *European Social Fund ('ESF')* – this aims to improve employment opportunities by supporting the costs of running vocational training schemes, guidance and counselling projects, job creation measures and other processes to improve the skills and employment potential of both employed and unemployed individuals;
- *European Agricultural Guidance and Guarantee Fund ('EAGGF')* – this finances projects to assist the restructuring and diversification of rural areas to promote economic growth, whilst maintaining the environment and rural heritage;
- *Financial Instrument for Fisheries Guidance ('FIFG')* – this finances projects to modernise the structure of the fisheries sector and encourage diversification into other sectors.

A region may be eligible for access to one or more of these funds, depending on whether it has been assessed as an Objective 1, 2 or 3 area (all UK areas have at least Objective 3 status):

- *Objective 1* – covers the most deprived areas (in the UK, these currently include Merseyside, Cornwall and the Scilly Isles, West Wales, the Welsh Valleys and South Yorkshire);
- *Objective 2* – covers areas facing industrial decline, rural areas, urban areas and areas facing decline in the fishing industry;
- *Objective 3* – covers the provision of assistance to education, training and employment.

Any project which is being considered for funding will be scored against various criteria linked with these objectives – projects will not be expected to meet all criteria but must be clearly designed to meet the most relevant in the circumstances.

Sources of Finance

Even if all the relevant criteria are met, there is no guarantee that funding will be provided. The assessment will usually include consideration of whether the proposed project:

- provides good value for money;
- complies with statutory planning requirements, including nature conservation;
- has a sound funding package already in place, but would not succeed without additional EU grant aid;
- contributes to at least one of the primary objectives;
- delivers quantifiable outputs and sets clear and attainable targets; and
- is of strategic importance and strengthens local partnerships.

Grants will generally be only the minimum amount necessary to secure the project. Funding can be provided for up to 75 per cent of the cost, but this will usually only be given for projects in regions with Objective 1 status. ESF grants are usually for 45 per cent to 65 per cent of the project cost, and EAGGF and FIFG grants are usually for 25 per cent to 50 per cent of the project cost. Applications can generally be made at any time, although some monitoring committees have established bidding rounds, but they must be made on correctly completed standard application forms. Grants are usually paid in instalments, in line with the progress of the project. The current cycle of Structural Funds programmes comes to an end in 2006 and a new cycle of Structural Funds programmes will be introduced for 2007 to 2013.

24.28   Technology

The DTI Grant for Research and Development is intended to help individuals and small and medium-sized businesses to research and develop technologically innovative products and processes. Grants available under the new scheme include:

- 60 per cent of eligible project costs up to a maximum grant of £75,000 for research projects;
- 35 per cent of eligible project costs up to a maximum grant of £200,000 for development projects;
- 35 per cent of eligible project costs up to a maximum negotiable grant of £500,000 for exceptional development projects; and
- 50 per cent of eligible project costs up to a maximum grant of £20,000 for micro projects.

Collaborative Research and Development grants are also available as part of the DTI's Technology Programme, which is designed to reduce the costs of bringing research and new technologies to market. Research projects must involve two or more collaborators and the level of grant support varies from 25 per cent to 75 per cent of the related costs. Details of both schemes are available from the Business Link (www.businesslink.gov.uk/).

The EU Framework Programme is also designed to support collaborative research and innovations in science, engineering and technology. Projects must involve international collaboration and include European partners. Further details are available from the DTI website (www.dti.gov.uk) and through Business Link (www.businesslink.gov.uk).

24.29   Enterprise Grants

Enterprise Grants are available to small and medium-sized businesses based in designated Enterprise Grant Areas. The maximum grant available is £75,000 on projects with up to £500,000 of capital investment, and the grants are intended to complement the availability of commercial finance. Projects can involve expanding, modernising or restructuring an existing business or setting up a new one. There is no formal requirement for job creation, although this can help to secure support, but there must be assurance that no jobs will be lost as a direct result of the project. A business is generally not eligible for the grant if:

- 25 per cent or more of its capital or voting rights is owned by another business (or jointly by several businesses), although exceptions may apply where the investment is held by public investment corporations, venture capital companies, or institutional investors; or
- it was set up by an academic institution and the institution has a shareholding of 25 per cent or more.

Details are available from Business Link (www.businesslink.gov.uk/) or the Small Business Service (www.sbs.gov.uk).

24.30   Regional Selective Assistance

Regional Selective Assistance grants are available in those parts of country designated as Assisted Areas and are discretionary grants to encourage firms to locate or expand in these areas. Projects must either create new employment or safeguard existing jobs and include fixed capital expenditure of £500,000.

Sources of Finance

Appendix 1

Useful Websites on Sources of Finance

Small Business Service	www.sbs.gov.uk
Business Link	www.businesslink.gov.uk
The Factors and Discounters Association	www.thefda.org.uk/
The Finance and Leasing Association	www.fla.org
British Business Angels Association	www.bbaa.org.uk
British Venture Capitalist Association	www.bvca.co.uk
Enterprise Investment Scheme Association	www.eisa.org.uk
Enterprise Advisory Service	www.govgrantsglobal.com
Association of Corporate Treasurers	www.treasurers.org/
ICAEW Finance and Management Faculty	www.icaew.co.uk/fmfac

Strategic Planning

25 Strategic Planning

25.1 The Need for Strategic Management

> **At a Glance**
> * Strategic planning and management should be used to assess the potential of the business and agree on long-term goals.
> * Strategic planning usually focuses around key marketing and financial issues.
> * Strategic management workshops can help to secure the commitment and involvement of every member of the executive team, and to develop a clear sense of collective responsibility.

25.2 Building for the Future

If a business is to be truly successful and achieve its maximum potential, its development needs to be carefully planned – it is rare for growth and success to happen, or to be maintained, accidentally. Strategic planning and management is therefore used to assess the potential of the business, identify any likely obstacles to success and develop plans to counter these, and agree on the business and financial goals for the medium to long term. The energy of management and staff can then be clearly focused towards the priorities and goals that have been agreed by the executive. Evidence of good strategic planning can also be helpful in recruiting talented executives and specialist staff for the future.

25.3 Market and Financial Issues

Strategic planning is usually focused around key marketing and financial issues. For instance, in terms of the business market, attention will be concentrated around:

* the nature of the products or services offered and the potential to develop new initiatives;
* the present customer profile and how this can be developed; and

- the way in which products and services are currently provided and whether this will need to be changed.

Key financial issues will include:

- the level of funding that will be needed to meet business objectives;
- the expected profitability and cashflow profile of the business; and
- the level of financial return that will be achieved for investors.

Strategic planning is a complex and demanding exercise and it is important that the directors or executive team are prepared to commit the necessary time to it. A considerable amount of preliminary research and other preparation will usually be required, as well as the time that needs to be devoted to consideration and discussion of detailed issues.

25.4   Strategic Management Workshops

The chief executive has a critical role to play in planning the growth and development of the business, but for a strategic plan to be turned into reality, it is essential that all directors or members of the executive team develop the belief, commitment and enthusiasm to make the plan actually happen in practice. Strategic management workshops can be a powerful tool in securing the commitment and involvement of every member of board or executive team, and also in developing a clear sense of collective accountability, improving motivation and teamwork and helping directors and executives with particular functional responsibilities to develop a broader view of the overall needs of the business. The purpose of such workshops is to address the issues which are vital to the future success of the business. These might include:

- creating a vision for the success of the business;
- taking stock of the business and assessing the opportunities available;
- evaluating strategic objectives;
- setting a quantum leap to be achieved; and
- establishing relevant initiatives.

Each of these is explored in more detail below. Ideally, workshops should be held away from the business premises to prevent participants becoming distracted by day-to-day practicalities and to enable them to focus on the matters in hand. If a series of workshops is planned, it is particularly important that the first of these is seen to be productive and successful in order to maintain enthusiasm and momentum for the rest of the programme. Some businesses therefore find it helpful to use outside consultants, in the early stages of the programme at least. The following steps will usually help to ensure the success of a workshop:

- only issues of strategic importance should be considered;
- a background paper to each item on the agenda should be circulated in advance so that everyone has the opportunity to consider the issues in advance of the workshop;

- a summary of the agreements reached, decisions made and action required should be circulated promptly after the workshop.

A skilled chairman will be needed to encourage everyone to participate fully, and to encourage them to express their views honestly, but without damaging relationships through undue or excessive personal criticism.

25.5   Preparing a Detailed Strategic Plan

At a Glance

* The preparation of a detailed strategic plan provides an opportunity to carry out an objective assessment of potential business opportunities, trends and developments.
* The process should begin with the development of a concise vision statement.
* The next stage is to carry out an objective, critical and realistic assessment of current performance.
* If a business has reached a plateau in its development and growth, a quantum leap will usually be needed to maintain progress.
* Strategic options should be identified and evaluated for each major element of the business and for the business as a whole.
* The organisational structure of the business may also need to be reconsidered.
* The objective should be to achieve an organisational structure that meets the needs of the business and also makes best use of the resources available.
* A manageable programme of new initiatives should be established to work towards achievement of the vision.

25.6   Opportunity for Assessment

The preparation of a detailed strategic plan provides an ideal opportunity to carry out an objective assessment of potential business opportunities, trends and developments, so that the directors or executives can decide on how best to respond to these. The relevant issues will vary depending on the nature of the business, but they might include:

- opportunities to increase market share, obtain market leadership or create niche markets;
- new market segments or geographical areas that would provide good distribution channels or new business opportunities;
- the expected impact on the business of:
  - changes in the general economic climate (eg the impact of exchange rates),
  - political changes (eg new legislation or changes in government policy),

    ○ social developments (eg as a result of demographic trends),
    ○ technological developments (eg the growth of e-commerce), and
    ○ consumer concerns (eg a growing awareness of environmental issues);
- an assessment of the strength of competitors in terms of products and services (eg product/service range, pricing, development and innovation, marketing and public relations, customer service); and
- an assessment of the strengths and weaknesses of the present business in the same areas.

25.7   Preparation of a Vision Statement

The process should begin with the preparation of a concise, single-page vision statement describing where the directors or executives see the business in (say) five years' time. This might summarise:

- the markets or geographical areas where market leadership will be achieved, maintained or enhanced;
- new markets or geographical areas which will be entered, either by acquisition or through organic growth;
- how the business will be seen by its customers and potential customers and how it will be differentiated from its principal competitors;
- the business goals for that period;
- the broad financial goals for that period (eg return on investment, profits from a particular market or area, average increase in earnings per share each year);
- future ownership plans (eg succession plans, potential merger, stock market listing within a specified period).

This will obviously be a commercially sensitive and therefore confidential document available only to the directors or executives, but key elements of the vision should be shared with management in briefing and planning meetings.

25.8   Assessing Current Performance

The next stage is to carry out an objective, critical and realistic assessment of the current performance of the business, and to compare this with the performance of the principal competition. The aim of this assessment is to identify opportunities in the existing business which can be capitalised on, attractive niche markets which could be created, new areas that should be explored, the need for changes to pricing structures and/or performance levels and the opportunity or need to reduce costs. Depending on the nature and circumstances of the business, particular areas to consider might include:

- current and forecast market share;
- performance of each product or service group;
- gaps in the range of products or services offered;
- niche market opportunities which exist or could be created;
- attractive opportunities in other markets or geographical areas;

- current pricing and discount structures;
- speed of delivery and quality of after sales service;
- the level of complaints or warranty claims and the efficiency of the process for dealing with them;
- the value of business lost through an inability to supply required volumes or to supply in time;
- opportunities for achieving cost efficiencies by sub-contracting services rather than providing them in house;
- the extent of research and development activities, and the results achieved;
- the current return on investment;
- staff morale and retention levels.

25.9   The Quantum Leap

A quantum leap can be defined as a dramatic improvement in business performance without any significant increase in commercial risk. If a business has reached a plateau in its development and growth, a quantum leap will usually be needed in order to maintain progress. The directors or executives will therefore need to build this into their vision of the business. It may not be possible to achieve the quantum leap immediately, but it can be incorporated into the vision as a medium- or longer-term objective if the directors and executives:

- genuinely believe that it will be achieved;
- are committed to making the necessary effort;
- are prepared to deal with the setbacks that will almost inevitably arise; and
- have the enthusiasm to motivate other management and staff.

Even if achievement of the quantum leap is a longer-term objective, it will usually be possible to agree on initiatives that can be taken immediately to put the business into a position to achieve the leap in due course.

25.10   Strategic Options

The strategic options for the business need to be identified and evaluated, particularly if the vision includes a quantum leap. There will usually be a huge range of strategic options open to any business, and much will rest on the willingness of the directors and executives to be innovative and to explore all the potential options. Depending on circumstances, strategic options might include:

- developing a series of detailed marketing initiatives to develop contacts with prospective customers;
- acquisition of another business to gain market share quickly;
- floating the business, or a particular element of the business; or
- seeking a merger with a competitor.

Strategic options may need to be evaluated for each major element of the business (eg for each subsidiary, division or department) and as well as for the business as whole.

Strategic Planning

25.11   Organisational Structure

The organisational structure of a business can be an important element in its growth, development and future success – at the two extremes it will either ensure the achievement of the vision for the business, or create and encourage internal politics and thus hinder growth and development. It is rarely advantageous for a business structure to remain unchanged for any length of time and it can be helpful to stand back and reconsider what the optimum structure would be where a number of changes have been made or forced on the business over a period of time, particularly where a number of smaller structural changes have been made or forced on the business over a period of time. There is no standard or ideal organisational structure for a business. Once again the options need to be reviewed critically and objectively and the end result should be designed to facilitate achievement of the vision for that particular business. Key issues to consider include:

- the degree of autonomy that should be given to each business element or unit;
- the co-ordination of services to individual customers and the relationship between customers and business units – for instance, all possible steps should be taken to avoid a situation where different business units within a company or group are in effect competing for business with the same customer;
- how units and individuals will be accountable for the achievement of targets;
- how performance will be measured and monitored;
- the role and efficiency of any central administrative function.

25.12   Staffing Issues

Having established an optimum organisational structure for the business, the individual strengths and weaknesses of key managers and staff should be reviewed. Changes to the structure may need to be made to capitalise on the strengths of individuals and to compensate for their weaknesses. In some cases it may be necessary to recruit new managers and staff from external sources to fill any obvious gaps in expertise or management skills. The objective is to achieve an organisational structure that meets the needs of the business and also makes the best use of the resources available. This part of the strategic process will often generate a certain degree of resistance to change and may therefore need careful handling. Input from non-executive directors and external consultants can be particularly helpful, especially where vested interests might otherwise detract from the main issues.

25.13   New Initiatives

A manageable programme of new initiatives should be established to work towards achievement of the vision (eg major quality initiative, review of customer satisfaction levels, preliminary search for a partner or acquisition candidate).

A director or executive should be given specific responsibility for each initiative and realistic targets should be set, against which to measure performance over the next twelve months. The budget should make realistic provision for the costs of these initiatives.

25.14   Preparing a Business Plan

At a Glance
* The preparation of a detailed business plan should flow naturally from the strategic planning process.
* The business plan should turn the overall vision into more detailed financial projections for the next three to five years.
* The tone of the document should be positive, but it should include a realistic assessment of potential difficulties and how these will be handled.
* The executive summary should explain clearly and concisely the purpose of the plan.
* Specific areas to be covered in the plan include:
  ○ the history of the business,
  ○ main products and services,
  ○ customer base and market analysis,
  ○ operation of the business,
  ○ organisational structure,
  ○ management and staff,
  ○ ownership, and
  ○ financial analysis.
* Actual performance should be measured against the plan on a regular basis.
* The plan should also be updated to reflect any significant changes that have been agreed.

25.15   Use of Business Plans

The preparation of a detailed business plan should flow naturally from the strategic planning process, in that it summarises much of the information gathered in that process and turns the overall vision into more detailed financial projections for the next three to five years. A business plan may be prepared initially for internal use, but provided that it is kept up to date, it can be useful for external purposes as well – for instance, to assist in securing additional funding from a bank or from a potential investor, such as a business angel or venture capitalist (see **24.20 BUSINESS ANGELS** and **24.21 VENTURE CAPITAL**). A condensed form of business plan may also be prepared by individual business units or departments from time to time – for instance, to support a request for approval of a new project involving a significant financial outlay.

25.16   Contents of a Business Plan

The contents of a business plan will usually comprise:

- contents list;
- executive summary;
- business issues:
  - history of the business,
  - main products or services,
  - customer base and market analysis,
  - operation of the business,
  - organisational structure of the business,
  - management and staff,
  - ownership;
- financial information;
- detailed appendices.

The length of the document will usually depend on its purpose and the intended readership, but the aim should be to present the relevant information clearly and concisely and to avoid the use of internal jargon that may be unclear or ambiguous to those outside the business. Wherever possible, the report itself should contain only summarised information and the supporting detail should be included as an appendix. The tone of the document should be positive, but where appropriate it should include a realistic assessment of potential difficulties and the plans to deal with these.

25.17   Executive Summary

Particular care should be taken over the drafting of the executive summary. It should be no more than a single page and should explain clearly and concisely:

- the purpose of plan;
- the business and its markets;
- success factors to date;
- any additional funding now required;
- projected turnover and profits for three (or possibly five) years.

25.18   History of the Business

This section should summarise the key events in the history of the business to date and in particular the successes and objectives that it has achieved. These should be linked with the current plans and objectives.

25.19   Main Products or Services

This section will usually include a description of the main products or services supplied by the business, the competitive position of the business in the market place, and how the current plans will build on the latest position to achieve development, growth and further success. Depending on the nature of the business, this section might also describe any particular technological strengths of the business, any intellectual property held that is critical to the business (and how this is protected) and activities in the field of research and development, including for instance the development cycle for new products or services.

25.20   Customer Base and Market Analysis

This will usually be a crucial element of the plan – however attractive new products or services may seem, there will be little merit in the initiative if the business cannot successfully market these to its existing customer base or attract new customers. This section needs to provide an honest assessment of the market place and the competition and explain how the planned marketing activities will achieve the market share predicted. The detail might usefully include:

- background information on the relevant industry or business sector – for instance:
  - its principal characteristics,
  - the main customers,
  - demand for products or services supplied by the business,
  - expected trends and developments over next five years;
- description of the present and potential market for the products or services supplied by the business – for instance:
  - existing market and market share,
  - potential new markets (or new segments of existing markets), including where these are and how they are changing or developing,
  - profile of customers and potential customers, including particular buying patterns and other relevant issues, such as seasonal factors,
  - customer service demands (eg product reliability, product quality, technical expertise, price),
  - interest shown to date in new products or services;
- an honest appraisal of current and likely competitors – for instance:
  - who provides the main competition,
  - any expected changes in competition,
  - an objective assessment of the strengths and weaknesses of the main competitors,
  - how the business compares with the competition and why it will succeed in gaining customers and/or market share;
- plans for marketing the business's products or services – for instance:
  - detailed plans for promotion and advertising,
  - procedures to identify potential customers,
  - conversion of potential customers into actual customers,
  - proposed sales and business development techniques (eg franchises, e-commerce),
  - pricing issues, including discount schemes or other incentives,
  - after-sales service and support.

25.21   Operation of the Business

The section of the plan relating to operation of the business will need to cover issues such as:

- how the detailed business operations are (or will be) carried out;
- any key operating advantages that the business has;
- the present facilities and operating capacity of the business, and any planned changes;
- the cost implications of the planned increase in business activities;
- the extent to which the business is reliant on key suppliers and how any potential risk is managed; and
- the principal commercial risks and how these are managed and controlled.

25.22   Organisational Structure of the Business

As explained at **25.11** above, the choice of organisational structure for the business can be a critical issue. This section of the business plan should outline the present structure of the business and, where relevant, explain any planned changes or improvements, together with the benefits that these are expected to bring.

25.23   Management and Staff

The section on management and staff should:

- identify each of the directors and give brief details of their experience and particular expertise;
- identify the key managers in the business, again with brief details of their experience and particular skills;
- explain how the business plans to retain key members of the executive and management teams;
- present an organisation chart and summarise the staffing of other functions;
- outline the policies and plans of the business for the recruitment, retention and remuneration of staff.

25.24   Ownership

The ownership section should give brief details of the extent to which the business is owned by the directors, managers and staff and summarise any other main shareholdings.

25.25   Financial Analysis

Financial information should always be presented in an accessible way. Summarised information only should be included in the body of the report – the detail should be given in the appendices, so that users are able to refer to this if they wish, but it does not obscure the key features to be highlighted in the report. Information included in the body of the report should usually comprise:

- key financial data (usually turnover and profit) for the last three (or possibly five) years;
- projections of the same data for the next three (or five) years;
- a succinct commentary on the key aspects of the financial information given in the report and appendices – in the case of financial projections this should include details of the assumptions used;
- summarised balance sheet for three (or five) years;
- summarised cashflow information for three (or five) years, showing when any additional funding is likely to be needed;
- sensitivity analysis to illustrate the likely impact on profitability and cashflow of failure to achieve key elements of the projections, and how the business would be able to respond to this;
- details of when borrowings will be repaid, or how investors could exit from the arrangement.

25.26   Detailed Appendices

The appendices should include the detailed profit and loss account, balance sheet and cashflow projections for the next three (or five) years, as well as actual information for recent years, to support the summary financial information included in the report itself. The projections should be prepared on a monthly basis for at least the first year – quarterly projections will usually suffice for future periods. Copies of relevant legal documents should also be included in the appendices (for instance, to show the detailed terms of significant contracts to which the business is committed).

25.27   Regular Monitoring and Updating

Actual performance should be monitored against the business plan on a regular basis – some companies will need to do this monthly, but for others a quarterly review may be sufficient. The objective of this review is to identify any significant deviations from the plan so that the directors or executives can take appropriate action to put the business back on course. The plan should also be updated as necessary to reflect any significant changes that have been agreed. The financial projections will usually need to be updated on a fairly regular basis (eg quarterly), particularly as these will provide an early warning of any potential funding problems. The main narrative of the plan may only need to be updated once a year, unless the business is regularly exposed to significant and rapid change.

Appendix 1

Useful Websites on Corporate Strategy Issues

Business Link	www.businesslink.gov.uk
Institute of Directors	www.iod.com
Chartered Institute of Personnel and Development	www.cipd.co.uk
Institute of Chartered Accountants in England and Wales	www.icaew.co.uk
Chartered Institute of Management Accountants	www.cimaglobal.com

26

Taxation

26 Taxation

26.1 Sources of Tax Law

At a Glance
* Tax law is set out in a variety of Acts of Parliament, many of them long-standing.
* A major project is under way to rewrite existing tax law to make it more accessible and understandable.
* Increasing use is made of secondary legislation to make changes or introduce new requirements.
* HM Revenue and Customs issues various statements to clarify the application and interpretation of the legislation and to identify areas where some relaxation of the provisions may be permitted.
* Extensive guidance is also available on the HM Revenue and Customs website.

26.2 Principal Parliamentary Acts

The following principal Acts of Parliament comprise the primary legislation setting out current tax law:

* *Income and Corporation Taxes Act 1988*;
* *Taxation of Chargeable Gains Act 1992*;
* *Value Added Tax Act 1994*;
* *Taxes Management Act 1970*;
* *Capital Allowances Act 2001*;
* *Income Tax (Earnings and Pensions) Act 2003*;
* *Income Tax (Trading and Other Income) Act 2005*.

Separate legislation deals with inheritance tax and social security contributions and benefits. Income tax must be imposed each year through the *Finance Acts*, although other legislation ensures continuity of administration for this tax. The annual *Finance Acts* are also used to make amendments to the main statutes. Continuity of the payment or deduction of tax is ensured by the *Provisional Collection of Taxes Act 1968*.

26.3   Tax Law Rewrite

A major project is currently under way to rewrite existing tax law in plain English to make it more accessible and understandable. The following legislation has been issued to date as part of the project:

- *Capital Allowances Act 2001*;
- *Income Tax (Earnings and Pensions) Act 2003*;
- *Income Tax (Trading and Other Income) Act 2005*.

A further Income Tax Bill has been published for public consultation, with comments requested by 31 May 2006. This deals with

- the charge to income tax, income tax rates, the calculation of income tax liability and personal reliefs;
- various other income tax reliefs, including loss relief, the enterprise investment scheme, venture capital trusts, community investment tax relief, gift aid and the gift of assets to charities;
- rules relating to trusts, the deduction of tax at source, manufactured payments and tax avoidance; and
- definitions for general income tax purposes.

The new income tax legislation will be complete once this Bill has been enacted and work is then expected to begin on the rewrite of the legislation relating to corporation tax.

26.4   Regulations, Orders and Statutory Instruments

Increasing use is now made of secondary legislation, and the Treasury and HM Revenue and Customs are empowered to make orders and regulations, usually by way of statutory instrument, provided that the draft is approved by the House of Commons before issue, or the instrument is subject to annulment by resolution of either of the Houses of Parliament.

26.5   Other Pronouncements

HM Revenue and Customs also issues other statements on how certain rules should be applied, how the requirements of the legislation should be interpreted and areas where they are willing to allow some relaxation of statutory provisions, usually where strict adherence would give rise to practical and administrative difficulties. Such guidance is set out in the following:

- Statements of Practice;
- Decisions;
- Interpretations;

- Extra-statutory Concessions; and
- Press Releases.

Further discussion and guidance on topical issues can be found in *Tax Bulletin*, which is issued six times a year and is available from HM Revenue and Customs website at www.hmrc.gov.uk. HM Revenue and Customs internal guidance manuals are now also available on the website, as is information on obtaining copies of the guidance listed above.

26.6 Corporation Tax

At a Glance

* Corporation tax is chargeable on the profits and gains of a UK-resident company, regardless of where they arise.
* Companies not resident in the UK are chargeable to corporation tax on profits arising in the UK from a business or trade carried on through a branch or agency.
* The definition of a company for corporation tax purposes includes certain unincorporated associations.
* Corporation tax is chargeable at a fixed rate for each financial year, which runs from 1 April to 31 March.
* Corporation tax is assessed on profits and gains arising in a corporation tax accounting period, which cannot exceed twelve months.
* Under the Corporation Tax Self-Assessment ('CTSA') regime, each company is required to calculate its own tax liability and notify this to HM Revenue and Customs.
* HM Revenue and Customs has a fixed period in which to enquire into the details submitted, although its powers are much wider where negligent or fraudulent conduct is uncovered.
* There are various rates of corporation tax to help minimise the tax liability of smaller businesses.
* Companies who are liable to pay corporation tax at the full rate must pay their tax in quarterly instalments.
* Smaller companies must pay their tax within nine months of the end of the relevant accounting period.
* The payment of advance corporation tax (ACT) on distributions has been abolished, but companies are still permitted to offset any unused ACT against their corporation tax liabilities.

26.7 Charge to Corporation Tax

Corporation tax is chargeable on the profits and gains of a UK-resident company, regardless of where those profits and gains arise. Companies not resident in the UK are also chargeable to corporation tax on any profits arising in the UK from a business or trade carried on through a branch or agency here. A company incorporated in the UK will usually be resident in the UK for tax purposes, and a company incorporated elsewhere will usually be regarded as resident here if central management and control is exercised from the UK. Additional rules apply under certain double tax arrangements to prevent a company being treated as resident in two different places. The definition of a company for corporation tax purposes covers both a body corporate and also an unincorporated association, subject to certain exemptions. Partnerships are not subject to corporation tax – each partner is instead required to pay income tax on his/her share of the profits of the partnership. Profits include chargeable gains arising on the disposal of assets but not dividends and distributions from UK companies which have a tax credit attached and are classed as franked investment income.

26.8   Corporation Tax Accounting Periods

Corporation tax is assessed on profits arising in a corporation tax accounting period and is chargeable at the rate fixed for each financial year, which runs from 1 April to 31 March. Where an accounting period straddles two financial years and different tax rates apply in those years, the profits must be apportioned between the financial years in order to calculate the tax payable. A company's first accounting period begins on the date on which it begins trading – this may be the same as the date on which it was legally incorporated, but will often not be. An accounting period is deemed to end on the earliest of:

- twelve months from the date on which the accounting period commenced;
- the company's accounting reference date;
- the date on which trade ceases, or the company ceases to come within the charge to corporation tax; and
- the date on which the company ceases to be resident in the UK for corporation tax purposes.

For tax purposes, therefore, an accounting period cannot exceed twelve months. If a company is required to prepare statutory accounts for a period of more than twelve months (for instance, in the case of its first accounts or on a change of accounting reference date), that period will be broken down for corporation tax purposes into an initial accounting period of twelve months and a subsequent period of less than twelve months, covering the remaining months of the statutory accounting period and ending on the company's accounting reference date.

26.9   Corporation Tax Self-assessment ('CTSA')

The Corporation Tax Self-assessment ('CTSA') regime came into effect for accounting periods ending on or after 1 July 1999. Under this system, each company is required to calculate its own corporation tax liability, notify this to

HM Revenue and Customs using a standard return form, and pay the amount due by the required date. The standard CTSA return form is normally due for filing within twelve months of the end of the corporation tax accounting period, although different filing dates apply in certain circumstances. Documentation supporting the calculations and the entries on the return must be prepared and retained by the company. HM Revenue and Customs has a right of access to the supporting documentation and has a fixed period during which it may enquire into the details shown on the return. Once this period has expired (or, if an enquiry has been opened, once this has been formally completed) the company's tax liability should be fixed. However, if negligent or fraudulent conduct is uncovered, HM Revenue and Customs is empowered to issue discovery assessments or determinations at any time up to 21 years after the end of the accounting period in which the negligent or fraudulent conduct was found. In the case of other errors and omissions, the time limit is six years from the end of the relevant accounting period.

26.10   Rates of Corporation Tax

In recent years, there have been three rates of corporation tax – the starting rate, the small companies rate and the full rate. These are applied as follows:

- the *starting rate* applies to companies with taxable profits below £10,000;
- where a company's taxable profits are more than £10,000 but less than £50,000 a marginal rate of tax applies;
- the *small companies rate* applies to companies with taxable profits between £50,001 and £300,000;
- a further marginal rate of tax applies where profits are between £300,001 and £1.5 million; and
- the *full rate* applies to companies whose profits exceed £1.5 million.

Profits for these purposes include franked investment income. Where the accounting period is less than twelve months, the limits are reduced proportionally. Special rules also apply to reduce the thresholds where a company has associated companies for tax purposes. 'Associated companies' in this context generally means that one company is controlled by the other, or both are under the control of the same person or persons. Controlled foreign companies ('CFCs') and close investment-holding companies ('CICs' – see **26.19** below) are not eligible for the starting rate or the small companies rate.

A separate non corporate distribution (NCD) rate was also introduced from 1 April 2004. This was equivalent to the small company rate and applied to profits distributed to an individual or a partnership by a company whose underlying tax rate would otherwise be lower than the NCD rate. The practical effect was to ensure that the starting rate applied only to profits that were retained within the company or distributed to another company. With effect from 1 April 2006, the starting rate has been abolished and, as a result, the non-corporate distribution rate will no longer be required.

The corporation tax rates for the financial years beginning 1 April 2006 and 1 April 2007 are:

	2006/07	2005/06
Starting rate	N/A	0%
Non-corporate distribution rate	N/A	19%
Small companies' rate	19%	19%
Full rate	30%	30%

26.11   Payment of Corporation Tax

For accounting periods ending on or after 1 July 1999, companies who are liable to pay corporation tax at the full rate must pay their tax in quarterly instalments. The first payment must be made six months and fourteen days after the start of the accounting period, and subsequent payments are the due at three-monthly intervals. Transitional arrangements apply for the first four years to help companies adapt to the new regime. Small companies must pay their tax within nine months of the end of the relevant accounting period.

26.12   Advance Corporation Tax ('ACT')

Prior to 6 April 1999, a company was generally required to account for advance corporation tax ('ACT') whenever it made a qualifying distribution, such as the payment of a dividend. If it received a dividend or other distribution on which ACT had been paid, the tax credit on this receipt could be offset against the ACT payable by the company. Any net ACT paid by the company could then be offset against its mainstream corporation tax liability for the period, subject to certain conditions and restrictions. Provisions in the legislation allowed any surplus ACT to be carried back to reduce the tax liability of previous years, or to be carried forward and offset against the corporation tax liability of future accounting periods. This system was abolished with effect from 6 April 1999, although a shadow ACT system still operates to enable companies which still have surplus ACT carried forward to offset this against future corporation tax liabilities in the same way, and to the same extent, as under the previous arrangements.

26.13   Close Companies

At a Glance
* The close company legislation was introduced to prevent individuals avoiding higher rates of tax by retaining income in companies under their control, but much of the original legislation has now been repealed.

* A close company is basically a UK-resident company which is under the control of five or fewer participators, or under the control of participators who are also directors (regardless of number).
* When assessing control, the rights and powers of associates must be taken into account.
* Net payments incurred by a close company in providing benefits or facilities to participators or their associates are generally treated as distributions and are not tax deductible for the company.
* A loan made by a close company to a participator or their associate is generally chargeable to tax in the accounting period in which it was made.
* Tax relief is generally given when such a loan is repaid, released or written off.
* Special tax rules apply to close investment-holding companies ('CICs').

26.14 Background to Close Company Legislation

The close company legislation was originally introduced to prevent individuals avoiding higher rates of tax by retaining income in companies under their control. The original legislation taxed shareholders on certain undistributed income through an apportionment of that income, but this was repealed by the *Finance Act 1989*. However, the original provisions on loans to, and benefits obtained by, participators have been retained and new provisions apply to certain investment-holding companies. Certain restrictions also apply to payments made by a close company to a charity under the Gift Aid scheme.

26.15 Definition of a Close Company

A close company is basically a UK-resident company which is under the control of five or fewer participators, or under the control of participators who are also directors, regardless of number. A company is also a close company if more than half of its assets on a notional winding up could be distributed between five or fewer participators or between director participators. A participator is:

* any person who has, or is entitled to acquire, share capital or voting rights in the company;
* a person entitled to participate in distributions by the company;
* a person entitled to have the income or assets of the company applied for his/her benefit; or
* a loan creditor (other than a banker in respect of money lent in the ordinary course of business).

A director is any person who occupies the position of director, regardless of title, and any person on whose instructions or directions the directors are accustomed to act (except where advice is given solely in a professional capacity). A manager in the company who holds or controls at least 20 per cent of the ordinary share capital of the company, either alone or with associates, is also regarded as a director for these purposes. The legislation specifies certain companies that cannot be regarded as close companies (eg a company which is not UK resident, a quoted company where more than 35 per cent of the ordinary share voting rights are held by the public, and a registered industrial and provident society). However, where a non-resident company would be a close company if it were resident in the UK, any UK company which controls it is deemed to be a close company.

26.16   Control

The control tests are expressed in the context of a single person and control by more than one person must be assessed by aggregation. In making the assessments, the rights and powers of any associates must also be taken into account. A person has control of a company if he/she exercises, is able to exercise or is entitled to acquire, direct or indirect control over the company's policies and affairs and power to appoint or dismiss the directors by ordinary resolution. A person is also regarded as being in control of a company if he/she is entitled to acquire more than half of the nominal or issued share capital or voting power of the company, or if he/she holds, or is entitled to acquire, issued share capital with a right to recover more than half of the company's income should it all be distributed. A person who is entitled to more than half of the net assets distributable to participators in a winding up is also regarded as being in control of the company.

26.17   Benefits Provided to Participators

The net payments incurred by a close company in providing any benefits or facilities (including accommodation, entertainment and domestic services) to the participators or their associates are treated as distributions. They are taxable in the hands of the recipient but are not deductible by the company for corporation tax purposes. There are certain exceptions to this general rule, particularly in respect of retirement and death benefits.

26.18   Loans to Participators

If a close company makes a loan, either directly or indirectly, to a participator or an associate of a participator, other than in the ordinary course of business, the loan is chargeable to tax in the accounting period in which it was made. Technically, the provisions apply even if the loan was repaid in part or in full before the end of the accounting period, although relief will usually be available in these circumstances. A company is treated as making a loan if the recipient incurs a debt to the company or assigns to the company a debt owed to a third party. A debt incurred for the supply of goods and services by the company in the normal course of business is not treated as a loan unless the period of credit given is more than six months or more than the credit period normally given to the company's customers. Small loans (basically those up to £15,000) may be made to a full-time employee of the company (including a director) provided that the recipient, together with any associates, does not hold more than 5 per cent of the ordinary share capital. However, in the case of directors, the provisions of the *Companies Act 1985* will also need to be taken into account (see **8.23** GENERAL PROHIBITION ON LOANS TO DIRECTORS). Tax on the loan is generally payable nine months and one day after the end of the accounting period in which it was made. If the loan has been wholly or partly repaid by this time, the company can take the appropriate relief for this in paying any tax that is due. If the loan is repaid after this date, relief is not given until nine months after the end of the accounting period in which the repayment was made. Different payment arrangements apply to loans that were made in accounting periods ending on or before 31 March 1996. With effect from 6 April 1999, relief is given when a loan is released or written off as well as when it is repaid, although a tax charge may still arise in some circumstances.

26.19   Close Investment-holding Companies ('CICs')

A close investment-holding company ('CIC') is a close company that exists wholly or mainly for the purpose of investment. Trading companies, commercial property investment companies and group holding, finance or property investment companies are amongst those that do not fall to be treated as CICs. A CIC is not eligible for the starting or small companies' tax rates and HM Revenue and Customs can in some cases restrict the entitlement of certain individuals to a tax credit in respect of distributions made by a CIC.

26.20   VAT

At a Glance
* VAT is charged on taxable supplies of goods and services made by a taxable person in the ordinary course of business and on certain imports of goods and services.
* All of the taxable supplies made by a person must be aggregated in determining whether the registration threshold has been reached.
* HM Revenue and Customs must be notified within a specified time limit once the registration threshold has been reached.
* The system also permits voluntary registration and voluntary deregistration (when taxable supplies fall below the deregistration threshold), and requires deregistration in certain circumstances.
* Anything that is done or provided for consideration is a supply for VAT purposes, although certain transactions and events are specifically deemed not to be supplies.

* The time of supply determines the period in which the related VAT must be accounted for.
* There are currently four categories of taxable supply: standard rate, lower rate, zero rate and exempt.
* A business which makes both taxable and non-taxable supplies will be partially exempt and must apply an apportionment process to calculate recoverable input tax.
* A taxable person must retain detailed VAT records and supporting documentation for at least six years.
* Special schemes are available for smaller businesses to help with cash-flow and administration.
* Local VAT inspectors make periodic visits to trading premises to confirm that appropriate VAT records are being maintained and that VAT is being accounted for correctly.
* Heavy penalties can be charged for offences and defaults in relation to VAT.
* The VAT rules in respect of property transactions are particularly complex.
* Specific VAT rules have been introduced in respect of electronically delivered services.

26.21   Nature of VAT

Value added tax ('VAT') is an indirect tax that is charged on taxable supplies of goods and services by a taxable person in the ordinary course of business in the UK. It is also charged on the import of goods into the UK from outside the EC, on the acquisition of goods from within the EC and on some imports of services. The tax is administered by HM Revenue and Customs ('HMRC') using a framework of registration and self-assessment, and there are heavy penalties for failing to comply with the relevant requirements, some of which are very complex. Broadly, a taxable person must charge VAT ('output tax') on all taxable supplies made and account for this to HMRC, but can deduct from the amount payable any VAT suffered ('input tax') on goods or services purchased or utilised in making those taxable supplies. The end result is that the tax is borne by the final consumer. VAT legislation is extremely complicated and only a broad outline of the main issues is given below.

26.22   Taxable Persons and Registration for VAT

The taxable unit is not the business as such, but the person who carries on the business. All of the taxable supplies made by a particular person must be aggregated in determining whether the VAT registration threshold has been reached, even though the supplies may be made in the course of several different businesses. Once a person becomes liable to register for VAT, tax must be charged on all supplies made by that person, although this does not extend to a business activity carried on by another person with which the first person is also involved. The expression 'person' is deemed to include a partnership and an entity with a separate legal personality, such as a company or trust. A taxable person must notify HMRC when their taxable turnover reaches the registration threshold (£61,000 with effect from 1 April 2006) on one of the following bases:

- at the end of any month, the value of taxable supplies in the last twelve months has exceeded the registration threshold – HMRC must be notified within 30 days of the month end; or
- there are reasonable grounds for believing that the value of taxable supplies will exceed the threshold in the next 30 days – HMRC must be notified before the end of the 30-day period.

A business can register voluntarily if it is making taxable supplies below the threshold or intends to make taxable supplies in the future. A taxable person may apply to be deregistered if taxable supplies in the next twelve months are expected to be below the deregistration threshold (£59,000 with effect from 1 April 2006). A person who ceases to make taxable supplies is no longer a taxable person and must notify HMRC of this fact within 30 days.

26.23   Definition of Supply

The principal charge to VAT is on supplies of goods and services made within the UK. There is no precise legal definition of supply, but it is apparent that:

- anything that is done or provided for consideration (in whatever form) is a supply for VAT purposes;
- anything that is done or provided for no consideration is not a supply, unless the law specifically deems it to be a supply – for instance, the law provides that a transfer of the property in goods, or of their possession, constitutes a supply, so the provision of goods will always constitute a supply.

The law also specifies that the following must be treated as supplies for VAT purposes, regardless of whether any consideration is involved:

- the transfer or disposal of goods that are business assets – there are exceptions for samples and business gifts costing less than £50; and
- the non-business use of business assets in respect of which input tax has been recovered.

Transactions and events that are specifically deemed not be supplies include:

- the transfer of a business as a going concern (subject to certain conditions);
- dividend receipts;
- compensation payments;
- loan repayments;
- grants (provided that the donor does not receive any benefit from the arrangement); and
- internal payments within the same legal entity.

26.24   Time of Supply

The time when a supply is deemed to arise is critical as it determines the period in which VAT must be accounted for. Slightly different rules apply for the supply of goods and the supply of services, and special rules apply for a number of specific supplies. The general rule is that the time of supply (or tax point) is the earliest of:

- the date on which the supply is made – referred to as the basic tax point;
- the date on which a tax invoice is issued in respect of the supply; and
- the date on which payment is received in respect of the supply.

In the case of a supply of services, the basic tax point is the date when the services are performed or completed. In the case of a supply of goods, the basic tax point is the date when delivery commences or, where there is no physical movement of goods, the date on which the goods are made available to the customer – for instance, in the case of a supply of land, the basic tax point will usually be the date on which legal completion takes place. If a tax invoice is raised within 14 days of the basic tax point, the date of issue of the invoice becomes the tax point in place of the basic tax point in order to simplify the accounting process. However, this 14-day rule cannot be used to override an earlier tax point, for instance where this has been triggered by a payment for the supply.

26.25   Categories of Supply and VAT Rates

There are currently four categories of taxable supply.

- *Standard rate:* The standard rate of VAT is currently 17.5 per cent of the value of the supply and this applies to all supplies that are not specifically allocated to one of the other VAT rate bands.
- *Lower rate:* A lower rate of 5 per cent applies in limited situations, including fuel supplied to domestic and charity users, the installation of central heating systems and home security goods provided under grants to pensioners and grant-funded heating measures for the less well off, and certain conversion work on domestic properties.
- *Zero rate:* Supplies that are zero-rated are specified in the legislation – broadly they include food, books, sewerage and non-industrial water services, transport, medicines and certain supplies of buildings for charitable or domestic use. The supplies are still taxable, even though the rate of tax is nil, and turnover in these goods or services therefore counts towards taxable turnover.
- *Exempt:* Exempt supplies are also specified in the legislation and in this case do not count towards taxable turnover. They include most interests in land, insurance, postal services (when supplied by the Post Office), financial services, education, health and welfare, burial and cremation, charity fundraising and cultural services.

In addition, certain supplies of services (essentially those made to a VAT-registered person elsewhere within the EC or to a person outside the EC) are regarded as being made outside the UK and therefore as being outside the scope of UK VAT (although they may come within the VAT regime of another country).

26.26   Partial Exemption

The rules on recovery of the input tax suffered by a taxable person on the purchase of business goods and supplies are very complex. Broadly, input VAT is only recoverable to the extent that it is attributable to taxable supplies and supplies made outside the UK which would be taxable (or in some cases exempt) if made within the UK. A business which makes only exempt supplies cannot register for VAT and consequently cannot recover any of the input tax that it suffers, whereas a business that makes only taxable supplies can recover all of its input tax (apart from that on certain items, such as business entertaining, which is never recoverable). A business which makes both taxable and exempt supplies will be partially exempt. In principle, such a business can recover all of the input tax suffered on purchases relating to the taxable supplies and none of the input tax suffered on purchases relating to the exempt supplies. Input tax suffered on supplies relating to both elements of the business must be apportioned between the two supply categories and only the element relating to taxable supplies will be recoverable. The *Value Added Tax Regulations 1995* (*SI 1995/2518*) set out a standard procedure for this apportionment, based on the proportion that taxable turnover bears to total turnover (adjusted where necessary for specified items that might potentially distort the figures). However, each taxable person may negotiate with HMRC to agree on the use of an alternative apportionment method if this can be justified. Written approval for this should always be obtained from HMRC.

26.27   Records and Returns

Each taxable person is required to keep, and to retain for at least six years, detailed records (with supporting documentation) of supplies made in the course of business, the output tax due on these supplies, and input tax suffered on the receipt of supplies of goods and services, imports and acquisitions. These must be used to complete quarterly VAT returns for submission to HMRC together with any payment due. Businesses are now able to file their VAT returns electronically if they wish. The return includes details of the total supplies made and obtained during the period, together with the output tax due and input tax suffered. The return must be submitted, and the payment made, within one month of the end of the return period. Where input tax exceeds output tax for the period, the return will generate a refund from HMRC. A business in an ongoing repayment position may apply to account for VAT monthly rather than quarterly. In addition, three special schemes are offered to small businesses as follows:

- a business with turnover up to £660,000 may apply to account for VAT on the basis of cash received and paid rather than on the basis of when supplies were made or received;

- a business with annual taxable turnover under £1,350,000 may apply at any time to use the annual accounting scheme – this allows the business to make one annual VAT return, but regular payments on account will usually have to be made during the year, based on an estimate of the expected liability; and
- under the flat rate scheme, a business with taxable turnover under £150,000 (and total turnover under £187,500) can opt to calculate VAT payments as an agreed percentage of turnover, in order to reduce the amount of administration and record-keeping required.

On the other hand, businesses whose net VAT liability exceeds £2 million are required to make monthly payments on account, and other businesses have the option of making monthly rather than quarterly payments if they wish.

26.28   VAT Inspections

Local HMRC offices make periodic visits ('control visits') to trading premises to inspect the VAT records and satisfy themselves that VAT is being accounted for correctly. The regularity of these visits generally depends on the size and complexity of the business. If an underdeclaration of VAT is detected, an assessment will be raised for the outstanding tax and interest and penalties may be charged. More serious action will be taken in the event of fraud or dishonesty.

26.29   Penalties

HMRC can charge heavy penalties for offences and defaults in relation to VAT. These include:

- failure to register – this usually attracts a penalty of a percentage of the net tax accrued from the date on which registration should have taken place, with the percentage ranging from 5 per cent to 15 per cent depending on how late registration is;
- failure to prepare and submit a return or pay tax by the due date – this may attract a default surcharge, with the possibility of additional automatic surcharges if a further default occurs within a period specified by HMRC;
- failure to preserve records – this attracts a fixed penalty of £500;
- dishonest evasion of tax – this attracts a penalty of up to 100 per cent of the tax evaded;
- breach of a regulatory requirement – this attracts a penalty of £5 per day (with a minimum penalty of £50 and a maximum penalty of 100 days), with the penalty increased to £10 or £15 a day for any subsequent breaches within a two-year period.

Misdeclaration penalties, together with default interest, can be charged for any underdeclaration of tax payable or any overstatement of tax refundable. Additional penalties can be charged in the event of repeated misdeclarations.

Taxation

26.30   VAT on Property

The VAT rules relating to property transactions are particularly complex. A broad distinction is made between commercial land and property, and that for domestic, residential or charitable use. In the case of commercial land and buildings, most grants of interest are exempt supplies for VAT purposes, except for the freehold sale of a new or uncompleted commercial building or civil engineering work, which is standard-rated. However, a landlord is generally given the right to elect to waive the exemption from VAT on other grants of interest in commercial land and buildings and therefore to charge VAT at the standard rate on any supplies made. Such an election will generally stand for at least 20 years and has the effect of making all future grants of interest in that land or property standard-rated for VAT. Most grants of interest in property for domestic, residential or charitable use are exempt supplies for VAT purposes, and a landlord has no right to waive this exemption. However, the grant of a freehold interest, or lease of more than 21 years, in a new domestic dwelling or new buildings for certain residential, charitable or communal use, or on the conversion of a previously non-residential building, will be zero-rated if the property is supplied by the person who actually constructed or converted it.

26.31   VAT and Electronically Delivered Services

In May 2002, the EU Council of Ministers confirmed that non-EU internet retailers wishing to sell electronically delivered services in Europe would in future have to register for VAT in one of the EU member states, to protect EU-based internet retailers, who are already obliged to charge VAT on sales to customers within the EU. The EC VAT on E-Commerce Directive amended the EU rules governing the place of supply of electronically supplied services with effect from 1 July 2003, with the result that non-EU businesses providing such services to EU customers could be required to register and account for VAT in each EU member state where they make supplies. In the UK, a special VAT scheme has been introduced to allow such businesses to register and account for EU VAT in a single member state of their choice and declare the tax due on a single electronic VAT return to that member state, which will then distribute the VAT due to the appropriate member states.

26.32   Deferred Tax

At a Glance
* Deferred tax is an accounting rather than a tax issue, and is relevant only in the context of financial statements.
* The profit or loss shown in a company's accounts can be very different to its taxable profit or loss, because of the effect of timing and other differences.

* Providing for deferred tax helps to ensure that the tax effects of timing differences are recognised in the accounts in the same period as the related gain or loss.
* FRS 19 *Deferred Tax* requires deferred tax to be accounted for on a full provision basis, subject to specific exceptions set out in the standard.
* Deferred tax should be measured at the average tax rates expected to apply when the timing differences reverse.
* Deferred tax assets and liabilities may be discounted, but there is no requirement to do this.
* FRS 19 includes clear rules on when deferred tax should be recognised in the profit and loss account and when it should be recognised in the statement of total recognised gains and losses.
* The standard also specifies how deferred tax should be shown in the balance sheet.
* Detailed disclosures must be given in the notes to the accounts, including a reconciliation of the actual tax charge with a notional tax charge, calculated by applying a relevant rate of tax to the profit or loss before tax.

26.33   Accounting for Deferred Tax

Deferred tax is an accounting issue rather than a tax issue and is relevant only in the context of financial statements. For accounting periods ending on or after 23 January 2002, the accounting treatment of deferred tax under UK accounting practice is set out in FRS 19 *Deferred Tax*. Prior to this, accounting for deferred tax was governed by the requirements of Statement of Standard Accounting Practice 15 (SSAP 15) *Accounting for Deferred Tax*. FRS 19 represented a considerable change in approach and has therefore had a significant impact on the profit and loss account and balance sheet of many entities. For information on obtaining copies of FRS 19 see the Accounting Standards Board ('ASB') website at www.frc.org.uk/asb.

Companies preparing IAS accounts (see **3.16–3.17**) must comply instead with IAS 12 *Income Taxes*, which deals with both current and deferred tax. Whilst the requirements in respect of current tax are broadly similar to UK accounting practice, those in respect of deferred tax are based on different accounting concepts and require deferred tax to be recognised in respect of many permanent differences as well as timing differences. This results in some significant differences in the accounting treatments required under FRS 19 and IAS 12, including those relating to:

  (i) revalued non-monetary assets;
 (ii) asset sales where rollover relief has been, or may be, claimed;
(iii) the unremitted earnings of subsidiaries, associates and joint ventures;
(iv) intra-group and foreign currency transactions;
 (v) share-based payments; and
(vi) certain aspects of business combinations.

The accounting treatment of deferred tax assets also differs under IAS 12, and the international standard does not permit discounting of deferred tax liabilities. The following paragraphs outline the present requirements under UK accounting practice.

26.34   The Nature of Deferred Tax

The profit or loss for the year shown in a company's accounts can often be very different to the taxable profit or loss that forms the basis of the tax charge for the year. As a result, the tax payable in respect of a particular accounting period may have little relationship with the accounting profit or loss shown for that period. Differences arise mainly for the following reasons:

- certain categories of income recognised in the accounts may be tax-free;
- certain categories of expenditure shown in the accounts may be disallowable for tax purposes;
- occasionally, tax allowances or charges may arise with no corresponding income or expenditure in the profit and loss account; and
- certain items of income or expenditure may be recognised in the accounts in one period, but be chargeable to, or allowable for, tax in a different period.

Some of these are classified as permanent differences because they will never become taxable or allowable for tax, or because there will never be corresponding income or expenditure for accounting purposes. Others are classified as timing differences because the tax effect will arise in an earlier or later accounting period than the accounting effect.

26.35   *Permanent Difference*

Permanent differences are defined in FRS 19 (see **26.33** above) as:

'Differences between an entity's taxable profits and its results as stated in the financial statements that arise because certain types of income and expenditure are non-taxable or disallowable, or because certain tax charges or allowances have no corresponding amount in the financial statements.'

They include items such as entertaining expenses, tax-free government grants and interest on tax due or receivable.

26.36   *Timing Differences*

Timing differences are defined in FRS 19 (see **26.33** above) as:

'Differences between an entity's taxable profits and its results as stated in the financial statements that arise from the inclusion of gains and losses in tax assessments in periods different from those in which they are recognised in financial statements. Timing differences originate in one period and are capable of reversal in one or more subsequent periods.'

Examples of timing differences include:

- tax deductions for the cost of a fixed asset (eg capital allowances) which are received before or after the cost of the asset is recognised in the profit and loss account (eg in the form of depreciation);
- pension liabilities which are accrued in financial statements in accordance with FRS 17 *Retirement Benefits* but which are only allowable for tax purposes when paid or contributed at a later date;
- interest charges or development costs which are capitalised in the balance sheet but are treated as revenue expenditure for tax purposes and are therefore allowed at the time that they are incurred;
- the gain recognised in the financial statements when an asset is revalued for accounting purposes, but which only becomes chargeable to tax if and when the asset is sold;
- general bad debt provisions made for accounting purposes, but which do not become allowable for tax purposes until they have been identified with specific debts.

Some timing differences will be short term and will reverse in the next accounting period, whereas others may take a substantial time to reverse (eg timing differences relating to pensions).

26.37   Methods of Providing for Deferred Tax

There are basically three methods of accounting for deferred tax in financial statements.

- *Flow-through:* No provision is made for deferred tax and the accounts therefore reflect only the tax liability arising on the profit or loss for the period. This treatment is straightforward to apply but fails to match tax reliefs and charges with the related income and expenses and can result in large fluctuations in the tax charge year by year.
- *Full provision:* The tax effects of all gains and losses recorded in the accounts are provided for in full. This method is also reasonably straightforward to apply, but it may result in significant liabilities being shown in the balance sheet, some of which will only arise in the distant future and even then may only crystallise if a particular transaction or event takes place.
- *Partial provision:* Provision is made in the accounts only for those tax liabilities that are expected to arise as a result of the reversal of timing differences. This has the advantage that the liabilities shown are those expected to arise in practice, but the drawback is that some highly complex calculations may be involved and the provision will often be based on very subjective financial projections.

26.38   The UK Position

For many years, the UK accounting treatment for deferred tax required the partial provision method to be used. The ASB reconsidered this accounting treatment in the light of developments in international accounting practice and con-cluded that:

- the relevant accounting standard (SSAP 15 – see **26.33** above) was developed in the context of a very generous corporation tax system operating at that time, which enabled many companies to postpone indefinitely some or all of their deferred tax;
- the recognition rules were very subjective and the need to anticipate future events was inconsistent with the principles underlying other aspects of financial reporting;
- the partial provision method was not appropriate for dealing with long-term deferred assets, such as those associated with provisions for retirement benefits;
- there were considerable variations in the way in which the standard was applied in practice, which had a detrimental effect on the comparability of financial statements; and
- the partial provision method was increasingly being rejected by standard set-ters in other countries.

FRS 19 (see **26.33** above) was therefore published to supersede SSAP 15 and requires deferred tax to be accounted for on a full provision basis, subject to some specific exceptions set out in the standard.

26.39   Recognition of Deferred Tax

Under FRS 19 (see **26.33** above), deferred tax should be recognised in respect of all timing differences that have originated but have not reversed at the balance sheet date, except in certain specific situations described in the standard. The detailed requirements may be summarised as follows:

- deferred tax should be recognised when allowances for the cost of a fixed asset are received before or after the cost of the asset is recognised in the profit and loss account;
- deferred tax should be recognised on timing differences that arise when a non-monetary asset is continuously revalued to fair value, and changes in fair value are recognised in the profit and loss account (eg where investments are 'marked to market');
- deferred tax should not be recognised on timing differences arising when other non-monetary assets are revalued unless the entity has, by the balance sheet date, entered into a binding agreement to sell the revalued asset and has recognised the gain or loss that is expected to arise on the sale;
- even where these conditions are met, deferred tax should not be recognised on timing differences arising when non-monetary assets are revalued or sold if, on the basis of all available evidence, it is more likely than not that the tax-able gain will be rolled over;
- tax that could be payable on the future remittance of past earnings of a sub-sidiary, associate or joint venture should be provided for only to the extent that, at the balance sheet date:
  - dividends have been accrued as receivable, or

○ the subsidiary, associate or joint venture has entered into a binding agreement to distribute the past earnings in the future (this is expected to be rare in practice);

• deferred tax assets should be recognised to the extent that, on the basis of all available evidence, it is more likely than not that they will be recovered – this is a complex issue and the standard includes a considerable amount of detailed guidance.

26.40   Measurement of Deferred Tax

Under FRS 19 (see **26.33** above), deferred tax should be measured at the average tax rates that are expected to apply in the periods in which the timing differences are expected to reverse, based on tax rates and laws that have been enacted, or substantively enacted, by the balance sheet date. This should not be read as a requirement to average the rates applying to individual types of taxable profits, or to taxable profits arising in different jurisdictions. The rate used should reflect the nature of the individual timing differences and the tax jurisdiction in which they are expected to arise. Average rates will usually only need to be calculated if the enacted tax rates are graduated (ie different rates apply to different levels of taxable income).

26.41   Discounting

Deferred tax assets and liabilities may be discounted to reflect the time value of money, but there is no requirement to do this. The decision on whether to discount or not is a matter of accounting policy. Where an entity considers it appropriate to adopt a policy of discounting, all deferred tax balances measured by reference to undiscounted cashflows, and for which the impact of discounting is material, should be discounted. FRS 19 (see **26.33** above) includes guidance on factors that are likely to be relevant to the consideration of whether a policy of discounting is appropriate, and on the discounting method and rates that should be used. Certain timing differences (eg provisions for pension liabilities) will have already been measured by reference to discounted cashflows and any related deferred tax provisions should therefore not be discounted further.

26.42   Presentation in Performance Statements

Deferred tax should be recognised in the profit and loss account for the period, except to the extent that it is attributable to a gain or loss that is or has been recognised directly in the statement of total recognised gains and losses. In this case, the attributable deferred tax should also be recognised directly in the statement of total recognised gains and losses. If, in exceptional circumstances, it is difficult to determine the amount of deferred tax relating to gains and losses recognised in the statement of total gains and losses, a reasonable pro-rata or other more appropriate allocation may be used. All deferred tax recognised in the profit and loss account should be included in tax on profit or loss on ordinary activities.

Taxation

26.43 Balance-sheet Presentation

Any deferred tax relating to a defined benefit asset or liability recognised under FRS 17 *Retirement Benefits* should be included as part of that asset or liability (see **21.25 FRS 17 RETIREMENT BENEFITS**; for information on obtaining copies of FRS 17 see the ASB website at www.frc.org./asb). Other net deferred tax liabilities should be classified as provisions for liabilities and charges and other net deferred tax assets should be classified as debtors, using a separate sub-heading where material. Deferred tax assets and liabilities should be shown separately on the face of the balance sheet where the amounts are so material in the context of total net current assets or net assets that readers may misinterpret the financial statements if separate disclosure is not given. Deferred tax debit and credit balances should be offset within these balance sheet headings only to the extent that they:

- relate to taxes levied by the same authority; and
- arise in the same taxable entity or in a group of taxable entities where the tax losses of one entity can reduce the taxable profits of another.

A company will therefore usually be able to offset deferred tax balances and this may also be possible where the companies in a group come within the same tax jurisdiction.

26.44 Disclosures

FRS 19 (see **26.33** above) requires a number of detailed disclosures to be given in the accounts, the main items being:

- the amount of deferred tax charged or credited in the profit and loss account, with an analysis of certain components if material;
- the amount of deferred tax charged or credited in the statement of total recognised gains and losses for the period, with a similar analysis of material components;
- the total deferred tax balance (before discounting, where relevant) analysed by each significant type of timing difference;
- where relevant, the impact of discounting on, and the discounted amount of, the deferred tax balance;
- the detailed movements between opening and closing deferred tax balances.

Additional disclosures are needed where certain deferred tax assets are recognised and where deferred tax has not been recognised on revalued assets. The notes to the accounts should also disclose the circumstances that affect the tax charge or credit for the period or may affect that of future periods. This disclosure must include a reconciliation of the current tax charge or credit on ordinary activities for the period to the current tax charge that would result from applying a relevant standard rate of tax to the profit on ordinary activities before tax. Either the monetary amounts or the rates may be reconciled and the basis on which the standard rate has been determined should be disclosed.

26.45   Tax Avoidance Schemes

> **At a Glance**
> * New disclosure rules have been introduced to require details of certain tax schemes and arrangements to be provided to HM Revenue and Customs.
> * Both scheme promoters and scheme users are required to make appropriate disclosures.
> * Separate rules apply on disclosure of the use of VAT avoidance schemes.

26.46   Notifiable Tax Schemes and Arrangements

As result of increasing concerns over the use of tax avoidance schemes and arrangements, new disclosure rules have been introduced in recent years to require information on the use of such schemes to be provided to HM Revenue and Customs. Schemes and arrangements are notifiable if:

* they meet the description of disclosable schemes and arrangements set out in relevant Treasury regulations;
* they result in an income tax, corporation tax or capital gains tax advantage; and
* the tax advantage obtained is the main benefit of the scheme or arrangement.

The Treasury regulations cover both schemes and arrangements connected with employment and schemes and arrangements relating to financial products.

26.47   Responsibility for Disclosure

The principal responsibility for disclosure to HM Revenue and Customs rests with the promoter of the scheme or arrangement. A promoter is defined as any person who designs, organises or markets such a scheme or arrangement, or otherwise makes it available, in the course of a relevant trade, profession or vocation. Disclosure must be made within a strict timetable. The scheme or arrangement will then be allocated a reference number by HM Revenue and Customs and the promoter must provide this reference number to all clients who implement the scheme. Users of the scheme or arrangement have an obligation to notify HM Revenue and Customs that they have used the registered scheme or arrangement, usually by including the relevant details on the appropriate income tax, corporation tax or P35 return. In some circumstances, the user of a scheme or arrangement will be responsible for making full disclosure of the scheme details to HM Revenue and Customs – for instance, this will usually apply where the scheme is provided by an overseas promoter, the scheme is developed in-house or the promoter is prevented from making disclosure to HM Revenue and Customs as a result of the rules on legal professional privilege.

Taxation

26.48 Disclosure Requirements

The required disclosures include:

- sufficient information to enable HM Revenue and Customs to understand how the scheme operates, including the significance of each step taken and the legal provisions on which the scheme relies;
- the name of the scheme (if any); and
- the name and address of the person making the notification.

26.49 Schemes to Avoid VAT

Separate disclosure requirements apply in the case of schemes designed to avoid VAT. In the context of VAT, tax avoidance is defined as including:

- paying less VAT than would otherwise have been due;
- claiming more VAT repayable than would otherwise have been due;
- creating an abnormal timing difference between when the customer accounts for input tax and the supplier accounts for output tax; and
- reducing the amount of irrecoverable input tax where exempt supplies or non-business activities are involved.

All businesses with an annual turnover of more than £600,000 are required to disclose the use of designated VAT tax avoidance schemes. Disclosure should be made in writing to HM Revenue and Customs, giving the name and address of the business, the VAT registration number and the scheme number of the designated scheme used. In addition, businesses with turnover of more than £10 million are required to disclose the use of any schemes or transactions which involve the hallmarks of tax avoidance, as specified in the legislation. In this case, the required disclosures include the hallmark involved, a description of the transaction, details of the goods or services involved, any relevant timing issues and the legal provisions relied on in order to obtain the VAT advantage. In each case, disclosure must be made in accordance with a strict timetable, and there are penalties for failure to make the necessary disclosures under either set of rules.

Appendix 1

Useful Websites on Taxation Issues

HM Revenue and Customs	www.hmrc.gov.uk
HM Treasury	www.hm-treasury.gov.uk
ICAEW Tax Faculty	www.icaew.co.uk/taxfac
Chartered Institute of Taxation	www.tax.org.uk
Institute for Fiscal Studies	www.ifs.org.uk
Taxation Web	www.taxationweb.co.uk
Taxation	www.taxation.co.uk
Business Link	www.businesslink.gov.uk
Institute of Directors	www.iod.com
UK Tax Directory	www.uktax.demon.co.uk

Treasury

Treasury

Treasury

27.1 Treasury Management

Treasury

> **At a Glance**
> * Treasury is essentially about the management of the balance sheet, funding and financial risk of a business.
> * Treasury activities require an understanding of how the financial markets work, how to manage relationships with them and how to use them to the company's advantage.
> * It is advisable to develop a written statement of treasury policy, even in a smaller business.
> * A framework should be established for the proper appraisal of proposed projects and investments.
> * It is also helpful to agree an overall policy on liquidity management.
> * There should be clear guidelines for the investment of any cash that is surplus to the working capital requirements of the business, and an agreed list of authorised investments.
> * The company should have a written policy for its banking arrangements.
> * Key performance indicators should be identified and actual performance in these areas reported regularly to management.
> * The Association of Corporate Treasurers provides detailed guidance, advice and training on treasury issues.

27.2 The Treasury Function

Treasury is essentially about the management of the balance sheet, funding and financial risk of a business. In the case of the balance sheet and funding, the key issues involve the capital structure of the business, including the mix of debt and equity, and liquidity or cashflow. Depending on the nature and size of the business, financial risk might include exposure to movements in interest rates and also to currency fluctuations, both in terms of import and export transactions and of any investments held overseas. In a smaller business, treasury management may well be included as part of the finance function, but in a larger, complex organisation, and especially one which is exposed to significant financial risk, treasury will usually form a separate function staffed by specialists in the field. Treasury activities require an understanding of how the various financial markets work, how to manage relationships with them and how to use them to the company's advantage. There is a vast range of financial products available today, and increasingly complex and sophisticated techniques are being developed in the sphere of financial risk management. Inevitably, some of these can bring their own additional risks with them, and an understanding of the underlying issues, together with a clear company policy on what is and is not acceptable, consequently becomes increasingly important.

27.3   Link with Corporate Strategy

Financial strategy is a key element of corporate strategy (see **25 STRATEGIC PLANNING**). It involves identifying and understanding the financial risk that the company faces, forming a view on what is likely to happen in the future and, in the light of this, taking appropriate decisions to mitigate against any potentially unacceptable levels of risk. Also the ongoing relationship between debt and equity, including future sources of funding for the business and acceptable rates of return, are an important feature of corporate strategy.

27.4   Link with Corporate Governance

The *Combined Code* requires the directors of listed companies to conduct an annual review (as a minimum) of the effectiveness of the company's (or group's) system of internal control and to report to the shareholders that they have done so (see **6 CORPORATE GOVERNANCE**). The guidance developed to help directors fulfil this requirement emphasises that internal control is one of the main elements in the management of risk, along with the transfer of risk to third parties (eg through insurance arrangements), the sharing of risk (eg through participation in joint ventures) and contingency planning. Companies are therefore encouraged to regularly review and evaluate the risks to which they are exposed, the aim usually being to manage and control business risk rather than to attempt to eliminate it completely. Treasury activities will be an important element of this risk management process.

27.5   Establishing Treasury Policy

Even in smaller organisations, it is advisable to develop a written statement of treasury policy. This should:

- identify the financial risks that the business faces;
- describe the risks to be managed through treasury management;
- set out the objectives of managing those risks;
- set out clear responsibilities for all staff involved;

- set out authorisation limits, and in larger treasury functions, dealing limits;
- specify the standards and procedures to be followed in treasury activities; and
- specify which banks and other financial markets may be used.

Most of these issues will need careful consideration at board level and the final policy document should be subject to board approval. It is also important to review the policy at least annually, so that appropriate changes can be made to reflect developments in business activities as well as any other relevant factors.

27.6   Project and Investment Appraisal

The proper appraisal of proposed projects and investments is an important element of treasury management. A framework should be established for this process and detailed rules laid down on how the appraisal process will operate and which appraisal methods should be used. Controls will also need to be introduced to ensure the consistency and integrity of assumptions and resulting financial projections, and the process should be designed to ensure that wider issues, such as the accounting and tax implications, or the potential impact on gearing, are not overlooked. For instance, in choosing between a leasing contract or outright purchase for a major new asset, the decision may need to take into account the potential impact on the balance sheet and gearing ratio of changes proposed in the Accounting Standards Board ('ASB') Discussion Paper *Leases: Implementation of a New Approach* and the subsequent joint ASB/IASB project on this issue, which proposes replacing the present distinction between an operating lease and a finance lease with a requirement to recognise the lessee's right to use the physical asset over the period of the lease as an asset in the accounts in all cases. The development of a new accounting standard on leasing is expected to be added to the IASB's agenda in the near future.

27.7   Liquidity Management

Liquidity management involves keeping control over the cashflows of the business – the detailed aspects are considered in more detail in **2 CASHFLOW MANAGEMENT**. It is helpful to agree an overall policy on liquidity management. For instance, in a group situation it will advisable to agree whether liquidity and cashflow should be managed at operating level (for instance, each subsidiary is responsible for its own banking arrangements and cashflow management) or whether overall control will be exercised at group level (for instance, it may be cost effective for the group as a whole to negotiate group banking arrangements, so that although each subsidiary maintains a separate memorandum account, all balances are combined for the purposes of calculating bank interest and charges). Other issues that may need to be considered in a group context include the solvency requirements for individual subsidiaries and the extent to which reliance should be placed on parent company guarantees or subordination of debt.

27.8   Investment Management

Clear guidelines should be established in advance for the investment of cash that is surplus to the working capital requirements of the business. There will usually be a cost for transferring surplus funds to a deposit or money market account and it is therefore important to establish that the return will be worth-while. Calculations should be carried out to identify the minimum amount that needs to be invested in order to achieve a return and thus to set a sensible guide-line above which funds should be considered for investment. There should also be an agreed list of authorised investments to avoid any unnecessary exposure to risk. The period of time for which the funds can be invested will depend on the company's financial commitments. An up-to-date cashflow forecast will help to establish when the surplus funds will need to be available for other pur-poses. Again, in a group situation, the level of inter-company funding, and any related charges, may be a significant issue and one on which a clear policy needs to be established.

27.9   Bank Relationships

Good relationships with banks and other investment or funding agencies are essential to the success of a business and need to be carefully managed. A clear policy should be set down for banking arrangements, including the company's cri-teria for the choice of bank and arrangements for a regular review of the services offered, with procedures for obtaining tenders from other banks where necessary. As noted above, this is an issue that may need to be considered at group level.

27.10   Measuring Performance

An essential element of good treasury management is the provision of good management information and in particular the regular measurement and assess-ment of performance. Key performance indicators should be identified for the treasury function as a whole, the aim usually being to achieve an appropriate balance between the effective management of financial risk and a realistic con-tribution to company profitability. Depending on the complexity of the treasury activities undertaken, measures might include accuracy of cash forecasting, compliance with controls, cost control (eg level of bank charges), investment returns achieved and hedging and/or dealing performance achieved.

27.11   Association of Corporate Treasurers

Detailed advice, guidance and training in treasury management issues, together with information on relevant qualifications, can be obtained from the Associ-ation of Corporate Treasures (Ocean House, 10–12 Little Trinity Lane, London EC4V 2DJ; *tel:* 020 7213 9728; *web:* www.corporate-treasures.co.uk).

27.12   Risk Management

At a Glance

* The identification, analysis and management of business risk is an essential element in the successful management of any business.
* A clear methodology should be developed for the identification and assessment of business risk, based on the specific circumstances of the business.
* Interest rate risk will be a particular issue in a business that is highly geared.
* Currency risk will be an issue if the business undertakes a significant element of import or export business, or holds substantial investments abroad.
* The accounting treatment of any hedging arrangements requires careful consideration.
* Procedures should be established for the regular monitoring of current financing arrangements and the development of a long-term financing strategy.

27.13   Need for Risk Management

The identification, analysis and management of business risk is an essential element in the successful management of any business. Listed companies in particular are now strongly encouraged to develop risk management policies and procedures for the purpose of internal control reporting under the *Combined Code* (see **6 CORPORATE GOVERNANCE**). Without the detailed process of identification and analysis of business risk, management cannot give due consideration to the extent to which that risk should be accepted and controlled, shared with other business partners or transferred to third parties. Risk management is also an ongoing process, not something that is carried out in the early stages of a business and then forgotten. As a business grows and develops, and surrounding economic factors change, the business will be exposed to new risks and early identification of these will enable management to respond accordingly.

27.14   Business Risk

The identification and management of business risk is considered in detail in the context of **6 CORPORATE GOVERNANCE**. It is helpful to develop a clear methodology for the identification and assessment of risk, based on the particular circumstances of the business. This should be subject to regular review so that new factors can be incorporated where necessary. Particular issues to consider include:

* the extent to which each category of risk is considered acceptable;
* guidelines on when risk should be controlled, shared, transferred or eliminated;

- reporting on the control of business risk; and
- assessing performance on the identification and control of business risk.

27.15   Interest Rate Risk and Currency Risk

Although they may arise in different situations and as a result of different factors, the process for managing interest rate risk and currency risk is virtually identical and they are therefore considered together here. Interest rate risk is a particular issue when a business is highly geared and interest cover is low, so that an increase in interest rates could have a significant adverse effect on profitability. A business may be exposed to currency risk if it undertakes a significant level of import or export business or if it holds substantial investments abroad, and particularly if it is involved with entities who operate in volatile economies. The risk management process involves:

- identifying the potential exposure of the business;
- assessing the likelihood of these risks crystallising;
- identifying acceptable methods of hedging against the risk;
- setting targets and limits for each type of exposure;
- agreeing on the specific instruments that can be used and when these should be brought into effect;
- specifying the approval procedures that must be followed; and
- measuring and assessing performance on a regular basis.

27.16   Accounting for Hedge Transactions

The accounting treatment of any hedging arrangements will also require careful consideration. Hedge accounting results in gains and losses arising on a hedge item being deferred and matched with those arising on the hedged item and it can therefore have a significant effect on reported financial performance. Consequently, its use is strictly controlled under accounting standards. Under FRS 26 *Financial Instruments: Measurement* and IAS 39 *Financial Instruments: Recognition and Measurement* hedge accounting can only be applied where strict criteria are met. These include formal documentation of the hedging relationship and the entity's strategy and risk management objectives in undertaking each hedge, and the satisfaction of certain effectiveness tests in respect of the hedge. If any of the criteria subsequently cease to be met in respect of the hedged item or hedging instrument, the use of hedge accounting must be discontinued. Not all UK entities are subject to FRS 26 at present – the standard currently applies to listed entities for accounting periods beginning on or after 1 January 2005 and to other entities from 1 January 2006 if they choose to adopt fair value accounting (see **11.68** above), but the ASB has already issued proposals for extending the scope of the standard in due course. For companies not required to adopt FRS 26, there are fewer rules and restrictions on the use of hedge accounting at present, although the requirements of SSAP 20 *Foreign Currency Translation* must be complied with where relevant.

27.17   Financing Risk

The management of financing risk involves assessing the financing arrangements that are currently in place and their impact on the business, managing the arrangements to avoid any unexpected reductions in funding (for instance, keeping loan covenants under constant review to ensure that none of these are accidentally breached), and developing a long-term strategy for the financing of the business. The long-term strategy should include consideration of any refinancing that may be needed (for instance, the need to renegotiate facilities or to identify the resources to repay loan commitments as they fall due) and the agreement of projected targets and limits for the various sources of funding that may be available to the business. As with other areas of risk management, performance should be measured and assessed on a regular basis.

27.18   Disclosure

At a Glance

* All companies, other than those that qualify as small, must give certain information about the use of financial instruments in the directors' report.
* The ASB's Reporting Statement *Operating and Financial Review* recommends the disclosure of detailed information on treasury issues.
* Accounting standards require listed companies and those adopting fair value accounting to give detailed disclosures on financial instruments and other treasury issues in the notes to the accounts, and other companies are encouraged to provide equivalent information where relevant.
* New disclosure requirements apply for accounting periods beginning on or after 1 January 2007.

27.19   Directors' Report

For accounting periods beginning on or after 1 January 2005, the directors' report should include information on the company's use of financial instruments, unless this information is not material for an assessment of the company's (or group's) assets, liabilities, financial position and results. There is a specific exemption from the disclosure requirement for companies that qualify as small and choose to take advantage of the option to prepare a modified directors' report (see **3.48** and **3.55** above). For all other companies, the directors' report should include an indication of:

* the entity's financial risk management objectives and policies, including the policy for hedging if hedge accounting is used; and
* the entity's exposure to price risk, credit risk, liquidity risk and cash flow risk.

Treasury

Practice has still to develop in dealing with these new disclosure requirements. In the meantime, directors may find it helpful to refer to guidance set out in FRS 25 *Financial Instruments: Disclosure and Presentation*, FRS 29 *Financial Instruments: Disclosure* and the ASB's Reporting Statement *Operating and Financial Review*, all of which are considered in more detail below. Whilst these documents deal primarily with details to be given by listed and other larger entities at present, they are aimed at providing information that is helpful to users of annual accounts and report, and so provide a useful source of information for directors preparing the new disclosures for the annual directors' report.

27.20   Operating and Financial Review

The ASB Reporting Statement *Operating and Financial Review* (see **11.89** above) is non-mandatory but sets out best practice on the presentation of qualitative information to analyse and explain the results and financial position of a company in its annual report. The guidance is directed primarily at listed and other larger companies, but others are encouraged to follow the recommendations where appropriate. The suggested disclosures are wide-ranging and include discussion of:

- the main factors and influences that may have a major effect on future results, regardless of whether they were significant in the period under review, including identification of the principal risks and uncertainties in the main lines of business, together with a brief explanation of the approach taken to managing these risks and the nature of the potential impact on the business;
- the capital structures of the business in terms of the maturity profile of debt, type of capital instruments used, currency and interest rate structure and comments on relevant ratios such as interest cover and debt/equity ratios;
- capital funding and treasury policies and objectives, including the management of interest rate risk, the maturity profile of borrowings and the management of exchange risk in terms of:
  ○ the manner in which treasury activities are controlled,
  ○ the currencies in which borrowings are made and in which cash and cash equivalents are held,
  ○ the extent to which borrowings are at fixed interest rates,
  ○ the use of financial instruments for hedging purposes, and
  ○ the extent to which foreign currency net investments are hedged by currency borrowings and other hedging instruments;
- an explanation of the purpose and effect of major financing transactions undertaken up to the date of approval of the financial statements;
- the effect of interest costs on profits and the potential impact of interest rate changes;
- the cashflows generated from operations and other cash inflows, including any segmental cashflows that are out of line with segmental profits;
- the business's liquidity at the end of the period, including:
  ○ the level of borrowings at the balance sheet date,
  ○ the seasonality of borrowing requirements,

- o the maturity profile of actual borrowings and committed borrowings facilities,
- o funding requirements for capital expenditure committed and authorised,
- o any restrictions on the ability to transfer funds within the group (eg exchange controls and tax consequences of transfers),
- o any breaches of loan covenants and measures taken or proposed to remedy the situation,
- o an indication of any current or proposed negotiations with lenders on the operation of covenants which have the effect of restricting the use of credit facilities.

27.21   FRS 13 *Derivative and Other Financial Instruments: Disclosures*

FRS 13 *Derivative and Other Financial Instruments: Disclosures* applies to:

- all banks and similar institutions; and
- all entities, other than insurance companies, that have one or more of their capital instruments listed or publicly traded on a stock exchange or market.

For most of these entities, the requirements of FRS 13 are superseded by those set out in FRS 25 *Financial Instruments: Disclosure and Presentation* (see **27.24** below). However, it remains in force for any banking or similar institution that does not fall within the scope of FRS 25 and does not voluntarily adopt the disclosure requirements of that standard, or of FRS 29 *Financial Instruments: Disclosures* (see **27.26** below). The disclosure requirements of FRS 13 are detailed and encompass both narrative and numerical disclosures, with the objective of providing information on the impact of financial instruments on the entity's risk profile, how the related risks might affect the entity's financial performance and financial position, and the action taken to manage the potential risks.

27.22   *Narrative Disclosures*

The narrative disclosures include:

- an explanation of how financial instruments create or change the risks that the entity faces in its activities;
- the directors' approach to managing those risks; and
- a description of the objectives, policies and strategies adopted for holding and using financial instruments to manage risk.

These disclosures are mandatory under the standard, although they can be given elsewhere in the annual report, provided that the financial statements include a cross-reference to where the information can be found.

27.23   *Numerical Disclosures*

The numerical disclosures are intended to assist in the evaluation of the entity's exposure to potentially significant risk. Separate requirements are set out for banks and similar institutions, other financial institutions, and other entities. The detailed disclosures cover:

- interest rate risk;
- currency risk;
- liquidity risk;
- fair values;
- financial instruments used for trading;
- financial instruments used for hedging; and
- certain commodity contracts.

A significant element of aggregation is encouraged to prevent key elements being obscured by detail. The standard includes illustrative examples of the disclosures, covering both straightforward and complex arrangements.

27.24 FRS 25 *Financial Instruments: Disclosure and Presentation*

FRS 25 *Financial Instruments: Disclosure and Presentation* was issued by the ASB in December 2004 (for information on obtaining copies, see the ASB website at www.frc.org.uk/asb). The presentation requirements of the standard apply to all entities (other than those adopting the FRSSE) for accounting periods beginning on or after 1 January 2005 but the disclosure requirements, together with the requirements of FRS 23 *The Effects of Changes in Foreign Exchange Rates*, FRS 24 *Financial Reporting in Hyperinflationary Economies* and FRS 26 *Financial Instruments: Measurement*, form a package of new UK accounting standards that apply to listed companies for accounting periods beginning on or after 1 January 2005, and to other entities for accounting periods beginning on or after 1 January 2006 if they choose to adopt fair value accounting (see **11.68** above), although adoption from 1 January 2005 is also permitted in this case. Entities who are not required to adopt FRS 26 are nevertheless encouraged to comply with the disclosure requirements of FRS 25 where appropriate.

27.25 *Detailed Disclosure Requirements*

The detailed disclosure requirements set out in FRS 25 are intended to provide information to help users of the accounts understand the significance of financial instruments to the entity's financial position, performance and cashflows, and also the amount, timing and certainty of future cashflows relating to the instruments. The disclosures therefore focus on market risk, credit risk, liquidity risk and cashflow interest rate risk. The standard does not prescribe the format, location or level of detail of the required disclosures, although guidance is provided on the issues that directors should take into account when making judgements on these. The required disclosures include:

- information on the extent and nature of the financial instruments, including significant terms and conditions that may affect the amount, timing and certainty of future cashflows;

- the accounting policies adopted, including the criteria for recognition and the basis of measurement adopted;
- information about the entity's exposure to interest rate risk, including contractual repricing or maturity dates, and effective interest rates;
- information about the entity's exposure to credit risk, including its maximum exposure to credit risk at the balance sheet date, without taking account of the fair value of any collateral, in the event of other parties failing to perform their obligations under financial instruments and any significant concentrations of credit risk;
- the fair value of each class of financial assets and financial liabilities in a way that allows this to be compared with the corresponding carrying amount in the balance sheet;
- details of financial assets pledged as collateral for liabilities and contingent liabilities, together with any material terms and conditions relating to them;
- details of any multiple embedded derivative features in compound financial instruments issued by the entity;
- for any defaults or breaches in the period in respect of loans payable at the balance sheet date, and any other breaches of loan agreements which permit the lender to demand repayment (unless the breach has been remedied, or the loan renegotiated, before the balance sheet date):
  - details of the default or breach,
  - the amount recognised at the balance sheet date in respect of the relevant loan, and
  - whether the default has been remedied or the loan renegotiated before the date on which the financial statements were authorised for issue; and
- detailed information in respect of any instruments that create a potentially significant exposure to risk, either individually or as a class.

A number of other detailed disclosure requirements apply in relation to the adoption of fair value accounting for financial assets and financial liabilities and also where hedge accounting has been applied.

27.26   FRS 29 *Financial Instruments: Disclosures*

The ASB published FRS 29 *Financial Instruments: Disclosures* in December 2005 (for information on obtaining copies, see the ASB website at www.frc.org.uk/asb). The standard applies for accounting periods beginning on or after 1 January 2007, although earlier adoption is encouraged, and supersedes the disclosure requirements of FRS 25 *Financial Instruments: Disclosure and Presentation* (see **27.24** and **27.25** above). If the standard is adopted for an earlier accounting period, this fact must be disclosed. Also, if an entity chooses to adopt the standard for an accounting period beginning before 1 January 2007, it has the option of adopting:

- only Appendix E (which deals with capital disclosures);
- all parts of the standard with the exception of Appendix E; or
- the entire standard.

Where an entity adopts FRS 29 for an accounting period beginning before 1 January 2007 and has not previously adopted the disclosure requirements of FRS 25, it need not provide comparative disclosures in the first financial statements prepared under FRS 29, although this exemption does not extend to the capital disclosures required by Appendix E. FRS 29 also supersedes FRS 13 *Derivatives and Other Financial Instruments: Disclosure* (see **27.21** to **27.23** above) for entities that comply with the new disclosure requirements.

27.27 *Scope of FRS 29*

At present, the disclosure requirements of FRS 29 apply only to entities that have adopted FRS 26 *Financial Instruments: Measurement* (see **27.24** above). The following are also specifically exempted from compliance with the standard:

- entities adopting the FRSSE (see **11.19** above);
- subsidiary undertakings (other than banks or insurance companies) where 90 per cent or more of the voting rights are controlled within the group, provided that the entity is included in publicly available consolidated accounts which comply with the detailed disclosure requirements of FRS 29; and
- a parent company in respect of its own individual accounts, provided that the company is included in publicly available consolidated accounts which comply with the detailed disclosure requirements of FRS 29.

However, as with FRS 25, entities not applying FRS 26 are encouraged to follow the disclosure requirements on a voluntary basis, adapted in line with their accounting policies for relevant transactions. The ASB has also issued proposals to bring all entities within the scope of FRS 26 in due course, and this would also bring them within the scope of the disclosure requirements of FRS 29. The disclosure requirements of the standard should also be applied to all types of financial instruments, other than those that are specifically excluded.

27.28 *Minimum Disclosure Requirements*

The standard sets out the detailed minimum disclosures that are considered necessary to enable users to evaluate:

- the significance of financial instruments to the entity's financial position and performance;
- the nature and extent of risks arising from the financial instruments to which it is exposed at the reporting date; and
- the entity's capital.

Given the wide variety of financial instruments available these days, the standard sets out only minimum disclosure requirements, with the implication that these may need to be expanded on, depending on the particular circumstances of the business.

27.29   *Balance Sheet Disclosures*

The minimum disclosures in respect of the balance sheet cover:

- an analysis of balance sheet carrying values by specified class of financial instrument, and additional information where fair value accounting has been applied to financial assets and liabilities;
- details of financial instruments that have been reclassified and the reasons for the reclassification;
- detailed disclosures on any financial assets that have been pledged as collateral;
- where an allowance account is used to record impairments of financial assets, a reconciliation of changes in the year for each class of financial assets;
- the existence of any multiple embedded derivatives in compound financial instruments issued by the entity;
- details of any defaults during the period in respect of principal, interest, sinking fund or redemption provisions on outstanding loans, together with:
  - ◦ the carrying amount of the relevant loan,
  - ◦ whether the default was remedied, or the terms of the loan were renegotiated, before the financial statements were authorised for issue; and
- details of any other breaches of loan agreements which allowed the lender to demand accelerated repayment, unless the breaches were remedied, or the terms of the loan were renegotiated, before the reporting date.

27.30   *Performance Statement Disclosures*

The minimum disclosures in respect of the entity's financial performance statement cover:

- net gains and net losses on financial instruments, analysed into specified categories;
- details of all material accounting policies in respect of financial instruments;
- detailed disclosures in respect of any fair value hedges, cashflow hedges and hedges of net investments in foreign operations; and
- disclosures to enable users to compare the fair values of financial assets and liabilities with their balance sheet carrying values, together with details of how fair value has been determined.

27.31   *Risk Disclosures*

The standard also requires the disclosure of detailed information (both qualitative and quantitative) to enable users to assess the risks to which the entity is exposed as a result of the financial instruments that it holds, and the policies and procedures used to manage these. In particular, the minimum disclosures set out in the standard cover various aspects of credit risk, liquidity risk and market risk.

27.32 *Capital Disclosures*

Disclosure requirements in respect of capital are set out in Appendix E to FRS 29 which is nevertheless considered to be an integral part of the standard. The overriding requirement is that an entity must disclose information that enables users of the financial statements to evaluate the entity's objectives, policies and processes for managing capital. The minimum disclosures specified in the standard are:

- qualitative information about the entity's objectives, policies and processes for managing capital, including (but not limited to):
  - a description of what is managed as capital,
  - if the entity is subject to externally imposed capital requirements, the nature of the requirements and how they are incorporated into the management of capital, and
  - how the entity is meeting its objectives for managing capital;
- summary quantitative data on what is managed as capital – for instance, some forms of subordinated debt may be regarded as capital, whilst certain components of equity may not be regarded as capital;
- any changes in the above details from the previous accounting period;
- whether the entity has complied during the period with any externally imposed capital requirements; and
- if it has not complied with such requirements, the consequences of the non-compliance.

The standard notes that the disclosures should be based on information provided internally to the entity's key management personnel. Also, aggregate disclosure may not be sufficient to provide users with useful information or may distort a user's understanding of the entity's capital resources. For instance, where capital is managed in a number of different ways or the entity is subject to a number of different capital requirements, due to the nature of its activities or to the different jurisdictions in which it operates, separate information may need to be provided.

27.33 Corporate Governance

Corporate governance disclosures in respect of risk management are considered in detail in **6 CORPORATE GOVERNANCE**.

Appendix 1

Useful Websites on Treasury Issues

Association of Corporate Treasurers	www.treasurers.org/
ICAEW Finance and Management Faculty	www.icaew.co.uk/fmfac
Institute of Credit Management	www.icm.org.uk/
Business Link	www.businesslink.gov.uk
Federation of Small Businesses	www.fsb.org.uk

Treasury

Table of Cases

Table of Statutes

Table of Statutory Instruments

Index

Numbers refer to Chapter and Paragraph Number (eg. 1.1). Appendix numbers refer to chapters (e.g. App 6 = appendix to chapter 6).